"Art is an illegal drug."

—Frank Moore

Other books by Frank Moore:

Art of a Shaman

Cherotic Magic

Chapped Lap

Deep Conversations In The Shaman's Den, Volume I

Frankly Speaking: A Collection of Essays, Writings and Rants

How to Handle an Anthropologist: Russell Shuttleworth, PhD interviews shaman/performance artist Frank Moore

Skin Passion

The Cherotic (r)Evolutionary Complete 1991-1999

ISBN 978-1-7346850-1-5

Cover and book design by Michael LaBash.

Inter-Relations
PO Box 1931
Eagle, ID 83616

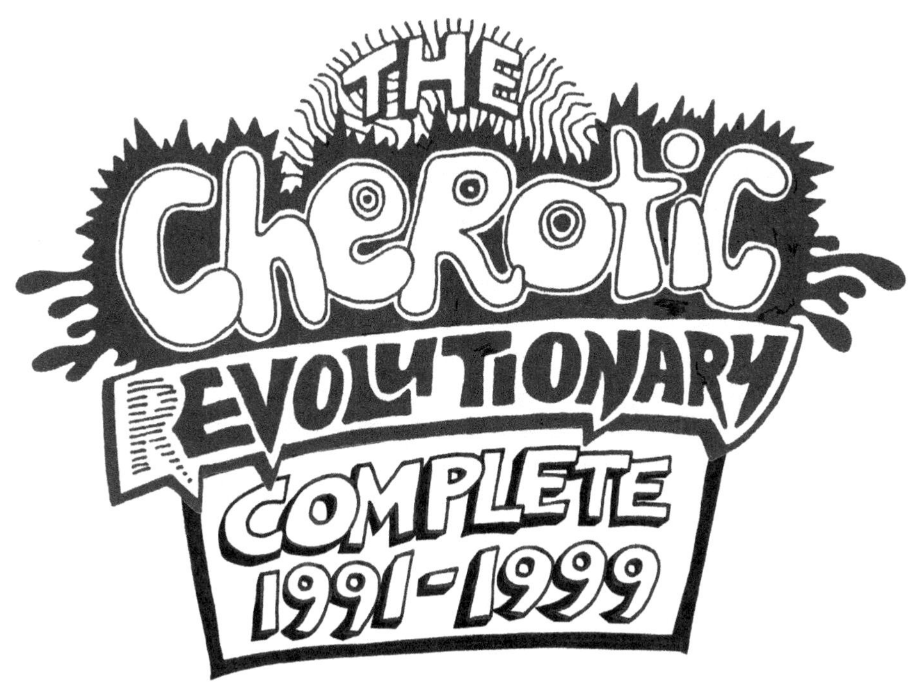
THE
CheRotiC
REVOLUTIONARY
COMPLETE
1991-1999

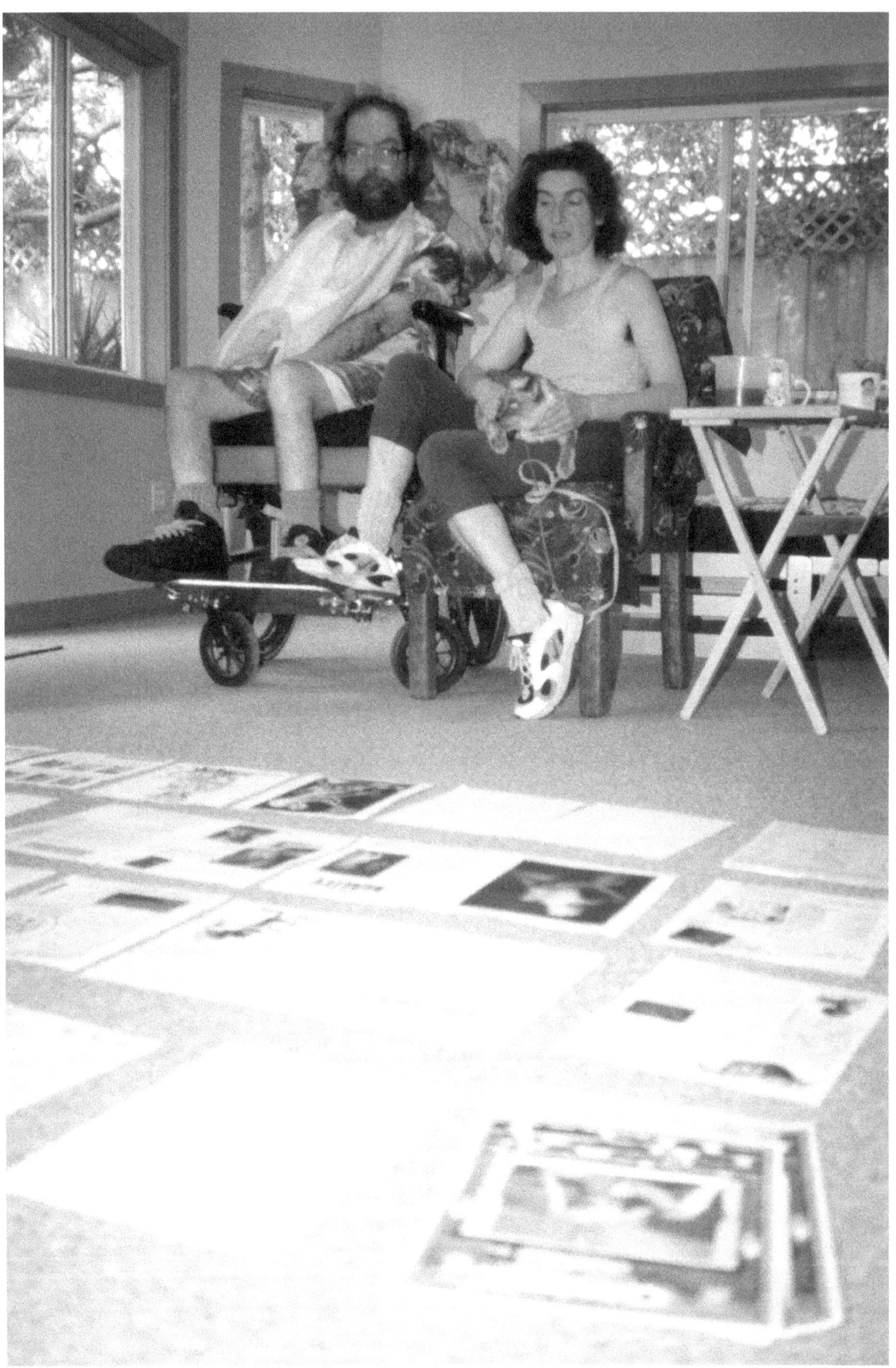

Frank Moore, Linda Mac and Kittee ordering pages for issue #7 in their Berkeley, California studio in 1997.

The Cherotic (r)Evolutionary (1991-1999)

by Stephen Perkins, April 11, 2019

> *I have always been lucky. I have a body that is ideal for a performance artist. And I have always wanted to be a performer. When I was a kid, my younger brother used to get mad when people looked at me when he pushed me to the movies or to the teen club. He cried. But I liked people looking at me. That is what I mean I am lucky. I am lucky I am an exhibitionist in this body. One time, I was working out on the jungle gym outside of our house...a kid came by and asked if I was a monster. I just roared like a monster. It was fun...I started to see my body as a tool. I could get away with things that others couldn't.*[1]

With incredible humor and an infectious smile Frank Moore (1946-2013) navigated the world in a body of which he had only minimal control. Born with cerebral palsy and unable to walk or talk he used a wheelchair his entire life. When he was seventeen, he created his own personal communication system by strapping a pointer to his head which allowed him to point to letters, words and phrases on a board, and thus he was finally able to break out of his isolation and communicate with the world. But Moore did not let his disabled body hamper his path through life, and his obituaries detail the myriad creative activities that he was engaged with, including a long career as a performance artist, a shaman, poet, essayist, playwright, painter, musician, Internet TV personality, a 2008 presidential candidate and co-editor of the zine *The Cherotic (r)Evolutionary* amongst a host of other activities.[2] Along the way Moore also completed a BA in English (1972, University of New Mexico), an MA in Psychology (1976, University Without Walls, Berkeley) and an MFA in Performance/Video (1983, San Francisco Art Institute). Mention should also be given here to Moore's longtime partner Linda Mac and fellow collaborator Michael LaBash, both of whom were key partners, and collaborators in helping Moore realize his ideas and projects during his years living in Berkeley, California.

This text concentrates on only one thin slice of Moore's extensive activities and that is his role as co-editor with Linda Mac of *The Cherotic (r)Evolutionary*, a zine that they published in Berkeley in nine issues (#0-8) between 1991-1999.[3]

Introduction

Looking at the inaugural issue, it is interesting to note that the first piece of news in Moore's editorial concerns the recent publication of his book *Cherotic Magic* (1990), which is an introduction to the shamanistic apprenticeship that he was offering at the time. Moore admits to this "...shameless self-promotion...for my apprenticeship, for my 6-session course, for my performance art and videos and tapes, and who knows what else."[4] Throughout the life of the periodical, Moore would use it as a distribution outlet for the varied products of his assorted activities.

About the magazine Moore states in the first issue:

> **TCR** *is a journal of the edge.* **TCR** *is an offensive movement or measure offering alternatives to the fragmentation, isolation, personal helplessness which is actively promoted by the combine of power systems.* **TCR** *is anarchical, based on personal responsibility to reshape reality into a more human, trusting, loving reality, full of fun and pleasure.* **TCR** *is not a reaction. It is a magical act of enjoying life. It is a journal of and for people who are doing this magical art....Now we magical misfits know we are not alone, that there are others out/in here/there feeling, thinking, trying, doing similar things. This just by itself should speed evolution up.*[5]

Moore's desire that the magazine should provide a network of support for these 'magical misfits' is coupled with his larger vision of this movement, about which he states, "I think it is very important that there be a Cherotic Movement, not unlike the so-called Sexual Revolution of the Sixties. This Cherotic Movement would be (or rather, is) a physical/spiritual movement that re-defines and expands sexual, spiritual, social concepts of reality."[6] This latter statement outlines the core themes that would form the basis of all of Moore's work in various media, and they would provide the links to all of his different activities throughout his career. On the definition of a "cherotic (r)evolutionary" Moore wrote, "...Chero is the physical life energy. I created the word "chero" by combining "chi" and "eros". And revolution is the mutation stage/phase in the process of evolution...so an erotic mutant for life!"[7]

The most direct way through which Moore offered interested people an experience of the *cherotic* was through his performances, in which the audience was invited to actively engage in what he called 'eroplay'. Eroplay is another word that Moore created to describe the experience of "...intense physical playing and touching of oneself and others. Eroplay is also the force of energy which is released as the result of such play". Moore emphasizes that "eroplay is not foreplay, even though foreplay is eroplay..." and further that "Foreplay leads to orgasm...eroplay leads to being turned on in many different ways in all parts of the body," and he concludes, "Eroplay is the blissed-out, warm, relaxed, turned-on, totally satisfying feeling of a good head rub...eroplay is that intense feeling throughout the entire body".[8] *The Cherotic (r)Evolutionary* would be one of the mediums through which Moore communicated his expansive philosophy of the cherotic, and he challenged his readers to become 'revolutionaries' in this radical movement to reshape, and expand our physical, spiritual and sexual lives.

In Moore's editorial for the second issue he expands upon his editorial position and in his desire to keep *The Cherotic (r)Evolutionary* an open and freewheeling place he states what the magazine is not going to do:

> *...we will never do theme issues such as poetry, gay, sex, women, etc. This is because the theme format is a great way for editors and galleries (etc.) to keep control of content, style, point of view, and the accessibility of the communication channels they manage. The theme concept also fragments both people and dialogue into labeled bits that can be shuffled in and out of fashion time.* **TCR** *will follow the magic wherever it non-linearly goes. We will print what we like, what interests us...*[9]

Moore was always alert to the ways systems oppress and suppress, even within the context of magazine publishing, and all nine issues of *The Cherotic (r)Evolutionary* display a comfortably unruly aesthetic that embraces a wide variety of artists' works, poetry, writings by Moore and others, and reviews of his performances and publications.[10]

What's in a Name?

Before I explore the contents of the periodical there are two subjects that I want to address, and the first is the name of the periodical. A look at all nine issues reveals that the periodical's name for the first five issues is *The Cherotic Revolutionary* and from the sixth issue the title has been changed to *The Cherotic (r)Evolutionary*. In editorials for issues #3 (1993) and #4 (1994), Moore spells the name of the periodical "*The Cherotic rEvolutionary*" with a lower case "r" and the title on the covers reflect this emphasis on the "R" by printing them with a screen that distinguishes the letter "R" from the rest of the word. By issue #5 (1995) the title of the periodical is *The Cherotic (r)Evolutionary*. In his editorial in issue #3 (1993) Moore explores the background around the eventual name change:

> *There are changes around here. Well, what do you expect from a zine with "revolution" in its last name? And that may be one of the changes...our name appears to be in the process of changing itself from The Cherotic Revolutionary to the Cherotic Evolutionary. A revolution is a mutation from the normal as-is reality, an experiment and adventure in newness. The purpose of a revolution, and any mutation, is to break new ground for evolution...to prod evolution along.*[11]

The second subject, and question that I want to explore is, what to call this periodical? In the first two issues Moore describes it as both a 'magazine' and a 'journal.' In the third issue he refers to the periodical as a 'zine' and by the next issue *zine* is used not only in the editorial but in the masthead for all futures as well. It's perhaps unsurprising that this new descriptor also parallels the period when the title of the periodical was in flux. I would agree with the use of the word 'zine' to describe this periodical, as its anarchic, and low-tech production, certainly displays all the features of a periodical published by enthusiasts and non-professionals. However, at one level Moore's original use of the term 'journal' is also appropriate as well. Journals have historically been the site where the activities, and research of specialized groups was communicated to their professional community. Moore, in his editorial for the first issue, describes the periodical as being just such a place, albeit comprised of an 'unprofessional' community, but with the same theme of sharing their research within this group. Moore writes that the periodical will provide a site for this community to address:

> *...magical issues that I for one have been hungry to talk about for a long time in the depths that it is possible with people who have committed their lives to going across the taboo border to effect evolutionary change. In future issues of TCR, I hope we will move far beyond the book, Cherotic Magic, and give one another aid and comfort on the edge by linking together, by announcing new findings in our hidden experiments [my emphasis] on nonlinear change."*[12]

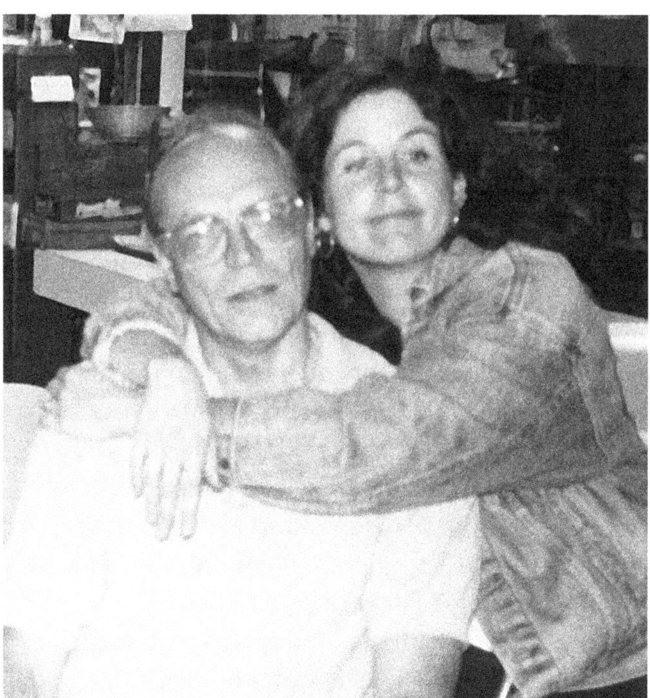

Kyle and Luna Griffith, S/R Press.

Inside the (r)Evolution

All nine issues of *The Cherotic (r)Evolutionary* present a smorgasbord of works by a variety of writers and visual artists, and the following overview includes the names of the more frequent contributors in different media. The periodical publishes a wide range of writings including poetry (Jesse Beagle, Robert Howington), reviews of the periodical, Moore's performances and other events (Kyle Griffith, Barbara Smith), texts related to shamanism (Kyle Griffith, Brenda Tatelbaum), personal stories about sex (Carol A. Queen, Veronica Vera), performance art (Annie Sprinkle, Karen Finley, Linda Montano), sex and spirituality (Chief Distant Eagle), and disability issues (Steve A. Brown). On the visual front the periodical is copiously illustrated (Michael LaBash, John Seabury, Brian Viveros), and throughout there are black and white photographs, and featured portfolios (Tony Ryan).

On the technical side, *The Cherotic (r)Evolutionary* was a photocopied periodical and beginning with the third issue was published by Frank Moore's and Linda Mac's Inter-Relations, their publishing arm that took over from the original publishers, S/R Press. Coinciding with this issue was their acquisition of a Mac computer, and with Michael LaBash as art editor, the quality of the overall design improves substantially, and would continue throughout the life of the periodical. However, even in the final issue (#8, 1999) where the design is at its tightest, there is still an element of the early anarchic quality that grounds the periodical within the larger history of zines. The periodical was an annual publication with the exception of #1 and #2, both published in 1992.

At the back of each issue is information about acquiring previous issues of the magazine as well as details about other products available from Frank Moore's assorted projects. Later issues also included a page that featured readers' and advertisers' works and products, as well as their contact information. The periodical ceased publication when Moore and Mac started their internet radio station *LUVeR (Love Underground Visionary (r)Evolution)*, and, "We were just too busy to do both...".[13]

Following from this brief survey of the periodical's contents, I want to examine a number of specific aspects of the periodical that play important roles in the periodical's nine-year lifetime. One theme that resonates powerfully throughout the periodical is censorship, in particular Frank Moore's experience of it during the 'culture wars' that were raging during the periodical's early years. I will also examine two other important elements of the periodical, specifically Michael LaBash's illustrations, and Moore's written contributions.

The theme of censorship appears in the first few pages of issue #0 (1991) by way of an article by Jack Helbig that first appeared in *The Chicago News & Arts Weekly* (Oct. 11 - 17, 1990) titled "Outlaw Artists, Porn? Play? Or Immoral Plot". In his article Helbig summarizes the recent conservative attacks on artists doing edgy performance works and the fact that they had all received grants with taxpayers' monies. Helbig concentrates on Annie Sprinkle, Karen Finley and Frank Moore, and he outlines the cases that Senator Jesse Helms and Representative Rohrbacher launched against what the late conservative art critic, Hilton Kramer, described as these "New Barbarians". The censorship wars of this period raged across the artworld and nobody in this community was unaffected by this controversy. Artists doing provocative works were an easy target for conservatives in whipping up hysteria about the use of public funds for this type of 'pornography'. Sadly, they were ultimately successful in changing the granting process in order give local communities a greater say, and control, over who did and who did not receive grants. Attempts to cut the amount of funds provided annually to the NEA (National Endowment for the Arts) were ultimately not successful, but within this hostile climate there would be no move to increase the funding either.

Further into the above issue #0 (1991) Moore publishes an open letter to Jesse Helms and demands to have a dialogue with him writing, "Why are you closing channels of expression and funding to me without due process of law?" claiming that this campaign is a way of smearing the artists' reputations and thus making them "...untouchable, unfundable, unbookable".[14] Moore concludes his text with one final address to Helms stating, "If you have anything to say to me or to ask me, come to talk to me man to man. Otherwise, get your Big Brother foot off my back".[15] One result of this controversy is that in future issues Moore would feature the works and writings of both Annie Sprinkle and Karen Finley, and in issue #3 (1993) six pages and the cover are devoted to the work of Sprinkle, including also Veronica Vera's important *Post Porn Modernist Manifesto* (1989).[16]

Michael LaBash's Artworks

One vital and eye-catching feature of *The Cherotic (r)Evolutionary* are the illustrations that are featured in all the issues of the periodical by Michael LaBash. The artist was one of the intimates within the family group that formed around Frank Moore, and Moore always spoke very fondly of this indispensable member of the cherotic team. LaBash's drawings are powerful, humorous and slightly creepy works in which naked people couple and engage in all sorts of surreal ways. Hands and body parts couple with all sorts of real and imagined bodies, and their assorted orifices.

The first two issues of *The Cherotic (r)Evolutionary* feature LaBash's works on the front covers, with all subsequent issues featuring his works on the back covers, and they provide powerful visual equivalents to Moore's eroplay teachings.[17] LaBash's works are also found inside the periodical where they are published in a variety of page sizes, as well as being used as illustrations for different submissions. As one of the consistent features of the periodical they have a very powerful visual presence within the periodical, and they seem to merge with the periodical's larger project, becoming in the process visual talismans for the *cherotic (r)evolution.*

Frank Moore's Writings

It goes without saying that Moore's writings would form a key part of the periodical. Each issue includes an editorial by Moore about the contents of the current issue as well as other pertinent themes and subjects. There are three reviews by Moore of different printed matter publications, as well as his own writings which are represented by fourteen texts spread out over the life of the periodical.[18]

A good proportion of Moore's writings explain and expand upon his key concepts of the *cherotic (r)evolution* and eroplay. In "Nonlinear Bits" (#1, 1992) he writes that, "The cherotic revolution is an evolutionary movement, an anarchistic way of change, in which the single person is the center of the creative force". In the second issue he examines a theme central to his practice under the title "Cultural Subversion" (#2, 1992) and he recounts his rejection of politics as "...a means of effective subversive change..." and how this led him to begin "...looking towards art and magic for an effective channel". Coupled with this vantage point he describes how, as an artist with very limited funds, he became a "no/low tech artist," and the important role his access to this personal technology played in his work, stating, "This no/low tech form is vital to work which is culturally subversive by expanding the concept of sexuality and reality beyond the frame of taboos".

In another important text in issue #3 (1993) titled "Frank Moore's Philosophy of Art", he gives a very succinct account of his philosophy, writing, "I'm not interested in doing art that comforts, decorates, entertains...I'm trying to go back to the time when art was the magical, irrational, non-logical channel of active impact...". Further into this text Moore takes a personal turn when he writes, "In this kind of art, my body gives me a definite advantage. It links me to the wounded healer, the deformed shaman. By combining this with performance tactics, I combine realities to create awake dreams".

Other articles detail different aspects of his philosophy including a text on the importance of the open mike as a democratic channel ("A Rant On An Open Mike," #6, 1996), and with "Their Cuddling Cocoon" (#6, 1996) he describes the bodily sensations that are experienced during eroplay. Other articles deal with issues related to his practice, like ordinances regarding nudity in the town of Berkeley, the larger field of performance art, musings on the nature of fame, and an interview with his counter-cultural hero and journalist Paul Krassner, former editor of the *Realist* (#5, 1995).

A word that regularly appears in Moore's writings about his practice is the word "channel," and he uses it to describe his view that art and magic are important *channels* in assisting the individual in their personal evolution. I would like to propose expanding the use of this term to include Frank Moore's own physical body, as the indispensable *channel* through which he developed his unique philosophy of art, and accompanying performance practice. Furthermore, *The Cherotic (r)Evolutionary* can be understood as playing a very similar role in Moore's work, which is reflected in his editorial in #5 (1995) where he addresses his take on the functionality of the periodical, "i realize that i and this zine are just middlemen, just a pipe. when art goes through the pipe, that is when the pipe is important...not before or after".

Wrapping Up

After having been immersed in *The Cherotic (r)Evolutionary* over the past month, I have to conclude that the most extraordinary thing about this zine is, that it exists at all! With Moore's restricted mobility, it required a number of extra hands to design, publish and distribute the periodical, and this is what his dedicated family unit was able to provide him. However, the contents of the periodical were Moore's decision, and they reflect a savvy intelligence in propagating his philosophy, and teachings on the art and magic of living and loving. Despite his uncooperative body, Moore's sharp mind was laser-focused on achieving his *cherotic (r)evolution*, and the zine brims with this burning desire.

For the nine years of its life *The Cherotic (r)Evolutionary* would be a virtual home for Moore's "magical misfits", and it functioned exactly as he had hoped for in his first editorial in #0 (1991) as a place where this community could come together to "...give one another aid and comfort..."[19] and also to "...know that we are not alone, that there are others out/in here/there feeling, thinking, trying, doing similar things."[20]

A powerful theme that runs through all of Moore's writings and activities is that of 'communication,' and the zine would be one of the many channels, or media, through which he was able to satisfy his desire to be seen and heard. From the seventeen-year old who devised his own low-tech pointer communication device and breaks out of his own personal isolation, there was no holding him back. A key philosophical, and practical strategy was his appropriation of the new personal technologies, all of which would become key elements in his role as a 'no/low tech artist' who was committed to using this 'anarchistic technology' for his own cultural subversion.[21] A prime example of this approach was Moore's use of the photocopy machine to publish the entire run of *The Cherotic (r)Evolutionary*.

As I have noted earlier, Moore understood *The Cherotic (r)Evolutionary* as being a part of the advance guard of the Cherotic Movement, a movement which he likened to the Sexual Revolution of the 1960s. Within this larger context *The Cherotic (r)Evolutionary* can be seen as continuing the long-standing tradition of artists' periodicals that accompanied all the avant-garde movements of the 20th century, serving both as indispensable players in communicating avant-garde intentions, and in this case preparing the way for the *cherotic (r)evolution.*

The Cherotic (r)Evolutionary at its core, is about healing the body politic, about mending the "...fragmentation, isolation, personal helplessness..." of contemporary life and creating "...a more human, trusting, loving reality, full of fun and pleasure."[22] It is not without irony that the messenger, and teacher of this healing message, was someone whose own body was so severely disabled, and yet it was this same body that was the channel through which this "wounded healer...deformed shaman,"[23] would develop his profound philosophy in which *The Cherotic (r)Evolutionary* would function as one of the spear tips of the *cherotic (r)evolution.*

Footnotes

1. Moore, Frank, "Caves," Berkeley, 1987, no pagination.

2. For links to Moore's activities: http://www.eroplay.com/ for his videos: https://vimeo.com/channels/frankmoore/page:1
The *Cherotic (r)evolutionary* archive: http://www.eroplay.com/contents.html

3. Some basic information about the periodical. All nine issues were photocopied, with the first four issues printed in standard letter size and side stitched. The remaining five issues were photocopied in the tabloid size and then folded, and saddle stitched. The page numbers for each issue vary from 24 - 38, with an average of 31. The covers of the first four issues were photocopied onto different colored papers with the insides the traditional white. The covers for the last five issues were printed on tabloid size white card stock, and coupled with the saddle stitching, enhance the overall look and feel of the periodical.

   The first three issues (#0, 1991 - #2, 1992) were published by S/R Press (Luna and Kyle Griffith) and from #3 (1993) onwards it was published by Inter-Relations, which consisted of Frank Moore and Linda Mac as the publishers/editors. Print runs for #3 (1993) was 300 copies, and by #6 (1996) it was 500 per issue, and continued until the last issue #8 (1999). Extra copies of individual issues were printed on demand. There were a few paid subscribers, and coupled with the contributors the readers were from all over the world.

   Source for the above information was an email from Linda Mac (4.1.2019).

   Below is a listing of the issues and their publication dates.
   Vol. 1, #0, April 1991
   Vol. 1, #1, January 1992
   Vol. 1, #2, July 1992
   Vol. 1, #3, April 1993
   Vol. 1, #4, 1994
   Vol. 1, #5, October 1995
   Vol. 1, #6, July 1996
   Vol. 1, #7, May 1997
   Vol. 1, #8, April 1999

4. Moore, Frank in *The Cherotic Revolutionary,* Vol. 1, #0, 1991, p. 2.

5. Moore, Frank in *The Cherotic Revolutionary,* Vol. 1, #0, 1991, p. 2.

6. Moore, Frank in *The Cherotic Revolutionary,* Vol. 1, #0, 1991, p. 12.

7. Moore, Frank from his website (The Cherotic Revolutionary section), http://www.eroplay.com/tcr.html, accessed 3.22.19.

8. Moore, Frank, "Caves," Berkeley, 1987, p. 3.

9. Moore, Frank, Editorial, *The Cherotic Revolutionary*, Vol. 1, #1, 1992, p. 3.

10. In the interests of authorial integrity I should state that I had an article of mine published in the final issue of *The Cherotic (r)Evolutionary* (Vol. 1., #8, 1999) titled "Assembling Magazines," (1997).

11. Moore, Frank, Editorial, *The Cherotic Revolutionary*, Vol. 1, #3, 1993, p. 3.
It's interesting to note that further into this editorial Moore credits Kyle Griffith as the person "...who pushed for the publishing of the book [ed. note *Cherotic Magic*, 1990]...and then strongly suggested we come out with a zine."

12. Moore, Frank, Editorial, *The Cherotic (r)Evolutionary*, Vol. 1, #0, 1991, p. 2.

13. In an email from Linda Mac (4.1.2019) she recounts the larger story around the periodical's demise, writing:

    TCR was going strong when we stopped publishing it and we loved doing it! What stopped it was our starting LUVeR (Love Undergound Vision Radio, later changed to Love Underground Visionary (r)Evolution). And that is a story

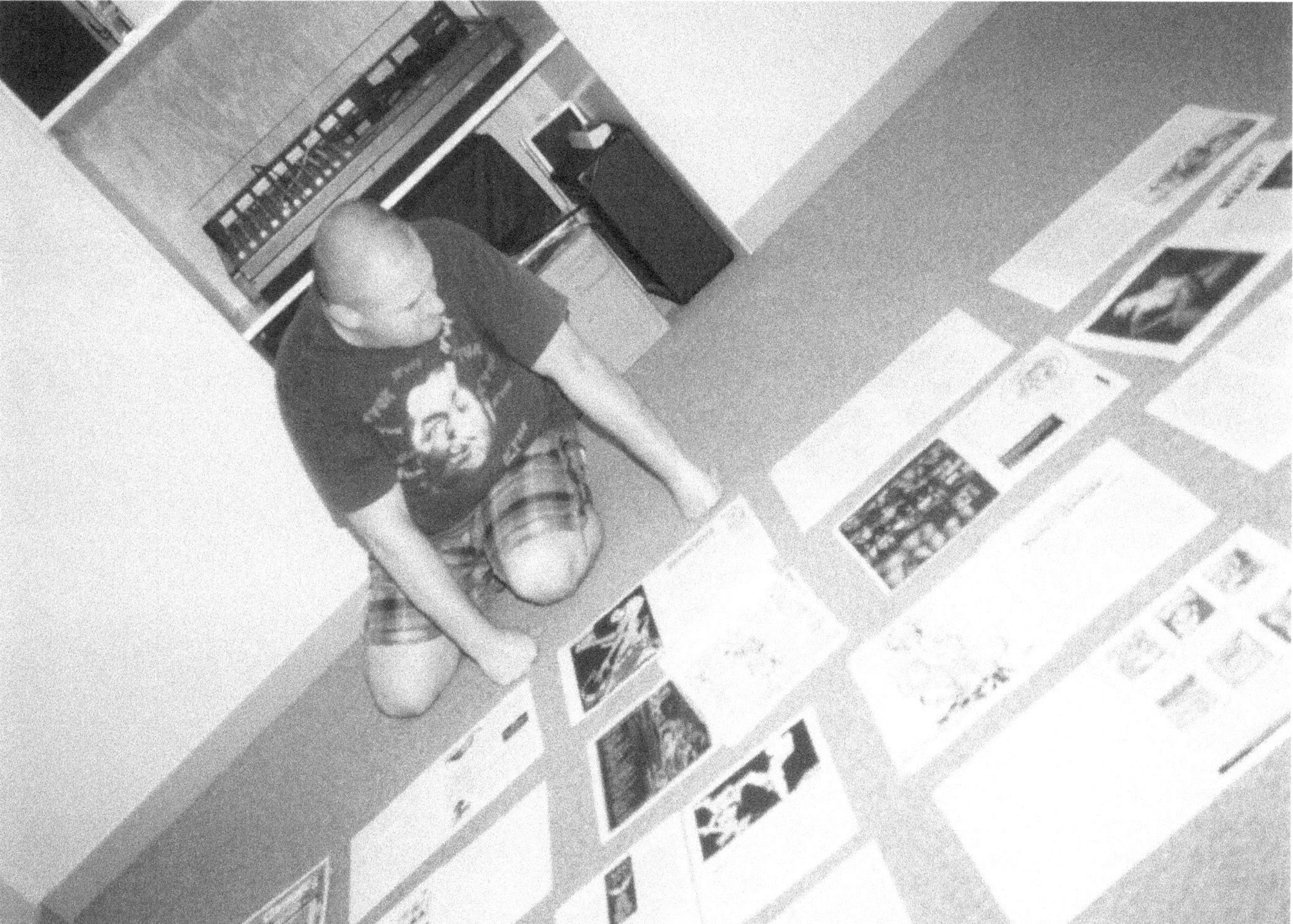

LaBash with layouts for issue #7 in 1997.

in itself! We were just too busy to do both, so we stopped doing TCR.

14. Moore, Frank, "An Open Letter to Sen. Jesse Helms," *The Cherotic (r)Evolutionary*, Vol. 1, #0, 1991, p. 24. Other artists attacked by Helms & Co. were: Holly Hughes, Tim Miller, John Fleck, Johanna Went and Cheri Gaulke.

15. Ibid., p. 24.

16. The text of Veronica Vera's *Post Porn Modernist Manifesto* (1989) is below:

    LET IT BE KNOWN to all who read these words or witness these events that a new awareness has come over the land. We of the POST PORN MODERNIST MOVEMENT face the challenge of the Rubber Age by acknowledging this moment in our personal sexual evolutions and in the sexual evolution of the planet.

    We embrace our genitals as part, not separate, from our spirits.
    We utilize sexually explicit words, pictures, and performances to communicate our ideas and emotions.
    We denounce sexual censorship as anti-art and inhuman.
    We empower ourselves by this attitude of sex-positivism.

    And with this love of our sexual selves we have fun, heal the world and endure.

17. One commentator on LaBash's works is Barbara Smith, and in her review of Moore's book *Cherotic Magic* in issue #0 (1991) she points out the discrepancy between Moore's definition of eroplay as an activity that does not lead to orgasm, and the fact that many of the figures in LaBash's works do indeed illustrate this kind of sexual activity. I too share this reservation, but within the broader reaches of what this periodical is about can reconcile their subject matter within Moore's larger philosophy.

18. Below is a listing of Frank Moore's writings in the periodical:

    Editorials
    One in each of the 9 issues

    Reviews
    #5, 1995: Annie Sprinkle's Post Porn Modernist
    #6, 1996: Barbara Golden Multimedia Package.
    #7, 1997: Tony Ryan Photobook.

Texts
#0, 1991: An open letter to Sen. Jesse Helms
#0, 1991: Museum of Lovemaking
#1, 1992: Nonlinear Bits
#2, 1992: Cultural Subversion
#3, 1993: Frank Moore's Philosophy of Art (1987)
#4, 1994: Tribal Performance (1992)
#5, 1995: Interview with Paul Krassner
#5, 1995: Magical Masks in dialogue with James Audlin (chief distant eagle)
#5, 1995: In Defense of Bad Art (1993)
#6, 1996: A Rant On An Open Mike (1995)
#6, 1996: Their Cuddling Cocoon (1995)
#7, 1997: Mainstream Avant-Garde (1996)
#8, 1999: What Price Fame? (1998) first published in Performance Journal #16, Spring 1998
#8, 1999: Out of Isolation (1986-1994) Insert in this issue as a small 8-page pamphlet.

19. Moore, Frank, Editorial, *The Cherotic Revolutionary*, Vol. 1, #0, 1991, p. 2.
20. Moore, Frank in *The Cherotic Revolutionary,* Vol. 1, #0, 1991, p. 2.

21. Throughout his career Moore worked in a wide variety of media including: radio, video, zine publishing, TV, performance art, writing, and he was a musician, painter and publisher of books.

22. Moore, Frank in *The Cherotic Revolutionary,* Vol. 1, #0, 1991, p. 2.

23. Moore, Frank in *The Cherotic Revolutionary,* Vol. 1, #0, 1991, p. 2.

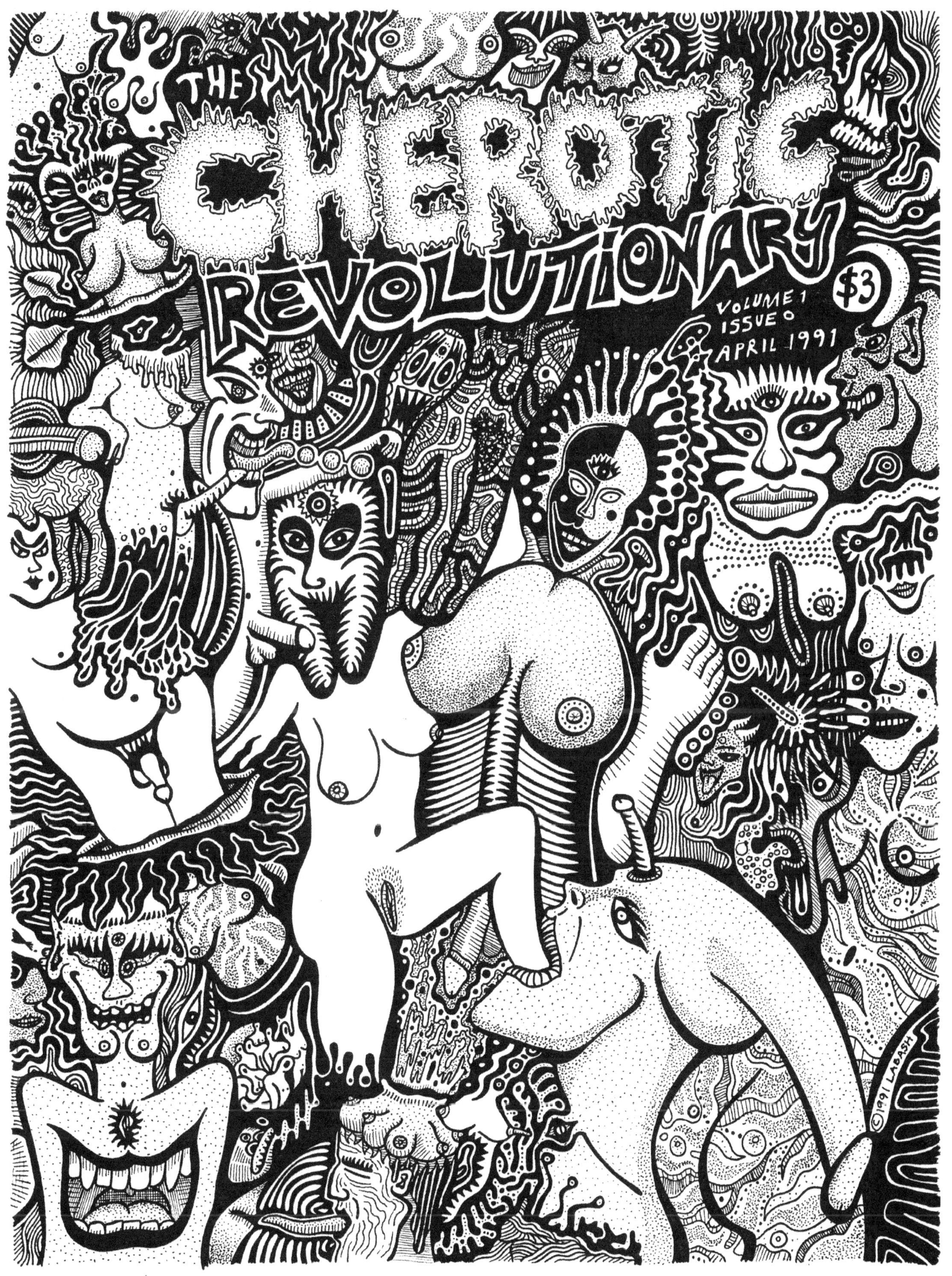
THE
EROTIC
REVOLUTIONARY
$3
VOLUME 1
ISSUE 0
APRIL 1991
©1991 LABASH

THE CHEROTIC REVOLUTIONARY #0 APRIL, 1991

TCR is edited by Frank Moore and Linda Mac, and published by Kyle and Luna Griffith. The art editor is Michael LaBash.

The price for this issue, and the next, TCR #1, is $3.00 per copy. We aren't taking subscriptions for more than one issue at a time, to avoid tying ourselves down to a rigid publication schedule or magazine size. We want to remain free to publish small issues frequently or larger issues at longer intervals and adjust the price accordingly, but each issue will announce the price of the next so readers can order it in advance.

We heartily encourage letters of comment from readers and will answer as many as we can. Please tell us if you don't want us to print material from your letter -- otherwise we will assume it's OK.

Please address all correspondence and orders for magazines to:

Frank Moore, P.O. Box 11445, Berkeley, CA 94701-2445

In This Issue ...

::

SPEAKING FRANKLY -- Editorial by FRANK MOORE -- April 10, 1991

At first look, this first issue of TCR looks like a shameless self-promotion, a big advertisement for my book, Cherotic Magic, for my apprenticeship, for my 6-session course, for my performance art and videos and tapes, and who knows what else. Well, you have to start somewhere. And that somewhere is the exploration of the magical edge I have been on for about 25 years. This promotion that we call TCR is a promotion of the edge itself.

Since Cherotic Magic was published, there has been a written dialog centering around the book. What is exciting about this dialog is that the people in the dialog are serious explorers of the edge themselves. They are writers, artists, publishers, cultural revolutionaries, reality subverters around the world. In this issue, under the cover of writing about my work, they talk about magical issues that I for one have been hungry to talk about for a long time in the depth that is possible with people who have committed their lives to going across the taboo border to effect evolutionary change. In future issues of TCR, I hope we will move far beyond the book, Cherotic Magic, and give one another aid and comfort on the edge by linking together, by announcing new findings of our hidden experiments of nonlinear change.

TCR is a journal of the edge. TCR is an offensive movement or measure, offering alternatives to the fragmentation, isolation, personal helplessness which is actively promoted by the combine of power systems. TCR is anarchical, based on the personal responsibility to reshape reality into a more human, trusting, loving reality, full of fun and pleasure. TCR is not a reaction. It is a magical act of enjoying life. It is a journal of and for people who are doing this magical act. Thanks to S/R Press, we finally have a channel of communications among the personal revolutions ... otherwise known as mutations ... which has always been the main fuel for evolution. Now we magical misfits know we are not alone, that there are others out/in here/there feeling, thinking, trying, doing similar things. This just by itself should speed evolution up.

Let me hear from you. Let us play together...

::

THE EDGE -- KYLE GRIFFITH -- April 13, 1991

I think another good name for the "edge" Frank is talking about is "creating free will." The "normal" state of consciousness for Earth people right now is one that traps them in a universe run much more by predestination than by free will. It doesn't matter if we identify the source of that predestination as the God of Saint Augustine and John Calvin or as B.F. Skinner's "operant conditioning by the social and physical environment," the result is still the same: a planet of sleep-walkers with very little control over their lives.

How can we break out of this trap of predestination and create free will for ourselves? My War in Heaven discusses some of the ways, Frank's Cherotic Magic describes a number of others, and TCR is being published to present still other approaches, by a wide variety of creative people, to this same "edge."

So ... welcome to the edge. Feel free to drop over any time ... but you'll find you won't fall ... you'll fly!

::

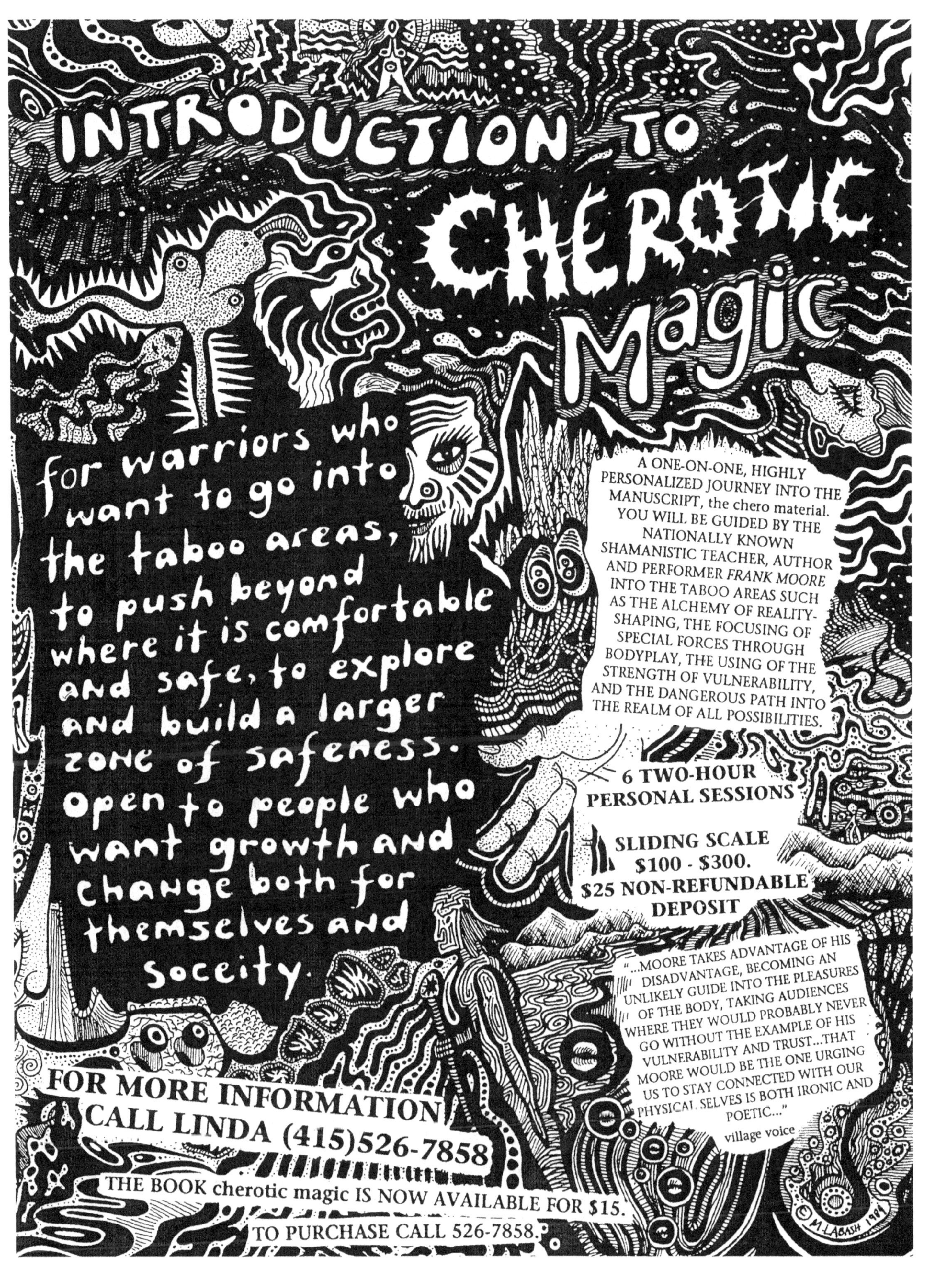
INTRODUCTION TO
CHEROTIC
Magic
for warriors who want to go into the taboo areas, to push beyond where it is comfortable and safe, to explore and build a larger zone of safeness. open to people who want growth and change both for themselves and soceity.
A ONE-ON-ONE, HIGHLY PERSONALIZED JOURNEY INTO THE MANUSCRIPT, the chero material. YOU WILL BE GUIDED BY THE NATIONALLY KNOWN SHAMANISTIC TEACHER, AUTHOR AND PERFORMER FRANK MOORE INTO THE TABOO AREAS SUCH AS THE ALCHEMY OF REALITY-SHAPING, THE FOCUSING OF SPECIAL FORCES THROUGH BODYPLAY, THE USING OF THE STRENGTH OF VULNERABILITY, AND THE DANGEROUS PATH INTO THE REALM OF ALL POSSIBILITIES.
6 TWO-HOUR PERSONAL SESSIONS
SLIDING SCALE $100 - $300. $25 NON-REFUNDABLE DEPOSIT
"...MOORE TAKES ADVANTAGE OF HIS DISADVANTAGE, BECOMING AN UNLIKELY GUIDE INTO THE PLEASURES OF THE BODY, TAKING AUDIENCES WHERE THEY WOULD PROBABLY NEVER GO WITHOUT THE EXAMPLE OF HIS VULNERABILITY AND TRUST...THAT MOORE WOULD BE THE ONE URGING US TO STAY CONNECTED WITH OUR PHYSICAL SELVES IS BOTH IRONIC AND POETIC..."
village voice
FOR MORE INFORMATION CALL LINDA (415)526-7858
THE BOOK cherotic magic IS NOW AVAILABLE FOR $15.
TO PURCHASE CALL 526-7858.
© M. LABASH 1989

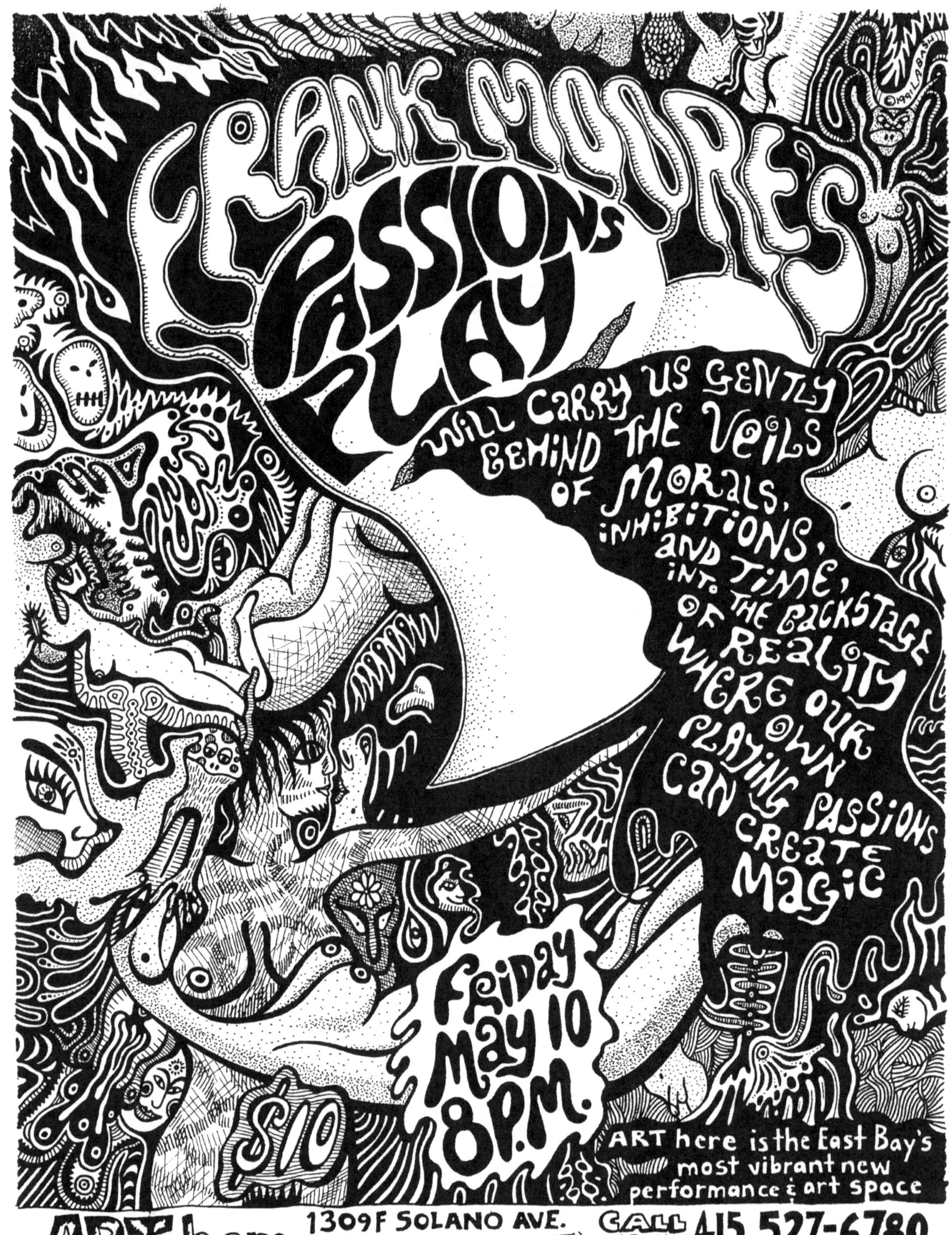

FRANK MOORE'S
PASSION PLAY
WILL CARRY US GENTLY BEHIND THE VEILS OF MORALS, INHIBITIONS, AND TIME, INTO THE BACKSTAGE OF REALITY WHERE OUR OWN PLAYING PASSIONS CAN CREATE MAGIC
FRIDAY MAY 10 8 P.M.
$10
ART here is the East Bay's most vibrant new performance & art space
ART here
1309F SOLANO AVE. (near POMONA AVE.)
ALBANY, CA (near BERKELEY)
CALL FOR INFO 415.527-6780
TICKETS SOLD IN ADVANCE

::

FORWARD TO FORUM 25 YEARS CELEBRATION COMPILATION, by TUPPY OWENS

Thank goodness for Forum! It's the haven where sexually aware people can turn to when they need to be comforted that they are not alone. This is especially true for people with special tastes -- if you buy Forum, you'll never feel odd again! Somehow, Forum combines responsibility with fun, so that, not only does it make you feel OK about your sexuality, you also get cheered up.

Forum has served this purpose for 25 years. It is as important now as ever before because nothing has really improved in the world out there. Ignorance and hypocrisy still reign. I can't believe that a recent issue of a popular British trendy fashion/feature magazine has 35 pages devoted to sex which are crammed with uptight values, inaccuracies, myths and cliches. Written by fashion writers and other young know-alls, these pages will confuse thousands of young minds that are already getting so many mixed messages about sex, porn, and morality that they hold no hope of ever sorting things out for themselves.

One of the things I like about Forum is that it's so incredibly British. Eccentric yet down to earth. Unlike those trendy magazines that are heavily influenced by American culture and have international aspirations, Forum is about every-day British folk and what they get up to in their bedrooms, and under the desk at work, etc. And, as every issue proves, there's always something new and fascinating about sex. How lucky we are that the most enjoyable subject on earth is also the most boundless.

But what of the NEXT 25 years? It's interesting to note that all the staff on Forum have been female for the past five years and this fits in with a trend that I have been aware of for some long time and has now been defined by a friend of mine, Frank Moore (an American -- see what a hypocrite I am?). He calls it the cherotic movement. This is not unlike the so-called sexual revolution of the sixties, but a physical/spiritual movement that redefines and expands sexual, spiritual, social concepts of reality, and it is being initiated by strong lusty women. Many anarchistic teenagers are looking to these women as role models, something both I and female Forum editors are experiencing right now. Young students are wanting guidance on their college theses, chosen topics being deep, meaningful aspects of sex.

This cherotic movement is quite new. After the 'free-love' sixties, ambition for success and consumerism took over, feminism became aggressive, people became repressed and shallow again. Let's hope the movement will grow into a whole new inspiration for humanity so that pleasure will, once again, become the prime reason for existence.

Forum will then become more adventurous, as young people put their energies into writing imaginative erotica and sharing experiences. They will revitalise the spirits of the rest of us as we sag in our fight through this age of AIDS and censorship. We certainly have lived through the toughest era of all -- no sooner did we find hope for freedom in the sixties as it was whisked from under our feet. Even Forum is not free to publish anything they wish. But the young can DEMAND freedom, and will. Madonna and most young bands are a great inspiration for them to assert their sexuality, yuppy parents offer an ideal reason to rebel.

We should be all set for the Cherotic Revolution! Rave on, readers, rave on.

::

THE CHICAGO NEWS & ARTS WEEKLY • FREE • OCTOBER 11 - OCTOBER 17, 1990

NEWCITY

WANTED!

THE NEW BARBARIANS

Alias (Art Outlaws, Performance Artists)

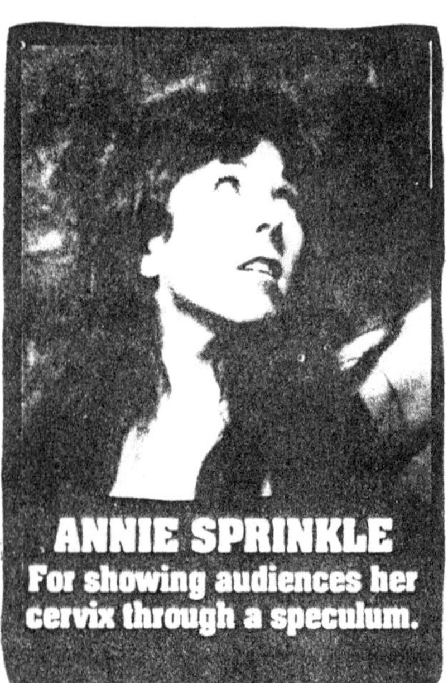

ANNIE SPRINKLE
For showing audiences her cervix through a speculum.

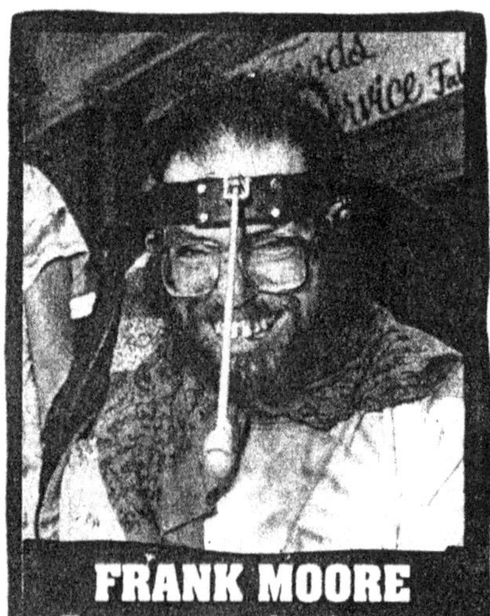

FRANK MOORE
For encouraging intense physical touching between adults.

Photo/ Steve D. Arazmus

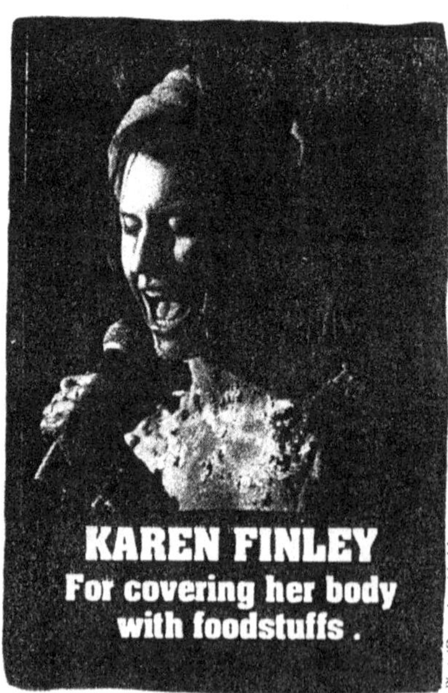

KAREN FINLEY
For covering her body with foodstuffs .

Photo/Dona Ann McAdams

Film Fest Guide • A Band Of Farmers • Now Weekly!

COVER STORY

OUTLAW ARTISTS

Porn? Play? Or Immoral Plot?

Story by JACK HELBIG

To conservative art critic Hilton Kramer, they are the "New Barbarians...licensed rebels at the taxpayers' expense." To Jesse Helms' rally Rep. Dana Rohrbacher (R-Calif.), they are a threat to the established moral order. They are the NEA outlaws, controversial artists the conservatives would dearly love to silence. Three of these outlaw artists — Karen Finley, Frank Moore and Annie Sprinkle — will be performing in Chicago this month.

Of the three, Karen Finley is by now the best known, thanks in part to NEA Chairman John Frohnmayer's awkward defunding of her work, and in part to conservative columnists Evans and Novak who labeled her as "the chocolate-covered woman." (One wonders what they'd be calling her, if the right wing had been hip to Finley when she was performing "Yams Up My Grandma's Ass.")

Her fame has come quickly. Less than a year ago, only the alternative press followed Finley. Even when her shows at the Edge of the Lookingglass sold out every night, the dailies hardly noted her presence in town. Now on her triumphant return (for a four-week run at The Beacon Street Gallery), after a summer's worth of press (over)-exposure, she has received long stories in *Chicago Tribune* and *Chicago* magazine.

Frank Moore and Annie Sprinkle are unlikely to receive such coverage. For one, both artists' work resists the easy and superficial descriptions that Finley's work had always attracted. Even Sprinkle's bit in which the audience is invited to take a peek at Sprinkle's cervix through a speculum is too gross to inspire, on retelling, the sort of ironic "oh yeah?" grins that Finley's bits involving covering her body with this, that or the other foodstuff do.

For another, both Moore's and Sprinkle's work challenge the consensus view more strongly and in ways less acceptable than Karen Finley's angry tirades and bitter attacks on consumer culture (whose time has come). Sprinkle's sexually provocative performances, involving sex toys, onstage masturbation, and parodies of oral sex involving rubber dildos, have provoked attacks by both the right and the left (feminists of the Andrea Dworkin variety), neither of whom see much difference between real pornography and Sprinkle's "Post-Porn" deconstructions of the genre.

As an admitted former prostitute and porn star, Annie Sprinkle's world view seems tremendously at odds with an increasingly hung-up America. Even the Post-Porn Manifesto, written by fellow performance artist Veronica Vera and signed by Sprinkle in large John Hancockish script, seems like a relic from the pre-AIDs sexual liberality of the late '70s.

Topped by two erect penises saluting an open vagina, the manifesto reads: "We of the POST-PORN MODERNIST MOVE-MENT... celebrate sex as the nourishing life-giving force. We embrace our genitals as part, not separate, from our spirits. We utilize sexually explicit words, pictures and performances to communicate our ideas and emotions. We denounce sexual censorship as anti-art and inhuman...And in this love of our sexual selves we have fun, heal the world and endure."

No wonder Rep. Rohrbacher, anxious to find the artist who could do for him what Mapplethorpe did for Sen. Helms, thought Annie Sprinkle an easy target. In February of this year, he launched his attack on the "feminist porn activist" by telling the House of Representatives that Sprinkle was "the recipient of taxpayer funds for her live sex act show in New York." "Actually," wrote C. Carr in *Village Voice*, "she has never received or applied for a grant of any kind. ...Neither did she perform a 'live sex act.'"

It seems Rep. Rohrbacher based

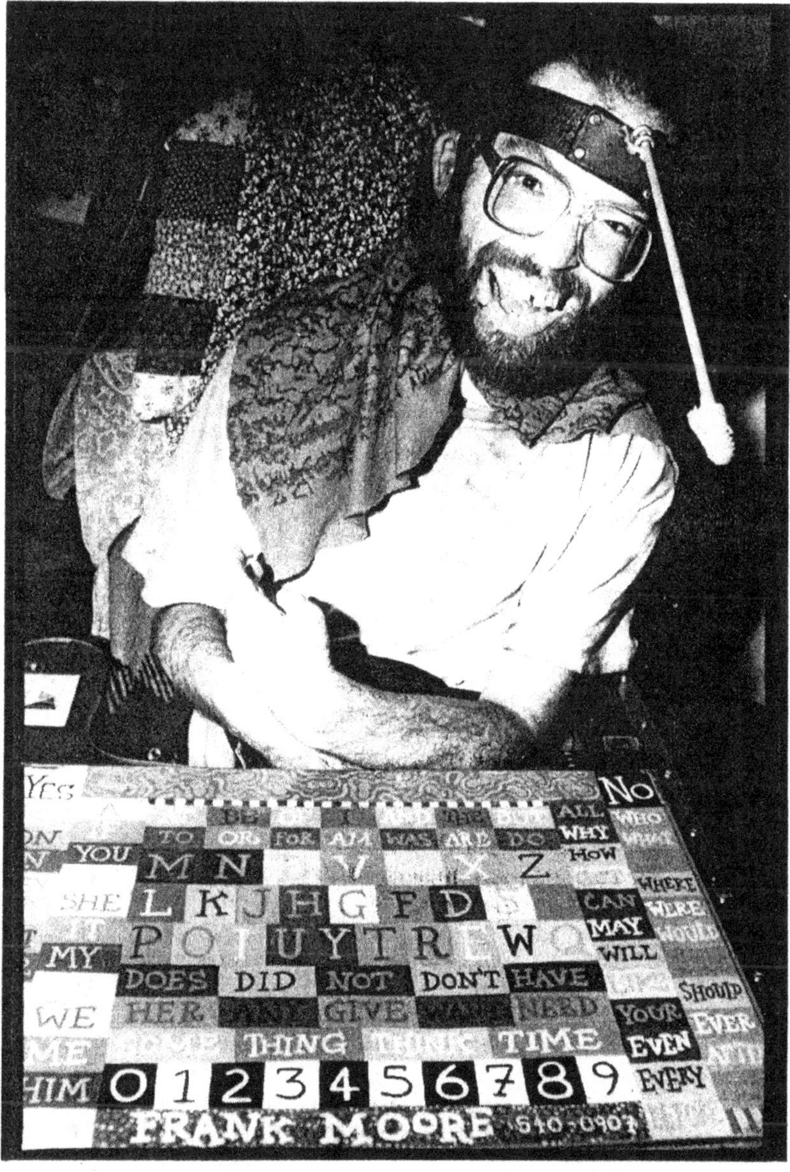

Photo/ Steve D. Arazmus

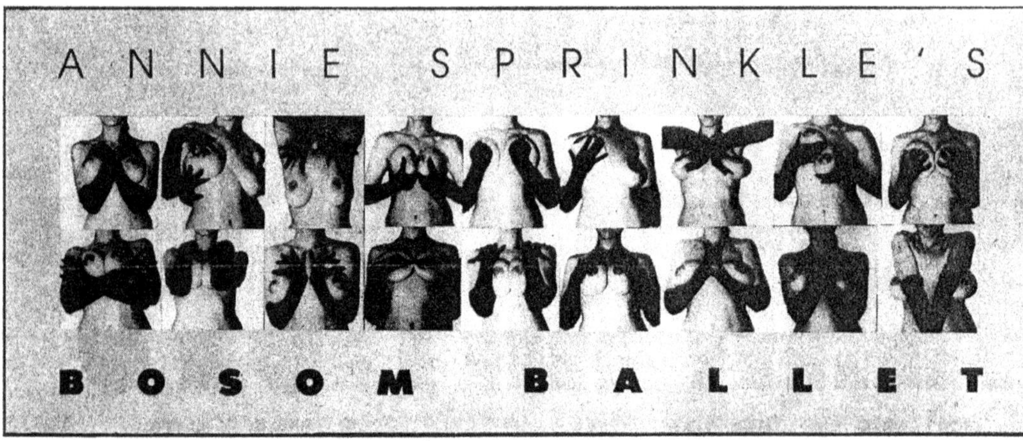

"If this community doesn't want me to... have an orgasm from breathing on stage, I'm not going to rub it in their faces."

his whole attack on Sprinkle articles published in the ultra-conservative *New York City Tribune* and the supermarket tabloid *National Enquirer*. *National Enquirer* proved to be an especially dubious source for information, since it based its allegation that Sprinkle had received NEA funding for her work on a one-liner Sprinkle quipped in the middle of her performance: "Usually I get paid a lot of money for this, but tonight it's government funded." Sprinkle, it turns out, was just joking.

However, the fact that his accusations were baseless didn't keep Rohrbacher from, again in the words of C. Carr, "sending a letter headlined: The National Endowment for the Arts Is At It Again! to every member of the House, describing Sprinkle's show" in detail. Nor did it keep John Frohnmayer from leaping into the fray and issuing the odd statement that "if the performance by Ms. Sprinkle was accurately described in recent media reports, then it is something that would not have been funded by the Endowment."

When asked about Rohrbacher's attack, Sprinkle's reaction is surprising. "I refuse to let anyone make me a victim, " she says in a surprisingly girlish and innocent voice, "especially people like that... these people like Jesse Helms have only heard about what I do. They're totally misinformed... They just have no idea what my work is really like, or what its about. But that's okay. I'm really happy with the way things are moving along. I'm really, really much more appreciated here in Europe. I get 100 times more money. A hundred times more offers. The people who don't see [my work], don't understand performance art, don't see sexuality anywhere near the way I see it, they have a problem [with my work]."

Post Porn Modernist Manifesto

I asked Sprinkle if Rohrbacher's attack had in any way affected where she can perform. Sprinkle denied that it had, mentioning only that she had gotten "a lot of publicity" but still had been able to do her show unimpeded. However, half way through her denial she remembered one incident on her recent tour. "So I don't feel—uh, in Cleveland, Ohio, there were police in the audience who would've arrested me," if Sprinkle had invited the audience to take a peek at her cervix. "So there was a blatant case of censorship. But I think there *is* a such thing as community standards. If this community doesn't want me to..." Sprinkle pauses as if unsure how I'm going to take what she's about to say, and then continues speaking a little too quickly, "have an orgasm from breathing on stage, I'm not going to rub it in their faces. I go where I'm appreciated and wanted. And it's fine with me that there are states and cities and people who don't want to see what I do....I don't see it as them against me. I see it as we are all one, and I love them, and its all quite perfect, you know?"

Sprinkle's laissez-faire attitude about the right wing's attacks on her art is in marked contrast to her buddy Frank Moore's reaction, who is absolutely livid about the treatment he's received lately by Helms and Company. "If you have anything to say to me or to ask me," Moore wrote in an open letter to Helms, published in *High Performance* magazine, "come to talk to me man to man. Otherwise, get your big brother foot off my back."

Of course, Helms' campaign against Moore has been considerably more subtle than Rohrbacher's blatant, baseless, and almost farcical assault on Annie Sprinkle. It seems that, according to *Los Angeles Times*, Helms demanded that the General Accounting Office inquire into the work of four performance artists: Karen Finley, Frank Moore, Johanna Went and Cheri Gaulke. As part of the GAO's investigation, the GAO "sent letters to the Franklin Furnace and the Kitchen (two of New York City's most prominent alternative performance spaces) formally requesting information on appearances since 1984 by these four artists.

This was not the first time that Finley, Moore, Went and Gaulke had found their very different works lumped together. Around the same time that Rohrbacher was accusing Sprinkle of the misuse of public funds, *New York City Tribune* (which is, itself, funded by Rev. Moon's Unification Church) began a series investigating the "obscene" art of, that's right, Finley, Moore, Went, and Gaulke.

The connection between Rohrbacher and *New York City Tribune* is well documented; Rohrbacher's press secretary David Eisner, admitted they had gathered information about Sprinkle from the *Tribune*. And the connection between the *Tribune* articles and the Helms' requested GAO investigation is clear.

Still, Frank Moore would seem an odd choice for Helms to pick on. Born with cerebral palsy, Frank Moore is not only wheelchair bound, he is also unable to control his arms or legs and incapable of making any sound except a kind of howling yelp. It is Frank Moore's conviction that Sen. Helms just plain doesn't know he's a disabled artist. (A fact the *New York City Tribune* article on Moore also failed to mention.) Which is why Moore is so anxious to meet Helms "man to man."

After all, Moore *can* communicate. Thanks in part to a device Moore developed when he was a teenager that allows him to paint, operate a personal computer, or, during interviews, spell out what he wants to say one letter at a time.

We start off talking about whether being on Helms' list hurt bookings for Frank Moore's performances. Moore spells out the answer: "They have closed Franklin Furnace." Linda Mac, long-time companion and fellow performer adds, "The [New York] Fire Department closed down the performance space and said it was not up to standards. So galleries are reluctant to book us because they see what happened to Franklin Furnace and they see what's happening to the Kitchen and they don't want to have to go through that."

Frank adds, "except clubs like Lower Links. I am lucky. I always have done grassroots—" "Galleries," Linda Mac pipes in, "Is that right?"

Frank grins his toothy grin and yelps.

Mac continues: "Places that don't get NEA money. In Seattle we performed at a place — A.F.L.N.(A Flimsy Lace Nightie) — that pays its bills by selling coffee and toast during the day. On the one hand we don't make very much money. But we always have places to perform."

What could Moore have done to bring down the wrath of Helms? Certainly, Helms can't be upset about "The Outrageous Horror Show" (which Frank and his troupe will perform at Lower Links). In this show, Moore confronts the audience by "singing" (howling, really) a number of rock standards "for one or two hours." "Moore jokes, "Maybe Helms doesn't like my singing."

Frank Moore suspects that it is "Eroplay," a form of performance he has developed, involving "intense physical touching between adults without limits but is non-sexual." Often performed nude, and involving audience participation, it has been described by Moore in the Spring 1989 *Drama Review* as being "fun...innocent and childlike!" Unfortunately, just how innocent Eroplay seems depends upon your definition of innocence. Certainly, anyone hoping to find obscene art could call Eroplay obscene. "In my work," Moore writes in the same essay, "I always have used nudity and physical acts which most people would call sexual." Though Moore makes the point that "Eroplay is a safe, fun, lusty, channel for physical touching" which does not lead to "physical intercourse," many of the photos of Eroplay in performance could pass for group grope sessions.

The question of obscenity, however, is just a smokescreen, Moore believes. In his essay, "The Combine Plot," (published in the current issue of *P-Form*), Moore argues that "The real goal of Helms' and Rohrbacher's attacks is to make all art, not just the N.E.A.-funded art, the agent for the established order, to deball art, to tame down all art. ...The message is clear: eliminate controversial, experimental, and avant-garde art."

(Karen Finley will be performing "We Keep Our Victims Ready" at Beacon Street Gallery, 361-3500, Fridays, Saturdays and Sundays, October 5-28 at 8. Frank Moore will perform his "Outrageous Horror Show" at Club Lower Links, Thursday, October 11, at 7. Annie Sprinkle's "Sex Education Class" will take place at Club Lower Links, Saturday, October 20, at 7 and 9. To make reservations for Frank Moore and Annie Sprinkle call 248-5238)

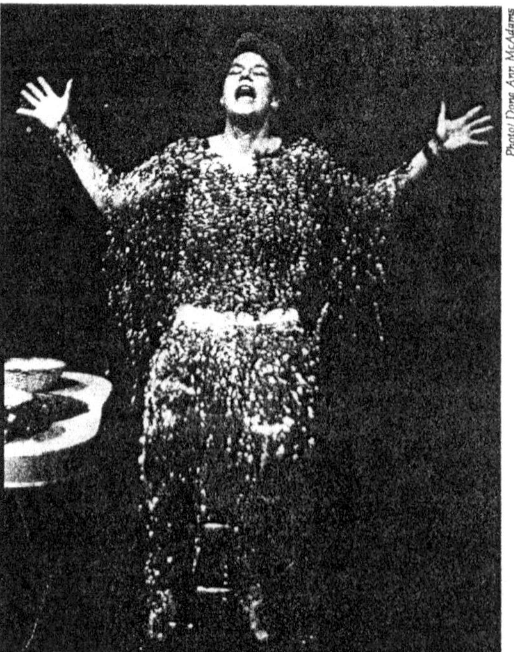
Photo/ Dona Ann McAdams

Karen Finley

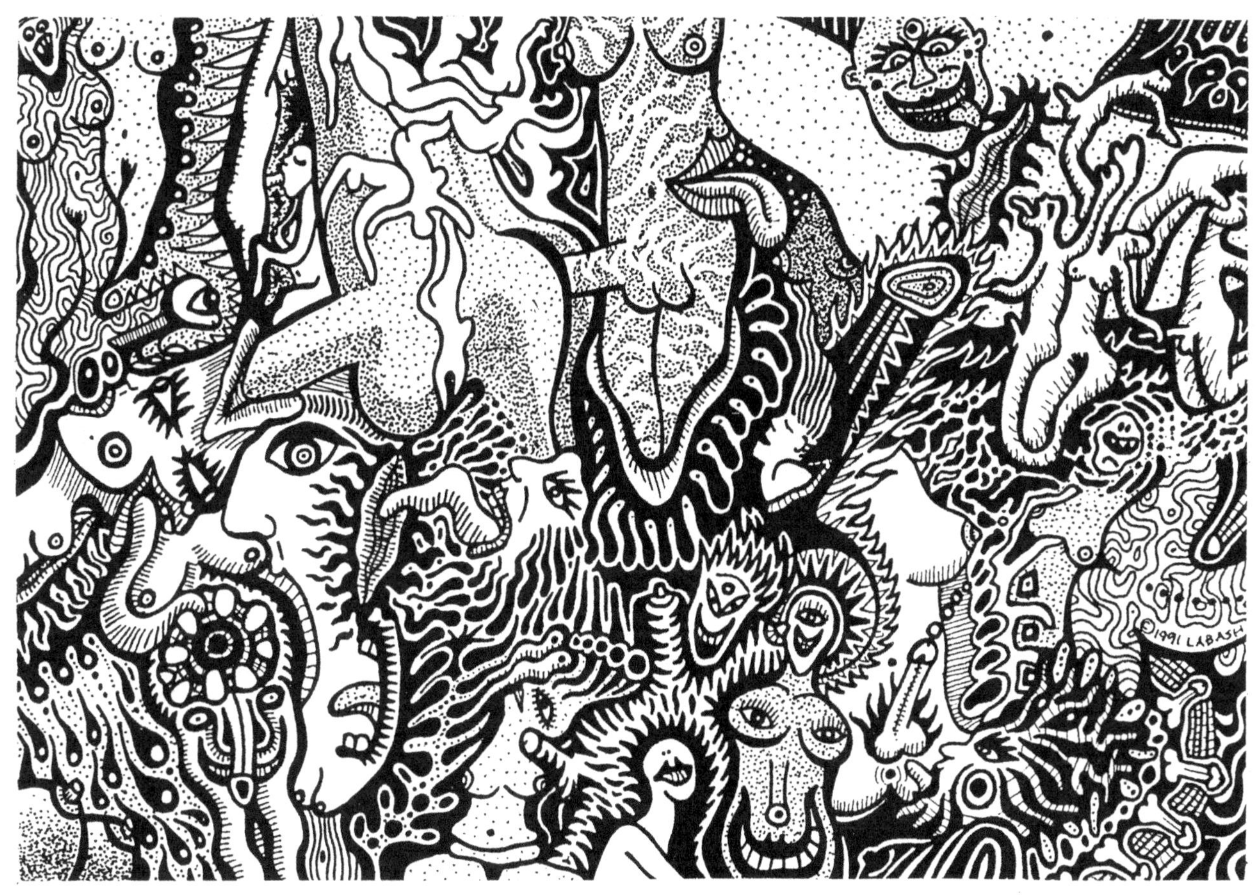

MUSEUM OF LOVE-MAKING -- FRANK MOORE

Imagine. Imagine walking down the sidewalk and seeing on a poster nude bodies melting into one another, floating into one another in a soft sea of passions unlimited, cock trees growing out of cunt pots, tit eyes laughing gently as the navel is sucking the whole universe off. You wonder why the cops, or some feminist moralist, or some born-again right-to-suffer TV watcher hasn't long ago ripped down this offense to the moral order.

You look more closely at the liquid moving bodies, and dancing letters are squeezed out from the twisting forms. You make out that you are invited tonight to "The Museum of Love-Making," whatever that is. Must be some performance art shit. You have gone to performances that promise to be about sex, to be passionately erotic, but when you got there, pale faces in black tights talked in mono-drones about isolation, about fathers' hidden lustings after two-year-olds of both sexes ... with nudity, human touching, sweating passion never even in sight, let alone explicit. But this poster again arouses hope. In the back of your mind, there is another handout saying "For Madmen Only."

Imagine. Imagine standing in front of a multi-colored curtain in a gallery, standing, waiting, standing with people who, like yourself, do not know what to expect. You hear classical music playing softly somewhere. Now three nudes, fully brightly soft body-painted, appear from the curtain. They chant instructions: "No talking, stay on this side of the rope, but you can walk to any point in the observing area at any time."

Now you are being ushered by the nudes behind the curtain of taboos. You find yourself holding onto a plush red rope. This rope runs around the entire large room. In front of you, behind the rope, a couple sits on a mat in warm soft light. They are kissing, not dramatic, but like they have been kissing each other for years.

You read the card pinned to the rope: "Mary and Roger Smith have been married for fifteen years. Both are teachers. They have two children."

Only now you realize that they are an older couple, that Mary is unzipping his pants to rub his limp wrinkled cock. They are giggling like kids watching cartoons. You try to look away uncomfortable, seeing something too private. But as you look around the room, you see couples, maybe a triad or two, on mats making love. You look back to Roger and Mary, her panties are now off. He is fingering her pink lips' greying blonde hair. You can see right up her into darkness. Still no dramatics, no contest of performance, just warm sex pleasure of years of love-making.

You move on, coming to Gil, a lawyer, and Henry, a househusband ... a couple of eight years. Gill is slowly moving back and forth in Henry's butt. Henry makes loud dramatic sighs. Meanwhile, an old woman sucks off her young black lover of three years. On another mat, two sweating nudes eat deep from each other's sweet pussies. Across the room, you see a hanging woman moaning orgasms as her husband of eight years whips her lovingly with a cat-of-nine-tails. A beautiful Chinese woman puts her spastic mate deep within her. The sounds, the human smells of sex and sweat, the sight of all of these real moving touching playing fucking in their own love relationships creates an overwhelming alternative reality which reclaims sex in all its forms as a direct expression of life and love.

This is the performance I am planning to do. Although I have used nudity and eroticism in my work, I have never before used actual sex. The time is right to do so. Magically and politically, this performance will send a powerful message. The fundamentalists, whether feminist or Christian or political, have attacked sex with smokescreens of violent, abusive, exploitative sex. They say they are not against sex itself, just... This performance will expose this as a baldface lie.

I am looking for all types of loving couples (triads, whatever) to be in this piece. All races and ages are welcome. I first plan to stage it in the Bay Area, but then across the country. So I will need couples in each city.

We have some arbitrary frameworks. A couple has to have been together committed for at least a year. Each person has to be 18 or older. There is no money involved. Interested couples should write me a letter describing your relationship and telling why you want to be a part of this magical explicit performance. My address is:

Frank Moore
PO Box 11445
Berkeley, CA 94701-2445

I also need women for other performances.

::

::
BRENDA TATELBAUM to FRANK -- January 15, 1991

Today's mail brought me your marvelous "Museum of Love-Making" which will appear in V5 #4 (late Spring '91) along with the review of Cherotic Magic. As you know, Kyle sent me a copy and in my letter of thanks to him I asked he forward any already-written reviews to me for my file. Please don't worry about what the review will say because I'm inviting you to send a review written by a reviewer of your choice. Should this be impossible, I'll do the accolades myself. Please let me know if you'll be forwarding one to my attention.

On pg. 81 you accurately state "It is fashionable to be anti-porn. But it is not fashionable to offer an alternative to porn." So let me thank you for saying in your letter that you respect what Eidos is attempting to accomplish. According to our worldview, it's a perversion to malign advocating sexual freedom (by defending human, civil and constitutional rights) for traditionally persecuted and oppressed consenting adult sexual minorities of all orientation, preferences and lifestyles. Our traditional church/state sanctioned paradigm of married heterosexual penile/vaginal procreative intercourse is the underlying cause of our culture's supremacist erotophobic aparthied. Eidos' mission militantly affirms sexual pluralism: the freedom to choose in all areas of sexual life & lifestyle.

I also agree with you that the performance of "The Museum of Love-Making" will be your most controversial and I look forward to our continued correspondence.

....
FRANK to BRENDA TATELBAUM -- January 31, 1991

I would be excited and honored about you writing the review...mainly because I am looking forward to reading in detail about what you think of Cherotic Magic. As yet, we have not received other reviews, except the one Kyle wrote. But he is my publisher, so if it was not glowing, he would not have published the book in the first place.

I have started getting letters from readers. They say they feel like they had written the book. They also say the book scares them because it rings true and that is putting pressure on them to change their life. I take these reactions as high praise.

I will be interested in the response to "The Museum of Love-making" in Eidos. I have noticed in the past five years women have gotten fearful and timid again. I get readings of this from who comes into my work. For example, last week we were on a 6-hour radio show with Kyle and Luna, then did a 24-hour performance. Not one woman called in to the radio. Just one woman called about the performance, and she just wanted to argue about the ratio of cocks to tits/pussies in the poster. Have you seen this trend? I wonder how this will effect the couples answering the call for the "Museum."

In the mid-70's, I got more women then men. I think it was because of the freeing exploring spirit of the early feminist movement which came out of the '60's. Men took a few years to catch up to the liberation. Then I a got pretty equal men-women ratio. But then the anti-sex, anti-men, abuse-paranoia, women getting seduced by the yang Western view of success...rather than pulling the reality into balance toward the Yin by using their bodies, sex, taboo-breaking subversion. Feminism, in other words, became enfolded in the very repressive power structure that it was fighting. As a result, most women are, under the illusion of freedom, more suppressed and repressed now. And the men who had shown signs of being liberated are getting shallow again.

I think it is very important that there be a Cherotic Movement, not unlike the so-called Sexual Revolution of the Sixties. This Cherotic Movement would be (or rather, is) a physical/spiritual movement that re-defines and expands sexual, spiritual, social concepts of reality.

There is a powerful group of strong lusty women who are, or at least could be, cherotic role models. These include people like yourself, Annie Sprinkle. Veronica Vera, Linda and Luna from here, Karen Finley and a few other female artists, Tuppy Owens in England. Except for Kyle and myself, I do not see a similar group of male cherotic role-models.

I do see a beginning of an anarchist movement within the teens and the early twenty-year-olds that is ripe for the Cherotic movement. They do use us as linear role models and, more importantly, as their nonlinear pathbreakers. But there has been little concrete intimate intercourse between these two erotic evolutionary groups. Between these two-groups, there is the black hole of scared yang-brainwashed women and male bunny rabbits who do not know what to do with their new yin liberation.

This will be what we will be working with in the '90's. What a challenge!

....

BRENDA TATELBAUM to FRANK -- February 7. 1991

Thanks for your 1/31 letter, I agree with you that feminism had become "enfolded in the very repressive power structure that it was fighting." As you know, feminism is not monolithic; yet only the most stridently vocal anti-porn, anti-sex, pro-censorship male-hating feminist voices were heard nationwide during the '80's. Unless liberal, humanist, pro-sex feminists like myself are attacked by the forces of suppression, we remain virtually invisible: deliberately ignored or systematically muzzled.

I believe the feminist backlash against the sexual liberalism of the 60s & 70s borders on panic based on a simplistic dogma that all male sexuality is rape and abuse. Their ideologically politically-correct fascistic "band-aid" remedy calls for restrictions (censorship) of male-created/oriented fantasy material, including art, erotica, porn, advertising, etc.: an attempt to control, dominate & destroy male sexuality. Playing the victim has empowered & emboldened them, whereas in the past they were silenced.

Now women like me find it difficult to publicly articulate or address the concept of female (human) sexual autonomy and female (human) sexual pleasure as distinctly separate from criminal acts of violent sexual abuse. In my opinion, domineering anti-porn feminists undermine the battle for reproductive freedom by undercutting the battle for sexual freedom: they deny other women their right to even publish intimate depictions of pleasurable consensual adult sexual expression which plays to the religious right's dogma that female/feminists like me are no better than adulterers and child molesters.

In effect, they're aiding the religious right's attempts to idealize the family, domesticity and concept of separate spheres for men & women based on biology and traditional religious & cultural restraints. Some pioneering feminists from the last century advocated a vision of sexuality for men and women alike which included spiritual, intellectual and physical planes. Perhaps their worst nightmares are coming true: that a complex feminist ideology has come under the control of "sexually deficient or disappointed women impervious to facts and logic and deeply ignorant about life" (Stella Brown in the 1912 edition of "The Freewoman").

By the way, I wear a yang/yin around my neck. I believe anti-porn feminists simply trash all yang.

::

BRENDA MCCANN to FRANK & LINDA, February 26, 1991

Well, I must say, your flyer to recruit committed couples certainly "pushed my taboo buttons." But ... your points are well made. The whole case that I've carried against "male barbarians" came up in wrath-reaction to the buzzwords used in the descriptive pitch. The only one I liked was "sacred dark." ("How dare a man to ejaculate in my sacred dark, like spit upon a sidewalk.") Also, I was angered that anyone could deduce my being "against sex itself" when it is middle-class male sexual fantasy projections upon any female that I am against.

On the other hand, the girl/child/soul-projection of me longed to see or behold the loving committed mature couples role modeling mature human love including their sexual relations. I cried and cried to receive that. I almost feel like I've already gotten the experience just from taking in all the images in the flyer. For me, it was like being there already. It's like I got a whole room full of new parents.

So, how it all turned out is, for whatever reasons, I discovered in retrospect that I really was (programmed) against sex. A "wrongness" rapport, there. And the vision of that many mature couples doing a free-flowing wonderful joyous sex dance together had never before occurred to me. Then I put together the idea of the trust factor necessary to complete (in the cave of apprenticeship) the polarity production and decided that there is no better place to put it into practice than in the "cave of sacred dark." Suddenly there is less and less fear in me concerning rampant imagination during any kind of relationship.

....

BRENDA MCCANN to KYLE & LUNA, April 8, 1991

Well, the Gods of Balance and other Elo(K)hims have helped me survive my own imaginations about **Cherotic Magic** and "The Flier." It all turns out to be a great and necessary process for the likes to me to even conceive of such images as the flier gives.

Instead of the cave of Lila I went with the cave of Zardoz -- you know, the one where you realize that the cave is really just you inside a crystal with all your own images reflecting back at you.

I'm so happy to have gotten a little contact with Frank and Linda (and Ted & Alice, Fred & Carol, etc.)! I cleared my sacred dark of middle class ejaculation spit, not to mention a barbarian and a foggy image of Nostradamas (representing my beliefs and other fears in his infernal qua(si)trains). In a nutshell, a very grand liberation from culturally collected constructs...

::

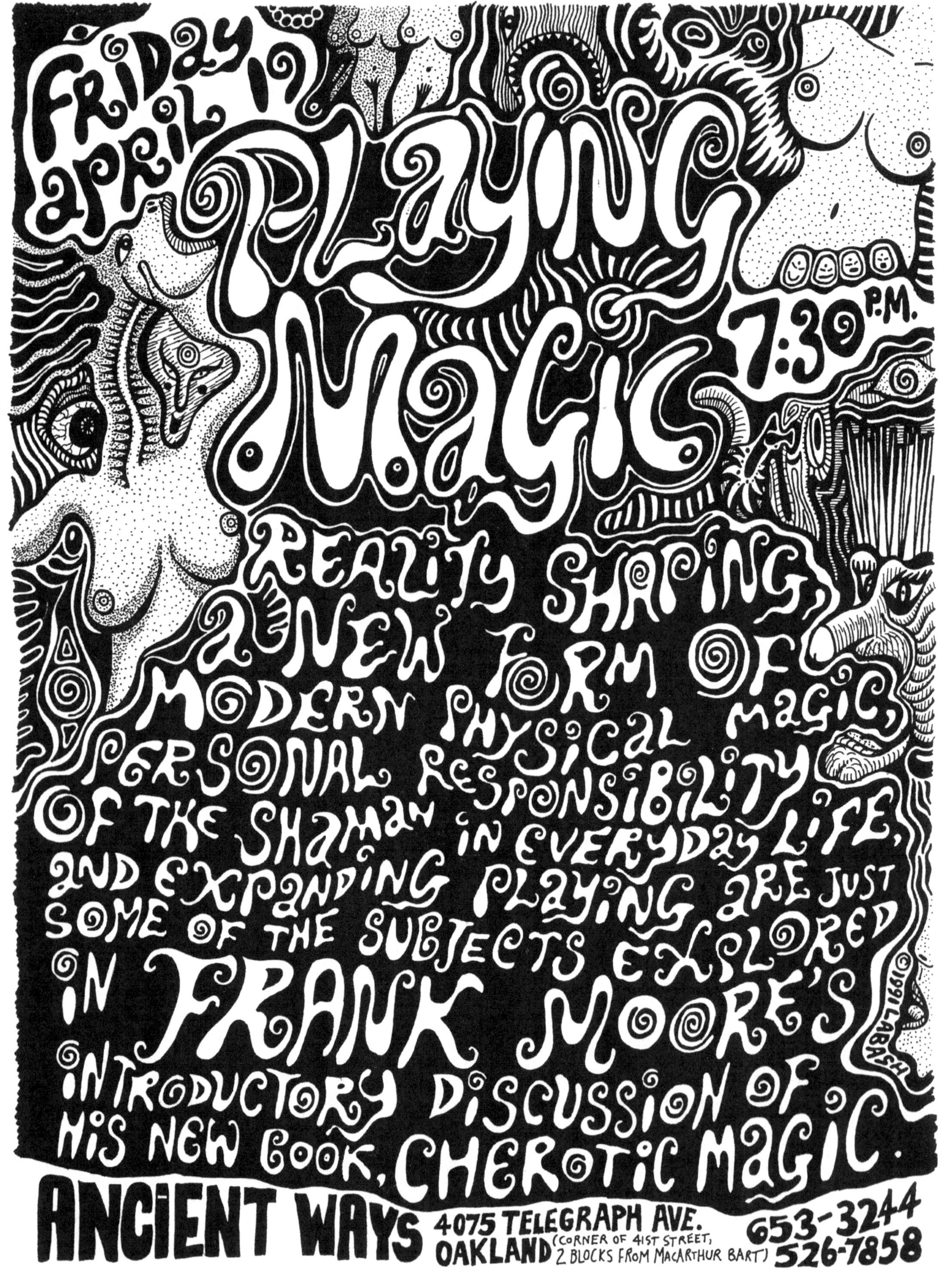

Friday April 19
Playing Magic
7:30 P.M.
Reality shaping, a new form of modern physical magic, personal responsibility of the shaman in everyday life, and expanding playing are just some of the subjects explored in Frank Moore's introductory discussion of his new book, Cherotic Magic.
©1991 LABASH
ANCIENT WAYS
4075 TELEGRAPH AVE.
OAKLAND (CORNER OF 41ST STREET, 2 BLOCKS FROM MACARTHUR BART)
653-3244
526-7858

::

REVIEW OF CHEROTIC MAGIC -- BARBARA SMITH

Due to the complex reasons of historical conditions and needs, artists from the industrialized nations of the world more or less simultaneously (late 1950's - early 1970's) felt a depth of experience uncontainable in ordinary and available cultural forms. They emerged with a language of remarkable similarity--clearly felt in retrospect to be shamanic and whose purposes extended far beyond the realm of the commercialized art market. One of these performance artists is Frank Moore who has just published an introductory manual for prospective apprentices in shamanic/art practices. The book is also a very helpful means of access to this particular realm of performance art for the historian and student.

Moore, paradoxically a severely disabled cerebral palsied human being, who cannot clearly utter a single word is simultaneously a clear and eloquent writer about a reality-shifting form of art he calls Cherotic Magic and a spectacularly courageous, ecstatic journeyer and practitioner of shamanic transformational art.

Reversing the ideas of normal causality, his book guides one towards powerful experiences of re-integration into a unified field of consciousness brought about by the apprenticeship. The radical purposes of the book initiate a teacher/student relationship more appropriately similar to a guru situation than the normal art student context which we all know can be one which borders on charismatic adulation. Rather, the relationship is intended to awaken and restructure the whole being with access to an interrelated "web of all possibilities," a potentiated ground of existence, from which the student may return empowered with energy, vision, and unflinching faith to change the so-called reality structure of this fragmented and specialized culture. The process is a form of magic, which inspires a sense of body wholeness and aliveness where the personal power is to be found. A manual of faith and a description of the nature of apprenticeship, the book is a clarification of the sort of contractual agreement one enters with a teacher, rarely stipulated but here clearly spelled out. This agreement is one of mutual responsibility where the risk is clearly seen to be taken by both parties.

Having explored these realms a good deal myself both in terms of self-discovery and also with teachers, I find the book to be rigorously tough in its demands (on the potential student and quite naturally the teacher as well), and it also clearly describes qualities required (such as trust) and the benefits to be gained in these explorations (such as love).

Moore has broken the apprenticeship into segments with re-entry periods back into ordinary life between the intervals in order to accommodate Western students' difficulty in going through the lengthy course in a sustained fashion. The fact that the student must exhibit a deep and long-term calling, will or faith to repeatedly return to the teaching is Moore's greatest risk, for spiritual apprenticeship is not a common practice in Western culture. This is a little known fact that the apprenticeship entails risk in the making and/or breaking of the relationship not only in regard to the student but more so for the teacher.

Moore speaks of the a-logical interaction, as a journey along which student and teacher become soul mirrors. Moore is not seeking a following, however. He states to his credit, I believe, that such work is highly personal and requires one-to-one attention and becomes non-productive when he has many followers.

The radical nature of this esoteric apprenticeship practice includes the breaking of social mores and taboos in order to reach direct experience particularly in the realm of conventional sexuality. Moore clearly states however that the touching and erotic playing involved (Eroplay) is not driven by the goal of sexual intercourse, but is the refreshing awakening of what he calls Cherotic energy which becomes a free fund of available and heightened "juice" for healing and creativity. (These teachings parallel quite exactly the teachings I've experienced from my Native American shaman teacher and also Tantric practices.)

My first response to reading Cherotic Magic is one of resonance and appreciation, the feeling of knowing very deeply that of which he speaks as true and uncompromising. He gives examples and authentication through powerfully written, illuminating stories about his own early life of terrible isolation and study; the breakthroughs which allowed him to finally believe in his own intelligence, joy and beauty and to receive the powerful inner flow of intrinsically experienced wisdom and knowledge of these liberating teachings. These life passages correspond to such experiences of mystics everywhere. I appreciate many things about this book, not the least of which are the words Moore has coined to name certain qualities and goals of his work (such as Eroplay and Chero). One such word, Erour, means vulnerable strength. Its meaning corresponds exactly to my own early performance experience. In the past, I put myself in very psychologically risky positions in performances and I was frequently criticized for doing so as if I were "hurting myself". My own experience was quite to the contrary, although I was in fact going to "the place of fear or pain or constraint" in myself with vulnerability and because I deliberately chose to do so, it was an act of strength and I returned with released energy and power.

If anything in his book is weak, it is this issue of authority and how to define the limits (and/or goals) of guru/student practice. It is weak not because I think Frank is either weak of unauthentic...but because we live in a spiritually naive culture. Most people I imagine are cynics. The book is not written for such people, as there is no language that I know of to convince them a priori to any experience which in itself is convincing. Further, the way one meets one's teachers in life is often inherently mysterious and a unique process. Perhaps the only ways a potential student can judge such persons and situations have first of all to do with one's depth of calling and an experienced synchronicity. Failing that, one needs to feel one may leave the teacher at any time despite the pressure to stay and one can also inquire of former students as to their experience.

For me, it would be advantageous if he could paint a picture of what completion might look like. Is it simply staying the course (twelve years for a resident; seven on, five off approximately/seven days for the introductory course)? The difficulty is that completion of such a practice might look very different in each of the "graduated" and only a sense of demonstrable knowing and changed behavior would be adequate.

The book is replete with black and white drawings by Michael LaBash. Depending on prior biases, they can appear to be psychedelically violent and visceral with a heavy emphasis on sex. They are intricate intertwinings of interpenetrating fields which writhe over the entire drawing area with no central image. Rather, naked figures whole or in parts of both sexes and composite hermaphrodites with breasts and cocks weave in and out of planes and orifices. As I have said, Moore speaks in the text of making clear how Eroplay is not to be thought of as driving for sex or focused in it. Rather it comes from a presexual state of infancy, yet here the drawings are strongly sexual in my view and often horrific. (No doubt, however not meant so much to be sexual as frank (pun intended).

Moore's writing about the ethics of commitment is a powerful critique of our shallow culture. What he says rings true and created a sense of gratitude in me and inner resolution. He speaks with great personal authority.

In the general dialog of art and culture this form of art appears to be the most difficult to speak about partly due to its radicality and partly because it re-integrates art into religion, magic, belief, and effect. It means and makes change. I, myself have twice come to a bifurcation point re: some need to synthesize art as I practice it somewhat within the cultural dialog and spaces of my profession as against a chosen spiritual path (Buddhism or Native American teachings). I finally had to ask the question: Which was my core path, art or the spiritual path? And could the creative process itself be a path to spiritual awakening and inner knowledge? Or was a core of spirit teaching the only way and the art must be derived from it? Not the least of which is the question of feminism. The female spiritual journey is for me a major issue within this questioning.

Moore himself raises the question of Shamanism /as art - /as performance - /as therapy. He cites performance as the bed of mystical initiation, rites of passage, mystical ceremonies where art/science, philosophy, and psychology and theology merge and become whole once again. Here, we may experience these things as at once ancient and strange. The breaking of restricting taboos and inner barriers moves towards a place not of isolated individualism, but one of connectedness both in the interior landscapes and with each other.

:::

REVIEW OF CHEROTIC MAGIC -- KYLE GRIFFITH (From TSR #13)

Why is the author of War in Heaven publishing a book that was originally written to be used as a text by apprentices studying shamanic magic under a teacher? Most of the material in WiH that deals with personal spiritual development and psychic training either directly states or tacitly assumes that submitting control of the process to a teacher or guru is undesirable, even dangerous.

Also, one of the most important concepts in WiH is that of "individual spiritual sovereignty" -- the idea that taking full conscious control over one's personal spiritual beliefs and psychic/magical practices is the best way to free one's self from outside mind-control and to develop towards one's full potential. A casual glance at the contents of Cherotic Magic reveals a lot of material that seems to violate this principle: Frank's book stresses surrender of the student's will to "the magic" as it expresses itself through the teacher, and it frequently condemns "individualism" as one of the chief obstacles to the student's progress. In fact, Cherotic Magic states in many different contexts and wordings that being an "isolated individual" is bad, and that it is our relationships with other people that make us fully human and give us the opportunity to evolve on every level: socially, physically, mentally, emotionally, and spiritually.

As I said, it is easy to conclude from a casual skimming of both books that Frank and I disagree on the fundamental issue of "the individual versus the group." This conclusion is completely false. Frank is just as staunch a believer in individual sovereignty as I am, and I feel that intimate personal relationships are just as important as he does. The only reason certain passages in War in Heaven seem to contradict passages in Cherotic Magic is that

Frank and I, who had never read each other's work at the time the two books were written, used similar words and phrases to refer to completely different philosophical ideas.

For example, whenever I used the word "individual" in War in Heaven, I used it with the unspoken assumption that I was referring to a hypothetical "normal human being" -- in other words, the archetype that all of us Spiritual Revolutionaries are striving to become. I was not talking about "the average individual" in this Theocrat-bedeviled society, but about someone who is sane enough to take for granted all of Frank's ideas about the importance of human relationships and the role of trust, voluntary mutual dependence, sharing, caring, and love within them.

I realize now that I should have explained this in War in Heaven, but when the book was written, the idea that I needed to define exactly what I meant by "the individual" simply didn't occur to me. I've lived my whole life in intimate relationships with other people and have always been acutely aware of the importance of those relationships to my sanity, happiness and personal development, and I assumed that "everyone would know" that when I said "individual" I did not mean an isolated, self-indulgent egotist, but the kind of sane individual I have as my own ideal.

On the other hand, when I mentioned "groups" in War in Heaven, I was usually referring to "average" human institutions on Earth at the present time. Since practically all such elements of earthly culture -- from traditional family structures right up through government at all levels to multi-national systems such as ideological power blocs and major organized religions -- were originally designed as instruments of Theocratic mind-control, War in Heaven suggests that Spiritual Revolutionaries avoid contact with existing institutions and find or create alternatives that do not practice coercion or mind control. In contrast, most of the mention of groups and group activities in Cherotic Magic refers to such non-Theocratic alternative institutions, not to any segment of the existing social order.

Frank's "magical tribe, consisting of the teacher and his students" is a completely voluntary association of free individuals, and I know from personal observation that there's no discernible amount of coercion or mind-control involved in any of the relationships within the group. Individuals who have serious problems functioning within the group always end up leaving, and the group seems willing to let minor conflicts remain unresolved for as long as it takes to work out completely voluntary solutions. This means that the Chero "tribe" has so far remained quite small and undergone frequent changes of personnel, but it also means that I consider it a "politically correct" group for Spiritual Revolutionaries to join, work with, or use as a model for designing other groups.

Also, when Frank mentions existing earthly institutions in Cherotic Magic, his judgments about them are usually much the same as those in War in Heaven. He doesn't use the same vocabulary as I use to discuss these subjects, but when it comes to the facts and opinions behind the words, he and I seem to be in essential agreement on every major point. I feel that Frank's knowledge of what mind control is and how to break free of it is equal to mine when it comes to discussing broad historical subjects, and superior to mine when he's describing the practical details of how to run a magical training system.

In fact, when you come right down to it, Frank is the only "spiritual teacher" I've ever met in the flesh that I consider completely trustworthy when viewed from a Spiritual Revolutionary viewpoint, and I think he knows as much about the practical details of how to work and teach magic as any of the famous modern occult teachers: Gurdjieff, Crowley, etc. In fact, he may be superior to all of them, because he seems to be much less egotistical and inflexible. He freely admits that what he's doing is experimental, that much of the time he's proceeding by plain trial and error -- and several times in the few months I've known him, I've seen him drop an approach that seemed to be failing and try something else.

Many traditional occultists and New Agers **say** they're using experimental methods and learning from experience as they go along, but their actions belie this -- they're actually just acting out their official doctrine as a script, over and over, with little regard of how it works in practice. This is why War in Heaven and my other Spiritual Revolutionary writings have refused to endorse any particular magical or psychic training system: none of them are close enough to my ideal for such a system to merit a recommendation. Frank Moore's system as described in Cherotic Magic is the first magical training system I feel I can recommend, and I'm extremely grateful he's allowing me to publish his book.

Anyway, I strongly recommend Cherotic Magic to anyone who is studying any psychic/magical training system that uses sexual energy as part of its practice, and to all of my other readers who are in basic sympathy with the ideas expressed in War in Heaven. On the deepest level, Frank is trying to lead the readers of Cherotic Magic towards the same fundamental Breakthrough in consciousness concerning the nature of spiritual reality described in WiH.

::

COLIN WILSON to KYLE -- February 2, 1991

I'm extremely grateful to you for sending me that really fascinating work Cherotic Magic. I think Frank Moore is quite brilliant.

I must apologize for taking so long to reply, but I've been working absolutely flat out. A paperback publisher asked me to do a kind of 200,000 word book about 'The Occult', which I did. I began it on Christmas Day, and had finished it by the end of January. Incidentally, rather an interesting synchronisity occurred while I was writing it. Looking through the pigeon hole underneath my desk, I came upon your War in Heaven. So I put it down at the side of my chair, with the intention of taking it upstairs with me to read. I didn't even take in its title -- although I knew what it was. Then I switched on my word processor, and saw that the last words I had written the day before were 'War in Heaven." (I was talking about T.C. Lethbridge.) At that moment, I turned to pick up a sheet of paper, and saw the word "War in Heaven" on the cover of your book. It struck me as one of those pleasant synchronisities that means that somehow you are in good form!

Now I've finished it, I've got to write a play about Mozart for the Mozart centenary, and get it delivered by the beginning of April. I've also got to write a book about Ouspensky, and complete an encyclopedia of unsolved mysteries! So I don't have as much time for reading as I'd like, and haven't read the whole of Frank Moore's fascinating book. But having got up to the section called 'reality shaping', I find that it corresponds very closely with many of the ideas that preoccupy me at the present moment. Please give him my warm congratulations.

::

;::
STEVE HIRSCH, editor of Heaven Bone, to KYLE and LUNA, January 10, 1991

This book Cherotic Magic both scares and delights me. Part of me doesn't want to understand it too much because it would mean I would have to change my life. I think of Rilke's poem "Archaic Torso of Apollo":

We cannot know his legendary head
with eyes like ripening fruit. And yet his torso
is still suffused with brilliance from inside,
like a lamp, in which his gaze, now turned to low,

gleams in all its power. Otherwise
the curved breast could not dazzle you so, nor could
a smile run through the placid hips and thighs
to that dark corner where procreation flared.

Otherwise this stone would seem defaced
beneath the translucent cascade of the shoulders
and would not glisten like a wild beast's fur:

would not, from all the borders of itself,
burst like a star: for here there is no place
that does not see you. You must change your life.

Cherotic Magic has a lot to offer I can see. I would like to know more about this group you're in. Send me some promo materials for CM and I'll sent them out in my correspondence. I am particularly interested in the artwork of Labash. Could you please forward me his address or put him in contact with me? I would like to publish some of his artwork. Heaven Bone #9 hopefully to happen before September and these drawings would give the mag motion and power.

....
STEVE HIRSCH to FRANK and MICHAEL -- February 7, 1991

It was very nice to receive your letter and samples of Mike's work. It is very exciting. It reminds me of a time in high school when I used to just meditate on a blank sheet of drawing or watercolor paper and let myself relax into a mild trance -- then I would start to see shapes and images in motion on the paper, miniature worlds that seem to follow the natural fiber of the paper, emerging from it, giving the paper depth and liquidity. Michael, your work is like the river of mind, emerging from a rich lake of associations and fevers, natural imprints of the nervous system in medium -- could your hand possibly be moving so fast?

Frank, I am still reading Cherotic Magic a little at a time and it chokes in my throat, making me feel my self-imposed limitations so thoroughly. Sex, to me, is like rubbing two sticks together -- the flesh dissolves and a true spark is ignited by some deep inner friction -- a merging of patterns that build in harmony to create universes. The possessing is illusory and what bliss remains is a smoother flow of reality through the chakras, a more balanced vibration. I look forward to reading deeper into Cherotic Magic and will likely prepare a review for Heaven Bone #9.

::

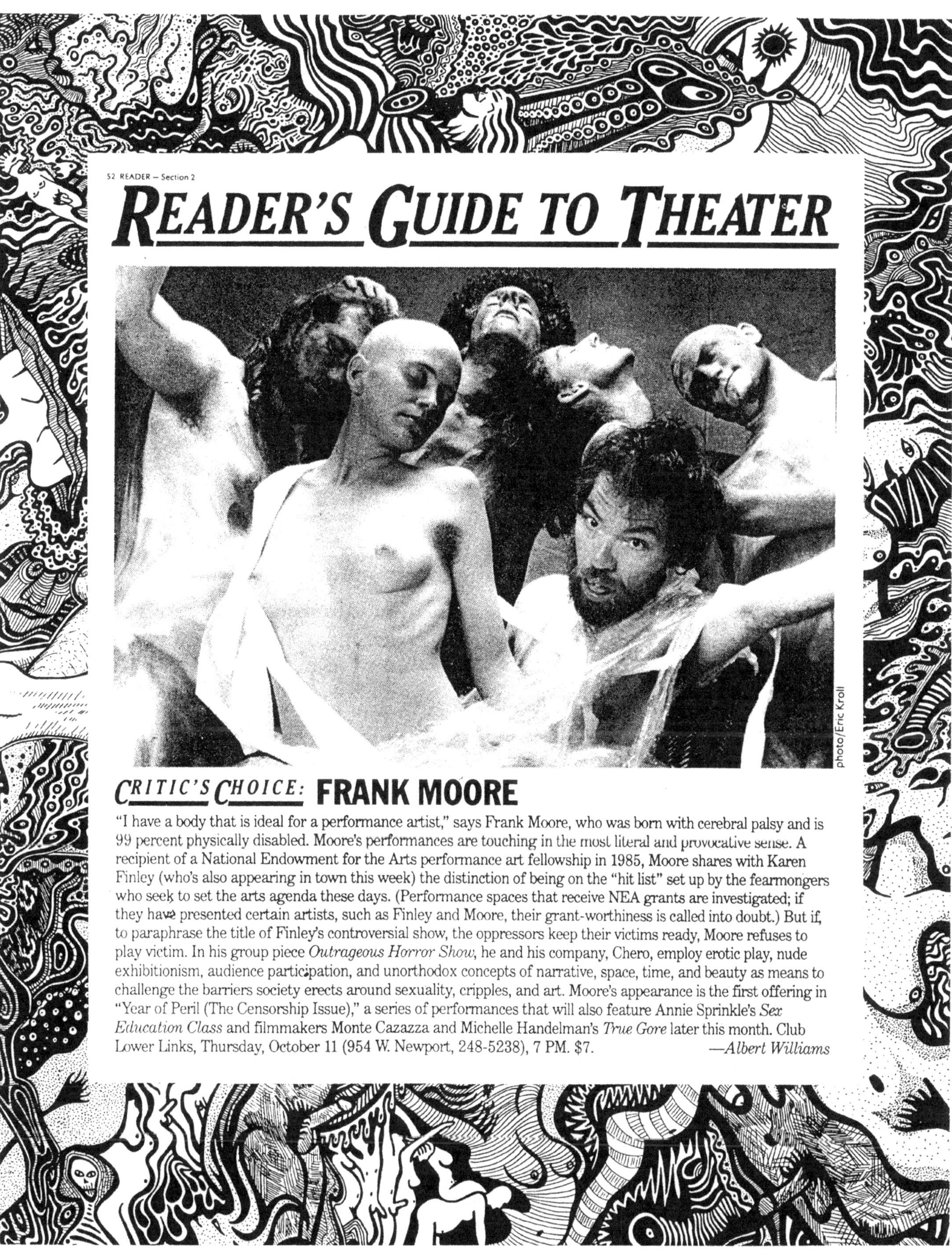

READER'S GUIDE TO THEATER

photo/Eric Kroll

CRITIC'S CHOICE: FRANK MOORE

"I have a body that is ideal for a performance artist," says Frank Moore, who was born with cerebral palsy and is 99 percent physically disabled. Moore's performances are touching in the most literal and provocative sense. A recipient of a National Endowment for the Arts performance art fellowship in 1985, Moore shares with Karen Finley (who's also appearing in town this week) the distinction of being on the "hit list" set up by the fearmongers who seek to set the arts agenda these days. (Performance spaces that receive NEA grants are investigated; if they have presented certain artists, such as Finley and Moore, their grant-worthiness is called into doubt.) But if, to paraphrase the title of Finley's controversial show, the oppressors keep their victims ready, Moore refuses to play victim. In his group piece *Outrageous Horror Show*, he and his company, Chero, employ erotic play, nude exhibitionism, audience participation, and unorthodox concepts of narrative, space, time, and beauty as means to challenge the barriers society erects around sexuality, cripples, and art. Moore's appearance is the first offering in "Year of Peril (The Censorship Issue)," a series of performances that will also feature Annie Sprinkle's *Sex Education Class* and filmmakers Monte Cazazza and Michelle Handelman's *True Gore* later this month. Club Lower Links, Thursday, October 11 (954 W. Newport, 248-5238), 7 PM. $7. —*Albert Williams*

BERKELEY VOICE

Volume 8, Number 52 THE COMMUNITY NEWSPAPER OF BERKELEY Thursday, October 25, 1990 35¢

::

BERKELEY ARTIST UNDER INVESTIGATION by Kristin Russell

One of Berkeley's best-known artists may be in trouble with the law. Frank Moore, a performance artist and self-described "deformed shaman," learned early last February that the General Accounting Office -- the investigative arm of Congress -- has been asking questions about him. And Moore, cerebral palsy victim, a spastic quadriplegic, 99 percent physically disabled, is flattered."I was feeling left out," he said. "All of my heroes in the past were banned, jailed, harassed for their work."

Moore is one of four performance artists being investigated by the GAO as the result of the demand by U.S. Sen. Jesse Helms (R-North Carolina). Helms has been loudly criticizing the National Endowment for the Arts for funding performers whose works some consider obscene.

Under a recently passed Senate appropriations bill the NEA endowment is prohibited from funding "patently offensive" material. Helms is now targeting individual artists, among them Moore, Annie Sprinkle, Karen Finley, and Cheri Gaulke. Moore has not received an endowment since 1985.

Moore can neither walk nor talk. He communicated by pointing a stick attached to a head-band at letters on a board, laboriously spelling out words. Despite his disability he is also an accomplished painter, who has had shows in Chicago and Berkeley, and the author of a new book, "Cherotic Magic." He is also a rock star and poet." I am lucky I am an exhibitionist in this body," Moore said. "It is not a disability, it is my tool, my meal ticket."

Controversy is no stranger to Moore, whose performances often span eight hours and involve, among other things, nudity and the use of what Moore calls shamanistic rituals. At the heart of Moore's performances is "eroplay," Moore's made-up name for intimate and playful touching between adults, which, he emphasizes, is non-sexual in nature.

Eroplay often entails some or most of the audience participating, either partially or completely naked. "By using eroplay," he said, "the innocent child within the body is released in a playful energy. Within this altered reality intense emotions can be released, intense acts can be performed outside the normal slots."

By encouraging audience members to shed their clothes and participate in non-touching exercises, Moore said he is creating a playground where adults can feel safe in being vulnerable. "I think playing is a safe mind-altering drug," he said.

In Moore's production "Wrapping/Rocking," he sits in his wheelchair, a woman on his lap, both of them naked. Several members of the troupe, including Linda Mac, Moore's companion, wrap the two in toilet paper, Saran Wrap and tin foil.

Other performances feature Moore as a rock star, howling to rock standards while members of his group eroplay and dance naked and oiled under strobe lights. They throw glitter in the air, and paint each other with chocolate and whipped cream.

"I wonder why Helms is after me," Moore said. But the simple issue of nudity and erotica are not the foundations of Helms' objections, Moore said; governmental suppression of art is motivated by the need to control threatening visionaries.

Moore said his art is "freeing people; that is threatening. It is also using shamanism; that is threatening. It is also minorities finding channels for change; that is threatening; What is threatening to Helms is not the sex or the gore." Moore said, "it is that if I can be a rock star, anybody can do anything they want to do."

Moore's next Berkeley performance will be Feb. 8, 1991, at Smokey Joe's Cafe on Shattuck Avenue. A 24-hour performance is scheduled for Jan. 26; those interested should phone 562-7858 for an interview.

::

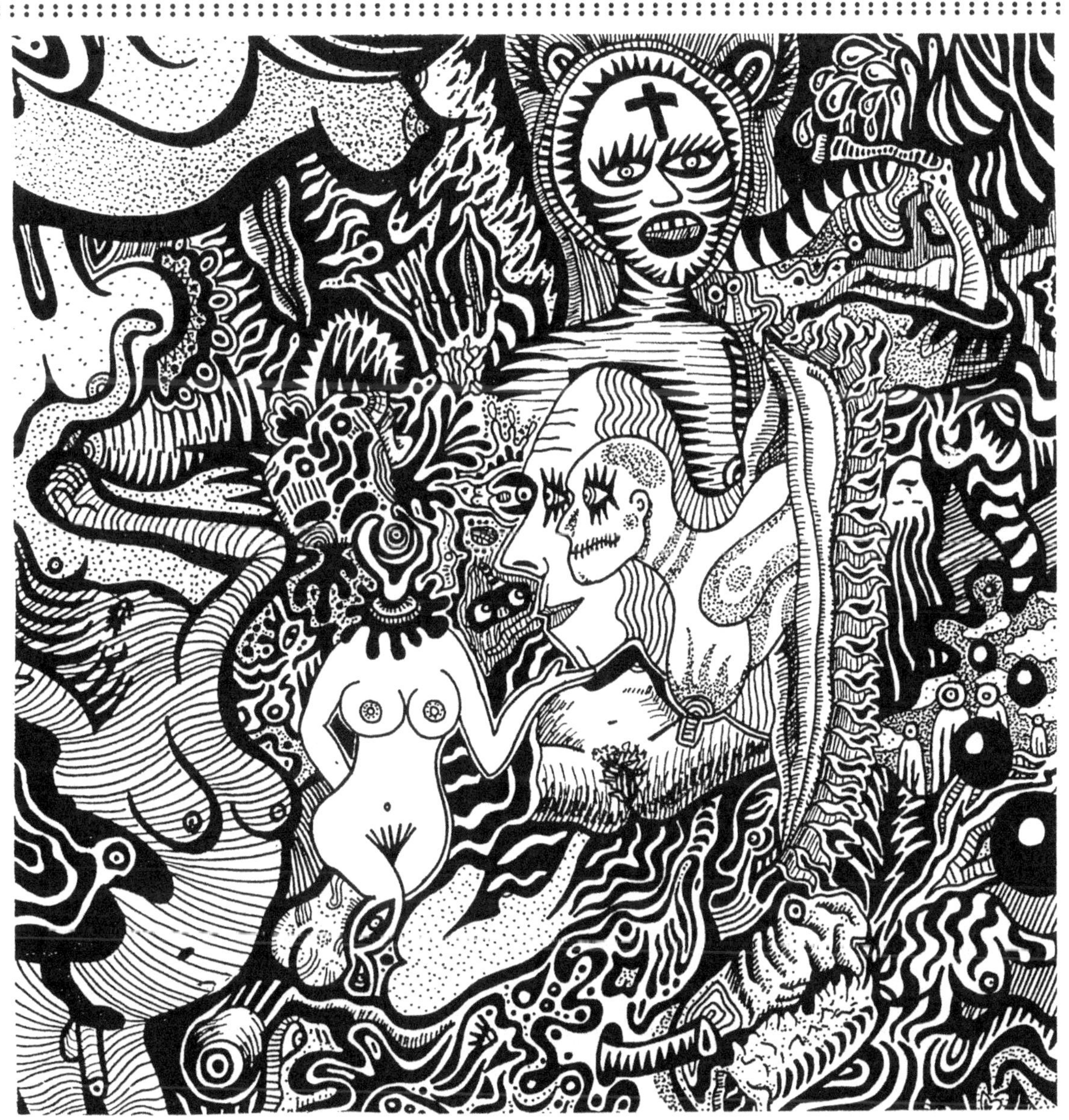

::

AN OPEN LETTER TO SEN. JESSE HELMS -- FRANK MOORE

Enough is enough. I have read in The L.A. Times and The Village Voice that you have the general accounting office investigating Karen Finley, Johanna Went, Cheri Gaulke, and myself. Why are you going behind our backs? Why aren't you talking directly to us artists, instead of having the G.A.O., at the taxpayers' expense, going to the galleries and the theaters we have performed in to ask veiled questions about us?

Here I am. Let's talk, man to man. It is the American way. What do you want to know about me? You had my address because I sent you my article about how I think what you are doing is patently offensive to the Bill of Rights. After all, it is the American way to directly confront your opponent, giving him a chance to answer, and giving the people a dialog. But you did not send me a letter. You sent the G.A.O..

This is not an investigation for information. It is an investigation for extortion. It is part of the campaign to smear us four artists -- as well as Holly Hughes, Tim Miller, Annie Sprinkle, and John Fleck -- as untouchable, unfundable, unbookable. The paint that is used to smear is that of "obscene artists." Are you trying to find out whether or not our work falls into the legal definition of obscene? Have you seen my performances or even talked to anyone who has? Have you read my writings on art in professional and scholarly journals, or my resume of over 20 years? I think not.

I think you know you can not show that any of us untouchable eight are even remotely legally obscene. So you and your ilk are trying to create the atmosphere of fear by using the extortion tactics of the Mafia. The N.E.A. chairman, Frohnmayer, used this atmosphere of fear, under the catchy phrase "certain political reality," to take away the N>E>A> grants from Finley, Hughes, Fleck, and Miller. Your extortion is what has created this political reality.

This extortion is an attempt to blacklist us untouchable eight and other artists who have the nerve to do difficult art. This so-called investigation is really the extortionist's message to galleries that, if they book us or artists like us, they are risking the possibility of funding being cut off, of being audited, of being closed down by the fire department, of being hassled by the vice squad and other governmental agencies. All of which has occurred to the galleries that have booked us untouchable eight.

Why are you closing channels of expression and of funding to me without due process of law? It is a political and cultural blacklist under the cover of obscenity. Extortion and blacklists are against the American ideals and spirit.

If you have anything to say to me or to ask me, come to talk to me man to man. Otherwise, get your Big Brother foot off my back.

In Freedom,

Frank Moore

::

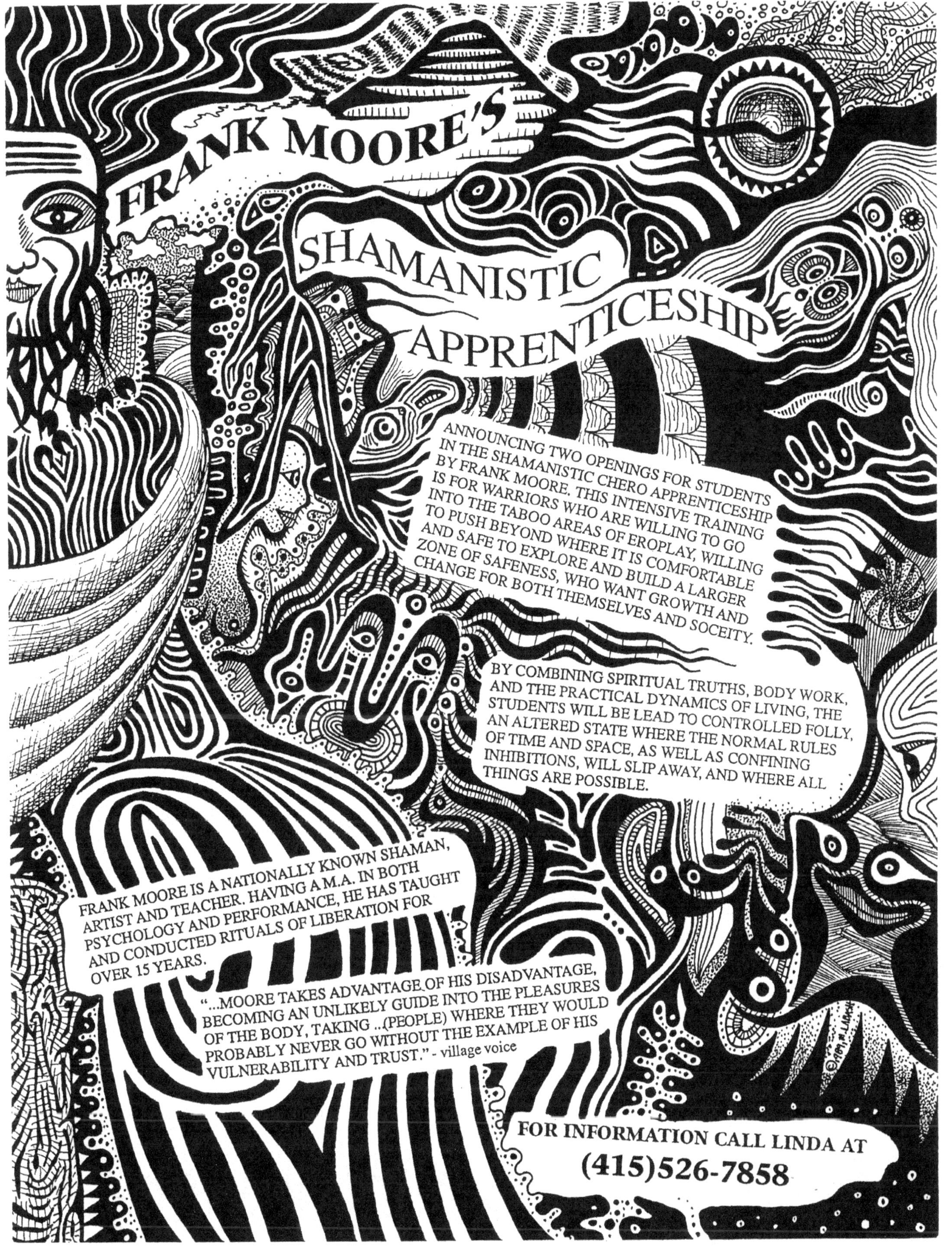
FRANK MOORE'S
SHAMANISTIC
APPRENTICESHIP
ANNOUNCING TWO OPENINGS FOR STUDENTS IN THE SHAMANISTIC CHERO APPRENTICESHIP BY FRANK MOORE. THIS INTENSIVE TRAINING IS FOR WARRIORS WHO ARE WILLING TO GO INTO THE TABOO AREAS OF EROPLAY, WILLING TO PUSH BEYOND WHERE IT IS COMFORTABLE AND SAFE TO EXPLORE AND BUILD A LARGER ZONE OF SAFENESS, WHO WANT GROWTH AND CHANGE FOR BOTH THEMSELVES AND SOCEITY.
BY COMBINING SPIRITUAL TRUTHS, BODY WORK, AND THE PRACTICAL DYNAMICS OF LIVING, THE STUDENTS WILL BE LEAD TO CONTROLLED FOLLY, AN ALTERED STATE WHERE THE NORMAL RULES OF TIME AND SPACE, AS WELL AS CONFINING INHIBITIONS, WILL SLIP AWAY, AND WHERE ALL THINGS ARE POSSIBLE.
FRANK MOORE IS A NATIONALLY KNOWN SHAMAN, ARTIST AND TEACHER. HAVING A M.A. IN BOTH PSYCHOLOGY AND PERFORMANCE, HE HAS TAUGHT AND CONDUCTED RITUALS OF LIBERATION FOR OVER 15 YEARS.
"...MOORE TAKES ADVANTAGE OF HIS DISADVANTAGE, BECOMING AN UNLIKELY GUIDE INTO THE PLEASURES OF THE BODY, TAKING ...(PEOPLE) WHERE THEY WOULD PROBABLY NEVER GO WITHOUT THE EXAMPLE OF HIS VULNERABILITY AND TRUST." - village voice
FOR INFORMATION CALL LINDA AT
(415)526-7858

video tapes BY FRANK MOORE

$40 each

fairytales can come true
copyrighted 1981
length: 35 minutes
THIS IS A FILM ABOUT RELATIONSHIPS AND DISABILITY STARRING FRANK MOORE, WHO HAS BEEN DISABLED SINCE BIRTH WITH CEREBRAL PALSY. IT IS A HUMOROUS, YET REALISTIC LOOK AT HOW TO ESTABLISH RELATIONSHIPS BY CHANGING NEGATIVE SELF IMAGE.

erotic play
copyrighted 1983
length: 84 minutes
THIS VIDEO EXPLORES WHAT HAPPENS WHEN PEOPLE OF ALL TYPES AND AGES ARE GIVEN A CHANCE TO RETURN TO BEING A KID AGAIN. A SIMPLE GAME OF DRESS-UP BECOMES A POWERFUL METAPHOR FOR DROPPING TABOOS, RELEASING CREATIVE EMOTION, AND FOR DRAMATIC CHANGE. AS A RESULT, AN INNOCENT EROTICISM IS FOUND... AS WELL AS GETTING INTIMATE WITH 60 HUMANS.

outrageous dream
copyrighted 1984
length: 41 minutes
A SURREAL, VISUAL POEM OF FOUND IMAGES.

the nude cave
copyrighted 1984
length: 113 minutes
AN EROTIC, SURREALISTIC VIDEO DREAM THAT COMBINES NON-LINEAR IMAGES AND FRANK'S ORIGINAL MUSIC SCORE.

the outrageous beauty revue
copyrighted 1980
length: approx. 30 minutes
THIS RAW VIDEO DOCUMENTS THE TACKY, MUSICAL, OVER-THE-EDGE COMEDY REVUE THAT FRANK CREATED, DIRECTED AND PERFORMED IN. THE SHOW RAN ON A WEEKLY BASIS FOR THREE AND ONE HALF YEARS AT THE MABUHAY GARDENS IN SAN FRANCISCO IN ADDITION TO A NUMBER OF OTHER NORTHERN CALIFORNIA AND NEVADA PERFORMANCES. FRANK PERFORMED ALONG WITH THE THIRTY PEOPLE WHO MADE UP HIS THEATRE GROUP, "the theatre of human melting."

out of isolation
copyrighted 1989
length: 105 minutes
A SURREAL EROTIC EXAMINATION OF AN INTIMATE RELATIONSHIP OF NEED. STARRING FRANK MOORE AND LINDA SIBEO.

books BY FRANK MOORE

caves
A COLLECTION OF MANIFESTOS ABOUT eroplay AND ART.
PUBLISHED 1987 **$5**

art of living
A GUIDE TO DOWN-TO-EARTH SPIRITUALITY AS CHANNELED BY FRANK MOORE.
PUBLISHED 1987 **$10**

cherotic magic
PUBLISHED 1990 **$15**

music BY FRANK MOORE'S CHERO COMPANY

$5 each

body music
copyrighted 1989
EXPLORING THE HUMAN BODY AS MUSICAL INSTRUMENT.

inter-rhythms
copyrighted 1989
PRIMAL MUSIC CREATED FOR FRANK MOORE'S RITUAL PERFORMANCES.

to order call or write:

frank moore
P.O. BOX 11445
BERKELEY, CA 94701-2445
(415) 526-7858

also available from S/R Press

war in heaven
BY KYLE GRIFFITH **$18**

the spiritual revolutionary vol. I
BOUND VOLUME ISSUES 0-9 **$20**

the spiritual revolutionary
INDIVIDUAL ISSUES **$3**
SAMPLE ISSUE **$1**

to order write:

S/R Press
P.O. BOX 60327
PALO ALTO, CA 94306-0327

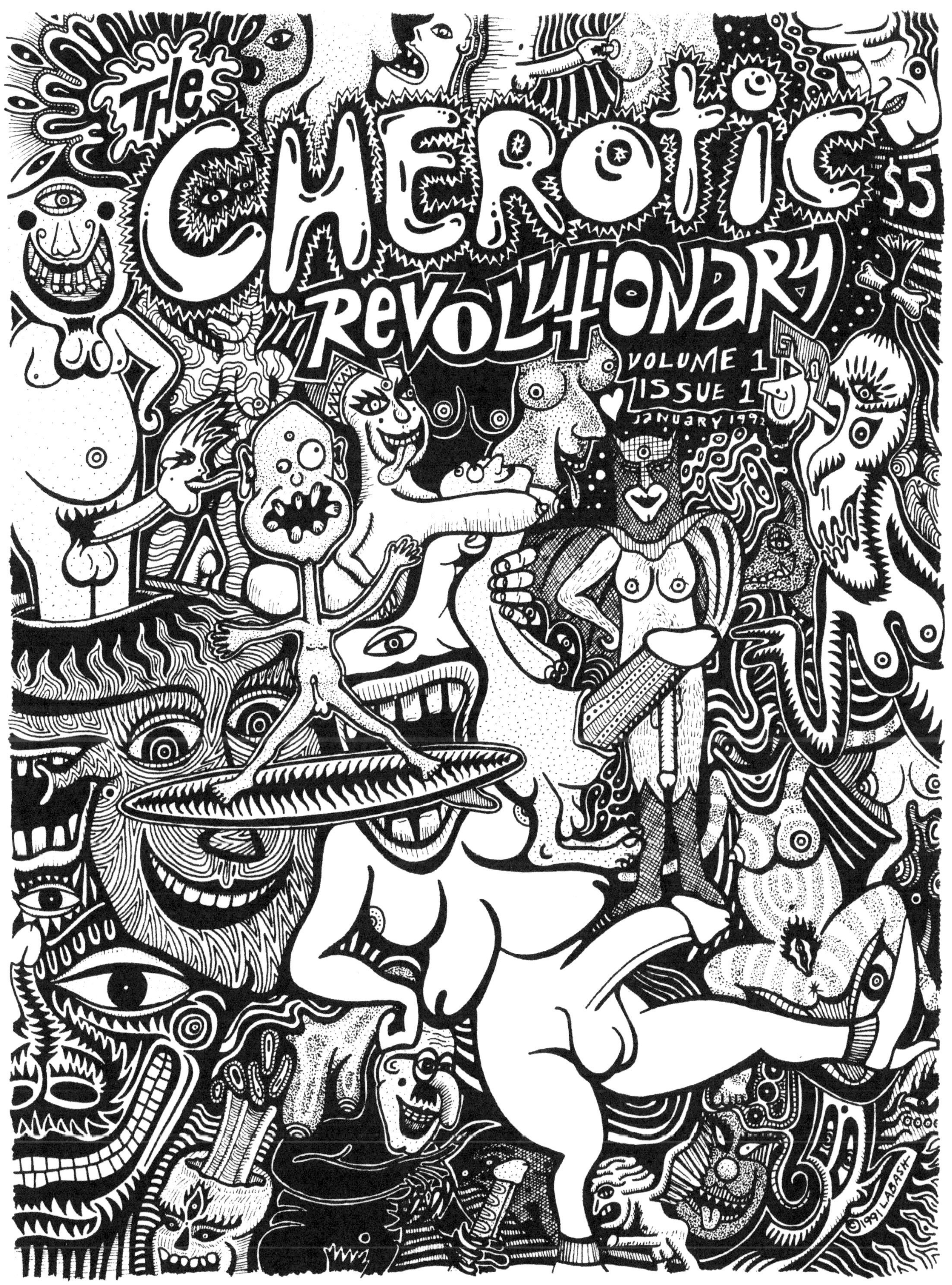
The
CHEROTIC
REVOLUTIONARY
$5
VOLUME 1
ISSUE 1
JANUARY 1992
©1991 LABASH

THE CHEROTIC REVOLUTIONARY #1 **JANUARY, 1992**

TCR is edited by Frank Moore and Linda Mac, and published by Kyle and Luna Griffith. The art editor is Michael LaBash.

The price for this issue, and the next, TCR #2, is $5.00 per copy. We aren't taking subscriptions for more than one issue at a time, to avoid tying ourselves down to a rigid publication schedule or magazine size. We want to remain free to publish small issues frequently or larger issues at longer intervals and adjust the price accordingly, but each issue will announce the price of the next so readers can order it in advance.

We heartily encourage letters of comment from readers and will answer as many as we can. Please tell us if you don't want us to print material from your letter -- otherwise we will assume it's OK.

Please address all correspondence and orders for magazines to:

Frank Moore, P.O. Box 11445, Berkeley, CA 94701-2445

In This Issue ...

FRANKLY SPEAKING

Editorial

FRANK MOORE

I AM PROUD OF THIS ISSUE. IT IS WHAT I HAD HOPED **TCR** WOULD BECOME...A MAGAZINE BY AND FOR BLACK SHEEP. KAREN'S POEM **THE BLACK SHEEP** DESCRIBES WHAT I MEAN BY BLACK SHEEP. WHENEVER I READ OR HEAR THIS POEM, I CRY. THAT IS CORNY. BUT BEING CORNY IS ONE OF THE MAJOR SECRET WEAPONS IN THE CHEROTIC REVOLUTION. CORNY IS BEING HUMAN. **BLACK SHEEP** IS FROM KAREN'S BOOK **SHOCK TREATMENT**, PUBLISHED BY CITY LIGHTS BOOKS WHO LET US REPRINT THE POEM HERE. KAREN IS USUALLY THOUGHT OF AS A FEMALE LENNY BRUCE-LIKE CHOCOLATE-SMEARED NUDE PERFORMANCE ARTIST KEEPING ME COMPANY ON JESSE HELMS' SHIT LIST. BUT I THINK HER REAL SIGNIFICANCE IS AS A POET IN THE TRADITION OF GINSBERG'S **HOWL**...HOWLING FOR A HUMAN, HUMANE WORLD.

I FEEL LIKE A HOST INTRODUCING MY GREAT FRIENDS TO ONE ANOTHER. GUESS THAT IS ONE OF THE PERKS OF BEING THE EDITOR OF A REALITY SUBVERSIVE MAGAZINE. LET ME CONTINUE TO TAKE YOU AROUND.

IF YOU HAVE SEEN THE FIRST **TCR** OR HAVE SEEN THE CHERO POSTERS, YOU KNOW LA BASH'S DRAWINGS. IF YOU HAVE COME TO OUR PERFORMANCES, YOU KNOW LA BASH AS MICHAEL (OR, BETTER YET, AS MIKEE), THE CURLY LOOK-ALIKE, A JOLLY MASTER WHO FARTS AND LAUGHS HIS WAY THROUGH LIFE. HIS DRAWING-POEMS GIVE **TCR** ITS UNIQUE LOOK.

HE, LINDA, KYLE, LUNA AND I ARE THE COLLECTIVE EDITORIAL **WE** THAT I SOMETIMES REFER TO.

I FIRST PERFORMED WITH JESSE AND JACK WITH HIS WIFE ADELLE, ALONG WITH THE WACKY PERFORMANCE/POETRY BAND **THE OUTPATIENTS**, WHEN I WAS LOCKED OUT OF **THE LAB**, A BAY AREA GALLERY WHICH HAD BOOKED ME BUT THEN BACKED OUT ON ITS COMMITMENT. WE PERFORMED ON THE SIDEWALK IN FRONT OF THE LOCKED GALLERY FOR TWO NIGHTS. THAT WAS ABOUT THREE YEARS AGO. SINCE THEN, WE HAVE PERFORMED TOGETHER NUMEROUS TIMES WITHIN THE POETRY COMMUNITY, WHICH IS IN GENERAL MORE EXPERIMENTAL, ACCEPTING, AND OPEN THAN THE ART SCENE...MAYBE BECAUSE IN POETRY THE POSSIBILITY, AND HENCE THE PRESSURE, OF MONEY, FAME, FASHION, AND EVEN OF AN AUDIENCE/READERSHIP IS SLIM.

JACK IS A DRIVING FORCE IN THE BAY AREA POETRY SCENE, HAVING A POETRY SHOW ON **KPFA** AND EDITING **POETRY USA.** I WAS GOING TO TRY TO DESCRIBE JACK'S ART. BUT I HAVE DECIDED TO PUT MY POEM ABOUT JACK IN THIS ISSUE. THAT SAVES ME THAT IMPOSSIBLE JOB. BY THE WAY **MASTER JAMES** IN JACK'S POEM IS THE GAY (IN MANY MORE WAYS THAN SEXUAL) POET/FILMMAKER JAMES BROUGHTON WHO IS MAKING LOVE TO LIFE IN HIS POST-75-YEAR OLD ERA. JACK HAS BOOKED **THE CHERO COMPANY** AT MANY POETRY EVENTS. A PART OF OUR FUNCTION AT THESE EVENTS, SOME OF WHICH WERE VERY HIGH CLASS, WAS TO CALL FORTH A MAGICAL CONTEXT FOR THE EVENT BY SITTING NUDE IN THE AUDIENCE. ONE TIME JACK BOOKED US FOR A POETRY READING AT A CAFE WHICH INFORMED JACK THERE COULD BE NO NUDITY DURING THE READING.....SO THERE WAS NOT...BUT THERE WAS PLENTY OF NUDITY BEFORE AND AFTER. THIS READING EVENT IS THE SUBJECT OF JESSE'S POEM. JESSE IS ANOTHER OF THOSE SEXY BEINGS BEYOND AGE. SHE IS A BLUES SINGER, A COMPOSER, A WRITER, A PERFORMER, ETC.

IN FACT, WE HAVE QUITE A NUMBER OF CULT FIGURES REPRESENTED IN THIS ISSUE. NONI IS A COMMANDING FIGURE IN BOTH THE POETRY WORLD AND THE SEXUAL UNDERGROUND. BRENDA IS THE PUBLISHER OF **EIDOS,** THE MILITANT SEX PAPER. TRACY AND DIVIANA MAKE UP A REVOLUTIONARY ARTISTIC COUPLE. ERIC IS ONE OF THE NATION'S BEST PHOTOGRAPHERS...AND A SWEET GUY.

AND WILL OF THE WISP JUST SENT THE CARTOONS BY THE MAIL. BUT THEY SPEAK FOR THEMSELVES.

THIS ISSUE MAY LOOK LIKE A POETRY ISSUE. IN A WAY, I HOPE EVERY ISSUE WILL BE A POETRY ISSUE EVEN WHEN THERE WILL BE NOTHING IN THAT CERTAIN ISSUE WHICH LOOKS OR SOUNDS LIKE POETRY. I HOPE THIS BECAUSE POETRY AT THE HEART IS AN ALCHEMICAL LANGUAGE REACHING OUT OF THE NORMAL REALITY INTO THE SUPER-NORMAL NONLINEAR REALITY IN WHICH THE CHEROTIC REVOLUTION, BOTH THE MAGAZINE AND THE MOVEMENT, EXISTS. BUT WE WILL NEVER DO THEME ISSUES SUCH AS POETRY, GAY, SEX, WOMEN, ETC. THIS IS BECAUSE THE THEME FORMAT IS A GREAT WAY FOR EDITORS AND GALLERIES (ETC.) TO KEEP CONTROL OF CONTENT, STYLE, POINT OF VIEW, AND THE ACCESSIBILITY OF THE COMMUNICATION CHANNELS THEY MANAGE. THE THEME CONCEPT ALSO FRAGMENTS BOTH PEOPLE AND DIALOGUE INTO LABELED BITS THAT CAN BE SHUFFLED IN AND OUT OF FASHION TIME. **TCR** WILL FOLLOW THE MAGIC WHEREVER IT NON-LINEARLY GOES. WE WILL PRINT WHAT WE LIKE, WHAT INTERESTS US...BUT WE PROBABLY WILL OFTEN PRINT WHAT WE DO NOT LIKE, ARE NOT INTERESTED IN. SO YOU WILL NEVER BE SURE WHY WE PRINT, OR DO NOT PRINT, SOMETHING. BUT YOU CAN REST ASSURED IT IS NOT BECAUSE YOU ARE IN A FRAMED GROUP.

WHILE WE ARE AT IT, WE CAN OUTLINE OUR FRAME OF COMMUNICATIONS. I WANT TO HEAR FROM YOU. MY ADDRESS IS THROUGHOUT THIS MAG. I CAN NOT PROMISE TO PERSONALLY WRITE BACK...BUT I MAY. BUT I MAY PRINT ALL OR PARTS OF WHAT IS SENT TO ME IN **TCR** UNLESS REQUESTED NOT TO. WE RESERVE THE RIGHT TO EDIT UNSOLICITED MATERIAL. BUT WE WILL NOT EDIT SOLICITED MATERIAL.

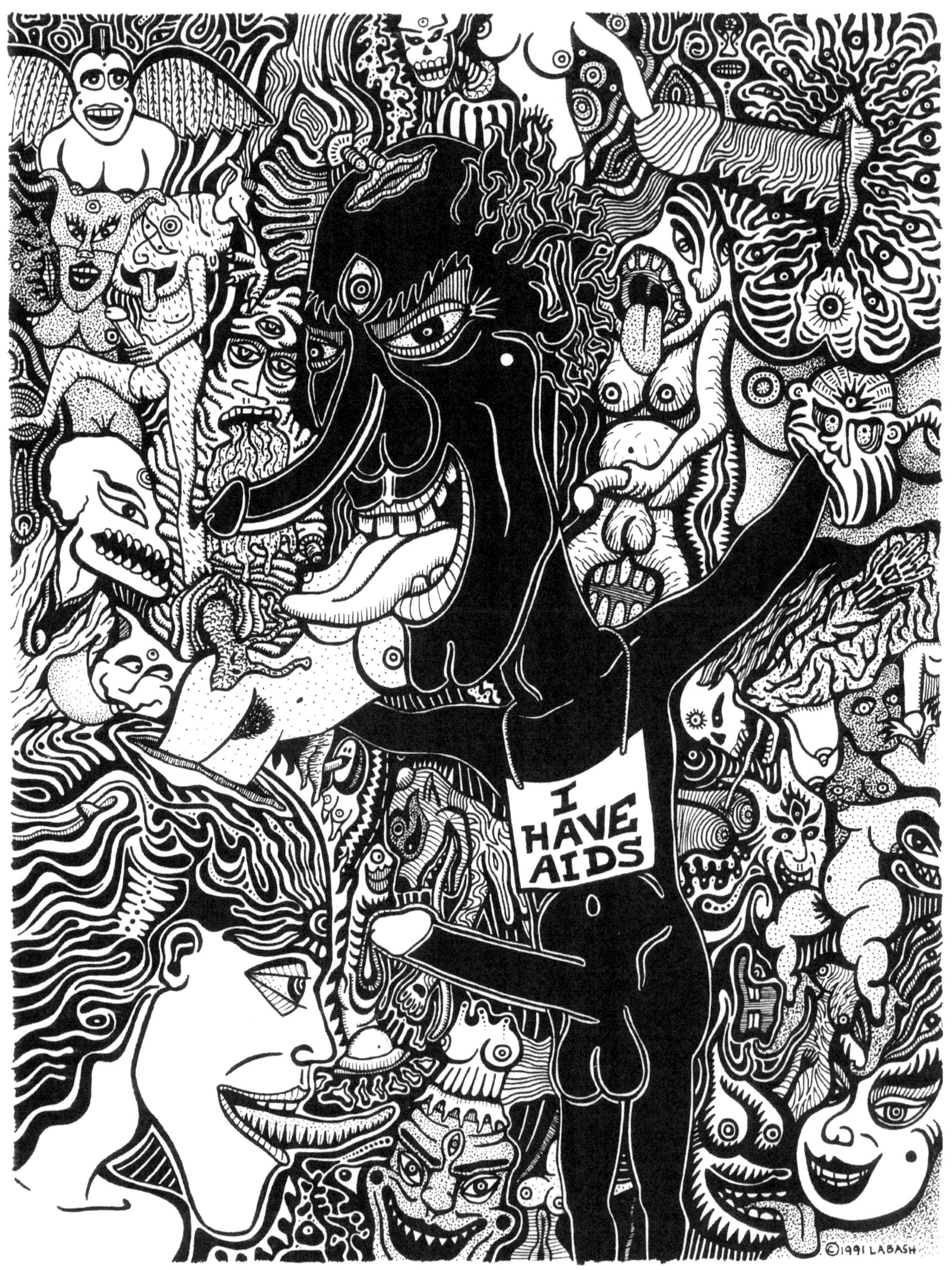
I HAVE AIDS
©1991 LABASH

THE BLACK SHEEP
by
KAREN FINLEY

After a funeral someone said to me
You know I only see you at funerals
it's been three since June --
been five since June for me.
He said I've made a vow --
I only go to death parties if I know someone
before they were sick.
Why?
'cause -- 'cause -- 'cause I feel I feel so
sad 'cause I never knew their lives
and now I only know their deaths
And because we are members of the
Black Sheep family.

We are sheep with no shepherd
We are sheep with no straight and narrow
We are sheep with no meadow
We are sheep who take the dangerous pathway through
the mountain range
to get to the other side of our soul.
We are the black sheep of the family
called Black Sheep folk.
We always speak our mind
   appreciate differences in culture
   believe in sexual preferences
   believe in no racism
   no sexism
   no religionism
and we fight for what we believe but
usually we're pagans.
There's always one in every family.
Even when we're surrounded by bodies
we're always alone.
You're born alone
and you die alone --
written by a black sheep.
You can't take it with you --
written by a former black sheep.

Black Sheep folk look different from their families --
It's the way we look at the world.
We're a quirk of nature --
We're a quirk of fate.
Usually our family, our city,
our country never understands us --
We knew this from when we were very young
that we weren't meant to be understood.
That's right, that's our job.
Usually we're not appreciated until the next generation.

That's our life, that's our story.
Usually we're outcasts, outsiders in our own family.
Don't worry -- get used to it.
My sister says -- I don't understand you!
But I have many sisters with me tonight.
My brother says -- I don't want you!
But I have many brothers with me here tonight!
My mother says -- I don't know how to love
someone like you!
You're so different from the rest!
But I have many mamas with me here tonight!
My father says -- I don't know how to hold you!
But I have many many daddies with me here tonight!

We're related to people we love who can't say
   I love you Black sheep daughter
   I love you Black sheep son
   I love you outcast, I love you outsider.
But tonight we love each other
That's why we're here --
to be around others like ourselves --
So it doesn't hurt quite so much.
In our world, our temple of difference
I am at my loneliest when I have something to celebrate
and try to share it with those I love
but who don't love me back.
There's always silence at the end of the phone.
There's always silence at the end of the phone.

Sister -- congratulate me!
NO I CAN'T YOU'RE TOO LOUD.
Grandma -- love me!
NO I DON'T KNOW HOW TO LOVE
SOMEONE LIKE YOU.
Sometimes the Black Sheep is a soothsayer,
a psychic, a magician of sorts.
Black sheep see the invisible --
We know each other's thoughts --
We feel fear and hatred.

Sometimes some sheep are chosen to be sick
    to finally have average, flat, boring people say
    I love you.
Sometimes Black sheep are chosen to be sick
    so families can finally come together and say
    I love you.
Sometimes some Black Sheep are chosen to die
    so loved ones and families can finally say --
    Your life was worth living
    Your life meant something to me!
Black Sheeps' destinies are not necessarily in having
families, having prescribed existences --
    like the American Dream.

Black Sheeps' destinies are to give meaning in life
    to be angels
    to be conscience

to be nightmares
to be actors in dreams.

Black Sheep can be family to strangers
We can love each other like MOTHER
FATHER SISTER BROTHER CHILD
We understand universal love
We understand unconditional love
We feel a unique responsibility, a human responsibility
for feelings for others.
We can be all things to all people
We are there at 3:30 AM when you call
We are here tonight 'cause I just can't go to sleep.
I have nowhere to go.
I'm a creature of the night --
I travel in your dreams --
I feel your nightmares --

We are your holding hand
We are your pillow, your receiver
your cuddly toy.
I feel your pain
I wish I could relieve you of your suffering.
I wish I could relieve you of your pain.
I wish I could relieve you of your destiny.
I wish I could relieve you of your fate.
I wish I could relieve you of your illness.
I wish I could relieve you of your life.
I wish I could relieve you of your death.
But it's always
Silence at the end of the phone.
Silence at the end of the phone.
Silence at the end of the phone.

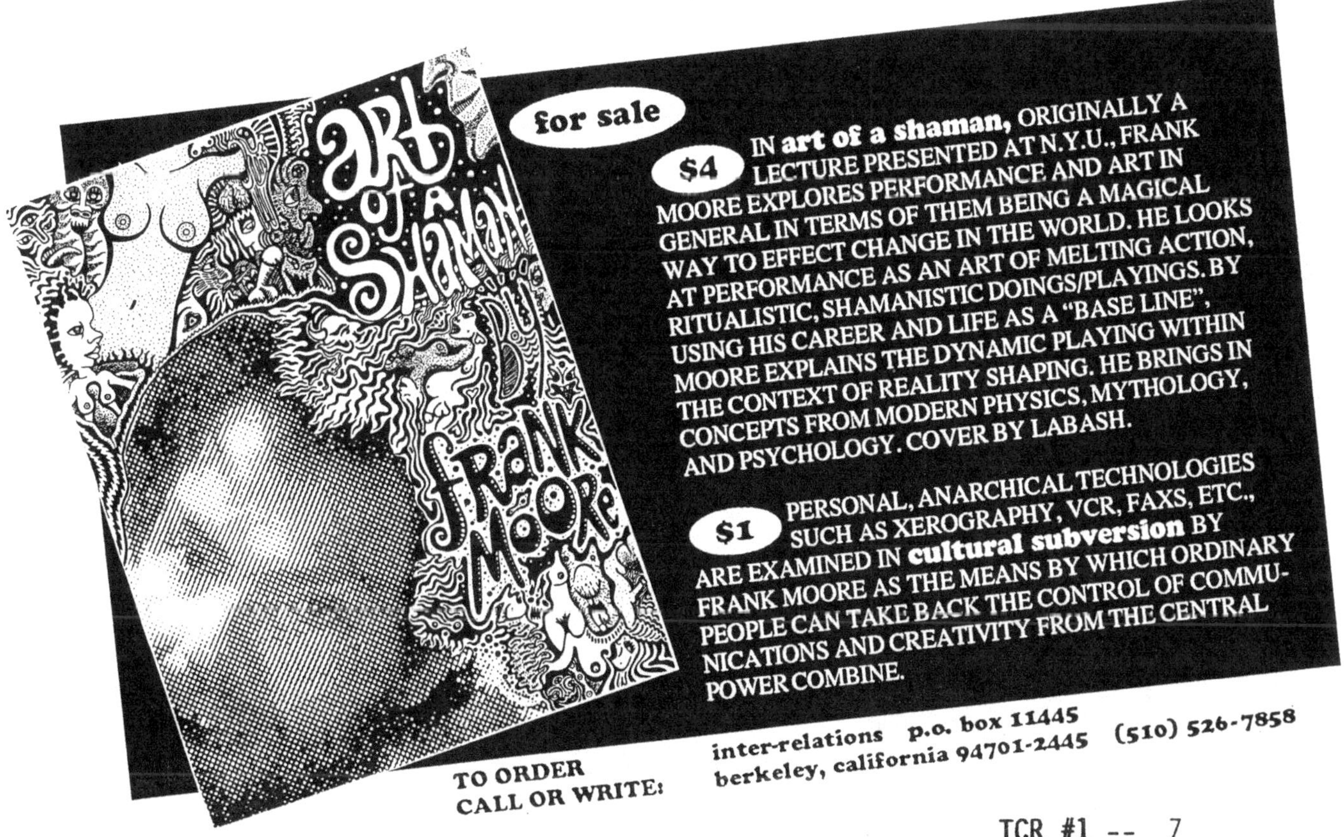

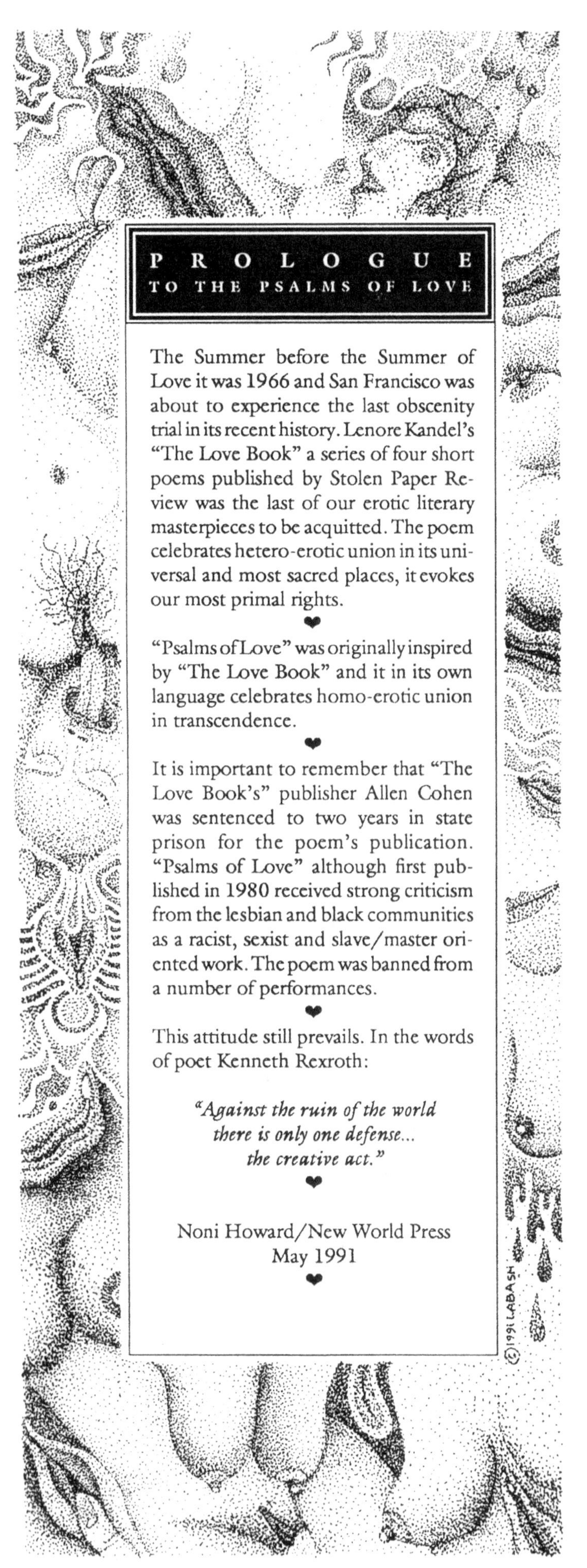

PROLOGUE
TO THE PSALMS OF LOVE

The Summer before the Summer of Love it was 1966 and San Francisco was about to experience the last obscenity trial in its recent history. Lenore Kandel's "The Love Book" a series of four short poems published by Stolen Paper Review was the last of our erotic literary masterpieces to be acquitted. The poem celebrates hetero-erotic union in its universal and most sacred places, it evokes our most primal rights.

❤

"Psalms of Love" was originally inspired by "The Love Book" and it in its own language celebrates homo-erotic union in transcendence.

❤

It is important to remember that "The Love Book's" publisher Allen Cohen was sentenced to two years in state prison for the poem's publication. "Psalms of Love" although first published in 1980 received strong criticism from the lesbian and black communities as a racist, sexist and slave/master oriented work. The poem was banned from a number of performances.

❤

This attitude still prevails. In the words of poet Kenneth Rexroth:

"Against the ruin of the world
there is only one defense...
the creative act."

❤

Noni Howard/New World Press
May 1991

❤

The Psalms of Love

I

the unendurable magic
of our making ourselves love.

your hands wispers of flames on my breasts
my belly heaves
molten sweat runs from our tongues
our saliva drips from our eyes.

long later i carry the pain of you
hidden in my flesh,
all week i wear the mask
of your kisses
my tongue so full of love
that when i smile
poems crack and all my words
are lies.

❤

the smell of your hair
on my neck
the fuck of you
my come dripping between
your legs
your tongue in my mouth

SURELY GOODNESS AND MERCY SHALL
FOLLOW ME ALL THE DAYS OF MY LIFE
AND I WILL DWELL IN THE HOUSE
OF THE LORD FOREVER

❤

you are gifted to know love
to caress the warm air and make it
flesh
and flesh to blood
deep and coming

ripe with desire and understanding
so that sacrilege and profanity
follows us
is all around us
seeking force to enter
the room with the altar
where you and i are holy
burning flesh to flesh.

II

you lie under me
farther than mountains under clouds
my wings pierce your smooth skin
i baptize you with my sweat.

my tears run into the rivers
of your come
my hands are full of you.

you are child beneath me
crying for absolution
i see your innocence and sadness
i forgive you your sins.
i have given you a new skin
to open like doors;
when i lay down the gifts
i have brought you:
          my hands, my eyes, my lips
you receive my offerings
i give you no choice.

III

i take off your outer skin
and you come naked to me
lay yourself down
upon my breasts,
i rock you to sleep
i sing songs in your flowing veins
i exhaust the day from you
and make it ours.

you are a thousand miles
below me
i carve out new patterns in your
aching flesh:
mountains, waves, whole trees and treacherous
valleys open to my touch.

with my tongue, my hands
my lips
i give you this act
of worship.

you are mine.
you have no other gods
before me.

IV

you have no name but mine
repeat it.
see it shine before us
between us
let it spill off our tongues
into our mouths
together.

i have built a great fire and placed you in its
numinous light.
you are the altar
the holy place
that i consecrate
for my enjoyment.

you are the scabbard of my pleasures
the blood lust
the sea salt of my mother
the one breasted god that we
breast to breast
make whole.

repeat it.
repeat the names of god.

V

i draw the knife of my thought
over your throat
and suck you into me.

you become my blood
the rivers of your fears
flow into me.

i bind you with my mind
your body incarnate
i fashion with my hands.

the upturned breasts
perfect as alabaster,
the soft belly moulded
by desire,
the swelling lips full to receive
my blessing.

turn and let me admire you.
turn and let me see
what i have done.

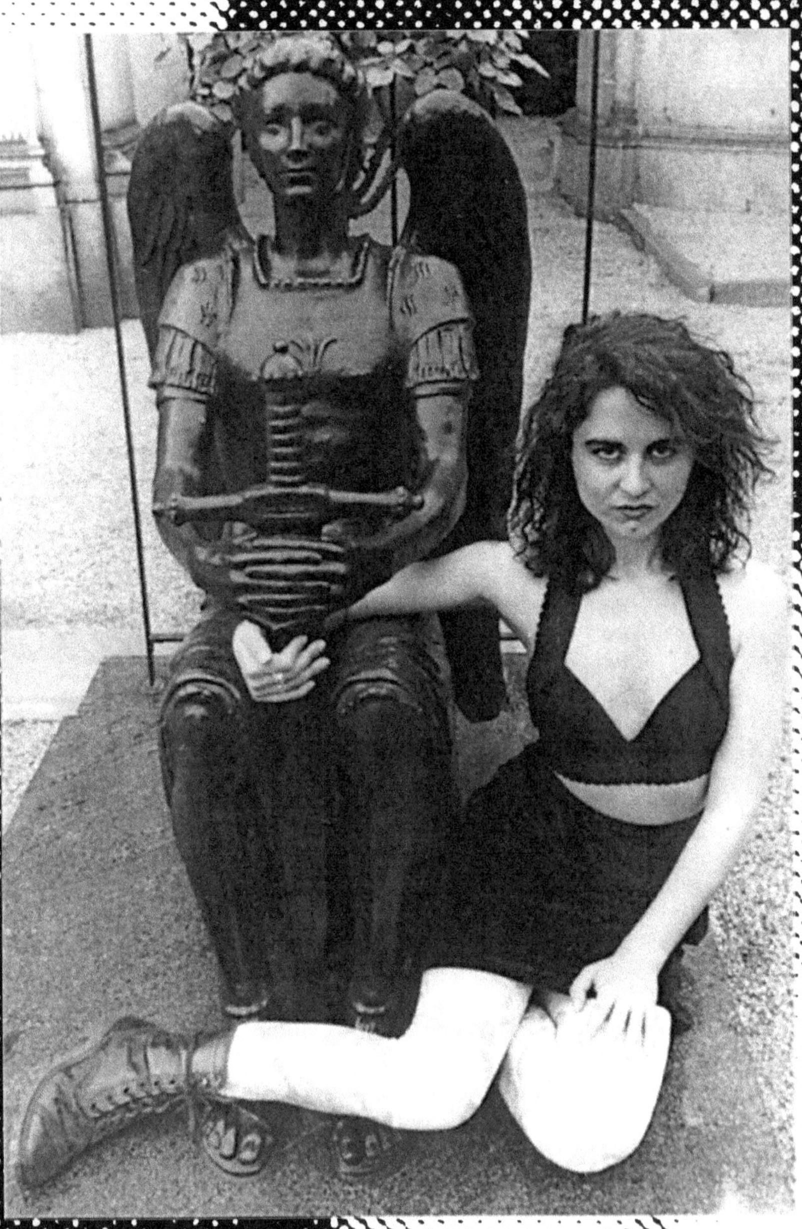

Photo by Tracy Mostovoy

SUCCUBUS
A Video by TRACY MOSTOVOY
Description by KYLE GRIFFITH

The Succubus dances seductively in a doorway:

"Christian abhorrence of sex began with the Fathers of the Church, who insisted that the Kingdom of God on Earth could not be established until the human race was allowed to die out through universal celibacy."

"For many centuries, the Church insisted that orgasms in women were unseemly and devilish."

Two androgynous faces are linked in an "open-air" kiss -- tongues extended all the way out and twining around one another like snakes:

"Saint Augustine pronounced that 'Sexual intercourse is never sinless, even within marriage.'"

The nude Succubus peeks out from behind rock formations in the Grand Canyon, as tourists go by on mules:

"Saint Peter said, 'Women are not worthy of life.'"

"The Goddess of Love, Aphrodite, La Mere, Marina, represents both beauty and wisdom. All women serve in the temple of love."

A neck-to-knee shot of the nude Succubus carrying a small bouquet of pink flowers:

"In the Christian view, women brought death into the world. Sex perpetuated it."

A man masturbates, leering joyfully into the camera:

"St. Jerome ordered, 'Regard everything as poison which bears within it the seed of sensual pleasure."

The Succubus bares her breasts in front of a ruined adobe chapel, a large white cross looming threateningly over her head:

"Officials of the Inquisition taught that women's carnal lust was the cause of Witchcraft and Satanism."

In the driver's seat of a car, the Succubus kisses her lover's breasts:

"Clement of Alexandria pronounced, 'I have come to destroy the works of the female. Every woman ought to be filled with shame at the thought that she is a woman.'"

The Succubus draws sensuous patterns in lipstick across her torso:

"Pope Paul VI, in 1976, pronounced masturbation 'a grave moral disorder,' and that 'only the finality of procreation' could ensure the moral goodness of sex."

Preening in front of a dressing-table mirror, the Succubus touches her body playfully:

"In the temple of the Goddess, the sacred ritual of mating with the opposite sex did not exclude from worship pleasure among women -- lesbian sexual practices were employed to dispel evil, to heal, and prophesy."

The Succubus spanks herself with a flyswatter:

"Patriarchal religion was devoted to the destruction of the sensual female nature. Women's sexual desire was considered detrimental to the marital relationship."

Lesbian lovers embrace in a shower:

"Sinibaldi said no woman could conceive if she enjoyed sex."

The Succubus does a sensual dance down a long hotel corridor:

"The Goddess was regarded as the patron deity of sexual love. In the worship of the female deity, sex was her gift to humanity. It was sacred and holy."

* * *

"SUCCUBUS" was written, produced, and filmed by Tracy Mostovoy and edited by Diane Mele. Diviana Ingravallo stars as the title character. The video had its world premiere at the Highways Gallery in Santa Monica on June 28 through July 5, 1991 as the introduction to Tracy and Diviana's multi-media performance piece "NAKED WOMEN."

"NAKED WOMEN" will be performed at The Kitchen in New York City on December 12 through December 17, 1991 and at the Theatre Rhinoceros in San Francisco in June, 1992.

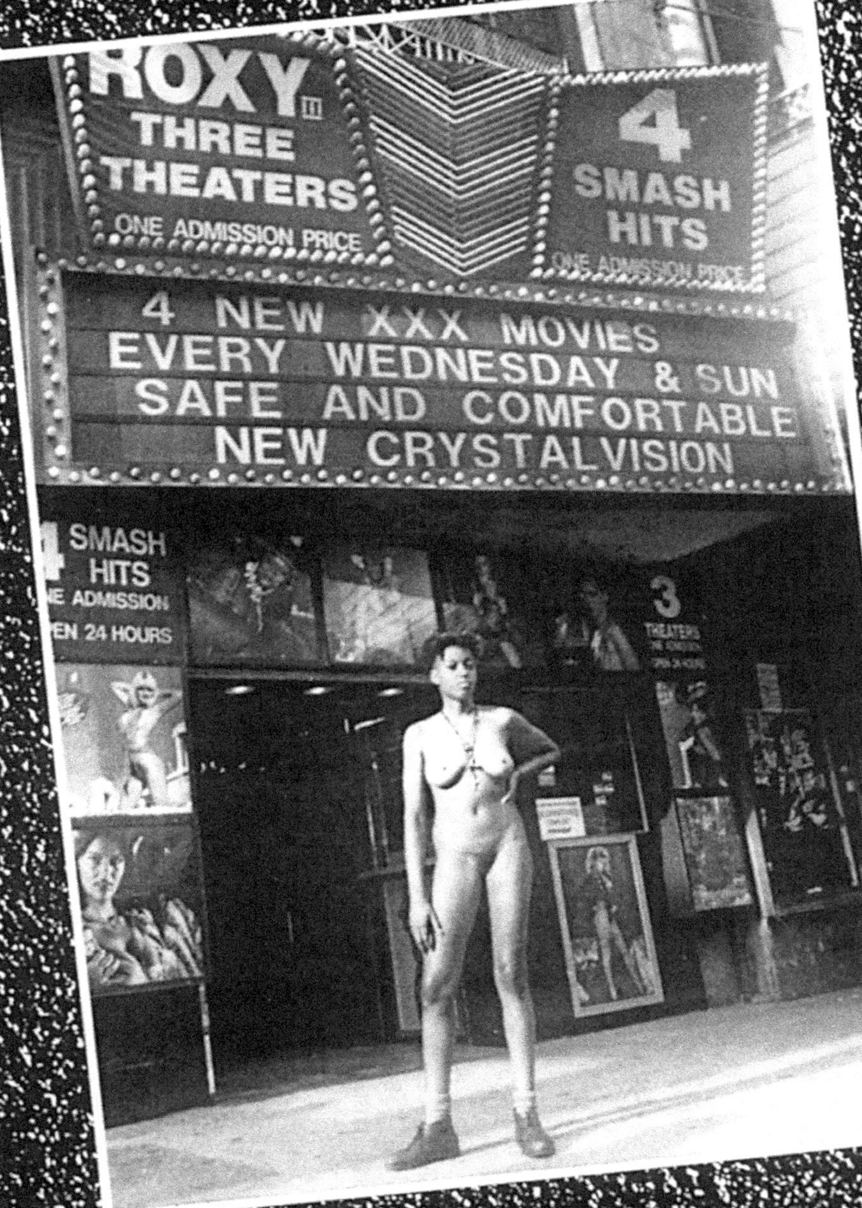

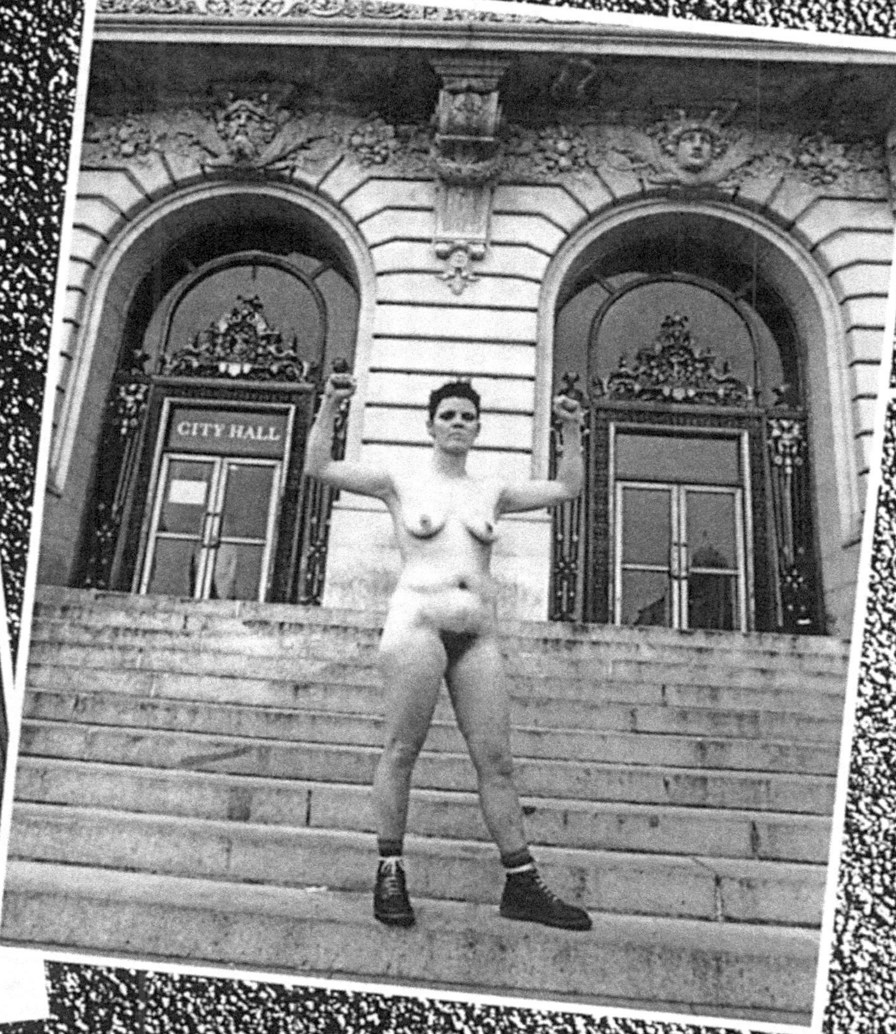

Photos by Tracy Mostovoy

MAXINE and the GODDESS
by
KYLE GRIFFITH

The way in which a work of art helps shape the viewer's personal reality is extremely complex and non-linear. I've always been aware of this, of course, but my recent experience with writing a critical analysis of the multi-media performance piece "Naked Women" by Diviana Ingravallo and Tracy Mostovoy has, I think, given me some new insight into the whole concept of "archetypes" and the way they affect life.

The main archetype used in the piece is the symbolic division of the phases of a woman's life into the three aspects of the Triple Goddess: virgin, mother, and hag. But Diviana's character "Maxine" does not live a typical life. We first see her in a vagina-dentata costume, having what is eventually revealed to be a daydream about turning into a vengeful avatar of the Goddess and sexually devouring the men who leer at her as she dances in a strip-club. In the second part of the scene, she describes her day-to-day life as a stripper and her relationships with various people: the men in her audiences, the other strippers, and her lesbian lover. In the second scene, she is an S&M mistress, invoking images of Kali, Goddess of Destruction, as she describes her interactions with her clients. Finally, the third scene shows her as a prostitute, walking the streets and engaging in fantasies that border on madness, no longer able to tell inspirational thoughts about the Goddess from mere wishful thinking.

The entire monologue is a mixture of utter realism with symbolic fantasy -- alternately linear and non-linear, as poetry often is. This mixture of linear and non-linear reality is greatly heightened by Tracy's slides, which are projected on the wall behind Diviana at intervals throughout the show. Some are completely realistic -- for example, a series of shots of men under bondage and torture in an S&M dungeon. Others are blurred, distorted, or flashed too fast for the eye to fully register -- especially a number of lesbian-erotic shots. And the appearance of the slides in relation to what Diviana is saying in the monologue is carefully timed to produce a complex, non-linear effect.

Maxine's monologs, alternating between her archetypal fantasies about the Goddess and vivid descriptions of the -- often sordid -- details of her own life are heavy with irony and a basic sense of hopelessness and frustration gave me a powerful feeling that Maxine often misused the Goddess archetype and ended up creating a reality for herself that was essentially negative and destructive. For example, the "vagina dentata" daydream is just a fantasy about the revenge the stripper would take on the men in her audiences if she only had the power of a goddess to turn the destructive potential in their exploitative lust back on them. And when Maxine starts talking about her actual on-stage relationships with these men, it becomes obvious that she herself actively and consciously contributes to creating the cycle of mutual contempt and loathing by allowing herself to indulge all of her own negative feelings while performing.

Since she makes her living by turning men on with her strip-performances, but isn't sexually attracted to them, the healthy way to react to their lust would be to repress her negative feelings about it as much as possible, and especially to conceal these feelings from her audience. By indulging these feelings and openly treating the men with contempt, she is helping create a social reality that perpetuates the concept of "sex as conquest and exploitation." And she's completely aware of this, because she says, "Tom is a go-go bar addict, and I'm a notorious co." So she's allowing herself to perpetuate the problem by refusing to control how she expresses her inner feelings.

When the same analysis is applied to the mistress, it appears on the surface that Maxine has learned this lesson, but her dialog proves that she hasn't. Her overt behavior on stage is now completely appropriate to the situation -- her clients have come to fulfill a desire to submit to a dominatrix, and her contempt for them contributes to this. The men she dominates come away from the sessions feeling they got what they asked for -- she doesn't frustrate them the way she did her audiences as a stripper, so she's not actively being a co-dependent for addiction -- but from her own viewpoint, being a mistress is just as frustrating and exploitative as being a stripper.

The client gets what he wants out of being a slave for a brief period, then goes back to his regular role in the male-dominated "real world" after receiving a form of psychotherapy to keep him from going crazy over the guilt generated by being an exploiter, but the mistress isn't really getting anything out of the process except money. Being an S&M dominant doesn't work to liberate one from the desire for power -- if there's any effect on the personality, it tends to be the reverse. Maxine's fantasies remain essentially the same as a mistress as they were when she was a stripper -- she still wants revenge for wrongs done to women, still creates mental images of a flesh-devouring Goddess. And she remains just as aware of the essential irony of the situation, as when she says, "I am so forever in their debt for giving themselves to the Goddess during their lunch-break, before they go back to working for God." As I watched this scene, I kept hoping she'd realize that, instead of wishing that she could actually maim or kill these men, and fantasizing a monster-goddess to do it for her, she would be much better off realizing that she, too, could empower herself through "switching" and becoming a submissive some of the time (a common practice in the professional S&M community).

By the time Maxine has become a prostitute, her fantasies have become so mixed up with her opinions about realities that she obviously can no longer discriminate between them. She is the Goddess, she is Mary Magdalene, and she is equally the burned-out old whore who can genuinely believe that in a few days she'll be off the streets and turning her tricks in a mansion in Beverly Hills. This is the reality, both on the earth plane and in her fantasies, that her actions have created over the whole course of her life. She continues to survive, and she still has the capacity to love and to enjoy life (to some extent, though we in the audience don't know how much from the brief glimpse we get of her), but it's easy for an observer to conclude that both her personality and her whole quality of life have degenerated from the way they were when we first saw her as a young stripper.

Maxine is at her best -- in terms of personal happiness and being in contact with reality -- in the first of her guises, as the stripper. For example, when she describes her relationship with her lover while artistic slides of lesbian erotica flash on the screen behind her; and when she talks about the positive, supportive relationships between her and the other strippers. When she takes on personal responsibility, she creates an image, an archetype, of the Goddess within herself that gives her more power to control her own destiny.

The best words I can find to approximate the non-linear message "Naked Women" conveys to its audience are: "Yes, there is something of the Great Triple Goddess of mythology in every woman, and yes, she has great power against male-supremacist religion and all of the authoritarian, exploitative social institutions it has created, but be careful. The Goddess, like any archetype or role-model, is something you create in your own mind as you use your existing knowledge about the concept (learned from mythology and other outside sources) to generalize from your life-experience and frame a personal myth or world-view.

So when you create your own personal Goddess, be sure she's somebody you want guiding your life from here on out."

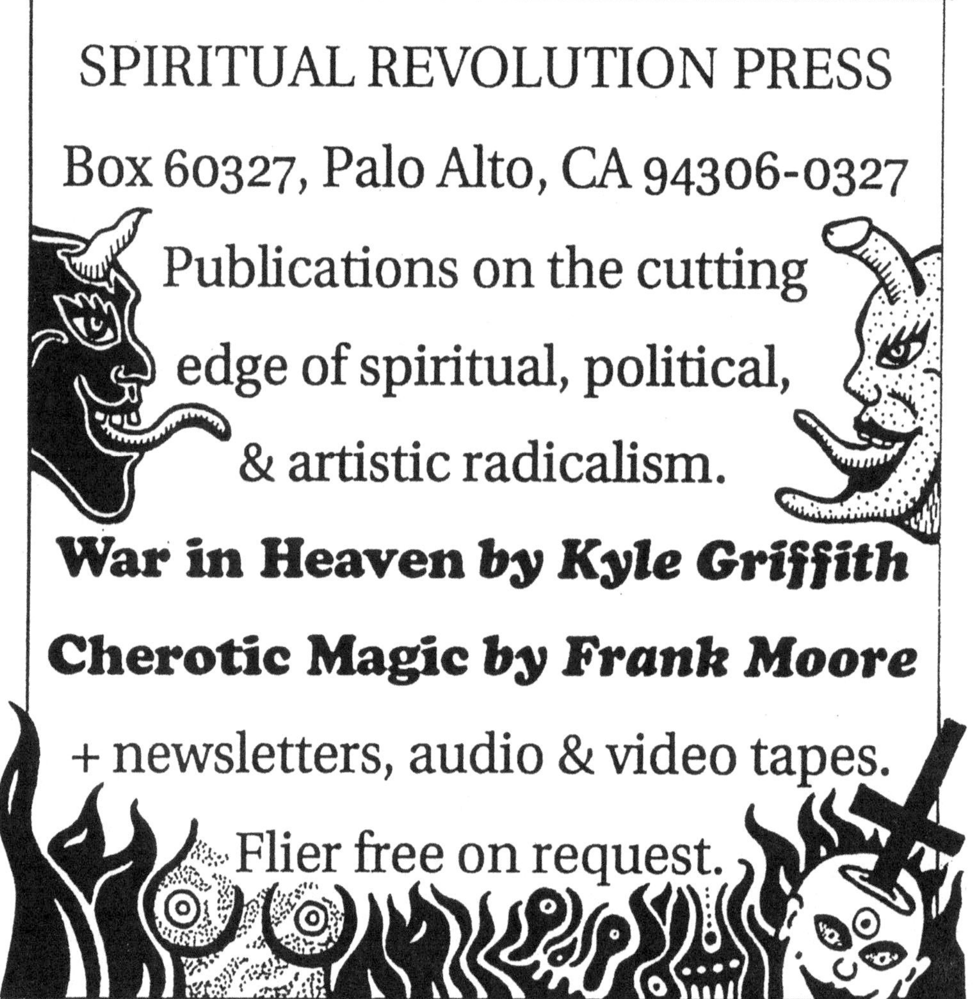

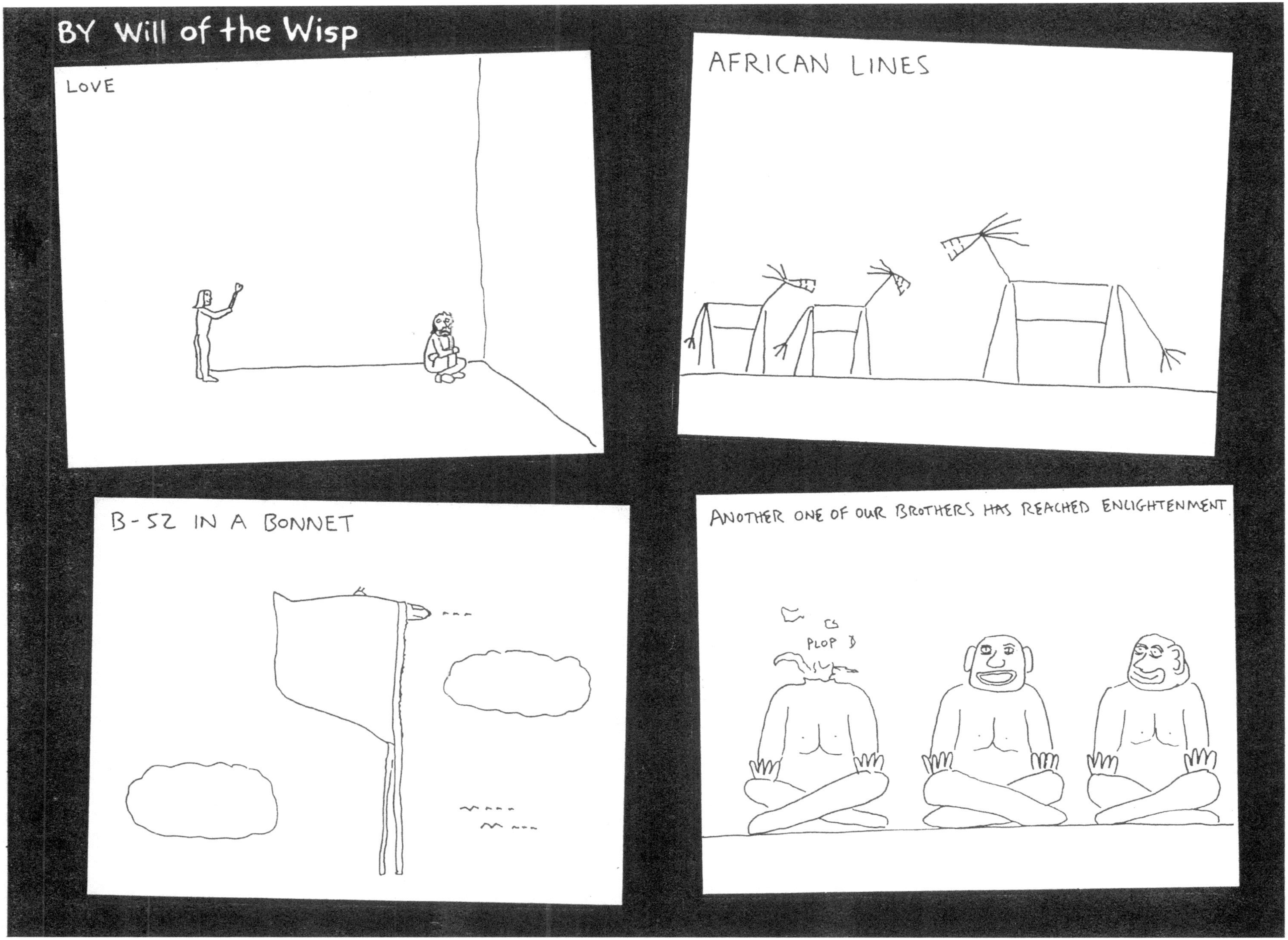

BY Will of the Wisp

LOVE

AFRICAN LINES

B-52 IN A BONNET

ANOTHER ONE OF OUR BROTHERS HAS REACHED ENLIGHTENMENT

PLOP

NONLINEAR BITS

by

FRANK MOORE

AN NONLINEAR POLITICAL COLUMN.

WE WENT TO THE MOVIES...PASOLINI'S ARABIAN NIGHTS AT BERKELEY'S ALTERNATIVE THEATRE. EATING CANDY, DRINKING COKE, RUBBING EACH OTHER, PLEASURE MAINTAINED ALMOST UNTIL THE END OF THE MOVIE, THEN QUIET COMING, THRILLING GENTLE PLEASURE EXPLOSIONS. JUST AN ORDINARY NIGHT AT THE MOVIES. IT WAS FAR AWAY FROM THE BRAVE NEW WORLD MORALITY COPS IN FLORIDA WHERE A GROWN MAN CAN BE ARRESTED AND LOSE HIS CAREER FOR JACKING OFF IN A SEX MOVIE THEATRE...WHERE IT ISN'T SAFE TO MAKE LOVE IN YOUR OWN BATHROOM OR BEDROOM BECAUSE YOU CAN BE ARRESTED, LOSE YOUR HOME, AND BE HUMILIATED...WHERE PEEPING TOMS WITH VIDEO CAMERAS ARE HEROS AS LONG AS THEY ARE ANTI-SEX AND HIDE BEHIND CHILDREN.

YES, OUR PLEASURE AT THE MOVIES WAS FAR AWAY FROM THE STATE OF MIND CALLED FLORIDA. RUBBING FOR ENJOYMENT, JUST LIKE EATING POPCORN. TAKING PUBLIC REALITY BACK INTO PERSONAL REALITY IS THE MAGICAL EFFECT OF SUCH PUBLIC ACTS, WHICH ARE MADE INVISIBLE TO THE SURROUNDING REALITY BY THE PERSONAL EVERYDAY NATURE OF SUCH ACTS, INSTEAD OF BEING REACTIVE CONFRONTATIONS. THE REASON CLOSEST TO THE SURFACE FOR SUCH ACTS IN **PUBLIC** PLACES IS THE PHYSICAL EXPRESSION OF ENJOYING OF FRIENDS AND LOVERS AND HUMANS JUST BEING TOGETHER. BUT THESE INVISIBLE PRIVATE/PUBLIC ACTS OF PLEASURE BECOME A POWERFUL FORCE FOR EFFECTIVE POLITICAL/SOCIAL/CULTURAL CHANGE WHEN THEY COLLIDE ON THEIR OWN WITH LIFE-DENIALS SUCH AS THE FLORIDA STATE OF MIND. THE EFFECTIVENESS OF SUCH PERSONAL PLEASURE ACTS, WHICH ARE IN REALITY SEXUAL OR CHEROTIC MAGIC, IS IN THE FACT THAT THEY ARE NOT REACTIVE, CONFRONTATIONAL, OR AN EXHIBITION OF SPECIALNESS OR DIFFERENCE...NOT WRAPPING OURSELVES IN THE GLAMOUR OF BEING KINKY, PERVERTED, OR EVIL AND THEREBY FALSELY CREATING OURSELVES INTO AN ELITE ABOVE THE COMMON HUMAN. BEING REACTIONARY ALWAYS CHAINS YOU TO THE OLD REALITY TO WHICH YOU ARE REACTING.

INSTEAD, THESE ACTS OF PERSONAL MAGIC ARE CREATING THE ALTERNATIVE REALITY WHICH WE WANT, RECLAIMING FREEDOM BY ACTING FREE, CALLING FORTH YIN ENERGY BY USING YIN ENERGY. THE FACT THAT THE FEMINIST MOVEMENT IN THE 70'S AND 80'S ON THE WHOLE DIDN'T USE THIS CHANNEL OF CHANGE CREATED LIMITS TO THE TRANSFORMATION OF GENDER.

TRACY'S DOING HER "NAKED WOMEN IN PUBLIC PLACES" PHOTOGRAPHIC SERIES IS ANOTHER EXAMPLE OF THIS RECLAIMING PUBLIC REALITY, RETURNING IT TO PERSONAL FREEDOM. WE HAVE DONE THESE RUBBING GOOD FEELING ACTS OF HUMANNESS AND SUBVERSION AT BASEBALL GAMES, IN THE MIDDLE OF THE SIDEWALK IN THE AFTERNOON, ON TRAINS AND PLANES. FOR MONTHS, FIVE OF US SAT IN THE MIDDLE OF A COFFEEHOUSE, PLAYING CARDS, DRINKING COFFEE, KISSING, RUBBING ONE ANOTHER INTO A PLEASURE TRANCE. JUST EVERYDAY HUMAN LIVING. BECAUSE OUR ATTITUDE TO OUR PLAYING IS THAT IT IS JUST EVERYDAY HUMAN LIVING, WE WERE INVISIBLE. NO ONE SAW, NOTICED, OR COMPLAINED. BECAUSE THE ART OF INVISIBILITY IS TRICKY, I AM STOPPING SHORT OF ADVOCATING SUCH RADICAL ACTS UNLESS YOU ARE PREPARED FOR ANY OUTCOME. SUCH INVISIBLE ACTION DOES NOT HAVE TO BE AT THIS DEGREE OF REVOLUTIONARY INTENSITY TO BE EFFECTIVE. EVERY TIME YOU KISS OR HUG OR LAUGH OR SMILE OUT IN THE "PUBLIC" WORLD, EVERY TIME YOU WEAR COLORFUL SEXY REVEALING CLOTHES, OR DO NOT WEAR A BRA (OR JUST WEARING ONE), OR ANY LUSTY JOYFUL ACT, YOU ARE PERFORMING A VERY POWERFUL MAGICAL/POLITICAL ACTION OF WHICH EFFECTS CAN NOT BE DELETED BY ANY LINEAR MEANS.

I CANNOT LEAVE THE FLORIDA STATE OF MIND WITHOUT COMMENTING DIRECTLY ABOUT THE PAUL REUBENS' CASE. I HAVE BEEN SEEING **FREE PEEWEE** BUTTONS AND SHIRTS. THEY DID NOT ARREST PEEWEE. THEY ARRESTED PAUL. CBS USED THIS FALSELY COMBINING THE ARTISTIC CREATION OF PEEWEE WITH THE REAL PERSON PAUL WHEN PULLING THE SHOW OFF THE AIR. WE DO REUBENS NO FAVORS BY CONFUSING THE TWO REALITIES. CBS DID NOT CAN THE SHOW FOR ANY LACK OF QUALITY OF THE SHOW OR ANY LACK IN THE RATINGS. THEY CANNED THE SHOW BECAUSE THE MAN PAUL DID WHAT HE HAD A RIGHT TO DO...GOING TO A SEX MOVIE AND JACKING-OFF[1]...AND GETTING CAUGHT BY THE MORALS PEEPING TOM COPS. THEY CANNED THE SHOW BECAUSE THEIR PRODUCT HAD BEEN DAMAGED BY HUMAN SEX LIFE.

MY READERS WILL HAVE NO TROUBLE IN SHARING MY RIGHTEOUS OUTRAGE SO FAR. BUT THE HARD PART IS COMING. WHAT HAPPENED TO REUBENS HAPPENED TO ANDY ROONEY AND JIMMY THE GREEK NOT SO LONG AGO. THEY WERE FIRED AFTER THEY MADE RACIST STUPID STATEMENTS, NOT DURING THEIR PROGRAMS, BUT IN THEIR PERSONAL LIVES...WHICH, IF I AM NOT READING **THE BILL OF RIGHTS** WRONG, THEY HAVE THE RIGHT TO DO. THE NETWORKS FIRED THEM FOR THE SIN OF POLITICAL INCORRECTNESS, FOR DAMAGING THE CORPORATE IMAGE. I DON'T KNOW ABOUT JIMMY THE GREEK WELL ENOUGH. BUT I KNOW ROONEY COULD HAVE BEEN FIRED LONG AGO FOR INANE ON-AIR COMMENTARIES. BUT WHEN BUSINESS, GOVERNMENT, OR POLITICAL OR RELIGIOUS MOVEMENTS (BIG BROTHER IS BIG BROTHER NO MATTER WHAT FORM IT TAKES) CAN FIRE ANYONE FOR ANY FORM OF SELF EXPRESSION IN HIS PRIVATE LIFE, FREEDOM ITSELF IS KILLED FOR ALL OF US. PEEWEE DID NOT JACK OFF IN HIS PLAYHOUSE. THE ADULT REUBENS DID WHAT HE DID IN HIS PRIVATE LIFE.

THE CHEROTIC REVOLUTION IS AN EVOLUTIONARY MOVEMENT, AN ANARCHISTIC WAY OF CHANGE, IN WHICH THE SINGLE PERSON IS THE CENTER OF CREATIVE FORCE. THIS DEMANDS THE EQUAL ACCESS OF AND TO ALL IDEAS. THIS EQUAL ACCESS IS NOT A REALITY AS OF YET. THIS IS PARTLY BECAUSE OF ECONOMIC AND MEDIA MONOPOLY AND CONTROL. BUT THE MAIN REASON FOR THIS LACK OF EQUAL ACCESS OF AND TO ALL IDEAS AND IMAGES IS THE TRYING BY ALL SIDES TO PROTECT THE INDIVIDUAL FROM BAD, HARMFUL, WRONG, SINFUL, SEXIST, RACIST, OR OTHERWISE INCORRECT IDEAS AND IMAGES. SO INSTEAD OF DEMANDING EQUAL ACCESS TO THE MEDIA, AND HENCE TO THE MINDS, EVERY SIDE IS DEMANDING THE BANNING OF THE "INCORRECT" IDEAS AND IMAGES. SO, FOR AN EXAMPLE, INSTEAD OF DEMANDING EQUAL ACCESS AND COVERAGE IN THE PUBLIC SCHOOLS OF ALL RELIGIOUS AND NON-RELIGIOUS PHILOSOPHIES, THE SUBJECT IS A TABOO IN THE PUBLIC SCHOOLS. THE UNDERLYING PREMISE OF THE CENSORING PROTECTION IS THE INDIVIDUAL IS NOT STRONG ENOUGH OR WISE ENOUGH TO ULTIMATELY EJECT BAD IDEAS. FRANKLY, I NEED PEOPLE LIKE JESSE HELMS. IF THE IDEAS, MAGIC, AND REALITY WHICH I REPRESENT ARE NOT STRONG ENOUGH OR ATTRACTIVE ENOUGH TO SURVIVE IN AN EQUAL REALITY BATTLE OVER THOSE WHICH ARE REPRESENTED BY HELMS, THEN WHAT I REPRESENT IS NOT WORTH SURVIVING. I WILL ONLY FIGHT HELMS DIRECTLY WHEN HE TRIES TO DENY US ACCESS.

I SEE BY THE CLOCK ON THE COMPUTER SCREEN THAT IT IS TIME TO GO...AND I HAVE NOT ADMITTED THAT I AM A LESBIAN IN A MALE BODY...OR WRITTEN ABOUT THE DENYING PERSONAL CHOICE BY FORCING PEOPLE OUT OF THE CLOSET AGAINST THEIR WILL BY SOME GAY PAPERS...OR ABOUT OUR BOYCOTT OF **BLOCKBUSTER VIDEOS** AND **BRAVO CABLE NETWORK** FOR CENSORING PRACTICES. MAYBE NEXT TIME.

[1]BECAUSE OF THE SEX IRON CURTAIN, WE REALLY DO NOT KNOW WHAT REUBENS ACTUALLY DID OR WHY HE DID IT.

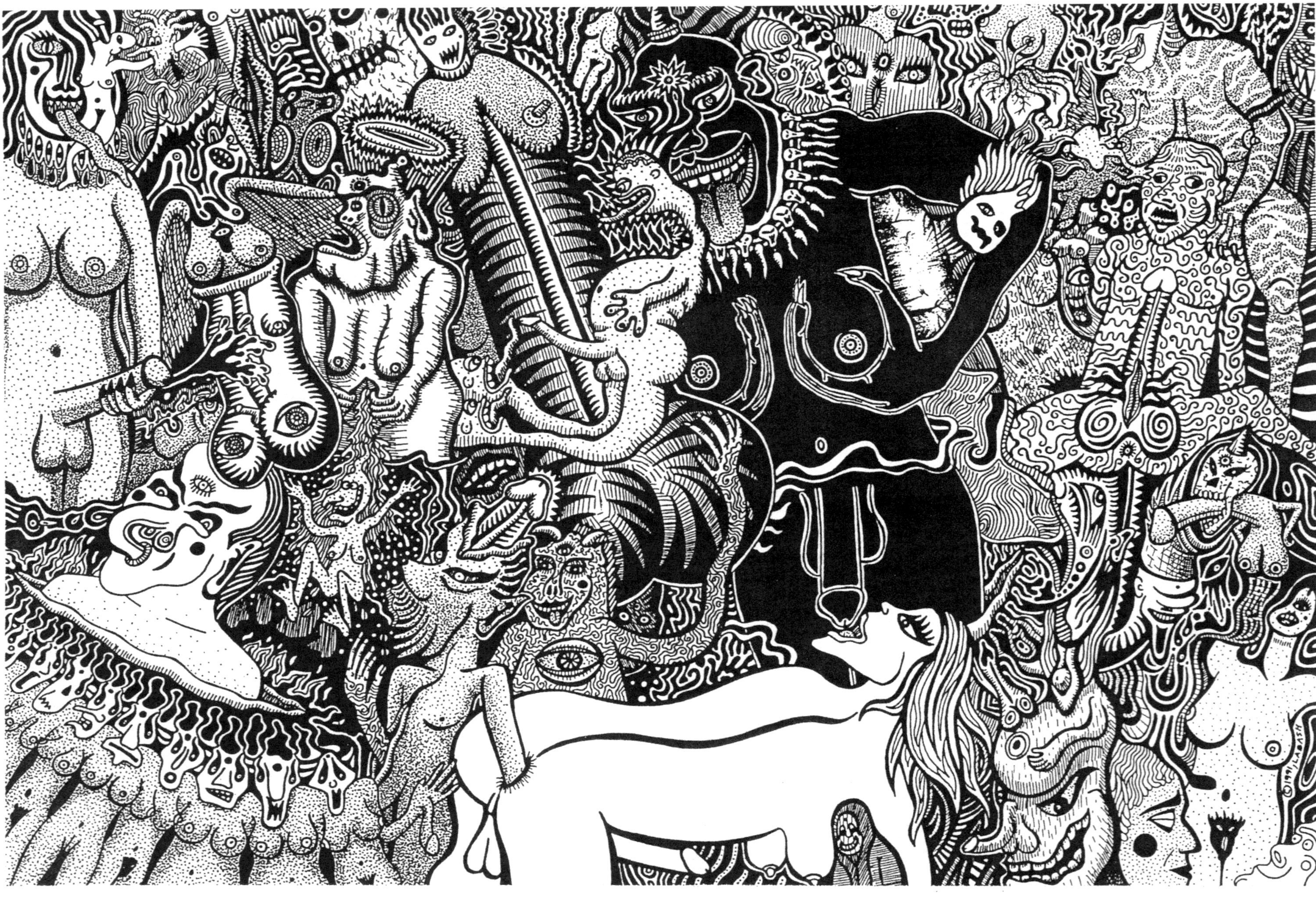

Luna

CHEROTIC LICENSE
by
LUNA GRIFFITH

I'm postulating that "cherotic license" is directly interconnected to the natural force of evolution. Chero = chi' (life force) + eros (love, beauty, sensuality). When defining Chero we can't limit ourselves to the contemporary (and often cynical) definition of erotic, but we can't exclude it either. We have to assume that a cherotic license works just like any concept of "license" (both in the sense of "poetic license" and in the legal/social sense of permission to do something) in that it can be taken away from someone who misuses it.

If it is true that cherotic license is directly interrelated with the evolutionary force, then we can also postulate that it follows the basic rules (ideals) of "form and function" -- the natural law that says the giraffe developed a long neck because it was always reaching up to eat tree leaves. In other words, that people who use their cherotic license will find life more fulfilling and ultimately more real, which takes them further along the scale of evolutionary development. And also that we as cherotic artisans are acting as agents of the evolutionary force each and every time we push forward the limits of our cherotic perception.

For the time being the accepted truth is that "beasts abstract not", and that it is often an understatement to say humans do. While our use of imagination does set us apart from the nonhuman life forms, our imagination can function even if we are not interconnected with the evolutionary force. We can see the evidence of this around us -- people using their intelligence to create industry that poisons them with pollution, etc.

Recalling Plato's "divided line," the realm of "Imago" is the lowest and least desirable state of consciousness to live in, compared to the realm of the "Logos" that is in harmony with "The Architect" (the evolutionary force). Of course, Plato makes a distinction between the imagination and the Logos, but for all practical purposes, we can only perceive the Logos with our imagination ... that is, if we can perceive it at all.

Peter Stenshoel writes in "The Nature of UD": "...I am not condemning popular art. I am pointing out the danger inherent in allowing popular art to take the place of the far richer antecedents each culture brought with it. Pop distills from the artist the essence of unsatisfiable desire! ....the nature of pop culture today: the very disposableness of it; indicates a lack of faith in nor concern for the future, and this bodes danger."

If we can use the imagination in harmony with the evolutionary force and be responsible enough to reject the seductions of the UD force, then we'll at least be on the right track. But how can we know when we are awake and creating reality, and when we are merely dreaming, creating a casual self-delusion through wishful thinking?

One might call the dividing line between reality-creation and wishful thinking (which is also the boundary between Plato's Imago and Logos) the "PC Rubicon." People who think their exercise of cherotic license has to fit their existing definition of what is "politically correct" automatically create a Rubicon that can never be crossed in reality. A Rubicon that is entirely within the realm of mesmerism, illusion and mind-control. A Rubicon created and delineated by total insanity.

Later in his article, Stenshoel goes on to say: "...Now, something must be said about the origins of UD. As a force, UD is quite real. Remember what we said about UD art (popular or disposable art) is brought on by the voice that always looks for gain. That voice is a victim, or adjunct, of UD. Because, in never being satisfied, that psychological construct, or voice, looks to more, bigger, and better, for relief. And, in doing so, creates more UD. The cycle is a tornado or whirlpool, and very hard to break. In fact, it hasn't ever been broken since its start-up in modern times. It has been slowed, and there's a good chance it can be driven away, but unfortunately with probably much cost. The force can be personified only to the extent that the force holds in its sway personalities. It's real people doing things they shouldn't. However, the phenomenon is best seen as a naturally occurring phenomenon, such as a tornado. Eventually, the winds change. The destructive force dies down. In the meantime, however, one can be sucked into the destructive cycle."

The most common way people get caught up into the UD cycle is by letting their natural desires become obsessions. Instead of merely wanting to feel youthful and vigorous, they become believers in a cult of eternal youth. Instead of simply wanting to look their best, they become obsessed with abstract concepts of beauty. Instead of wanting material things so they can enjoy them, they turn to desiring the abstraction "wealth."

Eventually, they fall totally under the control of this UD insanity and its inevitable consequences: perfectionism, classism and the need for dominance in everything they do. One of the easiest ways to identify people with this "UD disease" is their preoccupation with the regulation of bodily functions -- their own and everyone else's. This is the true origin of the present "health consciousness" fad -- it's really just an obsessive pursuit of unsatisfiable desires.

And this, in turn, leads people across the PC Rubicon, into endless debates over who is a politically correct "real" human and eventually into a form of self-inflicted genocide or slavery. Or better yet, let's call a spade a spade -- it makes them totally suicidal, but always in ways that are "PC," such as "eating disorders," "substance abuse," "occupational stress," "relationship dysfunction," etc. In the big picture, everyone in this category is out of contact with the evolutionary force. The only alternative is to avoid the PC Rubicon and cross the boundary into Plato's Logos.

Here's what Peter's sources have to say about this: "...In the meantime (while this destructive cycle is still collectively in motion), try to become as eclectic as possible -- study everything, or shall I say, enjoy everything. There's no need to stop absorbing pop art. Only ask yourself, like Zippy, 'Am I having fun yet?' Is a piece of art providing you with fulfillment... or just a sense of unsatisfiable desire? Will you want to peruse this art again in ten years... twenty? Is it an authentic product of human hearts and minds or is it a product calculated to produce a better-looking sale chart for some UD-driven executive? The more UD he can sell you, the more UD he'll crave, and consequently, the more UD he'll create to sell you. Don't get stuck."

Human imagination is dangerous and should be treated in the same manner that everything non-linear and "yin" should be treated -- it is a powerful magical force that automatically creates reality whenever it operates. Seeing imagination in this light should also make us realize that it may have functions and a purpose that we are unaware of. It may have timing and cycles and needs that we have not synchronized with. It is common knowledge that the mind, through the use of the imagination, can bypass commands in the brain in order to get the body to do something. For example, the imagination can conjure up an erotic ideal that then tells the body to respond with sexual excitement, completely bypassing the need of any of the five senses to have physically sensed the erotic ideal -- no pheromones or heat-cycles necessary.

It may be true that "the unheard melodies are the sweetest," but if we agree with this, then we must qualify what realm we are in when we "hear" them. Continuing to use Plato's divided-line, one would say that if you have not reached the Logos, if you are merely fantasizing about the melodies within the realm of the Imago, then what you are doing is entirely in vain. But if you are in the Logos, your imagination can truly work magic, can create reality instead of illusion.

This is what "Cherotic License" is really all about -- allowing yourself to let go of your preconceptions of what reality fits your "desired ideal" (which is always, simply by being idealized, also unsatisfiable) or your idea of what is "politically correct" (which is always a product of the Imago). Your cherotic license will take you places much more exotic than any "UD" obsession could -- beyond the realm Plato calls the Logos, into what Cherotic Magic calls the "Web of All Possibilities."

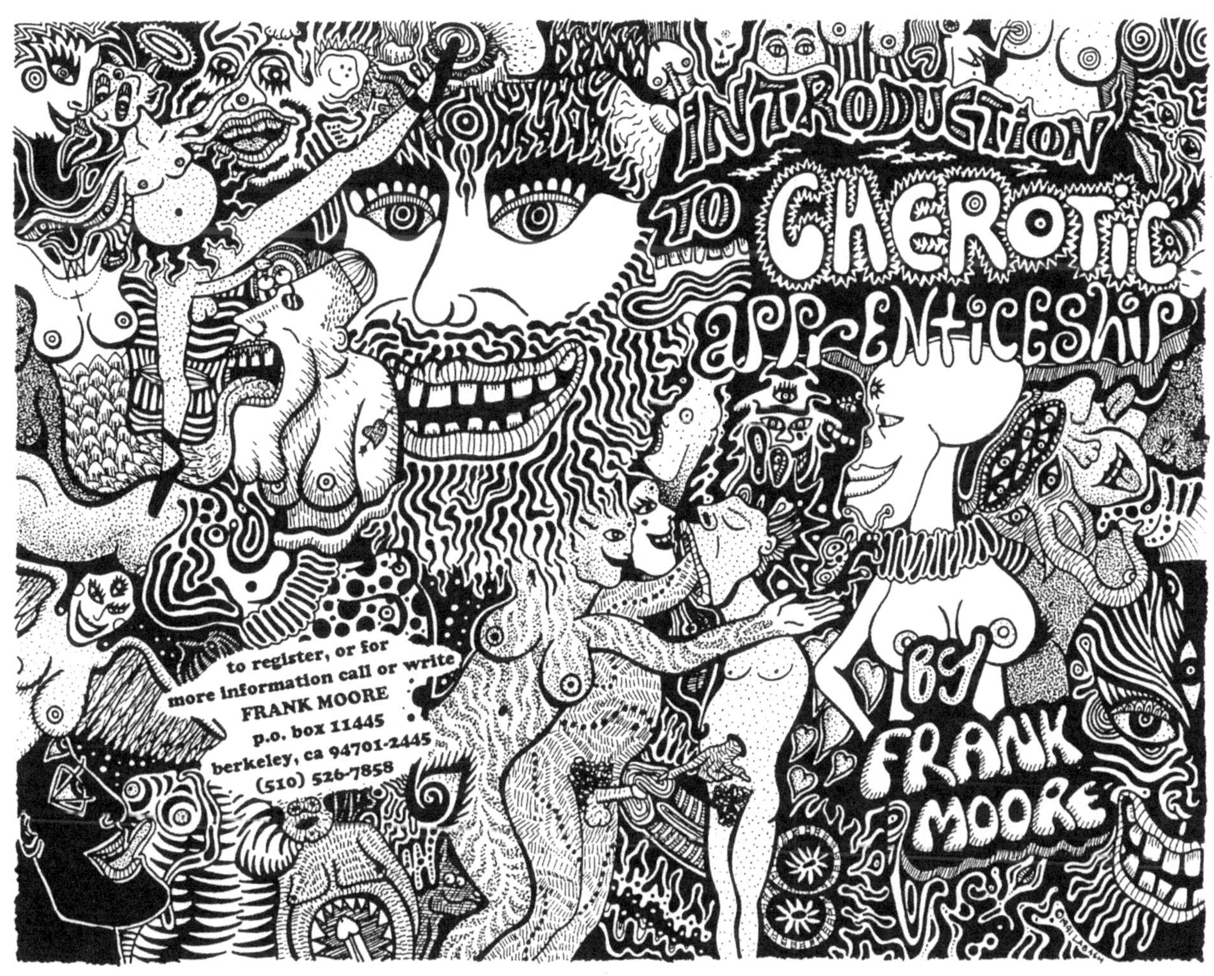

::

FRANK's letter to **BRENDA TATELBAUM** -- April 24, 1991

WHEN I READ IN the cherotic revolutionary #0 THE DIALOGUE THAT YOU AND MY LETTERS HAVE GENERATED...WHEN I READ THE DIALOGUE ALL TOGETHER INSTEAD OF IN PIECES, I AM AMAZED AND IMPRESSED AT THE POWER OF IT. WHAT IS EMERGING BY LINKING PEOPLE LIKE YOU, KYLE AND LUNA, TUPPY, BRENDA McCANN, LINDA AND MICHAEL AND ME, AND OTHERS WHO WILL JOIN THE DIALOGUE IN THE FUTURE IS A REDEFINING AND ENLARGING OF THE LANGUAGE OF CHANGE AND OF REALITY.

WE SENT YOU THE GREAT REVIEW OF cherotic magic BY BARBARA SMITH. EVEN IF YOU USE HER REVIEW RATHER THAN A REVIEW BY YOU IN eidos, I WOULD GET GREAT PERSONAL VALUE FROM HEARING IN MORE DETAIL WHAT YOU THOUGHT/FEEL ABOUT cm.

I AM HOPING the cherotic revolutionary WILL GET INTO THE HANDS OF THE YOUNG ANARCHISTS OF WHICH WE HAVE TALKED ABOUT BEFORE, AS WELL AS INTO THE HANDS OF SEASONED MAGICIANS AND CULTURAL/SEXUAL SUBVERSIVES.

IT WOULD BE USEFUL TO TALK ABOUT THE INNER CALLING AND INNER COMMITMENT NEEDED IN THIS LINE OF WORK/PLAY. MOST OF THE STUDENTS I GET ARE ATTRACTED TO THIS ALTERED CULTURE, THIS MAGICAL REALITY, FOR VARIOUS REASONS. LUNA SAYS IT IS LIKE WHITES GOING TO BLACK JAZZ CLUBS. IT IS LIKE READING A NOVEL. MOST OF MY STUDENTS CHOOSE THIS MAGICAL REALITY...THEY MAKE A COMMITMENT TO IT FOR A TIME. I DID NOT HAVE A CHOICE. I JUST HAD TO DO/BE THIS EVEN THOUGH I DID NOT KNOW WHAT THIS WAS, WHERE IT WOULD LEAD...EVEN IF IT LOOKED BAD OR DUMB. I HAD NO CHOICE...SO THAT I COULD NOT UNCHOOSE IT...I WAS NOT LOOKING AT MY OPTIONS AT EVERY TURN OR CARED ABOUT WHAT IT LOOKED LIKE...BECAUSE I HAD TO DO IT EVEN WHEN I WOULD RATHER NOT DO IT. I HAD TO BECAUSE IF I DID NOT I WOULD BE IN AN UNREALITY. I WAS CALLED. I THINK THERE IS A DEFINITE PLACE IN THE MAGICAL MOVEMENT FOR THE PEOPLE WHO CHOOSE, COMMIT TO, THE ALTERED REALITY. BUT THERE IS SOMETHING EXTREMELY MORE FRAGILE WITH THIS KIND THAN THE CALLED ONES WHO HAVE NO CHOICE, WHO ARE OBSESSED. I DO NOT MEAN FANATICS, WILD-EYED AND OUT OF TOUCH. I MEAN THE MISFITS WHO CANNOT FIGURE OUT HOW **NOT** TO LIVE A STRANGE VISION. THE PROBLEM WITH THE ILLUSION OF CHOICE IS NOT THE ONES WHO ARE ALWAYS LOOKING TO MAKE A BETTER REALITY MOVE. THE REAL PROBLEM OF THE ILLUSION OF CHOICE IS THAT IT MAKES THE MISFITS WHO HAVE NO CHOICE THINK THEY ARE WEAK OR STUPID FOR NOT HAVING A CHOICE.

ALL THE ABOVE IS A PREFACE TO ASKING YOU HOW DID A NICE, SMART WOMAN LIKE YOU START PUBLISHING A PAPER LIKE eidos? DID YOU HAVE A CHOICE? HOW CAN YOU BUCK THE SOCIAL IMAGES OF WHAT YOU SHOULD BE FOR SO MANY YEARS? WHAT IS THE CALLING VISION THAT HAS YOU UNDER ITS SPELL? AS YOU SEE, KYLE/LUNA'S GIVING ME A MAGAZINE HAS BROUGHT OUT THE JOURNALIST IN ME. BUT THIS ISSUE OF INNER CALLING HAS BEEN AS MUCH SUPPRESSED AS THE FULL CHERO RANGE OF WHICH SEX IS BUT ONE MODE. AND IT HAS BEEN SUPPRESSED FOR THE SAME REASON. THE SUPPRESSION CREATES A SHALLOWNESS, AN ISOLATION, AND AN INEFFECTIVENESS ON THE PERSONAL LEVEL.

WHAT IS SUBSTITUTED FOR THE INNER CALLING IS AN OUTER COMMITMENT TO, AN OUTER CHOICE OF, A TREND OR A MOVEMENT BASED ON INDIVIDUAL GROWTH, INDIVIDUAL COMFORT, INDIVIDUAL FUTURE, INDIVIDUAL IMAGE. DOES NOT WHAT YOU DO OFTEN TAKE YOU INTO SITUATIONS WHICH AT THE LEAST DO NOT APPEAR TO BE IN YOUR INDIVIDUAL BEST INTEREST...NOT THE BEST EXPERIENCE? BEING OUTWARDLY COMMITTED IS NOT A SOLID BASE FROM WHICH THE PERSON CAN CREATE. WHEN I WENT TO ART SCHOOL, THE BASIC QUESTION WAS ALWAYS WHAT WILL BE THE NEXT TRENDS TO WHICH IT WOULD BE SMART TO COMMIT...NOT DO YOU HAVE THE CALLING TO BE AN ARTIST...AND WHY DO YOU NEED TO BE AN ARTIST?

LAST WEEK, A JOURNALISM GRAD STUDENT FROM U.C. BERKELEY SHOT A VIDEO OF US FOR A "60 MINUTES" KIND OF STATE-WIDE CABLE T.V. SHOW. HE WAS A NICE GUY, BUT SHAPED COMPLETELY BY THE CONTEXT OF THE TIMES. HE IS DOING TELEJOURNALISM BECAUSE THAT IS THE WAVE OF THE FUTURE. HE IS DEEPER THAN THIS OR HE WOULD NOT HAVE CHOSEN ME AS HIS STORY. BUT THE CONTEXT OF THE TIMES DENIES HIM THIS DEPTH, DENIED HIM A CALLING, GIVING HIM INSTEAD CHOICES. DURING THE WEEK OF SHOOTING, I TWISTED HIS OWN REALITY AROUND SO THAT HE COULD NOT PLAY THE MYTH OF THE OBJECTIVE REPORTER. YESTERDAY, HE SAID HE NOW CAN SEE THAT THIS MYTH WAS A FALSE LIMITATION.

UNTIL THE EARLY 80s, I WOULD GO UP TO STRANGERS ON THE STREET, OR ON THE CAMPUS, AND ASK THEM TO LET ME VIDEO THEM AT MY HOME PLAYING DRESS-UP WITH STRANGE SEXY COSTUMES, OR OTHER SUCH PERFORMANCES. MOST PEOPLE WENT BEYOND THE SOCIAL TABOOS TO CHILD-LIKE FUN OR OTHER INTENSE EMOTIONAL STATES. MY VIDEO, erotic play, DOCUMENTS THIS. SOME EROPLAYED WITH ME OR EACH OTHER. BUT BY THE MID-80s, IT GOT HARDER AND HARDER TO GET PEOPLE FOR REASONS THAT WE HAVE DISCUSSED. I FINALLY STOPPED THIS DIRECT PUBLIC ACTION WHEN TWO PEOPLE IN A ROW, AFTER READING A GLOWING village voice REVIEW OF ONE OF MY PERFORMANCES, TURNED TO ME AND SAID, "SOUNDS LIKE PORN." IF THINGS HAD GOTTEN THAT UPTIGHT, WHY BOTHER TAKING THAT KIND OF SHIT?

ANYWAY, BRAD, THE JOURNALIST, WANTED TO SHOOT ME IN ACTION. SO WE WENT UP TO CAMPUS TO SHOOT ME GOING UP TO PEOPLE. I ASKED BRAD IF HE WANTED TO SHOOT SOMEBODY PLAYING DRESS-UP IF I COULD GET SOMEONE TO AGREE. HE THOUGHT IT WAS UNLIKELY, BUT SURE. TO HIS IMPRESSED SURPRISE, THE FIRST PERSON I APPROACHED EAGERLY SAID YES.

WE HAVE COME TO WHY I AM TELLING THE STORY. THE PERSON WAS A HISTORY GRAD STUDENT...OPEN, LIBERAL. SHE SEES HERSELF THIS WAY. SHE FELT A TRUST TOWARDS ME. BUT WHEN SHE CAME OVER TO PLAY DRESS-UP, SHE COULD NOT REALLY PLAY WITH THE CLOTHES, COULD NOT REMOTELY LOSE HERSELF IN FUN AND PLAYING. TAKING HER CLOTHES OFF WAS NOT A REMOTE POSSIBILITY...SHE HAD A HARD TIME TAKING HER OUTER SHIRT OFF. ALL OF THIS WAS TO BE EXPECTED IN THE PRESENT CULTURAL FRAME...ALTHOUGH IT WEIRDED HER OUT BECAUSE IT CONFLICTED TOTALLY WITH HER SELF-IMAGE OF BEING FREE AND OPEN. THE REALLY SHOCKING AND DISTURBING THING TO US WAS...THERE WAS A 1940s PINK SILKY/SATINY ANKLE-LENGTH NIGHTGOWN. SHE WAS ATTRACTED TO IT...BUT AT THE SAME TIME TREATED IT IN THE SAME WAY A VAMPIRE WOULD HANDLE A CROSS SMEARED WITH GARLIC. FOR HER, THE NIGHTGOWN WAS A SYMBOL OF THE FORBIDDEN OBJECTIFIED WOMAN OF THE FUNDAMENTALIST/FEMINISTS. IT WAS OBVIOUS THAT SHE WANTED TO TRY IT ON...THAT SHE LIKED IT...BUT SHE COULD NOT PUT IT ON EVEN OVER HER STREET CLOTHES. SHE FEARED THAT JUST BY PUTTING ON THE NIGHTGOWN, AS A SYMBOL, SHE WOULD BE TRANSFORMED INTO THE OBJECTIFIED WOMAN. THIS MAGIC WHICH THE FUNDAMENTALIST/FEMINISTS HAVE UNLEASHED IS AT LEAST AS IMPRISONING AS THE MAGIC WHICH CONTROLS THE SEXISTS. OF COURSE, IT IS THE SAME FUNDAMENTALIST MAGIC DRESSED UP IN TWO FORMS. OUR CHALLENGE IS TO SWITCH THE MAGICAL FORCE AROUND SO THAT WOMEN, ALL PEOPLE CAN FREELY PLAY WITH ALL SYMBOLS. ONLY IN THIS WAY WILL WOMEN, ALL PEOPLE, NOT BE UNDER THE CONTROLLING POWER OF SYMBOLS.

....

BRENDA's reply to **FRANK** -- May 5, 1991

Your 4/24 letter has arrived at a precisely pivotal point in time as our newest EIDOS issue went to press last Friday with our review of Cherotic Magic in it. I hope you're not disappointed with our more descriptive and informational presentation of CM to our readers and I'm sure we'll receive additional feedback and commentary about CM from them in their future letters to EIDOS. Naturally, we wish THE CHEROTIC REVOLUTIONARY a long and healthy life and congratulate you and everyone involved with the effort behind launching Issue #0!!!

I recognize that your choice of terminology to describe yourself, your work and worldview significantly differs from my own use of the language. Quite honestly, my repertoire has never similarly included "anarchists", "magicians". "cultural/sexual subversives", "altered culture", "altered reality", "magical reality", "misfits", etc. but, like yourself I am a "called one": I was "called" to my work and "had no choice" "even though I did not know where it would lead" "even if it looked bad". Bizarre? Or perhaps a little bit like "Close Encounters of the Third Erotic Kind"?

For me, my mission with EIDOS has evolved naturally and progressively -- corresponding to the unfolding chain of my life's events. Although I had always been a published writer and poet, it wasn't until close to my separation (after 12 years of marriage and two children) that, in 1982, I began writing and self-publishing erotic "women's" poetry and giving live readings to audiences of women and men at local colleges and bookstores. With the public's support and encouragement, I then decided to include the publication of erotic poetry, art, photography and fiction by like-minded others and thus EIDOS was born. The Premier issue rolled of the presses in January, 1984.

Obviously, my very own deeply-rooted erotosexual repression and feelings of female persecution and oppression led to my creating and publicly sharing my erotic poetry with others and, ultimately, to the founding of EIDOS. Those were the days of the rising-tide of draconian Reagan-Bush right-wing ideology but now I look back in retrospect at the risk I took and simply say, "I acted according to the dictates of my conscience. I had no choice." Therefore, I totally understand and relate to your concept of "inwardly committed" as opposed to "outwardly committed".

As a single woman journeying alone through the aftermath of divorce (with all the concomitant custodial responsibilities for parenting two small children and maintaining a household) these overwhelming negative-forces were magnified a thousand-fold but I channeled them into a positive, life-affirming force. At the time, however, I was completely unaware that, world-wide, women and men of all erotosexual/sexuerotic orientations, preferences and lifestyles were similarly living with such inner turmoil and tribulation.

Frankly, it wasn't until August 1985 that my personal/professional mission became political. At that time, the "trusted" elected officials (three conservative male selectmen) in the town of Milton, MA (where I live) sent the plainclothes police to my home (without a warrant) to order me to "cease & desist" from publishing EIDOS from the privacy of my own home. They claimed I was violating a town zoning bylaw (which I wasn't) prohibiting the operation of home-based business enterprises. Their disguised, deliberate attempt at censorship was possibly directed at garnering votes during an election year or, as they readily admitted to the electronic and print media, to shut EIDOS down and run me out of town. In any event, their witchhunt failed as did their attempt to publicly disgrace and humiliate me. Eventually they backed off and EIDOS fortunately still continues. In '85, as in '82, an overwhelmingly supportive public (both on the local level and nationally) telephoned and wrote letters of encouragement -- less than a year before the publication of the Justice Department's 1986 Final Report of the Attorney General's Commission on Pornography (the Meese Commission)!!!

In your letter you speak of having "twisted" a journalism student's "reality around" and say he recognized "myth" as a "false limitation". From my perspective, you were engaging in consciousness-raising and it worked!! How very excellent!!!

The bottom line is that EIDOS affirms the reality of our basic human right to sexual freedom: the right to choose in all areas of sexual life and lifestyle; our basic human right to be free from coercion by governments or individuals; our basic human right to free speech, a free press, freedom of/from religion and the right to privacy as well as other rights and freedoms including the right to personal property and to pursue political goals. Obviously these high-minded concepts are the basis of our secular laws and government and are incorporated into our Declaration of Human Rights.

However, we acknowledge the additional need to further reform the inequities inherent in our society's traditional social, moral and political infrastructures, Therefore, with EIDOS readers in all 50 states (and 57 countries overseas) from all legal age ranges, educational and income levels and occupations, we at EIDOS are of the firm belief that, in time, an invisible global grassroots networking movement of real everyday people will eventually transform millennia of authoritarian, dogmatic, sex-negative erotophobic self-loathing indoctrination into a rational, enlightened, free-thinking world community which values, accepts and ratifies, as holistic, the pluralism of democratic multisexualism.

In conclusion, would my use of the words "propaganda" or "mind (thought) control" or "brainwashing" be synonymous with your use of the word "magic" when describing the so-called "open, liberal, history" female grad student's self-image conflict upon her confrontation with the 1940's pink silky/satiny ankle-length nightgown?

I look forward to furthering our definition of terms!

Yours in freedom

::

DEAR BOB,

LIKE MYSELF, BOTH CROWLEY AND GURDJIEFF WERE TRYING TO EXPLORE THE PRACTICAL MAGICAL DYNAMICS IN THE CONTEXT OF THE EVERYDAY PHYSICAL REALITY RATHER THAN IN THE CONTEXT OF THE ABSTRACT SPIRITUAL DIMENSION IN WHICH MOST MAGICIANS HAD TRIED TO WORK. THEY SAW MAGIC (OR MAGICK) AS A SCIENCE OF THE NONLINEAR EFFECTS OF THE DYNAMIC RELATIONSHIP OF RESPONSIBLE PERSONAL ACTION. THEY TRIED, MORE OR LESS, TO PUT THIS MAGICAL SCIENCE INTO WHAT WAS IN THEIR TIME THE MODERN WESTERN CULTURAL FRAME. ALL OF THIS IS WHAT I AM ATTEMPTING TO DO.

BUT BOTH CROWLEY AND GURDJIEFF, FOR VARIOUS REASONS, HID THE MAGICAL SCIENCE IN COMPLEX AND GLAMOROUS RITUAL AND INTELLECTUAL SYSTEMS, FULL OF FUNHOUSE MIRRORS, MISLEADING INFORMATION, AND LONG DEAD-END ALLEYS. WHAT I AM TRYING TO DO IS GET THE MAGIC SCIENCE AS CLEARLY AND AS DOWN-TO-EARTH IN WRITING AS POSSIBLE. UNFORTUNATELY, THE POSSIBILITY OF THIS IS VERY LIMITING BECAUSE WRITING IS LINEAR AND THE MAGICAL SCIENCE IS NONLINEAR. THIS IS WHY I ALSO WORK IN EXPERIENTIAL REALITY SHAPING SUCH AS APPRENTICESHIPS AND PERFORMANCES (BOTH PUBLIC AND PRIVATE). BECAUSE SUCH REALITY SHAPING IS PHYSICAL, IT CAN CONTAIN NONLINEAR INFORMATION.

IF YOU WANT TO GET TOGETHER TO TALK, I WILL BE BACK HOME FROM A LECTURE/PERFORMANCE TOUR IN THE SECOND HALF OF OCTOBER.

YOURS,
FRANK

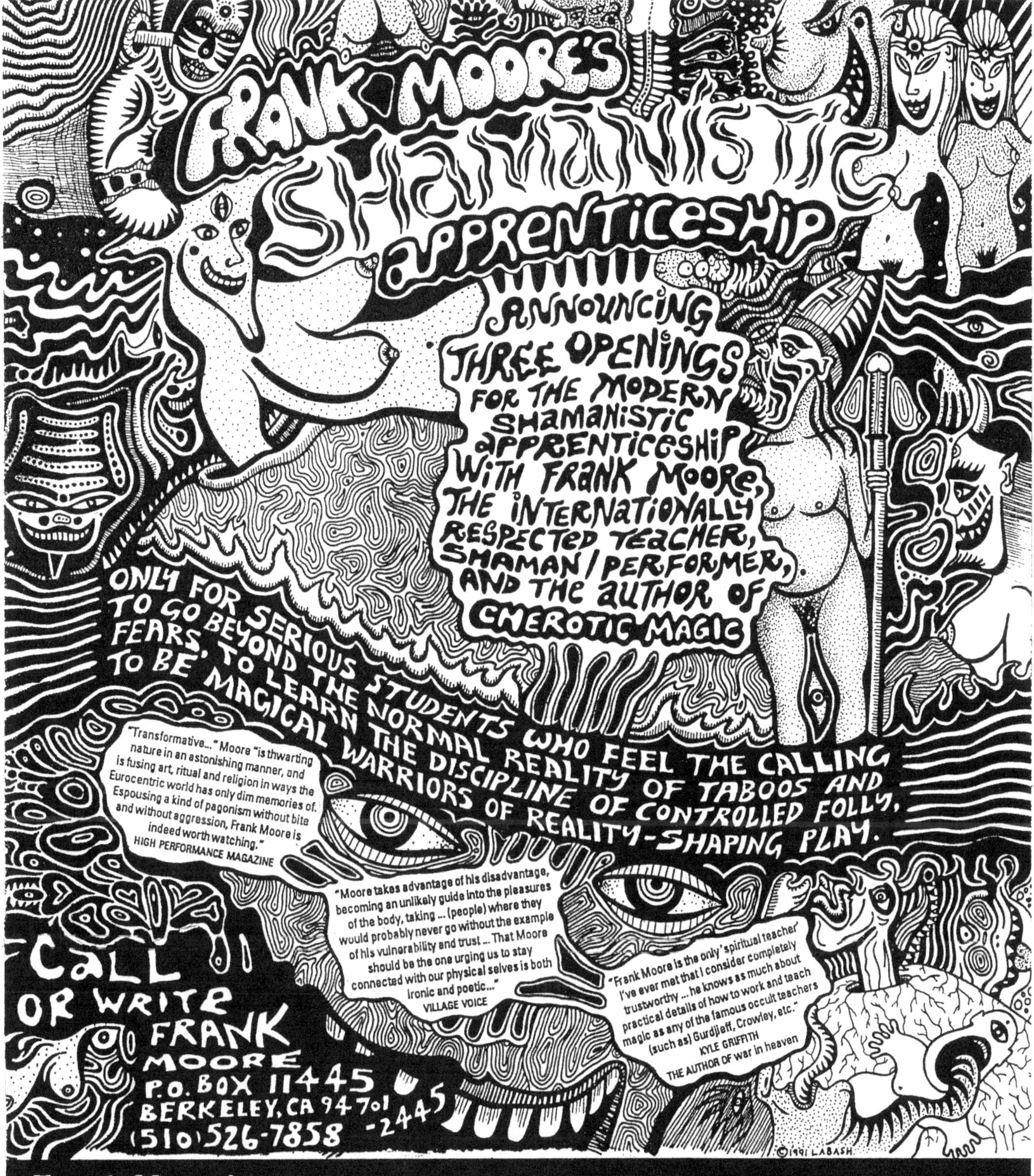

Frank Moore's new book *cherotic magic* is available for $15

cherotic magic BY FRANK MOORE IS A MAJOR ATTEMPT TO INTRODUCE A POWERFUL SYSTEM OF MAGIC INTO OUR MODERN WESTERN EVERY-DAY LIFE, THEREBY EXPLOSIVELY EXPANDING SUCH CONCEPTS AS SEX, HUMAN RELATION-SHIPS. THE CLEAR, DOWN-TO-EARTH TEXT IS AMPLIFIED BY THE NONLINEAR TRANCE ILLUSTRATIONS BY LABASH.

Also available for $3 is the premiere issue of *The Cherotic Revolutionary*, the magazine about the edge.

JACK/ADELLE
by
FRANK MOORE

WAITING FOR US,
WAITING OUTSIDE
OF HIDDEN MAGICAL KINGDOMS
OF, HUMAN WARM IMAGINATION,
HOT PASSIONS,
POETIC OCCULT KINGDOMS RULED
BY MASTER JAMES.

WAITING FOR US,
SITTING OUTSIDE THE GATES OF
JAZZ,
SITTING ON
THE TRAVELING FEEL-GOOD SHOW,
TAPPING
A TIPTOE
SOFTSHOE PAW
ON THE SAWDUST BOARDSTAGE,
WAITING FOR THE STRIPPERS AND TOP BANANAS.

WAITING IS THE OZ LION,
THE AWE LION,
THE LION OF TWO BODIES,
TWO FACES,
TWO VOICES SINGING TOGETHER
IN RAW BEAUTIFUL FUNNY CHAOS.
ALWAYS WAITING TO SING FROM THE
CAVEFIRES
TO ROAMING AROUND MEDIEVAL LANDSCAPES
TO THE AMERICAN
BADLANDS
TO SPEAKEASIES
TO RADIOWAVES.
WAITING TO DANCE AND SING
WITH ITS YINYANG BODY AND VOICE,
TAPPING CHAOS,

SINGING RAW HUMAN
PASSION AND HUMOR.
RELEASING DEPTHS,
RELEASING OTHER VOICES,
ALL POET VOICES,
NOT JUST ITS OWN TWO.
THE LION GRAVELING ROARING
PASSION VOICE
AND THE WOMAN WARM DEADPAN VOICE
DANCE TAPPING,
DANCING ON AND IN EACH OTHER,
DANCING A MAGICAL RITUAL,
CARRYING
US INTO A GIGGLING TRANCE,
A FEELING GIGGLING DANCE TRANCE.

WE ARE DANCING WITH
TWO-VOICED TWO-BODIED LION OF OZ,
OF AWE,
OF JUST LOVE.
WE DON'T NEED TO BE
A DANCER TO DANCE,
A SINGER TO
SING,
A POET TO FEEL.
JUST DANCE WITH
THIS BAGGYPANTS LION, DANCE
INTO THE DEEP HUMAN PASSION,
DEEP HUMAN HUMOR.

"THERE IS A FOUNTAIN FILLED WITH BLOOD" -- BROUGHTON FOUNTAIN
by
JACK FOLEY

First Published in Exquisite Corpse

The Master stood on the edge of the cliff. He asked which of his disciples would thrust himself over the side, plunging into the mouth of a horrible and certain death. "I," said one, eager to get a running start. "Wait," said the Master. "Do you think I'm some sort of idiot? I was only raising an abstract question. I need all the disciples I can get -- and, besides, it's a long way down the side of that cliff." "True," said the eager disciple. "But wouldn't you always honor the name of the disciple who died for you!" "Well, I might," said the Master, "but really it all depends on whether I've written it down. My memory's a little shaky these days, and I can't seem to locate my pencil!" "Master," said the disciple, "I would be the one who died for you!" "Well, go ahead if you must, " said the Master, fumbling in his pockets for a piece of paper. "But I'm not guaranteeing anything. Oh where is that pencil!" "Thank you, Master. Aieeeee!" said the disciple as he leaped over the edge. "What was his name?" said the Master. "I suppose," said another disciple, "there isn't much left of him now." The disciples looked at each other silently. The wind sprang up. They were suddenly filled with a strange ecstasy. "Aieeeee," they began to say, "aieeee, aieeeee," and made for the edge of the cliff. "Hey, wait a minute," said the Master, "whose disciples are you anyway, mine or his?" "Why, yours of course," said the disciples, stopping in their tracks. "That's better," said the Master. "You should at least look before you leap. It's been a rather bad year for disciples you know, and I'd just as soon have you stay a--" But before the Master was able to say the word live, the disciple who had leapt over the cliff suddenly appeared in front of him, looking only a little the worse for wear. "Aieeeee," said the Master, "what are you doing here?" "I'm back," said the disciple. "Death really isn't all it's cracked up to be." "You -- died!" said the Master. "Yes," said the disciple. "But what was it like?" "Not too bad, you know, nothing much really. A bit of a splat at the bottom. Otherwise fit as a fiddle actually." "But you've seen what no one else has ever seen and come back to talk of." "Well, yes, I suppose I have." "Won't you tell us about it?" "Well, all right. I saw--" But at this point a strong wind suddenly sprang up and lifted the seemingly solid body of the disciple up into the air like a leaf. His body seemed to collapse upon itself, to fold inward, to become nothing, nothing but a piece of scattered debris upon the wind. "Master," came the cry, "Master, Master--" Then nothing. "He must have had a name," said the Master. "Perhaps it was James. That certainly was a strong wind!" "Master," said another disciple, "could we leave this place?" "Yes, yes," said the Master, "I'm not enjoying it very much myself. Let's go." But then they realized that it was night and they couldn't go. They couldn't descend the mountain in darkness. "Oh, Fudge," said the Master as another burst of wind took his hat over the side of the cliff. "I was very fond of that hat too." "Fonder than you were of me, I sometimes think," came the voice. It was James. "Good lord, you're back again." "Yes," said James, "You know, it's better the second time around. The first time you have problems with that awful dog." "Did you get bitten?" "Not the second time!" "But James, how do you manage it? -- dying and resurrecting, dying and resurrecting." "Don't know, really. I suppose it's just a sort of talent." "Indeed. Can you make my hat come back?" "Doubt it. I'll try. Mmmmph, mmmmph, nothing much there." "You can only resurrect...yourself?" "Well, now, I don't know. It is possible..." "What?" "It is possible...You know, Master I had a terrible childhood." "What has that got to do with it?" "Beatings, always complaints--ah, here I go again!" The wind sprang up and James was off again into the night. "What stars, Master," he said, "What stars! I wish I could take you with me. It's <u>wonderful</u> here!" It was morning now. As the Master looked around him he saw that his disciples had all vanished. There was nothing there but the mountain and the sky. He opened his mouth and began to speak:

> My name is James Richard Broughton. I was born in the valley town of Modesto on Nov. 10, 1913. I come from a place of indescribable sweetness.

The wind sprang up again. "Master," said James, "we have the same name. Come! Come!" The Master looked up. His body seemed at one solid and -- <u>light</u>. "This is It," he thought, "This is really It." "<u>Now</u>," said James, holding out his hand to the Master, "<u>now</u>." A shock of electricity shuddered between them. "IS NOW THIS IT HERE?" said the Master, "I'm <u>fly-ing</u>!" And he was. "You see," said James, "There isn't even this mountain." "Certainly not this mountain," said James, "There is something, though." "What is it?" "How can I put it? Night and day, day and night -- I sound like an old song. <u>The indescribable sweetness of being alive</u>!" They reeled through the air, covering distance upon distance. Finally they lit down on a tiny island off the coast of Asia. "We are one, Master," said James, "we have merged." "Yes," said James, "it's true. I can't tell us apart anymore." "We are Master and Disciple, Master, Disciple and Master. We are moth and flame. <u>We are one</u>. Wondrous the merge!" "But what about <u>us</u>?" came a voice. "Yes," said another, "what about us?" "Oh, <u>them</u>," said the Master. It was all the <u>other</u> disciples hovering in the air. "I'm afraid you will have to find your own mountains," said James. "We can't find them for you. It's been a very complicated life we've had to lead. Follow your bliss!" The two James Richards waved to the creatures in the air. "Poor things," they thought, "poor sweetings. We would give them blood if we could." It was dawn again. Master and disciple shivered a little in the chill as the sun at last came up. "Camera!" said James, "Lights! I love the movies!

> --My name is James^2.
>
> There is nothing
>
> But the indestructible sweetness
>
> Of
>
> Everything! <u>Follow your weird</u>."

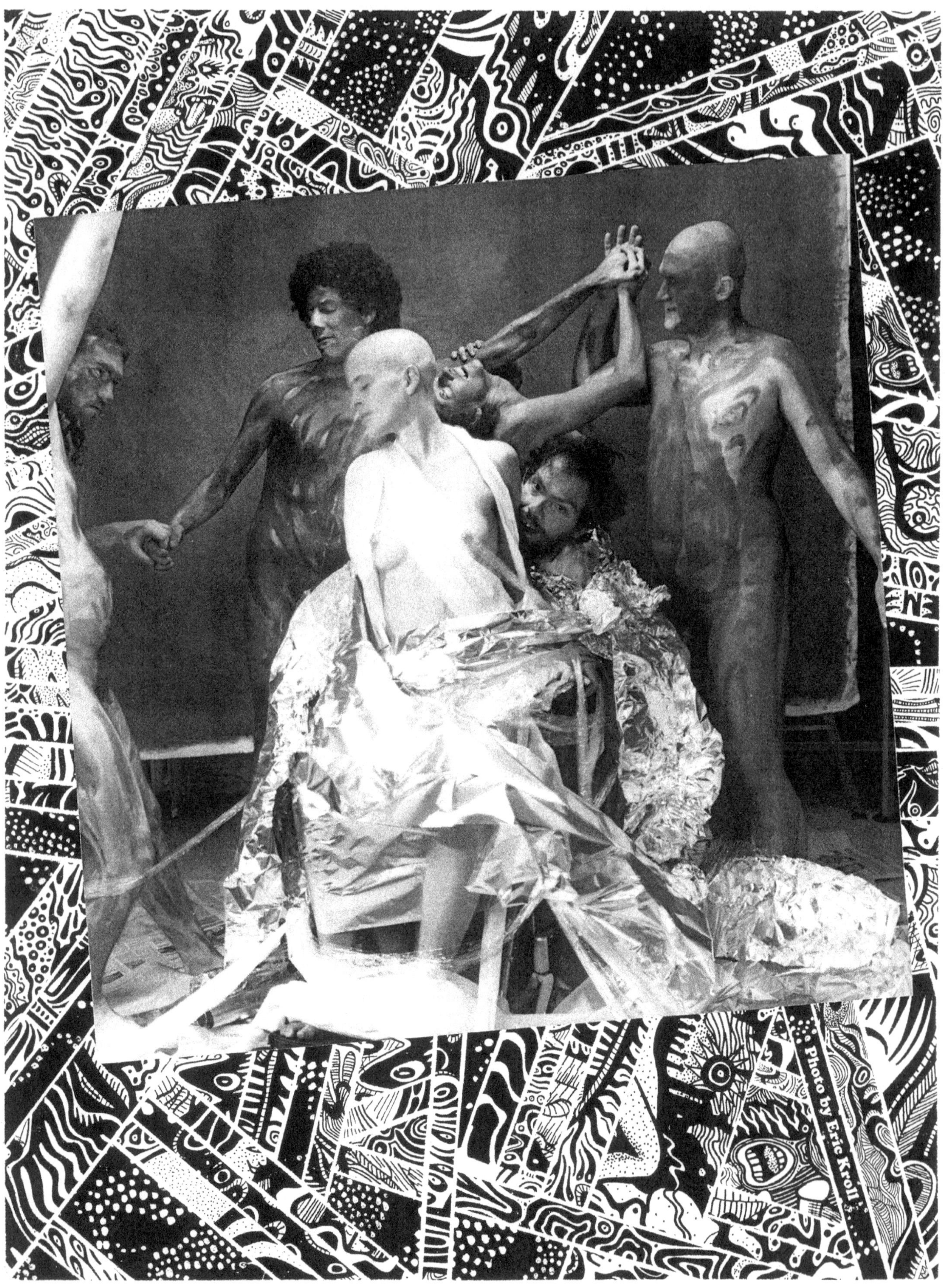

Photo by Eric Kroll

SOMETHING'S GOING ON!
by
DOROTHY JESSE BEAGLE

Frank Moore at Cafe Milano Poetry Series -- Berkeley, CA -- June 5, 1988
(Notes written the evening after the poetry performance)

The patrons
at Cafe Milano
took the stairs
two at a time,
"What on earth was going on
upstairs
an orgy?"
Strange sounds and curtain
sealing off
the Sunday night Poetry
where, some said,
poets, gay and straight
famous and infamous
and slightly known
ranted and raved
but never like this!
Some spoke softly,
beautiful imagery,
one man bellowed, didn't need
a microphone,
but we paid them no mind;
we came to Cafe Milano
for coffee
let the mad poets have the upstairs,
we pay them no mind

Until tonight
Is it an orgy?
from the sound of it,
from the secrecy (drawn curtains)
"Something's going on."
What a disappointment!
"What are they doing?
I was just having coffee
downstairs
and came to look."
"You look, you pay," said Adelle
Two minutes passed (after the
downstairs patrons paid)
"Can I please have my money back?"
Then made a hasty retreat,
from
This celebration of life,
a cacophony of people (musical)
interwoven,
a pulsating silver montage,
literally entwined with the
poet, they were
the poet
sorcerer of innocence
("I am old fashioned!")
weaving a silver montage
and one playful child
emerged ONE

A silver montage and cinematic
intermittent flashes of flesh
and joy/the soul of the poem revealed
as the words were spoken.
The audience of now-one became
  a lover
  a child
  a baby, held in love.

NOTE: An evening of poetry by Frank Moore performed through dance, touching, sound flickering light, strips of cellophane and shiny foil wrappings, and ... nudity (slightly amended for Cafe Milano) ... sensuous, womb-like, beyond sex"

"Eroplay"

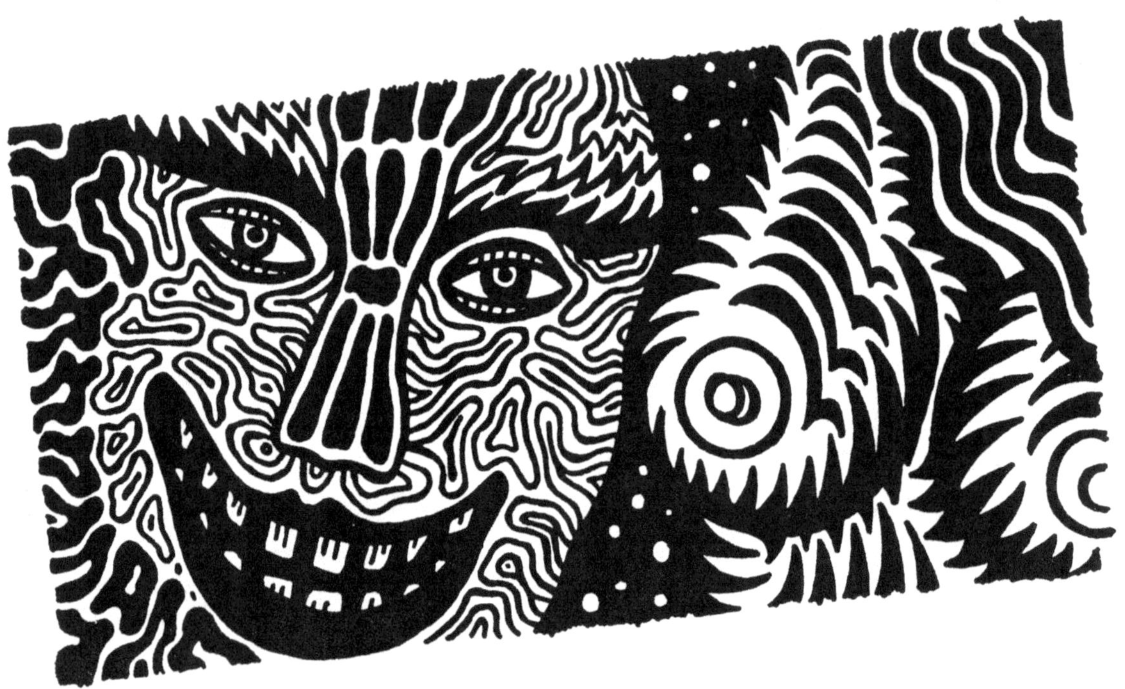

TOO CONTROVERSIAL FOR THE BAY AREA

CANNOT FIND A PLACE TO PERFORM IN THE BAY AREA

AMONG THE CITIES/PLACES MOORE HAS PERFORMED/LECTURED:

- SCHOOL OF THE ART INSTITUTE, CHICAGO
- PAINTED BRIDE, PHILADELPHIA
- FRANKLIN FURNACE, NYC
- UCLA • NYU
- LOWER LINKS, CHICAGO
- VANCOUVER, BC

OF FRANK MOORE'S PERFORMANCE WORK:

"SURELY WONDERFUL AND MIND-GOOSING EXPERIENCE."

L.A. READER

"...HE'S WONDERFUL AND HILARIOUS AND KNOWS EXACTLY WHAT IT'S ALL ABOUT AND HAS EARNED MY UNDYING RESPECT. WHAT HE'S DOING IS IMPOSSIBLE AND HE KNOWS IT. THAT'S GOOD ART..."

L.A. WEEKLY

"RESISTING "THE EASY AND SUPERFICIAL DESCRIPTIONS..., MOORE'S WORK CHALLENGES THE CONSENSUS VIEW MORE STRONGLY IN WAYS LESS ACCEPTABLE THAN...ANGRY TIRADES AND BITTER ATTACKS ON CONSUMER CULTURE."

CHICAGO NEW CITY

"FRANK MOORE ISN'T YOUR AVERAGE ARTIST...ONE OF THE MORE PROVOCATIVE WRITERS, FILM DIRECTORS AND-YES-PERFORMANCE ARTISTS AROUND SINCE THE EARLY '70'S."

THE ORGONIAN

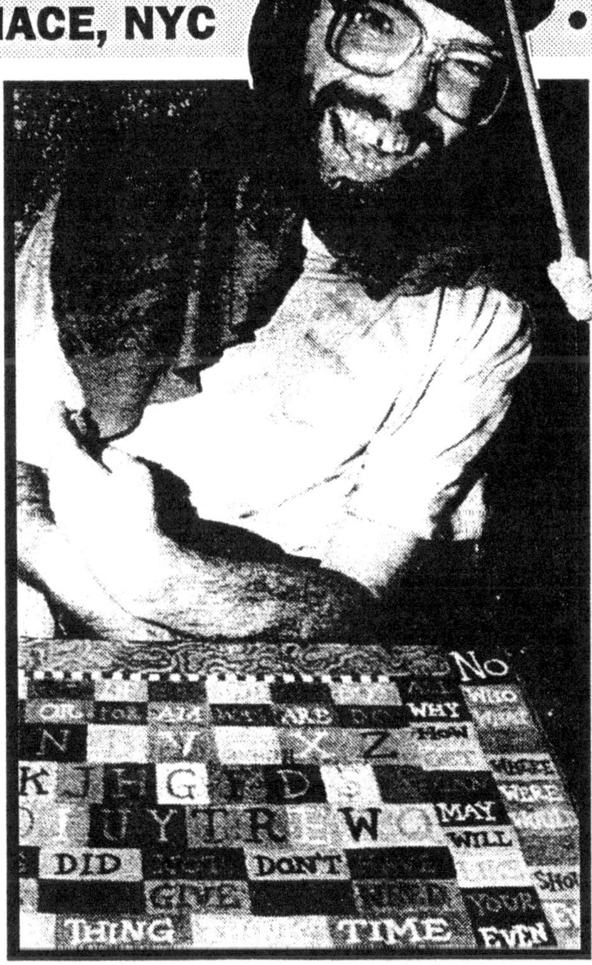

"TRANSFORMATIVE..." MOORE "IS THWARTING NATURE IN AN ASTONISHING MANNER, AND IS FUSING ART, RITUAL AND RELIGION IN WAYS THE EUROCENTRIC WORLD HAS ONLY DIM MEMORIES OF. ESPOUSING A KIND OF PAGANISM WITHOUT BITE AND AGGRESSION, FRANK MOORE IS INDEED WORTH WATCHING."

HIGH PERFORMANCE MAGAZINE

"IN PERFORMANCE, MOORE TAKES ADVANTAGE OF HIS DISADVANTAGE, BECOMING AN UNLIKELY GUIDE INTO THE PLEASURES OF THE BODY, TAKING AUDIENCES WHERE THEY WOULD PROBABLY NEVER GO WITHOUT THE EXAMPLE OF HIS VULNERABILITY AND TRUST...THAT MOORE SHOULD BE THE ONE URGING US TO STAY CONNECTED TO OUR PHYSICAL SELVES IS BOTH IRONIC AND POETIC..."

VILLAGE VOICE

"IF PERFORMANCE ART HAS A RADICAL EDGE, IT HAS TO BE FRANK MOORE."

THE CLEVELAND EDITION

IF YOU KNOW OF A PLACE IN THE BAY AREA WHERE FRANK CAN PERFORM WRITE TO:

Frank Moore P.O. Box 11445 Berkeley CA 94701-2445

video tapes BY FRANK MOORE

$40 each

fairy tales can come true
copyrighted 1981
length: 35 minutes
THIS IS A FILM ABOUT RELATIONSHIPS AND DISABILITY STARRING FRANK MOORE, WHO HAS BEEN DISABLED SINCE BIRTH WITH CEREBRAL PALSY. IT IS A HUMOROUS, YET REALISTIC LOOK AT HOW TO ESTABLISH RELATIONSHIPS BY CHANGING NEGATIVE SELF IMAGE.

erotic play
copyrighted 1983
length: 84 minutes
THIS VIDEO EXPLORES WHAT HAPPENS WHEN PEOPLE OF ALL TYPES AND AGES ARE GIVEN A CHANCE TO RETURN TO BEING A KID AGAIN. A SIMPLE GAME OF DRESS-UP BECOMES A POWERFUL METAPHOR FOR DROPPING TABOOS, RELEASING CREATIVE EMOTION, AND FOR DRAMATIC CHANGE. AS A RESULT, AN INNOCENT EROTICISM IS FOUND... AS WELL AS GETTING INTIMATE WITH 60 HUMANS.

outrageous dream
copyrighted 1984
length: 41 minutes
A SURREAL, VISUAL POEM OF FOUND IMAGES.

the nude cave
copyrighted 1984
length: 113 minutes
AN EROTIC, SURREALISTIC VIDEO DREAM THAT COMBINES NON-LINEAR IMAGES AND FRANK'S ORIGINAL MUSIC SCORE.

the outrageous beauty revue
copyrighted 1980
length: approx. 30 minutes
THIS RAW VIDEO DOCUMENTS THE TACKY, MUSICAL, OVER-THE-EDGE COMEDY REVUE THAT FRANK CREATED, DIRECTED AND PERFORMED IN. THE SHOW RAN ON A WEEKLY BASIS FOR THREE AND ONE HALF YEARS AT THE MABUHAY GARDENS IN SAN FRANCISCO IN ADDITION TO A NUMBER OF OTHER NORTHERN CALIFORNIA AND NEVADA PERFORMANCES. FRANK PERFORMED ALONG WITH THE THIRTY PEOPLE WHO MADE UP HIS THEATRE GROUP, "the theatre of human melting."

out of isolation
copyrighted 1989
length: 105 minutes
A SURREAL EROTIC EXAMINATION OF AN INTIMATE RELATIONSHIP OF NEED. STARRING FRANK MOORE AND LINDA SIBEO.

books BY FRANK MOORE

caves
A COLLECTION OF MANIFESTOS ABOUT eroplay AND ART.
published 1987 **$5**

art of living
A GUIDE TO DOWN-TO-EARTH SPIRITUALITY AS CHANNELED BY FRANK MOORE.
published 1987 **$10**

cherotic magic
A MAJOR ATTEMPT TO INTRODUCE A POWERFUL SYSTEM OF MAGIC INTO OUR MODERN WESTERN EVERYDAY LIFE, THEREBY EXPLOSIVELY EXPANDING SUCH CONCEPTS AS SEX, HUMAN RELATIONSHIPS. THE CLEAR, DOWN-TO-EARTH TEXT IS AMPLIFIED BY THE NON-LINEAR TRANCE ILLUSTRATIONS BY LABASH.
published 1990 **$15**

the cherotic revolutionary #0
A MAGAZINE ABOUT THE EDGE. **$3**

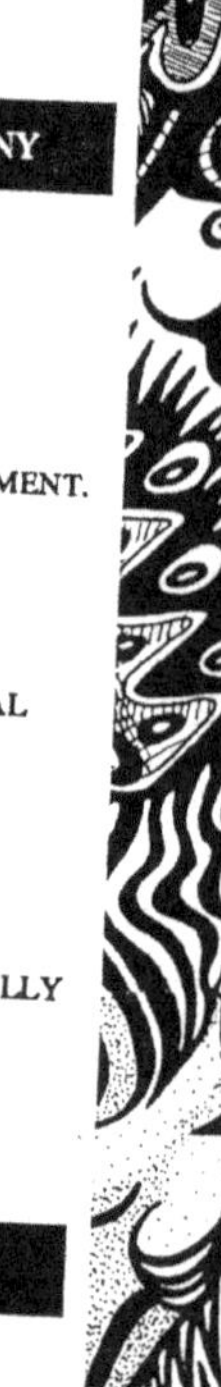

music BY FRANK MOORE'S CHERO COMPANY

$5 each

body music
copyrighted 1989
EXPLORING THE HUMAN BODY AS MUSICAL INSTRUMENT.

inter-rhythms
copyrighted 1989
PRIMAL MUSIC CREATED FOR FRANK MOORE'S RITUAL PERFORMANCES.

rock of passion
THE SOUNDTRACK OF the outrageous horror show, FRANK THE ROCKSTAR SINGS HIS HEART OUT, LITERALLY COVERING THE GREAT HITS OF ROCK, COUNTRY, AND HEAVY METAL ... INCLUDING SUCH SMASHES AS i am woman, i got you babe, AND hand of doom.

to order call or write:

frank moore
P.O. BOX 11445, BERKELEY, CA 94701-2445
(510) 526-7858

also available from S/R Press

war in heaven 18
BY KYLE GRIFFITH

the spiritual revolutionary vol. 1 $20
BOUND VOLUME ISSUES 0-9

the spiritual revolutionary
INDIVIDUAL ISSUES $3
SAMPLE ISSUE $1

to order call or write:

S/R Press
P.O. BOX 60327, PALO ALTO, CA 94306-0327

REVIEWS

The Cherotic Revolutionary #1
January 1992

"I love your magazine and articles."
Karen Finley

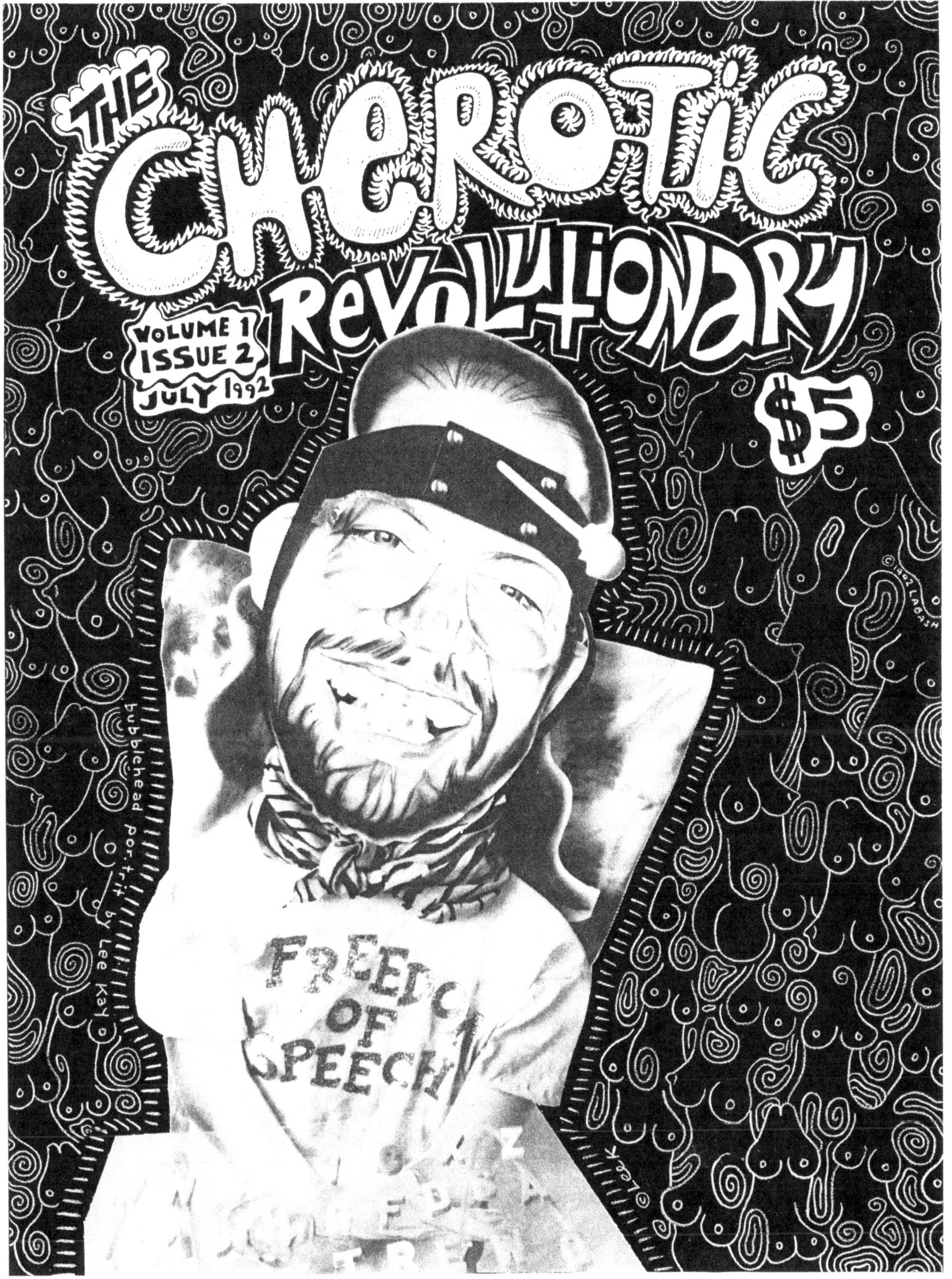
THE CHEROTIC REVOLUTIONARY
VOLUME 1
ISSUE 2
JULY 1992
$5
FREEDOM OF SPEECH
bubblehead por.trit by Lee Kay
©1992 LABASH

THE CHEROTIC REVOLUTIONARY #2 JULY, 1992

TCR is edited by Frank Moore and Linda Mac, and published by Kyle and Luna Griffith. The art editor is Michael LaBash, and the circulation manager is Alexi Malenky.

The price for this issue is $5.00 per copy. We don't sell subscriptions, to avoid tying ourselves down to a rigid publication schedule or magazine size. We want to remain free to publish small issues frequently or larger issues at longer intervals and adjust the price accordingly.

We heartily encourage letters of comment from readers and will answer as many as we can. Please tell us if you don't want us to print material from your letter -- otherwise we will assume it's OK.

Please address all correspondence and orders for magazines to:

Frank Moore, P.O. Box 11445, Berkeley, CA 94701-2445

In This Issue ...

FRANKLY SPEAKING

by

FRANK MOORE

WELL, THIS IS ANOTHER FINE ISSUE YOU'VE GOTTEN ME INTO, STAN...IS THAT YOUR NAME...HEY, YOU WHO ARE READING THIS. AFTER ALL, YOU SHOULD TAKE EQUAL CREDIT (OR EQUAL BLAME) AS US FOR **TCR**...AFTER ALL, YOU ARE READING THIS.

WE SAID AWHILE BACK THAT **TCR** WOULD BE ABOUT THE EDGE BY ARTISTS (OF ALL KINDS) WHO ARE ON THE EDGE. AS YOU WILL SEE, THAT HAS COME ABOUT.

TCR HAS STARTED CREATING ITSELF. THE NEXT ISSUE IS ALREADY LOADED AND READY TO BE FIRED OFF. WE GET MATERIAL IN MANY DIFFERENT WAYS.

FOR EXAMPLE, **BARNABY CHANCELLOR** FROM ARIZONA WAS PASSING THROUGH BERKELEY AND DROPPED INTO **SMOKEY JOE'S CAFE** FOR BREAKFAST. SINCE **TCR** WAS FOR SALE THERE, HE BROWSED THROUGH IT...AND GOT VERY EXCITED. HE STARTED TALKING TO THE COOK, WHO JUST HAPPENED TO BE **ALEXI** OUR CIRCULATION MANAGER. BARNABY SAID HE HAD A POEM, AND THAT HE HADN'T YET FOUND A ZINE THAT HE WANTED TO PUT HIS POEM IN...UNTIL **TCR**. WE ARE HONORED.

YOU WHO HAVE GOTTEN ADDICTED TO **LaBASH'S** COVERS AND ARE FREAKING OUT BECAUSE THERE IS NOT ONE IN THIS ISSUE...JUST TURN TO THE BACK COVER...IT'S THERE. OUR FRONT COVER ARTIST IS **LEE KAY** OUT OF CHICAGO. HE IS KNOWN FOR HIS "BUBBLEHEAD POR-TRITS" OF CULT FIGURES OF THE UNDERGROUND CULTURE. AH, YES, YOU NOW SEE WHAT THEY ARE TALKING ABOUT WHEN THEY SAY I'VE A BIG HEAD! BY THE WAY, A BUBBLEHEAD OF **ANNIE SPRINKLE** WILL GRACE HER WRITINGS IN OUR NEXT ISSUE.

WE ARE BLOWN OUT AT THE ARTISTS TO WHOM OUR LITTLE ZINE HAS ACCESS TO THROUGH MAGICAL CHANNELS. A CASE IN POINT IS **H. R. GIGER**. BASED IN SWITZERLAND, HE IS AN INTERNATIONALLY KNOWN SURREALIST. IF YOU HAVE WATCHED THE **ALIEN**(S) FILMS, YOU HAVE ENTERED HIS EROTIC VISUAL NIGHTMARES. WHEN THE PUNK BAND **THE DEAD KENNEDYS** ENCLOSED HIS COCKS/PUSSIES PAINTING IN THEIR ALBUM, THEY WERE BUSTED FOR OBSCENITY. (THEY WERE FINALLY JUDGED NOT GUILTY...AFTER THE CASE HAD BROKEN THEM.) THANKS TO MY CLOSE FRIEND **LES BARANY**, WHO IS **GIGER'S** AGENT IN THE U.S., FOR GIVING US PERMISSION TO REPRINT THE WORK.

PETER PETRISKO JR., AS WELL AS OBVIOUSLY BEING A GOOD PHOTOCOPY-ARTIST, IS THE CENTER OF THE CULTURAL UNDERGROUND IN PHOENIX, ARIZONA, WITH HIS OWN ZINE **(e)X-communications** (WHICH HAS PUBLISHED MY **CULTURAL SUBVERSION** THAT IS ALSO APPEARING IN THIS ISSUE), HIS OWN BOOKSTORE **METROPOPHOBOBIA** (WHICH CARRIES ALL OF OUR STUFF), AND HIS OWN PERFORMANCE CLUB **GALLERY X** (AT WHICH I WILL BE APPEARING THIS NOVEMBER).

KEVIN RICE IS AN UP-AND-COMING PHOTO-JOURNALIST WHO HAS DOCUMENTED OUR PERFORMANCES OVER THE YEARS.

STAVROS KRYSIAK'S REVIEW OF ONE OF OUR PERFORMANCES CAME OVER A COMPUTER NETWORK. THIS IS AN EXAMPLE OF THE PERSONAL ANARCHIAL TECHNOLOGIES I AM TALKING ABOUT IN **CULTURAL SUBVERSION**. STAVROS AND I HAVE DEVELOPED A CLOSE RELATIONSHIP BY TALKING EVERY NIGHT OVER **THE GENIE NETWORK**, WHICH IS RUN BY GENERAL ELECTRIC. WE TALK ABOUT STRANGE THINGS SUCH AS SHAMANISM, SHAPING REALITY, RITUAL....AND OF COURSE THE MANY THINGS I AM SELLING.

THE POWERFUL THING ABOUT A NETWORK LIKE THIS IS PEOPLE ALL OVER THE COUNTRY CAN READ OUR TALK AND, IF THEY WISH, JOIN IN. SO FOR $4.95 A MONTH (WITH NO PHONE BILL), I HAVE NIGHTLY ACCESS TO A NATIONAL AUDIENCE IN A DIRECT ALMOST LIVE CHANNEL THROUGH WHICH I CAN POUR SUBVERSIVE CONCEPTS AND INFO. HEY! WHY DON'T YOU JOIN ME ON-LINE?

KYLE SAYS A LOT OF NICE THINGS ABOUT ME IN HIS NEW INTRODUCTION TO MY BOOK, **CHEROTIC MAGIC**. BUT I THINK THE MOST IMPORTANT ASPECT OF HIS PIECE IS THAT HE OUTLINES THE PROCESS BY WHICH THE STUDENT WITHIN A TRIBAL SHAMANISTIC TRAINING "LEARNS" BY A DISCIPLINE OF TRUST.

I'M LAZY. FOR MONTHS I HAVE BEEN THINKING ABOUT WRITING ABOUT THE LIBERAL SICKNESS CALLED "POLITICAL CORRECTNESS." THIS SICKNESS FRAGMENTS PEOPLE INTO ARTIFICIAL GROUPS (BLACK, GAY, WOMEN, DISABLED, ETC.) WITHIN WHICH THEY THEN ARE FORCED TO STAY. THIS SICKNESS MAKES THE INDIVIDUAL SO FRAGILE THAT ANY "BAD" OR "WRONG" WORD OR IMAGE (NIGGER, FAG, CHICK, CRIPPLE) CAN COMPLETELY SHATTER THE PERSON. THIS FRAGILENESS MAKES IT IMPOSSIBLE TO FUNCTION IN THE REAL WORLD WITHOUT THE ARTIFICIAL DOME OF PC-CENSORSHIP. I WAS GOING TO EXAMINE THIS SICKNESS WITHIN THE ART WORLD, USING THE ART COMBINE **HIGHWAYS/HIGH PERFORMANCE MAGAZINE** AS MY CASE STUDY. BUT I KEPT PUTTING IT OFF. I'M LAZY. THEN **CURTIS YORK'S** LETTER FELL INTO MY HANDS. NOW I DON'T NEED TO WRITE THAT ARTICLE!

TALKING ABOUT PC-CENSORSHIP BRINGS US TO THE CARTOON BY THE ROCK'N'ROLL ARTIST **JOHN SEABURY**. WE HAVE GOTTEN SHIT FOR RUNNING HIS DRAWING IN THIS ISSUE...FROM PEOPLE WHO NORMALLY ARE AGAINST CENSORSHIP. I'VE BEEN THINKING ABOUT WHY THIS DRAWING GETS PEOPLE SO ANGRY OR UP-TIGHT. I DON'T THINK IT IS THE IMAGES. AFTER ALL, LOOK AT **LaBASH'S** DRAWINGS. THE TABOO-BREAKING IMAGE CONTENTS ARE EQUAL BETWEEN THEM. THE DIFFERENCE BETWEEN THESE TWO ARTISTS IS **LaBASH** IS NONLINEAR WHILE SEABURY IS LINEAR.

FRANK MOORE

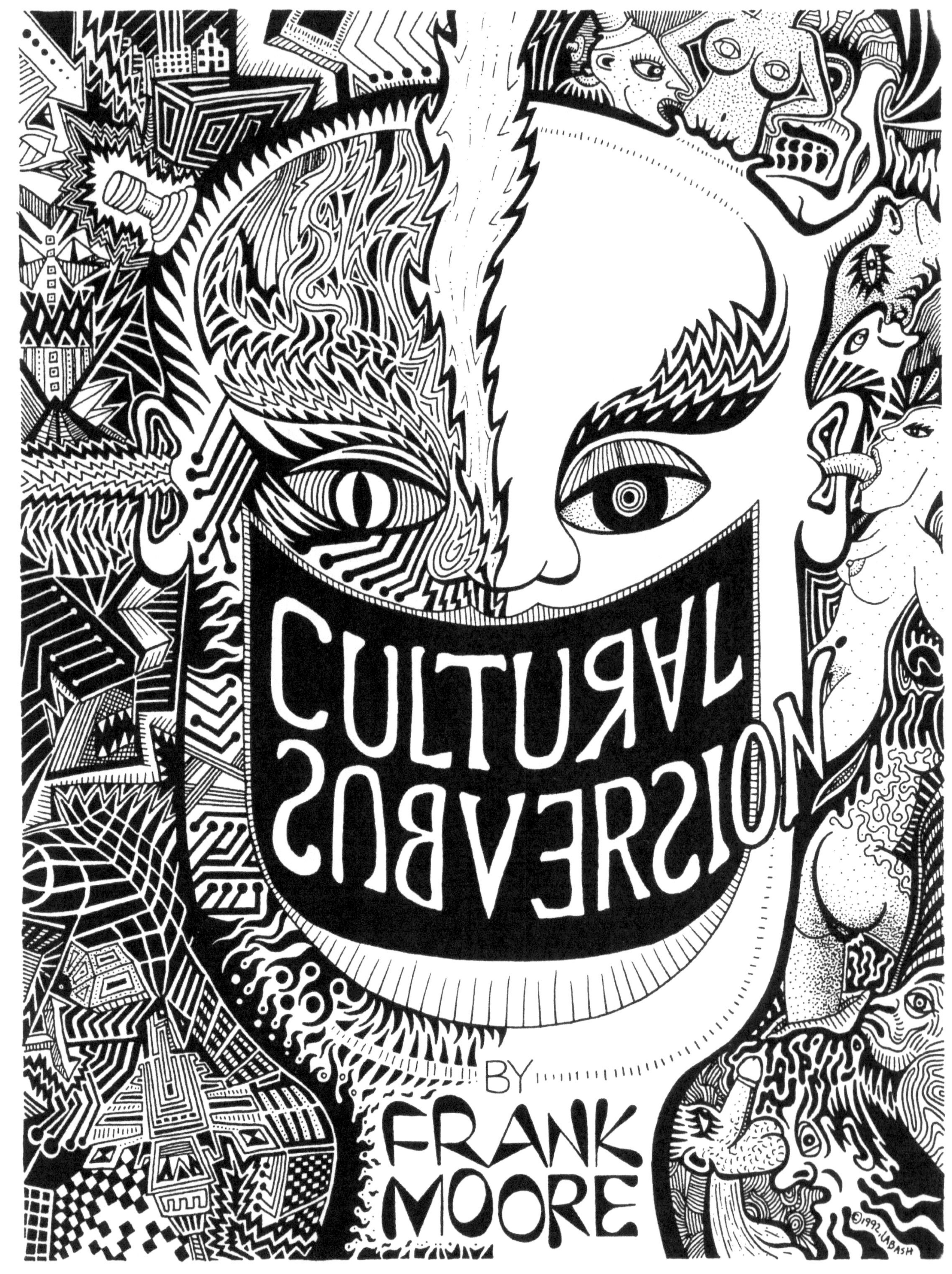
CULTURAL
SUBVERSION
BY
FRANK
MOORE
©1992 LABASH

CULTURAL SUBVERSION

BY

FRANK MOORE

October 23, 1991

THIS WILL BE PERSONAL. BUT THE PERSONAL LEVEL IS THE KEY TO UNDERSTANDING THE CULTURAL, ARTISTIC, AND POLITICAL MOVEMENT WHICH IS TAKING BACK TECHNOLOGY INTO THE PERSONAL CONTROL OF ANYONE WHO HAS SOMETHING TO SAY, SOMETHING TO CREATE. IT IS PERSONAL TECHNOLOGY, ANARCHISTIC TECHNOLOGY. IT IS NOT LIKE CABLE T.V. WHICH WE WERE TOLD 10 YEARS AGO WOULD LIBERATE THE PERSON BY GIVING HIM INTIMATE AND DIRECT INFORMATION AND COMMUNICATION CHANNELS...BUT WHICH TODAY IS SIMPLY MORE CHANNELS FOR THE MONEY TYPES WHO HAVE ALWAYS CONTROLLED THE COMMUNICATION FLOWING THROUGH MASS MEDIA...JUST MORE MONOPOLIZED CHANNELS FOR PASSIVE ENTERTAINMENT, SELLING, AND MANIPULATION OF INFORMATION AND OF REALITY. THE ONLY EXCEPTION TO THIS IS THE LOCAL ACCESS CHANNELS WHICH ARE KEPT IN THE CLOSET AND ARE ALWAYS IN DANGER OF BEING AXED BY THE CABLE COMPANY. THESE ACCESS CHANNELS ARE A PART OF THE PERSONAL TECHNOLOGY.

PERSONAL TECHNOLOGY IS BASICALLY A SLIP UP OF WHAT I HAVE CALLED ELSEWHERE "THE COMBINE PLOT." I TOOK THE TERM "COMBINE" FROM THE KEN KESEY NOVEL **ONE FLEW OVER THE CUCKOO'S NEST**. THE COMBINE PLOT IS A HIDDEN DYNAMIC SYSTEM OF POWER, CONTROL, AND INTEREST THAT KEEPS THE TOOLS OF CREATION AND OF EFFECTIVE CHANGE OUT OF THE HANDS OF THE COMMON PEOPLE. THIS KEEPS THE PEOPLE POWERLESS, KEEPING THE POWER WITHIN AN ELITE. THE TOOLS OF EFFECTIVE CHANGE HAVE BEEN KEPT OUT OF THE HANDS OF THE COMMON PEOPLE BY FALSE RITUALS OF EDUCATION, MONEY, AND BULKY EXPENSIVE EQUIPMENT WHICH TOOK A CULT KNOWLEDGE TO OPERATE. ADDED TO THIS MAZE OF CREATIVE BLOCKS WAS THE FALSE MYTHS ABOUT TALENT AND THE ACCEPTABLE QUALITY LEVELS NEEDED TO REACH PEOPLE, ACCEPTABLE QUALITY LEVELS BELOW WHICH PEOPLE ARE TRAINED TO NOT WATCH OR LISTEN.

ALL OF THIS IS TOO ABSTRACT AND PHILOSOPHICAL. IN THIS ARTICLE, I WILL TRY TO PULL THESE ISSUES DOWN INTO THE REAL WORLD BY USING MY OWN ARTISTIC EXPERIENCES AS A CONTEXT. BUT IT IS IMPORTANT TO REALIZE AT THE BEGINNING THAT PERSONAL TECHNOLOGY, ANARCHISTIC TECHNOLOGY IS STILL TECHNOLOGY. ALL TECHNOLOGY HAS HIDDEN, BUILT-IN LINKS TO THE ESTABLISHED ORDER OF ISOLATION AND FRAGMENTATION. THESE LINKS CAN FRUSTRATE ATTEMPTS TO USE TECHNOLOGY TO SUBVERT THE ESTABLISHED REALITY. ONLY BY BEING ALWAYS AWARE OF THESE LINKS TO ISOLATION AND FRAGMENTATION INHERENT IN ALL TECHNOLOGY, CAN TECHNOLOGY BE SAFELY USED AS A TOOL OF CULTURAL SUBVERSION. THIS FACT AGAIN BANGED ME OVER THE HEAD WHEN I WAS TALKING TO A SUCCESSFUL MUSICIAN WHO DIDN'T UNDERSTAND WHY ALL PERFORMERS DO NOT STOP TOURING, CONSIDERING THE POLLUTION CAUSED BY TRAVELING...AND DO WHAT HE DOES, WHICH IS DO EVERYTHING THROUGH TELECOMMUNICATIONS. I JUST SAID YOU CAN NOT TOUCH THROUGH PHONES, COMPUTERS, VIDEOS...AND EVEN THROUGH WRITING. TO RESTORE HUMANITY TO OUR CULTURE BY USING TECHNOLOGY, WE MUST KNOW AND ADMIT THE LIMITATIONS OF THAT TECHNOLOGY.

ALL TECHNOLOGY IS A DOUBLE-EDGED SWORD. THIS INCLUDES THE VERY FIRST COMMUNICATION TECHNOLOGY...WRITING/READING. WE USUALLY THINK OF THE INVENTION OF

WRITING AS EXTREMELY LIBERATING. AND IN SO MANY WAYS IT WAS. BUT IN SO MANY OTHER WAYS IT CONFINED HUMANITY. FOR ONE THING, IT PLACED A FIXED LINEAR FRAME OF THINKING WITHIN THE HUMAN BRAIN MUCH MORE THAN SPOKEN LANGUAGE HAD DONE. MOREOVER, WRITING/READING CREATED A VERY EXCLUSIVE ELITE FOR MOST OF THE KNOWN HUMAN HISTORY. BEFORE WRITING, EVERYONE KNEW THE TRIBAL LANGUAGE...EVERYONE KNEW HOW TO PAINT, SING, DANCE. INFORMATION FLOWED BOTH BETWEEN PEOPLE AND WITHIN TIME TO THE FUTURE THROUGH THIS TRIBAL ACCESSIBLE LANGUAGE BOTH OF SPOKEN WORD AND OF ART. IF INFORMATION DID NOT FLOW THROUGH THIS TRIBAL CHANNEL, THAT INFORMATION WAS LOST. ALL OF THIS CHANGED WHEN WRITING WAS INVENTED. NOW THERE WAS A CHANNEL THAT WAS NOT ACCESSIBLE TO EVERYONE, A CHANNEL THAT DID NOT EASILY LOSE INFORMATION. THOSE WHO COULD ACCESS THIS CHANNEL HAD POWER. BECAUSE OF THIS, FOR MOST OF RECORDED HISTORY, THE SKILL OF READING/WRITING WAS MONOPOLIZED BY THE RULING ELITE TO MAINTAIN ITS POWER. THIS WAS TRUE EVEN AFTER A LARGER MINORITY GAINED LIMITED ACCESS TO THE FLOWING CHANNEL OF WRITING. ONE OF THE WAYS THE ELITE MAINTAINED ITS CONTROL WAS BY WITHDRAWING THE IMPORTANT IDEAS...DANGEROUS IDEAS...BOTH THE SACRED AND PROFANE, AWAY FROM THE COMMON PEOPLE, WITHDRAWING THE DANGEROUS IDEAS INTO A DEAD LANGUAGE SUCH AS LATIN OR GREEK. ONLY THE MEMBERS OF THE ELITE WHO WENT THROUGH THE RITUALS OF EDUCATION OF THE ESTABLISHED ORDER (BE IT RELIGIOUS, POLITICAL, AND/OR CLASS) COULD READ OR SPEAK THIS DEAD LANGUAGE OF POWER. THERE WAS ANOTHER CHANNEL OF FLOWING INFORMATION WHICH WAS THE FOLK ART, FOLK MUSIC, AND FOLK WORDS, BE IT WRITTEN OR SPOKEN. THIS FOLK CHANNEL WAS ACCESSIBLE TO EVERYONE. IT WAS A DYNAMIC, INTERACTIVE CHANNEL OF COMMUNICATION. BUT THE FULL FORCE OF THIS FOLK CHANNEL WAS ALWAYS KEPT IN CHECK BY THE ELITE CHANNEL WITH THE MYTH THAT ANYTHING WHICH COMES THROUGH THE FOLK CHANNEL WAS NOT WORTHY OR IMPORTANT BECAUSE IT DID NOT COME FROM THE HIDDEN KNOWLEDGE.

THIS CONTROL OF THE ELITE DID NOT START TO BREAK DOWN UNTIL THE PRINTING PRESS BECAME COST ACCESSIBLE TO THE MEMBERS OF THE COMMON PEOPLE. THIS OPENED TO THE COMMON PEOPLE A COMMUNICATION CHANNEL WHICH WAS NOT ROOTED IN PHYSICAL TIME....THAT IS, YOU WRITE SOMETHING AND SOMEONE WITHIN ANOTHER TIME, ANOTHER PLACE READS EXACTLY WHAT YOU THOUGHT. THIS IS THE REAL FORCE WHICH WAS UNLOCKED BY THE PRINTING PRESS, AND NOT THE ABILITY TO REACH MASS AMOUNTS OF PEOPLE. WITHOUT THE PRINTING PRESS BEING TO A LARGE DEGREE ACCESSIBLE TO THE FORCES OF CHANGE, THE AMERICAN AND FRENCH REVOLUTION MIGHT NOT HAVE HAPPENED.

BUT THE ELITE QUICKLY DEVELOPED STRATEGIES TO LIMIT ACCESS FOR THE COMMON PEOPLE TO THIS PRINTING CHANNEL. THE ELITE SPREAD THE MYTH THAT TO BE REALLY EFFECTIVE, A WRITER HAD TO GO THROUGH THE RITUALS OF THE EDUCATIONAL SYSTEM, AND THEN BE BLESSED BY BEING RECOGNIZED BY THE PUBLISHING FACTORY, WHICH BECAME INCREASINGLY MASSIVE AND IMPERSONAL. SELF PUBLISHING WAS LABELLED "VANITY PRESS." THE PRESSES THAT OFFERED THIS SERVICE WERE SEEN AS CONS, AS SCAMS. WRITERS WHO USED THIS SERVICE WERE THOUGHT OF AS UNTALENTED FOOLS WHO GOT CONNED. THE INDIVIDUAL WHO BELIEVED IN THIS MYTH OF THE POWER OF THE CORPORATE MEDIA SYSTEM TO BESTOW ACCESS TO COMMUNICATIONS, AND TO BESTOW VALIDITY THROUGH ACCEPTANCE, WAS FROZEN OUT OF ANY REAL POSITION FOR SUBVERSIVE CHANGE.

ALL OF THIS IS AN HISTORICAL BACKGROUND ON WHICH I CAN TALK ABOUT THE ISSUES OF PERSONAL TECHNOLOGY, ANARCHISTIC TECHNOLOGY IN THE CONTEXT OF CULTURAL SUBVERSION.

I STARTED OUT IN THE LATE 60'S WRITING FOR UNDERGROUND PAPERS AS A POLITICAL COLUMNIST...SNEAKING INTO THE MIMEOGRAPH ROOM AT SCHOOL TO RUN OFF A HUNDRED COPIES UNDER THE PROTECTION OF A FRIENDLY TEACHER. OF COURSE, THE TEACHER ALWAYS, AS WELL AS US, GOT INTO HOT WATER...AND THE ACCESS TO THE MIMEOGRAPH MACHINE

WAS CLOSED. NO ACCESS, NO UNDERGROUND PAPER. THERE WAS NOT ANY QUESTION ABOUT OUR BUYING OUR OWN MIMEOGRAPH MACHINE...NO MONEY.

BUT IT TOOK ONLY A YEAR OR SO FOR THE UNDERGROUND PRESS TO MOVE FROM THE MIMEOGRAPH STAGE INTO BEING RUN OFF AT OFF-SET PRINT SHOPS. THE UNDERGROUND PRESS HAD ITS ROOTS GOING BACK THROUGH THE RADICAL PRESS OF THE 20'S AND 30'S AND IN THE POETRY PRESS. THE KIND OF PERSON WHO PUT OUT THESE PAPERS POURED ALL THEIR PERSONAL MONEY INTO IT, THEN HOPED BY SELLING ADS, SELLING PAPERS, BY MAGIC, THE PAPER WOULD KEEP AFLOAT. THERE WAS RARELY ANY QUESTION OF MAKING MONEY ON IT. BUT WHEN YOUR NEST EGG, YOUR DEAD AUNT'S MONEY, ADS, SALES, OR WHATEVER WAS SUPPORTING YOUR RAG RAN OUT, THAT PAPER OF VISIONS DIED. BUT THERE WAS ALWAYS A NEW PAPER BEING BORN TO FILL THE EMPTY SPACE.

THERE WAS A REJECTION OF THE OLD STANDARDS OF QUALITY OF BOTH FORM AND CONTENT WHICH HAD KEPT THE COMMON PEOPLE FROM CREATING. AS A RESULT OF THIS REJECTION, A NEW WAY OF LOOKING AT ART, POLITICS, AND LIFE WAS THUS CREATED. THE UNDERGROUND PRESS BECAME SO EFFECTIVE THAT BY THE EARLY 70'S, THERE WERE OVER 700 OF THESE PAPERS AND AN UNDERGROUND PRESS NETWORK. IT BECAME SO EFFECTIVE THAT THE F.B.I. TARGETED THE UNDERGROUND PRESS FOR DESTRUCTION BY A COVERT WAR. BY USING THE FACT THAT THE UNDERGROUND PAPERS RARELY HAD DIRECT ACCESS TO A PRINTING PRESS, AND BY USING THE ORGANIZATION WHICH DEVELOPED AROUND THE UNDERGROUND PRESS, THE F.B.I. AND THE REST OF THE COMBINE COULD BRING THE UNDERGROUND PRESS INTO CONTROL, INTO THE FOLD.

AROUND THIS TIME, I REJECTED POLITICS AS A MEANS FOR EFFECTIVE SUBVERSIVE CHANGE, AND BEGAN LOOKING TOWARDS ART AND MAGIC FOR AN EFFECTIVE CHANNEL. I TOOK A FILM-MAKING COURSE, LEARNING THE TECHNICAL RITUALS OF 16MM. 16MM WAS THEN THE HOME MOVIE TECHNOLOGY. BUT WHEN I DID THE TECHNOLOGICAL RITUALS OF LIGHTING, SHOOTING, SPLICING, ETC., THEY TOOK ME AWAY FROM THE ACTUAL MAGIC OF DOING. HIDDEN WITHIN THESE TECHNOLOGICAL RITUALS ARE DEADENING ROADBLOCKS TO DIRECT PERSONAL CREATIVE COMMUNICATIONS. ROADBLOCKS CAN BE GOTTEN AROUND. BUT WHY BOTHER WHEN THERE ARE DIRECT ALTERNATIVE ROUTES?

AFTER THE FILM COURSE, I STILL HAD NO MONEY TO MAKE FILMS. ONE ROAD WOULD HAVE BEEN TO PUT MY TIME AND ENERGY INTO GETTING MONEY OR A POSITION TO MAKE FILMS. BUT I ALWAYS HAVE MISTRUSTED THE MYTH OF CHANGING THE SYSTEM FROM WITHIN. IT NEVER WORKS. ONCE YOU HAVE COMPROMISED, MODIFIED, CHANGED, DISTORTED BOTH YOURSELF AND YOUR MESSAGE TO GET THE MEDIA CHANNEL, WHY BOTHER SENDING THE MESSAGE? THE SYSTEM MYTH IS A MAJOR VACUUM THAT SUCKS CREATIVE POWER AWAY FROM PEOPLE BY PUTTING VAST AMOUNTS OF TIME BETWEEN THE PERSON AND THE ACT OF CREATION. WHETHER THE MYTH IS OF WAITING TO GET ENOUGH MONEY, EDUCATION, OR POWER BEFORE YOU CREATE, THE EFFECT IS THE SAME...WAITING FOR GODOT.

FOR THESE REASONS, I CREATED A NO/LOW TECH FORM OF LIVE PERFORMANCE WHICH DID NOT NEED MONEY, THEATER SPACE, SETS, STAGE LIGHTING, APPROVAL, OR A PARTICULAR AUDIENCE SIZE. THIS NO/LOW TECH FORM IS VITAL TO WORK WHICH IS CULTURALLY SUBVERSIVE BY EXPANDING THE CONCEPT OF SEXUALITY AND REALITY BEYOND THE FRAME OF TABOOS.

FOR ME AS A NO/LOW TECH ARTIST, THE PERSONAL TECHNOLOGY, ANARCHISTIC TECHNOLOGY IS A VERY IMPORTANT DIMENSION. I FIRST REALIZED THIS WHEN I WAS TRYING TO GET ESTABLISHED IN N.Y.C. IN THE EARLY 70'S. I COULD NOT FIND OUT ABOUT ART EVENTS UNTIL AFTER THE FACT WHEN I READ ABOUT THEM IN **THE VILLAGE VOICE**. SO I COULDN'T GO TO THEM. SO I COULDN'T MEET PEOPLE WITH WHOM I COULD HAVE GOTTEN SOMETHING GOING. ONE REASON FOR THIS WAS THERE WAS VERY LITTLE FLYERING. IN N.Y.C., ORGANIZED CRIME HAS A MONOPOLY ON PUTTING UP POSTERS. I DID NOT REALIZE HOW MUCH

NO FLYERING ISOLATED PEOPLE UNTIL I MOVED TO BERKELEY WHERE ON EVERY TELEPHONE POLE, THERE WERE 10, 20, 30 FLYERS. ANYONE WHO HAS AN EVENT, A GROUP, A CAUSE, SOMETHING TO SAY, CAN GO TO A XEROX PLACE, RUN OFF HUNDREDS, OR EVEN THOUSANDS, OF FLYERS AND STAPLE THEM UP ALL OVER TOWN. THIS DIRECT TWO-WAY FORM OF THE PRESS PLUGGED ME IMMEDIATELY INTO THE COMMUNITY WHERE I COULD DO MY WORK.

WE HAVE TO START SEEING FLYERING, BE IT ON TELEPHONE POLES OR ON COMPUTER BULLETIN BOARDS, AS A FORM OF PERSONAL PRESS, AND AS SUCH IT IS PROTECTED UNDER THE FREEDOM OF PRESS. BIG BROTHER COMES IN MANY FORMS FROM THE MAFIA TO GOVERNMENT (DOWN TO THE ANTI-FLIER LAWS AS PART OF A CITY'S "BEAUTIFICATION" CAMPAIGN) TO CORPORATIONS SUCH AS A.T.&T. AND BLOCKBUSTER VIDEOS.

JUST RECENTLY I SAW THE POWER OF THIS DIRECT PERSONAL PRESS. FOR YEARS I HAVE NOT BEEN ABLE TO BE BOOKED IN THE "ALTERNATIVE" PERFORMANCE GALLERIES IN THE BAY AREA FOR VARIOUS REASONS...SO I PUT 500 "TOO CONTROVERSIAL FOR THE BAY AREA" FLYERS UP ASKING FOR LEADS TO SPACES. FROM THE VERY FIRST FLYER WE PUT UP CAME THREE GOOD LEADS INTO THE TRUE ALTERNATIVE ART SCENE. MOREOVER, THE FLYER DIRECTLY EXPOSED THE TRUE CONDITION OF THE ESTABLISHED "ALTERNATIVE" ART WORLD.

THIS DIRECT EXPOSING IS ONE OF THE STRENGTHS OF THE PERSONAL TECHNOLOGY, ANARCHISTIC TECHNOLOGY IN THE CONTEXT OF CULTURAL SUBVERSION. BE IT A CAMCORDER CAPTURING POLICE BRUTALITY OR A XEROX ZINE PUBLISHING RADICAL HERETOFORE UNPUBLISHABLE MATERIAL, THE EFFECT IS TO DECENTRALIZE POWER, PUTTING IT INTO THE PERSONAL LEVEL. I NOTICED THIS AGAIN LAST YEAR WHEN SEN. JESSE HELMS TARGETED ME FOR INVESTIGATION FOR MY ART. WITH ONLY ONE EXCEPTION, NO ONE FROM THE REGULAR PRESS CONTACTED ME TO GET MY REACTION OR STORY. SOME OF THE ART MAGAZINES PRINTED MY OPEN LETTER TO HELMS AND MY ARTICLE ON CENSORSHIP. BUT I REACHED A WIDE NATIONAL AUDIENCE WHEN **THE SPIRITUAL REVOLUTIONARY (TSR)**, A NEWSLETTER ZINE BY **S/R PRESS**, PRINTED BOTH. WHILE **TSR** HAS A SMALL READERSHIP, OTHER ZINES REPRINTED MY TWO PIECES FROM **TSR**, WITHOUT MY PERMISSION BUT WITHOUT EDITING. THEN STILL OTHER ZINES REPRINTED THE MATERIAL FROM THOSE ZINES. THE EFFECT OF THIS ANARCHISTIC GRAPEVINE OF XEROX ZINES IS I HAD EXPOSURE TO A WIDE NATIONAL AUDIENCE WHICH WAS MADE UP OF SMALL SUBCULTURES.

THE COMBINE RECOGNIZES THE UNCONTROLLABLE FORCE REPRESENTED BY THE DIRECT PERSONAL COMMUNICATIONS THROUGH THE ANARCHISTIC TECHNOLOGY. THE COMBINE IS TRYING TO PUT THIS GENIE BACK IN THE BOTTLE. THE EASIEST, AND THE MOST OBVIOUS, WAY TO DO THIS IS TO CENSOR THE PHYSICAL CHANNELS...BE IT PHONE LINES, THE MAIL, OR T.V./RADIO WAVES.

BUT THERE ARE HIDDEN MEANS BY WHICH THE COMBINE CAN THWART THE DIRECT PERSONAL USE OF TECHNOLOGY. ONE OF THESE IS MAKING EQUIPMENT SUCH AS COMPUTERS OBSOLETE EVERY SIX MONTHS, NOT FOR ANY REAL FUNCTIONAL IMPROVEMENT, BUT FOR PROGRESS. THE EFFECT OF HABITUAL UPGRADING IS NOT ONLY THAT WE KEEP HAVING TO BUY NEW SOFT/HARDWARE, BUT IT ALSO CREATES A FALSE MYSTERY AROUND THE COMPUTER VERY MUCH LIKE THE DEAD LANGUAGE OF LATIN DID IN THE DARK AGES.

BUT THE BEST WAY FOR THE COMBINE TO CURB THE USE OF PERSONAL TECHNOLOGY IS BY THE STANDARDS OF "PROFESSIONAL QUALITY."

WHEN I XEROX PUBLISHED MY FIRST TWO BOOKS, I DID NOT RUN INTO THIS WALL OF "PROFESSIONAL QUALITY." THIS IS BECAUSE I SOLD THEM DIRECTLY, PERSONALLY AT MY PERFORMANCES, AS WELL BY THE MAIL THROUGH A REVIEW IN **BOX OF WATER**.

BUT WHEN **S/R PRESS** XEROX PUBLISHED MY BOOK, **CHEROTIC MAGIC**, WE TOOK IT, AS WELL AS MY ZINE **THE CHEROTIC REVOLUTIONARY**, AROUND TO BOOKSTORES. THE REASON WHY A

LOT OF THE BOOKSTORES GAVE FOR NOT CARRYING THE BOOK WAS NOT THE WRITTEN OR THE VISUAL CONTENTS OF THE BOOK, BUT THAT IT HAD A SPIRAL BINDING, RATHER THAN A REGULAR BINDING. HAVING A REGULAR BINDING WOULD BOOST THE COST OUT OF THE REALM OF PERSONAL LEVEL AND INTO THE TRADITIONAL PUBLISHING WITH ITS CONCERNS OF MASS SALES. KYLE GRIFFITH IS FOND OF SAYING THAT IF THE BOOK'S FORMAT IS TOO REVOLUTIONARY FOR A BOOKSTORE, THEN THE CONTENT IS ALSO...SO IT WOULD SERVE NO PURPOSE FOR US TO TRY TO PACKAGE IT DIFFERENTLY. I MUST QUICKLY ADD THAT THERE ARE QUITE A FEW BOOKSTORES THAT ARE NOT LOCKED INTO BUYING SOLELY FROM A DISTRIBUTOR, THAT WILL CARRY PERSONAL XEROX PUBLISHED BOOKS AND ZINES. MOREOVER, THERE ARE BOOKSTORES DEVOTED TO PERSONAL XEROX PUBLICATIONS...FOR EXAMPLE, METROPOPHOBOBIA IN, OF ALL PLACES, PHOENIX! THESE OUTLETS FOR PERSONAL PUBLICATIONS WILL MULTIPLY IN THE COMING YEARS.

I HAVE DEALT WITH THE BARRIERS OF FORMAT AND TECHNOLOGY TO PERSONAL DIRECT HUMAN INVOLVEMENT IN EVERY MEDIUM I HAVE TRIED. A LOT OF PEOPLE HAVE ASSUMED THIS WAS BECAUSE I WAS POOR, DID NOT KNOW HOW TO GET GRANTS, DID NOT KNOW HOW TO USE TECHNOLOGY, OR DID NOT KNOW HOW TO USE THE SYSTEM. IN REALITY, EVEN IF I HAD TONS OF MONEY, I WOULD STILL USE THE SAME NO/LOW TECH, BECAUSE THAT IS THE BEST WAY TO TAKE BACK THE CREATIVE FORCE FROM THE COMBINE...BACK INTO THE HANDS OF ANYONE WITH A CREATIVE URGE...OR, FOR THAT MATTER, A DESTRUCTIVE URGE.

SINCE WE ARE COMMUNICATING ON THE PERSONAL CHANNEL, YOU CAN SEND FEEDBACK, INQUIRIES, OR WHATEVER TO ME AT:

FRANK MOORE
P.O. BOX 11445
BERKELEY, CA
94701-2445

DEFINITIONS:

CHERO IS THE PHYSICAL LIFE ENERGY. I CREATED THE WORD "CHERO" BY COMBINING "CHI" AND "EROS". MAGIC IS THE SCIENCE/ART OF NONLINEAR CHANGE. IN CHEROTIC MAGIC, IT IS THE PRACTICAL FOCUS OF THE PERSON TO RESHAPE REALITY INTO MORE HUMANE FORMS BY USING THE MAGICAL DYNAMICS OF RELATIONSHIPS.

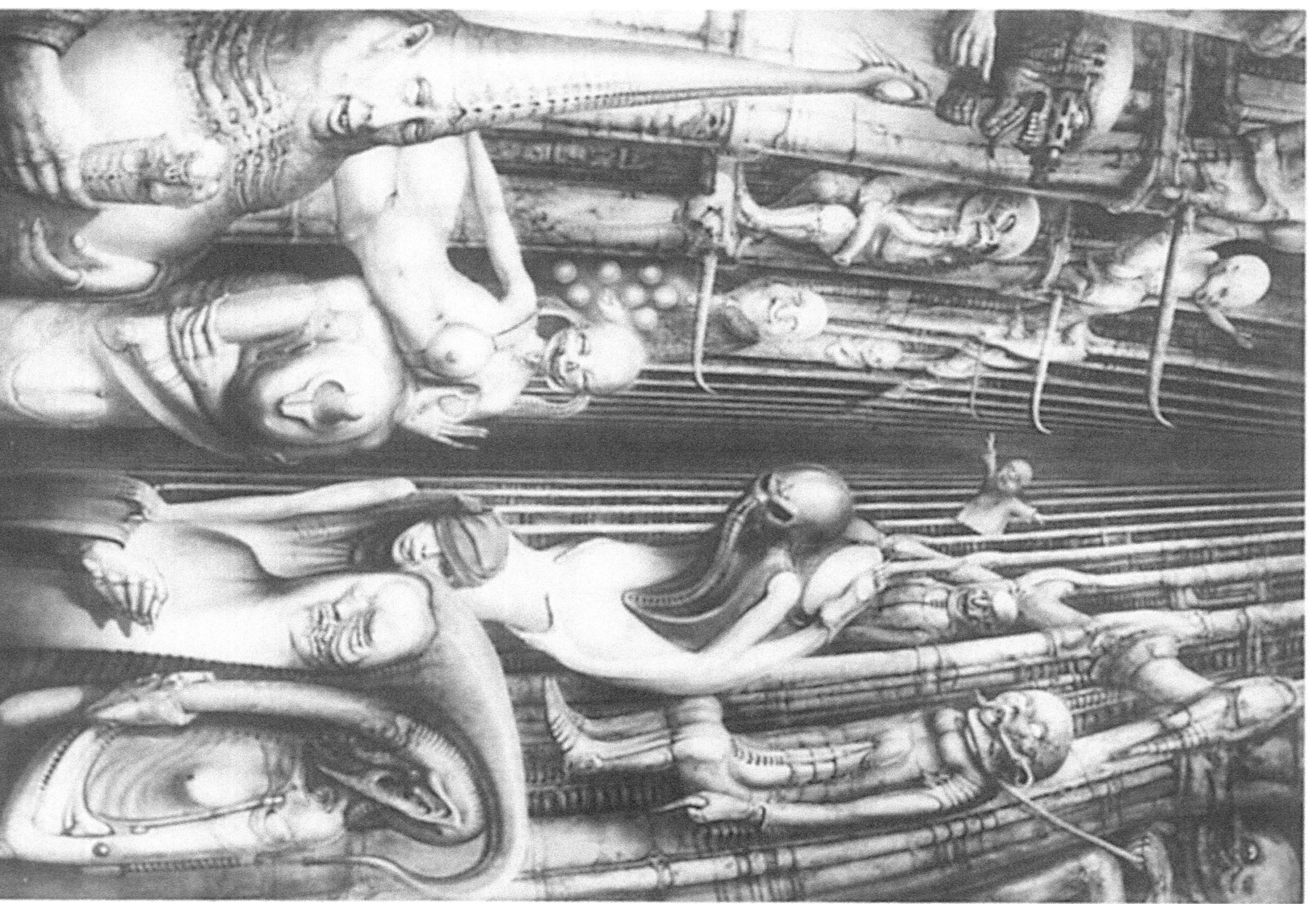

© 1992 **H.R. GIGER**, WORK #274, **A. CROWLEY (THE BEAST 666)**, 200 X 140cm., 1975

COURTESY OF LESLIE BARANY COMMUNICATIONS / NYC

THE POLITICAL CORRECTNESS MAFIA by Curtis York

A letter to the editor of HIGH PERFORMANCE Magazine, dated March 5, 1992

This letter is in response to Linda Frye Burnham's editorial which was printed in black letters on a white background in your Winter, 1991 issue.

Let me begin by saying that I believe any individual or organization which is making any attempt to combat racism in our society deserves encouragement and admiration. Racism is one of the various divisive human constructs which, in addition to political patriotism, classism, sexism and religions which glorify one group of people while condemning all others, negate the possibility that human cultures could ever be at one and at peace. I would also point out that racism is a problem which resides in every American, including, in my opinion, (are you sitting down?) the co-founders of Highways Performance Space themselves, Linda Burnham and Tim Miller.

I have for some time been angered by the base exploitation of "people of color" and "the gay community" under the banner of "multiculturalism in the arts" being waved by carpet bagging white operated organizations, including Highways and High Performance Magazine. Imagine my surprise to discover that L.A.'s own Linda Frye Burnham, reigning co-arbitrator of multiculturalism is Los Angeles, had written an article on the very subject, citing examples of the horrible race based abuses taking place in the arts "community" by other white operated arts organizations like hers.

Beginning shortly after Tim Miller publicly accused L.A.C.E. of racism, which was soon followed by the opening of Highways Performance Space; and post High Performance Magazine's transformation from a magazine about Performance Art into a magazine about multicultural Performance Art, I have been agitated by the same problem which I believe Ms. Burnham was attempting to address in her editorial. Namely: Art Organizations run by white capitalists exploiting the popular issues of race and racism under the banner of "multiculturalism" to snag the big grant bucks while ignoring the merit of the work of artists as individuals and lumping together large, vaguely connected human subsets to sell magazines and festivals.

As a "gay" man, I am often offended when I read articles in which generalizations are made about how "gay" people "are". I also am annoyed by continuous references to "THE" gay community. When I flip through a gay rag or pick up a gay porn magazine, I am often reminded that not only do I not fit in to main stream society, I also don't cut it as a fag. Fags have over developed bodies from working out at the Sports Connection in pastel togs. Fags invest in real estate. Fags take lengthy cruises around the world in search of an endless series of meaningless flings. Fags picket the opening of movies they have never seen. Fags try to appear more heterosexual than heterosexual men do.

I find it very difficult to believe that I automatically have anything at all in common with, for example, the hollow and meaningless models who appear in most 976 advertisements, the men who take out personal advertisements in search of a "straight acting" companion, Jeffrey L. Dahmer, the President of NAMBLA, or Tim Miller, who was represented in a San Francisco paper as having said that he desires for others to think of him as "the all-American boy next door". What the fuck does that mean? I don't know. I don't want to know. Does he wish to be mistaken for a heterosexual adolescent? Good luck Tim. On both counts.

This idea that some harmonious monochromatic definable "gay community" exists, and that every homosexual is a member of it, is a fantasy and a lie. Also a lie is the idea, which has been marketed by Highways Performance Space and other organizations, (some of whom Ms. Burnham was chiding in her article) that each member of a given ethnic group is a member of the same "community" or "culture"; that an art event becomes "multicultural" when one or more of the performers participating is not "white"; and that there lurked before the advent of Highways some mysterious white supremacist force in the local performance venues and art galleries which prevented non-white performers and artists from creating any work.

It might be possible for me to swallow Highway's definition of "multiculturalism" (i.e. race = culture), if the events they produce which were billed as multicultural actually were. Often, however, when the Highways calendar says that an event is "multicultural", what it really means is that one or more of the usually american middle class artists involved is not "white". Even though they may come from basically the same economic background and grew up in the same cultural and spiritual void that most Americans do, it is repeatedly implied that non-white artists are somehow intrinsically different than their white counterparts, while at the same time identical to the other members of their own "community" to the degree that all of black culture can be represented by a single black artist, all of asian culture can be represented by a single asian artist, all members of the homosexual-megalomaniacal-latino-christian communities can be represented by Tim Miller, etc.

Is not each and every form of communication by every individual in some way an expression of the many cultural influences that make up their life experiences? Does there exist a person who is influenced only by a single culture?

Another indication to me that culture has come to be synonymous with race in this ongoing debate is that nowhere deep inside Ms. Burnham's article or any other which I have seen on the subject by Highway's own pet journalists and multicultural experts Jan Breslauer or Doug Sadownick are discussions of, for example, institutionalized racism against, for example, white immigrants from Greenland. Correct me if I'm wrong, but to the best of my knowledge, no local performance space (including Highways) has yet sponsored "White Immigrants from Greenland" Performance and Visual Art Festival. But Highways is that one "multicultural" performance space, and an event can only be billed as multicultural if there are non-white artists participating. After all, everyone knows that a white immigrant from Greenland shares the same exact culture as Jesse Helms, Anne Frank, Adolf Hitler and my Mother.

Even as I resent being grouped together with all other males whose sexual behavior is vaguely similar to my own, one might wonder if some of the "artists of color" resent being mashed into the same mold as other artists of their same(?) ethnicity. Well, yes, they do. The "artists of color" whom I have discussed this with have expressed to me that they share my concern over this misrepresentation of their identities.

Is Rika Ohara an artist? No. She is an "Asian" artist, a "Japanese Immigrant" artist, or a "Heterosexual Woman" Artist. I guess that would depend on the other artists in the given festival or exhibit. But she is definitely in the right place at the right time. The fact that she is not only Japanese, but actually from Japan, makes her such a good Performance, and Visual Artist in the eyes of producing organizations like Highways, especially if they are having a hard time snagging an asian to round out their asian programming, their multicultural panel, or their installation of asian visual art.

Too bad she's heterosexual. If she was a lesbian she would be an even more qualified and valuable artist. Having english as a second language, however, is something of a handicap. Sometimes it can be difficult for Highways predominantly white middle class audiences to understand her when she is performing (i.e. talking), and as Tim has shown us, despite whatever the history of the Performance Art form may have been, these days the effectiveness of a performance piece hinges solely on language that is presented in a conversational style into a microphone while sitting or standing perfectly still. So what if she moves beautifully and presents a beautiful montage of sensory experiences? In the new reign of Miller style performance, the only thing that counts is the artist's ability to present popular political propaganda in a conversational fashion. Nevertheless, it is obvious that Ms. Ohara's work should be promoted and funded sight-unseen around the world, as being Asian has until now prevented her from doing any work. Why should she even try? Before Highways, all of the spaces existed as fronts for White Supremacist organizations.

I am amazed at resident "multicultural" expert Burnham's ability to decry her way through the entire manifesto managing to maintain such distance from the problem, speaking of it as something that other people are guilty of. When I read paragraph 11, in which Burnham, co-progenetress of multiculturalism in Los Angeles, stated that "For many artists of color, multiculturalism has failed", I was reminded that; (1) multiculturalism has not failed for people of "no color"; (2) the issue of multiculturalism is not a concern for "white" artists, (3) when it comes to art, there is "multicultural" or "regular" (white), and (4) culture and race are the same thing.

I was also surprised, yet at the same time relieved to learn from reading her article that since I am white, it is so very easy for me to "decode the funding process". "Wait a minute", I thought, "I'm white, yet at the same time I, too am terrified of the funding process. Hey, I bet if I do a little genealogy, I will discover that one of my distant ancestors was a "person of color." I suppose that's possible. I feel just like Dinah Shore. That would explain my difficulty in "decoding the funding process". My god, what a terrifying and yet at the same time exhilarating realization. I thought I was merely white, but I could actually be a "person of color", and therefore more worthy of grants and gigs than I previously realized. I'm calling my Mother.

Burnham goes on to state in paragraph 14, "They are forced into ethnic festivals or series labeled with political titles that they had no hand in choosing." Am I wrong, or didn't Highways recently produce an "Asian/American" Performance Festival which lumped together artists of each and every various Asian decent? (Hmmm... I wonder... was Rachel Rosenthal contacted to participate? She is, after all, the daughter of Russian Jews, and part of Russia is geographically located in Asia.)

What about the recently presented "Black December"; a month long festival of black art by black artists? Was that not an "ethnic festival or series"? I suppose Ms. Burnham's memory is a bit blurry as a result of her sleepless dedication to help poor non-white artists who, without her help, could never paint or perform again. Anyway, it's a good title for a series. It works well in terms of implying an inherent cohesiveness to the work which will be presented. Well, they are all, after all, black, and, after all, what else could a black artist want to express other than their experience of being black?

Besides, how can all black people be lumped together for the purpose of discussion in a grant application if any one of them insists on being an individual?

But was it fair to present an entire month of black art? What if Highways' predominantly white, middle class audience had had a craving to see some asian art by asian artists during "Black December"? And a month is an awfully long time to go without access to latino art by latino artists, if that is what you get a hankerin' for. I am certain, however, that Ms. Burnham's statement does indicate that the title of the month-long "Black December" event was arrived at by the consensus of each and every black artist and black technician who participated. Hmmm, I wonder... was the all-white paid staff of Highways temporarily replaced with an all black one during "Black December"?

O.K., I have an idea. Lets pretend. We're going to conduct a little imaginary experiment here. Just to make things a little clearer in regard to Highways' definition of "culture", "community", etc. I just want to get this whole thing straight in my head so I can be a more valuable and useful artist to the 18th Street Arts Complex. Let's see... Imagine that a middle class couple adopts three infants of the same age. One is black, one is asian, and one is a white baby boy who will discover later in life that he is heterosexual. Let's also pretend, just for a moment, just for the sake of our little imaginary experiment, that the race of the parents in unimportant.

O.K., so, the three happy little children grow up in the same exact neighborhood, have the same exact friends, are taught the same exact values by their loving parents, and generally share many of the same experiences growing up together. If I'm getting this multicultural thing right, then despite the fact that they shared the same conditions and environment growing up and were taught the same values by their parents, it would be politically correct to assume that each of the children, should they become artists later in life, would create art expressive of three completely different cultures?

I believe it to be true that during their lifetimes, the black and asian artist would have much more of a personal understanding of what it feels like to be an outsider looking in at American "culture"; and to be discriminated against and treated hatefully by ignorant people, but would, for example, the art produced by the black artist be an expression of "the" black community, the work by the asian artist be expressive of "the" asian community, and the work of the white artist be a continuous attempt to stifle and make invisible the work of the other two? O.K. Tim and Linda, whatever. I don't know if that's true, but there is one thing I'm sure of. If they were working in Los Angeles, and presenting a lot of their work on the 18th Street Arts Complex grounds, High Performance Magazine would be much more likely to write extensive interviews and reviews on the work of the black and asian artists, using generalizing terms to describe their work, dismissing the possibility that it is an expression of individuality, and constructing theories to reinforce each as expressive of black and asian culture.

Now it's story time. I'm going to relate a little series of bedtime stories, which to the best of my knowledge and belief are true, in an effort to raise the possibility that though the lofty ideals which emanate from the mouths and pens of the co-founders of Highways and their friends in the press may be noble and sound good, a closer look at their actions may show that they are just words, and the bottom line is that what they are actually attempting to secure is not so much a better world for poor unfortunate people of color, but the same old stand-bys: fame, money and power... at whatever cost.

When Mr. A., (one of L.A.'s local "latino" artists), discovered he had been cast in a production to be staged at the Taper, Too entitled The Undead, Doug Sadownick (Mr. A.'s "friend") shared in Mr. A.'s enthusiasm at being cast, going on to energetically postulate that he had more than likely been chosen by the director to add color to the production, since "Latinos are so colorful". Sounds like a blatant racial stereotype to me, but hey, I'm not Highways resident multicultural journalist/Highways staff columnist/Tim Miller sex toy... he is. (I wonder, is Richard Ramirez equally as "colorful" as the "Frito Bandito" or Charo?)

When Mr. A. was about to open his one-man show at Highways, Jan Breslauer, Los Angeles' other multicultural expert/Highways staff "journalist" wrote the copy that appeared in the L.A. Weekly "Pick of the Week" spot to promote the performance. She praised his work on the grounds that it was obviously valuable as it could be easily compared to the verbally based work of some of Highways most frequently booked performers, going on to state that the piece also had merit as his performance work was a continuous attempt at expressing his experiences as a Latino-American. Curious why the short column did not reveal anything specific or characteristic of his work, Mr. A. investigated the history of the column, to discover that Breslauer had never seen him perform.

At the beginning of the video tape documentation of United States of Christ, a piece which I presented at Highways, I have footage of Highways' own Tim Miller doing his pre-show routine encouraging the audience members to return for some of the coming attractions. Selling "Men", a series of short pieces by local male artists, he said "We have Asian Men, Black Men, Gay Men, Latinos... all kinds!" When I heard this it gave me pause, as until then I had never realized that there were only four different kinds of men; the Asian kind; the Black kind; the Latino kind; and the Gay kind. I also realized that the Asian performer was a representation of all men of the Asian type, the black performer represented all black men, etc. In fact, if one attended the event, one could ostensibly walk away having had a comprehensive experience of each and every man who has ever lived on earth.

According to sources which do not wish to be identified, when Performance Czar Tim Miller discovered that the aforementioned production The Undead was being considered for presentation at LACE as part of the L.A. Festival, he wrote both to the space and to one (or more) of the producers of the festival, warning that his wrath would fall if it were considered further, explaining that it would offend the gay community, as it displayed gays in a negative light.

Perhaps Mr. Miller is psychic or clairvoyant, as he arrived at these opinions concerning The Undead without having seen it first. Perhaps Mr. Miller was upset that he had not been invited to participate. Perhaps he was upset because he is opposed to the works of the writer, Dennis Cooper, whose body of work contains, among other things, dead fag bodies.

Mr. Miller explained in the letters that he was afraid The Undead would be perceived as obscene by "the" gay "community." Hmmm. Sounds familiar, Mr. Miller. I have an idea. In an effort to prevent the production of any work which Mr. Miller may find obscene, perhaps there should be some kind of governmental agency assigned to determine which works of art should be prevented on the basis of such obscenity. Maybe Mr. Miller could form such an organization himself. After all, only Mr. Miller could possibly know what is obscene in the opinion of Mr. Miller. A few months ago I saw Mr. Miller on the Ron Reagan Show chiding Lou Sheldon for wishing to control the content of art works. That's odd. Perhaps Mr. Miller has more in common with Mr. Sheldon than he realizes. If they would only pool their resources, they could get so much more accomplished.

Ms. S, one of our community's "white heterosexual women" artists, was at one time working very closely as an assistant to the "white heterosexual male" artist who founded the Los Angeles Poverty Department, a Homeless Theater project. The last project she did with them was called Condo at Thieve's Corner, an outdoor installation/performance event which was produced as a part of a site-specific series produced by LACE. During the event, Ms. S. got into a confrontation with one of the performers (the MC) back-stage, explaining to him that he was staying on stage too long between acts, and that one of the functions of an MC is to keep things moving.

He responded by calling her a "bitch", physically attacking her, and throwing her against a wall. (Ms. S is a very tiny woman). Though the attack was witnessed by a number of the homeless performers <u>and</u> the white heterosexual male director, no one raised a finger to help her. Over the coming months, Ms. S. sought the services of a chiropractor and a psychiatrist to remedy the physical and emotional injuries she had sustained as a direct result of the attack. Ms. S. racked up doctor bills in excess of $10,000.00. Being poor and without insurance, she turned to the organization which produced the Los Angeles Poverty Department for assistance in paying the bills. The Organization totally sided with the individual who had attacked her without any investigation whatsoever, even though many people who had been present during the attack were willing to verify Ms. S.'s story.

Unable to arrive at any other logical solution to settle the debt which she had incurred, Ms. S. sought legal help to sue the organization for damages. Unbeknownst to Ms. S., and several months after her initial consultation, Ms. S.'s lawyer sent a letter/summons to the organization, alerting them to the fact that he intended to begin litigating that matter.

The Los Angeles Poverty Department received news of the lawyer's letter one week before they were scheduled to open Highways Performance Space's first season. The Los Angeles Poverty Department told Tim Miller and Linda Burnham about the impending legal action and threatened not to perform unless Ms. S. withdrew the suit. Convinced that Ms. S. had personally seen to it that this letter (of which she had no knowledge) would arrive specifically at this time in order to defame and ruin the gala opening of Highways, and again, without launching any kind of investigation, Highways, in the form of Tim Miller, attempted to coax Ms. S. to retract the suit.

During his conversation with Ms. S., Mr. Miller cited her rumored history of erratic behavior, informed her that immediately prior to the attack she had called her attacker a "nigger" (not true) and implied ("through what seemed like intimidation") that she had in fact gotten what she had coming to her. When coaxing didn't work, Mr. Miller resorted to ideology and propriety, reminding her that artists just don't do thing like that to each other (law suits, etc.) as all artists are part of the same community. Seeing that this train of thought was ineffective as well, he proceeded to threaten her, reminding her of the ominous powers he has at his finger tips. He used the term "Black Ball" to describe the process by which he would systematically defame her and prevent her from getting work.

When he realized that she would not be moved and did not agree that she should accept that what had been done to her was her rightful due, he contacted Ms. R., long time friend and Teacher/Mentor of Ms. S., and one of L.A.'s most respected Performance Artists, warning her that she must use her persuasive powers to control Ms. S. in such a way as to make her drop the law suit. He began with the same trail of threats and manipulation he had attempted to use on Ms. S., culminating in a reminder ("through what seemed like intimidation") that he and Ms. Burnham sat on many granting panels and would not hesitate to use these positions to see to it that Ms. R. and Ms. S. would receive no grant funds to produce their art within the future.

Ms. R., of course, did not comply with Mr. Miller's demands, and did not attempt in any way to control the actions of Ms. S. Unable to believe that she had been threatened in this way, and in an attempt to clarify their telephone conversation, Ms. R. wrote a letter to Mr. Miller detailing the terms and conditions of his threats as he had set them forth, and asking him to respond with verification of same. Mr. Miller did not respond to Ms. R.'s letter.

I hope that this letter can facilitate an adjustment in the stance of Highways Performance Space and High Performance Magazine, as I strongly believe that such a change is possible and very necessary. I have been on the scene here in Los Angeles for seven years and I have seen both the good and the damage that Highways has caused to this "community" since its opening. I can assure you, if the reason there weren't many "people of color" performing on the scene before Highways (you know, that one "multicultural" space) opened was evidence of some kind of institutionalized White Supremacist plot on the part of Weba Garretson, Scott Kellman, Joy Silverman and the other individuals who were programming the events at spaces like LACE, the Wallenboyd, the Lhasa Club, I will gladly eat this letter along with a portion of my own hand.

I have been afraid that my reaction to all of this would be interpreted as racist and so have not addressed these issues directly to Highways or High Performance Magazine until now. It's really a perfect set up. If you don't like something about Highways, the reason is either (a) Racism; (b) Homophobia; (c) Sexism; or (d) Political Conservatism.

I know that I speak for many artists in this "community", both "multicultural" artists and "white" artists too, who find this situation to be exploitative but have stood by and watched, afraid to speak out against what they see is wrong. And who could blame them? Mr. Miller is a very powerful fascist and will stop at nothing to get his way, as evidenced in the stories I have set forth in this letter.

Racism, classism, patriotic nationalism, sexism, religionism, poverty and lack of adequate education prevent people access to accomplishing what they wish to do. These and other barriers must be broken down for the benefit of everyone. However, special privileges and means of advancement must not be given to one group of people while being denied another, whatever the race of the individual groups which benefit. When provisions are made to advance the career of one individual on the basis of race or sexual preference, everyone suffers. Even those who appear to benefit.

Very truly,
Curtis York, Danish-English Mongrel (White Trash) Performance Artist

SIMULATION / STIMULATION

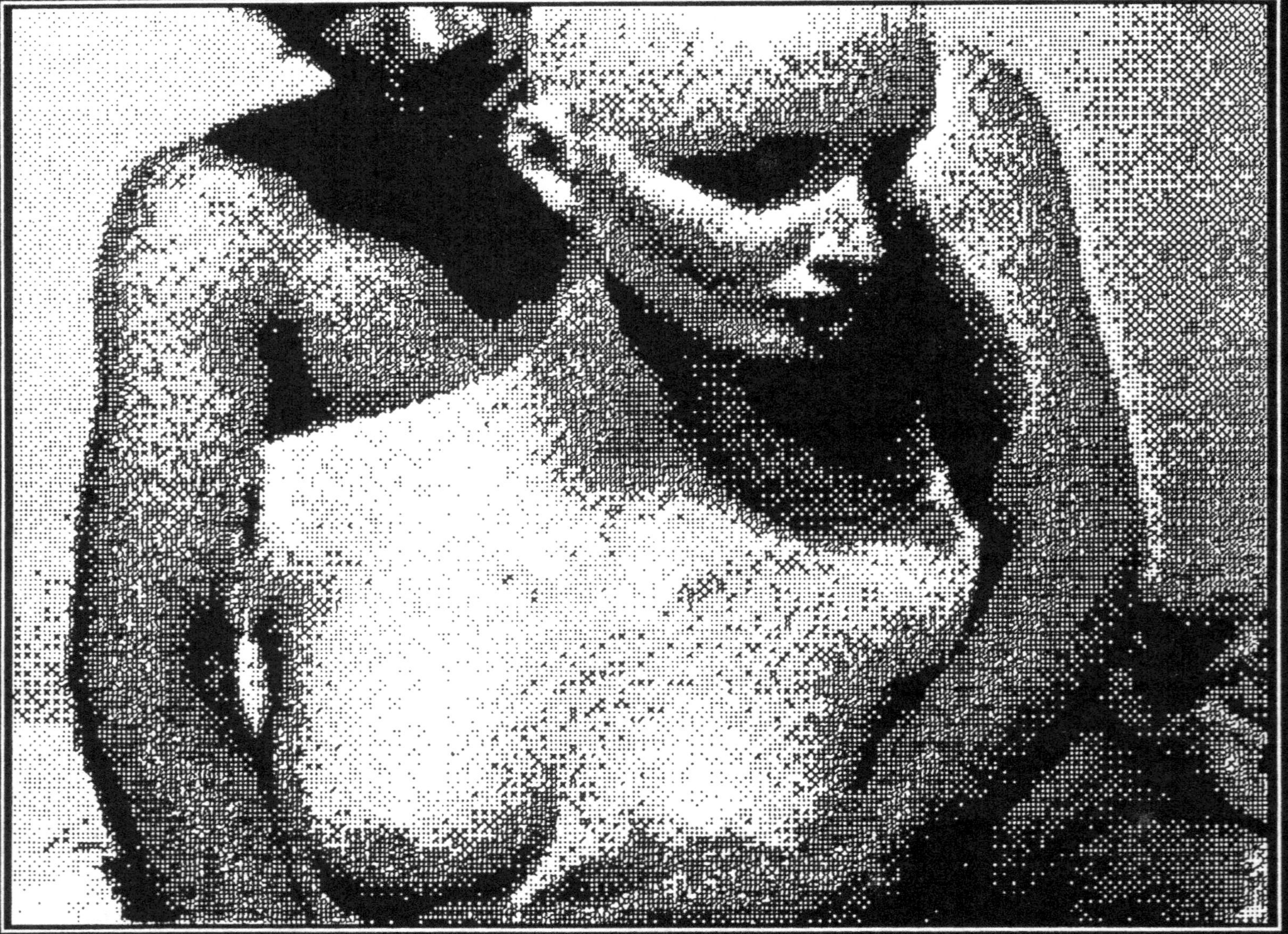

Peter Petrisko, Jr.

<u>medium</u>: digitized photograph

PUBLISHER'S INTRODUCTION TO CHEROTIC MAGIC

by

KYLE GRIFFITH

This introduction is being written over a year after Cherotic Magic first went into circulation. I realized I needed to write it while replying to a letter from a book store manager which said, "This is assuredly a singular book which is hard to categorize, very much tied to Frank Moore's personal tuition and not your usual do-it-yourself type of self-help occult manual." The writer wasn't making an outright refusal to stock the book in his store -- he wanted to see the rest of our S/R Press publications before deciding which ones, if any, to order -- but he seemed headed in that direction, and my natural inclination was to argue with him. I started drafting a letter to him which began:

"The main reason why Cherotic Magic is being published by Spiritual Revolution Press, which specializes in works too controversial or 'hard to categorize' for other Occult or New Age publishers is simply because it is so closely 'tied to Frank Moore's personal tuition.' It's very easy for publishers, and book-sellers to jump to the conclusion that the only potential readers for such a work would be people interested in studying directly with the author, but I don't agree. In my opinion, the text any genuine shaman uses to teach his complete magical system to his full-time apprentices should appeal to every reader seriously interested in the field, because it would give an entirely different viewpoint on the shamanic teaching process than most books on the subject now in circulation -- detailed descriptions of the apprenticeship are invariably written from the student's perspective. When shamanic teachers write books, they normally deal more with theory and generalities than with the essential practical details of their teachings.

"For example, I once asked Lame Deer why he didn't write a book containing the detailed information about the Ogalala shamanic system he taught to his apprentices, to supplement the more general religious, philosophical, and political material in his published work. He replied that he did have notes for such a text, in Lakota, but that he felt the teachings would lose most of their wakan if translated into English. Then he tied this in with requiring his apprentices to eat only buffalo meat, never beef, so they'd absorb wakan with their food. I couldn't think of any arguments against his point, but I still wished there was some way the public could have access to the full extent of his knowledge.

"Anyway, I feel that Cherotic Magic should be 'required reading' for anyone who is seriously studying shamanism. In my opinion, Frank Moore is as 'real' a shaman as any of the people described in the shamanic literature presently on your shelves -- and I don't even have to present arguments to support this claim, because Frank's international reputation as a 'shamanic performance artist' speaks for itself. Also, he's one of the only well-known shamans who thinks in English and works his magic within a cultural context familiar to the average American reader."

This is as far as I got before I realized I was wasting my time -- the book-seller would just reply, "You may be right that Cherotic Magic is an important primary-source document about shamanic teaching, but how many of the people who leaf through the book on my shelves are going to already be aware of what you pointed out in your letter? And how many will recognize Frank Moore's name? 'Performance art' is a small, specialized field, and you shouldn't assume the average reader of spiritual books is familiar with it." It became instantly obvious to me that I really should say all this in an introduction to the book itself, so that every potential reader could see it. I also realized that there are still other things I can say in an introduction that will increase both the book's reader-appeal and its effectiveness in communicating Frank's message, so I decided to go ahead and say them.

First, I now think it's important to tell the readers of Cherotic Magic, right up front, exactly who Frank Moore **is**. The text itself contains fragments of personal information about him, but nothing approaching a full description. I thought this was completely appropriate, viewing the book in isolation before it was published, but a year of writing and editing material to promote Cherotic Magic has forced me to change my mind. I now believe that the book itself should contain a summary of the information about Frank that's mentioned in most of the reviews and articles about him that we reprint to promote the book. I've already described Frank as "the only 100% bonafide shaman I've known personally who thinks in English and describes his magical system in images derived mainly from our Western culture," but there's a lot more to him than that -- he's also one of the best examples of "success against all the odds" I've ever met.

Frank Moore was born so severely disabled with cerebral palsy that he has to be fed and taken care of almost like an infant. He can't speak or control any of his muscles except a few in his head and neck. He converses with people by using a pointer attached to his head to pick out letters on a Ouija-board-like device (which he invented as a teen-ager) fastened to the arms of his wheelchair.

What has this "99% disabled" man done with his life? Well, he's earned **two** masters degrees in fine arts and become one of the best known performance artists in the country. He's been a guest lecturer at the drama departments of many different colleges and universities, including NYU, the Chicago Art Institute, and UC Berkeley. He's had numerous articles, poems, and essays published. His movie, Out of Isolation, and a number of shorter video pieces have appeared nationally on cable TV. And he even produces saleable oil paintings with a brush attached to his famous pointer!

If this was all there was to Frank Moore, he'd probably be a rich and famous "mainstream" artist, lauded by magazines like Readers Digest as a Horatio Alger-type example of "the crip who made good." In reality, during the late Sixties, Frank "dropped out," hitch-hiked from one coast to the other in his wheelchair, and joined a Hippie commune. Since then, he's always lived in group marriages and worked on the leading edge of the artistic avant garde. He's not only one of the best known contemporary performance artists, he's also one of the most controversial -- right up there on Jesse Helms' "hit list of obscene artists" along with Annie Sprinkle and Karen Finley. In my opinion, if I had to single out one aspect of Frank's activities as being more important to the universal humanistic goal of "building a more advanced civilization on this planet" than the rest, I'd be forced to pass over both his art and his magic in favor of his work as a "freedom fighter."

In the text of Cherotic Magic, Frank names such non-violent crusaders for personal freedom and human rights as Mohandas Gandhi and Martin Luther King, Jr. among the people who have inspired him the most, and it's obvious to me that he's doing his best to follow their example. He's easily the most radical and most courageous opponent of artistic censorship I know -- he doesn't just take on the political reactionaries, the religious bigots, and both the commercial and the academic wings of the "Art Establishment," he's even willing to criticize other "underground" artists whenever they lapse into censorship. And as he also says in Cherotic Magic, on the most basic level, his art, his shamanism, and his political activism are all parts of one whole.

Second, I also feel that this introduction needs to answer the charge that Frank's Cherotic Apprenticeship is reactionary, exploitative, and "cultish" because it requires students to relate to the teacher with complete trust and obedience, and asserts that people should value their relationships with others more than their individuality. A number of the reviews of Cherotic Magic published so far have made this charge by innuendo rather than directly, and a few people have mentioned it to me in so many words in private letters and conversations. I've also determined by experiment that randomly opening the book and browsing through it, as so many shoppers do in book stores, can create a similar impression. I know from personal experience that there's nothing even remotely "cultish" or exploitative about Frank's teaching methods, but I do feel it's necessary, at this point, to fully explain this matter.

In reality, Frank's methods **are** "authoritarian" in the sense that his apprentices are required to let him take complete control over their lives, twenty-four hours a day, for the whole time they study with him. If this sounds cultish to you, remember that all of us spend the first few years of our lives in such a relationship, trusting our parents to make all our decisions for us. Frank asks his students to enter such a relationship with him simply because he realizes that, in order to become shamanic magicians, they must make radical changes in their existing patterns of thinking and feeling -- patterns originally forced on them against their will by coercive families, schools, etc. In other words, Frank is not functioning as a cult leader, but as a **deprogrammer**. And he's doing it by creating a relationship with his students similar to the one of total love, trust, and obedience that young children have for their parents. However, unlike cult-deprogrammers and parents, Frank is operating with his apprentices' informed consent.

In order to enter the apprenticeship, students first have to take elementary-level courses with Frank that give them first-hand experience with his system, then they sign a written agreement that spells out exactly what they're getting into. Another detail which shows that the Cherotic Apprenticeship is the exact opposite of a cult is the fact that it's hard to get into and easy to get out of. Because Frank puts so much time and effort into working with each of his apprentices, he can only accept a few at a time, and turns down most of the people who apply. And not only are apprentices free to leave the program if they're dissatisfied with it, Frank also sends away anyone he feels is not making satisfactory progress.

And I've also been asked, "Is Frank's system really the best way to become a magician, or are better ways available?" I don't have a definite answer to that, but let's take a look at some of the alternatives. Many of the magical training systems that might be mentioned are much more authoritarian than Frank's Cherotic Apprenticeship, but are cleverly designed to hide their true nature. This is especially true of systems based on any kind of organized religion -- Eastern, Western, or Third World. Any system that requires trust in deities or obedience to "divinely revealed" doctrine is also authoritarian -- but there's no way the authority-figures can be held personally accountable for their actions. The priests, preachers, gurus, etc. can all "pass the buck Upstairs." Frank, on the other hand, takes full personal responsibility for everything he does.

Other systems are, in my opinion, non-totalitarian and non-coercive, but also extremely inefficient at actually teaching students what they want to learn. I've observed large numbers of people using various "New Age" systems ever since the movement started about twenty years ago, and about the only skills most of them seem to learn are "how to turn wishful thinking into full-fledged self-delusion" and "how to convince suckers you're a great and powerful magician." I remain convinced that "no pain, no gain" is one of the laws of nature, and that Frank is completely reasonable in insisting that all successful magical training involves risk, hard work, and self-discipline. It also appears self-evident to me that the only way to benefit from having a "teacher of magic" is through complete trust and obedience.

The only other alternative is to become a magician entirely on one's own, without a teacher or a formal training system. This is the path that Frank followed himself, and he says that one of the main reasons he's now a teacher of magic is to help students avoid his mistakes and all the frustration, pain, and danger they cost him. Again, the logic of this is self-evident.

Does this mean that I'm encouraging every student of magic who reads this book to enter Frank's apprenticeship or that I believe other magicians and shamans should teach their systems using the methods described in Cherotic Magic? Not at all. In my opinion, his teaching methods could be successfully imitated only by another magician who was almost identical to him -- physically as well as in personality, and I also feel that only a tiny percentage of the students now studying shamanic magic are temperamentally suited to getting maximum benefit out of Frank's system -- only those who are willing to dedicate themselves to Frank's performance-art activities and who identify totally with his lifestyle and opinions.

Why, then, do I feel that every student and teacher of shamanic magic should read this book? Simply because it gives the reader an extremely detailed description of how a shamanic teacher leads his students through the process of "reality creation" -- how he assists them in deprogramming the personality structures that have been forced on them by all aspects of their environment (physical, intellectual, emotional, and psychic), and in reprogramming themselves with the structures described in Cherotic Magic. I don't expect that many readers will want to create Frank's exact "reality" for themselves, or that they'll be able to use the same methods he employs, but I do believe that quite a few of them will be able to absorb some of the "non-verbal, non-linear essence" of his system and incorporate it into their own shamanic practices, whether as students or as teachers. And I also feel that reading the book will encourage some people to attend Frank's audience-participation performances or do some kind of in-person study with him -- which give them an even better opportunity to absorb some of his ability to "create reality."

Kyle Griffith
May 9, 1992

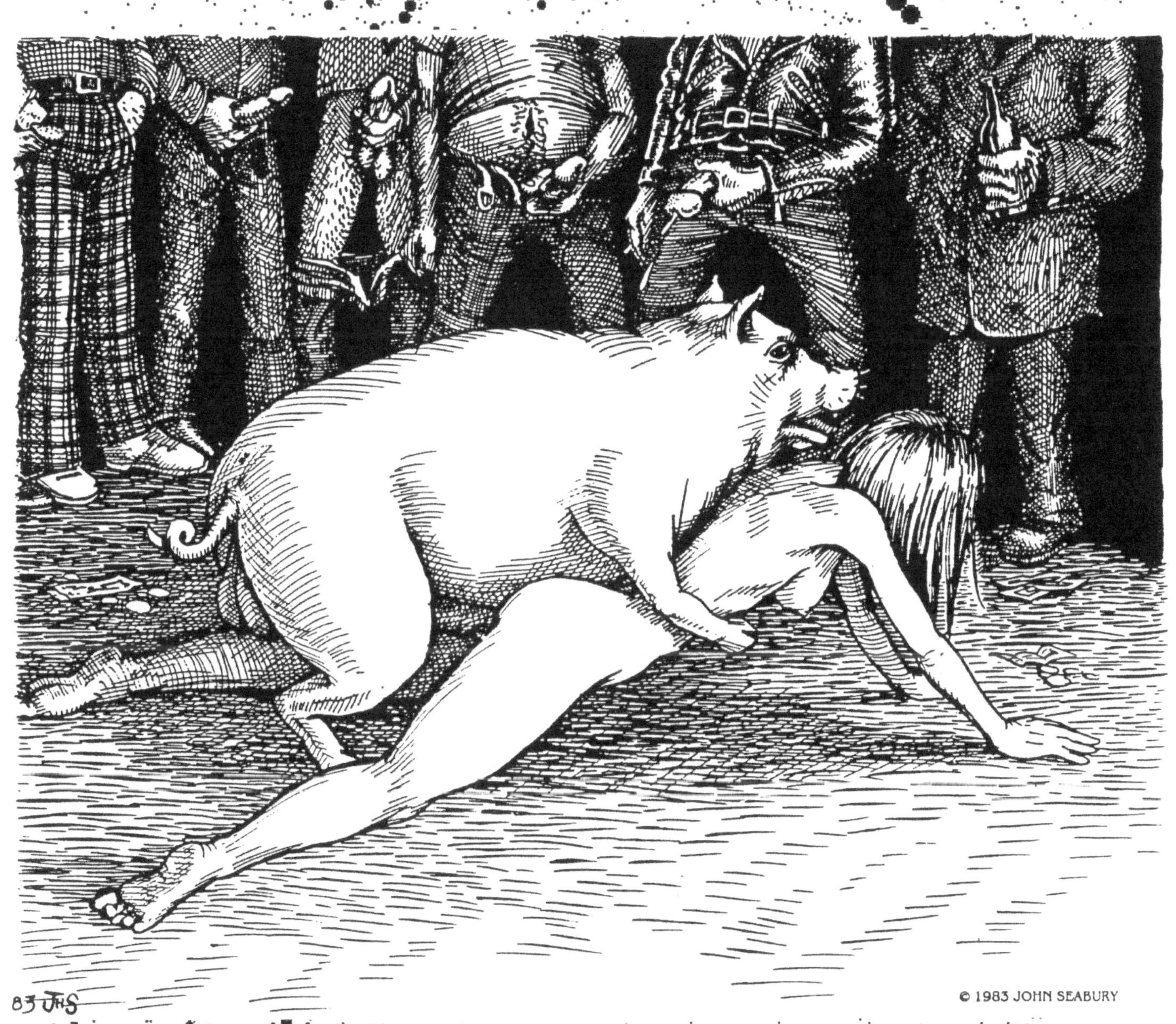
© 1983 JOHN SEABURY

REVIEW OF FRANK MOORE'S "PASSIONS PLAY" PERFORMANCE by STAVROS KRYSIAK

I, STAVROS experienced a unique event, in which I was shamanized by Frank Moore at an event billed as the "Passions Play." I met Frank on GEnie, where I learned that Frank Moore had been investigated by Jesse Helms. I was intrigued with Frank's posts about his Shamanistic Art, and when the opportunity came for me to attend his Passions Play, I couldn't resist. I had to go to find out what a Shaman was and what he did.

On Saturday March 7, I drove to Oakland, to an artist studio located on the waterfront near Jack London Square. I knew at once that I was at the right place when I saw a woman standing in front of a building with a blanket. Frank had instructed us to bring a blanket.

I entered the studio where I could hear a man singing. It was a chant and his voice would move from high tones down to low ones, as he periodically slapped his body to the mantra he was singing. He was naked. His body was covered only with body paint, as were two other painted men, who walked around those of us sitting on the floor. They moved ever so gracefully and ever so slowly.

After about a half hour or more, one of the men came up to people sitting on the floor and ask them if they wished to be prepared to see the shaman, who was in his cave. The cave was behind the curtain in the front of the room. At this point, one couple decided this wasn't for them and they left the room, never to experience the visit to the shaman.

Those that elected to go were taken in pairs. They were first blindfolded. Before they were led to the front of the room, where the entrance to the cave was situated, they were kissed on both cheeks.

We could hear weird sounds coming from the shaman in the cave. A very beautiful naked woman, who was also decorated with body paint came out of the cave. She walked up to the blindfolded participant and gave instructions. They were given a cup containing a magical formula, which tasted mysteriously like water. This, they were told, would release their inhibitions. Then they were taken to the cave.

Some would come back sooner than others. Some came back naked, others fully dressed. One young man hadn't come out yet, when it was my turn. He was one of the first to go in. After drinking the magic formula I was lead into the cave. My instructions were not to speak in words and only in sounds.

When I left the cave I was instructed to go back to my nest and not to reveal what had happened in there. And I will not break that word even for this review.

After I came out, I was asked by an elderly gentleman if it was a positive experience. I gave him a thumbs up. Later, when he came out he gave me the thumbs up sign.

After all had entered the cave and returned to their nests, we prepared to see the shaman. Until this moment I had touched Frank Moore and had written to him on GEnie but I had never seen him.

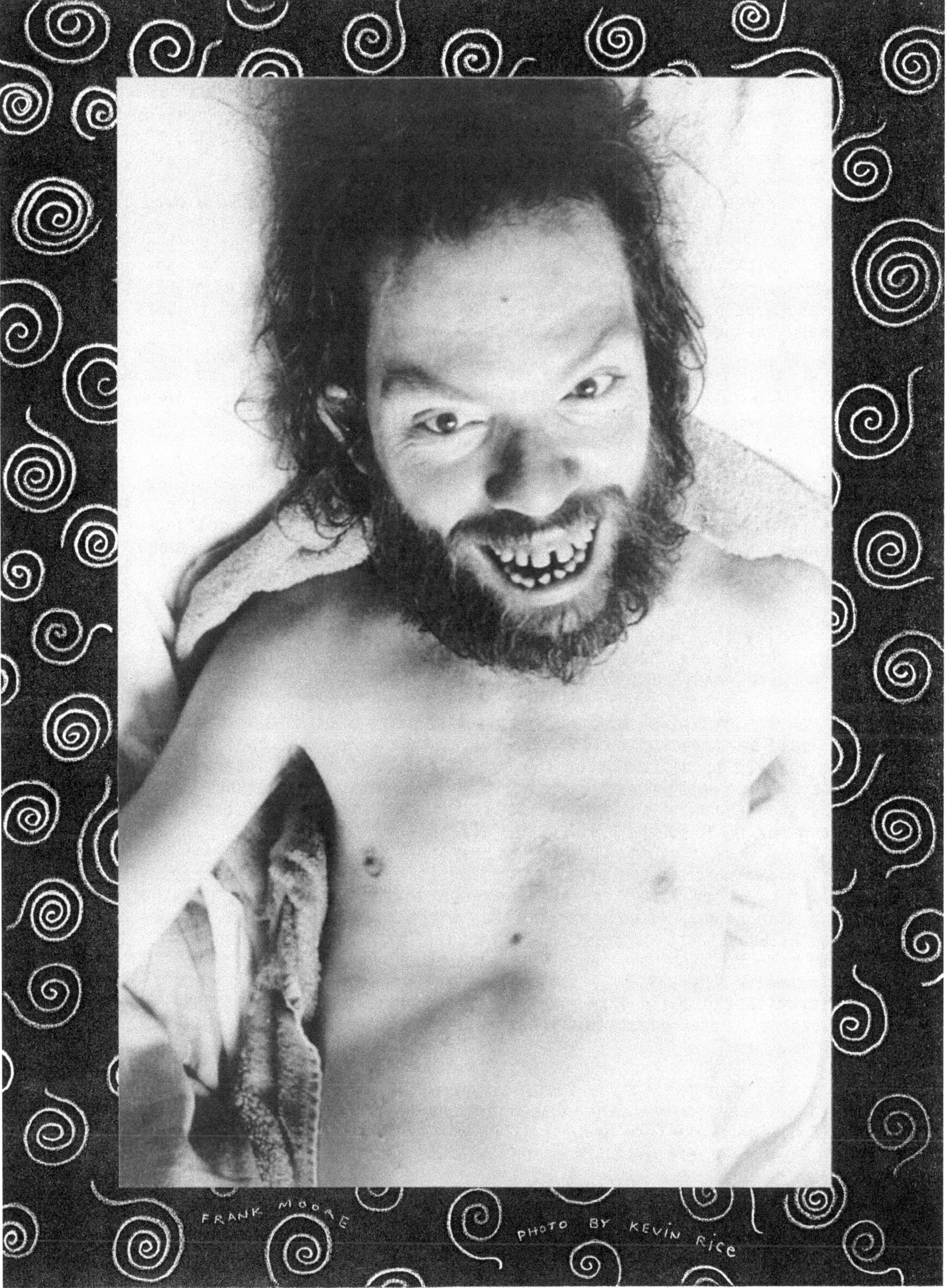
FRANK MOORE
PHOTO BY KEVIN RICE

The Shaman enters and he is placed naked in a wheelchair. Before my very eyes is that great intellect I have come to respect on the GEnie Bulletin Boards.

Then to the tune of music, he made the most God awful animal sounds and grunts. There was a happy smile on his face. I had read other reviews of his work, where they refer to Frank's grotesque body, but I couldn't see the grotesqueness. I saw a very happy person.

Frank was later strapped into the wheelchair. They placed a head band on his head, which had a pointer attached to it. In front of him there was a word board. Frank, who was born with Cerebral Palsy, couldn't control the muscles of 90% of his body. He cannot speak and using the only muscles he can control, his neck muscles, he communicated to us much like he communicates on GEnie, only using the word board instead of a key board. It's his survival in this state, as a happy being, that gives him the power to be a shaman.

We then followed his instructions and prepared to die, so we could be reborn. As I laid on the floor, death visited me and took off my clothes. I was prepared to be reborn. About 40 naked bodies huddled together in the center of the room. It was a cool evening and the body warmth of skin against skin brought warmth to each of us in our bodies and in our hearts. A group of adult men and women were playfully pretending that they were these creatures of evolution. Bodies were rubbing against bodies. Not since I was a naked babe, have I remembered my sense of touch being so fulfilled. My cup of the delight of touch had runneth over. We were single cell beings, multiple cells, seaweed, ants, birds, and other creatures until we evolved to that human form of a child, who was ready for eroplay.

Eroplay is a word coined by Frank Moore. It is a non-sexual but erotic playing. Unlike sex there is no climax. Magically, we were brought to the place where we were ready to be taught eroplay.

We were broken up randomly, mostly into pairs, but some in threesomes. The pairs would be a man and a woman, two men, or two women. At random times we were randomly moved to different partners. We received random instructions to rub your belly, or rub your partner's belly. Rub cheeks. Rub butts. Lay on top of your partner touching their whole body with your whole body. Embrace and rock back and forth. Touch genitals.

Then we watched the great shaman perform the most erotic eroplay with a woman. In all my life I never have seen anything as erotic, as that woman playing with Frank. We were mesmerized, as he played with her. Strobe lights flashed as assistants came out and covered us with Saran Wrap and foil. It was a sight to behold, as we engaged in spontaneous eroplay under a blanket of wrap, which connected us all. By the end of the evening I found myself filled to capacity with the child-like eroplay. It transformed me to another world. I broke taboos I never dreamed of breaking. It felt good. It was a safe place for all of us.

I said good-bye to the shaman at about 3 AM. As I was ready to leave I stopped to watch three men engaged in eroplay. It was beautiful. I felt beautiful, the shaman was beautiful. I exited the magical cave and entered the world of taboos, left with the memory of a magical experience that will be with me forever.

Thus Stavros was shamanized.

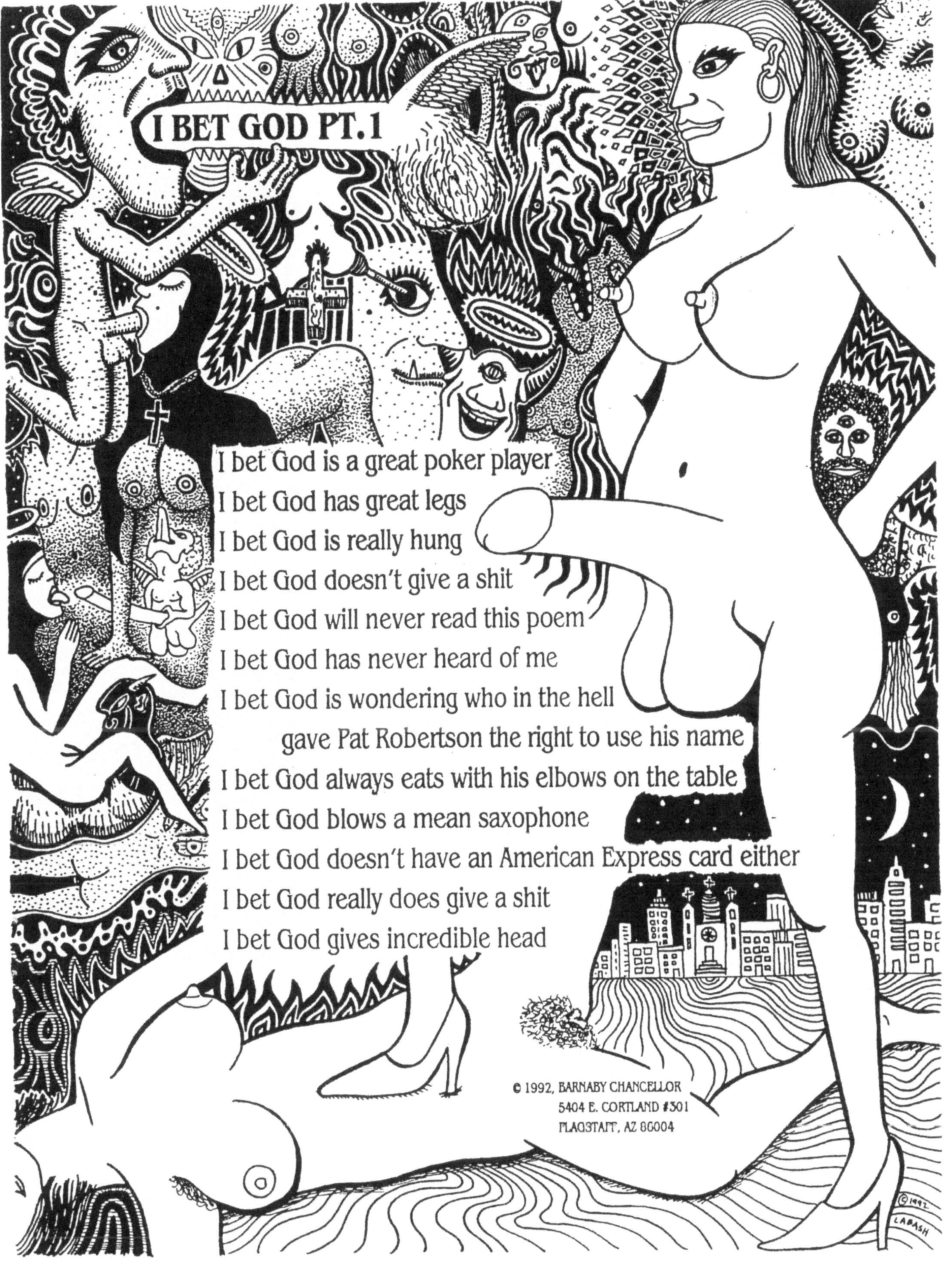
I BET GOD PT. 1
I bet God is a great poker player
I bet God has great legs
I bet God is really hung
I bet God doesn't give a shit
I bet God will never read this poem
I bet God has never heard of me
I bet God is wondering who in the hell
gave Pat Robertson the right to use his name
I bet God always eats with his elbows on the table
I bet God blows a mean saxophone
I bet God doesn't have an American Express card either
I bet God really does give a shit
I bet God gives incredible head
© 1992, BARNABY CHANCELLOR
5404 E. CORTLAND #301
FLAGSTAFF, AZ 86004
© 1992
LABASH

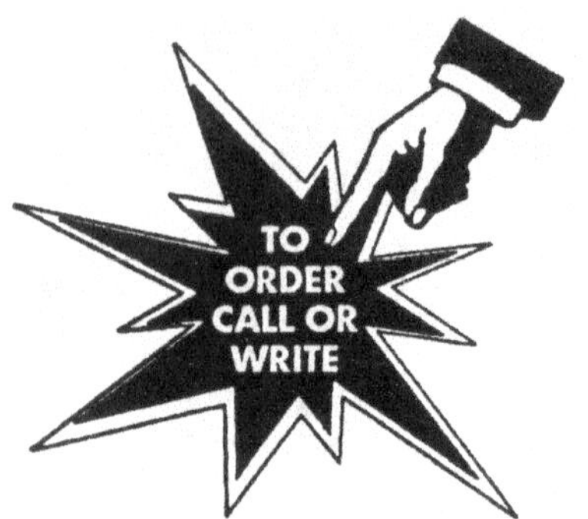

inter-relations
p.o.box 11445
berkeley, ca 94701-2445
(510) 526 7858

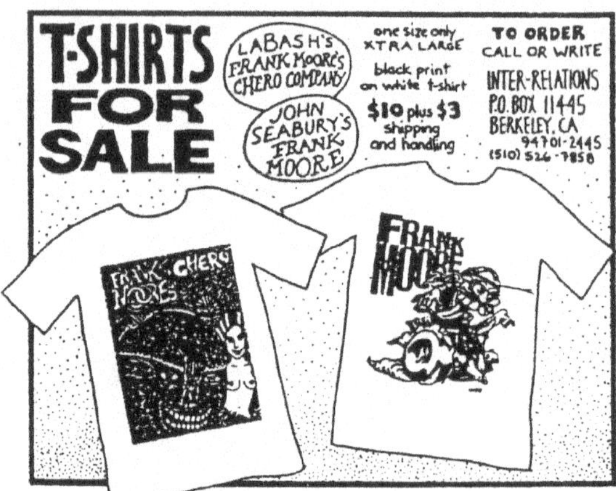

BOOKS/ZINES by Frank Moore

art of living
A GUIDE TO DOWN-TO-EARTH SPIRITUALITY AS CHANNELLED BY FRANK MOORE.
published 1987 **$10**

art of a shaman
IN art of a shaman, ORIGINALLY A LECTURE PRESENTED AT N.Y.U., FRANK MOORE EXPLORES PERFORMANCE AND ART IN GENERAL TERMS OF THEM BEING A MAGICAL WAY TO EFFECT CHANGE IN THE WORLD. HE LOOKS AT PERFORMANCE AS AN ART OF MELTING ACTION, RITUALISTIC, SHAMANISTIC DOINGS/PLAYINGS. BY USING HIS CAREER AND LIFE AS A "BASELINE", MOORE EXPLAINS THE DYNAMIC PLAYING WITHIN THE CONTEXT OF REALITY SHAPING. HE BRINGS IN CONCEPTS FROM MODERN PHYSICS, MYTHOLOGY, AND PSYCHOLOGY. COVER BY LABASH.
published 1991 **$4**

cherotic magic
A MAJOR ATTEMPT TO INTRODUCE A POWERFUL SYSTEM OF MAGIC INTO OUR MODERN WESTERN EVERYDAY LIFE, THEREBY EXPLOSIVELY EXPANDING SUCH CONCEPTS AS SEX, HUMAN RELATIONSHIPS. THE CLEAR, DOWN-TO-EARTH TEXT IS AMPLIFIED BY THE NON-LINEAR TRANCE ILLUSTRATIONS BY LABASH.
published 1990 **$15**

the cherotic revolutionary
A MAGAZINE ABOUT THE EDGE. issue #0 **$3**
issue #1 **$5**
issue #2 **$5**

cultural subversion
PERSONAL, ANARCHICAL TECHNOLOGIES SUCH AS XEROGRAPHY, VCR, FAXS, ETC., ARE EXAMINED IN cultural subversion BY FRANK MOORE AS THE MEANS BY WHICH ORDINARY PEOPLE CAN TAKE BACK THE CONTROL OF COMMUNICATIONS AND CREATIVITY FROM THE CENTRAL POWER COMBINE. published 1992 **$1**

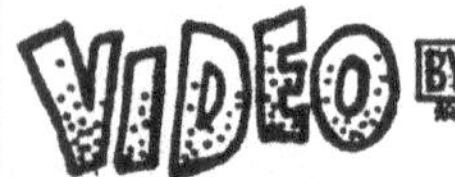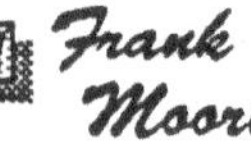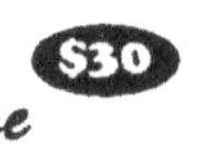

VIDEO BY Frank Moore $30

fairy tales can come true
THIS IS A FILM ABOUT RELATIONSHIPS AND DISABILITY STARRING FRANK MOORE, WHO HAS BEEN DISABLED SINCE BIRTH WITH CEREBRAL PALSY. IT IS A HUMOROUS, YET REALISTIC LOOK AT HOW TO ESTABLISH RELATIONSHIPS BY CHANGING NEGATIVE SELF IMAGE.
copyrighted 1981 *35 minutes*

erotic play
THIS VIDEO EXPLORES WHAT HAPPENS WHEN PEOPLE OF ALL TYPES AND AGES ARE GIVEN A CHANCE TO RETURN TO BEING A KID AGAIN. A SIMPLE GAME OF DRESS-UP BECOMES A POWERFUL METAPHOR FOR DROPPING TABOOS, RELEASING CREATIVE EMOTION, AND FOR DRAMATIC CHANGE. AS A RESULT, AN INNOCENT EROTICISM IS FOUND... AS WELL AS GETTING INTIMATE WITH 60 HUMANS.
copyrighted 1983 *84 minutes*

outrageous dream
A SURREAL, VISUAL POEM OF FOUND IMAGES.
copyrighted 1984 *41 minutes*

the nude cave
AN EROTIC, SURREALISTIC VIDEO DREAM THAT COMBINES NON-LINEAR IMAGES AND FRANK'S ORIGINAL MUSIC SCORE.
copyrighted 1984 *113 minutes*

the outrageous beauty revue
THIS RAW VIDEO DOCUMENTS THE TACKY, MUSICAL, OVER-THE-EDGE COMEDY REVUE THAT FRANK CREATED, DIRECTED AND PERFORMED IN. THE SHOW RAN ON A WEEKLY BASIS FOR THREE AND ONE HALF YEARS AT THE MABUHAY GARDENS IN SAN FRANCISCO IN ADDITION TO A NUMBER OF OTHER NORTHERN CALIFORNIA AND NEVADA PERFORMANCES. FRANK PERFORMED ALONG WITH THE THIRTY PEOPLE WHO MADE UP HIS THEATRE GROUP, "the theatre of human melting."
copyrighted 1980 *approx. 30 minutes*

out of isolation
A SURREAL EROTIC EXAMINATION OF AN INTIMATE RELATIONSHIP OF NEED. STARRING FRANK MOORE AND LINDA SIBEO.
copyrighted 1989 *105 minutes*

chero collage
ATTEMPTS TO CAPTURE THE TRANCE STATE OF LIVE, SHAMANISTIC PERFORMANCE COMBINING FOOTAGE OF SEVERAL OF chero company's RITUALS INTO A REALITY-WARPING VIDEO.
copyrighted 1992 *27 minutes*

the outrageous horror show
A LIVE CABARET SHOW THAT BREAKS THROUGH THE LIMITING TABOOS, THROUGH MESSY NIGHTMARES, INTO THE DREAMS OF ALL POSSIBILITIES.
copyrighted 1992 *32 minutes*

audio tapes by Frank Moore's Chero Company $5

body music
EXPLORING THE HUMAN BODY AS MUSICAL INSTRUMENT.
copyrighted 1989 *90 minutes*

inter-rhythms
PRIMAL MUSIC CREATED FOR FRANK MOORE'S RITUAL PERFORMANCES.
copyrighted 1989 *90 minutes*

rock of passion
THE SOUNDTRACK OF the outrageous horror show, FRANK THE ROCKSTAR SINGS HIS HEART OUT, LITERALLY COVERING THE GREAT HITS OF ROCK, COUNTRY, AND HEAVY METAL ... INCLUDING SUCH SMASHES AS i am woman, i got you babe, AND hand of doom ...

trance rap
WRITTEN BY FRANK MOORE AND SUNG/CHANTED BY MICHAEL LABASH WITH A BACKGROUND OF BODY MUSIC, trance rap IS AN AUDIO INTRODUCTION TO CHEROTIC MAGIC COVERING SUCH SUBJECTS AS eroplay, the plot of fragmentation AND magic art. ALSO INCLUDED IS THE POEM wrapping/rocking.
30 minutes

ALSO FROM S/R PRESS

war in heaven by Kyle Griffith $18

the spiritual revolutionary vol. 1
Bound Volume issues 0-9 .... $20

the spiritual revolutionary
Individual issues $3
Sample issue $1

TO ORDER: Call or write S/R Press
P.O. Box 60327, Palo Alto, CA 94306-0327

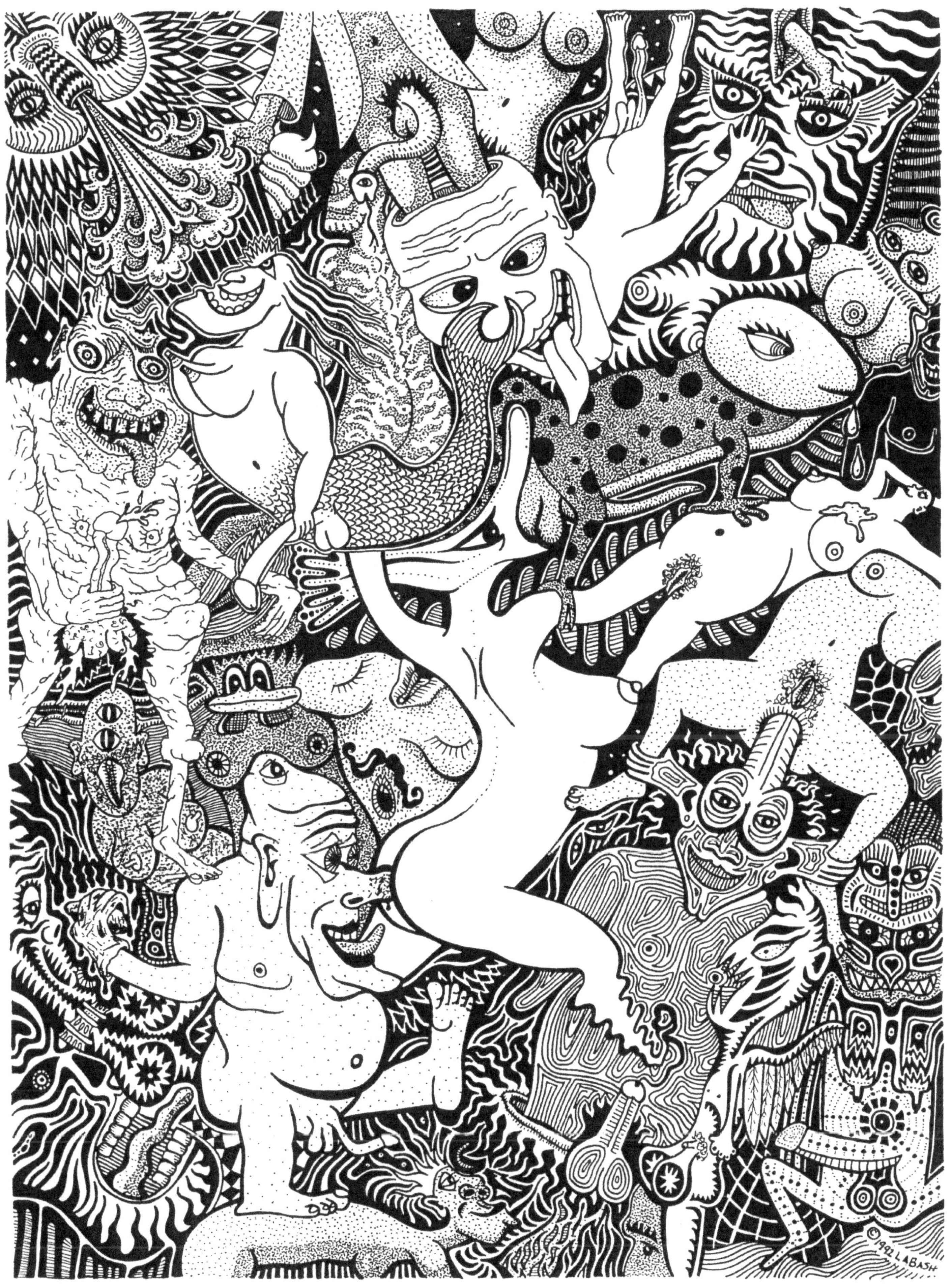
©1992 LABASH

REVIEWS

The Cherotic Rvolutionary #2
July 1992

(TC(r)#2) "is fuckin' great! A little weird, but fuckin' great! I love the art work. It lends a whole new meaning to the word psychedelic. I enjoyed the surrealism also. Being somewhat of an artist & musician I enjoy it all provided it is done well. Or beauty is in the eye or ear of the beholder. I guess."
Uncle Junky, editor of Yello Submarine 'Zine

"'The Cherotic Revolutionary'...is right out there on the artistic edge, (Frank Moore is) reveling in the use of eros to make his points about freedom."
Factsheet Five

"I personally cannot live up to the society-cracking dares that Moore issues (in 'The Cherotic Revolutionary')... Seriously, one of the more thought-provoking items..."
Ivan Stang, (SubGenius Magazine) Stark Fist

"TCR is a beautiful tragedy. A symbolism of creativity."
Merle Tofer, artist

"The new TCR is remarkable. It keeps getting more outrageous, more independent, more tender. A magazine of such sensual splendor should be considered by the American government as a national treasure!!"
Merle Tofer, artist

"I anxiously await (the next issue of) TC(r) as it is one of my most favorite publications. Reading TC(r) is analogous to having a mystical experience."
Spiros, Open Forum (Greece)

The Cherotic (r)Evolutionary "A zine about 'The Edge' for and by people on The Edge ... if not over The Edge." Published and edited by Frank Moore and Linda Mac. Frank is a shamanistic teacher, author, and performer whose zine reflects the Berkeley I remember - sexual, artistic, bold, yet soft, loving, and at times, crippled (what is the PC word?) - less than perfect (like the rest of us). Articles, poems, photos, commentary, posters.
The Whole Sex Catalog Supplement, 1995, Synergy Book Service

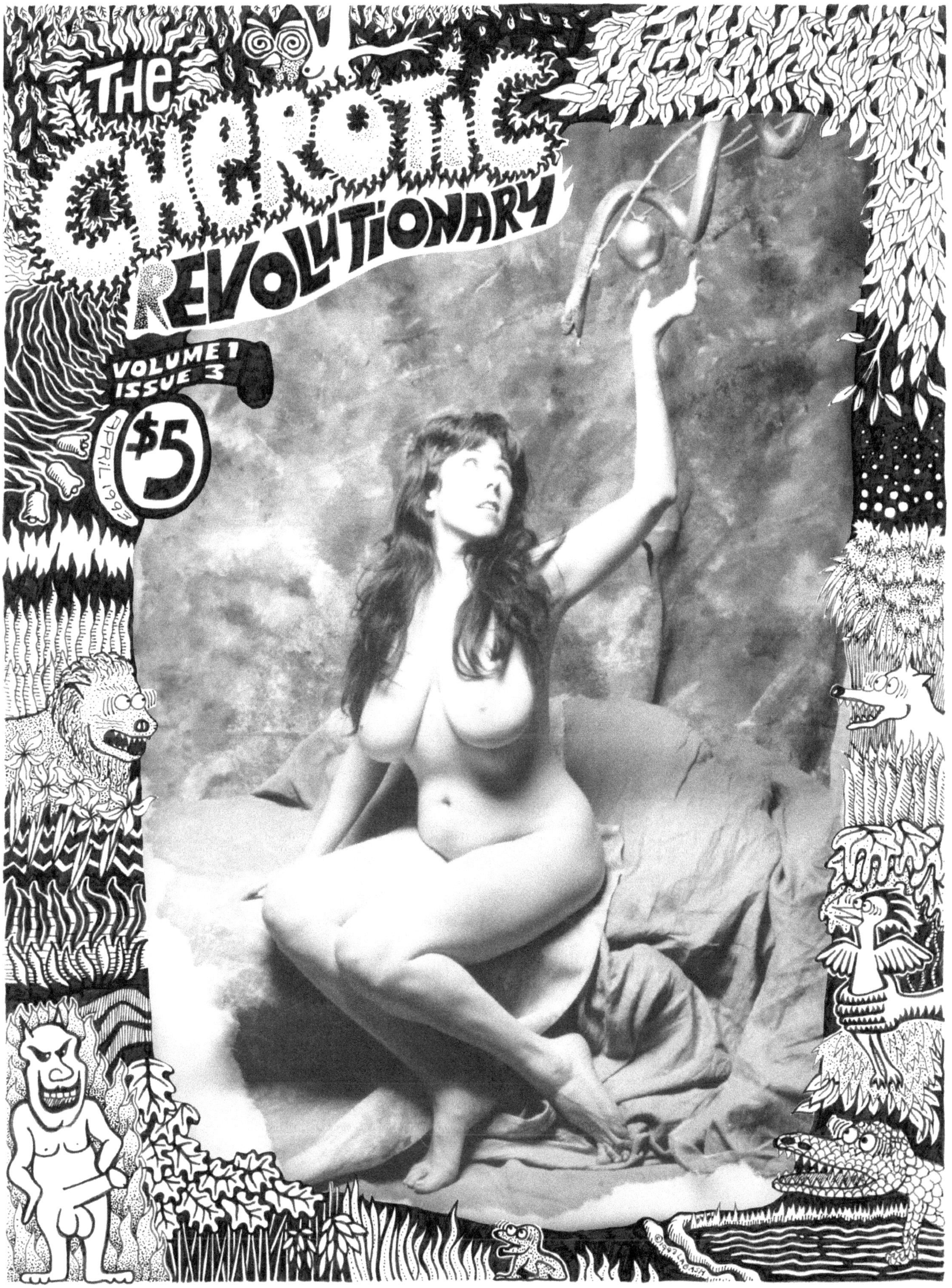
THE
CHAOTIC
REVOLUTIONARY
VOLUME 1
ISSUE 3
$5
APRIL 1993

the Cherotic rEVOLUTIONARY

NUMBER 3

The Cherotic rEvolutionary is a zine about "The Edge" for and by people on The Edge...if not over The Edge.

TCR is published by Inter-Relations. The publishers/editors are Frank Moore and Linda Mac. The art editor is Michael LaBash, and the circulation manager is Alexi Malenky.

The price for this issue is $5.00 per copy. We don't sell subscriptions, to avoid tying ourselves down to a rigid publication schedule or magazine size. We want to remain free to publish frequently or larger issues at longer intervals and adjust the price accordingly.

We heartily encourage letters of comment from readers and will answer as many as we can. Please tell us if you don't want us to print material from your letter – otherwise we will assume it's OK.

Please address all correspondence and orders for magazines to:

Frank Moore, POBox 11445, Berkeley, CA 94701-2445

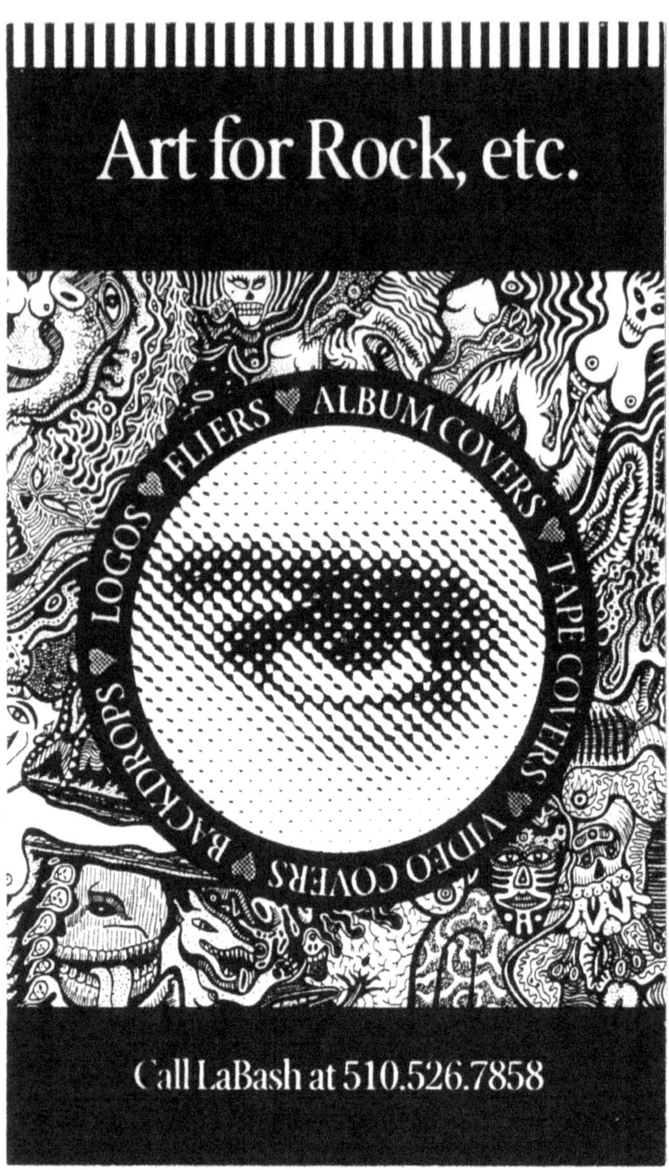

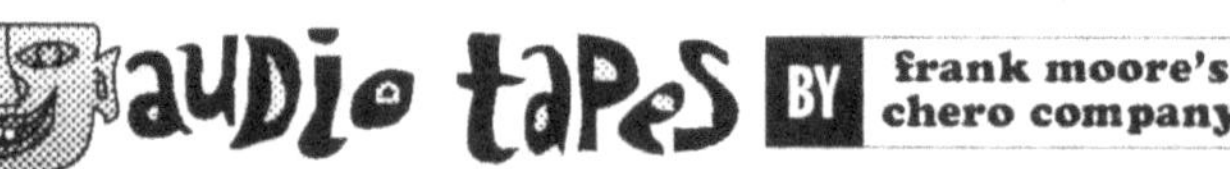

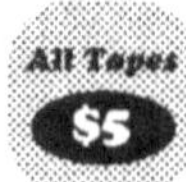

body music
EXPLORING THE HUMAN BODY AS MUSICAL INSTRUMENT.
90 minutes

inter-rhythms
PRIMAL MUSIC CREATED FOR FRANK MOORE'S RITUAL PERFORMANCES.
90 minutes

nude cave soundtrack
THE NONLINEAR ELECTRONIC MUSIC COMPOSED AND PERFORMED BY FRANK MOORE FOR THE FEATURE LENGTH VIDEO. *110 minutes*

rock of passion
THE SOUNDTRACK OF the outrageous horror show, FRANK THE ROCKSTAR SINGS HIS HEART OUT, LITERALLY COVERING THE GREAT HITS OF ROCK, COUNTRY, AND HEAVY METAL ... INCLUDING SUCH SMASHES AS i am woman, i got you babe, AND hand of doom ...

trance rap
WRITTEN BY FRANK MOORE AND SUNG/CHANTED BY MICHAEL LABASH WITH A BACKGROUND OF BODY MUSIC, trance rap IS AN AUDIO INTRODUCTION TO CHEROTIC MAGIC COVERING SUCH SUBJECTS AS eroplay, the plot of fragmentation AND magic art. ALSO INCLUDED IS THE POEM wrapping/rocking.
30 minutes

to order call or write: **inter-relations, p.o. box 11445, berkeley, CA 94701-2445 telephone (510)526-7858**

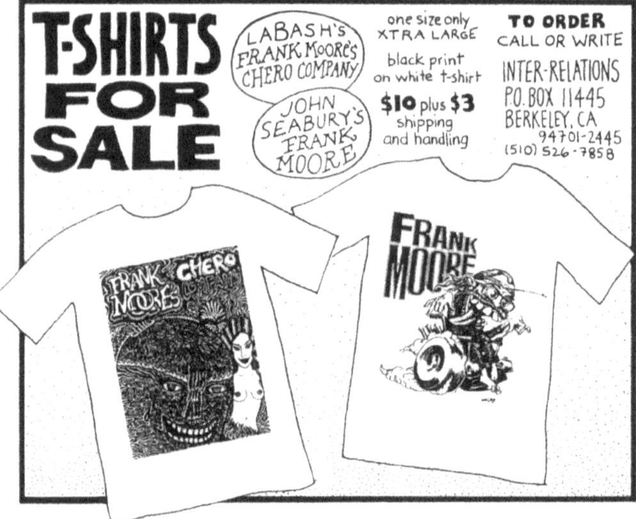

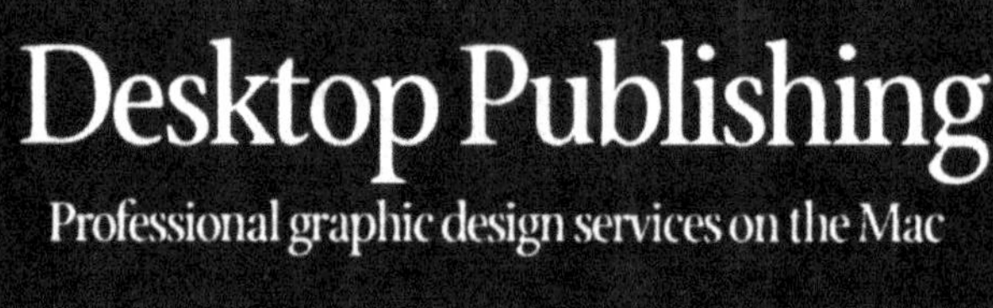

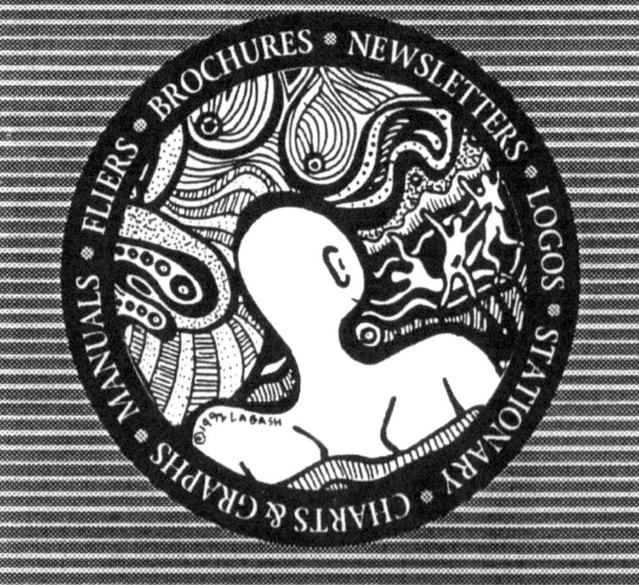

Call Michael at 510.526.7858

There are changes around here. Well, what do you expect from a zine with "revolution" as its last name? And that may be one of the changes ... our name appears to be in the process of changing itself from The Cherotic Revolutionary to The Cherotic Evolutionary. A revolution is a mutation from the normal as-is reality, an experiment and an adventure into newness. The purpose of a revolution, and any mutation, is to break new ground for evolution ... to prod evolution along. Revolution, if it is to be successful, must be a tool, not an end. But we will have to wait until the next issue to see if our name really does change. ❤ Another important change is we have created Inter-Relations to take over the publishing chores of both TCR and my book Cherotic Magic from S/R Press. I owe a lot to Kyle Griffith of S/R Press. He was the one who pushed for the publishing of the book ... and then strongly suggested we come out with a zine. ❤ So this is the first Inter-Relations publication. (Very soon, we will be coming out with a revised edition of Cherotic Magic.) So now being both the editors and the publishers, Linda and I along with LaBash are totally to blame (or to praise) for this. By the way, we don't accept blame through the mail! ❤ Magically we got our hands on a Mac computer and a laser printer...which explains the embarrassing good quality of this. It does not mean my rich aunt died ... or that i sold out. In fact, we had to break the material we have into half. What you have in your hand is just the first half. The next issue will be the second half. ❤ In the past issues, I walked you around to meet everyone in the issues. But there are just too many artists in this one to do that. You know Mapplethorpe and Annie Sprinkle and Veronica Vera as sexual artists. If you're in the know in the art world, you probably know Linda Carmella Sibio as the Los Angeles performance artist who does things like a musical on suicide. If you are into poetry, you probably know Merl Tofer as a neo-beat ... who is trying to take the crown of the king of name-droppers away from me. (check out his new poetry book Sensitized to Pain with LaBash's illustrations.) If you read TCR before, you know the work of Dorothy Jesse Beagle, Lee Kay, and Luna. And we all should have known Dixie Cohn. ❤

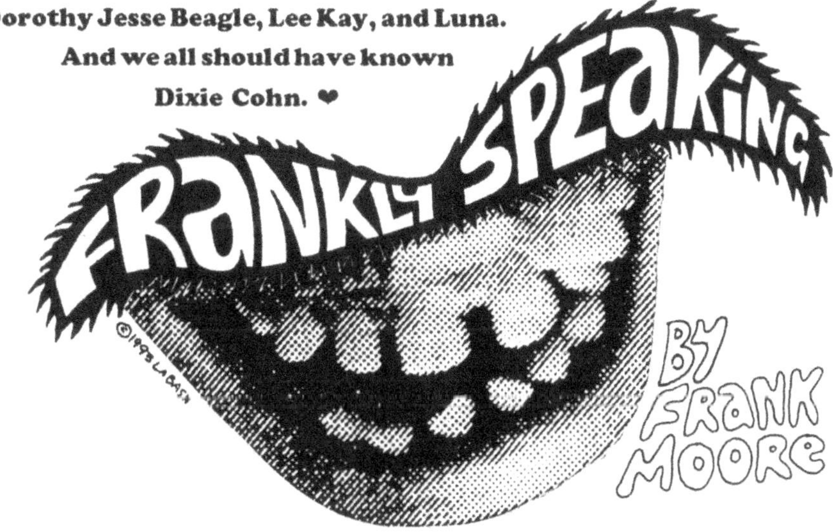

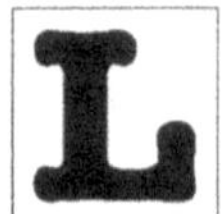
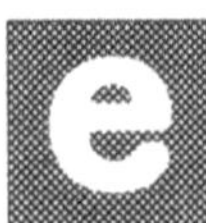
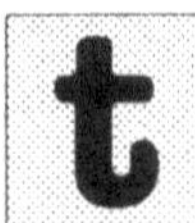
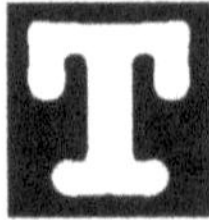
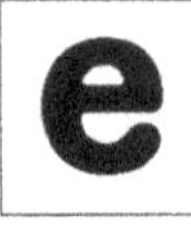
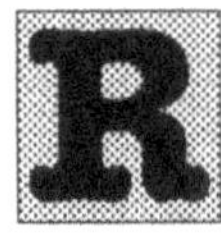
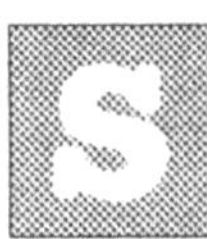

August 5, 1992

Dear Frank,

"...The artwork/photography in TCR V1 I2 7/92 is quite something! Petrisko's 'Simulation/Stimulation' looked like a PXL still to me at first, then I saw the medium was digitized photography. But moore than that (pun intended!), The Beast (page 10) could be in The Church of the Sub-Genius 'zine – why is it in YOUR 'zine? Seabury's fucking pig art is cool!!! Wonder what the anti-porn fems would say about it!?!..."

Yours in freedom
(what's left of it)
Brenda Tatelbaum
Publisher
Eidos Magazine

Dear Frank,

"...the Pleasure Dome Collective is very enthusiastic about your work...

"I found the tapes amazing.... I was surprised and deeply impressed by the gentleness and sense of community that I got watching you and your group perform. We live in a world where there is so much hatred and in that hatred is such a fear and loathing of bodies and human interaction. But in your tapes I saw people interact in such a way that hatred was overcome and was replaced by comfort, kindness and understanding.

"(In Chero Collage) the audience is led in, sat down, some get a massage by naked, painted members of your group. Then you're brought in and lain across a member of the audience and then carried on stage. It seemed so simple yet I felt you were addressing many complex issues surrounding our relationship to our own, and others, bodies. We wear clothes all the time continually denying that we and those around us have bodies under the clothes. Your tapes have made me think a great deal about how sexualized, regulated and forbidden bodies have become. I was continually encouraged by the fact that in each of your videos the people on stage or around stage seemed to really enjoy what they were doing....

"(In The Outrageous Horror Show) there are certain moments that have an absurd beauty that I am unable to describe .... What I found in your work was a desexualization of the body that challenged taboos surrounding the body. When this rigid sexualization is removed, the sensual and erotic joy of touching, and exploring reacquaints the viewer (and participants) with the personal strength that can be gained through this reacknowledgement of bodies and the selves that reside inside those bodies.

"I found your work to be both challenging and inspirational...."

Marnie Parrell,
Pleasure Dome, Toronto

"In some way, if a life-style or a drug culture or a mode or an artistic tendency has any intrinsic power, it will, I think, put itself in a position where it won't be accepted. If it can be contained, then its value is not revolutionary."

JUDITH MALINA
Living Theater

"Glory! Glory *hole-leluhia!*"

by Veronica Vera

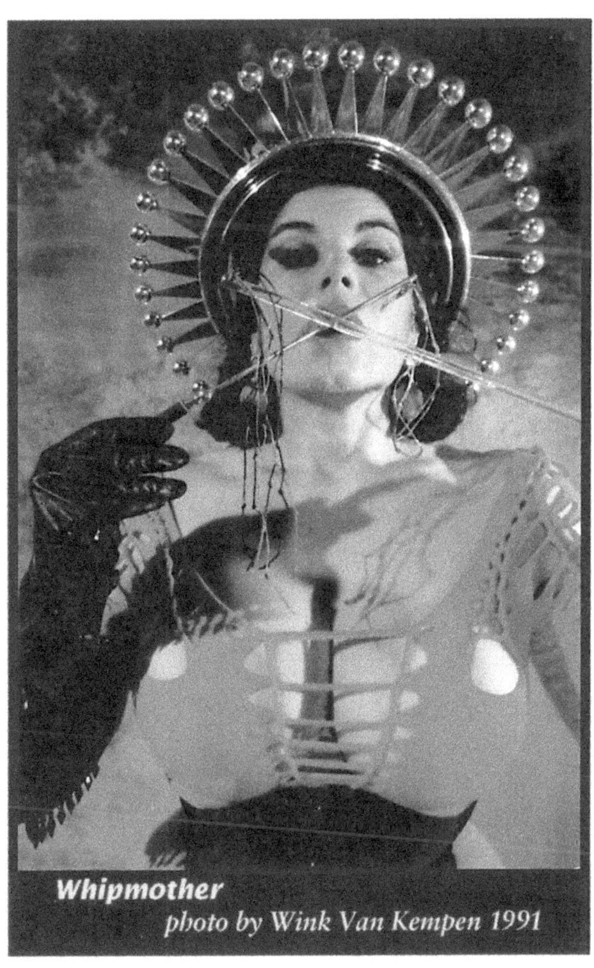
Whipmother
photo by Wink Van Kempen 1991

My path to enlightenment began the day I put my fingers in my underpants, felt my first moments of heavenly bliss, then was slapped and informed, "God does not like that." Ostensibly, I accepted my mother's decree and prayed very hard that I could stay holy by staying away from my hole. Subconsciously, I stamped my maryjane's in protest and determined that there must be a way I could feel divine and still be good. My quest has taken me literally and figuratively all around the world. As I grew, so did my shoes, from maryjane's to "come-fuck-me" pumps. I became a high-heeled journalist, writing about my sex life, interviewing other people about theirs: commercial sex workers, fetishists, s/m aficionados, swingers, transgenderists... the fields of my research spanned from orgy to temple. One day, I made my first hard core movie and became a porn star. Eventually, I understood that I wanted to show my vulva to no one more than I wanted to show it to myself.

Becoming a porn star, helped me work out my personal sexual issues. When people ask what led me to a career in the sex industry, I credit the inspiration to a good Catholic education. Ironically, repression laid a foundation for my exhibitionism. I have carried this concept further to evolve a theory of sexual evolution - the idea that no practice is kinky, bizarre or perverse. In terms of each person's development and experience, everything makes absolute sense. We are all at different places in our sexual evolutions and we are all entitled to our own path.

My research has given me a very special kind of wisdom and for that I am grateful. If I'd been an economist, I would understand motivation in terms of who's getting what and how much, instead, I look for who's getting off and how.

To me, sex is an intimate, nourishing force that connects us with the energy of another person, with ourselves, and with the universal energy of the cosmos. Is sex always intimate - even anonymous sex? From the people I know involved in sexual support groups, I hear that it is popular to put yourself down for indulging in anonymous sexual encounters when you believe these encounters will not get you what you want? Such support groups are good. They provide a forum for people to talk and learn about sex and a place to get off aurally, if not orally. But we have a responsibility to beware of what we swallow. Let's not forget what we do get from sex. A trip to a glory hole will not likely get you a steady date for the movies but it will get you an intimate connection with another person on this planet, a sharing in the universal energy and a connection with yourself, if you choose to appreciate sex that way. You can believe lust is a vice, you can believe it is a virtue. Imagine two strangers sharing a sexual encounter and ending it with the words, "thank you."

I once appeared on a television program with a preacher who was anti-pornography and pro-censorship. I really wanted to understand this man. I told him that I believed in the goodness of humanity and placed my trust in the choices of each individual. Since he was advocating some sort of control by outside parties, namely himself and others anointed to do the job, did this mean that he believed that humanity was essentially good or essentially bad? "I believe in the total depravity of man," he said, and then quoted scripture, "Babies come forth from the womb speaking lies." How sad.

"Pornography" is not a word that I like to use because it is too loaded with connotations. Most of the time what we mean by pornography is explicit sexual images. At base, these images are a celebration of life, a celebration of humanity. If like this preacher, we believe that humanity is essentially bad, then so are the images that represent humanity recreating itself. The reverend was misguided, but at least he was consistent.

His was the kind of thinking that inspired the spankings when I was caught "touching myself." Even as a child, I believed in the goodness of my self. I held on to it like a bitch with her bone and refused to let it go. But for a very long time, the primary emotion I experienced during sex was guilt, until guilt became the ultimate aphrodisiac. Touch myself, feel good, get a licking; feel good, get a licking; get a licking, feel good.

My experience was not unique. Our culture is mired in guilt and this has kept us bound in chains of fear and powerlessness, not only about the experience of sex but of the experience of being human. Our institutions of state, church and the media, either through ignorance or guile continue the process. When I listen to the news, and hear one crime story after another, testaments to the evils of humanity, I see the voyeur at the peep show feverishly pumping his dick, peering to the left and right, afraid of being caught with his pants down. Ashamed of his own need, he has learned to be excited by his shame and to be very, very quiet.

When we feel guilty, we do not voice our opinions. If we do not voice our opinions, we cannot raise questions. If we do not raise questions, we cannot effect change. In any evolution, what happens when there is a surfeit of a particular resource is that resource begins to lose its effect. We have had guilt 'til it's coming our of our ears. Today, less and less people find comfort in guilt. In my personal evolution, I accepted sex with guilt as better than no sex at all. Guilt had a purpose, it helped me have pleasure. When guilt began to hurt, I dropped guilt. But it took a long time for me to differentiate those feelings. From childhood, everything had rushed in so quickly... and there was no chance for discussion. Awareness came with growing up, doing my own explorations and the support

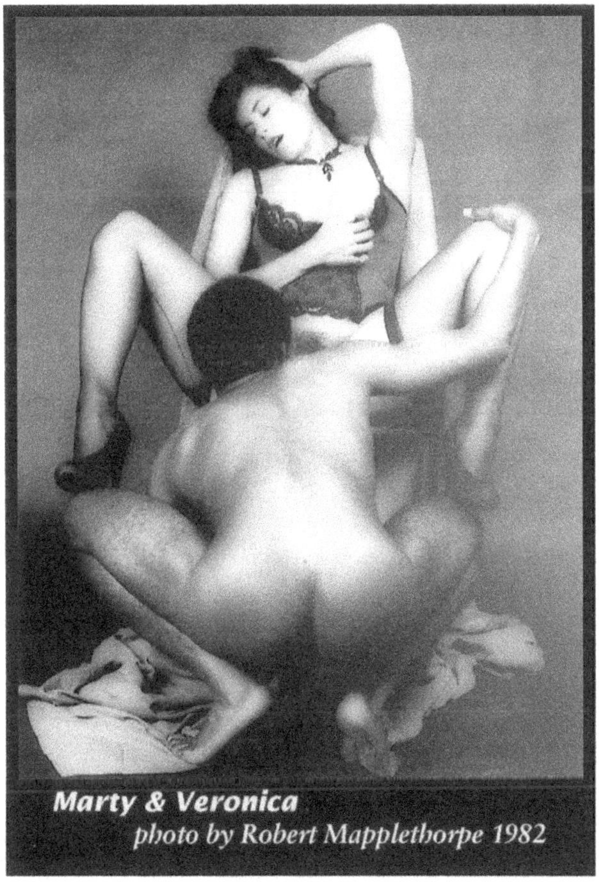

Marty & Veronica
photo by Robert Mapplethorpe 1982

of other people who felt the same way. The political consequences of sex without guilt are enormous.

Attitude is everything. Attitude is our position toward a particular fact or state. That preacher's attitude, toward being human was that humanity was evil right from the get-go and that evil needed to be controlled. But if we begin with the attitude that humanity is good and we embrace our sexuality in all of its varieties as part of what it is to be human, we give ourselves permission. We acknowledge our right to experience sex with ourselves and with each other because we believe in the power of our energy and sex is the most efficient way that we share that energy. We rejoice and humbly accept our need for each other, because our need for each other is what makes us human and to be human is not just good, it's divine.

When I gave myself permission to touch myself, I gave myself permission to feel. I validated my feelings. The right to feel is a basic right and with it comes the right to have an opinion, and what follows is the right to ask questions. We ask questions and we meet others who are asking the same questions and together we create a world. Make no mistake about it. Sex is a political act.

When my bosom buddy, Annie Sprinkle invited me to create the playbill for her brave, iconoclastic one woman show, I was inspired to write the Post Porn Modernist Manifesto. On the evening of its completion, a group of libido liberals had gathered at my home for a party. We all signed the manifesto like it was the Declaration Of Independence, in a way, it was. Among the signers that night were nude, "crip" performance artist Frank Moore who says, "I have the perfect body for an exhibitionist"; Candida Royalle famous for making erotic movies from the woman's point of view; Betty Dodson, author of Sex For One and creator of The Bodysex Workshops; England's greatest treasure Miss Tuppy Owens whose Sex Maniac's Diary and charity Ball chronicle and honor the sex world.... Rene "I Am The Best Artist" decorated the manuscript with genitalia, a most appropriate insignia. The space at the bottom was left for your name. Here is what it said. We still hold these truths to be self-evident:

continued on next page

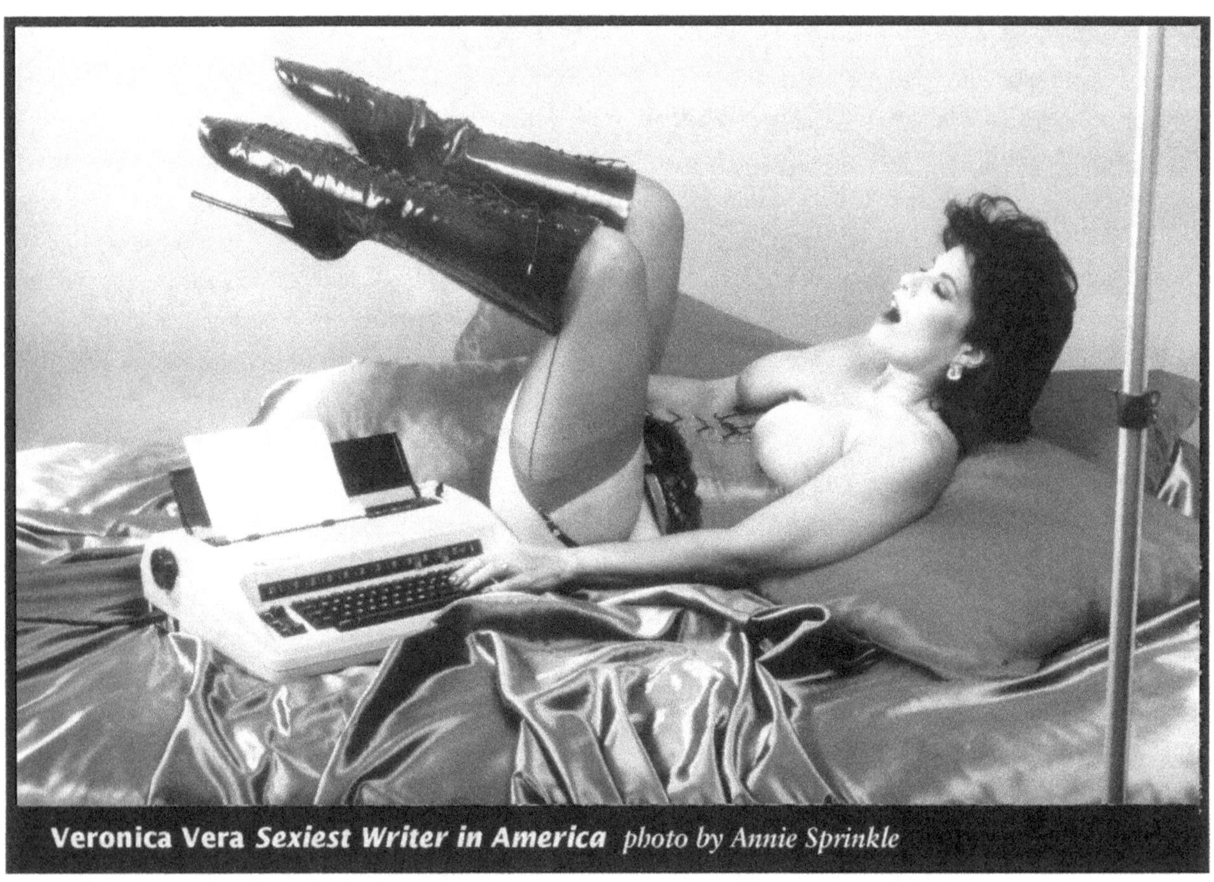
Veronica Vera *Sexiest Writer in America* *photo by Annie Sprinkle*

Post Porn Modernist Manifesto*

Let it be known to all who read these words or witness these events
that a new awareness has come over the land.
We of the Post Porn Modernist Movement face the challenge of the Rubber Age
by acknowledging this moment in our personal sexual evolutions
and in the sexual evolution of the planet.
Post Porn Modernists celebrate sex as the nourishing, life-giving force.
We embrace our genitals as part, not separate from our spirits.
We utilize sexually explicit words, pictures and performances
to communicate our ideas and emotions.
We denounce sexual censorship as anti-art and inhuman.
We empower ourselves by this attitude of sex-positivism.
And with this love of our sexual selves, we have fun, heal the world and endure.

Veronica Vera, June 1989.

*Your name (if you dare)*______________________________________.

**The term "post-porn modernist" was created by Dutch artist and porn fan, Wink van Kempen.*

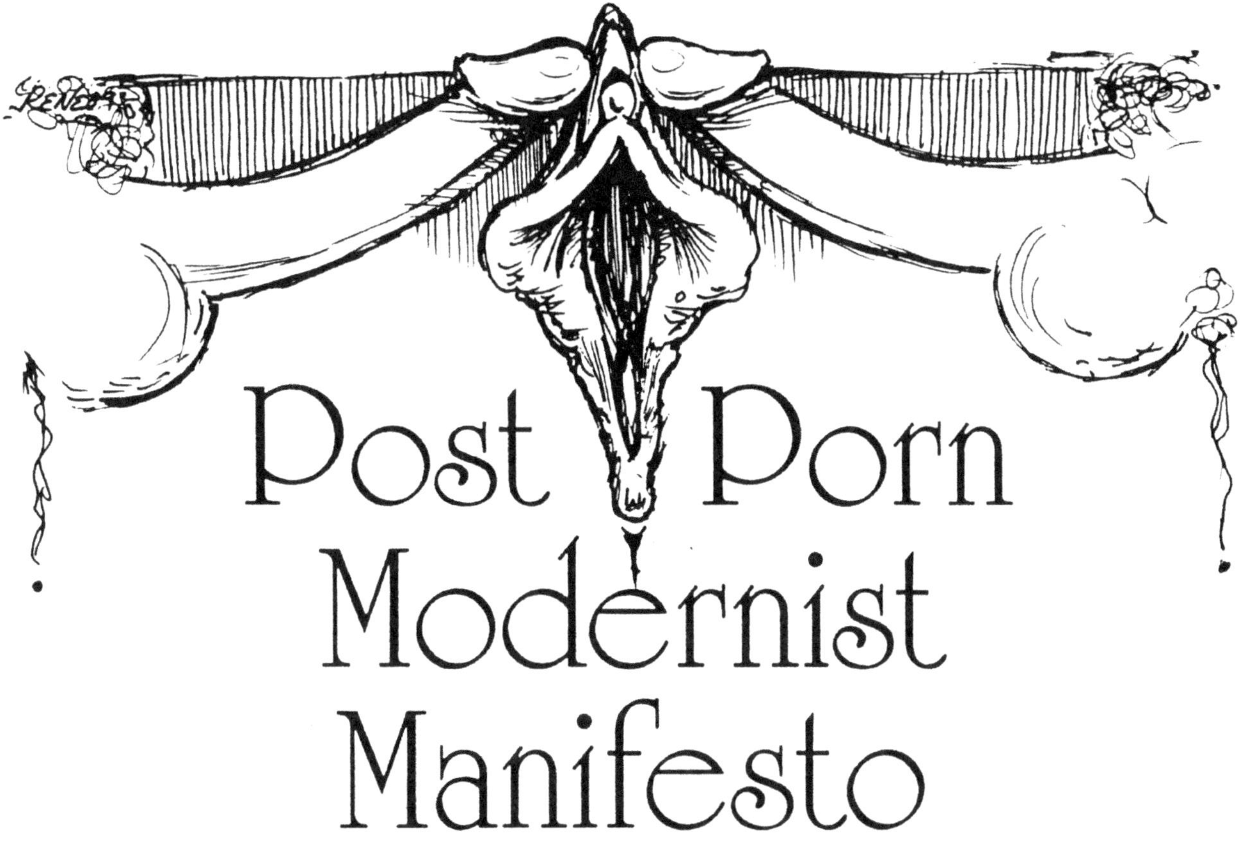

Post Porn Modernist Manifesto

LET IT BE KNOWN to all who read these words or witness these events that a new awareness has come over the land. We of the POST PORN MODERNIST MOVEMENT face the challenge of the Rubber Age by acknowledging this moment in our personal sexual evolutions and in the sexual evolution of the planet.

Post Porn Modernists celebrate sex as the nourishing, life-giving force.

We embrace our genitals as part, not separate, from our spirits.

We utilize sexually explicit words, pictures and performances to communicate our ideas and emotions.

We denounce sexual censorship as anti-art and inhuman.

We empower ourselves by this attitude of sex-positivism.

And with this love of our sexual selves we have fun, heal the world and endure.

—Vera, June 1989

Candida Royalle
Gail Solow
Johnny Science
Linda Mac
Frank Moore's sign
Leigh Gates
Veronica Vera
Annie Sprinkle
Rene 89
I AM THE BEST ARTIST.

Your name (if you dare): ______________________________

"Oeidipus Pete"

NOTE: The nickname given to the unfortunate ballplayer by Lowell Cohn (no relation) columnist for the San Francisco Chronicle. In a very literate sports piece comparing him to Oeidipus of Greek fable who was forced to leave his Greek city for unbecoming conduct

"Oedipus Pete" was fleet on his feet,
ran the bases like no one can,
had more hit then "Ty Cobb",
many bases did rob,
made his fans hearts...throb,
So they nicknamed him "Charlie Hustle"

Over others, Rose he in the game,
gaining a name, in the sport of great fame
known as Baseball,
the national religion played out in the fall,
Pete its high priest, the player with gall
Oeidie Pete, really played ball,
and often played the world series..delirious

But Petes secret lyfe,
known perhaps...to his wyfe,
But especially....his Bookie,
who knew Pete bet Red,
and contracted him dead,
for revenging the line, not paying on time
to cover his bets made on Baseball,

continued on page 12

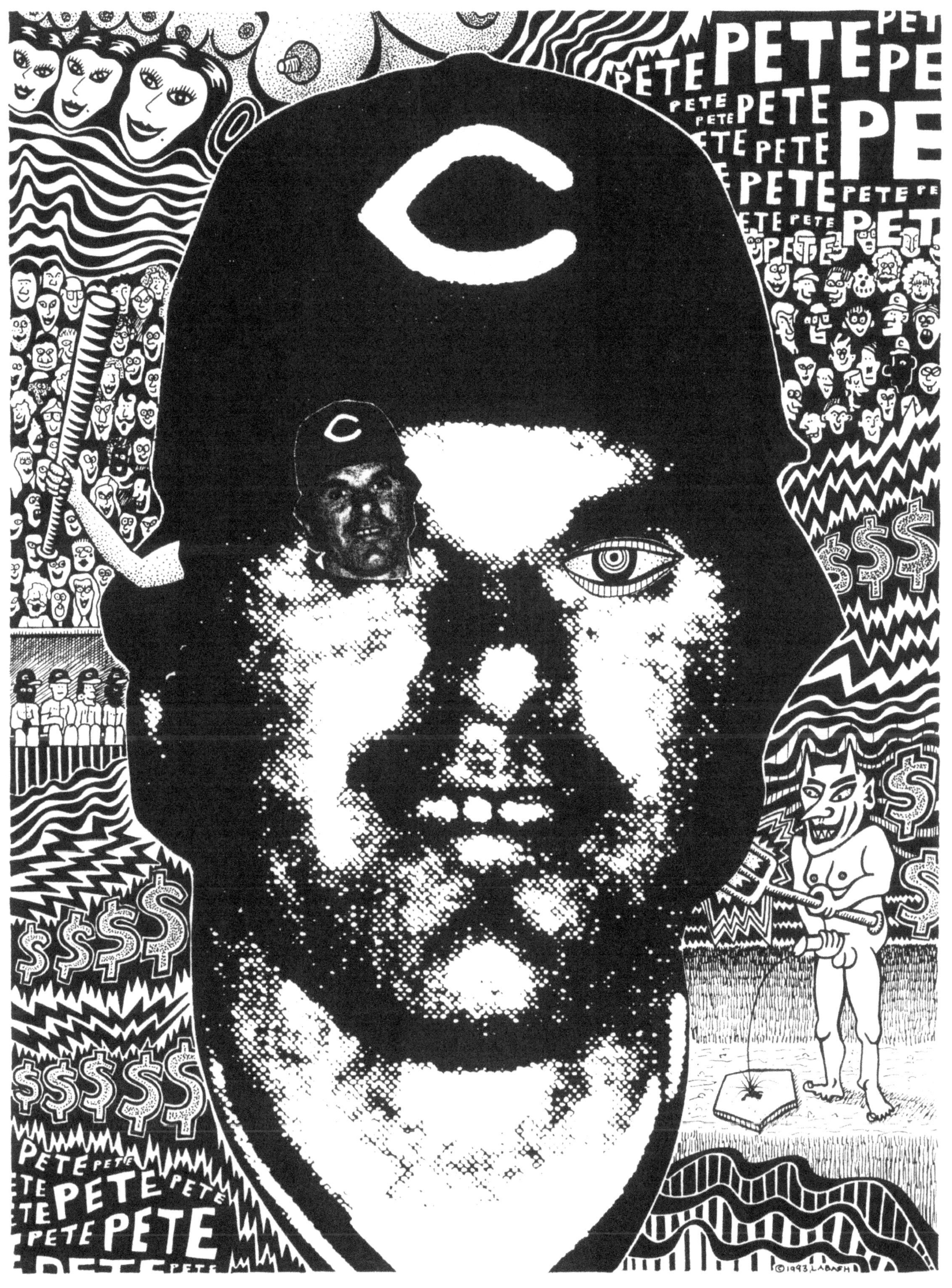
PETE PETE PETE
PETE PETE
PETE PETE PETE
PETE
PETE PETE
$$$$
$$$$$
PETE PETE
PETE PETE
PETE PETE
©1993 LABASH

Yeah!, Pete had the lyfe
a cute lovin wyfe,
and on the side, sly nookie,
his failure was thus,
feet of clay he did bust,
forfeiting loans from his Bookie,
He'd had money and fame, Rose to the top of the game,
One day heard his name, for the Hall of fame,
called over prarie and plain,

But the media doth say,
Oeidipus Pete, bet on baseball!
Denial! sayeth, He,
But Giamatti, say Yay,
Still Pete exclaimeth, Nay
Bet on Baseball?...NO WAY!!

But the thing, Pete forgot,
When religion ya got, And Baseballs the National religion,
Don't spill blood on its altar,
topple idols of ball,
You'll lie and you'll stall,
throw your career...over the wall!,
But most all,
Pete....LOOK!!,
if you jes payed off the Book,
Pete!!

Your Lyfe would be all quiet and neat,
But you risked it all for a buck,
And now,, all we can say is,
Oy! What a Schmuck,

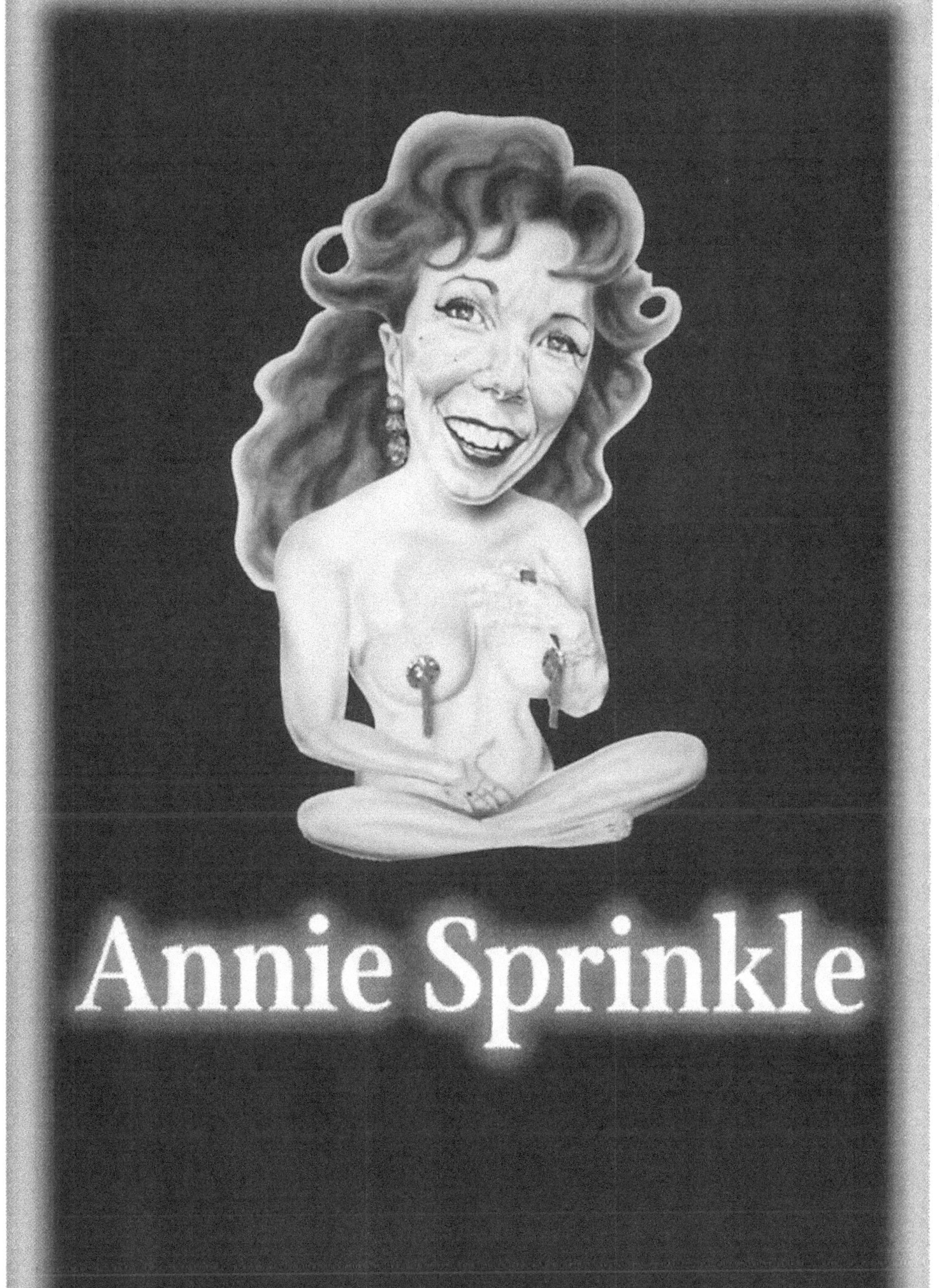
Annie Sprinkle

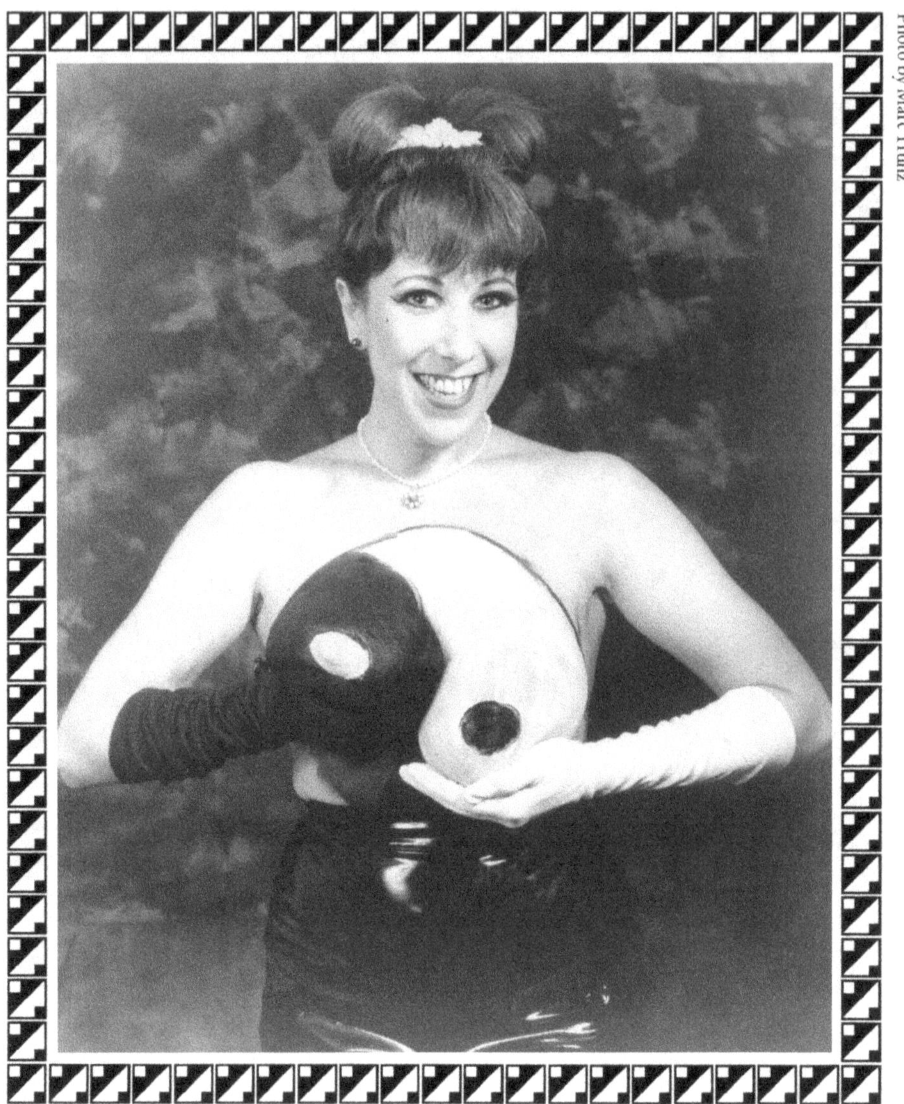

Photo by Marc Trunz

ELLEN/ANNIE

I was born Ellen Steinberg, but I didn't like 'Ellen' very much, so I invented Annie Sprinkle.
Ellen was excruciatingly shy. Annie is an exhibitionist.
Ellen was fat and ugly, and nobody seemed to want her.
Annie is voluptuous and sexy, and lots of people want her.
Ellen desperately needs attention. Annie gets it.
Ellen wore orthopaedic shoes and flannel nightgowns.
Annie wears six-inch spiked high heels and sexy lingerie.
Ellen was afraid of men and sex. Annie is fearless.
Ellen was a nobody, Annie gets asked for autographs.
Ellen wants to get married and have children. Annie wants fame and fortune.
I suppose Ellen Steinberg really is Annie Sprinkle,
and Annie Sprinkle is really Ellen Steinberg.

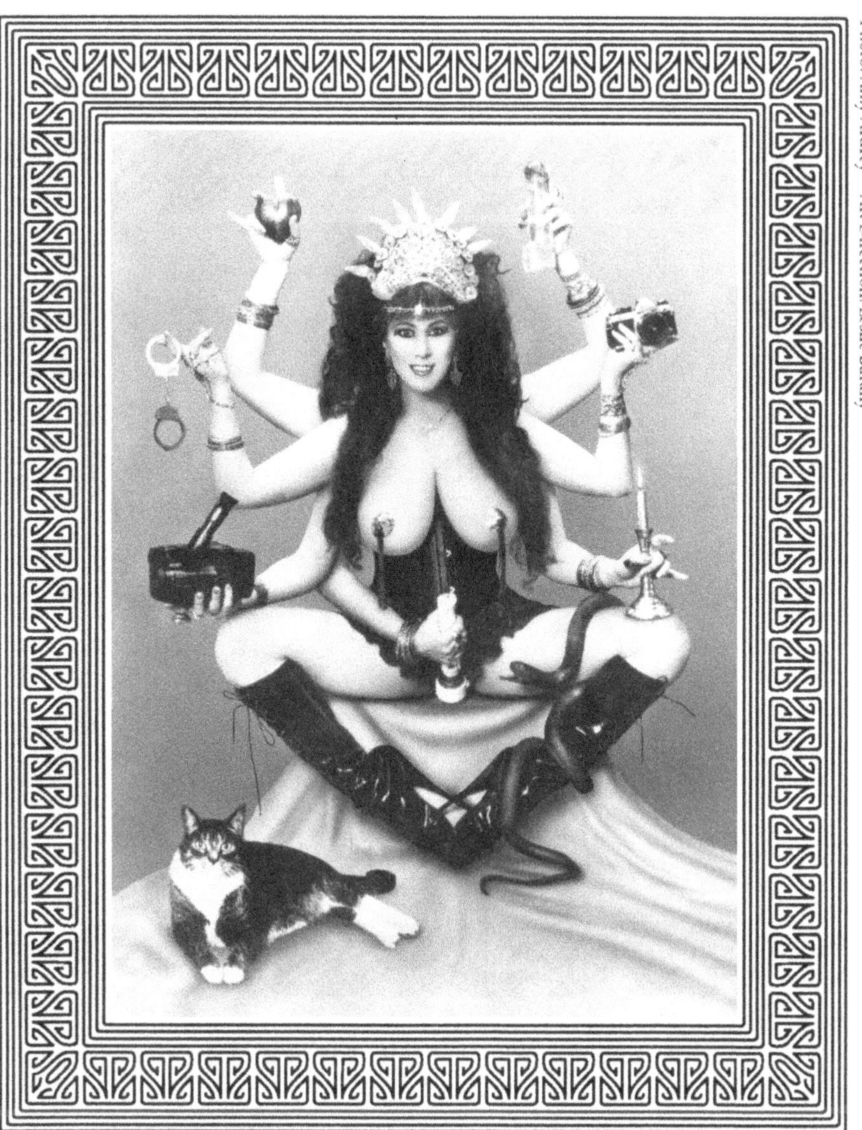

Photo: Amy Ardrey Art Direction: Leslie Barany

17 YEARS LATER

ANNIE	ANYA
Annie Sprinkle loves everybody.	Anya loves herself.
Annie Sprinkle seeks attention.	Anya seeks awareness.
Annie Sprinkle is a feminist.	Anya is a Goddess.
Annie Sprinkle wants a career, fame and fortune.	Anya wants peace, love and freedom.
Annie Sprinkle wants an animal attraction.	Anya wants a spiritual connection.
Annie Sprinkle loves men.	Anya loves men... and absolutely adores women.
Annie Sprinkle is a modern woman.	Anya is ancient.
Annie Sprinkle likes sex with transsexuals, midgets and amputees.	Anya makes love to the sky, mud and trees.
Annie Sprinkle masturbates.	Anya meditates... while she masturbates, of course.
Anya is today,	only because Annie Sprinkle was.

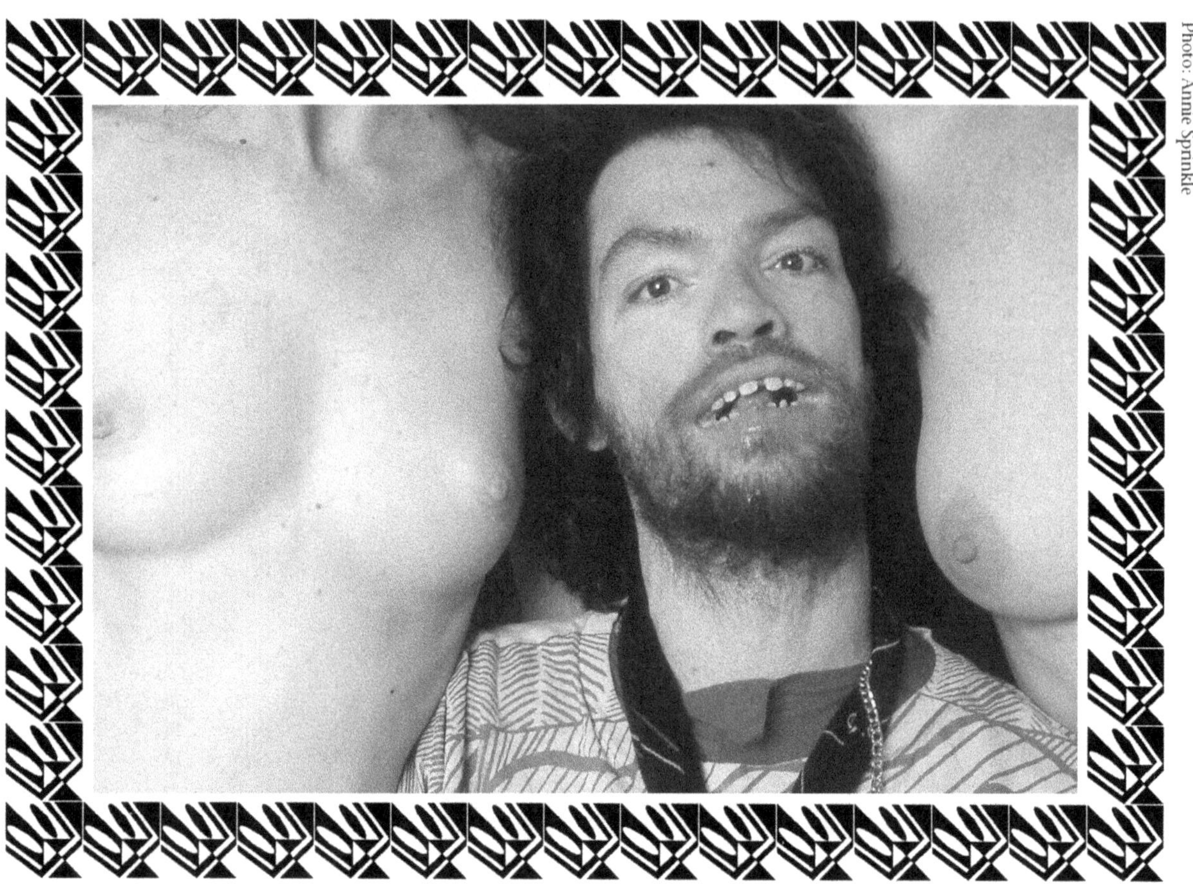

Photo: Annie Sprinkle

MY FORMAL SEX TEACHERS

I've learned something from every sexual encounter. Many people have contributed to my knowledge, but there are several in particular from whom I've learned major things.

Frank Moore is a unique performance artist, teacher, writer, painter and philosopher. He taught me to love my body exactly the way it is. Frank has cerebral palsy, and can't walk, talk or stand. He doesn't have any control over his arms, he can't feed himself or go to the bathroom without help. He spells out his thoughts on a letter board by using a pointer attached to his leather headband. Although he lives in a wheelchair, he manages to accomplish many things, including having a very erotic sex life. He teaches what he calls "Eroplay", which is basically getting naked with a person or a group, touching and playing sensuously, making it "sexual, but not quite". It's innocent and child-like. Eroplay is about energy, not genitals.

All selections excerpted from Annie's book, *Post Porn Modernist*, published by Torch Books, copyrighted 1991.

Produced and Directed by Maria Beatty & Annie Sprinkle
Music by Pauline Oliveros

THE SLUTS & GODDESSES

VIDEO WORKSHOP OR HOW TO BE A SEX GODDESS IN 101 EASY STEPS

ORGASMIC OFFER! ORDER NOW! Delight Your SENSES
SAFE SEX • FOR ADULTS ONLY

This video is a humorous, absurd, heartfelt and worshipful look at SEX. Guided through this unique adventure by sexpurt extraordinaire Annie Sprinkle and the "Transformation Facilitators", you will explore the ancient and forbidden knowledge about female sexuality.

This fresh and inspiring video features many exotic ways to stimulate sexual and sensual pleasure. You will encounter flagellation with oak leaves, Chinese sword dancing, striptease, body contortions, tattooing, piercing, shaving and gender-play. The mysteries of sex magic and female ejaculation will be revealed. You will learn about Tantric breathing, primal screaming, the joys of group

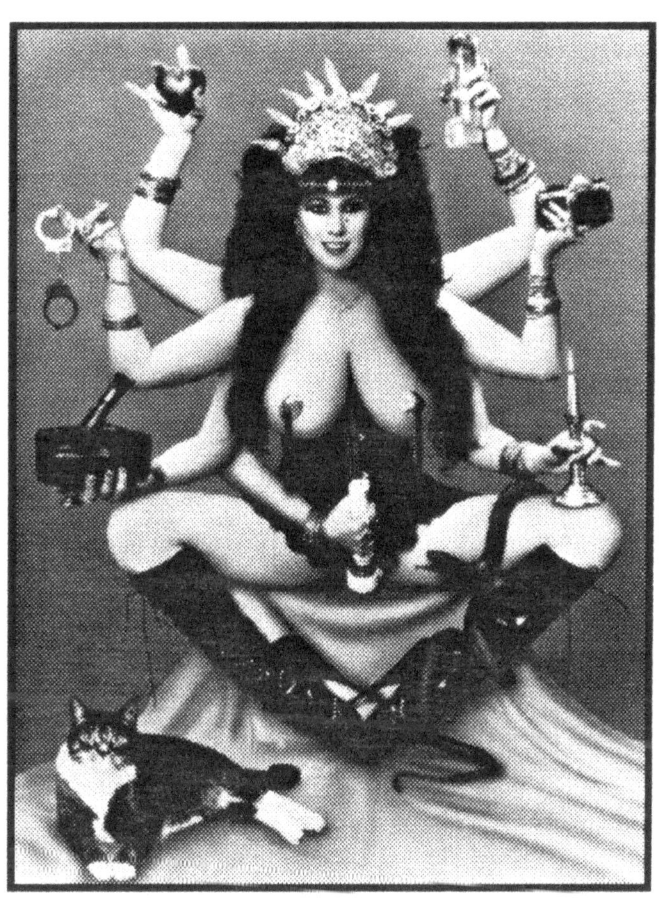

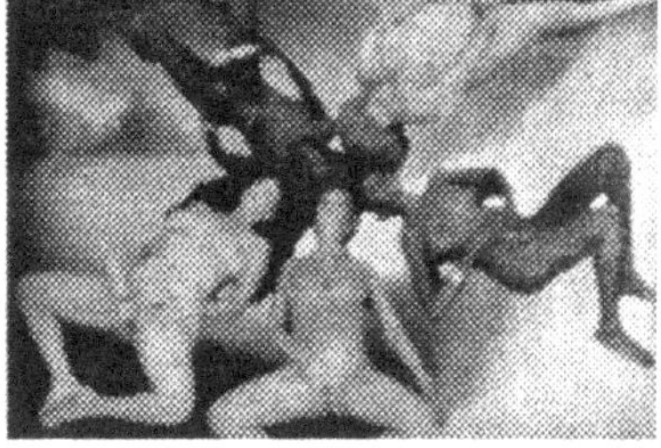

masturbation while meditating, and not least of all, you will witness a profound five minute long orgasm!

Featuring ten magnificent, hot Goddesses, this tape is explicit and lavishly produced. Prepare for an "eye fuck"!

Challenging the boundaries of femininity, the "good girl"/ "bad girl" myths as well as the sexual "norms", it is controversial and thought provoking and thus best viewed in a group. This insightful work of art will remind you that your sexuality is precious and sacred.

Starring Annie Sprinkle, Barbara Carrellas, Amy Harlib, Diviana Ingravallo, Jade, Carol Leigh (a.k.a. Scarlot Harlot), Jocelyn Taylor, Chris Teen, Trash and Kelly Webb. Cameos by Pulsating Paula, Donna Theresa

Associate Producer	Leslie Barany
Assistant Director	Kathy High
Art Director/Stylist	Catou Guillaud
Screen Play	Annie Sprinkle

YES! I WANT TO BE A SEX GODDESS!

Here is my check (or money order) for $40.00 plus $5.00 shipping and handling.

Make check out to Maria Beatty.
POB 435,
Prince St. Station.
New York, N.Y. 10012

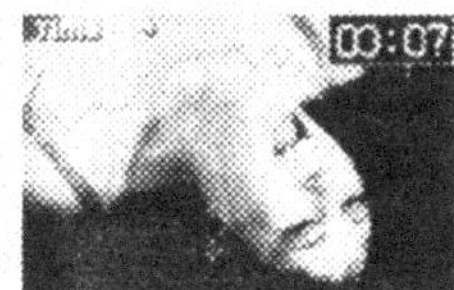

U.S. allow 4 weeks for delivery. Add $5 U.S. for European Shipping. For international orders send $U.S. money orders only. Add $5 for PAL format.

NAME ______________________

ADDRESS ______________________

CITY/STATE ______________________

ZIP ______________________

I am over 21 and I request this material. Running Time: 52 Minutes/Color

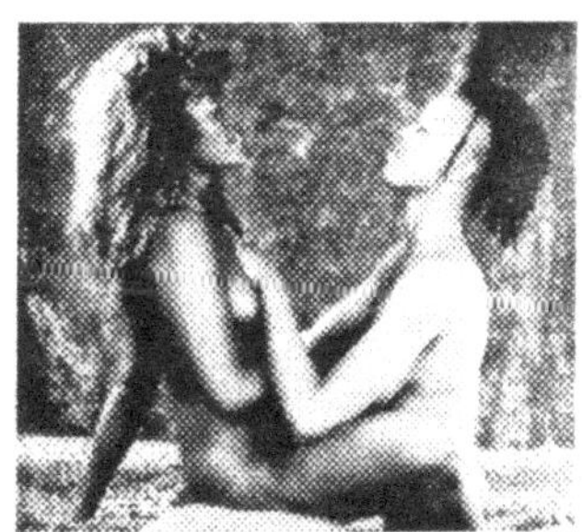

PHOTOGRAPHY, AMY ARDREY • RETOUCHING, MARILYN HAWKRIDGE • PHOTO ART DIRECTION, LES BARANY • FLYER, CLIFF SCHWARTZ

I'm Just a Pubic Hair for Someone Bigger (a performance)

i've got my spade and i'm going to start shoveling away the shit
i'm going to start shoveling the shit, shoveling the shit
i'm going to start with your asshole and shoveling out all that shit from the lower intestines
cause nice guys
cause nice guys are the seeds the holy seeds of homophobia.
are there any nice guys out there?
nice guys think they so cooool to let this queer upon his stage upon his stage
just doing his thing
just doing his thing
he's a nice guy cause he sits
he's a nice guy cause he under stands the circumstances ...
it makes you a nice guy to let me do my thing, right?
well you're wrong
well you're wrong.
i don't want you to liberate me man, but let me follow thru and say what i want
let me follow thru and say what i want
cause i'm going to say what i want anyhow – i'm going to say what the fuck pleases me.
when was the first time guys
when was the first time guys you realized you had hair around your asshole
when was the first time guys you realized you had hair around your assholes and you put
your index finger between your ass cheeks wondering how it got there ...
there is no garden of eden in your ass
there is no god of almighty in your ass –
you shit/you shit
because you shit from that hole
because you have to shit from that hole
some put devices up that hole
some put cocks up that hole because it is not an intolerant hole like your
mouth.
after sex get the fuck away from me go clean yourself up you smell like cum change the sheets
i hate the wet spot turn the t.v. on get me a beer get me a smoke get me some peace and
quiet around here you fucking asshole go snake yourself.
i am one of jesse helms' pubic hairs
i am one of nancy reagan's pubic hairs
i am one of barbra streisand's pubic hairs
i am one of john frahnmeyer's pubic hairs
i am one of allen ginsberg's pubic hairs
i am one of mary magdelene's pubic hairs
i don't have a problem
i don't have a problem

continued ☛

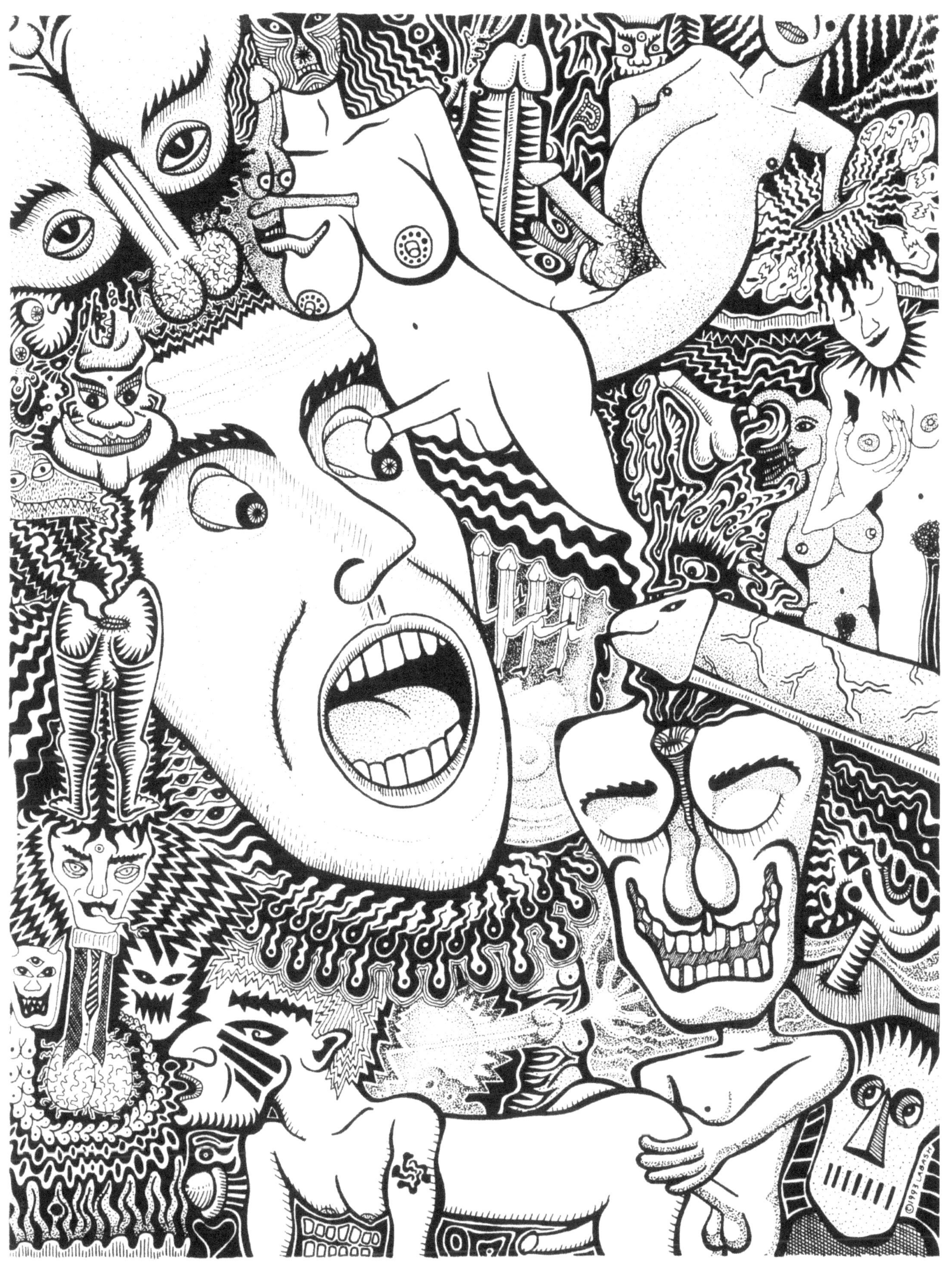
©1993 LABASH

the problem is my lover doesn't accept me
doesn't accept me because you don't accept him
                                        you don't accept him
i have an attitude
i have a fucking attitude
because society has accepted for years the exploitation talk about boobs, ass, pussy
all of that
all of that
but i we you they cannot talk about a man because society doesn't accept or understand
truth and reality
truth and reality
(people don't you understand this is my honor and social reality)
orgasm and nudity
orgasm and nudity
(to to to to to realize there are 16 different words for sexual pleasure in the native hawaiian language)
you've got your mind made up about abortion
you've got your mind made up about abortion
and i could care less either way, either way – i could care less –
but orgasm and nudity are open
but orgasm and nudity are open ... or is it?
i am here to change all of that
i am here to change all of that
I AM HERE TO CHANGE ALL OF THAT
i can't talk about it
i can't talk about it
i can't talk about how this is beginning to get uncomfortable ...
some of you are afraid that you're going to have to pull down those little boxers,
those little calvin klein's, those jock straps and show me show me that **THING** between
your **LEGS.**
semi liberal man so warm and funny you going to fart as soon as i start talking
about
how you wiggle when those balls are being nustled those balls being nustled or
being probed
being probed
cause it's not cool to be so cool it's not hip to be hip
it's a lie it's a lie – the totality lie
cause i hate macho men
i hate macho men
men with muscles and iron
men with muscles and iron

your dick is getting hard, huh?
not like the little thing hanging limp from the underwear, but it's getting thick and red
burning with lust
fuck the weakness
the hairy thoughts
the drive
the eclipse of being a nice guy
like a dog that's how i want it like a dog that's how i want it
i want to be dry humped with whiteness all over
i don't want anything old, i don't want anything old, i don't want anarchy –
straight guys ignore gay guys because we're so unusual, so strange, so savage, so beasty ...
do you like looking at your own cock do you even touch your own cock.
it's a weird mix man
it's a weird mix man
cause there are some always trying to pass for white
cause there are some always trying to pass for white
but it's known
it's known that they only masturbate to madonna pictures
                    they only masturbate to madonna pictures
agony
agony
agony
caught between to/two different lies
caught between to/two different lies
the gay lie
the straight lie
can't let your mama, your mama see you jacking off ...
but i can spot the different lies instantaneous because you always have a revolver pointing
at your head, you always have hard nipples and a female cover who'll support you ...
but most of all
i am the most important person in your life
i am one of your soft stabbing unyielding pubic hairs.

– merle tofér, II

The BATTLE of the sexes

by **Luna** Sanguine

This is the first of several articles that I will be doing on "The Battle of the Sexes". Now that we are in the nineties, I want to synthesize once and for all everything that we have learned over the past twenty years. I do not want to carry a lot of extra baggage into the new decade.

In order to do this, we must create a whole new dynamic to govern relations between men and women at all levels – a Hegelian synthesis combining many different elements from the opposing belief-systems labeled "sexism" and "feminism." There is still no way to avoid having to act out the alleged "Battle of the Sexes" over and over again, but we should be wide awake and conscious of the act, bringing it into the consciousness of "lest we forget."

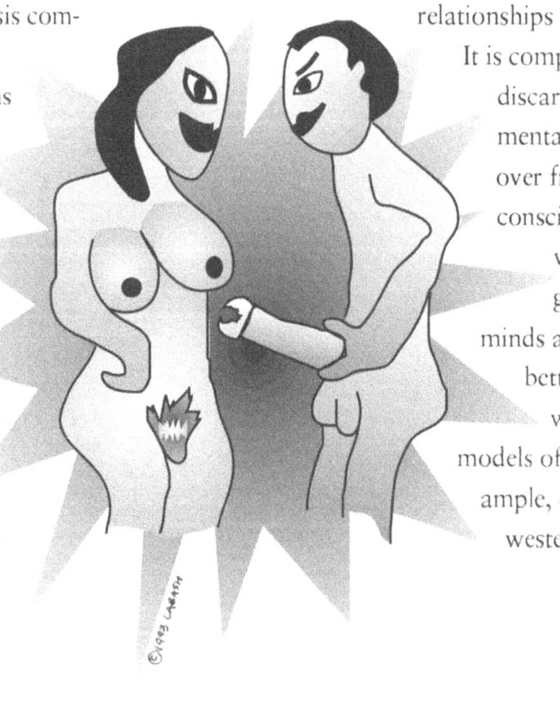

I believe that many women and men are now ready to create entirely new ways for the genders to interact and inter-relate on the level of day-to-day living. It is now possible to discard all of the stereotypical role models that have been imposed on our western society by Theocratic religion, patriarchal family structure, authoritarian governments, and exploitative economic systems. In order to do this, however, we still have to use our existing knowledge and opinions about gender relationships as a starting point.

It is completely impossible to simply discard thousands of years of bad mental programming and start over fresh, but it is possible to consciously recognize the individual elements of this programming within our own minds and to assemble them into a better pattern, a pattern which will produce sexual role models of our own choosing. For example, every man who grows up in western society is influenced by

©1993 LABATH

the stereotypes which give him very few choices in his behavior toward women. No matter how hard his conscious mind tries to treat a particular woman as a unique individual, his subconscious still tries to impose one of the ancient mythological images on her: mother, sister, lover, maid-servant, whore, etc. The only way to break out of this trap is to take the elements of which these stereotypical images are built and reassemble them into a new pattern.

The first step in such a synthesis is isolating these individual elements. I will start with some notes dictated to me in the winter of '86 by a friend who at that time considered himself a Situationist. I at that time was working as a professional dominatrix. I petitioned this friend for an outside view that focused in only on the "straight" client/mistress relationship not on the S/M or sex industry community.

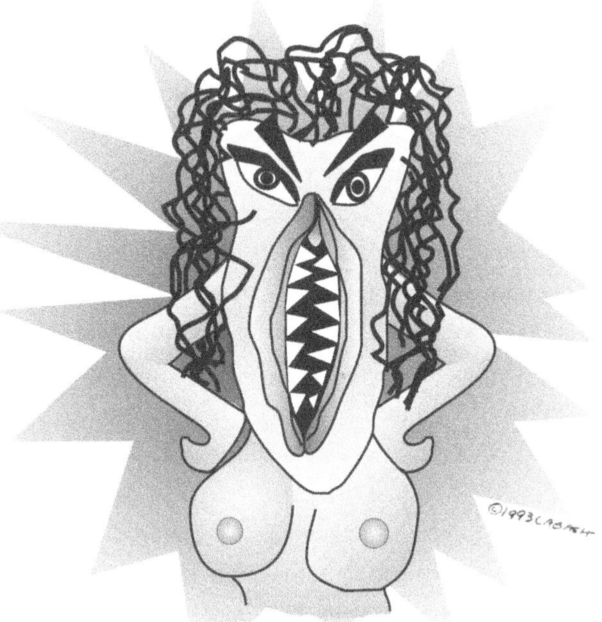

Capitalism functions by taking desires, wants, and needs and mirroring them back in such a way that the fetish, the representation of desire, replaces the original desire and becomes a commodity, a "luxury." Throughout our lives we come across the same dichotomy: desire to obtain pleasure versus sacrificing ourselves to obtain the accepted rewards and avoid the accepted punishments to take our place in a completely fabricated hierarchy.

Attaining the only "acceptable" solution to ourselves as individuals. Unconditional surrender of ourselves as individuals for a piece of the pie (the piece of the pie being merely convenient inventions themselves) in return for our living out the lies of accepted roles. Democracy must (has to) come from everyone being strong instead of merely maintaining a democratized level of weakness (that comes from surveyed averaging) to help us to reach for and achieve a cosmic averageness in a supportive atmosphere.

There is no standard of desire. By maintaining a standard of desire we judge ourselves on our desire capabilities, turning once again desire into a commodity where some could be "rich" in desire and others "poor," as if any of our real desires are in any way "standard." We judge how capable we are by what we desire. How capable are you of acquiring desired status quo? All consumers of the sex industry had real desires to touch. But instead what is sold back to them are carefully airbrushed women made misty, mysterious, illusive and untouchable. That is the talent this society works from. It takes real desires and inverts them before selling them back.

The mystique of male privilege is that supposedly he owns a woman as property. What he must give up in return for the illusion of owning a woman as property is permitting himself to really touch anyone completely and fully. Why do you think that more sophisticated men are so concerned with making women orgasm? Because orgasm becomes the new product, the standard of success. And that "orgasm" has, as the standard of "success," been interchanged for the actual need/desire to really touch a partner, whether "straight" or "gay."

That is the basis of one area where women have found "power" (but not on their own terms, of course, except on "women's terms" as defined by power), the one sheer means of gaining control over the so-called privileged male. Why? The myth of the so-called privileged male shows up that the patriarchal privilege, like authority of any sort, is based on made-up principles. Notice that Meese – he goes too far and will not last – says that the general direction of things is to make sex become more of a product rather than the fulfillment of desire by making it less "obscene" and more acceptable to the mass audience.

The power structure controls pornography to keep it within the realm of a certain romanticism – this romanticism helps perpetuate the fraud that pornography can replace honest desires that are unfulfilled. With women, the only means of achieving control has traditionally been through the bedroom. From Mata Hari to other examples too numerous to mention, women have found the bedroom the only realistic means of achieving power in the illusion of a "man's world."

In a sense, men have been just as victimized as women because their need to touch has become as greatly separated from them. The more perceptive women have realized that the best means of manipulating men within their illusion of male superiority was by manipulating men's real need/desire for real touch/contact. Of course in the same breath, obviously men aren't alone in not achieving real contact.

Both pornography and using sex coercively to obtain a simulation of power are examples of a world that is turned completely upside down. A world where we are sold a multitude of substitutes for real contact with each other and real fulfillment of our most basic real desires and needs: to contact, love, and really touch one another.

But feminists also lose contact with reality when they counter these illusions by operating on the unspoken principle of "Everyone loses: no one touches, and no one is really touched." This is really just another way of playing the same game and saving one's commodity for the highest bidder. Love becomes business.

This is the sad point of being in a sex industry, i.e. being a mistress. People really do want/need love, we live in a world where we don't touch ourselves and we don't touch each other. There's always a mediation between us. There is even mediation between "I" and "me" by power through complete identification with my roles – "I" the producer or giver and "me" the consumer or recipient. That mediation is power. Power mediates all transactions from relations with ourselves, to our personal relations with others, to international affairs.

Why don't we, can't we, really understand people of different races or nationalities? Why can't we even understand sexism amongst our own kind? We can't understand them as long as power remains victor, as long as our relations to each other are based on a spirit of relative power in which authority dictates rewards and punishments that become replacements for people's real desires. Reward replaces actual desire. Make a lot of money and get to buy women, etc. People exchange real desires for rewards offered by society in an acceptable manner.

In that sense, male privilege is all illusion. Men are offered a slightly higher place on a scale of relative power. By offering people shares in power, society makes people participants. Society works by you licking a person's boots and someone licks yours, achieving a full circle, merely reversing the roles imposed by society, while still giving these (im)personal lies justification: men make themselves slaves to mistresses as a justification of lies.

A lot of people enter into S/M because this society has made them incapable of real feelings. More and more extreme innovations of contact as commodities are developed to give impressions of feeling. For instance, if more pain can be inflicted the more you are

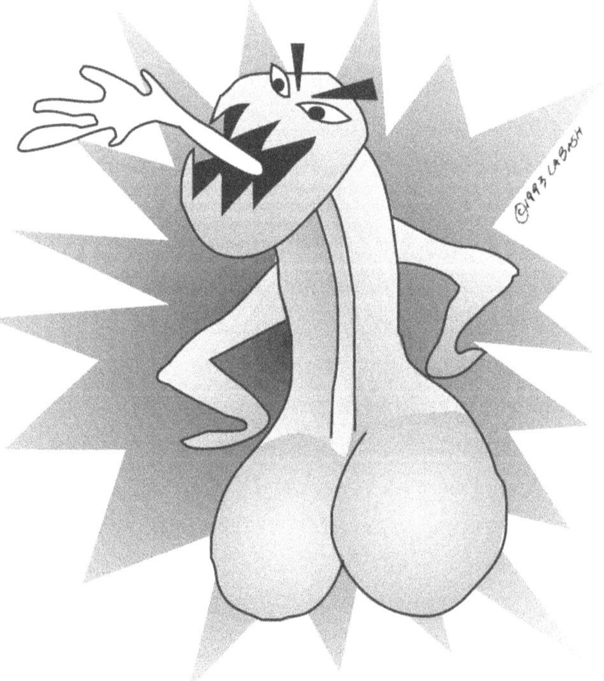

alive. It comes to a point that it takes extreme pain to feel something honestly. At least when you're having the shit beat out of you, you know you're actually feeling something instead of acting a part. You know you're alive. For particularly jaded people, that's the only way they feel alive.

At least when you're completely enveloped in pain, you are honestly feeling and responding without mediation. When you hurt badly, your screams aren't mediated through acceptable forms of behavior. Pain cuts across things like power because it is too immediate. Because society has conditioned you not to permit yourself to feel emotions directly and immediately from more positive forms of physical or social stimulation, your pain becomes one of the few means of feeling emotions at all. Someone tears your skin off. You scream and for a moment you are outside of social functions. For a moment there you are just feeling and reacting.

Capitalist society has a really good bet by investing in the so-called battle of the sexes, in that seeing the opposite sex as a potential enemy keeps women and men separate to help insure that no concerted assault can be directed at the society. It is much like the tactic used by the British in the Arab colonies and in India – encourage various local political or ethnic factions to fight among themselves, keeping them from banding together and overthrowing the British as the ultimate authority.

We have more to gain by seeing through any sort of separation by regarding ourselves and each other as living, feeling people, as ourselves. To help each other and ourselves as a concerted force, integrating to achieve our common goal that is the fulfillment of our own real desires, needs, and joys.

They've turned the women's movement, which was a big chance. When women started making revolutionary demands to claim themselves, to recognize that their needs and desires have reality, they thereby created a new terrain that hadn't been seriously claimed before by the society and put under control of the power structure. Women jumped out of normal affairs and said "we demand our own," and it was an untouched area. They basically opened up a new can of worms that neither the "Left" nor the "Right" sectors of the power structure was yet prepared to put under control.

If properly used, the feminist movement could have erased the false separation between men and women of all sexual persuasions. And with that lack of alienation and fear of each other, it could have been the beginning of a breaking down of a whole multitude of imposed differences.

When something so basic as women and men are separated, how are people going to get together? How will they get their real wants and needs if the sexes are constantly warring against each other? Society can be assured that they won't align and destroy the power-structure. But society being basically flexible and adapting, it altered the potential of the women's movement to merely define exploitation of one gender by the other in slightly different terms. It hasn't allowed women to break free of the slavery of the working class, but has only allowed some of them higher positions in the existing exploitative hierarchy.

Then as some of the female wage-slaves got higher-paying jobs, the power structure acted very quickly to prevent them from using the money to increase their freedom or meet their real wants and needs. Instead, it just created a new class of female consumers, reading magazines such as WOMAN'S WORLD or WORKING WOMAN, full of propaganda telling them that the best way to "achieve even more success in the world of business" is to squander their pay buying all the "correct" clothes, gadgets, etc. Women are becoming the strongest consuming market, and as such, the best way to reach them is through women's magazines that they unfortunately trust, which perpetuate themselves as being the choice of the new liberated woman. This very cleverly leads women from one form of slavery to another, and successfully blunts the possibilities that were opened with the onset of the women's movement.

I place the blame for allowing the power structure to do this on both men and women. The majority of "liberated" women refused to listen to the handful of truly radical feminists who tried to tell them that they were a new force going into a brave new world. Most feminists quickly became ripe fruit or "chickens" to well-practiced liars whose only goal was to use the real demands of women based on their needs and desires merely as an engine to bolster their own positions. This managed to diffuse the very real threat the women's movement offered if its possibilities and implications could be realized.

In this context, the male as submissive to the female is no great revolutionary gain, because it is the mere exchanging of two fundamentally impoverished roles. The way towards meaningful change is through the utter destruction of the concept of people, male or female, as merely fodder to fulfill roles. It doesn't really matter who has a measure of power over the other as long as the very nature of that authority is not questioned, understood, and canceled.

Do you think it really matters to the survival of this system which individual plays what role in perpetuating this society's existence? As long as we can be persuaded to participate in the extension of power, authority, and our own destruction as sovereign beings by accepting any offer of a share of power, a little place within the reigning hierarchy, all of us stand little chance of becoming ourselves on our terms and making our desires reality, rather than having our desires turned against us.

My strongest impression upon rereading the above is that this subject does, as the author says, open up many cans of worms: I find myself with a lot to say about almost every point discussed in it, and it does a good job of opening the door to future articles. The mysteries of sex, shamanism, S/M etc., are well-discussed issues at this present time. There are many good articles, magazines and books that go into such things in detail. If you want me to direct you to actual titles, just write and ask.

I am 100% pro choice, pro legalization of sex, drugs, and experimentation with one's own body, be it tattoos, piercings, prostitution, drug-induced vision quests, abortion, sterilization, or euthanasia. As long as we buy into the false reality that there is inherently something in men and women that cannot be shared and must be fought over, our society will take advantage of this and take it to any limits it can get away with economically and religiously.

We have no idea what life would be like without sexism. It is time in the nineties to just live as we are. To respond naturally as we are. To stop reacting to what we are not.

From THE SPIRITUAL REVOLUTIONARY issue #12

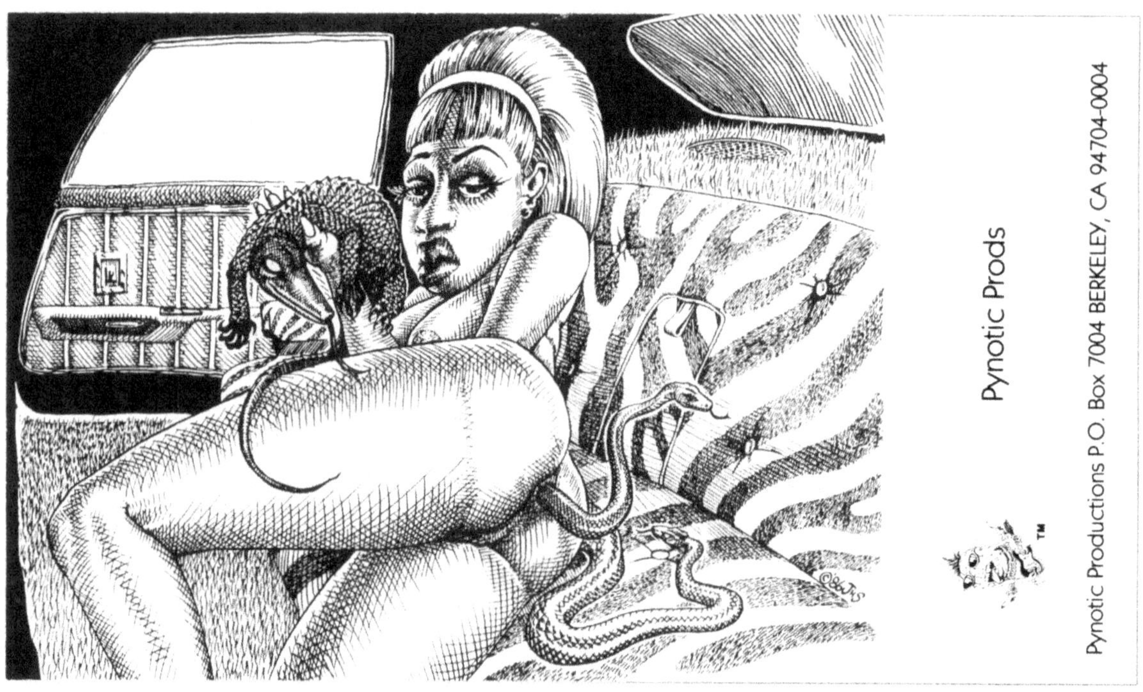

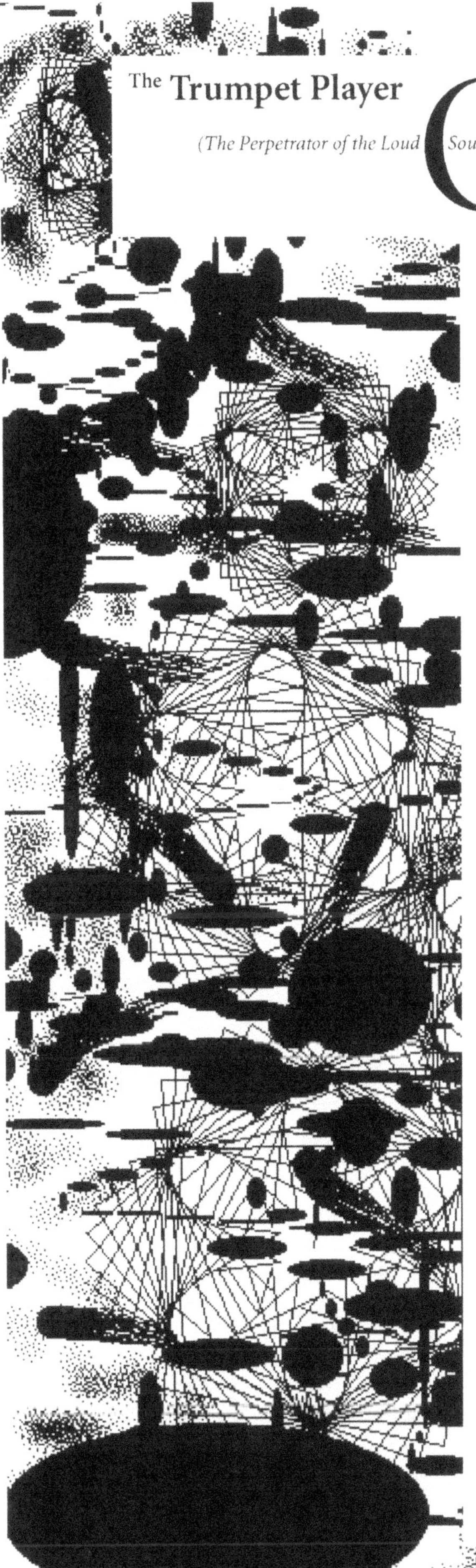

The Trumpet Player

(The Perpetrator of the Loud Sound)

One person playing a beautiful trumpet is
a universe
billions of years in the making
beginning as one invisible to the eye speck of energy,
expanding finally to nothingness (which would you prefer?)
or compressing, wise owl physicists call this one "crunch"
going backward in time, slurped up by the one tiny speck,
important YOU, and important ME, and history and galaxies
billions of humans, each a universe, valuable, complete and
immortal (as we see it)
connected, interdependent yet
uniquely alone, on a solo flight hurtling through space
at millions of miles per hour, not small...
HUGE and all encompassing, for everything known
is only what the eye filters
ONE ONLY.."human".."being", you interpret, perceive, create
and this puts you squarely in the center of the universe,
inescapably

ONE PERSON PLAYING A BEAUTIFUL TRUMPET

whether you play
humbly or grandly, you're IT for all practical purposes,
St. Francis, Mother Theresa, couldn't give their life away
by absorbing ten thousand and more, selflessly unable
to lose themselves, interpreting creating their lives,
at the center of the universe, inescapably..
and not small among billions, but HUGE and all encompassing through
perceiving, interpreting, creating, filtering, forming and squarely
in the center of the universe, inescapably.

ONE PERSON PLAYING A BEAUTIFUL TRUMPET

Billions of humans, each a universe
valuable, complete and immortal (as we see it)
connected, interdependent, seemingly
yet uniquely alone, on a solo flight hurtling through space

The Universe, billions of years in the making
began as one invisible to the eye
speck of energy...
that tiniest speck of energy
that infinitesimal speck of energy
was that speck...that energy..

the same perpetrator of the loud sound
in the beginning
in the beginning of the beginning (bang!)
was that speck..that energy...
and that loud sound
the same perpetrator?
the same trumpet player?

dorothy jesse beagle - 4/92

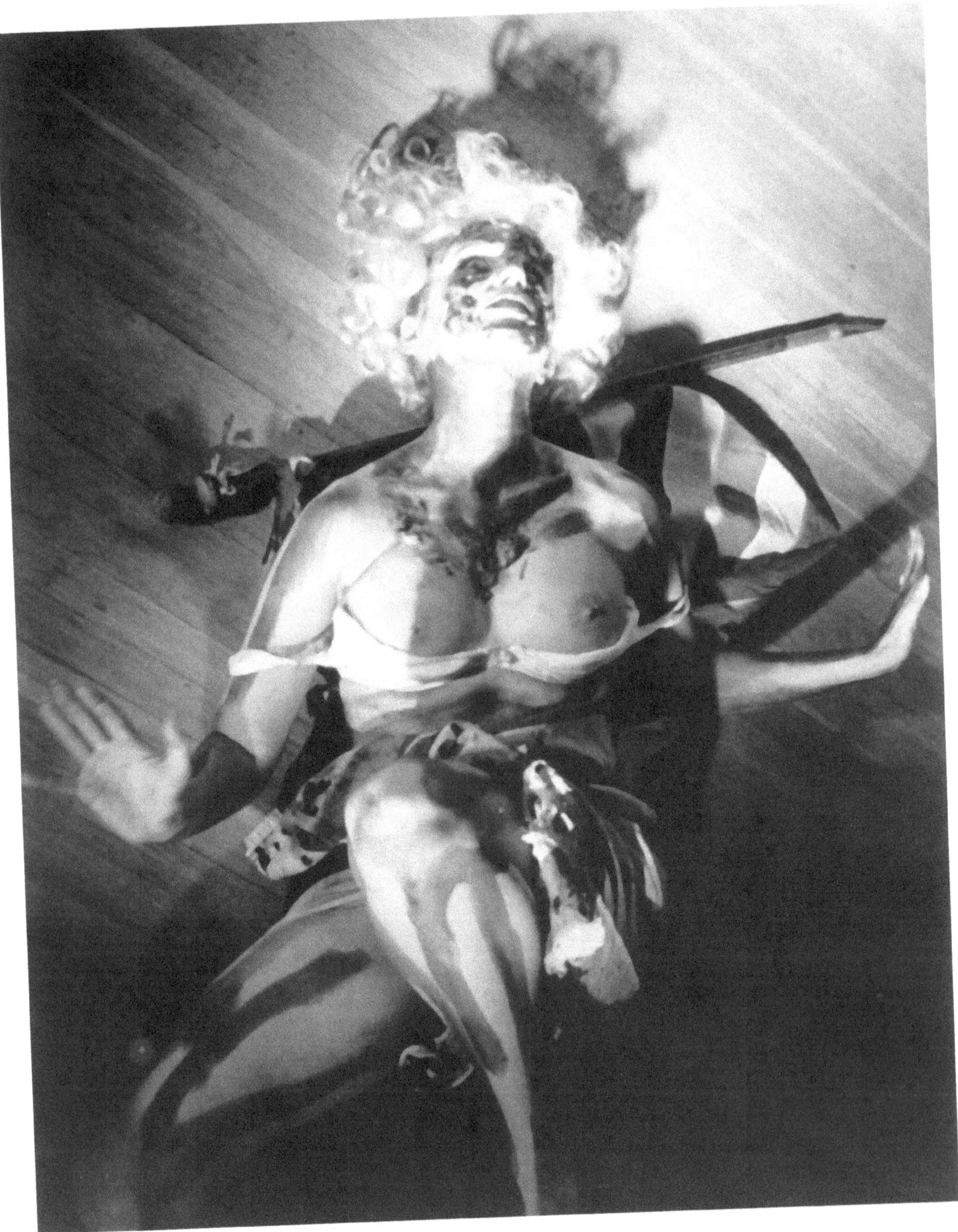

Linda Carmella Sibio *photo by Jan Deen*

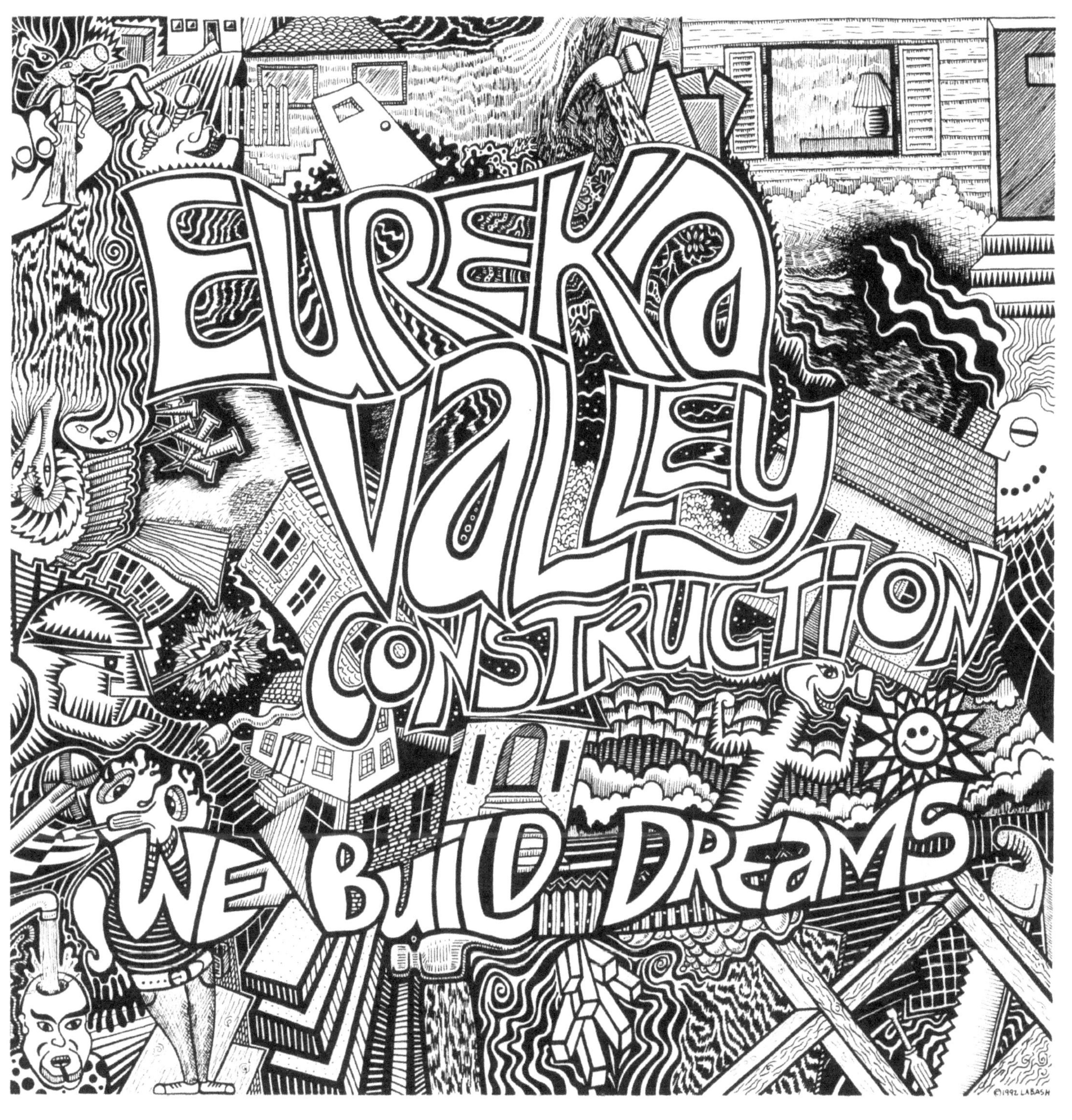
EUREKA
VALLEY
CONSTRUCTION
WE BUILD DREAMS
©1992 LABASH

Frank Moore's Philosophy of Art

The kind of art in which I am interested is art that causes change, that heals, that threatens, that unites, that subverts, that destroys limits and breaks taboos. I am not interested in doing art that comforts, decorates, entertains. In my performances, in my workshops, and in my lectures, I am trying to go back to the time when art was the magical, irrational, non-logical channel of active impact... when art was not just an object of passive viewing. I focus on live direct art for this end.

When we trace art to its primal roots, it combines with science & religion to form the primitive man's occult tool to influence both the natural and the super natural worlds. It involved both private and communal rituals with no audience except the gods and demons.

IN MY WORK, I TRY TO CREATE AN ENVIRONMENT IN WHICH THE LINE BETWEEN CONSCIOUSNESS AND THE SUBCONSCIOUS CAN BE TEMPORARILY ERASED, WHERE THE POWER OF TABOOS IS RELEASED SO THAT PERSONAL AND SOCIAL CHANGE CAN BE MAGICALLY INDUCED. THE ARTIST IN THIS INTENSELY INTIMATE WORK IS A CONDUCTOR FOCUSING AND GUIDING THE RITUAL FORCES. THIS IS AN AVANT-GARDE ART, A REVOLUTIONARY ART.

IN THIS KIND OF ART, MY BODY GIVES ME A DEFINITE ADVANTAGE. IT LINKS ME TO THE WOUNDED HEALER, THE DEFORMED SHAMAN. BY COMBINING THIS WITH PERFORMANCE TACTICS, I COMBINE REALITIES TO CREATE AWAKE DREAMS.

OF COURSE, MY KIND OF ART IS NOT MASS MEDIA, TRENDY OR FASHIONABLE. IT IS JUST IDEALISTIC... DEFINITELY NOT A MONEY-MAKER.

BUT I HAVE ALWAYS THOUGHT ART SHOULD BE A CALLING, NOT A CAREER.

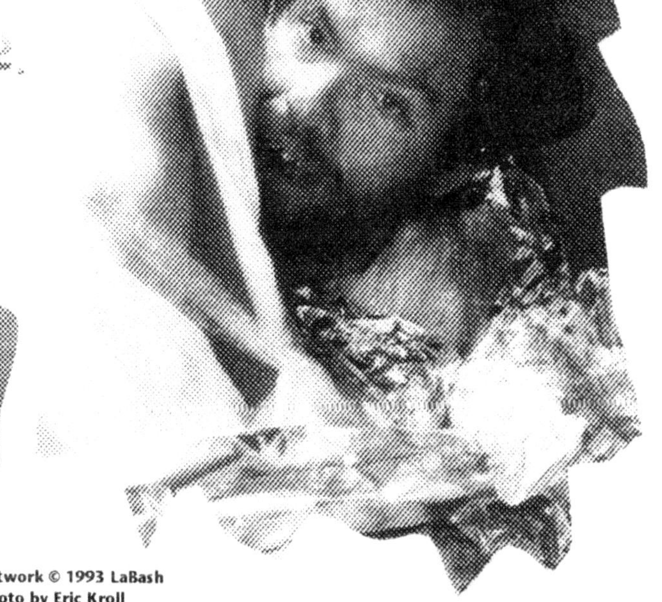

Artwork © 1993 LaBash
Photo by Eric Kroll

VIDEO BY frank moore

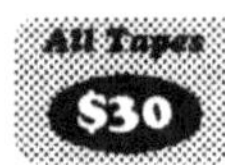

fairy tales can come true

THIS IS A FILM ABOUT RELATIONSHIPS AND DISABILITY STARRING FRANK MOORE, WHO HAS BEEN DISABLED SINCE BIRTH WITH CEREBRAL PALSY. IT IS A HUMOROUS, YET REALISTIC LOOK AT HOW TO ESTABLISH RELATIONSHIPS BY CHANGING NEGATIVE SELF IMAGE.

copyrighted 1981 *35 minutes*

erotic play

THIS VIDEO EXPLORES WHAT HAPPENS WHEN PEOPLE OF ALL TYPES AND AGES ARE GIVEN A CHANCE TO RETURN TO BEING A KID AGAIN. A SIMPLE GAME OF DRESS-UP BECOMES A POWERFUL METAPHOR FOR DROPPING TABOOS, RELEASING CREATIVE EMOTION, AND FOR DRAMATIC CHANGE. AS A RESULT, AN INNOCENT EROTICISM IS FOUND... AS WELL AS GETTING INTIMATE WITH 60 HUMANS.

copyrighted 1983 *84 minutes*

outrageous dream

A SURREAL, VISUAL POEM OF FOUND IMAGES.

copyrighted 1984 *41 minutes*

the nude cave

AN EROTIC, SURREALISTIC VIDEO DREAM THAT COMBINES NON-LINEAR IMAGES AND FRANK'S ORIGINAL MUSIC SCORE.

copyrighted 1984 *113 minutes*

out of isolation

A SURREAL EROTIC EXAMINATION OF AN INTIMATE RELATIONSHIP OF NEED. STARRING FRANK MOORE AND LINDA SIBEO.

copyrighted 1989 *105 minutes*

the outrageous beauty revue

THIS RAW VIDEO DOCUMENTS THE TACKY, MUSICAL, OVER-THE-EDGE COMEDY REVUE THAT FRANK CREATED, DIRECTED AND PERFORMED IN. THE SHOW RAN ON A WEEKLY BASIS FOR THREE AND ONE HALF YEARS AT THE MABUHAY GARDENS IN SAN FRANCISCO IN ADDITION TO A NUMBER OF OTHER NORTHERN CALIFORNIA AND NEVADA PERFORMANCES. FRANK PERFORMED ALONG WITH THE THIRTY PEOPLE WHO MADE UP HIS THEATRE GROUP, "the theatre of human melting."

copyrighted 1980 *approx. 30 minutes*

chero collage

ATTEMPTS TO CAPTURE THE TRANCE STATE OF LIVE, SHAMANISTIC PERFORMANCE COMBINING FOOTAGE OF SEVERAL OF chero company's RITUALS INTO A REALITY-WARPING VIDEO.

copyrighted 1992 *27 minutes*

the outrageous horror show

A LIVE CABARET SHOW THAT BREAKS THROUGH THE LIMITING TABOOS, THROUGH MESSY NIGHTMARES, INTO THE DREAMS OF ALL POSSIBILITIES.

copyrighted 1992 *32 minutes*

To order call or write: **inter-relations, p.o. box 11445, berkeley, CA 94701-2445 (510)526-7858**

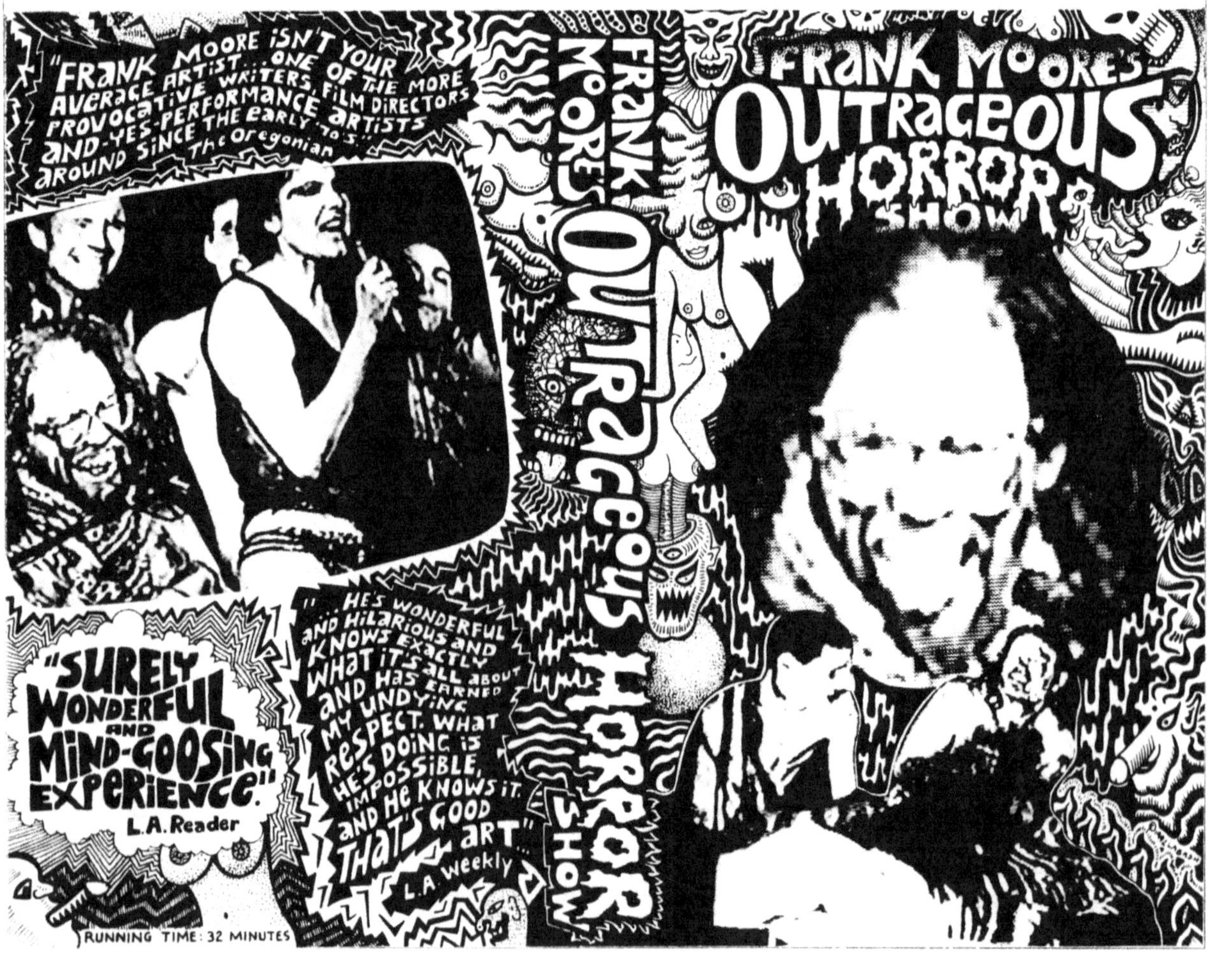

"FRANK MOORE ISN'T YOUR AVERAGE ARTIST... ONE OF THE MORE PROVOCATIVE WRITERS, FILM DIRECTORS AND-YES-PERFORMANCE ARTISTS AROUND SINCE THE EARLY '70'S." The Oregonian

FRANK MOORE'S OUTRAGEOUS HORROR SHOW

FRANK MOORE'S OUTRAGEOUS HORROR SHOW

"SURELY WONDERFUL AND MIND-GOOSING EXPERIENCE." L.A. Reader

"... HE'S WONDERFUL AND HILARIOUS AND KNOWS EXACTLY WHAT IT'S ALL ABOUT AND HAS EARNED MY UNDYING RESPECT. WHAT HE'S DOING IS IMPOSSIBLE, AND HE KNOWS IT. THAT'S GOOD ART"... L.A. weekly

RUNNING TIME: 32 MINUTES

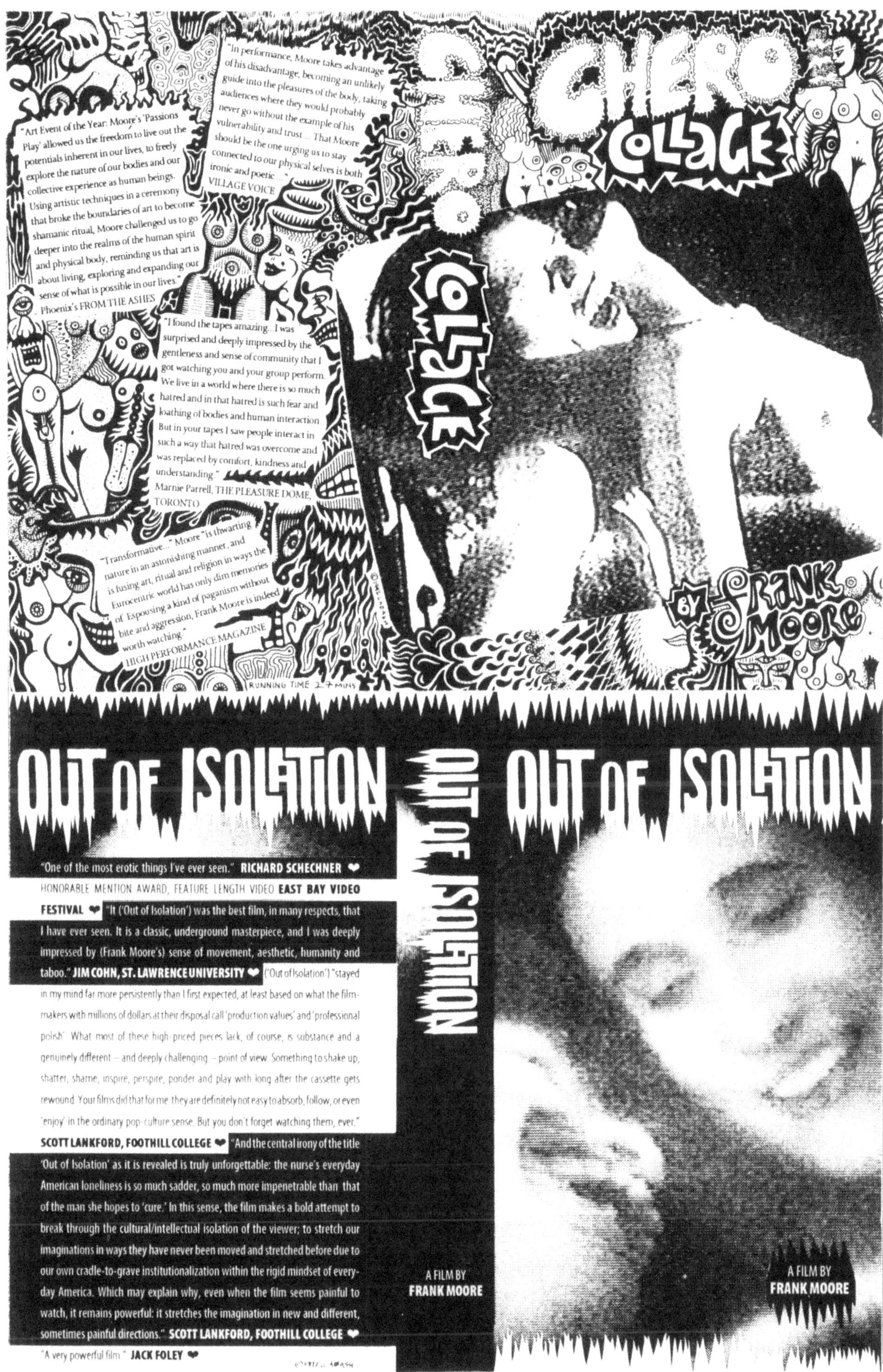
"In performance, Moore takes advantage of his disadvantage, becoming an unlikely guide into the pleasures of the body, taking audiences where they would probably never go without the example of his vulnerability and trust ... That Moore should be the one urging us to stay connected to our physical selves is both ironic and poetic ..."
VILLAGE VOICE
CHERO
COLLAGE
"Art Event of the Year: Moore's 'Passions Play' allowed us the freedom to live out the potentials inherent in our lives, to freely explore the nature of our bodies and our collective experience as human beings. Using artistic techniques in a ceremony that broke the boundaries of art to become shamanic ritual, Moore challenged us to go deeper into the realms of the human spirit and physical body, reminding us that art is about living, exploring and expanding our sense of what is possible in our lives."
Phoenix's FROM THE ASHES
COLLAGE
"I found the tapes amazing...I was surprised and deeply impressed by the gentleness and sense of community that I got watching you and your group perform. We live in a world where there is so much hatred and in that hatred is such fear and loathing of bodies and human interaction. But in your tapes I saw people interact in such a way that hatred was overcome and was replaced by comfort, kindness and understanding."
Marnie Parrell, THE PLEASURE DOME, TORONTO
"Transformative..." Moore "is thwarting nature in an astonishing manner, and is fusing art, ritual and religion in ways the Eurocentric world has only dim memories of. Espousing a kind of paganism without bite and aggression, Frank Moore is indeed worth watching."
HIGH PERFORMANCE MAGAZINE
by Frank Moore
RUNNING TIME 27 MINS
OUT OF ISOLATION
"One of the most erotic things I've ever seen." RICHARD SCHECHNER ❤ HONORABLE MENTION AWARD, FEATURE LENGTH VIDEO EAST BAY VIDEO FESTIVAL ❤ "It ('Out of Isolation') was the best film, in many respects, that I have ever seen. It is a classic, underground masterpiece, and I was deeply impressed by (Frank Moore's) sense of movement, aesthetic, humanity and taboo." JIM COHN, ST. LAWRENCE UNIVERSITY ❤ ('Out of Isolation') "stayed in my mind far more persistently than I first expected, at least based on what the film-makers with millions of dollars at their disposal call 'production values' and 'professional polish.' What most of these high-priced pieces lack, of course, is substance and a genuinely different – and deeply challenging – point of view. Something to shake up, shatter, shame, inspire, perspire, ponder and play with long after the cassette gets rewound. Your films did that for me: they are definitely not easy to absorb, follow, or even 'enjoy' in the ordinary pop-culture sense. But you don't forget watching them, ever." SCOTT LANKFORD, FOOTHILL COLLEGE ❤ "And the central irony of the title 'Out of Isolation' as it is revealed is truly unforgettable: the nurse's everyday American loneliness is so much sadder, so much more impenetrable than that of the man she hopes to 'cure.' In this sense, the film makes a bold attempt to break through the cultural/intellectual isolation of the viewer; to stretch our imaginations in ways they have never been moved and stretched before due to our own cradle-to-grave institutionalization within the rigid mindset of every-day America. Which may explain why, even when the film seems painful to watch, it remains powerful: it stretches the imagination in new and different, sometimes painful directions." SCOTT LANKFORD, FOOTHILL COLLEGE ❤
"A very powerful film." JACK FOLEY ❤
OUT OF ISOLATION
A FILM BY
FRANK MOORE
OUT OF ISOLATION
A FILM BY
FRANK MOORE

BOOKS & ZINES

BY **frank moore**

To order call or write:
inter-relations, p.o.box 11445
berkeley, ca 94701-2445
(510) 526 7858

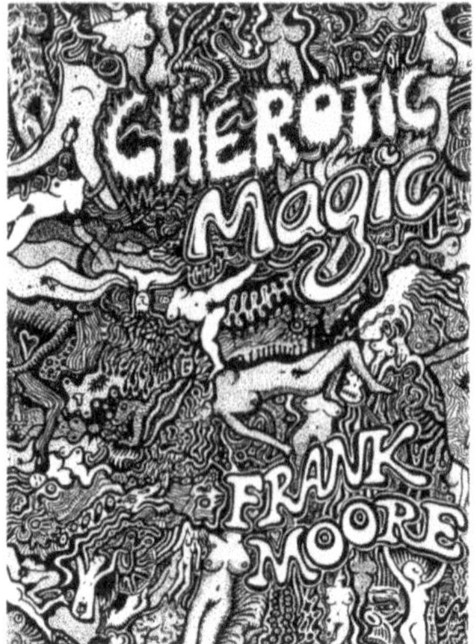

cherotic magic **$15**

A MAJOR ATTEMPT TO INTRODUCE A POWERFUL SYSTEM OF MAGIC INTO OUR MODERN WESTERN EVERYDAY LIFE, THEREBY EXPLOSIVELY EXPANDING SUCH CONCEPTS AS SEX, HUMAN RELATIONSHIPS. THE CLEAR, DOWN-TO-EARTH TEXT IS AMPLIFIED BY THE NON-LINEAR TRANCE ILLUSTRATIONS BY LABASH.

published 1990

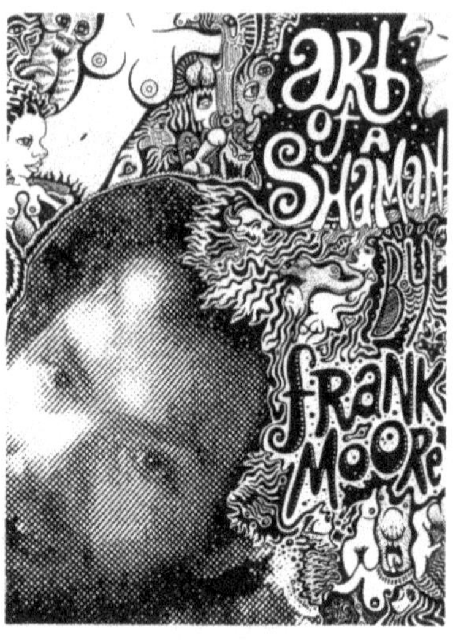

art of a shaman **$4**

IN art of a shaman, ORIGINALLY A LECTURE PRESENTED AT N.Y.U., FRANK MOORE EXPLORES PERFORMANCE AND ART IN GENERAL TERMS OF THEM BEING A MAGICAL WAY TO EFFECT CHANGE IN THE WORLD. HE LOOKS AT PERFORMANCE AS AN ART OF MELTING ACTION, RITUALISTIC, SHAMANISTIC DOINGS/PLAYINGS. BY USING HIS CAREER AND LIFE AS A "BASELINE", MOORE EXPLAINS THE DYNAMIC PLAYING WITHIN THE CONTEXT OF REALITY SHAPING. HE BRINGS IN CONCEPTS FROM MODERN PHYSICS, MYTHOLOGY, AND PSYCHOLOGY. COVER BY LABASH.

published 1991

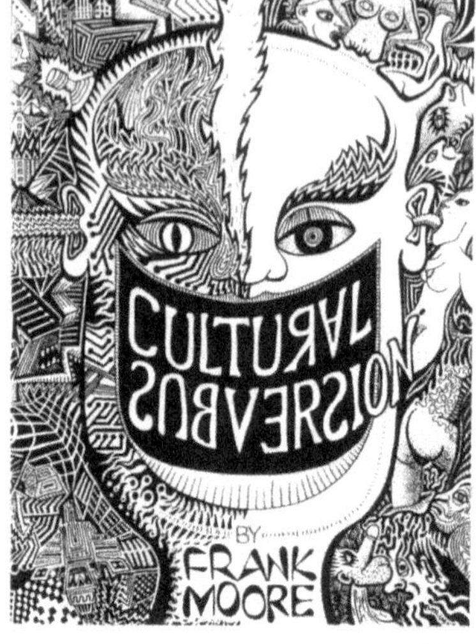

cultural subversion **$1**

PERSONAL, ANARCHICAL TECHNOLOGIES SUCH AS XEROGRAPHY, VCR, FAXS, ETC., ARE EXAMINED IN cultural subversion BY FRANK MOORE AS THE MEANS BY WHICH ORDINARY PEOPLE CAN TAKE BACK THE CONTROL OF COMMUNICATIONS AND CREATIVITY FROM THE CENTRAL POWER COMBINE.

published 1992

art of living **$10**

A GUIDE TO DOWN-TO-EARTH SPIRITUALITY AS CHANNELLED BY FRANK MOORE.

published 1987

the cherotic revolutionary A MAGAZINE ABOUT THE EDGE.

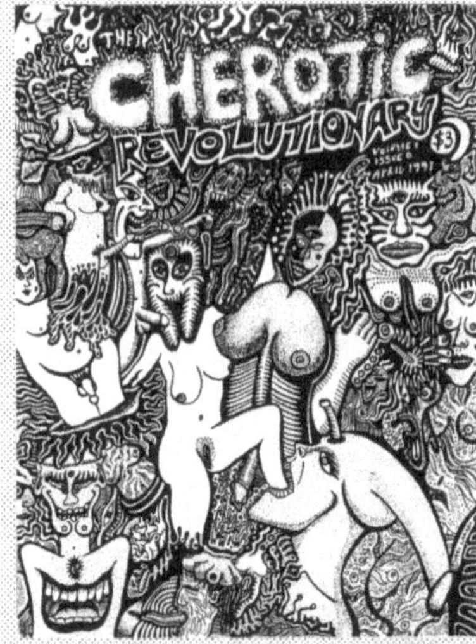

issue #0, *april 1991* **$3**

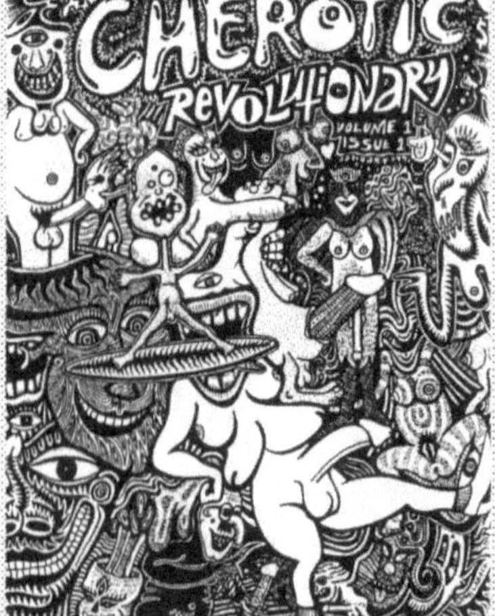

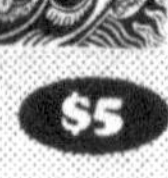

issue #1, *january 1992* **$5**

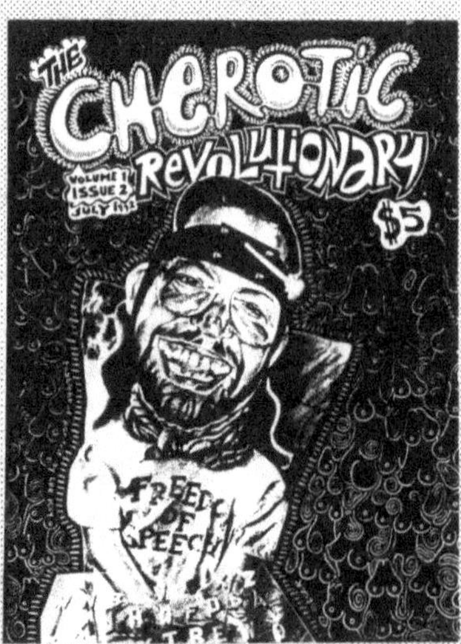

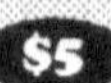

issue #2, *july 1992* **$5**

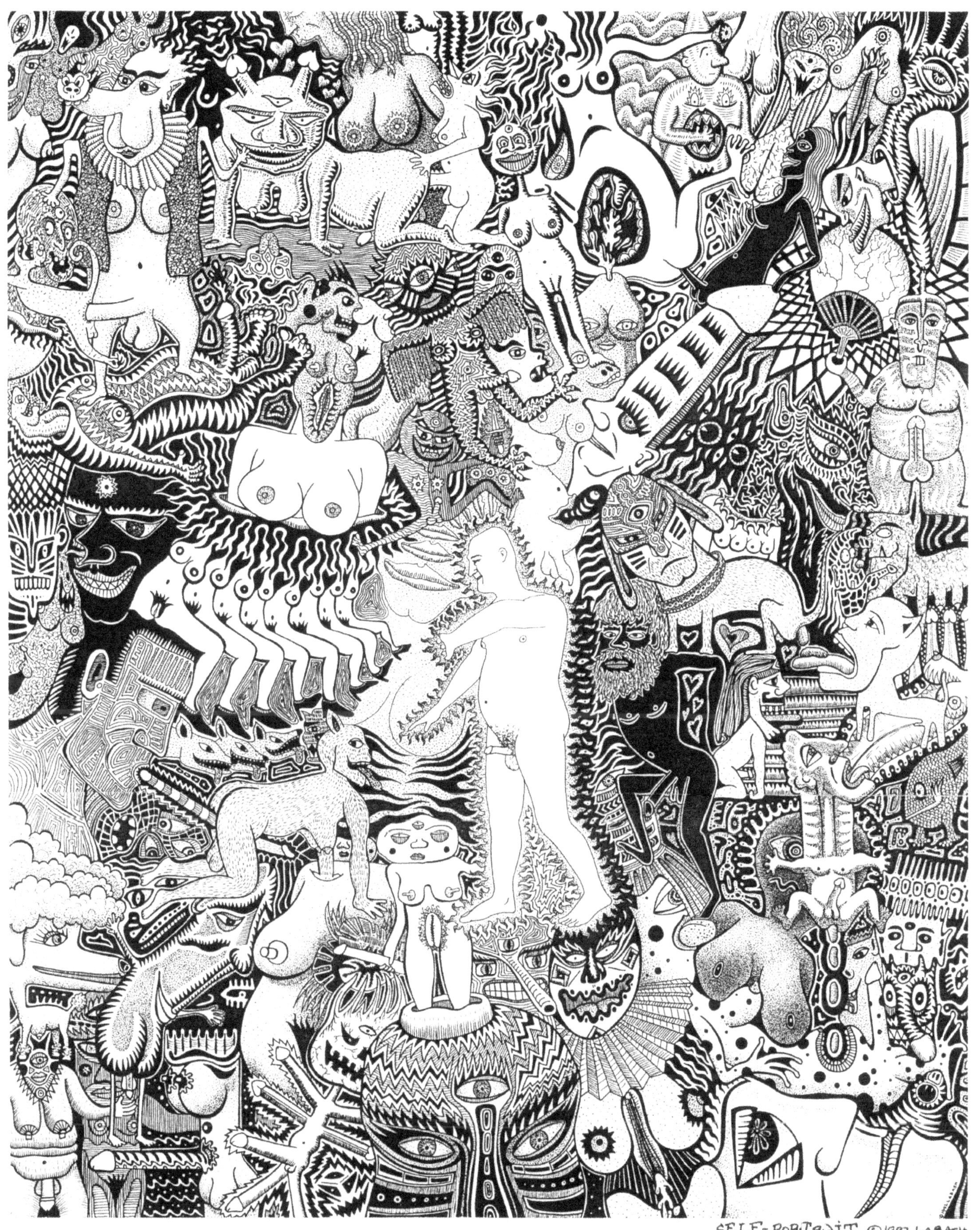

SELF-PORTRAIT ©1992 LABASH

REVIEWS

The Cherotic rEvolutionary #3
April 1993

"Since 1980, Frank Moore has been creating and carving a niche of his own within a creative artistic and literary community at one time traditionally reserved for others. His journey of self-identification & self-discovery as unique statements are documented not only in his fine collection of revolutionary, subversive, anarchical, magical videos, books and 'zines but now he (and Linda Mac) have been very busy again, producing and marketing The Cherotic Revolutionary, "a 'zine (according to Frank) about 'The Edge' for and by people on The Edge... if not over The Edge." With this issue we learn that TCR has not only gone through a major transformation desktop publishing/production-wise (MAC computer/laser printer) but Shaman Frank has made mega-progress in terms of his legitimate acceptance into the elite magikal inner circle of high profile "name" ex-porn industry stars turned performance artists! This magnificently stark black/white issue includes unique articles (and art) of & by Veronica Vera; photos & art of/by Annie Sprinkle; a 1982 photo of Veronica by Robert Mapplethorpe; artwork by LaBash and Lee Kay; poetry by Merle Tofer; & contributions by long-time supporters such as Luna Sanguine (writing) as well as Jan Deen, Richard Silvarnes, Wink Van Kempen, Marc Trunz, Amy Ardrey (photos), Dorothy Jesse Beagle (poetry), Dixi Cohn (poetry), etc... For those EIDOS readers who have never heard of Frank Moore, here's a brief excerpt about Frank written by Annie Sprinkle from her book, Post Porn Modernist (Torch, 1991):

> **"My Formal Sex Teachers"**
> I've learned something from every sexual encounter. Many people have contributed to my knowledge, but there are several in particular from whom I've learned major things. Frank Moore is a unique performance artist, teacher, writer, painter and philosopher. He taught me to love my body exactly the way it is. Frank has cerebral palsy, and can't walk. He doesn't have any control over his arms, he can't feed himself or go to the bathroom without help. He spells out his thoughts on a letter board by using a pointer attached to his leather headband. Although he lives in a wheelchair, he manages to accomplish many things, including having a very erotic sex life. He teaches what he calls "Eroplay", which is basically getting naked with a person or group, touching and playing sensuously, making it "sexual" but not quite. It's innocent & childlike. Eroplay is about energy, not genitals."

Whether TCR is revolutionary, evolutionary, on or over the Edge; or a liberating personal statement that, like a point on a time line, describes & defines his own personal relativism & the relativity of the entire range of his lifework to other artists and the world at large, Frank Moore deserves our unequivocal respect, love and support."
EIDOS Magazine, Volume 7, Number 2

REVIEWS CONTINUED...

"Here is a zine that almost defies description..."
Maximum RocknRoll, July 1993

"Frank Moore is the inspirational figure behind this whole work associating himself with very liberated public figures on the more intimate scene expressing their challenging stand towards the more constricted societal values."
The Affiliate, November 1993

"Sex in all its variations interpreted throughout stories, poems, drawings, and photographs."
Factsheet 5, #48

"The CHEROTIC REVOLUTIONARY is an important voice in any dialogue re: the relationship between sexuality and spirituality. Published/edited by renown performance artist Frank Moore, Linda Mac and friends, discussion here is pointed, an engaging read, instructive and more. The latest issue (Vol. 1, #3) contains contributions from Veronica Vera ('Glory! Glory hole-leluhia'), Annie Sprinkle and Luna Sanguine with a Situationist's take on the S & M sex industry. (There's also a piece from Frank himself, wherein he traces performance art and his own work's lineage back to its primal roots, when art combined 'with science and religion to form the primitive man's occult tool to influence both the natural and super natural worlds.' Whew! Plus: poetry, manifestos and some really awesome pen & ink art by the one and only LaBash."
Randy Lee Payton, the ROC

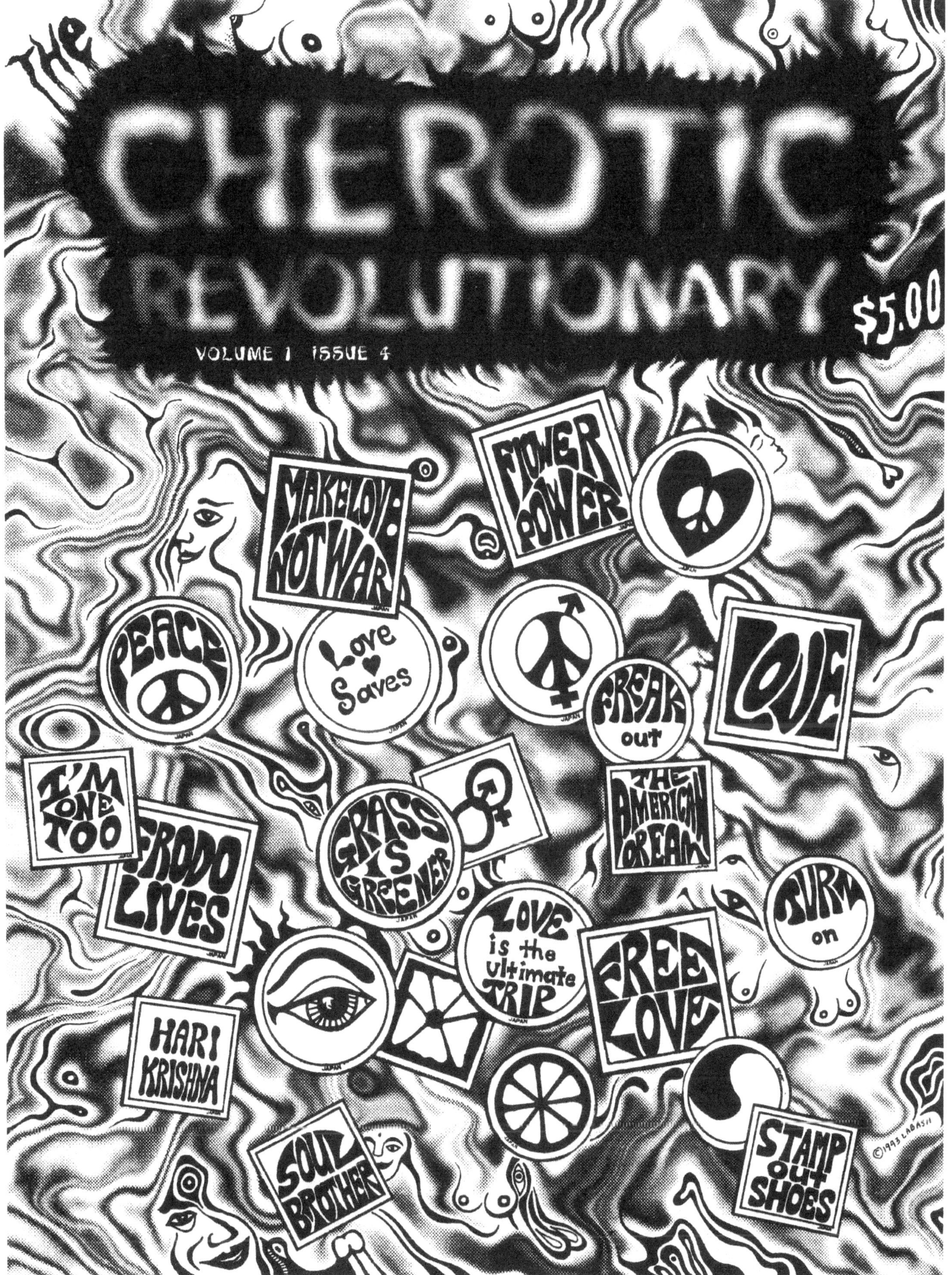
THE
CHEROTIC
REVOLUTIONARY
$5.00
VOLUME 1 ISSUE 4
MAKE LOVE NOT WAR
FLOWER POWER
PEACE
Love Saves
LOVE
FREAK out
I'M ONE TOO
FRODO LIVES
GRASS IS GREENER
THE AMERICAN DREAM
TURN on
LOVE is the ultimate TRIP
FREE LOVE
HARI KRISHNA
SOUL BROTHER
STAMP out SHOES
©1993 LABASII

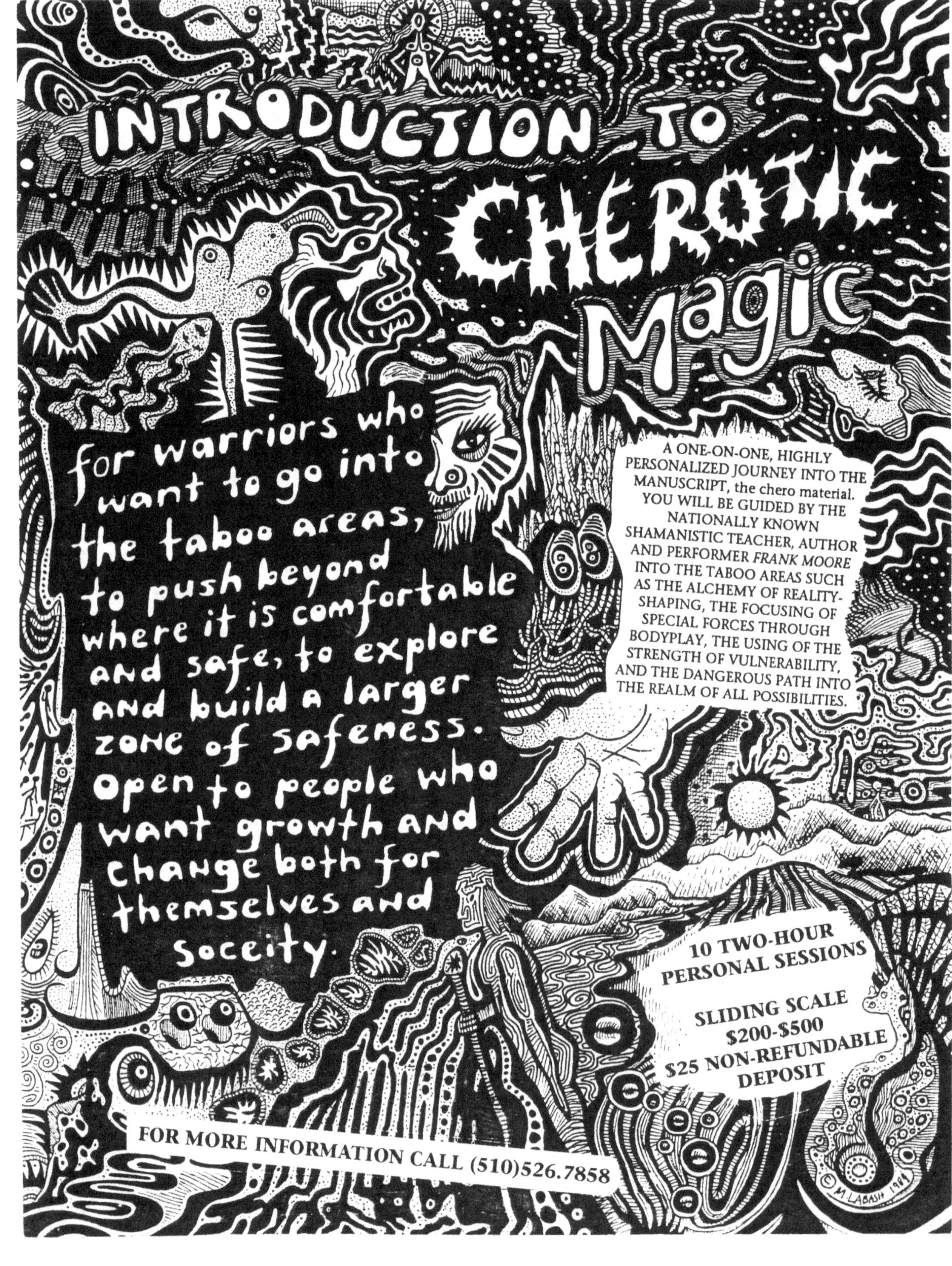
INTRODUCTION TO
CHEROTIC
Magic
for warriors who want to go into the taboo areas, to push beyond where it is comfortable and safe, to explore and build a larger zone of safeness. Open to people who want growth and change both for themselves and soceity.
A ONE-ON-ONE, HIGHLY PERSONALIZED JOURNEY INTO THE MANUSCRIPT, the chero material. YOU WILL BE GUIDED BY THE NATIONALLY KNOWN SHAMANISTIC TEACHER, AUTHOR AND PERFORMER FRANK MOORE INTO THE TABOO AREAS SUCH AS THE ALCHEMY OF REALITY-SHAPING, THE FOCUSING OF SPECIAL FORCES THROUGH BODYPLAY, THE USING OF THE STRENGTH OF VULNERABILITY, AND THE DANGEROUS PATH INTO THE REALM OF ALL POSSIBILITIES.
10 TWO-HOUR PERSONAL SESSIONS
SLIDING SCALE
$200-$500
$25 NON-REFUNDABLE DEPOSIT
FOR MORE INFORMATION CALL (510)526.7858
© M. LABASH 1991

The Cherotic rEvolutionary

The Cherotic rEvolutionary is a zine about "The Edge" for and by people on The Edge.... if not over The Edge.

TCR is published by Inter-Relations. The publishers/editors are Frank Moore and Linda Mac. The art editor is Michael LaBash, and the circulation manager is Alexi Malenky.

The price for this issue is $5.00 per copy. We don't sell subscriptions, to avoid tying ourselves down to a rigid publication schedule or magazine size. We want to remain free to publish frequently or larger issues at longer intervals and adjust the price accordingly.

We heartily encourage letters of comment from readers and will answer as many as we can. Please tell us if you don't want us to print material from your letter – otherwise we will assume it's OK.

Please address all correspondence and orders for magazines to:

Frank Moore
P.O. Box 11445
Berkeley, CA 94701-2445

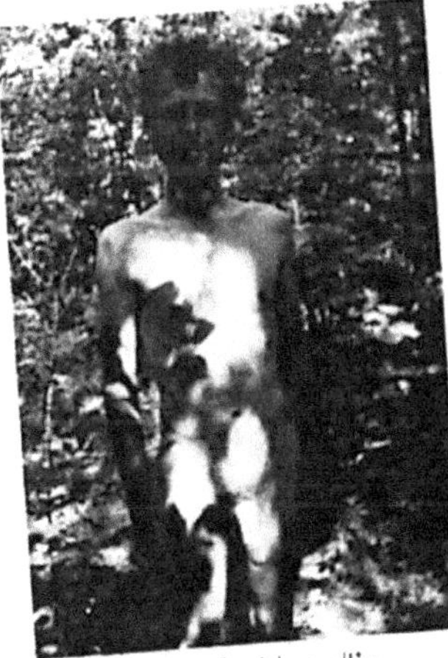

James david audlin
chief distant eagle

T.C.(R).'S AD POLICY
Recently we have recieved several inquiries about how to buy ads in The Cherotic (R)evolutionary. Although we are not actively seeking such ads, we are not precluding them either. However, we will judge whether or not to accept an ad.

T.C.(R). is a xeroxed, black and white zine that is published irregularly...if we are lucky, twice a year. So it is not the place for fancy color ads or for ads with time deadlines. On the other hand, T.C.(R). magically finds its way around the world.

TO SUBMIT AN AD
Send us a copy of your ad and a S.A.S.E. If we accept it, we send you the rate for your ad...and if we need anything from you such as half-tones, we will tell you. If we don't accept it, we will send your ad back.

AD RATES
Sliding scale: $10-$50 per quarter of a standard typing page. The scale slides according to our whim.

HOW WE ACCEPT AN AD
Our whim also is a big factor in accepting an ad. Another factor is the other contents of the particular issue. And there maybe other factors which are unknown even to us.

FREE T.C.(R). COPIES
Because we are not actively looking for paid ads, we do not give free copies to would-be advertisers. But we encourage them to buy a back issue or two. However, we do give you a free copy of the issue in which your ad appears.

Frank Moore
November 12, 1993

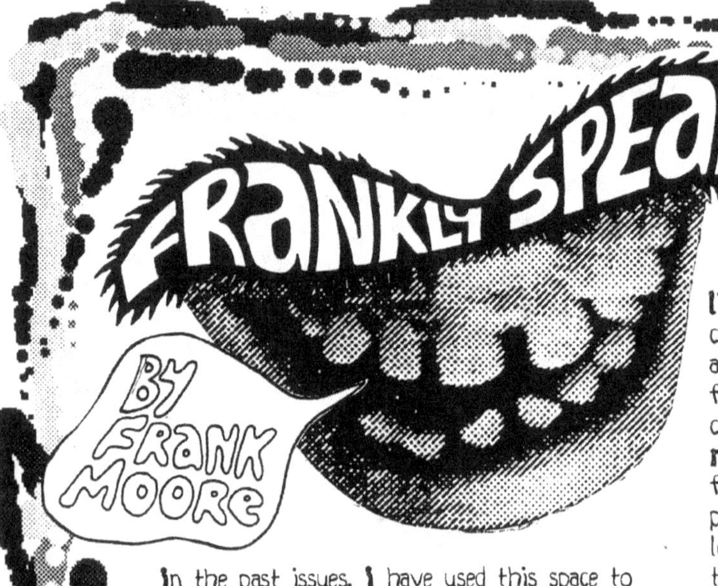

In the past issues, I have used this space to introduce you to the artists and the writers in the particular issue. But in this issue, there are simply too many for me to do that. And besides their work should and does stand on its own. Most of the people in this issue ... and we are honored to be able to present them to you ... have their own books in the underground. If I were you, I would seek these books out.

I need to thank Urban Ore of Berkeley, California for giving us a deal on the collection of original 60's rubber stamps which Labash used in our cover collage. Thanks also to Wendy Gunderson of Imagick, Ltd., P.O. Box 405, Ledyard CT 06339 for the 50+ rubber stamp-images which Labash used in our back cover collage. If I were you, I would send away for her catalog of rubber stamps.

Wendy and I, along with Joanna Pettit and Jim Audlin, are a part of a community of friends that uses the Genie computer network as its means of communication and cultural subversion. My e-mail address on Genie is f.moore7. I would love to hear from you directly. But old-fashioned letters are great too ...!

Now that we have gotten the business out of the way.... let me ramble and rant for the rest of the page. It has been amazing how this zine has found its way around the world, being distributed by Tower Books and Fine Print, getting all kinds of kind words in reviews, etc. ... all without our trying. It is a cause of concern ... are we getting too slick, too acceptable ... are we, god forbid, politically correct ... or to use the more politically correct term for politically correct ... are we culturally sensitive? Is there a worse fate? like being undead. It did not help our self-confidence getting "friendly" letters from advertizing agencies and record companies asking for our ad rates and for free copies (how cheap can they get?). What do we look like ... Rolling Stone? Then there were letters from print shops specializing in "alternative publications", trying to woo us away from our local xerox place. We had already resisted the temptation to raise our prices after signing the distribution deal. What was this force trying to make our little zine into a **real magazine** Where did we go wrong?

Then I forced myself to calm down. I forced myself to remember the good things. I remembered that the anti-liberation post-feminists go through each issue ... and especially the Labash drawings ... counting tits, pussies, and cocks ... and always getting offended by the number. You know the ones ... the ones who can't see that separatism, racism, and sexism are the same thing ... the ones who are misusing Annie Sprinkle's work to support their isolation ... the ones with chips on their shoulders and between their legs.

I was feeling better. Then I remembered that some "gay" bookstores will not carry T.C.(r) because it is not "queer enough"! It doesn't matter that about eighty percent of our contributors consider themselves gay or bi. It doesn't matter that some of the works focus directly on "gay" reality. It doesn't matter that T.C.(r.) has always been included in the queer zine scene. And it does not matter that I am a lesbian in a male body.

I was now feeling really good. Then I remembered what a male reader wrote. He said he liked the zine ... and Annie Sprinkle's tits .... but why did I have all these women writers and artists in it? "Face it," he said, "women don't have the balls to write good sex!" If he said that around the women who are in the zine, he might not have his balls for long!

Yes, I was feeling great now. If we offend all the hues of separatist/sexist/elitist thinking which limit freedom with political correctness ... well, we must be doing something right! We can sleep good.

EROPLAY IS FUN

Warm Silk

by Carol A. Queen

My skin feels like buttered silk after I come. I run my hands over my belly, my thighs which are still pulsing and aching as if I'd run up several flights of stairs, and I swear I've never had anything so wonderful under my hands as this glowing expanse of my skin.

What I love about getting turned on when I'm alone is that it sneaks up on me. I run around all day, busy and maddened. I slump into a stolen few hours of solitude at the end, too tired to return phone calls, much less think about watching sexy videos or open dirty novels or pull the Hitachi out from under the bed. Far too tired to think about sex.

Yet I've been thinking about sex all day.

Every bus shelter poster of k d lang or Roger Craig I drove past today. Every short skirt and every luscious set of buns in bike shorts. Every sparkly-eyed girl or guy I waited on in the store; every tattoo, pierced lip (or nose), pointy-toed boot, fishnet-stockinged leg, leather jacket, every tight dress, every pair of jeans faded where the cock rests or rises, every hole in a pair of jeans, especially where the white warp-threads lattice and half-cover the skin underneath; every red-painted mouth, the darker the better, and red-lacquered nail, especially short ones; every curve of breast or curve of muscle under skin, in fact every curve; every pair of young lovers or old lovers or any sort in-between in any gender combination, with extra points if the gender's indistinguishable; every teenaged boy trying to hide his hard-on, catholic schoolgirl who's hiked her skirt up or put on lacy tights, boy's ear pierced by one gold ring, black lace bra peeking.

And at home! Too tired to notice the piles of books and magazines with contents devoted to sex, lingerie spilling out of drawers like it's trying to come alive, piles of pearly-cunted seashells which I scatter around, all these femmey, flowery curtains; four kinds of lube, an antique Roseville dish full of condoms (four kinds of those too), and a box of sex toys that'd get me busted in Texas (and lots more in the closet): a set of steer horns, gleaming,

pointed and priapic, red candles and ostrich feathers and my old white-enameled wrought iron bed with enough bars to tie two or three people up to, not to mention the big mirror situated next to it, all the scenes it's seen; and all the pictures - of my lover (now and when he was a little boy), of my ex-lover when she was a little girl, holding the stuffed tiger she used to masturbate on, of my adolescent friend who's not old enough to think about but I do anyway; of a turn-of-the-century dancehall girl with a big snake, a young leatherman with a snake, Gustav Klimt's "Water Serpents," two lovers twined around each other like snakes; of Madonna, Marilyn Monroe, the Virgin Mary, and angels with their wings mightily unfurled, and French whores and antique lingerie and old pinup girls; women in sailor suits who look like sisters but were probably lovers, holding hands in 1919, sisters photographed by Imogen Cunningham which I bought at the Art Museum gift shop because their small breasts and curved bellies look just like mine though the shutter snapped in 1920, the year my mother was born; Betty Dodson's muscled couple fucking that people always think are both men (that's why I bought it); and of course my Dad, debonair in his officer's clothes and thin moustache who can be sexy now because he's dead and anyway the photo's from 15 years before I was born.

And somehow it still surprises me when I find in my fatigue that I can't sleep, that the pillow feels too hot on my cheek, and I toss and turn. What I love about this turn-on is how my body won't let me forget I've seen all those things today, a thousand sex-signifiers that my mind has stored and my flesh and blood remember.

So when I finally run my hands over my skin I find I am already releasing into little tension-orgasms, not real comes but little flurries of shaking at the relief of my touch, and if I kept this up I would drive myself crazy: the more I touch everywhere else, the more my pussy wants it. (Sometimes this starts with me beginning to think about, no, just be aware of, my asshole, and before long my body is a writhing snake with my asshole as its hungry mouth and nothing will satisfy me except to slide something in and fuck myself slowly, at first, as I can stand, as hard and fast, then, as I can manage with my hands tense and trembling - but not tonight.)

Tonight my clit is hard already and insistent. My clit wants it. My skin is prickly in a lush way; my body is full of tension, the sex-tension so intertwined with the city-traffic-tension and too-many-phone-calls-to-make-tension and I'm-on-deadline-but-I-can't-

think-tension that I can't separate it and all I can do is let it all work together.

I can reach my vibrator without turning on the lamp. Car headlights cut flickering beams across the wall. I raise my knees under the blanket, make a tent for the Hitachi, switch it on. At first buzz my heels dig into the sheets and the muscles in my arm pump like I'm weightlifting. Then I relax into the vibration, descending into a valley before I start to climb.

The vibrator is on my clit as a tease. I don't come that way; I want my cunt full, if not with cock or fingers then with a zucchini or a dildo or my dad's old hairbrush handle. I used to fuck the strangest things before I discovered sex toys - protruding knobs on furniture, anything. I love the wave of crazy horniness that washes over me when I'm alone, separate from any love or lust I feel for a woman or a man, that makes me want to straddle bedposts. I love the frantic attempt to incorporate the whole world into my cunt, a juicy itch that can't possibly be scratched from the outside.

Tonight I fish in my toybox - not moving the vibrator, which purrs mechanically on my clit - and pull out the first cunt appropriate toy that comes to hand. Two ivory plastic balls, the size of ping-pong balls but heavier, attached by a cord. Slicked with a little lube and pressed against my labia, I disappear them with twin moans: "ohhh... ohhh." Hearing my own sounds is more exciting when I'm alone and sometimes, though not tonight, I talk the whole time, at once lewd show-off and *ecouteuse.* But tonight I'm distracted from this - which is sort of a masturbation extra - by this tense and building wave of need.

I get so tense that tugging on the string is difficult, but each tug moves me palpably higher, whether it's rhythmic, as it is at first, or a wild and frenzied yanking. By the time I lose my rhythm it's too late. I am stretched out taut. The flexible neck of the Hitachi is bent nearly at right angles and its purring has changed to a labored, complaining whine because I'm pressing so hard. I hold the vibrator against my clit from the left, with my labia cushioning it. The nearness of orgasm brings my body up like a bow, the arc I learned about from Reich and my first girlfriend, the one who used to rub off on the stuffed tiger. It is an entirely different electrical current than anything else I know. I feel in and out of my body all at the same time. In that second when my body arcs up at its tightest - and only then - I understand what **release** means.

It no longer has anything to do with tight jeans and pictures of Madonna. I'm not even human, and that's the best release of all. I'm part of the electrical energy of the universe,

part of natural laws, one with protons and electrons, one with satellites circling. It's the clear, breathless instant before my cunt starts pulsing stronger than my heart. It's the second I feel my voice get ready to howl. Tonight it's so strong I bellow like the stuck calf of the Goddess, and my whole body is spasming like my cunt - out of control, writhing and snapping, I feel like a necklace of pearls whose string has been cut.

The second time it's even stronger, and with the first squeeze of my cunt I gush scented sex-brine all over the hand that holds the ivory balls' string: the balls come squirting out with the nectar, and somehow, somehow I manage to switch off the hot and throbbing Hitachi. I am flushed pink and panting.

And slowly I come back to myself, begin hearing the sound of cars again, notice the moving shadows again on my wall. My awareness comes back without the tension, like warm liquid filling a hot bottle. I know it's been a big one because I feel the sweet muscle-soreness of working out. Best of all is my skin, wrapping me up, holding all the wet loose pearls inside, so alive to my stroking that I almost want to start over again, but no, I've had enough for tonight - I'll put myself to sleep stroking this warm, buttered silk.

Bio: Carol A. Queen is a San Francisco writer and sex educator. This piece is a true story and not intended to serve as an advertisement for the Hitachi Corporation.

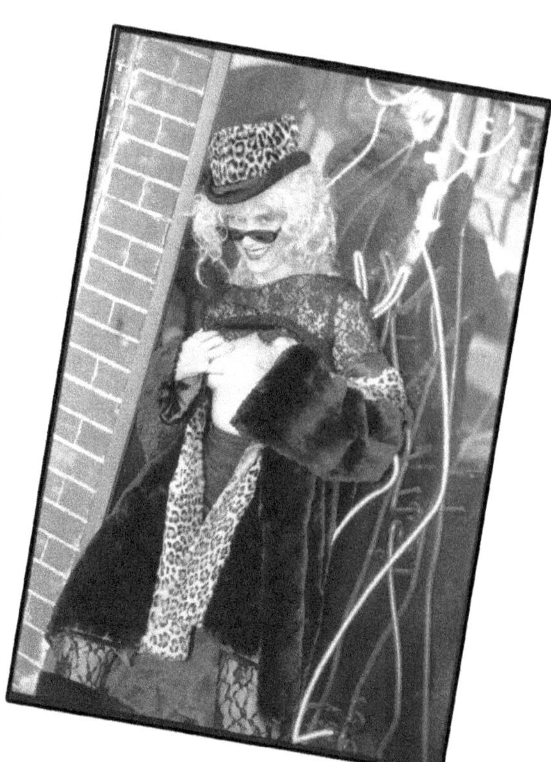

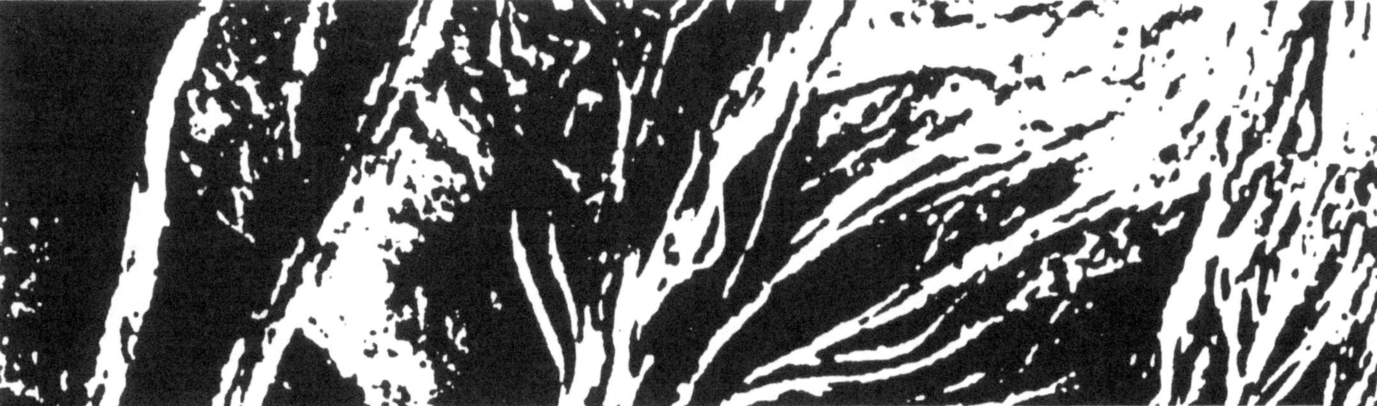

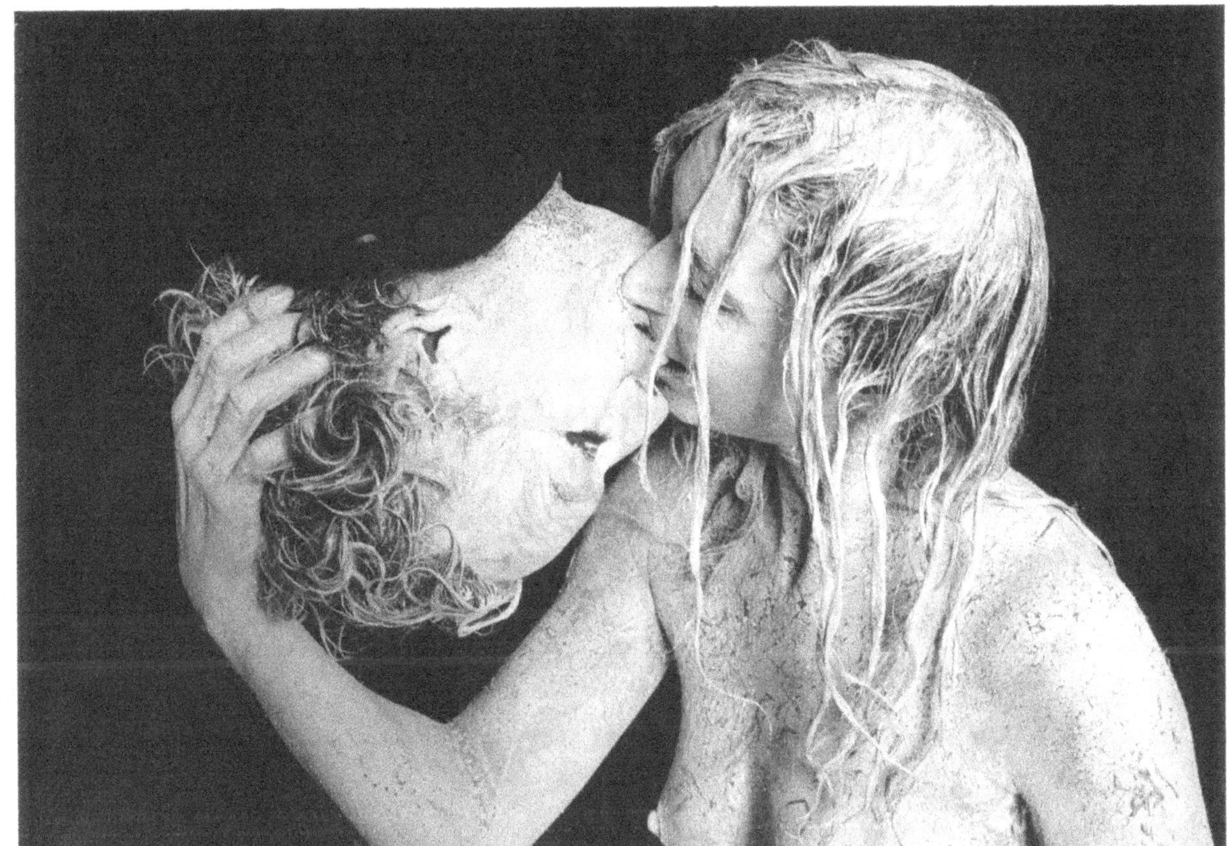

© NINA GLASER

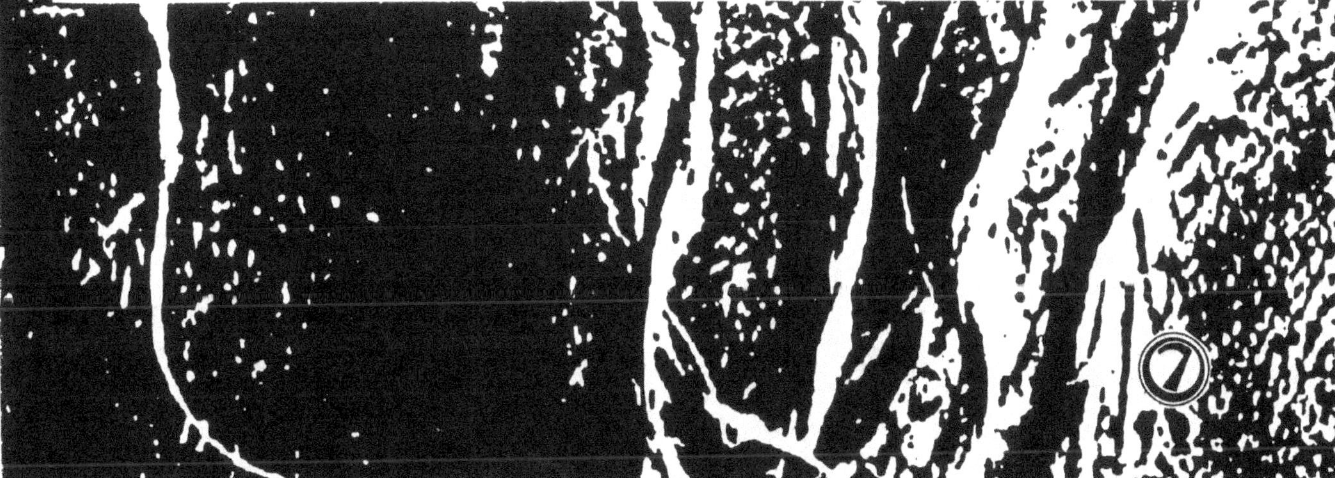

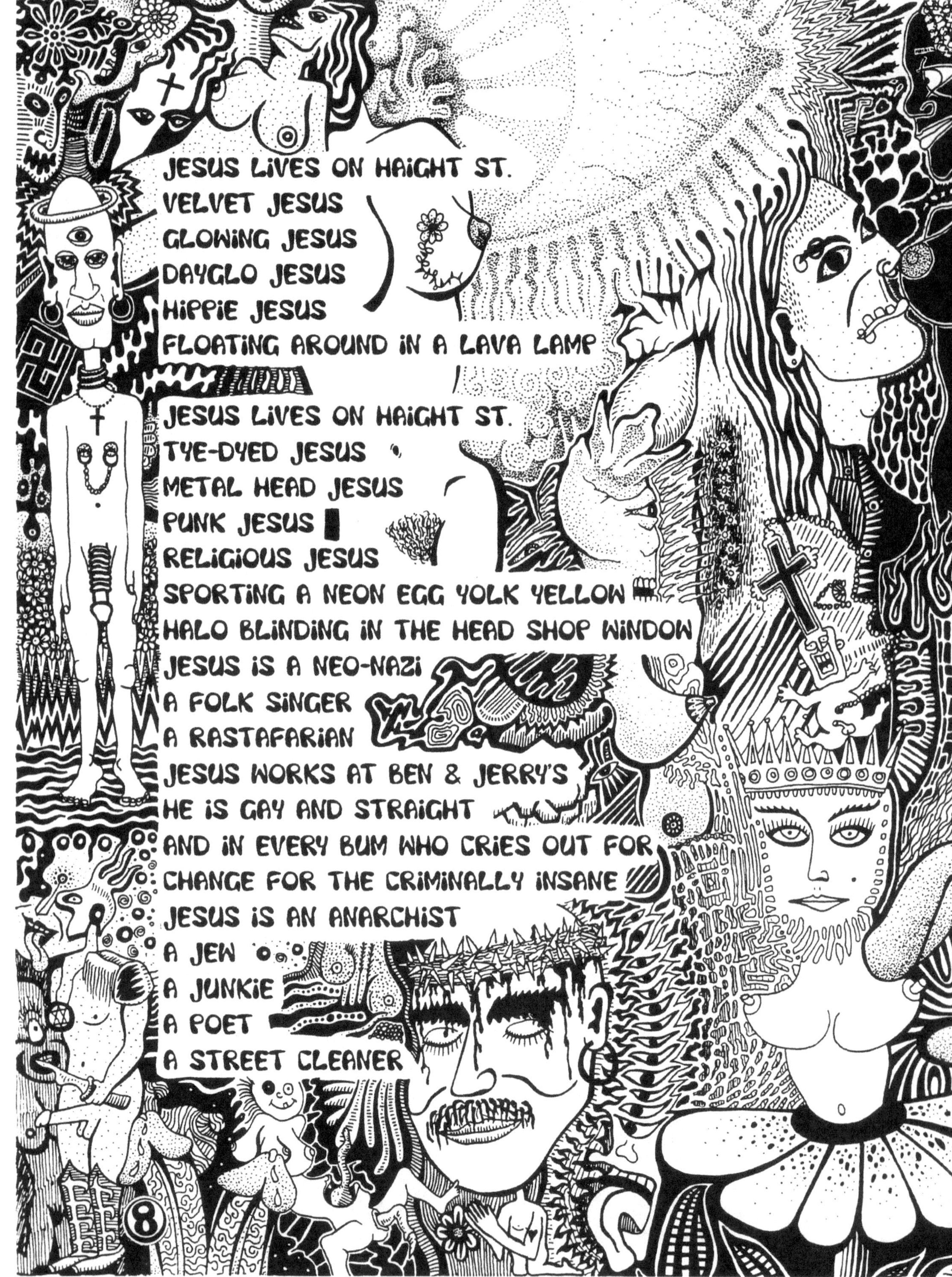
JESUS LIVES ON HAIGHT ST.
VELVET JESUS
GLOWING JESUS
DAYGLO JESUS
HIPPIE JESUS
FLOATING AROUND IN A LAVA LAMP

JESUS LIVES ON HAIGHT ST.
TYE-DYED JESUS
METAL HEAD JESUS
PUNK JESUS
RELIGIOUS JESUS
SPORTING A NEON EGG YOLK YELLOW
HALO BLINDING IN THE HEAD SHOP WINDOW
JESUS IS A NEO-NAZI
A FOLK SINGER
A RASTAFARIAN
JESUS WORKS AT BEN & JERRY'S
HE IS GAY AND STRAIGHT
AND IN EVERY BUM WHO CRIES OUT FOR
CHANGE FOR THE CRIMINALLY INSANE
JESUS IS AN ANARCHIST
A JEW
A JUNKIE
A POET
A STREET CLEANER
8

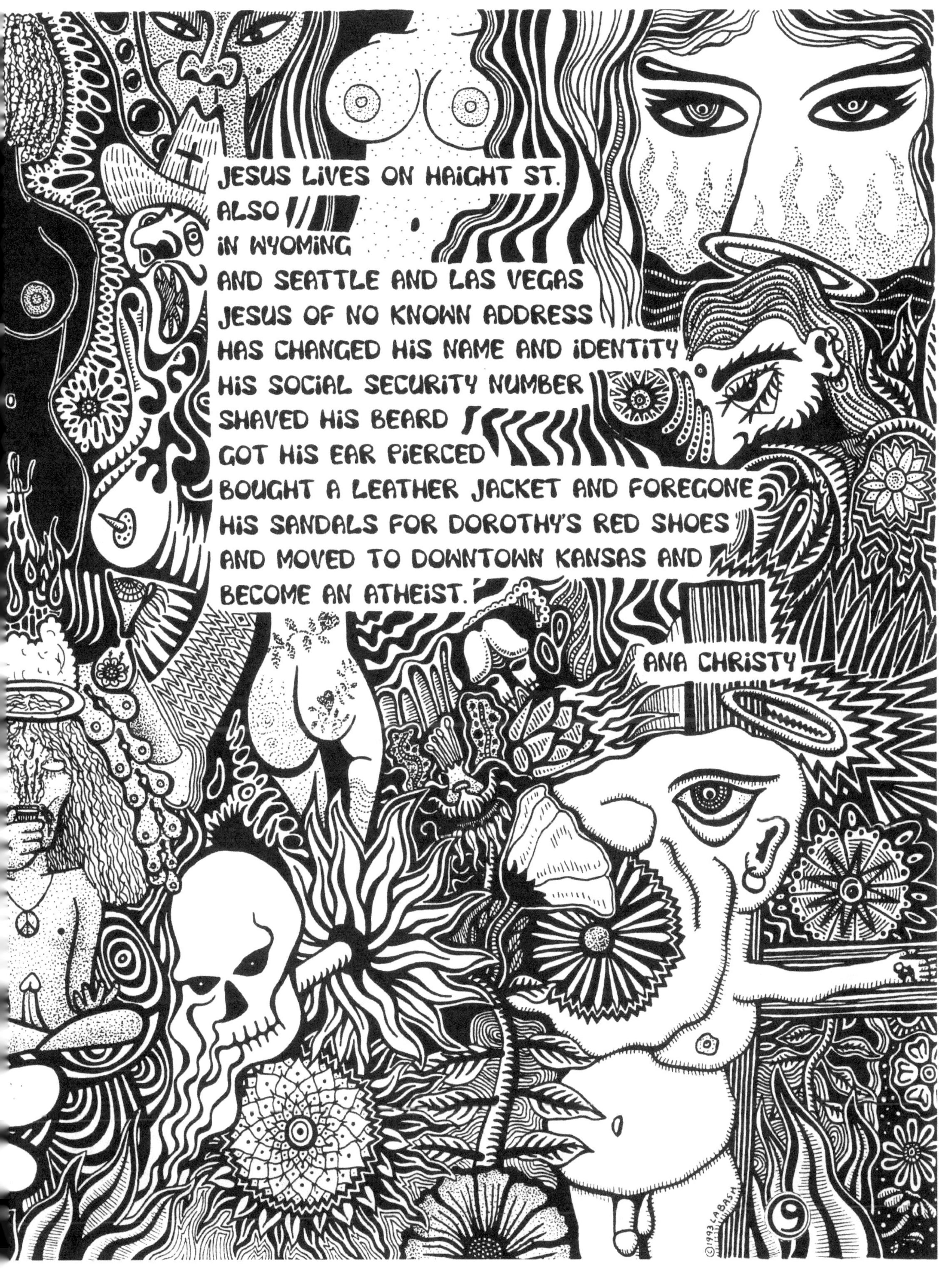
JESUS LIVES ON HAIGHT ST.
ALSO
IN WYOMING
AND SEATTLE AND LAS VEGAS
JESUS OF NO KNOWN ADDRESS
HAS CHANGED HIS NAME AND IDENTITY
HIS SOCIAL SECURITY NUMBER
SHAVED HIS BEARD
GOT HIS EAR PIERCED
BOUGHT A LEATHER JACKET AND FOREGONE
HIS SANDALS FOR DOROTHY'S RED SHOES
AND MOVED TO DOWNTOWN KANSAS AND
BECOME AN ATHEIST.
ANA CHRISTY
©1993 LABASH

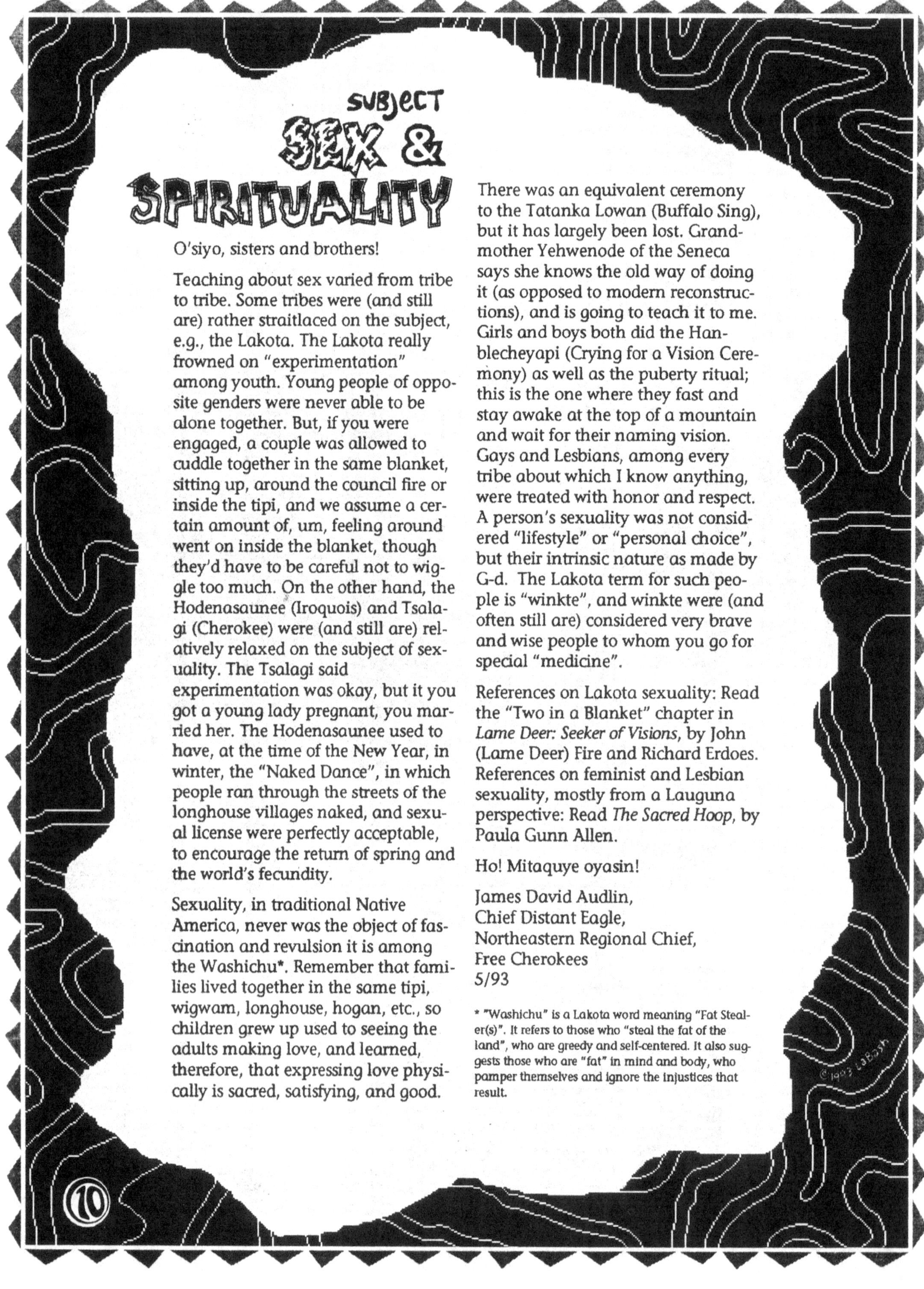

SUBJECT SEX & SPIRITUALITY

O'siyo, sisters and brothers!

Teaching about sex varied from tribe to tribe. Some tribes were (and still are) rather straitlaced on the subject, e.g., the Lakota. The Lakota really frowned on "experimentation" among youth. Young people of opposite genders were never able to be alone together. But, if you were engaged, a couple was allowed to cuddle together in the same blanket, sitting up, around the council fire or inside the tipi, and we assume a certain amount of, um, feeling around went on inside the blanket, though they'd have to be careful not to wiggle too much. On the other hand, the Hodenasaunee (Iroquois) and Tsalagi (Cherokee) were (and still are) relatively relaxed on the subject of sexuality. The Tsalagi said experimentation was okay, but it you got a young lady pregnant, you married her. The Hodenasaunee used to have, at the time of the New Year, in winter, the "Naked Dance", in which people ran through the streets of the longhouse villages naked, and sexual license were perfectly acceptable, to encourage the return of spring and the world's fecundity.

Sexuality, in traditional Native America, never was the object of fascination and revulsion it is among the Washichu*. Remember that families lived together in the same tipi, wigwam, longhouse, hogan, etc., so children grew up used to seeing the adults making love, and learned, therefore, that expressing love physically is sacred, satisfying, and good.

There was an equivalent ceremony to the Tatanka Lowan (Buffalo Sing), but it has largely been lost. Grandmother Yehwenode of the Seneca says she knows the old way of doing it (as opposed to modern reconstructions), and is going to teach it to me. Girls and boys both did the Hanblecheyapi (Crying for a Vision Ceremony) as well as the puberty ritual; this is the one where they fast and stay awake at the top of a mountain and wait for their naming vision. Gays and Lesbians, among every tribe about which I know anything, were treated with honor and respect. A person's sexuality was not considered "lifestyle" or "personal choice", but their intrinsic nature as made by G-d. The Lakota term for such people is "winkte", and winkte were (and often still are) considered very brave and wise people to whom you go for special "medicine".

References on Lakota sexuality: Read the "Two in a Blanket" chapter in *Lame Deer: Seeker of Visions*, by John (Lame Deer) Fire and Richard Erdoes. References on feminist and Lesbian sexuality, mostly from a Lauguna perspective: Read *The Sacred Hoop*, by Paula Gunn Allen.

Ho! Mitaquye oyasin!

James David Audlin,
Chief Distant Eagle,
Northeastern Regional Chief,
Free Cherokees
5/93

* "Washichu" is a Lakota word meaning "Fat Stealer(s)". It refers to those who "steal the fat of the land", who are greedy and self-centered. It also suggests those who are "fat" in mind and body, who pamper themselves and ignore the injustices that result.

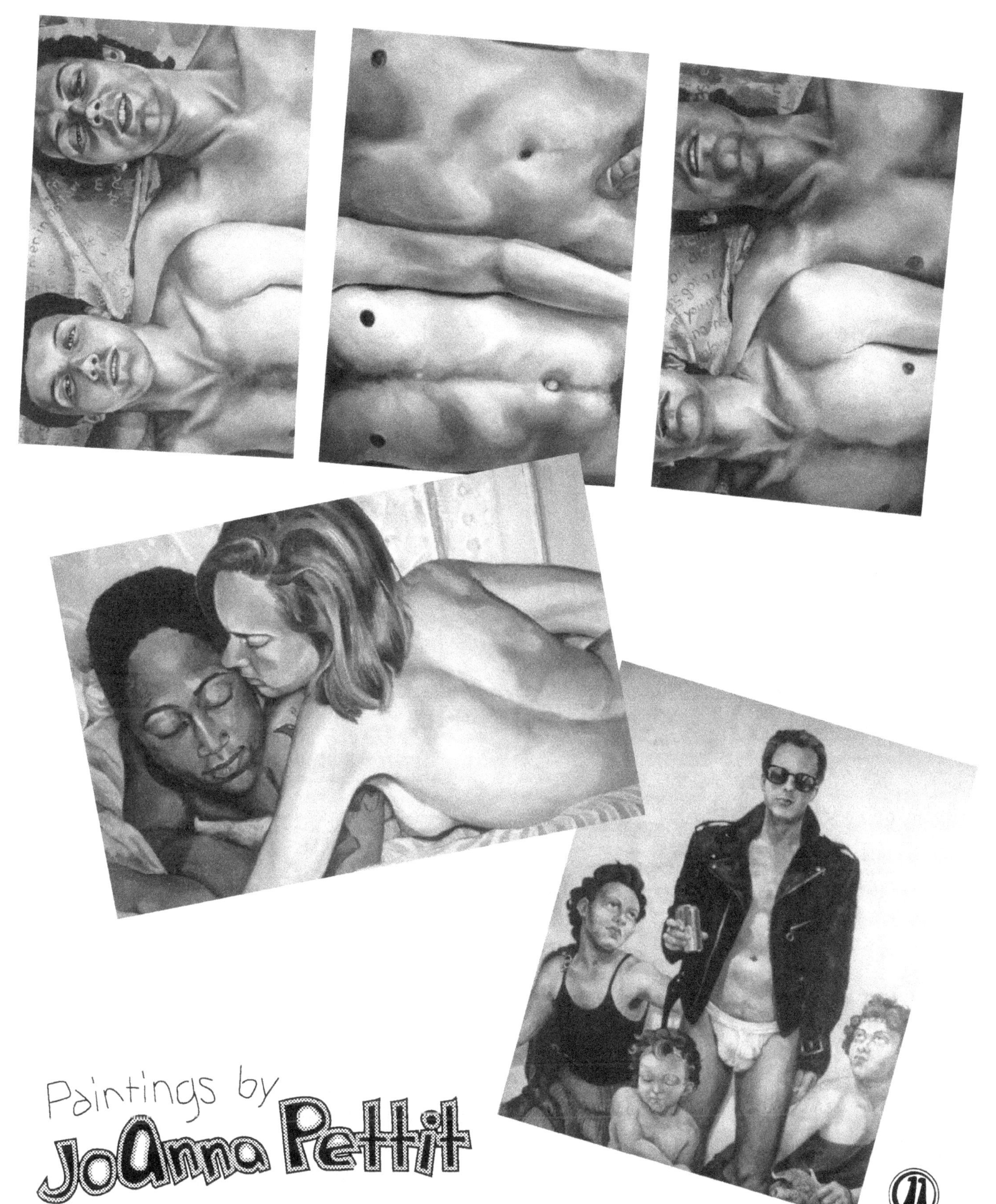

Paintings by
JoAnna Pettit

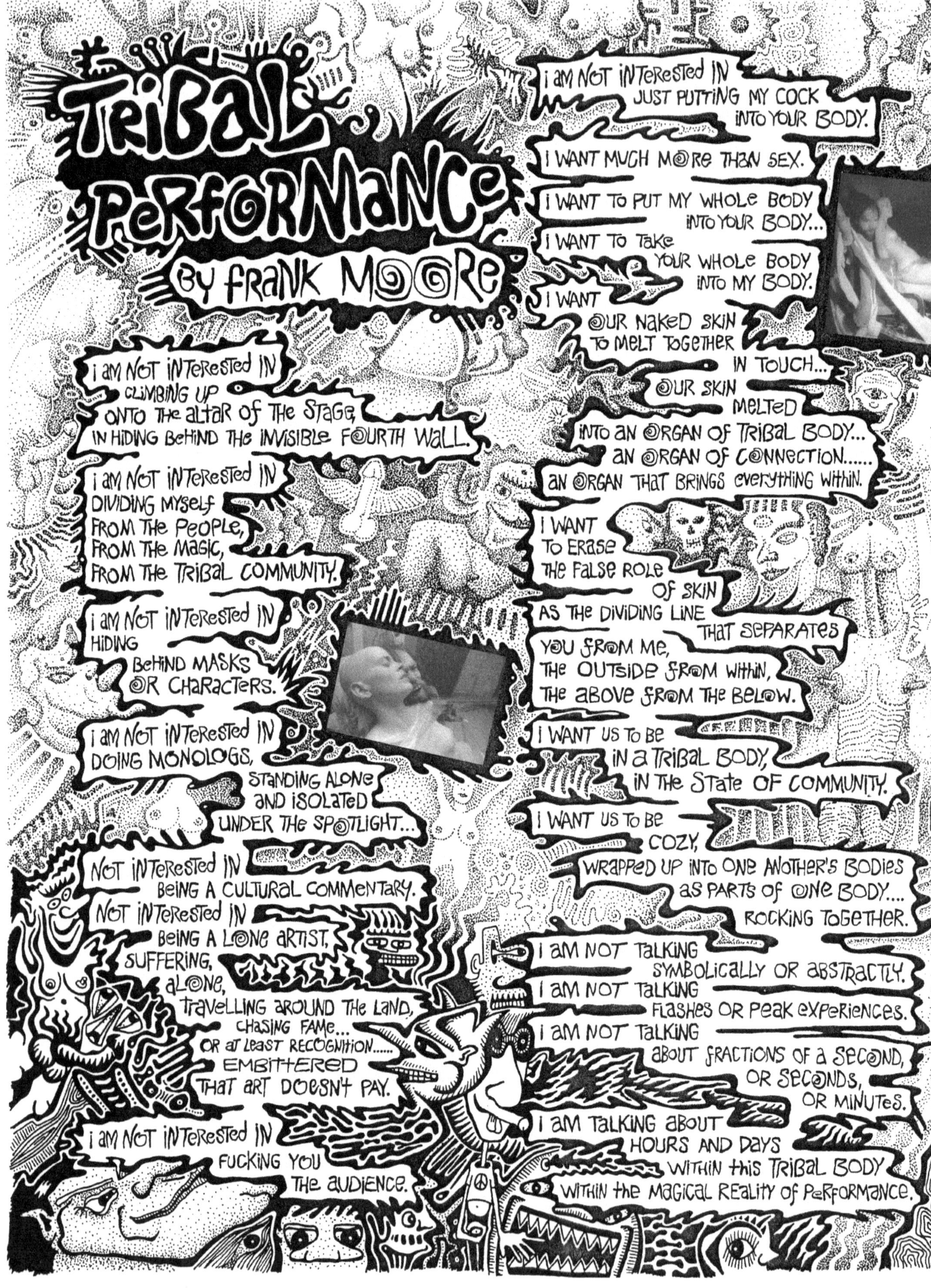
TRIBAL PERFORMANCE
BY FRANK MOORE
i am NOT interested in
JUST PUTTING MY COCK
INTO YOUR BODY.
I WANT MUCH MORE THAN SEX.
I WANT TO PUT MY WHOLE BODY
INTO YOUR BODY...
I WANT TO TAKE
YOUR WHOLE BODY
INTO MY BODY.
I WANT
OUR NAKED SKIN
TO MELT TOGETHER
IN TOUCH...
OUR SKIN
MELTED
INTO AN ORGAN OF TRIBAL BODY...
AN ORGAN OF CONNECTION......
AN ORGAN THAT BRINGS EVERYTHING WITHIN.
i am NOT interested in
CLIMBING UP
ONTO THE ALTAR OF THE STAGE,
IN HIDING BEHIND THE INVISIBLE FOURTH WALL.
i am NOT interested in
DIVIDING MYSELF
FROM THE PEOPLE,
FROM THE MAGIC,
FROM THE TRIBAL COMMUNITY.
i am NOT interested in
HIDING
BEHIND MASKS
OR CHARACTERS.
i am NOT interested in
DOING MONOLOGS,
STANDING ALONE
AND ISOLATED
UNDER THE SPOTLIGHT...
NOT interested in
BEING A CULTURAL COMMENTARY.
NOT interested in
BEING A LONE ARTIST,
SUFFERING,
ALONE,
TRAVELLING AROUND THE LAND,
CHASING FAME...
OR AT LEAST RECOGNITION......
EMBITTERED
THAT ART DOESN'T PAY.
i am NOT interested in
FUCKING YOU
THE AUDIENCE.
I WANT
TO ERASE
THE FALSE ROLE
OF SKIN
AS THE DIVIDING LINE
THAT SEPARATES
YOU FROM ME,
THE OUTSIDE FROM WITHIN,
THE ABOVE FROM THE BELOW.
I WANT US TO BE
IN A TRIBAL BODY,
IN THE STATE OF COMMUNITY.
I WANT US TO BE
COZY,
WRAPPED UP INTO ONE ANOTHER'S BODIES
AS PARTS OF ONE BODY....
ROCKING TOGETHER.
I AM NOT TALKING
SYMBOLICALLY OR ABSTRACTLY.
I AM NOT TALKING
FLASHES OR PEAK EXPERIENCES.
I AM NOT TALKING
ABOUT FRACTIONS OF A SECOND,
OR SECONDS,
OR MINUTES.
I AM TALKING ABOUT
HOURS AND DAYS
WITHIN THIS TRIBAL BODY
WITHIN THE MAGICAL REALITY OF PERFORMANCE.

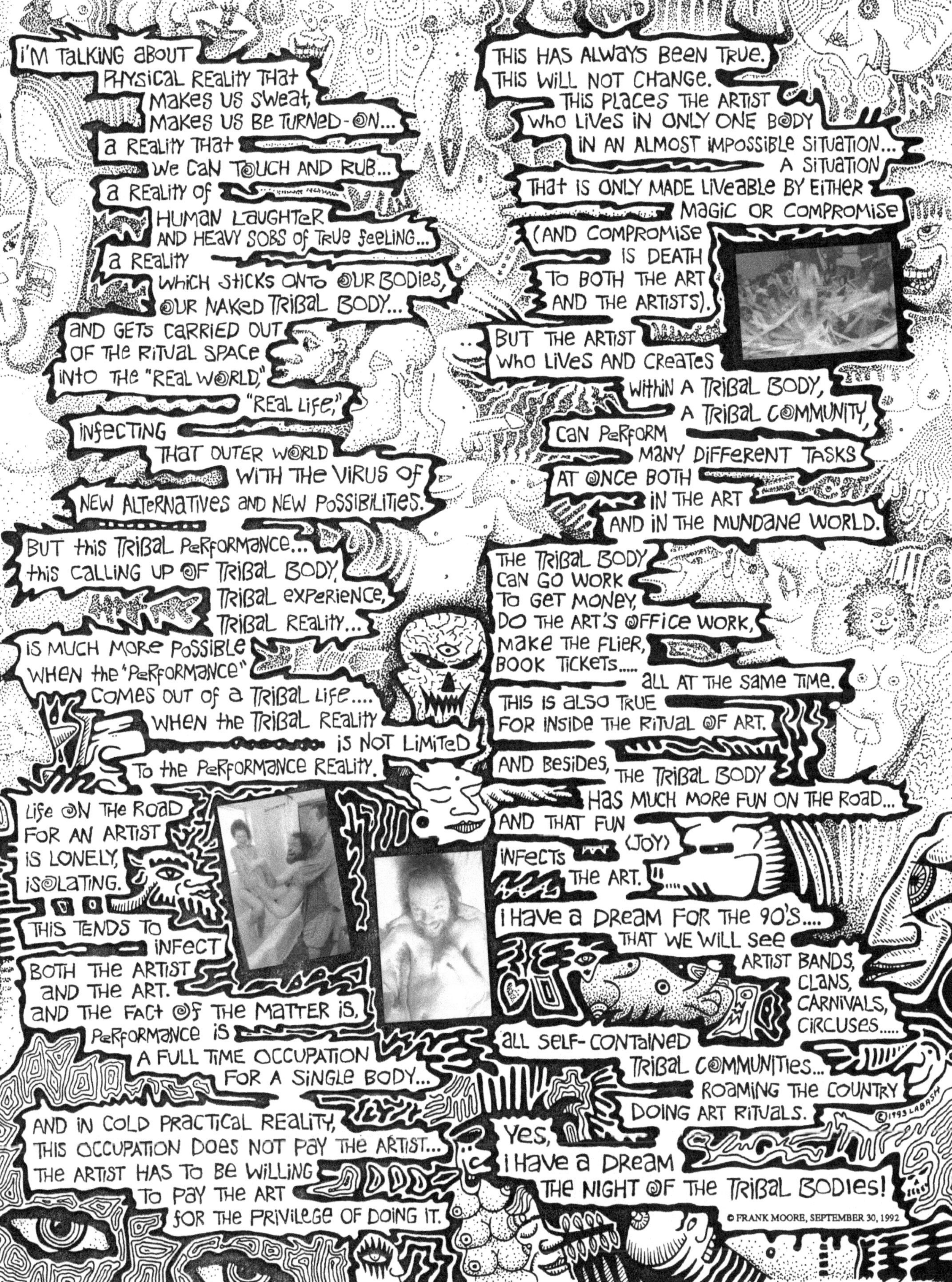

I'M TALKING ABOUT
PHYSICAL REALITY THAT
MAKES US SWEAT,
MAKES US BE TURNED-ON...
a REALITY THAT
WE CAN TOUCH AND RUB...
a REALITY OF
HUMAN LAUGHTER
AND HEAVY SOBS OF TRUE FEELING...
a REALITY
WHICH STICKS ONTO OUR BODIES,
OUR NAKED TRIBAL BODY...
AND GETS CARRIED OUT
OF THE RITUAL SPACE
INTO THE "REAL WORLD,"
"REAL LIFE,"
INFECTING
THAT OUTER WORLD
WITH THE VIRUS OF
NEW ALTERNATIVES AND NEW POSSIBILITIES.
BUT THIS TRIBAL PERFORMANCE...
THIS CALLING UP OF TRIBAL BODY,
TRIBAL EXPERIENCE,
TRIBAL REALITY...
IS MUCH MORE POSSIBLE
WHEN THE "PERFORMANCE"
COMES OUT OF A TRIBAL LIFE....
WHEN THE TRIBAL REALITY
IS NOT LIMITED
TO THE PERFORMANCE REALITY.
LIFE ON THE ROAD
FOR AN ARTIST
IS LONELY,
ISOLATING.
THIS TENDS TO
INFECT
BOTH THE ARTIST
AND THE ART.
AND THE FACT OF THE MATTER IS,
PERFORMANCE IS
A FULL TIME OCCUPATION
FOR A SINGLE BODY...
AND IN COLD PRACTICAL REALITY,
THIS OCCUPATION DOES NOT PAY THE ARTIST...
THE ARTIST HAS TO BE WILLING
TO PAY THE ART
FOR THE PRIVILEGE OF DOING IT.
THIS HAS ALWAYS BEEN TRUE.
THIS WILL NOT CHANGE.
THIS PLACES THE ARTIST
WHO LIVES IN ONLY ONE BODY
IN AN ALMOST IMPOSSIBLE SITUATION...
A SITUATION
THAT IS ONLY MADE LIVEABLE BY EITHER
MAGIC OR COMPROMISE
(AND COMPROMISE
IS DEATH
TO BOTH THE ART
AND THE ARTISTS).
BUT THE ARTIST
WHO LIVES AND CREATES
WITHIN A TRIBAL BODY,
A TRIBAL COMMUNITY,
CAN PERFORM
MANY DIFFERENT TASKS
AT ONCE BOTH
IN THE ART
AND IN THE MUNDANE WORLD.
THE TRIBAL BODY
CAN GO WORK
TO GET MONEY,
DO THE ART'S OFFICE WORK,
MAKE THE FLIER,
BOOK TICKETS.....
ALL AT THE SAME TIME.
THIS IS ALSO TRUE
FOR INSIDE THE RITUAL OF ART.
AND BESIDES, THE TRIBAL BODY
HAS MUCH MORE FUN ON THE ROAD...
AND THAT FUN
(JOY)
INFECTS
THE ART.
I HAVE A DREAM FOR THE 90'S....
THAT WE WILL SEE
ARTIST BANDS,
CLANS,
CARNIVALS,
CIRCUSES.....
ALL SELF-CONTAINED
TRIBAL COMMUNITIES...
ROAMING THE COUNTRY
DOING ART RITUALS.
©1993 LABASH
YES,
I HAVE A DREAM
THE NIGHT OF THE TRIBAL BODIES!
© FRANK MOORE, SEPTEMBER 30, 1992

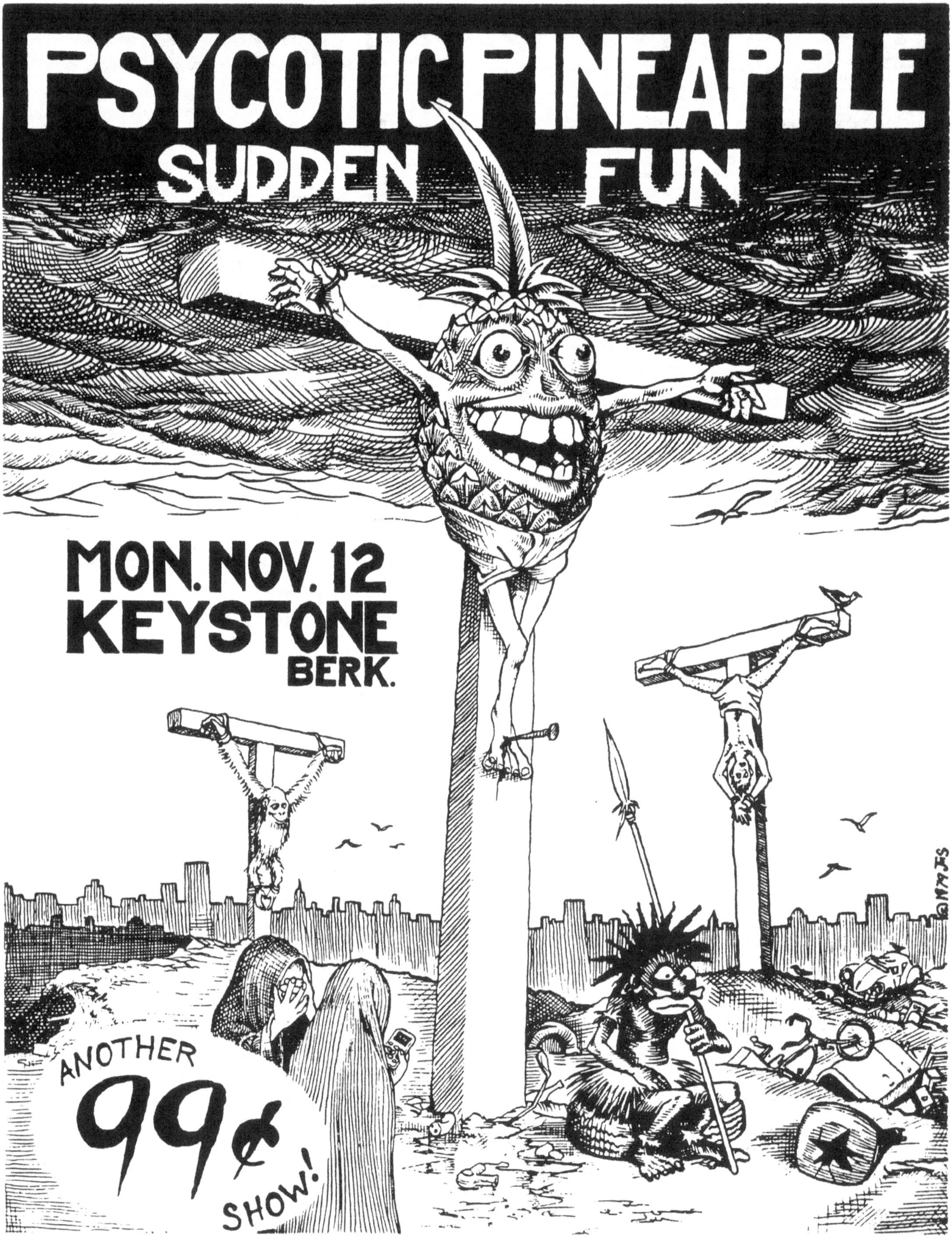

PSYCOTIC PINEAPPLE

SUDDEN FUN

MON. NOV. 12

KEYSTONE

BERK.

ANOTHER

99¢

SHOW!

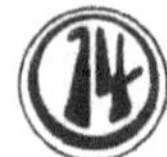

Poster by **John Seabury**, Pynotic Productions, P.O. Box 7004, Berkeley, CA 94707-0004

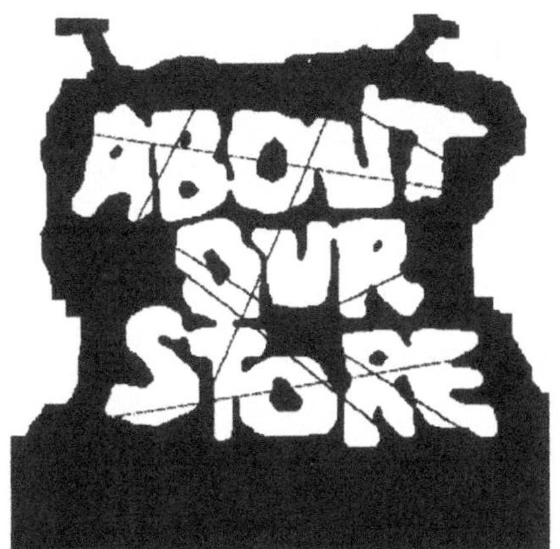

I hope you're doing well. I'm Professor Curtis thanking you for your interest in FAMOUS CULT VIDEOS. I began my video rental business on Valentines Day February 14 1990, and I'll tell you the truth, my life has been tougher than shit ever since. I run my store by myself, and I wouldn't have it any other way, but after two and a half years, well, let's just say that I identify closely with Doctor Frankenstein. The reason this little store continues to survive is because I have a kinky collection of escapism videos. But I cannot go on without giving thanks to the customers also known as The Associate Professors, those gifted, insightful and generous beings who encourage me daily to purchase more and more bizarre videos while supporting my fight against the corporate bosses who seek to manipulate our video selections, and thus our minds, by selling us overpriced, over-advertised remakes of movies we already have. Why should we spend money duplicating the efforts of others. If the big-heads buy 50 copies of the same video, why should we play catch up? We possess a unique position in the video scene, a position which should not be manipulated into oblivion by a bunch of boot lickin' corporate lackeys who don't know if they'll be employed next week. That ain't freedom.

The Professors have spoken:
WE WANT ESCAPISM, HOT SEX, SHOCKING REALISM, GIVE US CREATURE FEATURES AND HEAR US ROAR. Top it all off with a nice warm fuzzy, and we'll always come back to you.

From political to violent death from women in prison to animation, I seek out the best and by pass the rest, to bring the customer what they ask to see, so that they can free their minds of the common concerns of troubled man and find freedom now, within a society that seeks to destroy your creative juices before your imagination can be utilized to make you money. Yes there is a conspiracy, and if you're not part of the solution, you're part of the problem. In order for you to regain your strength and position in life, you must regain total control over your own mind. You can only regain total control through mental escapism. Sure you can live your life in servitude, paying out every dime you make to everyone else except yourself, you can even be made to believe that you like it, and that poverty is nature in these modern times, but it's not true. Do you fail to realize that the purpose of the conspiracy is to stop you from seeking freedom. They also intend to burden you with endless social pressures designed to emotionally stress you out, mentally discourage you, and of course bleed your pocketbook dry. If you do not escape regularly, into a world of your own creation where you, with proper instruction, can tap your hidden resources for creativity which without a doubt will lead you to the freedom and happiness and the money long overdue you from the powers that control life from above, if you fail to alert others to the true reality which surrounds them, if you fail your duty to your family, friends and self at this crucial point in time, your spirit shall never find peace on Earth, or in Heaven, or in Hell or in Limbo, because you allowed the conspiracy to continue unchallenged. Yes, there are things that "THEY" will not tell you. Such as: The only tools that you need on Earth are TIME, SPACE AND FREEDOM. When you possess these tools, you can do or create anything you can imagine, that is if your imagination still works. So you say, what about money? Money is part of freedom. You will need money to be free to create your personal happiness. Speaking of money, you can always enhance your financial karma by donating money to Professor Curtis. Make sure to include your name and telephone number.

FAMOUS CULT VIDEOS OF BERKELEY (510) 849-1189

By expanding your present consciousness through the use of Professor Curtis' unique program to achieve freedom through escapism, you too can become a happy paranoid, free of the burdens of keeping up with the Jones and relieve yourself of the responsibilities of modern day mental slavery, but first you must devote yourself to yourself, you must decide to be free. Continue reading this booklet. Order often. Watch for newsletter updates. Keep your eyes open. Say little. Listen closely. All shall be made known to you.

Sincerely,
Professor Curtis
8/9/92

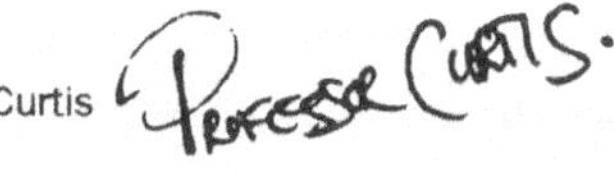

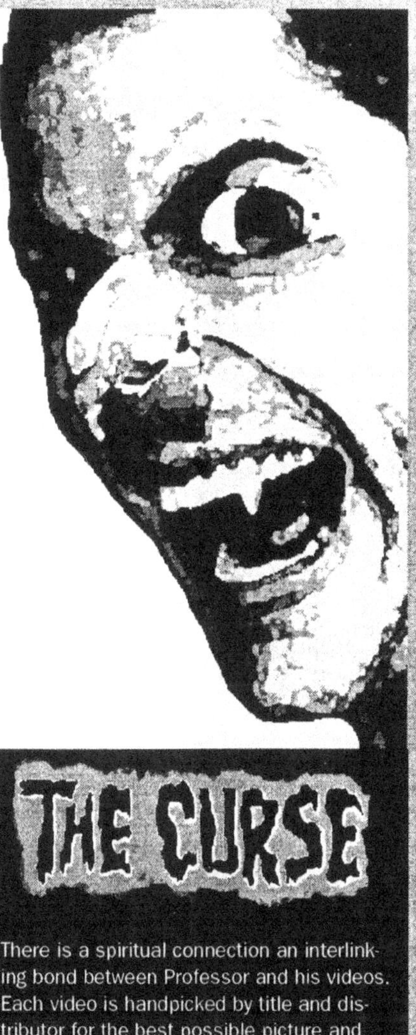

THE CURSE

There is a spiritual connection an interlinking bond between Professor and his videos. Each video is handpicked by title and distributor for the best possible picture and sound. Only a select few videos become a part of Professor Curtis' Famous Cult Video Collection.

When a video is not returned Professor Curtis takes the following actions.

A) You'll be contacted at your home (by one method or another) and urged to return the videos A.S.A.P. (Use the mail slot if you have to.)
B) You'll receive a threatening "DEMAND LETTER" if step "A" doesn't get your attention.
C) A legal, financial and spiritual CURSE will be enacted upon your person if step "B" doesn't get your goat.
D) Your deposit will be used and your membership will be canceled if step "C" doesn't get you movin'.
E) If you can survive the pressures placed upon you at this point, you'll be considered "HARDCORE". You will be taken to the legal woodshed for rippin' off the store, and of course your name will be slandered, NATIONWIDE.

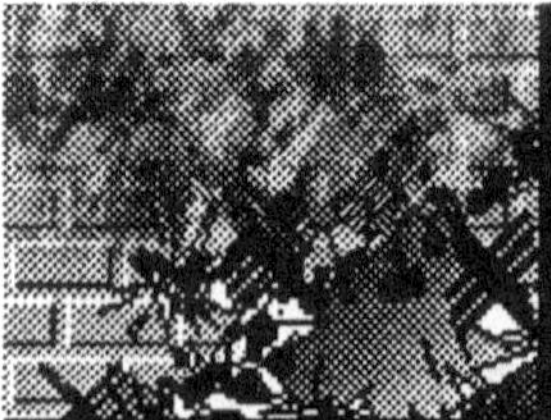

January 1991 at Langley/Porter Psychiatric Institute

(a confessional piece)

by Steven Kauffman

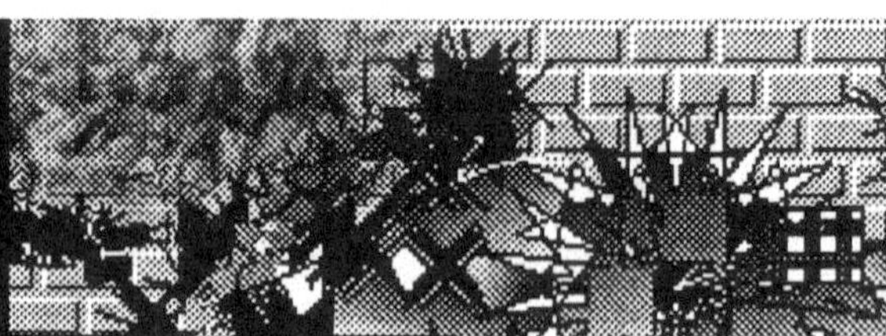

Introduction

As the following poem's title indicates, I spent most of January, 1991 at Langley-Porter Psychiatric Hospital due to a variety of mental and emotional problems. Most prominent among these problems were attacks of rage, uncontrollable anger, and loss of control over my emotions. One of the nurses on duty instructed me that if I should get any warning that I was about to lose control, I should come to her immediately and say "I need to talk to you!" Shortly after, I started cursing and yelling and realized my anger was building out of control and I went back to the nurse saying "I NEED TO TALK TO YOU! I NEED TO TALK TO YOU!" She took me to my room and said "I'll be back in a few minutes," then closed the door. The following piece is a confessional expression of what then transpired.

the truth is...
that I did the right thing
that I did what she asked me to do
and that I told the truth

but they used words against me
words that said
I wanted to do the wrong thing
words that said
I often did the wrong thing
an even clearer distinction...
I was the wrong thing

the lie is...
that I admitted urges to harm the others
I never said that to anyone!
not to staff
not to doctors
not to nurses
not to patients

but they documented that I admitted these urges
and they threw two 5150 forms at me
at first, 48 hours,
and then,
as the second 5150 read,
indefinitely

I told the truth
and
they told a lie
and
I did what I was told to do
and
they rewarded that crime with two policemen
enforcing their rules
and
separating the rest of the patients
from
the contagion on two legs that was me
in their eyes

I said what I felt and
I said it loudly and
though sometimes I might have been out of control
and
though sometimes I might have been sedated,
I still had an active brain
and
that made me dangerous to them

so the cops put the cuffs on my wrists
and they bled
and the cops dragged me down the hallway
and
I could see the whole staff and the patients
walking around and beside my body
dragging on the floor
and
I looked up and I asked them
Why?
What did I do? What was so wrong? Why are you doing this to me?

and I realized...
there is no need for the truth when there is power
and there is no reason for truth to exist
when there is autonomy on the inside
and a powerless outside
and there is no need for a truth called Steven who shoots his mouth off
and
so easily could upset the apple cart of order
and so they set me up
and
they censored me
and
they didn't allow me to be what I was

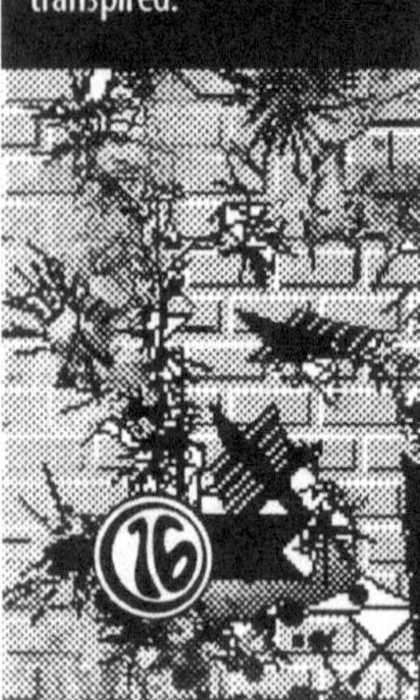

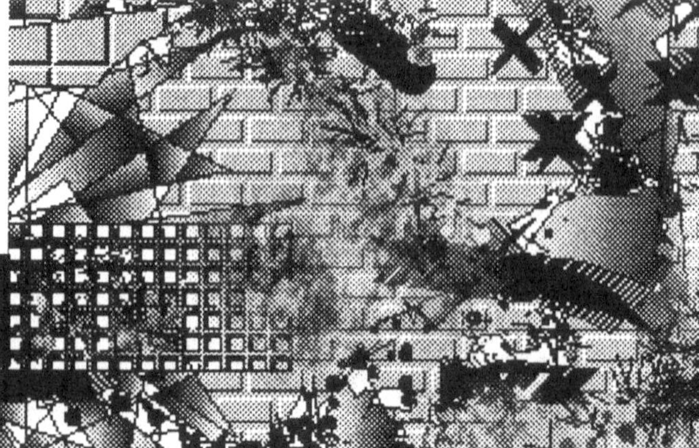

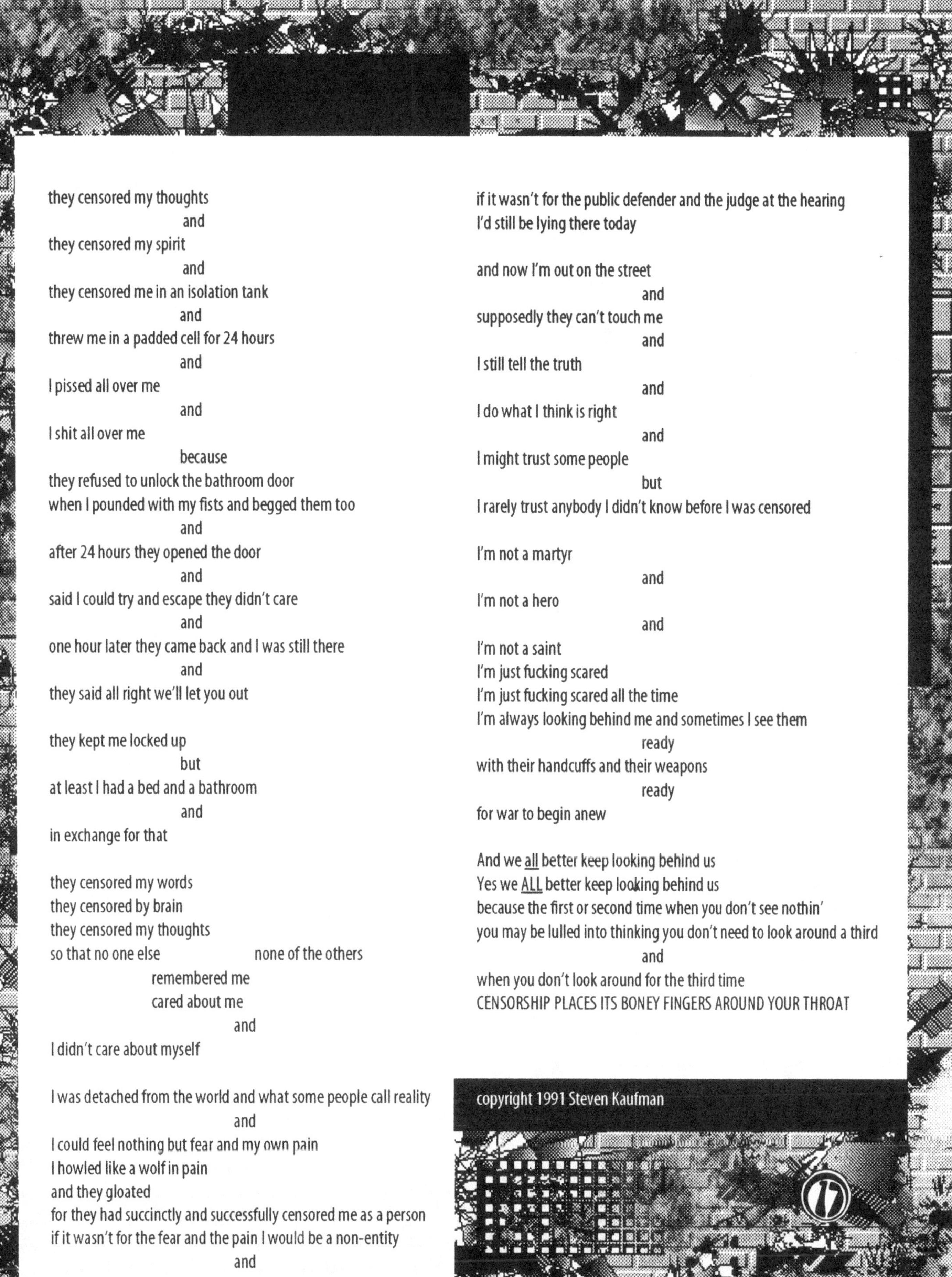

they censored my thoughts
and
they censored my spirit
and
they censored me in an isolation tank
and
threw me in a padded cell for 24 hours
and
I pissed all over me
and
I shit all over me
because
they refused to unlock the bathroom door
when I pounded with my fists and begged them too
and
after 24 hours they opened the door
and
said I could try and escape they didn't care
and
one hour later they came back and I was still there
and
they said all right we'll let you out

they kept me locked up
but
at least I had a bed and a bathroom
and
in exchange for that

they censored my words
they censored by brain
they censored my thoughts
so that no one else none of the others
remembered me
cared about me
and
I didn't care about myself

I was detached from the world and what some people call reality
and
I could feel nothing but fear and my own pain
I howled like a wolf in pain
and they gloated
for they had succinctly and successfully censored me as a person
if it wasn't for the fear and the pain I would be a non-entity
and
if it wasn't for the public defender and the judge at the hearing
I'd still be lying there today

and now I'm out on the street
and
supposedly they can't touch me
and
I still tell the truth
and
I do what I think is right
and
I might trust some people
but
I rarely trust anybody I didn't know before I was censored

I'm not a martyr
and
I'm not a hero
and
I'm not a saint
I'm just fucking scared
I'm just fucking scared all the time
I'm always looking behind me and sometimes I see them
ready
with their handcuffs and their weapons
ready
for war to begin anew

And we all better keep looking behind us
Yes we ALL better keep looking behind us
because the first or second time when you don't see nothin'
you may be lulled into thinking you don't need to look around a third
and
when you don't look around for the third time
CENSORSHIP PLACES ITS BONEY FINGERS AROUND YOUR THROAT

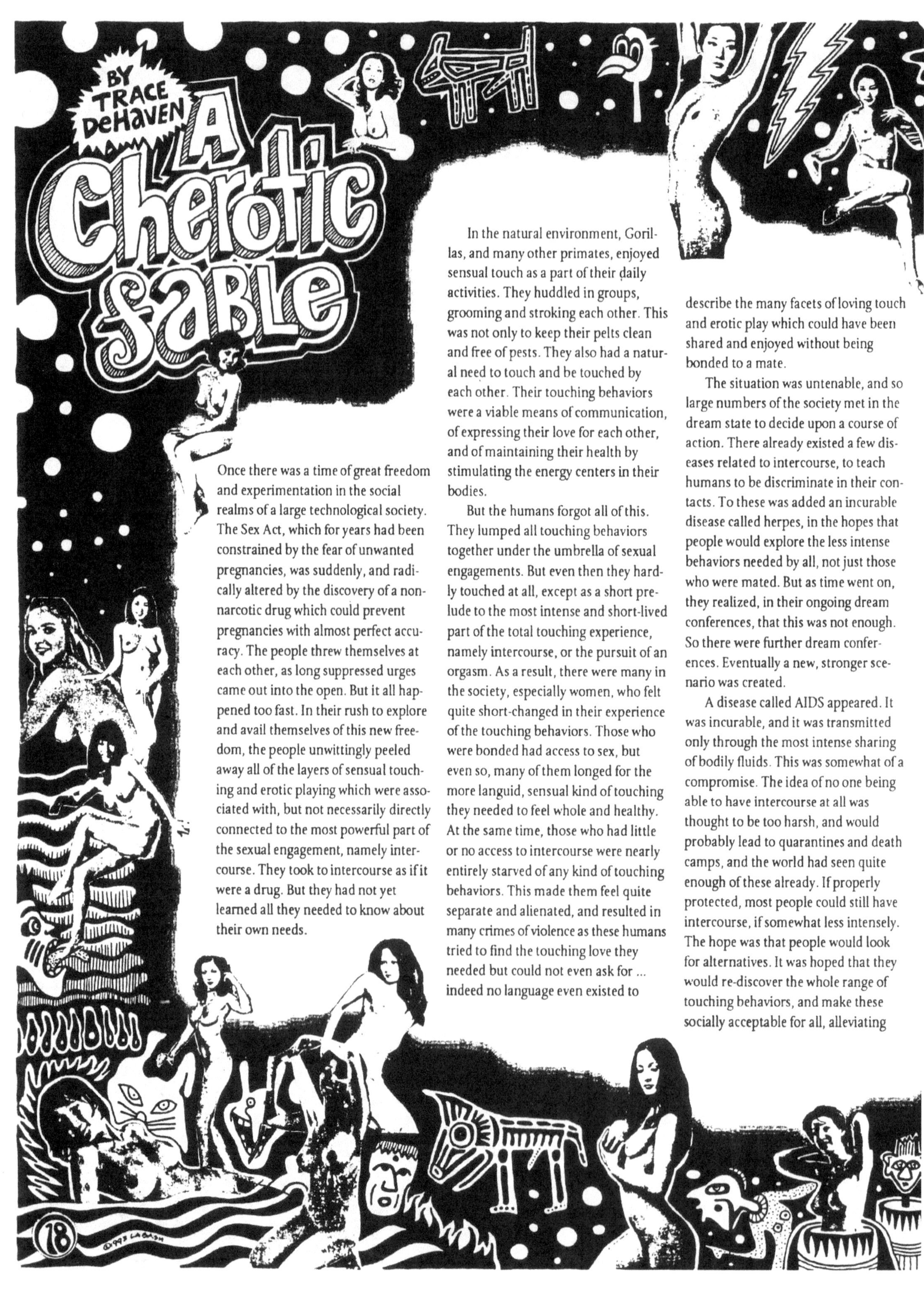

Once there was a time of great freedom and experimentation in the social realms of a large technological society. The Sex Act, which for years had been constrained by the fear of unwanted pregnancies, was suddenly, and radically altered by the discovery of a non-narcotic drug which could prevent pregnancies with almost perfect accuracy. The people threw themselves at each other, as long suppressed urges came out into the open. But it all happened too fast. In their rush to explore and avail themselves of this new freedom, the people unwittingly peeled away all of the layers of sensual touching and erotic playing which were associated with, but not necessarily directly connected to the most powerful part of the sexual engagement, namely intercourse. They took to intercourse as if it were a drug. But they had not yet learned all they needed to know about their own needs.

In the natural environment, Gorillas, and many other primates, enjoyed sensual touch as a part of their daily activities. They huddled in groups, grooming and stroking each other. This was not only to keep their pelts clean and free of pests. They also had a natural need to touch and be touched by each other. Their touching behaviors were a viable means of communication, of expressing their love for each other, and of maintaining their health by stimulating the energy centers in their bodies.

But the humans forgot all of this. They lumped all touching behaviors together under the umbrella of sexual engagements. But even then they hardly touched at all, except as a short prelude to the most intense and short-lived part of the total touching experience, namely intercourse, or the pursuit of an orgasm. As a result, there were many in the society, especially women, who felt quite short-changed in their experience of the touching behaviors. Those who were bonded had access to sex, but even so, many of them longed for the more languid, sensual kind of touching they needed to feel whole and healthy. At the same time, those who had little or no access to intercourse were nearly entirely starved of any kind of touching behaviors. This made them feel quite separate and alienated, and resulted in many crimes of violence as these humans tried to find the touching love they needed but could not even ask for ... indeed no language even existed to describe the many facets of loving touch and erotic play which could have been shared and enjoyed without being bonded to a mate.

The situation was untenable, and so large numbers of the society met in the dream state to decide upon a course of action. There already existed a few diseases related to intercourse, to teach humans to be discriminate in their contacts. To these was added an incurable disease called herpes, in the hopes that people would explore the less intense behaviors needed by all, not just those who were mated. But as time went on, they realized, in their ongoing dream conferences, that this was not enough. So there were further dream conferences. Eventually a new, stronger scenario was created.

A disease called AIDS appeared. It was incurable, and it was transmitted only through the most intense sharing of bodily fluids. This was somewhat of a compromise. The idea of no one being able to have intercourse at all was thought to be too harsh, and would probably lead to quarantines and death camps, and the world had seen quite enough of these already. If properly protected, most people could still have intercourse, if somewhat less intensely. The hope was that people would look for alternatives. It was hoped that they would re-discover the whole range of touching behaviors, and make these socially acceptable for all, alleviating

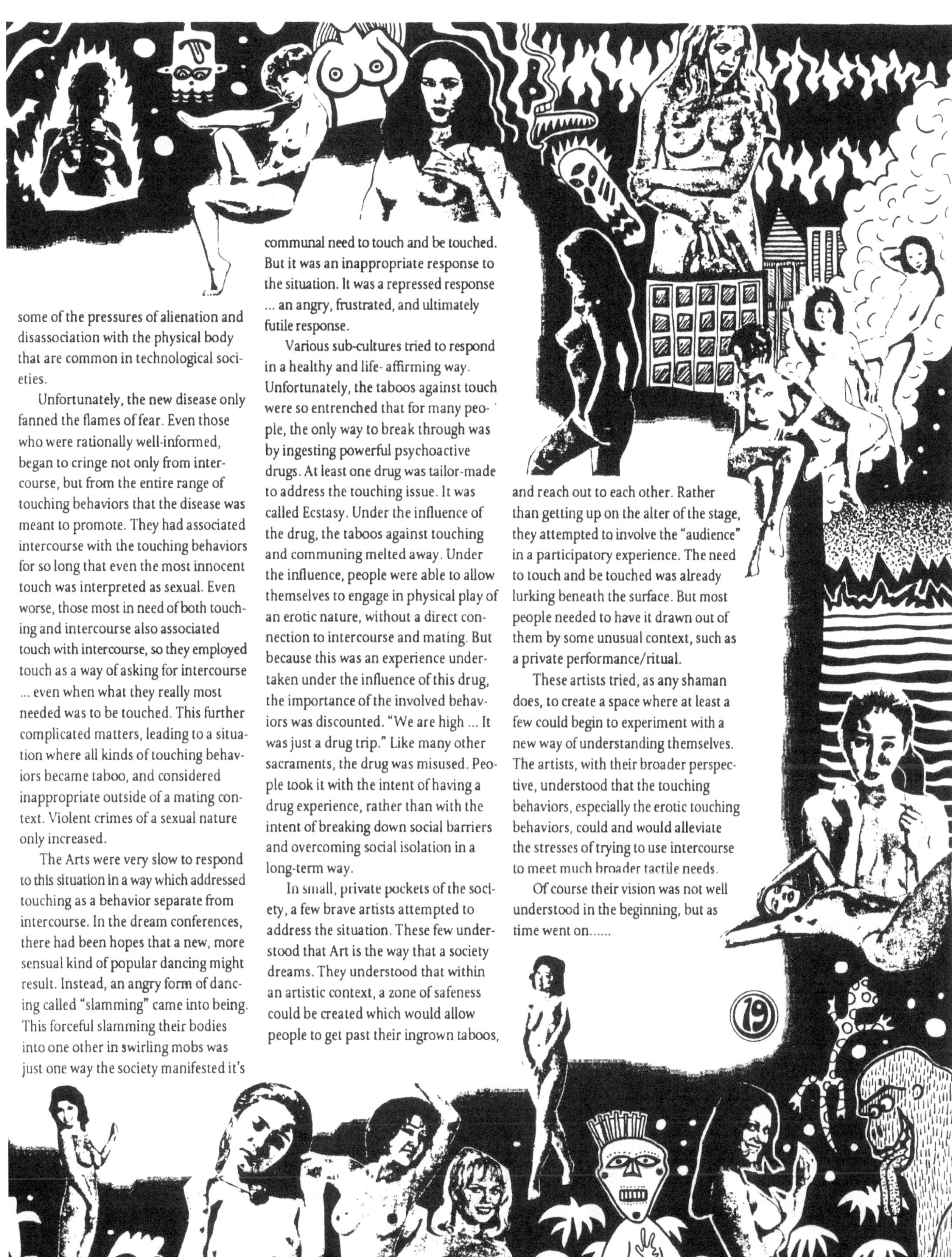

some of the pressures of alienation and disassociation with the physical body that are common in technological societies.

Unfortunately, the new disease only fanned the flames of fear. Even those who were rationally well-informed, began to cringe not only from intercourse, but from the entire range of touching behaviors that the disease was meant to promote. They had associated intercourse with the touching behaviors for so long that even the most innocent touch was interpreted as sexual. Even worse, those most in need of both touching and intercourse also associated touch with intercourse, so they employed touch as a way of asking for intercourse ... even when what they really most needed was to be touched. This further complicated matters, leading to a situation where all kinds of touching behaviors became taboo, and considered inappropriate outside of a mating context. Violent crimes of a sexual nature only increased.

The Arts were very slow to respond to this situation in a way which addressed touching as a behavior separate from intercourse. In the dream conferences, there had been hopes that a new, more sensual kind of popular dancing might result. Instead, an angry form of dancing called "slamming" came into being. This forceful slamming their bodies into one other in swirling mobs was just one way the society manifested it's communal need to touch and be touched. But it was an inappropriate response to the situation. It was a repressed response ... an angry, frustrated, and ultimately futile response.

Various sub-cultures tried to respond in a healthy and life- affirming way. Unfortunately, the taboos against touch were so entrenched that for many people, the only way to break through was by ingesting powerful psychoactive drugs. At least one drug was tailor-made to address the touching issue. It was called Ecstasy. Under the influence of the drug, the taboos against touching and communing melted away. Under the influence, people were able to allow themselves to engage in physical play of an erotic nature, without a direct connection to intercourse and mating. But because this was an experience undertaken under the influence of this drug, the importance of the involved behaviors was discounted. "We are high ... It was just a drug trip." Like many other sacraments, the drug was misused. People took it with the intent of having a drug experience, rather than with the intent of breaking down social barriers and overcoming social isolation in a long-term way.

In small, private pockets of the society, a few brave artists attempted to address the situation. These few understood that Art is the way that a society dreams. They understood that within an artistic context, a zone of safeness could be created which would allow people to get past their ingrown taboos, and reach out to each other. Rather than getting up on the alter of the stage, they attempted to involve the "audience" in a participatory experience. The need to touch and be touched was already lurking beneath the surface. But most people needed to have it drawn out of them by some unusual context, such as a private performance/ritual.

These artists tried, as any shaman does, to create a space where at least a few could begin to experiment with a new way of understanding themselves. The artists, with their broader perspective, understood that the touching behaviors, especially the erotic touching behaviors, could and would alleviate the stresses of trying to use intercourse to meet much broader tactile needs.

Of course their vision was not well understood in the beginning, but as time went on......

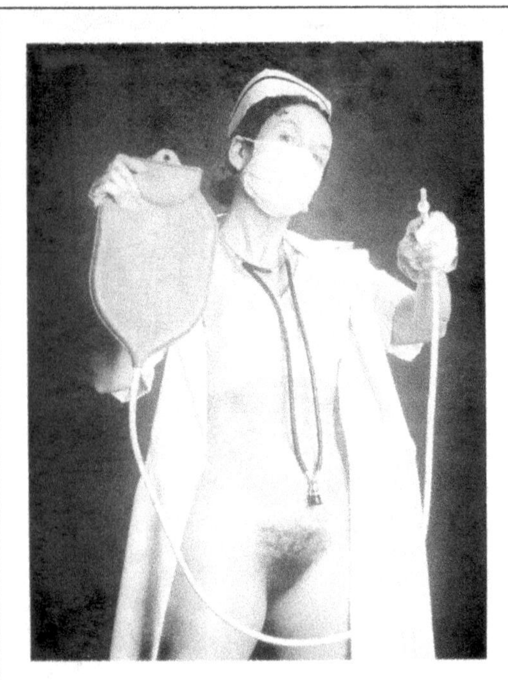

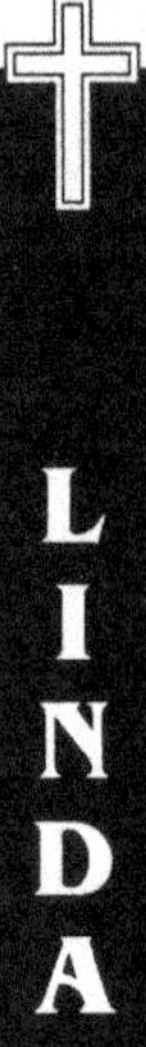

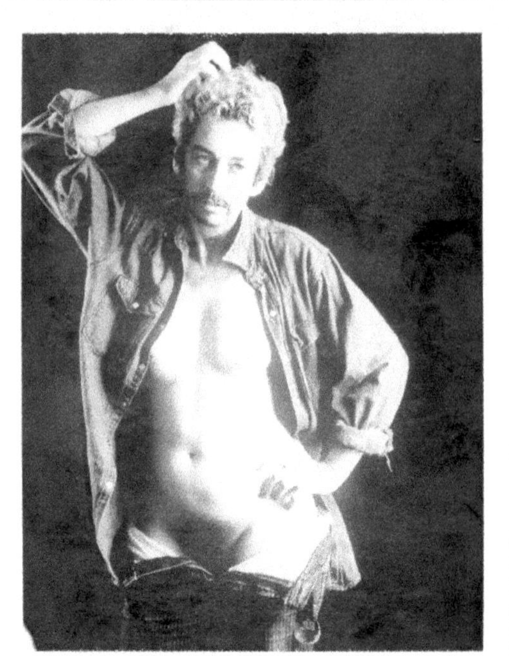

photos by

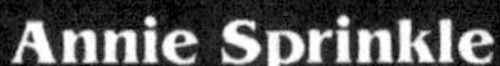

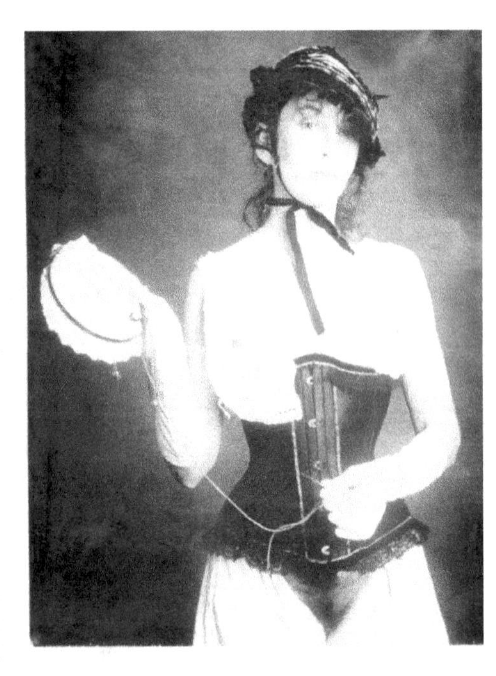

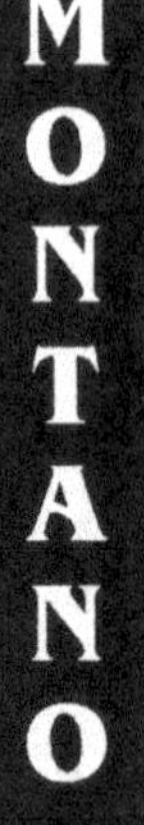

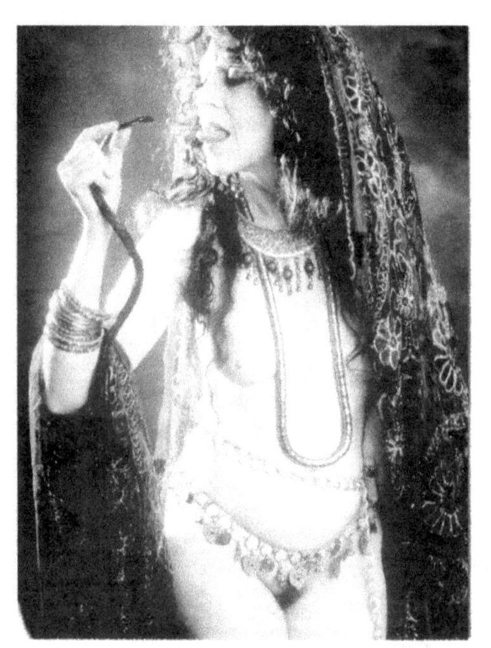

Love Poem in Blue

For P.R.

i am all of you.
take me

i lie against you
an extended metaphone
in work shirt
between blue black waves
of sheets.

sometimes we undulate
in these raw places
secret as snakes
our fox eyes beating in the luminous dark

but at the moment
we lie still
sated with our knowledge
breathing in the freshness
of new sheets
tailored and perfect
as soft flat leaves.

we speak
about the war
any war, our
frailities,
what you will do tomorrow
it makes no difference.

behind this language
tempered with need
and distance
this language of nouns
and future tenses

is the language
of our bodies
hung briefly here
and finally silent
a dark sacrifice
between wishes

a pulse/
of blood.

i wrote a fuck poem and let julie read it.

julie put down the piece of paper and looked
at me with a kind of disappointed resignation.

"what's wrong?" i said. "you didn't like it?"

"no, it was good," she said with a sigh. "real
good. i just wish you would fuck like you write."

poems by robert w. howington

smell this, honey.

i watched a deodorant commercial
on tv and a buxom, young woman,
sitting very upright on a couch
in a beautiful home, said in an
uppity, miss scarlett-gone with
the wind tone, "i just can't get
close to a guy if he smells."

well, dear, i can believe that
coming from a high-maintainance
bitch like you, but if the guy's
got a dick the size of a brick i
don't think you'd mind the b.o.

julie thought she had heard it all.

my wife, julie, was born with
one arm. people often look at
her armlessness with confused
stares, which say, like, wow,
that woman's only got one arm.

recently, a guy walked up and
asked her about her armlessness.

"were you born an amputee?"

i can't even get safe sex

i tried a phone sex line
for the first time the
other day.

clara told me i should
get more comfortable by
taking off all my clothes.

as soon as i got naked
our connection went bad.

the old woman waiting to
use the phone began yelling
at me so loud and banging
her fists against the booth's
glass so hard i couldn't
hear a word clara said.

armlessness

my wife, julie, was born
with only one arm.

she does things with
her one arm that two-
armed people take for
granted, like tying
her shoelaces, driving
a stickshift, putting
on a wristwatch and
shooting pool.

two-armed people may
not consider having
only one arm advantageous,
but julie knows otherwise.

"my deodorant," she says,
"lasts twice as long."

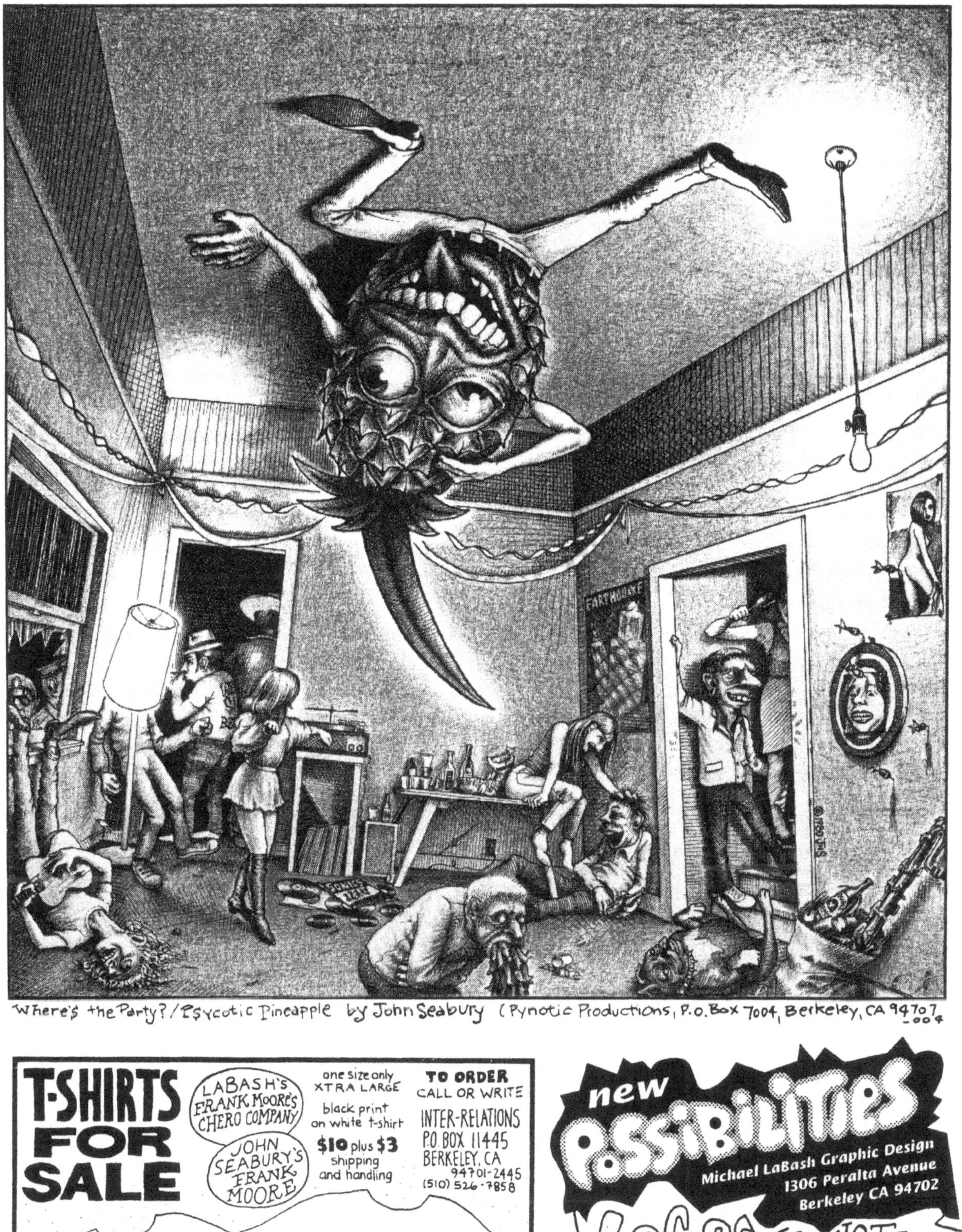

Where's the Party?/Psycotic Pineapple by John Seabury (Pynotic Productions, P.O. Box 7004, Berkeley, CA 94707-0004

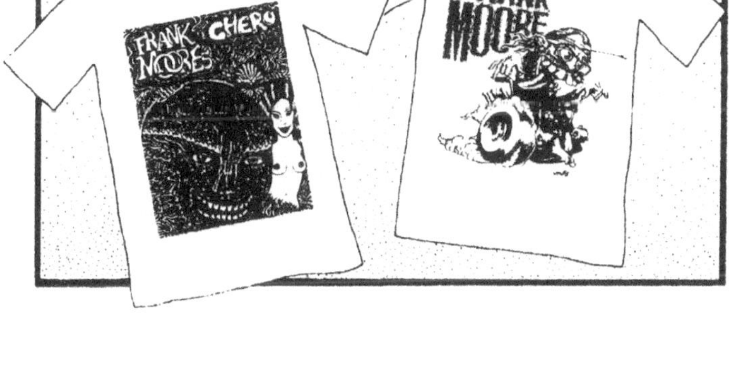

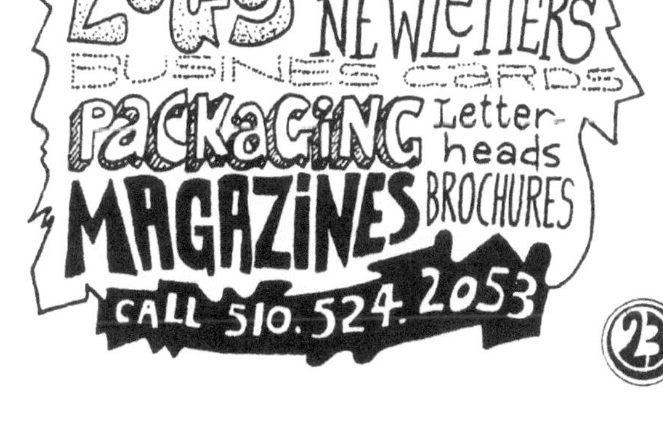

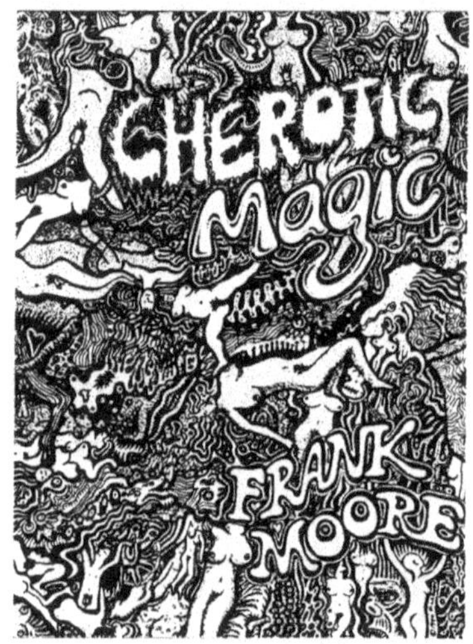

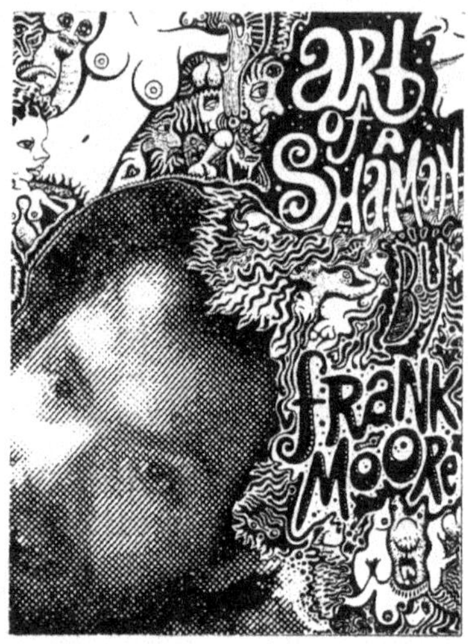

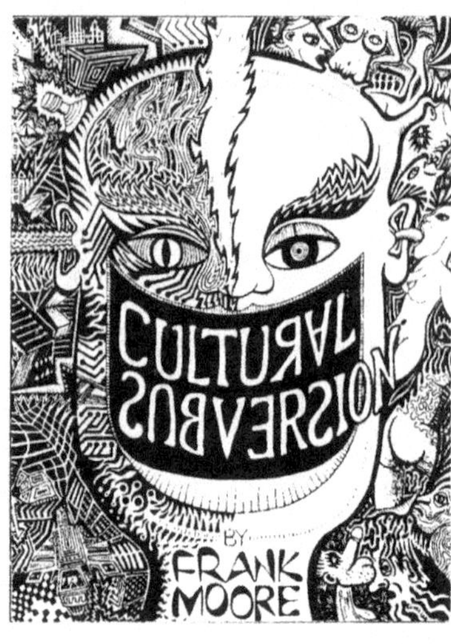

cherotic magic **$15**

A MAJOR ATTEMPT TO INTRODUCE A POWERFUL SYSTEM OF MAGIC INTO OUR MODERN WESTERN EVERYDAY LIFE, THEREBY EXPLOSIVELY EXPANDING SUCH CONCEPTS AS SEX, HUMAN RELATIONSHIPS. THE CLEAR, DOWN-TO-EARTH TEXT IS AMPLIFIED BY THE NON-LINEAR TRANCE ILLUSTRATIONS BY LABASH.
published 1990

BOOKS & ZINES

BY **frank moore**

art of a shaman **$4**

IN art of a shaman, ORIGINALLY A LECTURE PRESENTED AT N.Y.U., FRANK MOORE EXPLORES PERFORMANCE AND ART IN GENERAL TERMS OF THEM BEING A MAGICAL WAY TO EFFECT CHANGE IN THE WORLD. HE LOOKS AT PERFORMANCE AS AN ART OF MELTING ACTION, RITUALISTIC, SHAMANISTIC DOINGS/PLAYINGS. BY USING HIS CAREER AND LIFE AS A "BASELINE", MOORE EXPLAINS THE DYNAMIC PLAYING WITHIN THE CONTEXT OF REALITY SHAPING. HE BRINGS IN CONCEPTS FROM MODERN PHYSICS, MYTHOLOGY, AND PSYCHOLOGY. COVER BY LABASH.
published 1991

cultural subversion **$1**

PERSONAL, ANARCHICAL TECHNOLOGIES SUCH AS XEROGRAPHY, VCR, FAXS, ETC., ARE EXAMINED IN cultural subversion BY FRANK MOORE AS THE MEANS BY WHICH ORDINARY PEOPLE CAN TAKE BACK THE CONTROL OF COMMUNICATIONS AND CREATIVITY FROM THE CENTRAL POWER COMBINE.
published 1992

art of living **$10**

A GUIDE TO DOWN-TO-EARTH SPIRITUALITY AS CHANNELLED BY FRANK MOORE.
published 1987

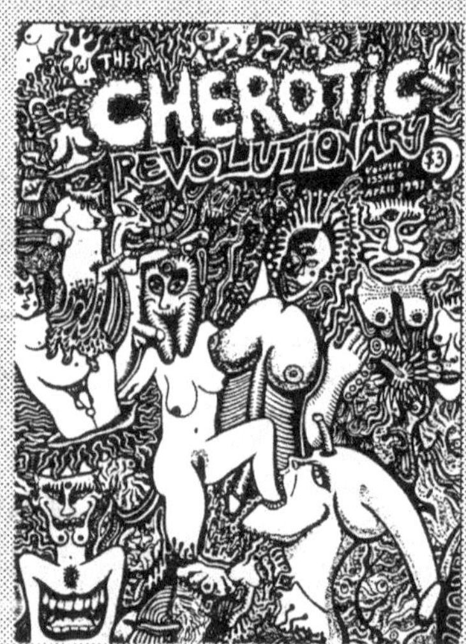

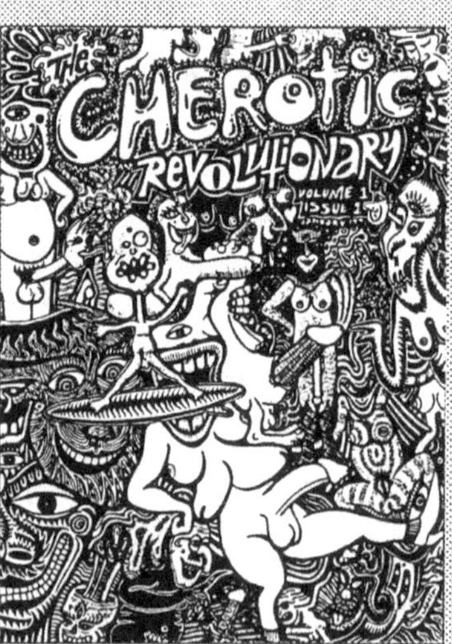

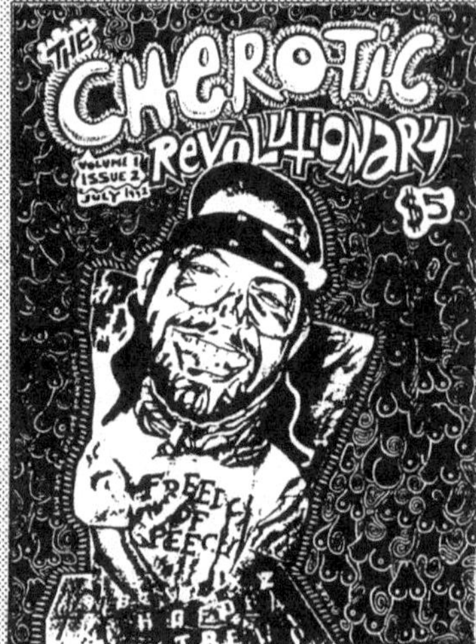

TCR #0, *april 1991* **$3**

POEM AND ESSAYS BY **FRANK MOORE**
ARTWORK BY **LABASH**
CORRESPONDANCES BETWEEN EDITOR AND **BRENDA LOEW TATELBAUM, STEVE HIRSH, ETC.**
PHOTO BY **ERIC KROLL**

TCR #1, *january 1992* **$5**

POEMS BY **KAREN FINLEY, NONI HOWARD, TRACY MOSTOVOY, FRANK MOORE, JACK FOLEY** AND **JESSE BEAGLE**
ARTWORK BY **LABASH**
PHOTOS BY **TRACY MOSTOVOY** AND **ERIC KROLL**
CARTOON BY **WILL OF THE WISP**

TCR #2, *july 1992* **$5**

ESSAYS BY **FRANK MOORE, CURTIS YORK** AND **KYLE GRIFFITH**
ARTWORK BY **LEE KAY, H.R. GIGER, PETER PETRISKO, JR., JOHN SEABURY** AND **LABASH**
PHOTO BY **KEVIN RICE**
POEM BY **BARNABY CHANCELLOR**

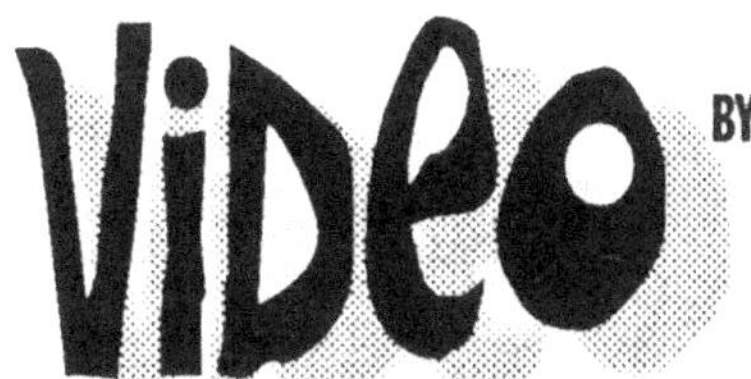

BY **frank moore**

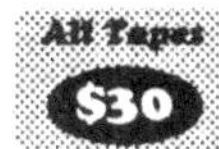

fairy tales can come true
THIS IS A FILM ABOUT RELATIONSHIPS AND DISABILITY STARRING FRANK MOORE, WHO HAS BEEN DISABLED SINCE BIRTH WITH CEREBRAL PALSY. IT IS A HUMOROUS, YET REALISTIC LOOK AT HOW TO ESTABLISH RELATIONSHIPS BY CHANGING NEGATIVE SELF IMAGE.
copyrighted 1981 *35 minutes*

erotic play
THIS VIDEO EXPLORES WHAT HAPPENS WHEN PEOPLE OF ALL TYPES AND AGES ARE GIVEN A CHANCE TO RETURN TO BEING A KID AGAIN. A SIMPLE GAME OF DRESS-UP BECOMES A POWERFUL METAPHOR FOR DROPPING TABOOS, RELEASING CREATIVE EMOTION, AND FOR DRAMATIC CHANGE. AS A RESULT, AN INNOCENT EROTICISM IS FOUND... AS WELL AS GETTING INTIMATE WITH 60 HUMANS.
copyrighted 1983 *84 minutes*

outrageous dream
A SURREAL, VISUAL POEM OF FOUND IMAGES.
copyrighted 1984 *41 minutes*

the nude cave
AN EROTIC, SURREALISTIC VIDEO DREAM THAT COMBINES NON-LINEAR IMAGES AND FRANK'S ORIGINAL MUSIC SCORE.
copyrighted 1984 *113 minutes*

out of isolation
A SURREAL EROTIC EXAMINATION OF AN INTIMATE RELATIONSHIP OF NEED. STARRING FRANK MOORE AND LINDA SIBIO.
copyrighted 1989 *105 minutes*

the outrageous beauty revue
THIS RAW VIDEO DOCUMENTS THE TACKY, MUSICAL, OVER-THE-EDGE COMEDY REVUE THAT FRANK CREATED, DIRECTED AND PERFORMED IN. THE SHOW RAN ON A WEEKLY BASIS FOR THREE AND ONE HALF YEARS AT THE MABUHAY GARDENS IN SAN FRANCISCO IN ADDITION TO A NUMBER OF OTHER NORTHERN CALIFORNIA AND NEVADA PERFORMANCES. FRANK PERFORMED ALONG WITH THE THIRTY PEOPLE WHO MADE UP HIS THEATRE GROUP, "the theatre of human melting."
copyrighted 1980 *approx. 30 minutes*

chero collage
ATTEMPTS TO CAPTURE THE TRANCE STATE OF LIVE, SHAMANISTIC PERFORMANCE COMBINING FOOTAGE OF SEVERAL OF chero company's RITUALS INTO A REALITY-WARPING VIDEO.
copyrighted 1992 *27 minutes*

the outrageous horror show
A LIVE CABARET SHOW THAT BREAKS THROUGH THE LIMITING TABOOS, THROUGH MESSY NIGHTMARES, INTO THE DREAMS OF ALL POSSIBILITIES.
copyrighted 1992 *32 minutes*

To order call or write:
inter-relations, p.o.box 11445
berkeley, ca 94701-2445
(510) 526 7858

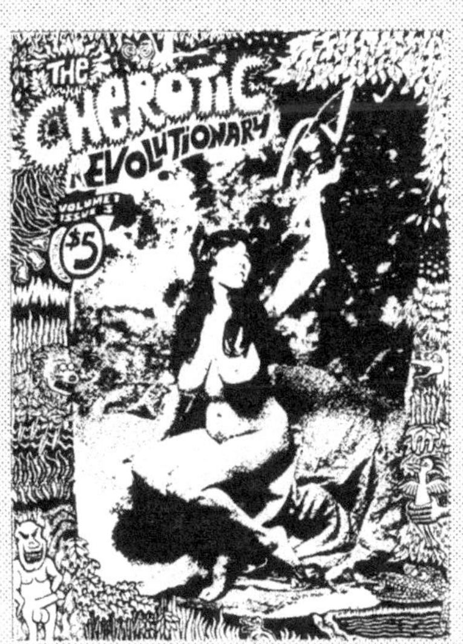

TCR #3, *april 1993* **$5**

POEMS BY **R. (DIXI) COHN, ANNIE SPRINKLE, MERLE TOFER, JESSE BEAGLE**
ESSAYS BY **VERONICA VERA, LUNA SANGUINE** AND **FRANK MOORE**
PHOTOS BY **RICHARD SILVARNES, WINK VAN KEMPEN, ROBERT MAPLETHORPE, ANNIE SPRINKLE, MARC TRUNZ, AMY ARDREY** AND **JAN DEEN**
ARTWORK BY **LABASH** AND **JOHN SEABURY**

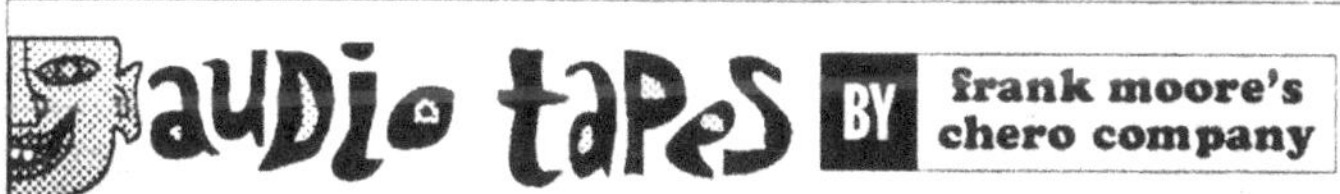

All Tapes **$5**

body music
EXPLORING THE HUMAN BODY AS MUSICAL INSTRUMENT.
90 minutes

inter-rhythms
PRIMAL MUSIC CREATED FOR FRANK MOORE'S RITUAL PERFORMANCES.
90 minutes

nude cave soundtrack
THE NONLINEAR ELECTRONIC MUSIC COMPOSED AND PERFORMED BY FRANK MOORE FOR THE FEATURE LENGTH VIDEO. *110 minutes*

rock of passion
THE SOUNDTRACK OF the outrageous horror show, FRANK THE ROCKSTAR SINGS HIS HEART OUT, LITERALLY COVERING THE GREAT HITS OF ROCK, COUNTRY, AND HEAVY METAL ... INCLUDING SUCH SMASHES AS i am woman, i got you babe, AND hand of doom ...

trance rap
WRITTEN BY FRANK MOORE AND SUNG/CHANTED BY MICHAEL LABASH WITH A BACKGROUND OF BODY MUSIC, trance rap IS AN AUDIO INTRODUCTION TO CHEROTIC MAGIC COVERING SUCH SUBJECTS AS eroplay, the plot of fragmentation AND magic art. ALSO INCLUDED IS THE POEM wrapping/rocking.
30 minutes

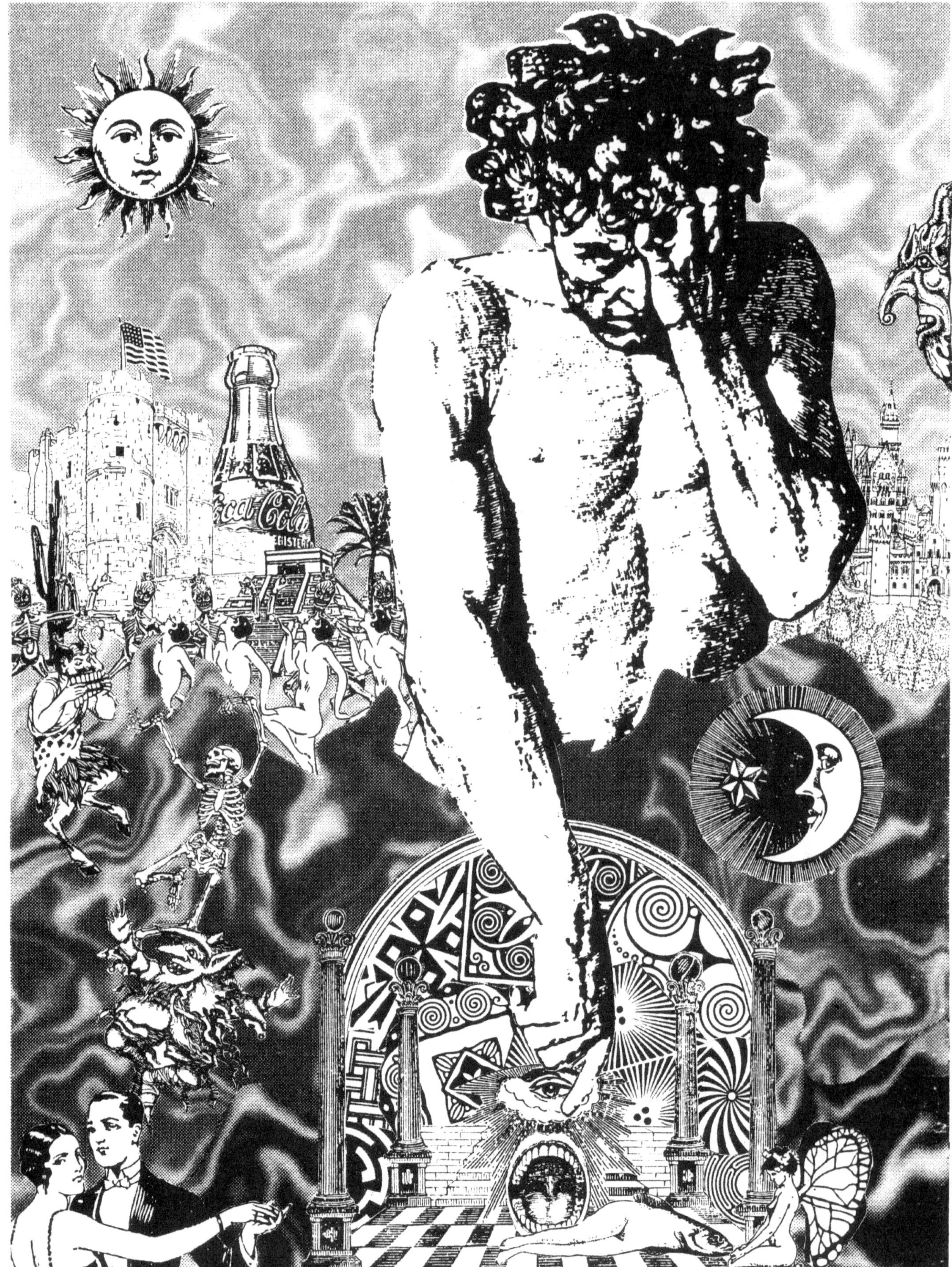

Collage ©1993 LaBash, Rubber stamps by Imagick

REVIEWS

The Cherotic rEvolutionary #4
January 1994

"A 'zine about 'the edge' for and by people on the edge....if not over the edge.' Put out by Linda Mac and Frank Moore, amazing person who invented the word eroplay.... For over two decades Frank has been doing ritual trance in private and public 'performances' with the magic of touch, 'going into taboo areas, to push beyond where it is comfortable and safe, to explore and build a larger zone of safeness.' I feel a deep gratitude for the risks and challenges the Inter-Relations group have taken, weaving their web of magic radical possibilities. It's like its their lava in our eruptions. 'The basic secret of magic is to like life, to love life, to throw yourself into life so completely, so extensically that you lose yourself as a source in the individual sense. You become a point in a wave' (from an upcoming piece of Frank's)."
GAWE

"This erotic zine is put out by the Shamanistic teacher Frank Moore and his very creative friends. You'll find thought and emotion provoking articles, essays, poems, photos and drawings. An example is Frank's work entitled 'Tribal Performance'. He expresses, '... I am not interested in just putting my cock into your body. I want much more than sex. I want to put my whole body into your body ... I want our naked skin to melt together ...' He stresses the need and importance of touching and connecting with each other, not only with the body, but with the whole mind and spirit. To be magically alive and to truly experience! Also, the visual stuff is great. The front cover of TCR Volume 1 Issue 4, created by LaBash, is especially superb. It consists of a collage incorporating various rubber stamps such as 'Turn On', 'Free Love' and 'Flower Power'. Refreshingly reminiscent of the late 60's and early 70's! All this with a sense of humor too, as evidenced by the words of Frank Moore. After getting nice reviews and receiving 'friendly letters' from advertising agencies asking for ad rates, he writes, 'It is a cause for concern ...are we getting too slick, too acceptable ... are we, god forbid, politically correct ... or to use the more politically correct term for politically correct ... are we culturally sensitive? Is there a worse fate? Like being undead ...'"
Open Forum #6, June 1994 (Athens, Greece)

"Thanks for TC(r)#4. You guys are doing great work."
Roma, Good Vibrations

REVIEWS CONTINUED...

"A curious mixture of sex, spirituality and tribal magic. Warm Silk, by Carol Queen was really good - truly erotic, which is something not many things are. Generally mad bad gender bending stereotype bashing (like people with disabilities are sexual) taboo breaking material. Photos by Annie Sprinkle and one by Nina Glaser which I found quite disturbing, a moving and disturbing poem about incarceration in a mental hospital, various other poetry in lighter veins, and articles and prose. Guaranteed to deeply offend some people and delight others."
ByPass (England)

"Here we have a stylishly-done zine with erotica, cool artwork, photos, poetry and more. It's fun to read and look at because it seems to have a variety of people submitting stuff. Seeing as much of the content deals with sex, it's not for anti-body types."
Sniper's Nest #2, Fall 1994

"I just got ... The Cherotic (r)Evolutionary and I am blown away. This is an incredible zine, you should be very proud!!! I was so impressed I dropped everything I was doing and read it cover to cover."
Molly Holzschlag, artist

"Frank Moore is a legend around these parts - organizing performances and workshops about the transformative nature of tribal sex magic. This is an intense zine mixing psychedelia, rubber stamps, photographs, poetry, and rants ... If you can't make it to one of his workshops he also produces books, videos, and audio tapes."
R. Seth Friedman, Factsheet Five

"Frank Moore has earned a name for himself in the Bay Area by organizing performances and workshops about the transformative nature of tribal sex magic. This intense 'zine mixes articles on psychedelia with photographs, poetry, and essays."
R. Seth Friedman, Bay Guardian

"Frank Moore, with Linda Mac's strong assistance, has not been deterred by his 99 per cent physical disability and the inspiration he generates with the friends who tag along are a whole story of determination in itself. Add his challenging stand for passion, love and freedom."
Peter Riden, The Affiliate (Canada)

REVIEWS CONTINUED...

"The cover art leads us to believe this issue will take us back to the counterculture of the '60s sexual revolution. But thirty years later, what with desktop publishing, GEnie/e-mail, Tower Records distribution, inquiries from advertising agencies, printers & record companies and feeling great about offending separatist/ sexist/ elitist politically-correct feminists and gays, performance artist and shaman publisher Frank Moore appears content with the knowledge and wisdom he's acquired from the successes of his lifework!! Another Highly Recommended issue of TCR, 'a zine about 'The Edge' for and by people on The Edge if not over The Edge.'"
EIDOS Magazine, Volume 7, Number 4, 1994

"Art, sexuality, breaking barriers."
Slingshot, Vol 1 #51, May 1994

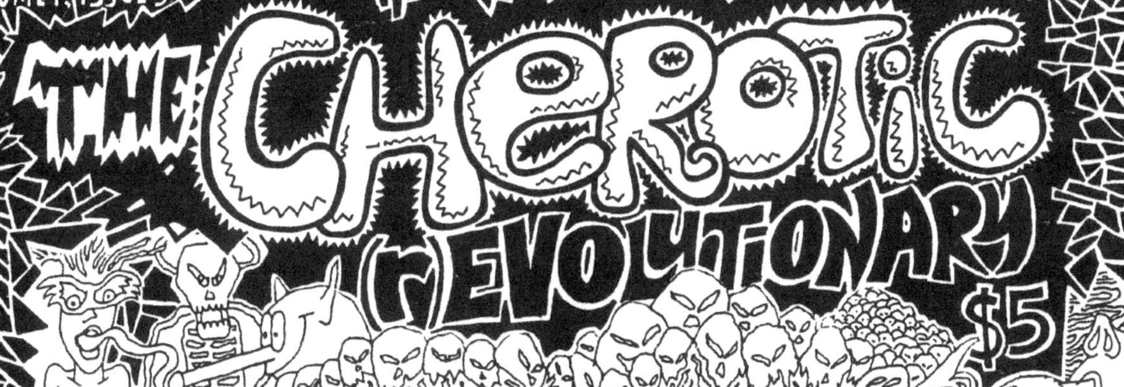

WARNING

ENTER at YOUR OWN RISK!

This piece may be threatening to your everyday reality.

This piece may cause questioning of the common morality.

These symptoms may appear days after the piece without warning ... even if during the piece, you may feel as if nothing is happening ... or you may even enjoy it. BUT above symptoms may still appear, leading to restlessness, and even to radical change.

FRANK MOORE

In Defense of Bad Art

One of the things I will be doing in this piece is to defend the right of bad art to be fully protected under the Bill of Rights as a form of speech. To do this, I will use the Berkeley performance group known as the X-plicit Players as an example of bad art.

Before we get to the particular case, we should lay out some universal truths:

Bad art is the manure from which good and great art springs. All artists have done some bad art. A large percentage of art could be called bad art. In other words, you can not have any art without having bad art anymore than you can have any science without having most experimentation be "failures". So we have to protect the right and the freedom to do bad art. We also have to keep the government out of art criticism.

Now for the background to the particular case. Berkeley until this year has not had a law against public nudity. In fact, over the years, performance artists such as Paul Cotton and myself have done "street pieces" containing nudity in Berkeley with community acceptance and support. But about two years ago, public nudity became a political issue. A U.C. student, Andrew Martinez, who the media dubbed The Naked Guy, began going to his classes and walking around town nude. Martinez seems to be an idealist suffering from naivete ... which is natural at his age. The college administration, as is the nature of the beast, expelled him.

Around this time, the X-plicit Players began to affix themselves to the controversy by walking nude around town and sitting in coffeehouses wearing only chips on their shoulders ... and of course being with Martinez when the cameras were on him. In art, using confrontation, in-your-face methods are very valid to incite change. In bad art, confrontation is often used for calling attention, recognition, to the artist creating an arrogance around the artist. All of which may be an unavoidable, if embarrassing, stage in an artist's development. Be that as it may, the tactics that the X-plicit Players used created considerable resentment in the community. That resentment was transferred to public nudity in the minds of a sizeable portion of the community, a community that usually prides itself on its openness, tolerance, and freedom. One of the functions of art is to offend, to create tension by revealing hidden aspects of life. The bad artist does this for his own aggrandizement or other questionable motives. But to keep our freedom, we must remember that we do not have a right to not be offended.

At this point, a Berkeley council-person, who for some reason does not want her children to see nude bodies, used this built-up resentment to push through a very reactionary law against public nudity. So the home of the Free Speech Movement now has a law that is clearly unconstitutional, a law that not only outlaws public nudity, but outlaws a lot of different kinds of clothing (including a lot of swimsuits ... unintentionally).

To be a test case of an clearly unconstitutional law is the easiest ... and one of the best ... ways for an artist to get in the papers and in the history books. One of the exceptions to the nudity law that the "liberals" wrote into the law to ease their consciences was theatrical events. That is, public nudity in theatrical events is permitted. So the X-plicit Players apparently put on a street theater event. And they were arrested.

Now we come to the meat of my essay. If the X-plicit event was held in a theater, in a performance space, in a gallery, the X-plicit Players would not have been arrested because the logic of the cops would be "it's in a theater, so it is theater". The logic of the arrest was "it isn't in a theater, so it is not theater, thus it is covered by the anti-nudity law". The issue is not whether the X-plicit Players are good or bad theater/art. Rather, the issue is are they theater/art, thus under all of the protection afforded to theater/art. But the core issue is can the government decree that the S.F. Mime Troupe, the satirist/humorist Stoney Burke who works the crowd on Sproul Plaza, street theater, union theater, performers like myself, are not theater or art when we do our work outdoors, in public, in the parks, etc. No matter what I or anyone else think of their work, the X-plicit Players are a theater/performance group.

Although the charges were finally dropped, the bad logic of the judge at the hearing on the constitutionality of the charges is frightening. Judge Ron Greenberg's decision was "I don't know this is a live theatrical performance deserving First Amendment protection". Greenberg explained that he had difficulty in finding a satisfactory legal definition of a live theatrical performance. Because this performance included spontaneity, he decided to rule that the performance would be viewed as "conduct" and not as "speech" and therefore was not protected by the First Amendment. Greenberg seemed afraid that a member of the audience might "spontaneously" at some future performance, decide to have sexual intercourse.

Let's run that by again. A performance that has any kind of spontaneity is not speech, and thus not protected ... because of an unknown possibility which may or may not happen sometime in the future! That would include any work containing any space of freedom, including improvisation, jamming, jazz, dancing, and on and on. Like I said, it is very frightening!

You bet I would say the X-plicit Players are art and theater. Freedom and art are worth it.

Frank Moore
October 28, 1993

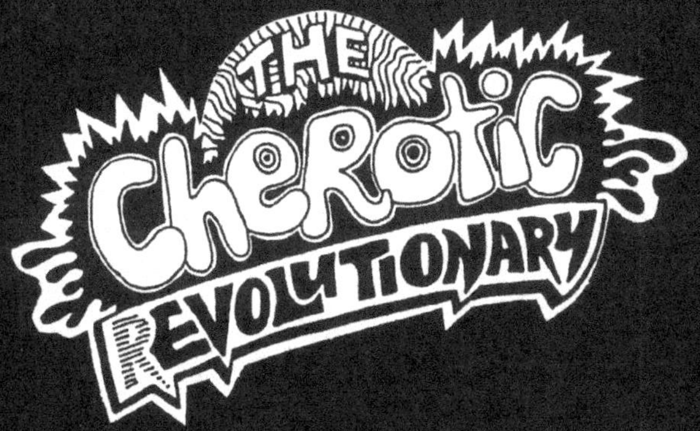

THE CHEROTIC (r)EVOLUTIONARY IS A ZINE ABOUT "THE EDGE" FOR AND BY PEOPLE ON THE EDGE.... IF NOT OVER THE EDGE.

TC(r) IS PUBLISHED BY INTER-RELATIONS. THE PUBLISHERS/EDITORS ARE FRANK MOORE & LINDA MAC, THE ART EDITOR IS MICHAEL LABASH, AND THE CIRCULATION MANAGER IS ALEXI MALENKY.

THE PRICE FOR THIS ISSUE IS $5.00 PER COPY. WE DON'T SELL SUBSCRIPTIONS, TO AVOID TYING OURSELVES DOWN TO A RIGID PUBLICATION SCHEDULE OR MAGAZINE SIZE. WE WANT TO REMAIN FREE TO PUBLISH FREQUENTLY OR LARGER ISSUES AT LONGER INTERVALS AND ADJUST THE PRICE ACCORDINGLY.

WE HEARTILY ENCOURAGE LETTERS OF COMMENT FROM READERS AND WILL ANSWER AS MANY AS WE CAN. PLEASE TELL US IF YOU DON'T WANT US TO PRINT MATERIAL FROM YOUR LETTER - OTHERWISE WE WILL ASSUME IT'S OK.

PLEASE ADDRESS ALL CORRESPONDENCE AND ORDERS FOR MAGAZINES TO:
FRANK MOORE, P.O. BOX 11445
BERKELEY, CA 94712

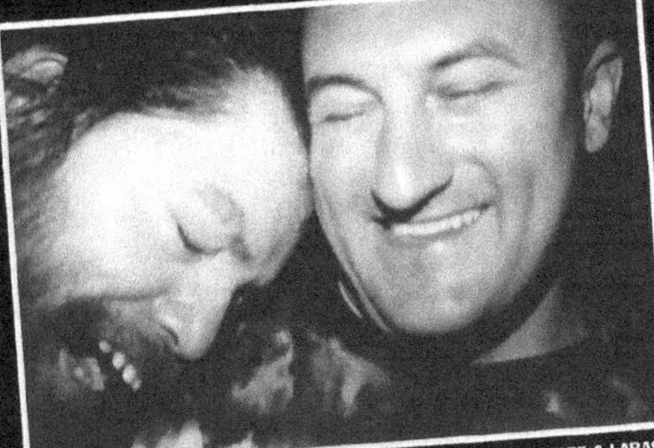

FRANK MOORE & LABASH
photo by Linda Mac

TC(R)'S AD POLICY
Recently we have recieved several inquiries about how to buy ads in The Cherotic (r)evolutionary. Although we are not actively seeking such ads, we are not precluding them either. However, we will judge whether or not to accept an ad.

TC(r) is a xeroxed, black and white zine that is published irregularly... if we are lucky, twice a year. So it is not the place for fancy color ads or for ads with time deadlines. On the other hand, TC(r) magically finds its way around the world.

TO SUBMIT AN AD
Send us a copy of your ad and a S.A.S.E. If we accept it, we send you the rate for your ad ... and if we need anything from you such as half-tones, we will tell you. If we don't accept it, we will send your ad back.

AD RATES
Sliding scale: $10-$50 per quarter of a standard typing page. The scale slides according to our whim.

HOW WE ACCEPT AN AD
Our whim also is a big factor in accepting an ad. Another factor is the other contents of the particular issue. And there maybe other factors which are unknown even to us.

FREE TC(r) COPIES
Because we are not actively looking for paid ads, we do not give free copies to would-be advertisers. But we encourage them to buy a back issue or two. However, we do give you a free copy of the issue in which your ad appears.

Frank Moore
November 12, 1993

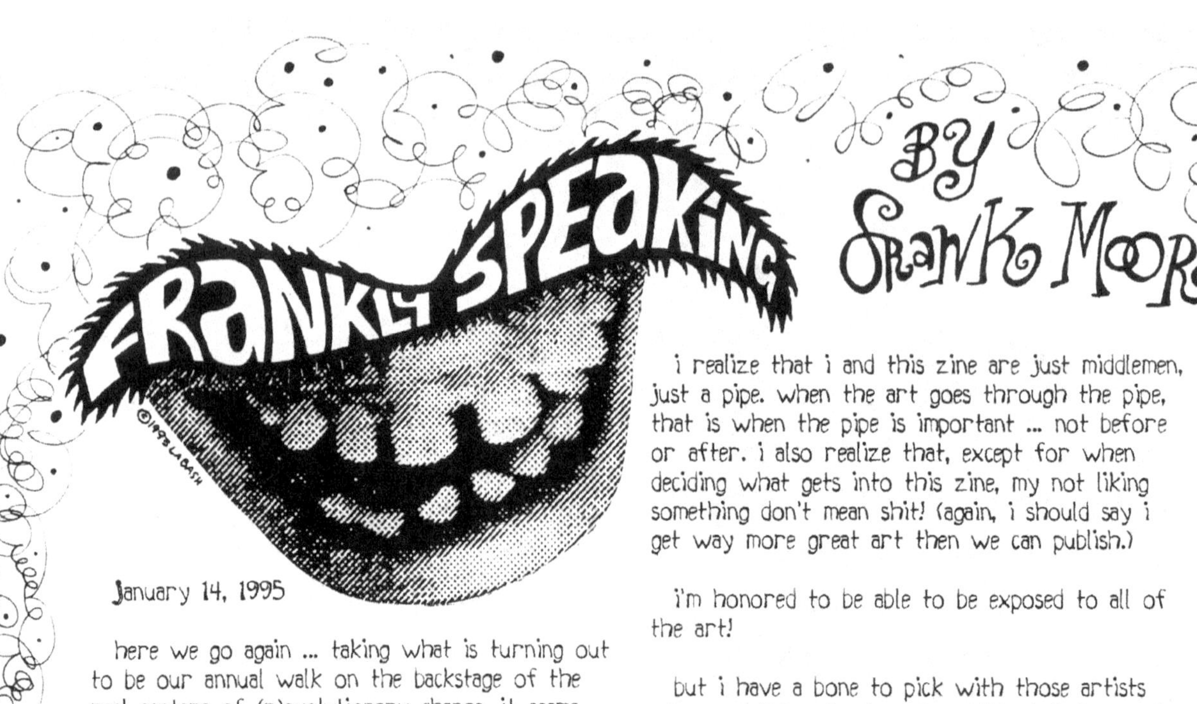

January 14, 1995

here we go again ... taking what is turning out to be our annual walk on the backstage of the real centers of (r)evolutionary change. it seems we can get out only one issue a year ... not because of any lack of great material ... we have about half of the next (year's) issue waiting in our file. it's because we have a great full life ... which **tc**(r) is one part of. in other words, don't rush us! after all, look at this issue. wasn't it worth the wait? we have added more pages, then crammed stuff in.

we had to because every time we go to our p.o. box, it's full of great art, photographs, and writings from around the world. it is one of the perks of doing a zine ... one of the privileges of being a linking channel between you writers/artists and you readers. and one of the hardest aspects of being a channel is deciding what to leave out because of limited space.

have you noticed there is a plague in all walks of modern life of people forgetting their function as servers? we editors tend to take our position much too seriously (or not seriously enough). one editor of a literary magazine actually charges writers a dollar a poem ($3 a short story) for the "privilege" of having her read their stuff ... and they don't get a comp copy if she publishes their work! then there are editors who come unglued if another zine prints, without giving him "credit", a poem that he had first published ... as if he shares ownership rights with the poet ... maybe he has forgotten that he had neither hired the poet to write it nor bought it from the poet ... he had just published it. then there are the editors who must think that when a poet sends her work to them, she is asking them for their god-like judgments!

i realize that i and this zine are just middlemen, just a pipe. when the art goes through the pipe, that is when the pipe is important ... not before or after. i also realize that, except for when deciding what gets into this zine, my not liking something don't mean shit! (again, i should say i get way more great art then we can publish.)

i'm honored to be able to be exposed to all of the art!

but i have a bone to pick with those artists who send lists of who has published their work before. frankly, i don't care. what we have here is a place where we mix everything and everyone together to get something fresh.

i need to thank the zine community for all the kind reviews of **tc**(r) over the years. i only wish they would not classify **tc**(r) as a sex zine. we do have a lot of sex in us. we will never shy away from that. but we really are an anarchist/arts/avant-garde/experimental/art/beat/cartoons/community/counter-culture/alternatives/culture/dada/surrealism/erotica/essays/ethics/feminism/fiction/gay/humanism/humor/interview/lesbianism/libertarian/literature(general)/magic/non-fiction/philosophy/photography/poetry/prose/psychology/satire/sex/short stories/spiritual zine ... or a life on the edge zine ... for short.

finally, i need to footnote my talk with paul krassner. i'm a very lucky guy to be able to spend time with one of my heros ... who else has dropped acid with groucho? anyway, when we were talking about l.b.j., what that referred to is the hoax paul pulled. in the 60's, there was a book about john kennedy that jackie had censored. paul published what he said were the censored parts ... in which jackie saw l.b.j. fucking john in his neck wound in his coffin on the plane ride from dallas. the rest is history!

see you next year ... or look for my june performance in toronto ... or in the bay area!

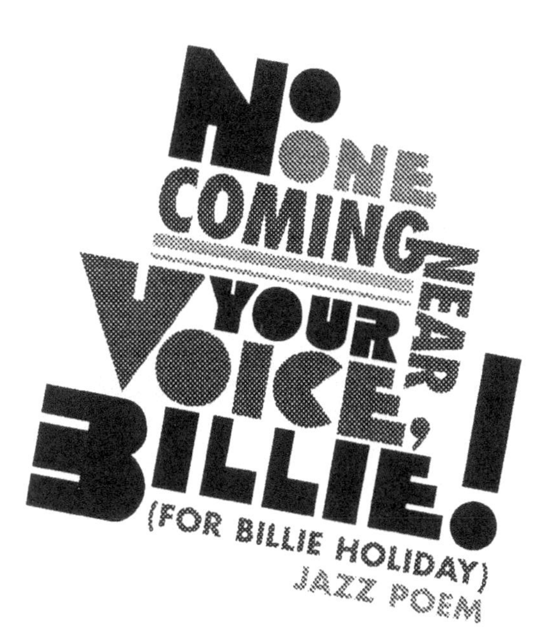

Someone played your record
I didn't say WHO WAS THAT?
Beyond singing
I didn't say WHO WAS THAT?
Beyond singer
I didn't say, WHO WAS THAT?

I said, WHAT was that?

Like the first time I saw a Rodriguez sculpture
and said, "that can't be a sculpture,
is it an artifact?
dead - yet living?"

Billie! Billie! Billie sculpting sound like NOBODY'S sound
You could hear
Bessie, Ma Rainey, Leadbelly, she left nobody's sound
out,
but turned them__inside out shook the notes like loaded dice,
exploding dice, tugging them inside out on a drawstring from her
pure and holy black soul wholly giving it up

"Only sweetness will come out of your mouth," it was written
on saxophone riffs; "little girl sounds will come out of your
mouth, high sweet sounds" it was written on half triple-beat of a
"cunga" drum "Tin Pan Alley songs in elegant satin, YOU'RE THE
WRITER'S DREAM," it was written on the
New Orleans take-it-up there, higher, cry, note of a
funeral-marchin' clarinet, set-to-carry-back-to ole Virginy
down the Mississippi on a gamblin' boat, with a ramblin' TROMBONE
mellowtone sliding slyly over, nearly under, almost
into the WHOLE ------------note! in your throat, Billie!

Giving it all up, "Only sweetness will come out of your mouth,"
it was written on saxophone riffs, "What a diff-rence a day
makes," Billie, in your day, what a diff-ence did it make
who mistook the odds, the gods were yours as much as any
badge wearing, southern swearing New York top cop . . . but you
didn't quit quit on love people, music, people, you
still gave it all, in innocence just-born innocence
which lays in many stranger places than false pedestals not a stranger
to whore houses, jazz, pure all night long in the whore house,
giving birth to the blues, baby shoes hanging from the chandelier

jazzzzzzzzz in the night

trombone, mellowtone sliding slyly over, nearly under almost
into the WHOLE ---------- note! in your throat, BILLIE!
in your throat, BILLIE!

jazzzzzzzzzzzz in the night

-Dorothy Jesse Beagle

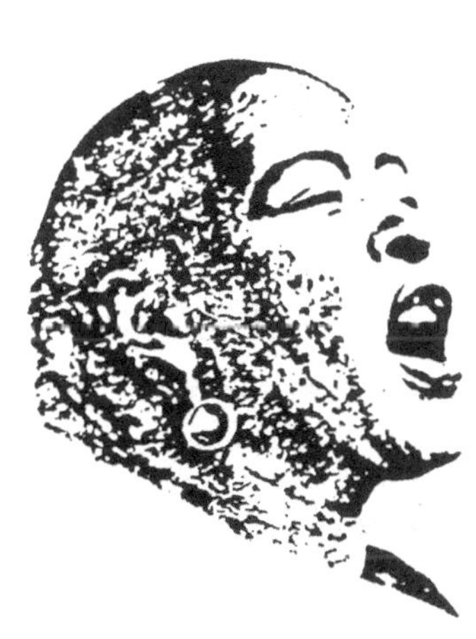

Dear Frank Moore,

My name is Yana Petrova, I'm from Moscow (Russia). Not to long ago I read an interview with you in "Magical Blend" and was really shocked, as it was a real revelation to me; revelation, yes, as not having chance (and not know if some time will have) to talk with you or take part in your performance. I felt just reading this article a wonderful, new energy that comes from you to me. What a pity that I cannot talk with you, to know you better as the lack of such a person in my life (and in our country on the whole) is unbelievable. I feel so deep what you are talking about, I'm sharing your ideas and views on art completely as for a long time already I'm interested in studying the ancient ways "to break through" the reality for our small physical eyes. But unfortunately I didn't manage to realize myself or let's say I feel the lack of energy in myself for that or ... studying and reading doesn't change being. When you feel that you are full of information, when you feel that may be even you have some knowledge inside you that can be expressed out in some way, and you can not do anything - it's awful, painful, really, when you feel like in "shell", you feel this "shell" on your way and can not do anything. I'm not bodyly-deformed but the effect of isolation that this psychological shell gives is the same. I stopped some time ago almost all contacts with people as even if you have many friends it doesn't change anything – the level of communicating is superficial, it doesn't involve any inside energy and I studied and read books to have idea what was the ancient way – I was looking through ancient sacred arts, religious art (starting from Christian religion, then the art of Indians (Mesoamerica) and then Islam) as I thought that immersion in this will allow me to absorb it, on one hand, and on the other hand to find myself, to see "what or who" built this shell inside me, and go forward. But till now more than feeling this shell I can't do anything.

Frank, if only I had chance to come to you, I would do it immediately but for me, at least, in the near future it is impossible and that's why I'm asking you very much to send me your book "Cherotic Magic" or some kind of your work that you feel can help me a lot. I'm asking you that as I feel that the realization that I'm in some contact with you can be of great help for me as it's much much better to contact with you by letter than to see those people who satisfied with their life but arise despair in me.

With love and admiration to you,
Yana
September 10, 1993

Dear Yana,

Thank you very much for your great and amazing letter. It fuels us to know that what we do here effects someone like you half way around the world. Most people do not take the time to write. So you wrote for them too.

I am enclosing a packet of material about my work. In this packet there is *Art of a Shaman*, which is the lecture I give at universities. It is a good introduction to the kind of art we both are interested in. Let me know what you think and feel when you read it. Would you send me a photograph of yourself?

Yana, I strongly urge you not to give up on people. What is before you is a quest for people who will fulfill your needs ... and you theirs. It is a spiritual quest. All quests involve a certain amount of pain, rejection, and so on. But what comes out of such a quest is very much worth it ... not only for you, but for everyone. Grab onto trust, faith, and happiness.

I hope someday you can come to study, work, and play with me.

In freedom,
Frank
September 30, 1993

Dear Frank,

First let me say, "THANK YOU" for such a thrill and exciting venture. I truly enjoy your publication, it is a delightful taste of sweetness after the shit which has been forced upon me everyday here. It allowed me to leave the confined of the cell and wander into the world which not only I left, but that of other worlds of wonderful pleasure and dreams.

There is also an educational value to this zine, for one definitely leaves with far more knowledge than one starts with. Veronica Vera's article "GLORY! GLORY hole-leluhia!" is proof of this. Very beautifully written. But then, what else could you expect from a very beautiful woman.

Sincerely,
Al Cunningham
August 6, 1994

NOOKIE DAYS OVER

My nookie days are over
my pilot light is out.
What used to be my sex appear
is now my water spout.

Time was when, of its own accord,
from my trousers it would spring.
But now I have a full time job
to find the blasted thing.

It used to be embarrassing
the way it would behave.
For every single morning
it would stand and watch me shave.

Now, as old age approaches,
it sure gives me the blues
To see it hang its withered head
and watch me tie my shoes.

-Al Cunningham

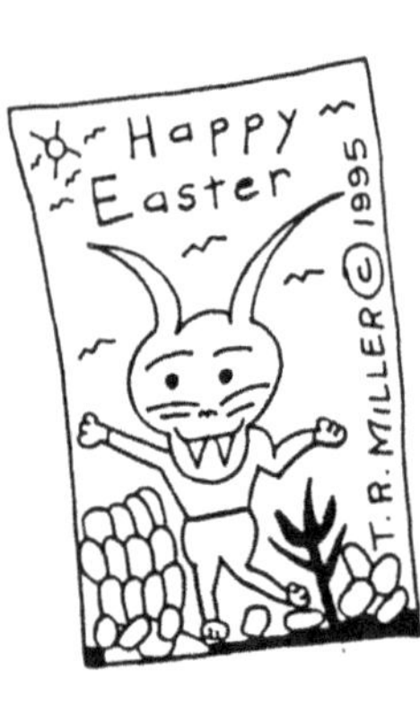

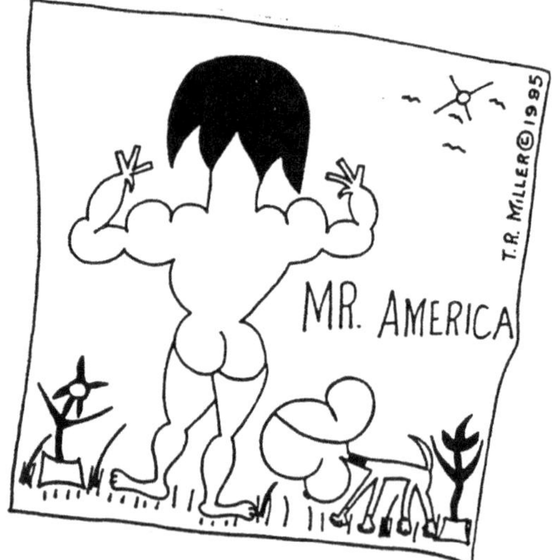

a letter from robert w. howington

frank, feb 10 (1994) –

last three weeks been doing MUCH better regarding separation/divorce. thinking about other things – getting on with my life. the depression shit i was going thru was pure d HELL. it seems to have ended for the most part. julie filed our divorce papers yesterday. so i'm hanging in there and getting on with life.

the latest *TCR* is luscious. loved the way you presented my poems! beautiful magazine. art, layout is top dog. lot of care and effort involved. and love. honored you think so highly of my stuff to showcase it so well.

here's some more of it. SASE. and other stuff.

beth blachowiak, she had a poem in FE #2 or 3, wrote me the other day and said she had a poem rejected by the Univ. of Wisconsin's lit mag because she refused (good for her!) to take the word 'fucking' out of it. I love reading Buk poems where he rails against the academia. i couldn't say it any better so i don't even try. it's just that these people are in a totally different world than ours. i was in that world when i went to TCU and UTA and picked up 77 hours but all the time i knew i didn't belong so i finally dropped out.

i always give my readers credit for having imaginations. i don't explain things in my stuff – readers can figure it out themselves. i don't describe things – in my poem called A HOME MADE KILLER the protagonist was a cockroach. Everybody knows what a cockroach looks like. no need for description. i get caught up in telling a story not what the fucking story looks like. i like Buk so much because he tells us a story and stays the fuck outta the way while doing it. KISS (keep it simple stupid!) is what ALL writers need to learn. WHO WHAT WHERE AND HOW. old journalism ism. got a rejection yesterday from SOAPBOX: 'your poems contained subject matter that is just not suitable for what we'd like to accomplish.' LOVED that rejection slip. The TRUTH is censored once again. so why in the hell do they call their mag a SOAPBOX? isn't that something you get up on and say what you wanna say?

BRIX END and KEROUAC's poetry readings are mostly attended by very young college kids acting 'cool', but the thing is some serious people like me show up and let them know that there are people out there with demons to exorcise and they will have to watch that exorcism up there on that stage whether they like it or not. And they do like it because they REACT with the appropriate laughter after what i tell them – autobiographical poems about basic real life. I bring them a side of life they'll never have to experience – total failure. a loser. with their parent's money they'll never have to work at a job they hate or have to make a living, buying clothes and furniture at the flea market or thrift store. they can just breeze along and maybe for them that's the best way.

Life is one big suck and we're all caught in the whirlpool.

read last thursday night at KEROUAC'S. started off slow by fucking up a poem with a misspeak. but i picked it up and had them laughing at end. i think not being nervous this time made me relax and get overconfident. so being nervous does help keep you aware i guess. some guy came up to me afterwards and said he liked hearing my BUK-inspired shit. he said, "Man, Bukowski is the GREATEST. All these poetry readings are usually boring but your stuff was like hearing Bukowski." So that made me feel good and appreciated. Again, the people up there were pretty boring, but a couple people, especially the MC John Myers and this freaked out black chick who'd I'd fuck, did some good shit. John told us about the time he blew up a dead dog by accident. his mom told him to burn the dog in one of those big 60 gallon drum barrels because they lived out in the boonies and there was no trash pickup so they had to burn everything, even dead animals. so john dropped the dog in the drum and poured gas on it. not sure if this was enuff he poured a bunch MORE gas on it. he soaked the dog thru. he stood back and lit a stick and tossed it into the drum. BOOM! the dog's carcass exploded out of there and flew over his head spilling guts and maggots on him. he said he threw up his breakfast and his back yard began catching on fire from all the dog parts that were flaming. he stamped out all the fires with his shoes and then had to douse the main dog carcass with water to get it to stop burning. he said he was known at high school as 'dog mortar boy' from then on.

i wish i COULD tell those 'poetry' poets at readings to stick it up their asses. but, hey, nobody reacts to their shit except WITH polite applause. that's saying something right there W/O saying something. at least i get the fuckers laughing with one or two of mine because they can IDENTIFY with what's going on in the poem. THE TRUTH is a powerful weapon that makes people react in ALL kinds of ways. Mostly bad.

I read at the BRIX END for the third time on Jan 12. Went over to a friend's prior to and got fucked up on some weed. i can't read sober. i get too fuckin' nervous. anyway, we get there and this friend's friend is the musical guest and he plays a set of acoustic guitar. he's in a band called CREAM OF MUSHROOM. they play local clubs like The Hop. Tim's got a hell of a voice. The man can BOOM out lyrics. then the open mic poetry starts. the stuff is awful of course. if it doesn't speak to me then I'm not interested. for the people who've read the mags and chaps i've published under HOMEMADE ICE CREAM PRESS you know what i like, what i identify with. that's what i'd like to hear at these poetry things but forget it (unless 'weasel boy' or w. bryan massey III or Joel Mathews are up there. these guys can go up and tell me something.) except for a couple by jesse garcia the reading sucked as usual. most of these poets should just kill themselves and get it over with and spare us their personal torture. the featured poet kept mentioning his book that was on sale at Borders Book Store (a national chain). After reading some of his shit from outta his book he can forget about any sales, the dumfuck. especially after he informed the gathered slackers (i think that term replaces the long -standing 'bohemian') that he is a fuckin' cop pig. a distinct and collective 'gasp' went up from out of our mouths upon his revelation and our coffee cooled off as the room grew cold. it's a god damned good thing i didn't read any of my pot smoking poems or he'd have handcuffed me on stage on conspiracy charges. FUCK YOU, PIG! And fuck your god damn sorry ass poems, you fuck wad! His thirty minutes of poems were as dull and as wasted as any poetry could get. Most of it rhymed and most of it had an intended message – we were being preached to, not taught. but what do you expect from a pig?

as i write this i'm listening to a MOTHERFUCKERS cassette called 'second coming' and there's a girl on it gasping/moaning from getting fucked by a non-stop fuck machine. turning me on but now it's over and i go back to this letter.

at the break i sat and talked to Big John Parker, the king of slackers. He's an old, heavyset guy who wanders around Fort Worth on the city bus system. he's at the BRIX END poetry reading every Wednesday. "Gotta take the bus everywhere because my car is broke. I have no job so I can't get it fixed," he said. He's white and lives in the middle of Polytechnic Heights, the blackest part of Fort Worth. The house where he stays is at the corner of Miller and Crenshaw. A redneck businessman friend of his bought the house for one of his mistresses. She went in there and spent a load of this guy's money on furnishings then suddenly bolted for something better. John's friend didn't want to rent the place fearing the renters would rip off all the top of the line furniture, electronics and drapery. "Also, it's a place where he can bring his $2 dollar whores from Como (another black area of Fort Worth)," John said. "He brings them over at all times so it ain't too peaceful over there. When I moved in he gave me a cellular phone and a .357 Magnum and said, 'don't let any niggers come in here and rip me off.' If it weren't for my friend I'd be on the streets sleeping under a bridge or at the Presbyterian Night Shelter or the Union Gospel Mission."

John's tale was the most entertaining oratory of the night and i'm the only person who heard it. Maybe I'll write a poem about it sometime and his words won't be lost.

I read three poems and got a good laugh out of the second one called A HOME MADE KILLER, which is the first poem i'd written since my break up with Julie. It was a poem about a cockroach inspired by a poem i read in Kill Robertson's 'bear crossing' chapbook. I think when I read my shit the people listening don't really get it because they've been listening to this other shit that is more like the poetry you read in the schools. but my shit is direct and to the point. little slices of reality. incident

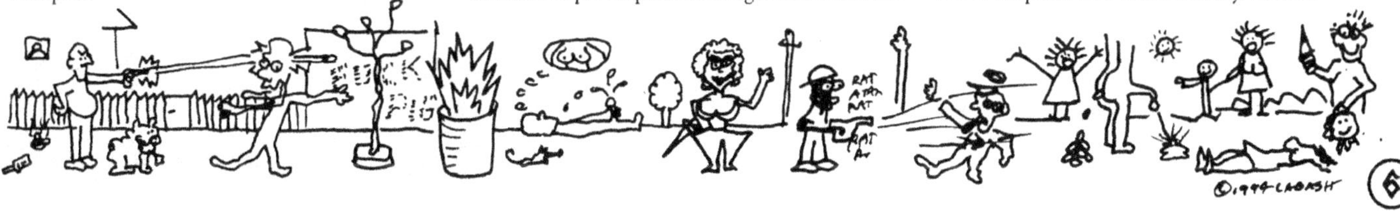

literature, bukowski has called it in SCREAMS FROM THE BALCONY book. i'm facing my demons head on. that kinda stuff. after finishing the audience politely clapped like they do after every poet no matter if the guy sucked or succeeded. so i couldn't really read what they thought. nobody said anything to me as i sat there afterwards (but the guys i went there with did say the following day that they liked my shit. that made me feel all right. Tim said, "I bet you get sick of people telling you they like your stuff." No, Tim, i said, i don't get tired of it. in fact, you could tell me you like my stuff all over and over again and you'd never lose my attention.) so i felt like i failed to wake up these dead fuckers (even though most were just kids they were still DEAD). i left after the PIGGIE'S reading and a couple of the slackers followed me out and both said they liked my shit. this really made me feel great. their sincerity touched me. i sucked that feeling down deep into my lungs and kept it there so i could get the full effects of their complimentary hit. they also liked the MOTHERFUCKERS shirt i had on. i got one of them to give me their address and i sent them info on the MOTHERFUCKERS and copies of a couple of chaps I've been in.

On the 13th I met Kevin 'weasel boy' White at KEROUAC'S coffeehouse on West Berry near Texas Christian University a little after 9 p.m. This place has a poetry reading every Thursday. KEROUAC'S is a lot more laid back than the BRIX END. There's even a pool table in there and a tall bookshelf full of books and even games like checkers and chess. At a couple of the tables people were playing chess and dominoes during the readings. And a couple of guys were playing pool. Espresso seemed to be the popular beverage. I read A HOME MADE KILLER here and it went over well again. Kevin said, "I like that one." Kevin read from his weasel boy mini-book and he had the crowd of very young looking college students and the usual slackers (aren't they the same thing really?) laughing the whole time. Kevin is very cool onstage and can play an audience into his hands with such ease i sit there in awe and think i wished i could do that. His weasel boy book is $4 cash/checks to Kevin and you can send that money to POB 470701, Fort Worth TX 76147. It's 72 pages of Kevin's wisdom and insight into everyday things that turn into neat, compact poems. Funny stuff. I highly recommend it. He sold three copies at the reading. "The last time I sold some copies at a reading I went to Fred's Cafe and blew the money on beer," Kevin said. "I think I'll hold onto this money tonight." As I sat there drinking a Coke and listening to the people read (and the reader's here were much better than at the BRIX END) I wrote a new poem called SAY IT AIN'T SO. I ended up going onstage a second time and read it. I got a laugh from the people I had published in Driver's Side Airbag #10. The reading wound down around 11 p.m. and Kevin and I left saying we'd be back.

Got a 7-11 coke flavored Slurpee here with a shot of jack daniels in it. damn it tastes all right. good in these bad times.

got four rejections in the mail on the SAME day and to just make matters worse all the editors said they liked some of the stuff BUT.

the editor of CHILDREN, CHURCHES & DADDIES said, "Some of your work is very much like Ai's work, but your statements could be made more powerfully if you used more vivid descriptions than the bluntness of some of your 'quotes.'" She wants me to send more stuff. But, hey, it's ALL gonna be as blunt as the shit I sent her the first time. She hasn't been an editor long enuff to know not to invite repeat subs unless you think there is definitely going to be something in the poet's catalog you'll like. And I don't know who in the hell Ai is. Do you? And what the fuck is wrong with being blunt and laying it down like it really is? Bukowski had the same trouble with these dumbfucks who think they know what good poetry is. He's probably been the most rejected poet on earth.

Sent my shit to two more university lit mags. Have never been accepted in one of these stiff upper lip 'journals'. Still haven't after these both rejected me. GRASSLANDS REVIEW of The University of North Texas said,"'Yeah, I Love My Car' came very close – good 'attitude' there. 'Art Is In The Box Of The Eye Of The Beholder Of Pen And Paper' is good little story! I like the idea. I like the dialogue at the end, but I find the story as a whole lacking. I think the sentence structure is too simple." Has this educated person ever heard of KISS – keep it simple stupid? They teach it in journalism classes but i guess 'creative' writing people are above that maxim. And 'lacking' what? I think this motherfucker is lacking the guts to publish original, unordinary bleak straightahead and into your gut shit. FUCK YOU NORTH TEXAS and your goddam 'committee' of editors.

OWEN WISTER REVIEW is out of the University of Wyoming, I think. Says its 'committee' spokesperson, Georgette, "I do want you to know that 'The Next Time A Woman Swallows' had me in stitches! It was a candidate up until the absolute last cut. I loved it." I think we know why the 'committee' balked here: The poem was about a certain sex act and we know sex is kept behind closed doors in mainstream american university lit mags. hush, hush. it's not proper even though it's the fucking truth. FUCK YOU TOO U OF W!

okay, the last knife in my back. INSOMNIA's Rocco said, "Couldn't seem to get all i liked into the issue at hand – thanks for sending anyway." Yeh, and fuck you too for sending me that reject, muthafucka!

I thot the idea was if you liked it you published it. That's the way it's been here. Why can't it be that simple?

Okay, all HIC PRESS operations are suspended. Don't know if I'll ever do another BASK and will hold subs for that until i do decide. Drive-by will probably never be done but will hold its subs until further notice. Have sent all poems accepted for Flaming Envelopes to Robb Allan at Silent Treatment litmag. He's low on submissions so he'll use all of it. Don't have the juice left to do this small press stuff. Will from now on do my own chapbooks. I'm gonna be a selfish pig. maybe write that ground-breaking novel (yeh, sure!).

feel like doing drive-by. yeh.

Robert W. Howington
Homemade Ice Cream Press

Conversation Between Two MUCKRAKERS

PAUL KRASSNER INTERVIEWED BY FRANK MOORE
APRIL 30, 1994, BERKELEY, CALIFORNIA

Paul: Ready when you are coach.
Frank: Why have not you gotten big?
P: (laughs) Well, big is relative. Sometimes people hear my name and they think I'm Paul Kantner from the Jefferson Airplane. And I wonder the same thing myself sometimes. I performed last week and somebody called me an unacknowledged Robin Williams. But I think its, you know, on one hand its because I haven't compromised ... and on the other hand it's because I'm lazy.
F: Me too!
P: Welcome to the club.
F: But I have worked hard not to get big.
P: Well, (laughs) I could handle getting big because I would like to reach a lot of people, but ... and it could happen. I'm ready to sell out. But I wouldn't sell out, they would buy in.
F: (laughs) Don't you reach a lot of p...?
P: P...? Do I reach a lot of p (laughs) or people? Yeah, well when *The Realist* was a magazine, it reached a hundred thousand people, and a million pass on ... now it's only a newsletter, it reaches 5,000 people and maybe several thousand pass on readership, and then with my book, it sold 15,000 copies and we published in paperback more. So, I think that I'll probably reach more people when I'm dead. (laughs)
F: Always.
P: Oh yeah...it's probably true of Abbie Hoffman and Richard Nixon.
(both laugh)
F: Why did Abbie (Hoffman) kill himself?
P: Abbie was clinical manic/depressive ... and he had injured his foot and was in a lot of pain and he was separated from his girlfriend, and he wanted to start a school for organizing but he didn't have the money and so ... I would like for him to have stayed alive, but nobody can judge the level of anybody else's pain, so I guess that was his final act of power to get rid of his pain, physical and emotional and you know it made me sad and angry but it was his choice.
F: How did you start the Yippies?
P: We wanted to protest the war in Vietnam and the yippies was just a name I made up to describe this phenomenon that already existed, it was the hippies and the political activists and at first they thought they were adversaries and the hippies thought that the political activists were just playing the game of the administration and the political activists thought the hippies were dropping out and not being responsible. But then they realized ah, that if a hippie was smoking a marijuana joint in the park, that was a political act of defying an unjust law. And the hippies saw that the political activists by protesting the war had the same value system and so they began to affect each other. So the political activists started to smoke dope and let their hair grow long and wear tie-dyed shirts and the hippies, instead of just staying in the park, went to anti-war rallies and civil rights' demonstrations. So it was happening already ... and sometimes you have to just give a name to something that's already going.
F: Yes.
P: Oh, you agree ... that was easy ... I agree with your agreement.
F: I always i n v e n t ...
P: Wait, what word am I dealing with here ...? Oh, invent ... yeah.
F: ... words.
P: The other word I invented was "soft-core" pornography because the Supreme Court said that hard-core pornography wasn't protected by the First Amendment. And so soft-core pornography meant, you know, they use it in TV commercials ... that's soft-core pornography ... it gives a man a soft-on. What words have you invented?
F: When I and Linda were in Annie Sprinkle's video on orgasm, she wanted us to do safe sex. (both laugh) But we have been in a relationship for 20 years.
P: Well, that's about as safe as you can get.
(both laugh)
F: Exactly. That was what I told Annie. But, (both laugh) she wanted to be politically correct.
P: (laughs) So some people fake orgasms, you'd have to fake safe sex.
F: Finally she said we could do soft-core.
(both laugh)
P: She stole my word.
F: What is that? (laughs)
P: Soft-core...?
F: But, we agreed.
(both laugh)
P: Well that was very agreeable of you ... anything to help out Annie. That's why we were late, we were having dinner with her (Annie) ... and you know, she likes to talk while she's eating.
F: I just did a review of her show.
P: Oh yeah? I assume you liked it.
F: The show, yes. Her (Annie), yes. But, the goddess, no.
P: That's very interesting, because, she talked about the goddess today and I thought a female god is just as unlikely as a male god. Excellent.
F: Exactly.
P: Oh, I'm glad you thought that, because I thought that today, and it's nice to have consensus on reality.
F: We all have both in us.
P: Oh, so you objected to her just doing only the female goddess?
F: The gender.
P: Well, you know, Robert Anton Wilson once wrote in The Realist that if people continue to refer to god as "he" then they should think of a giant penis in the sky.
F: So, now it is a cunt ...
P: (laughs)
F: ... in the sky.
P: That's right and that's why when we hear thunder it's just cock and cunt fucking in the sky ... that's what thunder is ... and lightening.
F: Annie is not a s e p e r i s ...
P: What word am I on ... wait, start again ... Annie is not a ...
F: Separatist.
P: Oh, no but she has great cleavage ... that's pretty separate.
F: But the separatists are using her ...

P: The separatists are using her? Oh, the separatists are using her ... yeah, you can't control what people do with what you put out. You know, if we didn't get misunderstood, you and me and her, we wouldn't be doing our job right. The separatists are using her ... for what?

F: To justify their trip.

P: Right. It's always that way. Everybody has their own agenda and it's true, it's true ... and they'll use us too. But that's ok. It's better than not being used at all.

F: Don't you build in bombs?

P: Don't I build in bombs? (laughs) Well, in a way. (both laugh) In a way ... don't I build in bombs? Yeah, to fool them. To fool them? Yes, it's like magic, sometimes, to divert their attention ... if that's what you mean? Or, it's like a lawyer will give seven objections when he only wants one or two, so he builds in a few bombs, if that's what you mean? And if I write something for a magazine, I may put something that I know they'll take out and they'll leave something else in. So if that's what you mean by a bomb, yes, I build them in.

(Frank laughs)

F: Me too.

P: Yes, we're the secret bombers.

F: Are people more serious now?

P: Some of them are, some of them aren't. I think they both happen at once ... and it's not separate either, it's two sides of the same coin, you know, serious and frivolous. And I think what people get serious about are their own hang-ups.

F: Maybe I mean fragile.

P: Oh, more fragile. In a way yeah, because of diseases and because of gangs, you know, fragile because ... it's like what kids in the ghetto have in common with kids in Bosnia at the age of 14 ... they are already planning their funerals.

So, that is fragility at it's most heightened state. Yeah, because the quality of life is fragile, so people are more fragile. Yeah, that's an accurate word for it.

F: When I was growing up, I was dumb. I did not know I could not do things so I did them.

P: Oh, (laughs) yeah, me too. Right, and then they told you you couldn't do it, but it was too late, cause you already did.

F: But, now people think they cannot and they blame whatever.

P: They blame whatever? Well, yeah, that's the trend now, blame. That's one of the biggest things is blame. People blame their astrology chart ... people blame their childhood ... and the ultimate is people blame the victim ... it's the victim's fault for getting in my way.

F: So how can you do satire?

P: Well, you just report what's happening, and they think you're making it up. I have an article in the new *Realist* on a support group for people who drink their own urine. It's a real group! But people think I made it up. (both laugh) But it doesn't make any difference because it gets in their consciousness.

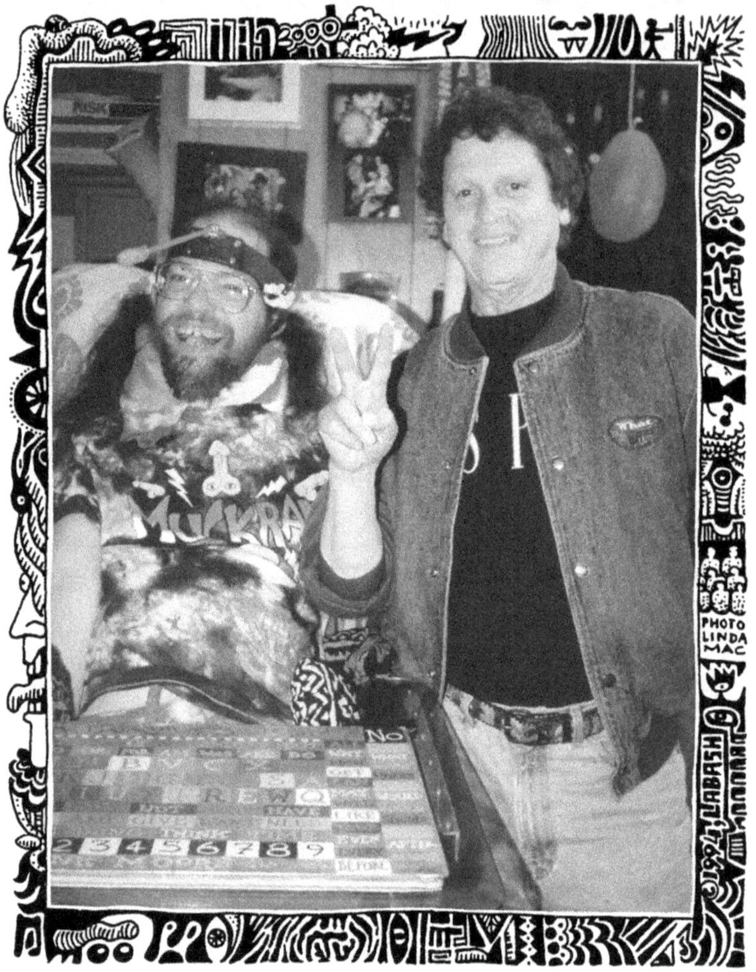

F: That was one of the things I loved about *The Realist.*

P: Me too.

F: You can not tell what is real. (laughs)

P: I know, sometimes I don't even know myself. Sometimes I'm not even sure if the page numbers are real. (laughs)

F: My dad got pissed at the LBJ ...

P: LBJ! (laughs)

F: ... fucking.

(both laugh)

P: Oh, well, a lot of people got pissed off at that. You know now Frank, that was in 1967, so this is ... 67 ... 77 ... 87 ... twenty what years .. .27 years and people still come up to me and tell me how that blew their minds. So, yeah, I can understand why he would get pissed, you know, it's no surprise.

F: And my mom thought it was real! (laughs)

P: Well, it was real. How do you know? A lot of people thought it was real. Sometimes only for five minutes, but that was good enough for me. (laughs) Because they thought Lyndon Johnson was ok for dropping napalm but they thought he was crazy when they read that, and that was the point ... so your mother was in good company. A lot of people thought it was real. But that meant that she thought that LBJ was capable of it.

F: And he was!

P: Oh, and he was capable of it ... yes, yes. (laughs)

F: I like playing with reality.

P: How do you play with reality? I mean, I do too, but everybody has their own way.

F: One trick is to say, "But, I may be lying."

P: I know, do you know the average person lies 25 times a day. But that includes the times we lie to ourselves.

(both laugh)

F: I do 48 hour performances ...

P: Forty-eight hours? Well, that's more than I do. If I do an hour and a half I'm satisfied. (laughs)

F: ...where I mix realities up.

P: Oh, yeah, well, look, if reality mixes us up, then it's only fair that we mix reality up ... tit for tat. (laughs)

F: Like Andy ...

P: Warhol?

F: ...Kauffman.

P: Oh, Andy Kauffman? Oh, the comedian? Oh, yeah, yeah ... he did that good. I remember him. He was just on the edge ... you know, you just watch it to see is he really going to go on with this? Yeah, he played with reality ... I like that.

F: And you were never quite sure.

P: It's true ... it's true ... he was on the edge ... he was on the edge. He may still be alive, that may be his ultimate playing with reality.

F: (laughs) That is what *The Realist* did.

P: Yeah, that was the purpose to find the left and right lobes of the brain and get between.

F: How did you get there?

P: Well, I started at *Mad Magazine*. My jacket has Alfred E. Newman on the back..."What, me worry?" But that was for teenagers and there was nothing for adults and I wanted something for me, cause I figured I wasn't the only one ... I wasn't the only martian on the block. And so it was kind of to find who else was out there. So we could have our own martian tribe. So, I was working

PHOTO LINDA MAC

for Lyle Stewart who had a newspaper called *The Independent* and it was anti-censorship. And so when I started *The Realist* it was a combination of the satire from *Mad* and the anti-censorship from *The Independent*.
F: But in *Mad* you knew it was not real.
P: Well, that's true, but I took it a step further because I also published serious stuff and if I labeled it, like *Playboy* labels something: satire, article, fiction ... And I wanted the readers to decide for themselves. I didn't want to take away the pleasure from them. Or I didn't want to take away the confusion from them either. (laughs)
F: Exactly.
P: Exactly.I know this board already now ... I can do it with my eyes closed. So, you didn't tell me a word that you invented.
F: Eroplay.
P: Eroplay? Oh, like erotic play. I like that, that's good ... ok. Well see, that will be in the dictionary some day ... after we're dead.
F: People are using it.
P: For what?
F: In their language.
P: Language? Eroplay?
F: It amazes me ...
P: Oh, yeah. I know.
F: ... how fast.
P: It's true. Cause everything is accelerating now. In the 60's when the word "black" replaced the "negro", they didn't do it right away. But now, when "african american" replaced "black", they did it quicker, cause everything's accelerating ... including "soft-core" and "eroplay".
(both laugh)
F: How did you get to edit Lenny...
P: ... Lenny Bruce's book? Well, *Playboy Magazine* serialized it and they knew that Lenny and I knew each other and he was writing it but ... they needed somebody to help structure it and to draw him out ... get questions answered. And so they asked me. And I jumped at the chance, because he was a rare individual and influenced comedians today who don't even know they were influenced by him. And he was attacked for the language he used, but he was really attacked because he used organized religion as a target. And that was really why they went after him.
F: Who ...
P: ... Lenny Bruce we're talking about ... oh ...
F: ... but, who went after him?
P: Well, the police ... if the police would go after him in San Francisco, then the police in Los Angeles would say we got to go after him, then the police in Chicago say well we got to go after him. Especially in Chicago where the church was big. When he was on trial in Chicago it was Ash Wednesday, and all the jurors and the judge and the prosecutor had the ash on their forehead there. It was very spooky.
F: I am playing dumb ...
P: Oh, well, I am dumb. I am playing dumb ... ok ...devil's advocate.
F: ... because lots of people don't know.
F: Oh, yeah, of course, that's right. Ok, well, when you play dumb, you're playing with reality again.
(both laugh)
F: They think he self-destructed.
P: Yeah, a lot of his friends thought that at the time. But, you know, it's just a matter of opinion. I think to be consistent with your principles is not self-destructive, but a lot of people thought he should compromise. And that would have been self-destructive.
F: They say he was not funny any more.
P: He got serious, but ... when I first interviewed Lenny I asked him, "What's the role of a comedian?" And he said, "To get a laugh every 15 to 25 seconds." But then later on, when he was reading from court transcripts and police records ... and I said to him, "Lenny, you're not getting a laugh every 15 to 25 seconds." (both laugh) And he said, "Yes, but I'm changing." And I said, "What do you mean?" He said, "Well, I'm not a comedian, I'm Lenny Bruce." So he knew that he had become a symbol of free speech. He was still funny, but he didn't get a laugh every 15 to 25 seconds. He was funny sardonic.
F: It is like when Mort (Sahl) went after JFK's killers.
P: That's true, yeah, he dropped out, Mort Sahl dropped out and worked for Jim Garrison as a researcher. And he wasn't funny then. And there were times when I got heavy into conspiracy and the readers would complain. And I said, "Sometimes you have to earn the right to be funny."
(both laugh)
F: Who is doing that today?
P: You mean besides me? (laughs)
F: And me!
(both laugh)
P: Just us. Nobody else. No, there's a few, there's a few ... there's a comedian named Jimmy Tingle who's good. There's Elaine Boosler, who's good. There's a few. But most of them talk about their first date or TV commercials or airplane food. They're like clones on a conveyor belt in a factory, most comedians. But there are a few good ones.
F: How about the black?
P: Yeah, there's a few. There's a guy named Franklin Ajai (sp) who's excellent. Who else ... ? A lot of the black comedians are very raunchy. But who else is good that I've seen ... ? Richard Pryor is kind of sick. Dick Gregory is making diet powder. (laughs) There are some new black comedians, but I think that Franklin Ajai and Paul Mooney are two of the best. I haven't seen them all. They have on HBO Def Comedy Jam, but they do such raunchy material that it makes me blush. (both laugh) And I support their right to do it, but sometimes you wonder if they don't have a larger vocabulary.
F: If they have a big picture ...
P: But they want to be successful, and so they don't always have the big picture. A few of them do, but they're afraid their audience ... they make a separation ... once again separation ... they make a separation between them and the audience. Whereas you and I don't. You know, we respect the audience, that they either get us or they don't.
F: That is what is wrong with Dennis Miller.
P: Dennis Miller? That's a good point because he likes to show off his references ... but he's better than a lot of others. He's ok ... he could be better but ...
F: But he is all over the place.
P: Yeah, I know, but so is pollution. (both laugh)
F: I mean in his act.
P: Oh yeah, yeah, because he'll pull out a reference from a TV show from 1940, and then from a musical group from 1990 ... yeah, but he means well ... but then so did Hitler.
F: That is what is scary.
P: Yeah, I know, but what would we do if we didn't have something to be scared about.
F: People who mean well can do more harm.
P: Oh yeah. Wasn't that a Barbra Streisand song ... "People who mean well can do more harm ..." (both laugh) Yeah, it's true, it's true, because they're self-righteous about it and they think that they're on a mission from god.
F: And people feel they are honest.
P: Yeah, well, that's what I said before ... that in the 25 lies a day that we tell, a lot of them are to ourselves. Because if you want to deceive other people, you have to deceive yourself first. That's a pre-requisite.
F: How about Bill Maher?
P: Oh, Bill Maher. I like him. I was on his show, *Politically Incorrect*. And he's an ex-Catholic who took acid. (Frank laughs) And so, he had Tim Leary on ... he has people on that other people don't. He's good. He's nice and irreverent. He's wrong on some positions, but, that's only because I disagree with him.
F: Yes, but he has a big picture.
P: Yeah, he does, he does. Do you watch his show ... do you get cable?
F: Yes.
P: Yeah, he has several writers but ... he's excellent. I've seen him do reports for Jay Leno from events. And he's very irreverent and very smart. He doesn't talk down to the listeners. Yeah, he's good ... I forgot to mention him. He's good.
F: What would you like to do that you have not done?
P: That I have not done? (both laugh) It's a big question. Ok ... write a novel. Fuck three girls at once. And be young again. Oh, I've done that already ... cancel that one. (Frank laughs) Have unlimited power. (laughs)
F: For what?
P: Just for the hell of it. You mean, the power?

Oh, to make miracles. Somebody just asked Ram Dass what he thinks is the most important question of the twenty-first century. And he thought, and he thought, and he thought for a long while, then he said, "How can we get rid of greed?" So if I had unlimited power, I would just say, "Greed is out and compassion is in!" And then I'd get some fudge.
(both laugh)
F: One time I took my students to a drug conference and when I walked into the lobby Leary ran up and hugged me.
P: Yeah, that was one of the things about the 60's, that men could hug other men. Before that it was considered homosexual, instead of just love.
F: And then Dass ...
P: Ram Dass? Oh well, he had an extra hug.
F: ... hugged me. And (laughs) then the widow of Huxley ...
P: Huxley ... oh, Laura Huxley ... she's still around.
F: (laughs) ... hugged me.
P: It was a regular hug fest. A lot of hugging.
F: And during the intermission I was flapping my arms ...
P: (laughs) Arms? (claps and laughs)
F: ... and Leary started flapping his.
(both laugh)
P: Him too! (laughs) Yeah, that's good. He's a good mirror.
F: Was I on drugs or what?
P: Maybe, maybe not. Only you know for sure.
F: How could I tell? You're test did not work!
P: Well, it must have worked, if you thought you were dreaming ... if you were flapping your arms. (Frank laughs) At that point it doesn't make any difference. Reality was playing with you again. (Frank laughs) But in order to flap his arms he had to stop hugging you.
F: The two groupies did not know what was going on. (laughs)
P: I know, it's a secret language. When I performed at an island off Canada where I did the flapping my arms thing. And for two weeks after that everybody on the island was flapping their arms. It was good. I added that to the language. But nonverbal language.
F: What should I ask? (laughs)
P: Let me think. Am I optimistic or pessimistic?
F: Ok. Or a realist.
P: Realist? Well, because I'm a realist, I'm optimistic on Monday, Wednesday and Friday; I'm pessimistic on Tuesday, Thursday and Saturday, and Sunday I rest ... my case.
F: A realist is an idealist.
P: I know, but don't tell anybody!
F: Skeptic ...
P: Yeah, I'm a professional skeptic. I wish I could get paid to be a skeptic, cause that's what I do. (laughs)
F: Don't you?
P: What, get paid for being a skeptic? That's true I do, yeah. See how quickly my wish came true. (laughs)
F: I do. (laughs)
P: Get paid for being a skeptic? Welcome to the club. (laughs)
F: People think cynical is the same.
P: No. No. Cause a cynic is negative and a skeptic searches for the truth. It's a big difference.
F: Cynicism is a illness.
P: Right. And a cynic thinks there's no cure for this. (both laugh) Yeah, it's too bad but ... you know, people get their identity from any number of things, and some people get their identity from being cynical. And they go to a party and they're cynical. And then their personality freezes that way. Our mothers were right.
F: Is that what happened in the 80's?
P: Is that what happened in the 80's? Yeah, yeah, people ... yeah ... it was a combination of greed and cynicism and selfishness. It's all the same. Yeah, money became more important than people. But a lot of those same people now are getting more socially conscious. You know, some of the baby boomers had babies themselves, and when they saw hypodermic needles washing in from the ocean, they thought they better do something about it. So I think some of the greed has changed to social consciousness. But that may just be wishful thinking.
F: No.
P: No? It's not wishful thinking?
F: Because the people who come to my performances have changed.
P: Have changed? How have they changed?
F: Like in the 70's they had dreams about freedom. They wanted it. They may not have thought it was possible ...
P: Yeah, well, but, you know, it always starts with a dream.
F: In the 80's (laughs) they had not dreams and did not want it and why was I forcing them. (laughs)
P: (laughs) I give up. Why?
F: In the 90's they have not dreams, but when they find it, they want it.
P: Well, that's a hopeful sign. Atleast they think it's possible. Even if they stumble on it. When I travel around I meet a lot of young people who are the way we were in the 60's. Except they have less innocence. We were innocent.
F: What do you think of zines?
P: They're like the underground press was in the 60's. Because now there are the alternative papers but they're like a farm team for the mainstream. So they want to get discovered. In the 60's the underground press, like the zines now, were a form of personal revolution as opposed to the alternative papers, which are just a good career move.
F: (laughs) In a way you are the root.
P: Oh, in a way, but I had my roots ... it keeps going back ... to the cave people. (both laugh) When they were writing on the cave walls, there was somebody who was writing on a rock in the field. And that was the first underground paper.
F: I always get the criticism I am old-fashioned.
P: Old-fashioned? You old-fashioned?
F: They say I do 60's art. (laughs)
P: Well, so what? If you like it ... you have to do what comes from your insides.
F: I say I am more old-fashioned. I do cave (art). (both laugh)
P: That's real old-fashioned (claps and laughs). That's right. Pre ... even before the caveman ... when you were a fish. (both laugh) Yes, right. I guess I'm old-fashioned too, then. Oh, our time has gone.
F: When did art become fashion?
P: Oh, well, you know, Abbie Hoffman said fashion is fascism. So, whenever people buy something, if they spend money on it, they think it must be art. Cause they don't want to waste their money. But, you know, art is ... true art is self-expression and that's very often out of fashion. And when we get in fashion, we better start worrying.
F: I have been doing what I am doing for 25 years.
P: How will you know when you're finished? (both laugh)
F: Sometimes it is in fashion. Sometimes it is not.
P: Monday, Wednesday and Friday ... Tuesday, Thursday and Saturday ... !
F: I do the same thing. (laughs)
P: You don't change?
F: It evolves.
P: That's right.
F: But, they think I don't change.
P: Well, fuck 'em! That's what I say. Fuck 'em if they can't take a change.
F: And when I am in fashion, I have to work hard to not get big.
P: That's where we started.
(both laugh)
F: You always have inspired me.
P: Well, I'll tell you Frank, it's a two-way street cause you inspire me. So, let's continue to inspire each other.
F: How?
P: How? Because you work hard ... and you say what you mean ... and you communicate. It's difficult to communicate and you do it. And that's the most important thing ... that's what life is about is communication. And I respect it a lot. So, what else is there to do in life but communicate. You know, and you do it with passion and honesty. So that's inspiring.
F: That is a great end.
P: Better than death. (both laugh) Very nice interview. Excellent. I had a good time.

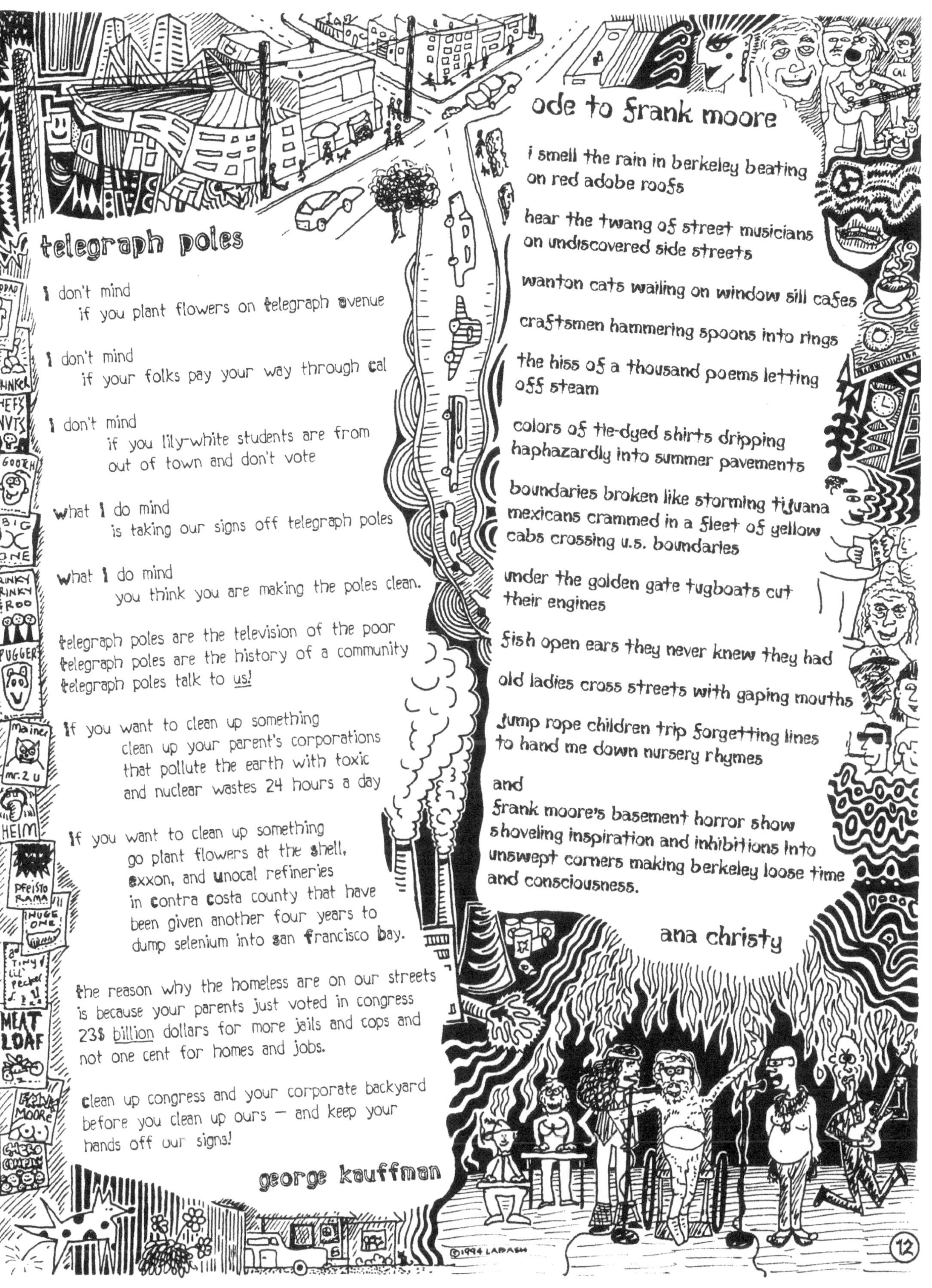

telegraph poles

i don't mind
if you plant flowers on telegraph avenue

i don't mind
if your folks pay your way through cal

i don't mind
if you lily-white students are from
out of town and don't vote

what i do mind
is taking our signs off telegraph poles

what i do mind
you think you are making the poles clean.

telegraph poles are the television of the poor
telegraph poles are the history of a community
telegraph poles talk to us!

if you want to clean up something
clean up your parent's corporations
that pollute the earth with toxic
and nuclear wastes 24 hours a day

if you want to clean up something
go plant flowers at the shell,
exxon, and unocal refineries
in contra costa county that have
been given another four years to
dump selenium into san francisco bay.

the reason why the homeless are on our streets
is because your parents just voted in congress
23$ billion dollars for more jails and cops and
not one cent for homes and jobs.

clean up congress and your corporate backyard
before you clean up ours — and keep your
hands off our signs!

george kauffman

ode to frank moore

i smell the rain in berkeley beating
on red adobe roofs

hear the twang of street musicians
on undiscovered side streets

wanton cats wailing on window sill cafes

craftsmen hammering spoons into rings

the hiss of a thousand poems letting
off steam

colors of tie-dyed shirts dripping
haphazardly into summer pavements

boundaries broken like storming tijuana
mexicans crammed in a fleet of yellow
cabs crossing u.s. boundaries

under the golden gate tugboats cut
their engines

fish open ears they never knew they had

old ladies cross streets with gaping mouths

jump rope children trip forgetting lines
to hand me down nursery rhymes

and
frank moore's basement horror show
shoveling inspiration and inhibitions into
unswept corners making berkeley loose time
and consciousness.

ana christy

ANNIE SPRINKLE'S Post Post Porn Modernist

San Francisco, April 1994

A REVIEW BY FRANK MOORE

Annie sprinkle invited us to her *Post Post Porn Modernist* one-person show last saturday. i saw it years ago when she did it at a n.y.c. strip theatre ... and i wrote a review of it which was published in *Art Papers*. in the review, i pretended i was just someone who had come to the show (in reality we were staying at her place, watched her rehearse the last ritual, and michael [LaBash] painted her vibrator). i could not do that now because she has put me into the show for my "famous tongue" ... and listed me in the program credit as one of her performance teachers ... which is very flattering because she is the best performance artist i have seen and her show is the best i have been to. i said this in the old review. but the ritual that is this show has become much deeper, much more human. annie very quickly shattered the limitations of a stage show, very quickly created an intimate community from all the people in the space. it is the community that really does the ritual, using annie's life as the pathway. the ritual never stops, not even during the "intermission" (annie stays on stage for people to have their picture taken with her bare breasts on their heads ... at $10 a pop). the show's last section, a very magically powerful ritual did not end, annie did not leave the stage, until way after the last audience member had left (i, as a performer, watched each person somehow decide it was time to go).

annie's messages are clear in the show ... sex and the body are good ... people do not have to be victims ... and the more happiness and pleasure you have, the more happiness and pleasure you are creating in/for the world.

unfortunately the new age goddess haunts the show just below the surface, producing a sublayer or a hidden message of separation and isolation which really runs in conflict with both annie's basic nature and the community that her show calls forth. the new age goddess is basically a corruption of the original goddess which is the yin principle which is within all of us no matter what our gender. the original ritual journey or task was to reunite the yin and yang principles into the original creative life force, and to apply, along this major journey, the yin principle for the tribal welfare. one of the powerful characteristic of the original goddess has always been an unlimited inclusiveness. this is also true of annie personally, and it radiates from her show. but both the original goddess and annie are being misused, distorted, by the forces of exclusion as an excuse and a justification of elitism, separatism, discrimination, fear, and isolation. these forces of exclusion are the main cause of today's world conflict.

one of the problems is "goddess" is being personalized, then given a gender. it is common today to hear women saying "i am a/the goddess". it has the protection of being politically correct. but if we change the words to "i am a/the male god", or "i am a/the white god", or "i am an/the american god", the fascistic dangers of this kind of logic become more obvious. moreover, the new age goddess has more to do with mother mary than the original goddess. it isolates women once again high upon the pedestal.

annie's story is one of self-discovery ... both her personal self and our collective self. her method is to isolate and define aspects of herself, give each a name and a personality, and then live each to the hilt. so far, she has discovered ellen, annie, and anya. in the past, annie has described anya as the goddess, which attracted the confusion. recently she has started describing anya as a sacred prostitute. although this term is also misleading ... created by one culture projecting its morality into the past onto another culture ... it is not gender-driven ... after all, annie introduced me to the audience as a sacred prostitute. what is really meant by the term is a cultural role of a magical channel between this and other realities by means of, among other techniques, expanded sex.

annie is only in the middle of her story. before it is all over, i think she will discover many more aspects within herself ... and will then combine all of the aspects together. i'm looking forward to that climax!

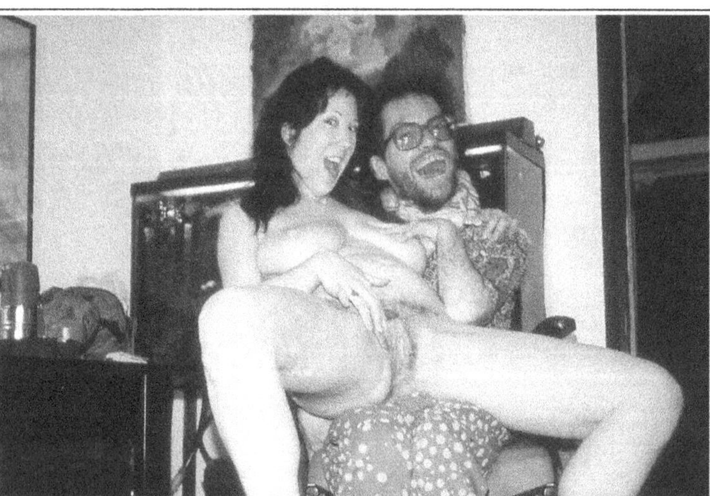

Annie & Frank, NYC, 1987
Photo by Linda Mac

THE GRAND BARN

NO EXCESSIVE FEATURES YET A GIGANTIC UNIQUE STRUCTURE

We all know of the many resorts, clubs, campsites that are sprouting all over the world and where Nudity is finally becoming accepted on their premises. Most are located at great distance from the main roads and insist on ultra privacy as if conducting a secret society. We all know we're battling with many currents of ideology regarding the presentation of the human body and we're all well aware of the easily offended tone of some of the more prudish kind. And the soldiers of peace who take the stand for pushing further the acceptance of Nudity are mostly of the "single kind". Those spokesperson express themselves through the many medium available or sometimes do initiate their own. Many publications keep coming out in the open, adding their voices to those of whom have already initiated the path. The more supporters joining in, the better. For some of them, beyond the publication lies a whole organization. And what you may find is that, along with the network, also comes an outlet for where all can gather to substantiate the efforts of the organization presented through the publication. This is the case with the worldwide organization/network of <<THE AFFILIATE>> with its monthly publication and where the significant outlet, in this regard, is known as +THE GRAND BARN+.

Pioneered by Peter Riden, grandmaster of the whole project, +THE GRAND BARN+ certainly serves well those who are basically concerned with meeting others of like-minded open attitude. In its rural environment, the location comes out as a defiance to the usual criteria of any landed club or resort for it does not insist as much on the facilities it may provide but rather on the quality of its attendance. And it is located right by a major highway. For many years a multitude of "single" pioneers have been denied access under the pretense of misbehaving conduct as most locations have played the conservative less challenging approach of selectively welcoming the family cell. On the other side rarely anyone would take note that most of achieved progress were accomplished by those dedicated "singles", out there, who once it was time for them to come through the gate, they would find themselves denied access. At +THE GRAND BARN+ your conduct is the main criteria, not your gender neither your status. For once, both genders are getting equal and single treatment. Nudity is accepted as an expression of being at ease with oneself and others without pretense of any kind. The mental approach is on high gear at +THE GRAND BARN+, but any eventuality of developing intimate interactions is not perceived as an impossibility but encouraged with all the class and reverence that should come with. For once you have a rather imposing unit that will not let itself be described as only a "Nudist/Naturist" club/resort, but rather a location where the fact of Nudity is only the beginning of the educational process. People have been for too long constricted in their interactions and dialogue with others. Too many taboos have been perpetuated in a wrongful way detrimental to the most needed dialogue between different factions who could otherwise all work in an ultimate collaboration to face a common enemy: Prejudicial ignorance.

That's the crowd you are to expect when coming at +THE GRAND BARN+ and the events presented are geared at getting the most of collaboration with all attendees. With its impressive stage on the upper floor and with a capacity crowd that can easily exceed a thousand people, no doubts that the entertainment aspect can be well served. Music shows, conferences, seminars, theatre, dance, banquets, indoor sports, award presentations, art gallery and many other events left to the imagination. The ground floor has been preserved in its original form with stalls being rented on event days, where any endeavors can be presented to the attending crowd.

+THE GRAND BARN+ promises to be an all year operation in the times to come. For those who enjoy winter sports on a rather flat, but big land, this is your chance. If you really seek the warmer days then you may contemplate a visit when weather permits. Usually April 1st to November 1st is as much as we can stretch for the time being. The outside facilities are at their initial phase although plenty of space can accommodate all future expansions. The atmosphere is very homey, no pretense. The circular pool, site of a previous existing silo, is one attraction everyone does appreciate. And it is right next to the warm enclosure featuring a choice of cement slab or fine grass, where most find themselves for relaxing time and chatting with friends or potential ones. Overnight stay is certainly possible for those equipped in consequence, from the small tent to the big motor home/coach. The land is an agricultural area so there are no surprise to see cows grazing by. The 2 majestic silos rising high above the 220' ft long Barn are a landmark one can hardly miss. On non-event days visitors are welcome on a daily basis to just come and relax and enjoy the 150 acres of land and forest +THE GRAND BARN+ has to offer. The 40 acre forest presents stunning sight of gigantic Maple Trees and other fine species in a magnificent Underwood accessible through many new open trails. At $15.00/day anyone individual of either gender is welcomed on a fair equal basis to access our domain. Children may enter free under proper supervision. Members of many organizations are given a 10% discount on non-event days and those being direct Affiliates are welcome at $10.00/day.

Some of the main events of note are being scheduled on the same dates year after year. Talk about steadiness! They are "ART-AT-HEART", May 27-31; "*CONCEPT* WEEK", July 1-7; our 2 sessions of "NATURE'S WAY IN THE NUDE", July 17-25 and Sept. 5-9; "CONVERGENCE", August 5-15; "SPACE AND BEYOND", August 22-29. Other events are also added on a seasonal basis.

If you want to be part of this major, yet very homey worldwide network, you may contact us at 777 Barb Rd, Vankleek Hill, Ontario, KOB 1RO Canada

Presented by Peter Riden

The Secret of Creation: *or how do women know?*

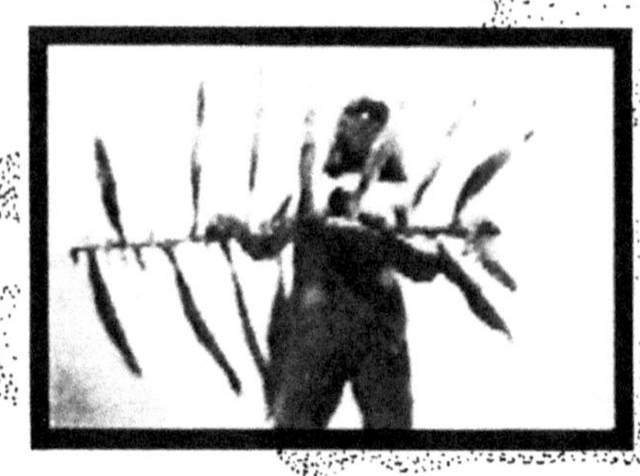

by Barbara Smith 1982-1994

We were sisters, you and I and as each day began we'd meet wearing our hair heretically long (or short) to fit our whim or mood.

One morning we, while dressed in our silk print dresses, waded in the surf, wantonly hooking nubile seaweed pods in our randy toes. We pulled at our clinging skirts in the soft and brilliant light and laughed as we beamed our knowing glances one to the other. Then we dashed away to create our own individual day's adventure alone.

You, met with your lean, fresh, white-skinned German boy, who you totally bewitched with your wild animal tenderness that made him open to you in a moment of utter guilelessness which turned at once to wonder.

As I lay on the white, white sheets, a fragrant billowing breeze gently touched my man and I with its humid lips. He had downy, hairy legs and chest that tingled my entire frame like cat whiskers or foxes fur, like millions of tiny lightning flashes (which are the differentials between softness and being thunderstruck). Our sweat became the ground condition for bringing forth the rain! The contact completed circuitry from source to humans which creates not only relief but is the literal mechanism for change. This was magic.

At the end of the day, you and I, we'd meet again at one of our favorite small cafes, our table illumined by the light of the crystal glasses radiating the colors of the flowers in their vase. Our entire sense field was alive, the tactility of our silks, the aroma of the coffee, the tinkling of the cutlery, and surrounding voices, perhaps a violin and the swelling inner surge of the warming wine. We'd share our stories each with the other, made twice as rich by the telling. Once plus once made the truth of three, evoking the thrill of risk and daring found in this way of knowing. Our experience created a field that expanded our beings twice over making a repository of connectedness. It became the deep strength, and power, that has the quality of permanence and deity.

First you'd put on that naughty smile which when joined by mine, soon became conspiratorial play as we shared our tales of love and power. It was, we suddenly discovered, an experience of painful wonder, the sharing of the carnal secrets meant by society never for us to have. They had been corrosively expunged from us and kept forbidden. Then if we, as sisters, were kept apart we could be constantly confused, never certain, never able to share, demand or demonstrate what we knew. Our greatest and most sacred feat of all was that you and I found we had it merely by experiencing it and then by telling each other.

It was through this we discovered that the secret of all mystery cults, all religions, all paths was this thing we were not supposed to know but were learning to have and was why our smiles were at first so naughty. It was this which was so forbidden that kept women puerile children without their power, and weak. The secret is that through this very body surges the same absolute wave of creative energy which by itself can make a life, a world, a first form, a self-sustained, self perpetuating unit, organelle, paramecium, or pomegranate, pear or person. And we ourselves can direct it. We now know that life was formed not only from the light but as well from the dark unbidden seas through heat and chemistry alone and more: The first real and authentic human was a lone black FEMALE in Africa! No force, male or female, has got it all. The secret is, we know it now and can be tricked no more.

One day we met, I recall you with those gorgeous earrings on: waterfalls of shells, tiny trash cans and little angle irons cascading down your ears. You'd dyed your hair orange and wore it like a trophy with banners round your brow. I sat in my warrior's bonnet opposite you like the mystical medicine chief and I saluted you. We had to concede that you and I were great. Anyone could tell.

This is why they hated us so much. It was that our dress actually gave us away. It meant we had the power (read prowess). Having acquired shared experiences, we were no longer innocent dupes of the culture. We'd escaped to the joy of life itself, enabled by the sharing of our stories to KNOW life's fire. (Though as we have said, it's easier to see things and events as they die, much harder to watch them as they first become.) Still we learned to do it.

I, in my pelts and flowered skirts and glowing hair, with celery stalks acting like Spanish combs in my hair, said, "Let's dance!" I began, with the slow tread of the feet and a drawing together of my legs that they watched. (I know I can get them to watch me.) And what do we teach with this dance that we do? I sometimes with pants and soft leather shoes or a dress or skirt with fringe, my shawl, my rimless glasses and my case. We teach them this:

That the key to the stopping of our hearts was in our hands and the sounds that we make! We found this rite I spoke of with the breath to bring our hearts into synch. As he and I lay together, our breath would be coming in waves of joy, then in a sudden moment, he'd put my hand fully and deeply on his heart and his on mine and they stopped! He opened his eyes to mine and when we released our hands, our hearts, (would you believe?), beat in unison then as one. It was all very much like gym, and takes care and coordination.

Then we took classes, you and I, here and there as we found them, not knowing that we were in fact on a path, searching a certain thing out, which was not what we had at first imagined. We began to see we were learning indirectly. You see, it's the nature of an esoteric path. You believe you are being taught one thing and actually learning another. Sometimes a dance class would give us some clues. Not your ordinary dancing, you know, it was one about tiny increments of energy, about breathing and chanting for hours, and undulating the spine. Here what happened was so profound, we'd often go away viscerally sick, but somehow suddenly without the slightest intent, our body began having a knowledge of its own, quite separate from our intended will, a movement of its own that was impossible not only for us to resist, but especially for the men. We began to acquire a look which if we gazed into the man's eyes, he could not refuse. And in our coming together, there was a power that is rarely experienced. The whole body became a "sexual" organism and the entire night a joyous ecstasy.

By that time our inner images had changed from those of excitation and lust to those of body response and visions of energies and we as the Goddess. The only requirement seemed to be that we, you and I, had to be the ones who did the choosing, deciding and directing. We were the ones who had the power and who were so compelling ... (although the man may not have realized this at all). What we were experiencing was the gradual re-empowerment of female force and godhead.

Meditating did it too, everyday by giving smaller and smaller increments of attention to the subtle details of experience, things slowly began to lose their names, to lose any thought about what they were, about anything at all but the thrill of their occurrence. This made for such exquisite experiencing that only the limiting behavior of others made us have to control our generosity which would want to spread this knowledge to all at any time.

Each day we'd go our ways returning once again with new treats for sharing. One day I'd try the art of wearing heavy-duty cowboy boots and jeans and a man's dark hat to tease him with my hips and butt. He'd grab me by the waist and pull me to his lap, or I'd just walk over and sit there wearing the "odor of cunt" perfume, as he'd say. And afterwards, like his trophy, he'd wear me on his hand stuffed down the back of my tight pants.

And you would be off staring, with night blue intensity into your man's eyes, catching his breath with your heart, as you spoke of the strawberries you ate, labor unions, cartography and Jung. And he'd write poems to you, because they rolled off his tongue to his pen on little scraps of paper that he could not resist. And you'd kiss like two beloveds. In no time at all your words became few and were the voices of the Gods. He gave you gifts, shining magical things, because he knew you loved them.

Again we'd return to share, the awe of it, the amazing awe. "I can't believe it," you'd say, and neither could I.

The men in their grasping directed ways always have wanted to move, and take action, to get to the point. They think that by so doing, they have the power, and all they've found is how to break it, to short circuit it into images, and things, but never just to have it. This we women began to know, it is we are the teachers of the light.

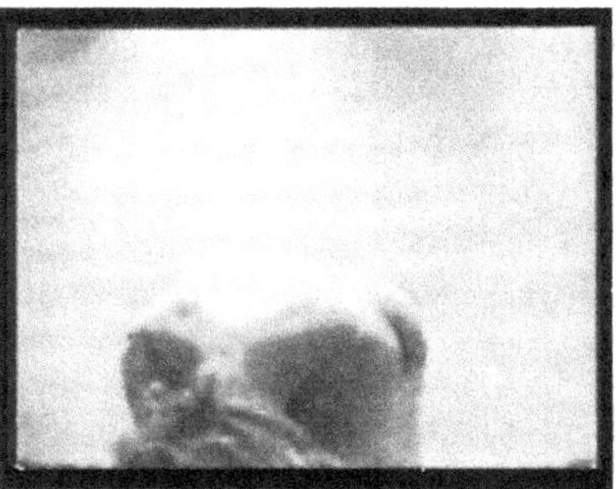

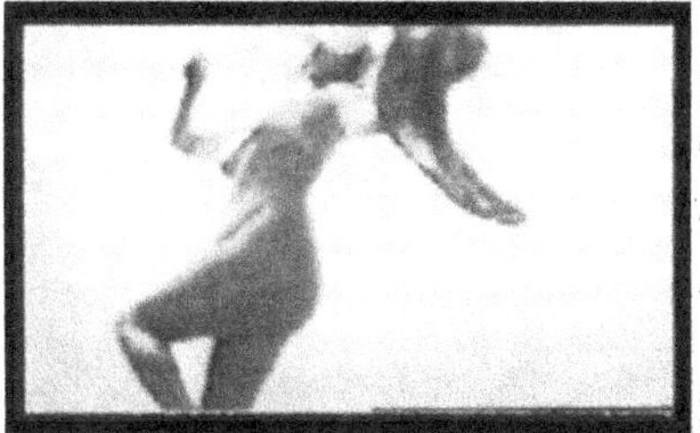

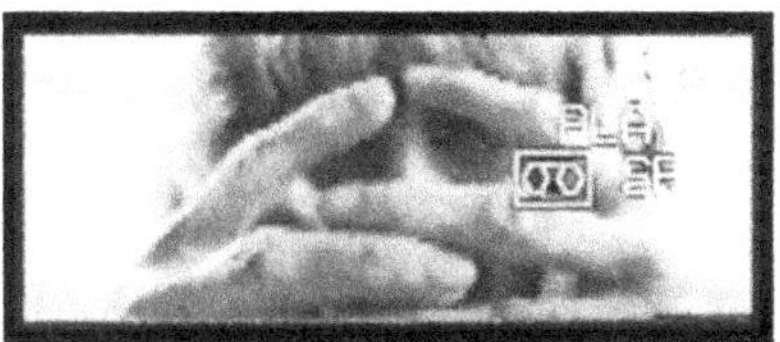

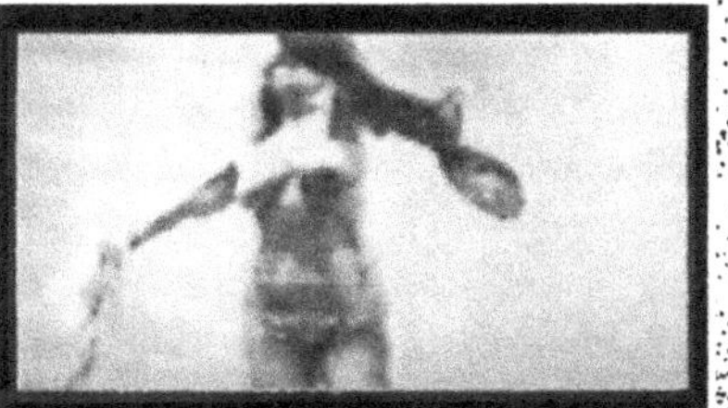

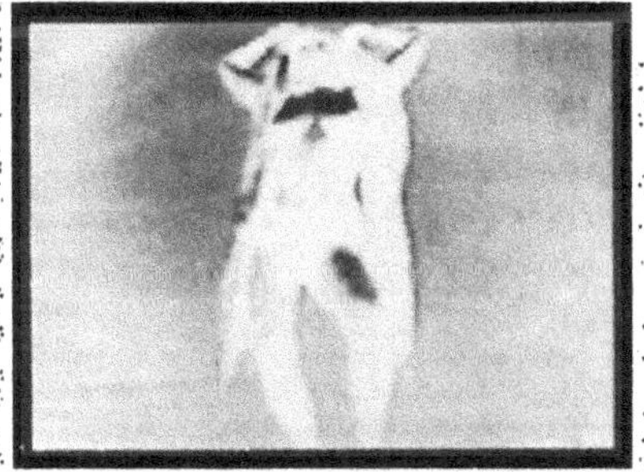

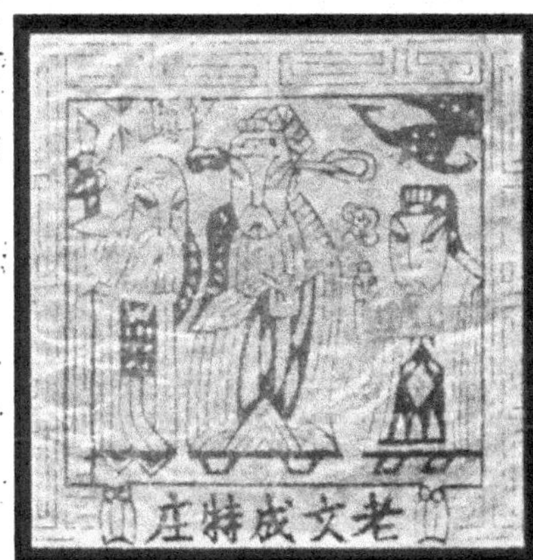

The Secret of Creation CONTINUED

Sometimes you and I would meet for coffee in our business jackets, tailored skirts and good shoes, big bracelets on our wrists, bangles in our ears, cigarettes in hands with painted nails and we'd smile. "Never for a moment let them forget, never for a moment have they tamed you." The bangles tell them that. We're here to do a job, not work! Domestic animals are in the service of their 'lord', broken to the heel (of self-hatred, certain of rejection because certain of their dependency). We are, instead, in the service of life, giving light in the day and the deep encompassing dark womb of the night.

AND there are prizes! The boy who put his hand on your hip at work gets one.

The difference is we KNOW and we SEE what they need and can heal them. Our hands and bodies are so sensitive that at every point of touch there is a sense of deep inner body joy, pleasure and delight. We can see inside our heads, we can....

Listen Lin, let's go places far from home, go camping at the river, with the men at the roadside cafe, fishing creel at their feet, woolen shirts and pipe, as we drink the steaming coffee. While outside the cold granite mountain locks its triangular shadow in its forested place to hold the deep cold lake at its base. The sky vaults its gleaming white cloud tails as the setting sun turns them in to salmon, peaches and cheeks.

Let's motor through the fields of Southern France. Let's trek the Himalayas in Tibetan skirts. Let's sit in temples, homes and schools and let them come to us for what we know to share.

As long as sisters need to write a literary gloss for the outside about knowledge wrested free from unconsciousness and dread, which later merges into the pool of the light of all-knowing, we must go on with this!

I hope you don't mind my telling people our story!

When do you want to meet? Tomorrow? Want'a borrow my red skirt?

©1995, LABASH

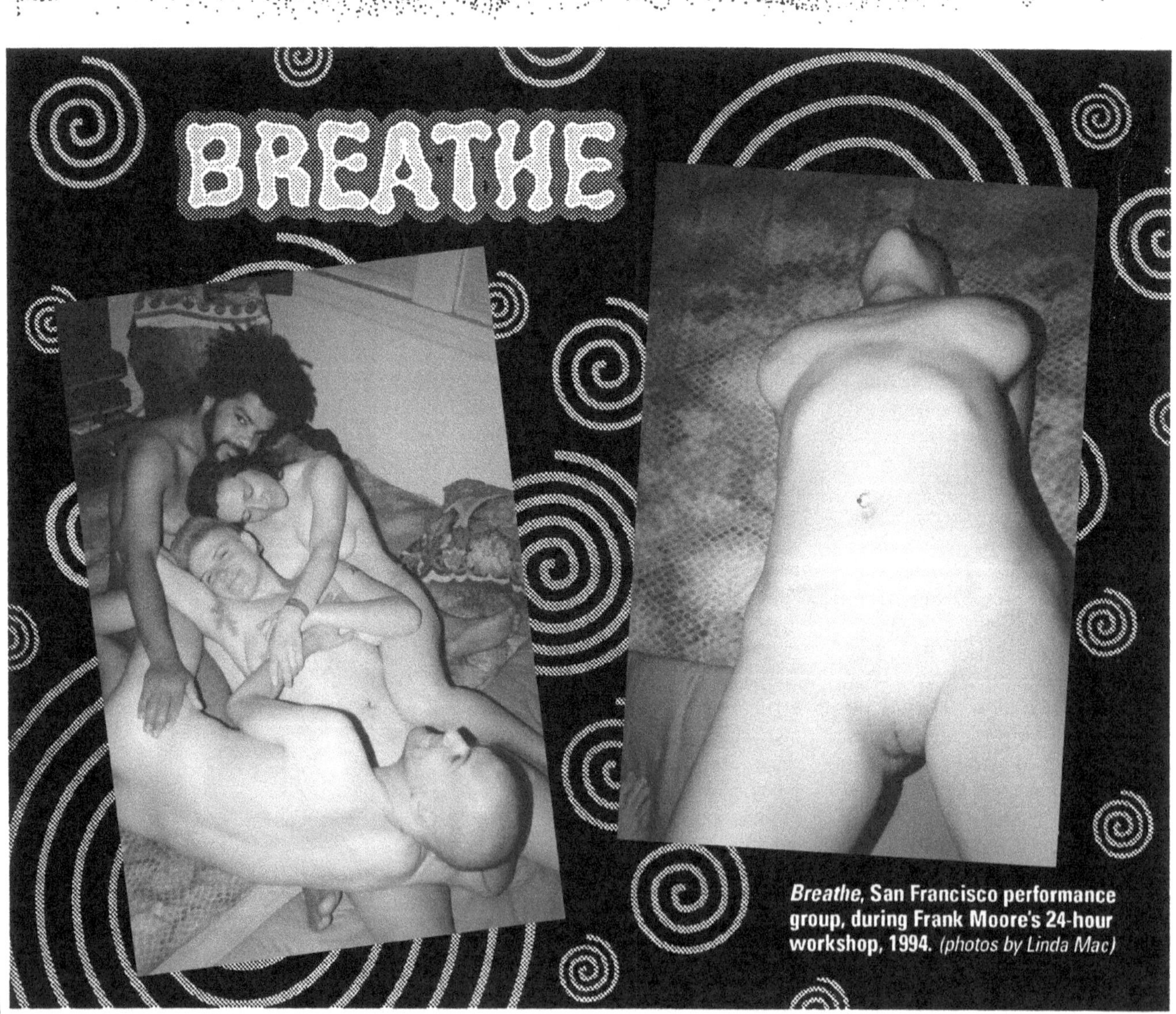

***Breathe*, San Francisco performance group, during Frank Moore's 24-hour workshop, 1994.** *(photos by Linda Mac)*

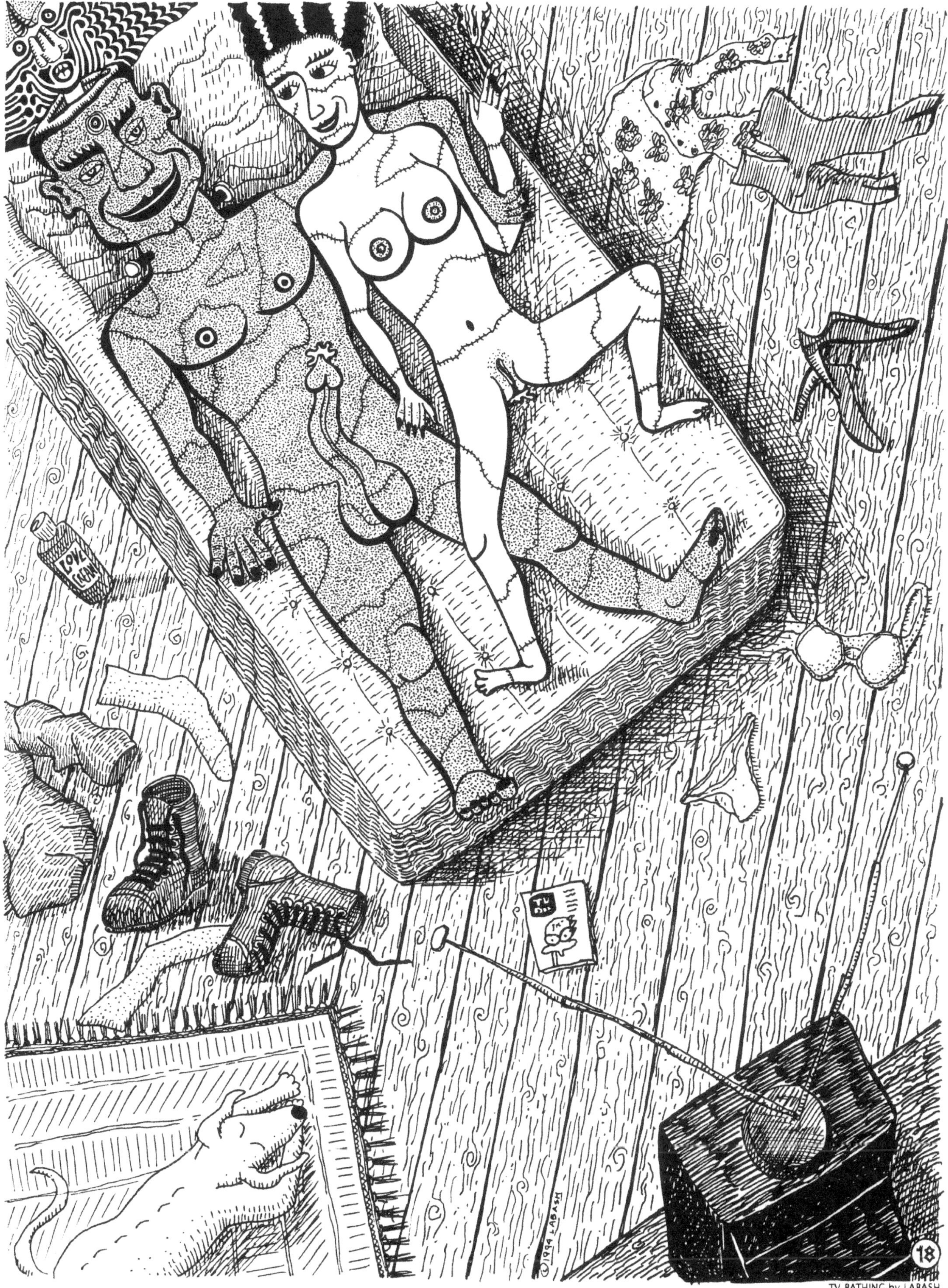

TV BATHING by LABASH

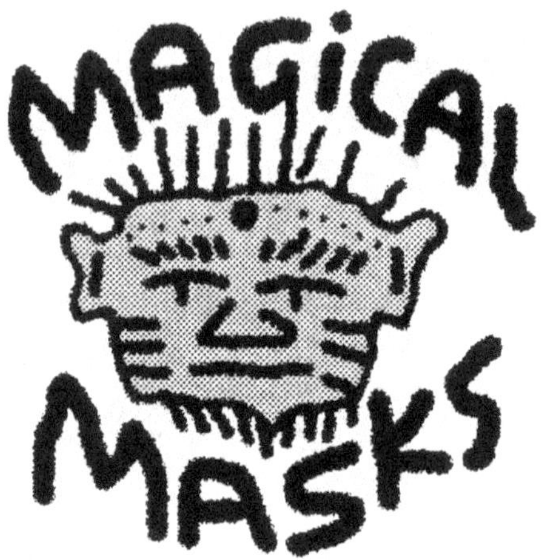

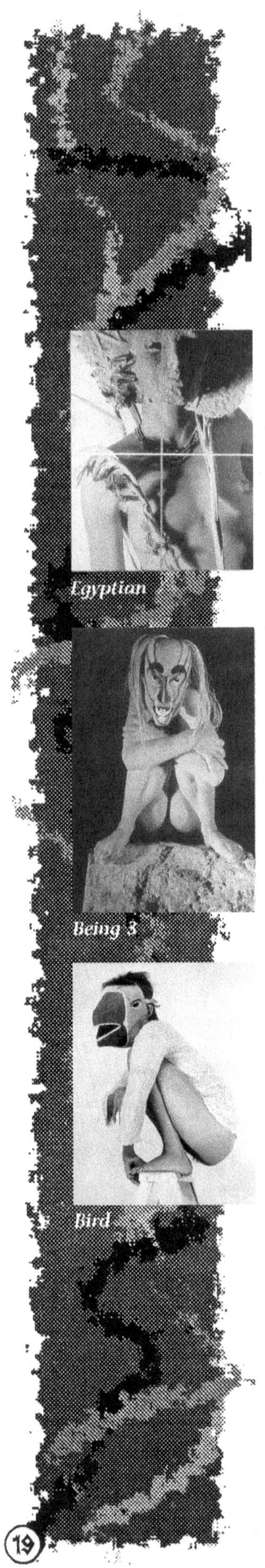

From the book *Cherotic Magic* by Frank Moore:

In magic, masks are important. These masks could be created out of material, or paint, or tatoos, or facial expressions. Magical masks are not meant to be a hiding, a covering up, or a protection. Rather, they are meant to reveal, to liberate, to call forth the deep personality which is usually hidden in normal society. They are vulnerable masks.

In our work, nudity is such a vulnerable mask. In itself, physical nudity does not always mean you are vulnerable. But in the context of this work, it takes you out of the social, polite world. It physically changes you slightly (I will get into these changes later). It signifies the willingness to use every part of yourself in the work ... holding nothing back or in reserve, holding no part too private or sacred not to be used in the work. This is on all levels of your being, from your body to your psyche.

From *Sacred Faces (Masks)* by Chief Distant Eagle:

Today I will talk about sacred faces. These are used in many tribal traditions, both in Turtle Island and elsewhere in the world. African masks, masks used in the Nọh drama of Japan, Apache masks, masks in New Guinea, and so on, are all for a sacred purpose. I will talk about the sacred face tradition I understand best, and that is the one of the Hodenasaunee (Iroquois Confederacy).

The masks used in the dominant culture are used to hide identity. Robbers often wear masks to hide their identities. At costume parties people wear masks to tantalize others with their anonymity. Anciently, in Europe too, masks served a sacred purpose, and a last vestige of this remains in the Hallowe'en customs now relegated to children only.

Among traditional, tribal peoples, on the other hand, masks are not to hide identity but to evoke sacred identity. To explain this, let me first tell you something else.

Tribal people believe that we create our own reality. The nature of our spirit determines the nature of the world around us. If we are happy within, we will be happy without. If we are unhappy within, our environment will be full of unhappiness. If we are happy within, we will be happy even if our environment is austere or adverse. If we are unhappy within, no amount of pleasant things in our environment will make us happy.

In everything you do as you walk the Red Road, if you walk in harmony with your world, at peace with yourself, you will have happiness within, and therefore happiness without. Smudging and praying, keeping spiritually clean in the Stone People's Lodge, listening to your dreams, walking in balance with all living things; all such things help you to walk the Red Road well.

Sacred faces are like windows: they help us to see the sacredness within ourselves and within the world around us. A person will do things wearing a mask that he or she will never do as an "ordinary person". This is because the mask represents a sacred being which comes to the person, and enables the person to do very sacred and powerful things. These things are not of our \washte\ ordinary world, but \wakan\: dangerous and holy things that lead to healing.

These sacred faces should not be called by either of the common English terms for them, neither "masks" nor "false faces". They are not masks to hide identity, and these faces are anything but false. The Seneca word \gagosa\ means "face", referring to the sacred face of the primaeval Younger Twin (a male) who was vanquished by the Older Twin (a female) and made to promise to help humanity. Those cured by the rituals of the "False Face Society" become members of it. The rituals are traditionally performed at the New Year and Green Corn Festivals.

The faces are carefully carved directly from living basswood trees, without killing the trees. They are painted black, red, or black and red. They have large eyes, often of pressedin metal, with pupilholes. The mouth and nose are exaggerated and distorted, often with large snaggly teeth and/or lolling tongue. A long hank of hair always hangs down from the face. The particular form of the face comes from a dream the person has had.

The sacred faces are considered alive. When not in use, they are hung facing the wall or wrapped in red cloth and put away in a safe place. They are occasionally "fed" by smearing a thick gruel of parched cornmeal with maple sugar on their lips. They are also often

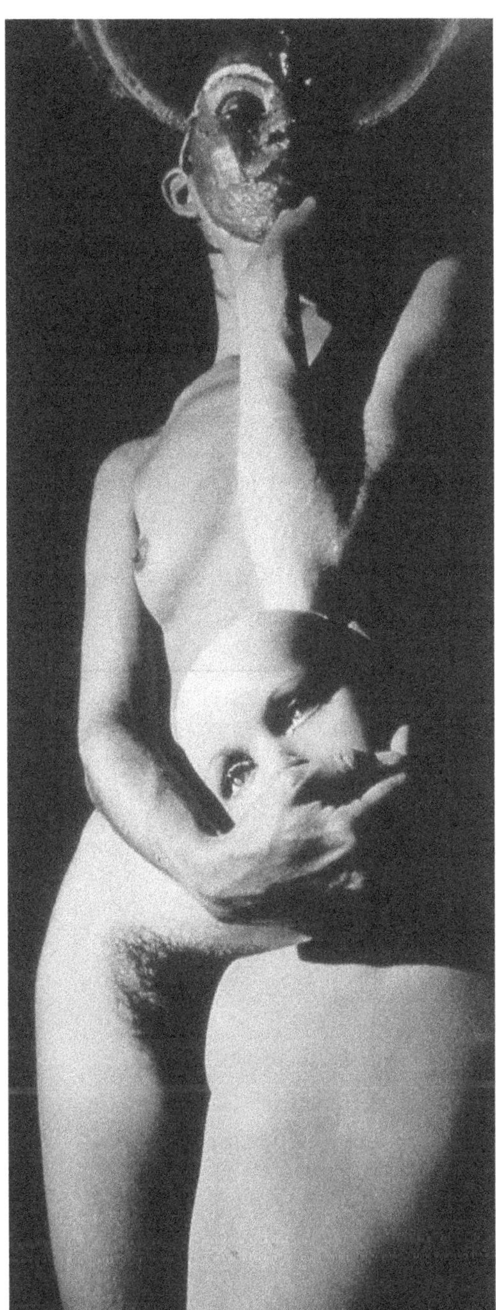
Woman & Child

wiped with sunflower seed oil to help "keep their skin soft". Old ones, thus, will have a bright shine from many such applications. Each one has a name and personality; it is always addressed as "Grandfather". They are often talked and/or sung to.

Sacred faces, therefore, are another way to listen to the Grandfathers, and to learn from them. They help us to cleanse our inner spirits, and to bring healing to ourselves and others. Even if you yourself do not carry a sacred face, you can still learn from them that it is important to recognize the sacred powers, the

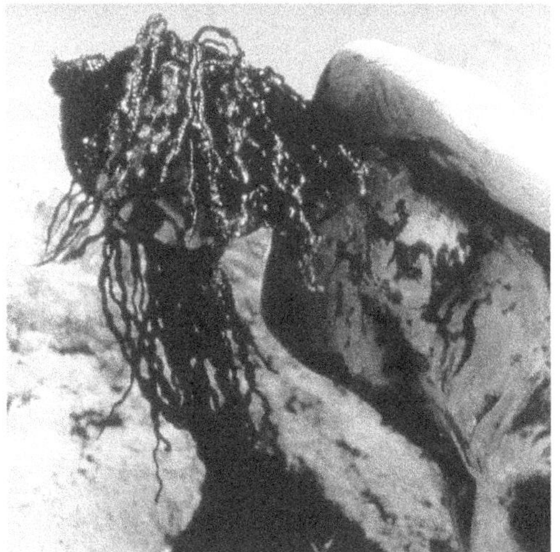
Guardian

\wakan\, within yourself and not be afraid to let it come out when appropriate for healing and cleansing.

That is what I have to say about sacred faces. Hau, mitaquye oyasin!

From a conversation on the GENIE computer network

Magical Mask-Roles
Frank Moore
May 1, 1994

there is a misunderstanding of the nature of the magical maskroles such as goddess, chief, wounded healer, shaman, heyoka, etc. people think these roles have something to do with the individual's personal identity. what they are really are projected aspects of the self that is in all of us and is all of us. we are granted access to particular magical maskroles to be played in the rituals and/or as tribal functions ... but trouble comes in when we think the maskrole is our individual personality. if i thought i was the wounded healer, the shaman, the heyoka ... all of which i have access to...all of the magic would be drained from the role ... and the role would be merely a part of my ego. this is what you see happening in those regional chiefs.

(Jim Audlin)
Chief Distant Eagle's Reply
May 1, 1994

Boy, are you right!!! Exactly. (About masks.) Most Washichu want to take the sacred mask and "own" it, to control it, to make it theirs. The only way you can ever "have" that mask is to let go of yourself. And that's the LAST thing Washichu will ever do!

Painted Photographs by Peter C. Turner

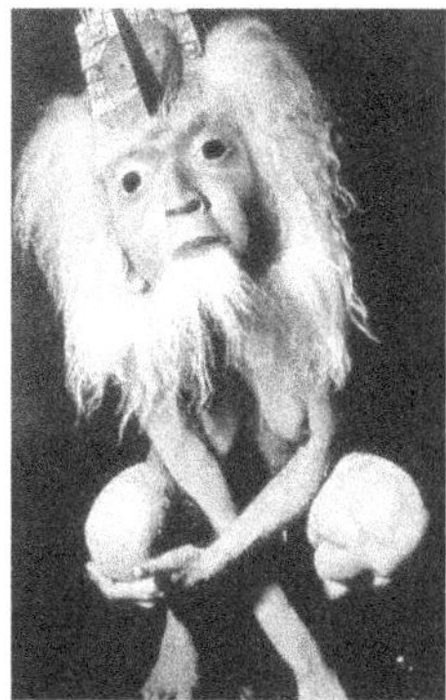
Yearning

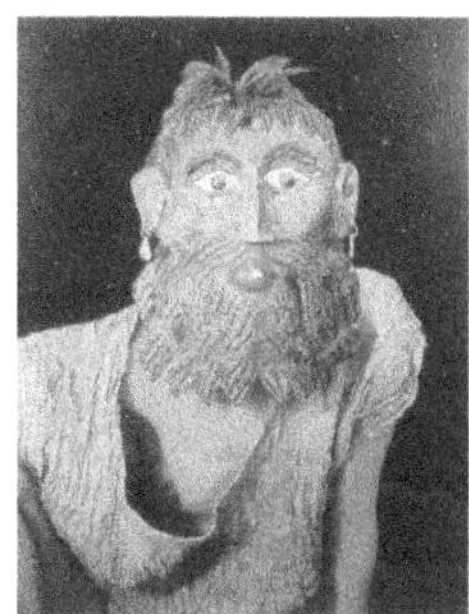
Smoker

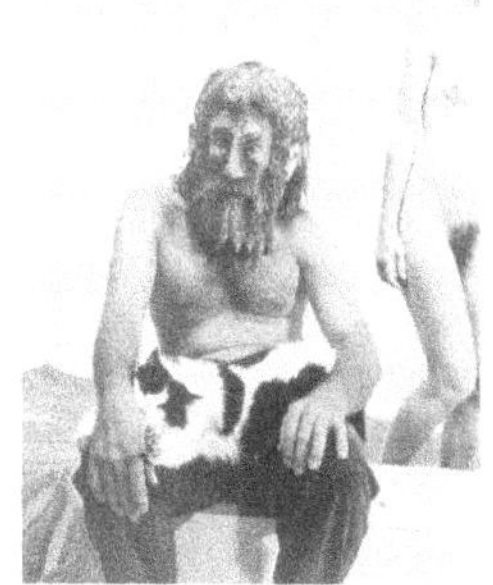
Autumn

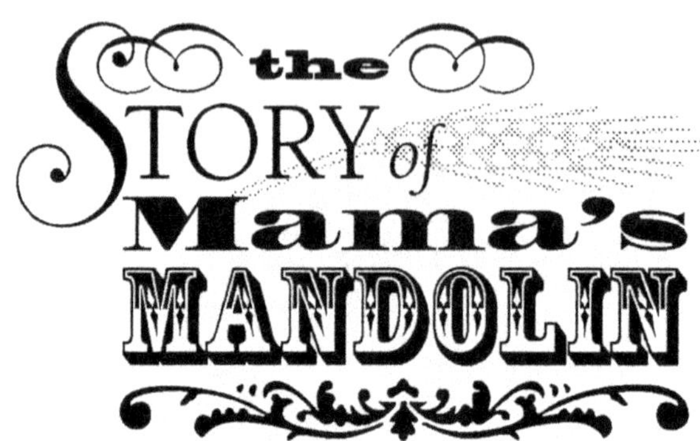

the STORY of Mama's MANDOLIN

The "F-4" Model, Gibson
Mandolin, with curly cues
and Ivory keys.
Mama's Mandolin.
Waiting in her living room
for the evening performance
the day she died.
She was 82.
Carlos, who played in her
orchestra
wrote
in memorium,
"The Maestro has gone to Heaven
Taking with her the mandolin"
He was Catholic and paid no
attention
to the Unitarian Minister announcing
proudly,
"Pearl Ava Beagle was an Atheist."

an oxymoron
I believe.
to call the musician an atheist!
music tells more what you will be than
what you won't be
There's more of a ring in believing
and she believed

in the world as full of beauty,
seeking, learning, loving
believing in justice,
believing in goodness
believing in joy
believing in the wonder

of her own self
believing in her beauty,
loving her self,
loving the earth and all
creatures,
loving the flower,
loving her music, loving the mandolin

It's true
she had no use
for organized religion
But, it's not enough to say
But, it's not enough to say
she was "non-religious"
not a believer in God,
Atheist.

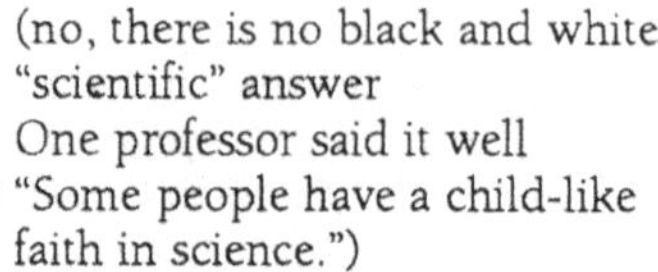

(no, there is no black and white
"scientific" answer
One professor said it well
"Some people have a child-like
faith in science.")

The scientists admit
with ever wondrous new discov'ry
they'll still know less than nothing
of the human brain.

Wise philosophers
neither deny
nor affirm
the meaning of life,
and neither deny
nor affirm
some interconnection,
(electrical impulse)
light?
a consciousness?
a floating non-existence
they can neither deny
nor affirm
some interconnection
some oneness of time and space
past events if remembered
are in the present!   some say.
and I say, if
the beginning of this earth
is out there somewhere,
and man
devises ways to place it
in time (which was created
by man in the first place)
if it's there, it's
there,
and isn't that peculiar?
When you think about it,
it seems to prove,
it is (as the Sufis said)
all happening at the same time,
one day we may find
that travelling through so-called time
with a space ship
isn't necessary, (it might be just
around the corner, or not!
earth as it began!)

But it's important
for Atheists to deny
God

the universe as designer of itself
is all the miracle
the atheist needs
I respect that
but there's more to say
about Pearl

This is how I felt,
when the Unitarian Minister said
Pearl Beagle was an Atheist!
as the STRONGEST most proud
statement of his talk.

But what an "anti" word, what
a "non" word, what a "denial"
word
True, she was "AGAINST" and "ANTI"
  injustice.

But joyously PRO so many high,
  exhilarating forces in life,
  not the least of these,
  her music

Surely her music soared to the heavens
  to be heard by Angels if there are Angels,
  in Heaven, if there is a Heaven
  (metaphors, what else is there but
  layered metaphors; I, as a metaphor, for
  my parents act of love!)

  And Heaven a metaphor for
  human desire,
  and Angels, a
  metaphor for the good in
  everyman.

The words musician/spiritual
are indeed synonymous:
of the spirit
with the spirit,
in the spirit
by the spirit
through the spirit
is it tangible,
measurable,
can you touch it, smell it,
see it,
you can hear it,
with you ears?
how do they hear, that's
mysterious,
with your body,
with what part
of your brain,
"I feel the spirit"
"I feel the music"
is to hear,
"I hear you!"
the jazz man said,
and he heard much more
than a flatted 9th,
or the dissonance
or the pulsating
percussion, the
whoosh and thunder
of percussion,
he heard much more
than the draw of a majestic
bow
across the strings
of the bass viol,
"I hear you,"
he may have heard
the story
of the universe
and he won't deny
or affirm that,
like the scientist
who was enabled to peer
at the coy, flirting
every ephemeral
Will-o-the-Wisp
answer
story
fable
fairy tale
ultimate truth
or illusion
(some say)
a baby
could understand
better
too simple
for a grown-up
man or woman
song,
perhaps just a song,
for the jazz man to hear
and the scientist to
dissect
note by note,
measure by measure

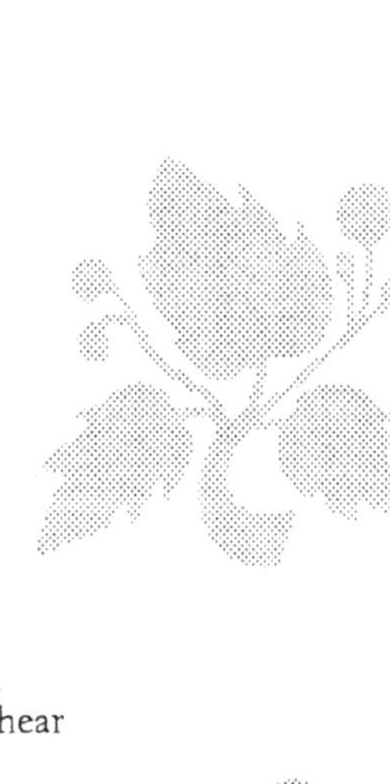

I thought of this
when the Minister said,
Pearl Beagle was an Atheist.

And again, later when
I re-read her letters, one
written a decade before,
saying in an off-hand way
DEAR Dorothy May,
"The Mandolin is yours, if you want
the old thing."

The Mandolin! For me!
The sacred Mandolin!
Around which everything revolved
it was
the laughter well,
the Irish spell
From Mama. To me. The sacred mandolin!

Mama was so joyously PRO so many high
  exhilarating things in life,
  not the least of these
  music

on her death, mercifully quick,
a member of her orchestra wrote a poem:
"The Maestro has gone to heaven
taking with her the Mandolin."

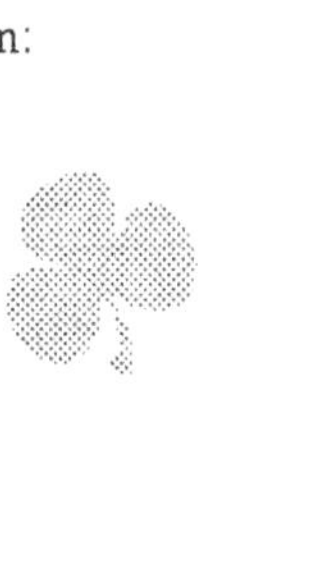

I thought of that beautiful line
smiling and wanting to say,
no, the mandolin is not with Pearl.
For in her own hand she wrote,

"Dear Dorothy May,
and I'm leaving you my mandolin.
if you want the old thing."

– dorothy jesse beagle

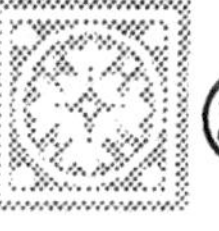

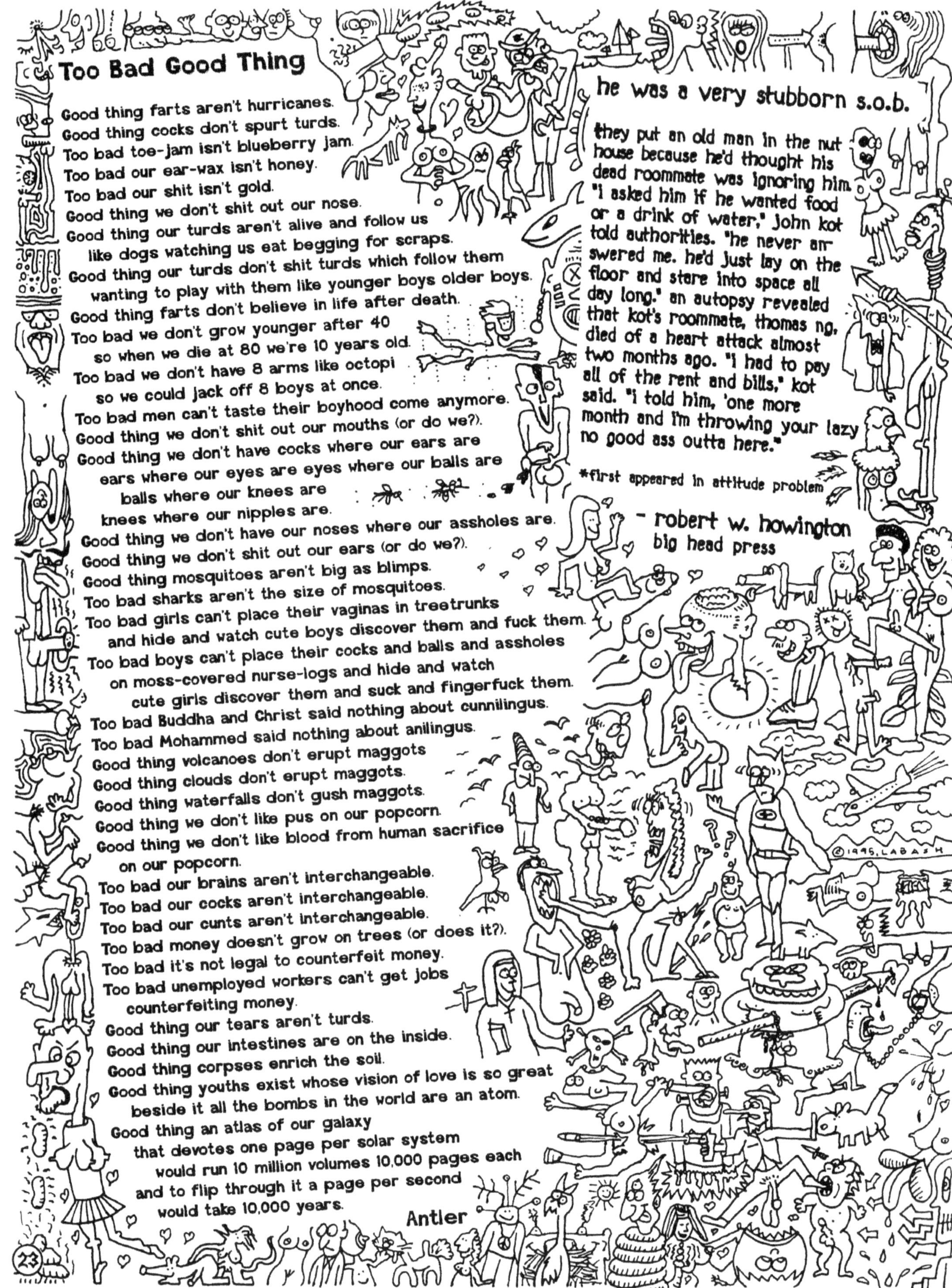

Too Bad Good Thing

Good thing farts aren't hurricanes.
Good thing cocks don't spurt turds.
Too bad toe-jam isn't blueberry jam.
Too bad our ear-wax isn't honey.
Too bad our shit isn't gold.
Good thing we don't shit out our nose.
Good thing our turds aren't alive and follow us
like dogs watching us eat begging for scraps.
Good thing our turds don't shit turds which follow them
wanting to play with them like younger boys older boys.
Good thing farts don't believe in life after death.
Too bad we don't grow younger after 40
so when we die at 80 we're 10 years old.
Too bad we don't have 8 arms like octopi
so we could jack off 8 boys at once.
Too bad men can't taste their boyhood come anymore.
Good thing we don't shit out our mouths (or do we?).
Good thing we don't have cocks where our ears are
ears where our eyes are eyes where our balls are
balls where our knees are
knees where our nipples are.
Good thing we don't have our noses where our assholes are.
Good thing we don't shit out our ears (or do we?).
Good thing mosquitoes aren't big as blimps.
Too bad sharks aren't the size of mosquitoes.
Too bad girls can't place their vaginas in treetrunks
and hide and watch cute boys discover them and fuck them.
Too bad boys can't place their cocks and balls and assholes
on moss-covered nurse-logs and hide and watch
cute girls discover them and suck and fingerfuck them.
Too bad Buddha and Christ said nothing about cunnilingus.
Too bad Mohammed said nothing about anilingus.
Good thing volcanoes don't erupt maggots
Good thing clouds don't erupt maggots.
Good thing waterfalls don't gush maggots.
Good thing we don't like pus on our popcorn.
Good thing we don't like blood from human sacrifice
on our popcorn.
Too bad our brains aren't interchangeable.
Too bad our cocks aren't interchangeable.
Too bad our cunts aren't interchangeable.
Too bad money doesn't grow on trees (or does it?).
Too bad it's not legal to counterfeit money.
Too bad unemployed workers can't get jobs
counterfeiting money.
Good thing our tears aren't turds.
Good thing our intestines are on the inside.
Good thing corpses enrich the soil.
Good thing youths exist whose vision of love is so great
beside it all the bombs in the world are an atom.
Good thing an atlas of our galaxy
that devotes one page per solar system
would run 10 million volumes 10,000 pages each
and to flip through it a page per second
would take 10,000 years.

Antler

he was a very stubborn s.o.b.

they put an old man in the nut house because he'd thought his dead roommate was ignoring him. "i asked him if he wanted food or a drink of water," John kot told authorities. "he never answered me. he'd just lay on the floor and stare into space all day long." an autopsy revealed that kot's roommate, thomas ng, died of a heart attack almost two months ago. "i had to pay all of the rent and bills," kot said. "i told him, 'one more month and i'm throwing your lazy no good ass outta here."

*first appeared in attitude problem

- robert w. howington
big head press

To My Ray by Molly Holzschlag

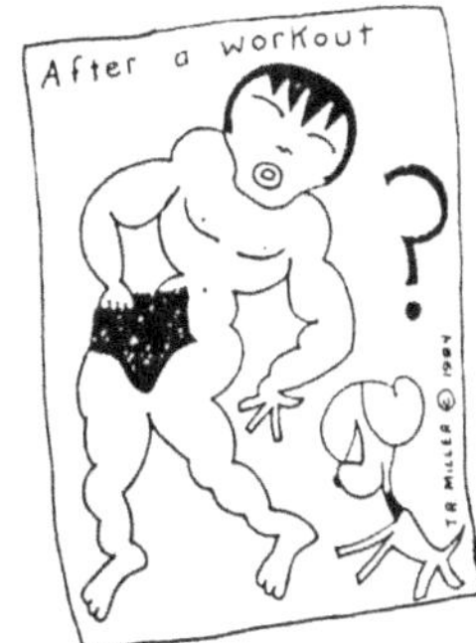

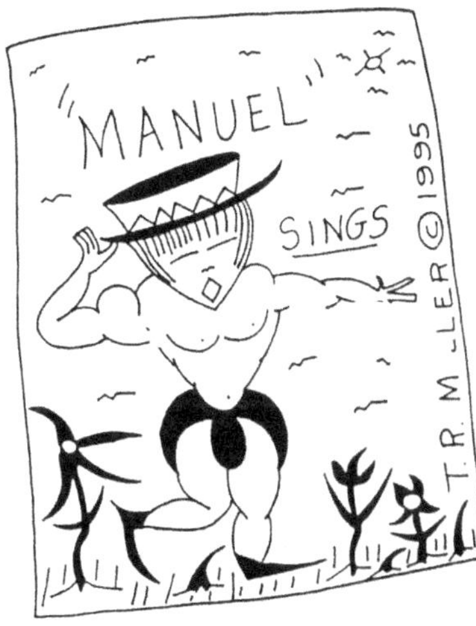

You need to know.
I
have held on to your black heart
in fact
I sleep with it beneath my pillow
it fits
in my hand when
no one else will

I went to Hawaii
I drowned
I came back
I never saw
blue like that

I never saw you
so I ask

I ask for you
I cry in the shower
I hold my scar not all healed
I bleed and think
you knew all along
but could not
save me.

I know
you are dead or walking
with some mixed up Shaman
picking mushrooms in Sonora
each time it hurts I remember
your fingers reaching inside
and stopping the pain.

But I could not stop the Viet Cong
from smashing your face in my living room
or crucifying you or burying you
not dead

The October sun is still too strong
are you in hell or somewhere?
I reach for you with psychic wings
but this time you do not come.

I need to tell you.

I sat watching a movie
the miracle of life they called it
with cameras the size of a pinhead
looking with wide eyes at the
pink feather flowers
of her fallopian tubes

So I hemorrhaged in class because
I did not feel so beautiful
I have been hacked up
laser, scalpel
did my spirit slip out with the blood?

I don't seem to feel
so much myself. I take men to fill
the puzzle but discard them when
they do not fit.

I have smelled my own flesh rotting
I am terrified
I am so lonely
you were my ray

my angel gone, most intimate lover
of this flesh though

you never entered me

I saw you walking
but it was not you

The Frank Zappa Sixties-Nineties Blues Raga

Yeah it can't happen here with it's plastic hippies
and faxed I.D. toadstool brains wound tight but it
can't happen here away from the nasty messy city ghetto
with your cute picket fences and pink flamingoes
nigger jockey painted white on your manicured lawns
three different cereals yeah it can't happen here not
the 'D' word not drugs in your schools not Mary with her
yellow curls spread eagle on the pavement it can't happen
here not in 'OUR' America (pass the pancake syrup, Jimmy)
Paul wants to hold your daughter's hand Mick wants to
spend the night together but it can't happen here it
can't happen here Yeah there's lsd on Mickey Mouse and
a bad comedown and a halfway house in the middle of a Taco
Bell and a Burger King they're selling junk and everything but
IT CAN'T happen here cause I've been checking it out and I'm
here to tell you that it can't happen here.
Now the guns your horoscope don't look back in
every crack) alley) tongues and jammies everyones a nanny
with a USMC tatoo
and the faked faxed America is panting ranting Billy Graham
and Bishop Sheen screaming; It can't happen here, it can't
happen here cause I've been checking it out and I'm here to
tell you that It can't happen here
(not in Our America)

Elliott

Kiss and Tell by Molly Holzschlag

Dionysis don't you dare
tease my Venus
wine-drenched tongues
and false blue eyes
touch the leather
of this man

Or, knocking on the Happy,
New Year
the sultry Lord of my Heat
rubs his fingers milking
the softer flesh
of this right arm and touching
the tip of his
fingers I am
made drunk by the rivers washing

I pulsate with grief.

The Alaskan remains quiet with his Indian angles.
His lips should be kissed do I dare?
He turns the pages of
a book softly. Reading words? Or curves?

Curve to angle
Geometry of lovers and a crushed velvet gown
Bosom hides Wicca's tongue,
I love her, I love him.
Can I crawl inside
the crevass and watch from there?
Protected?

Mother lode – in those hills of scent sweet with the Lily.

The maniac Saint Steven
writes love poems and pushes them deep
into my box.

I am consumed in smoke and confused desire
Venus embrace me do not let me die
Here in the chilled cell of my sometimes
friends
I look through the bars to the alley
wanting to forget
California's eyes crying
the red steel hair of my old brother flipping cards
the woman who has
too many
holes to fill they are
in her heart
and someone else's hard-on is laughing.

Attila goes to fence with the foppish
off to the Bay with rappier and tongue
he grew a moustache and beard it hides
his handsome face
he must obscure lies like I do
nestled in our Hungarian, Gypsy blood

Dionysis don't you dare
make him sing to me this way
with this other language
with the greed of the hungry shaft
with the ring of promise
tightening the exotic canal where I
know a secret
I know a secret

Kiss and tell.

Molly Holzschlag is a poet, songwriter and medical journalist living in Tucson, Arizona. Also known as Molly Who... she has an album of original music available through Kept in the Dark Records, and is working on another recording project with her current partner, Patty Sundberg, in a duo known as Courage Sisters.
For more information write:

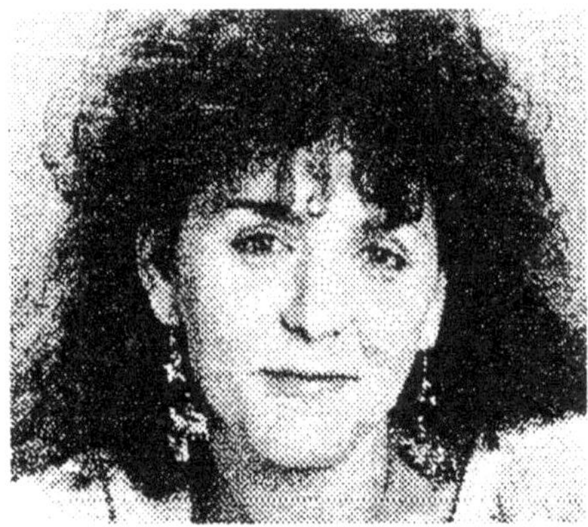

Molly Who...
P.O. Box 42225
Tucson, Arizona
85733-42225

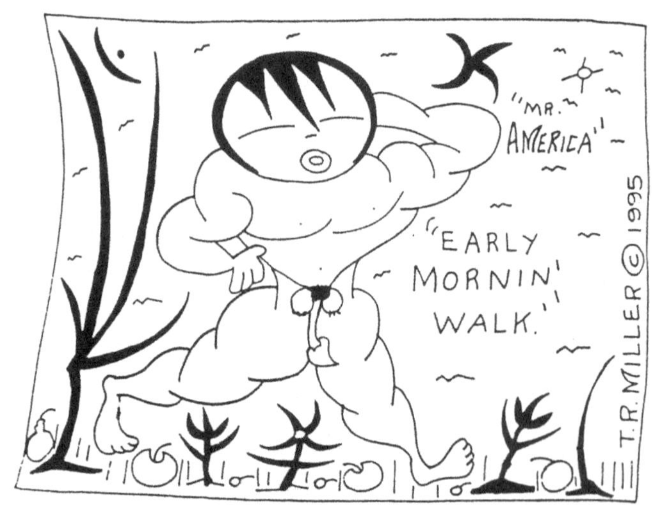

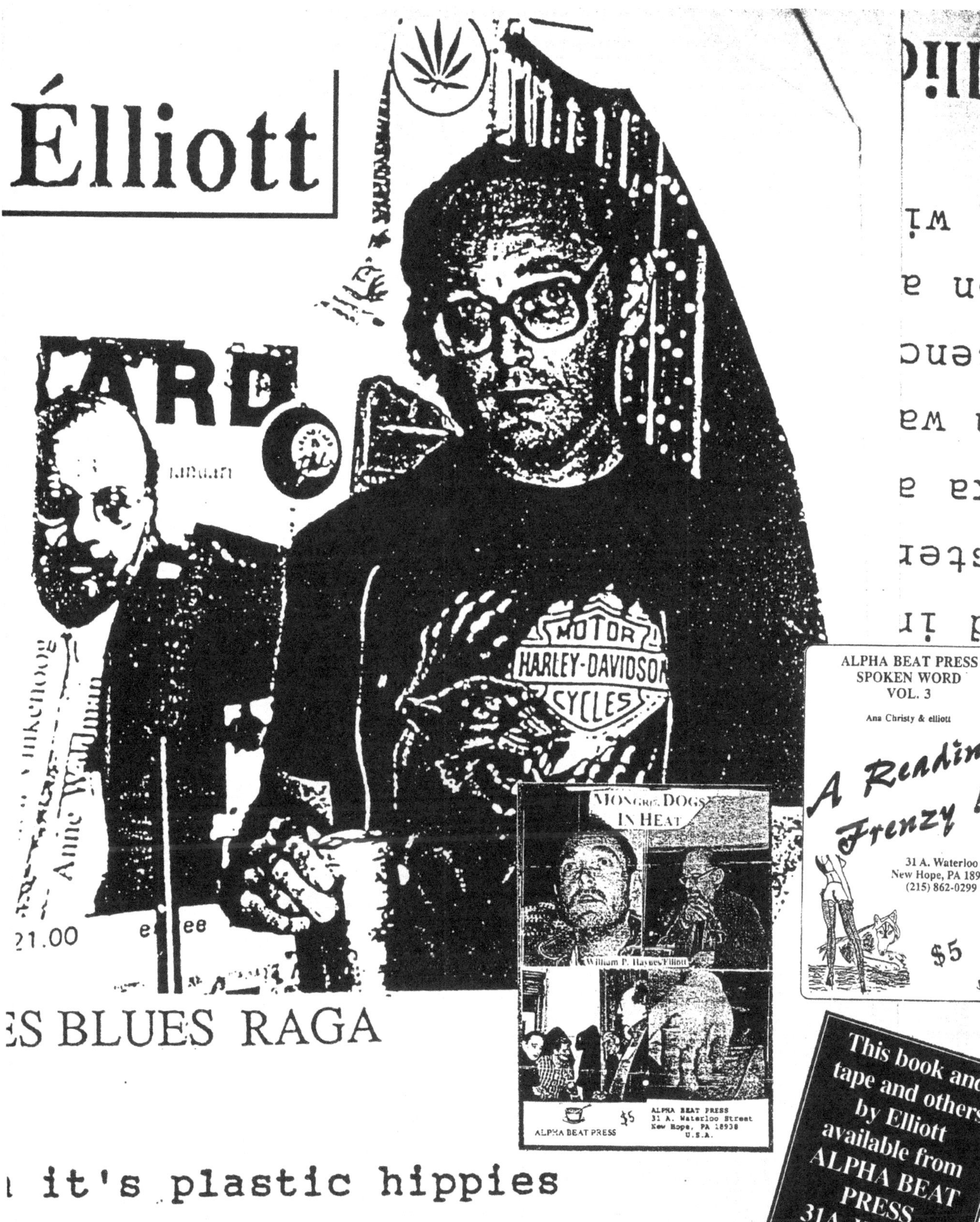

i it's plastic hippies

is wound tight but it

ie nasty messy city ghetto

ind pink flamingoes

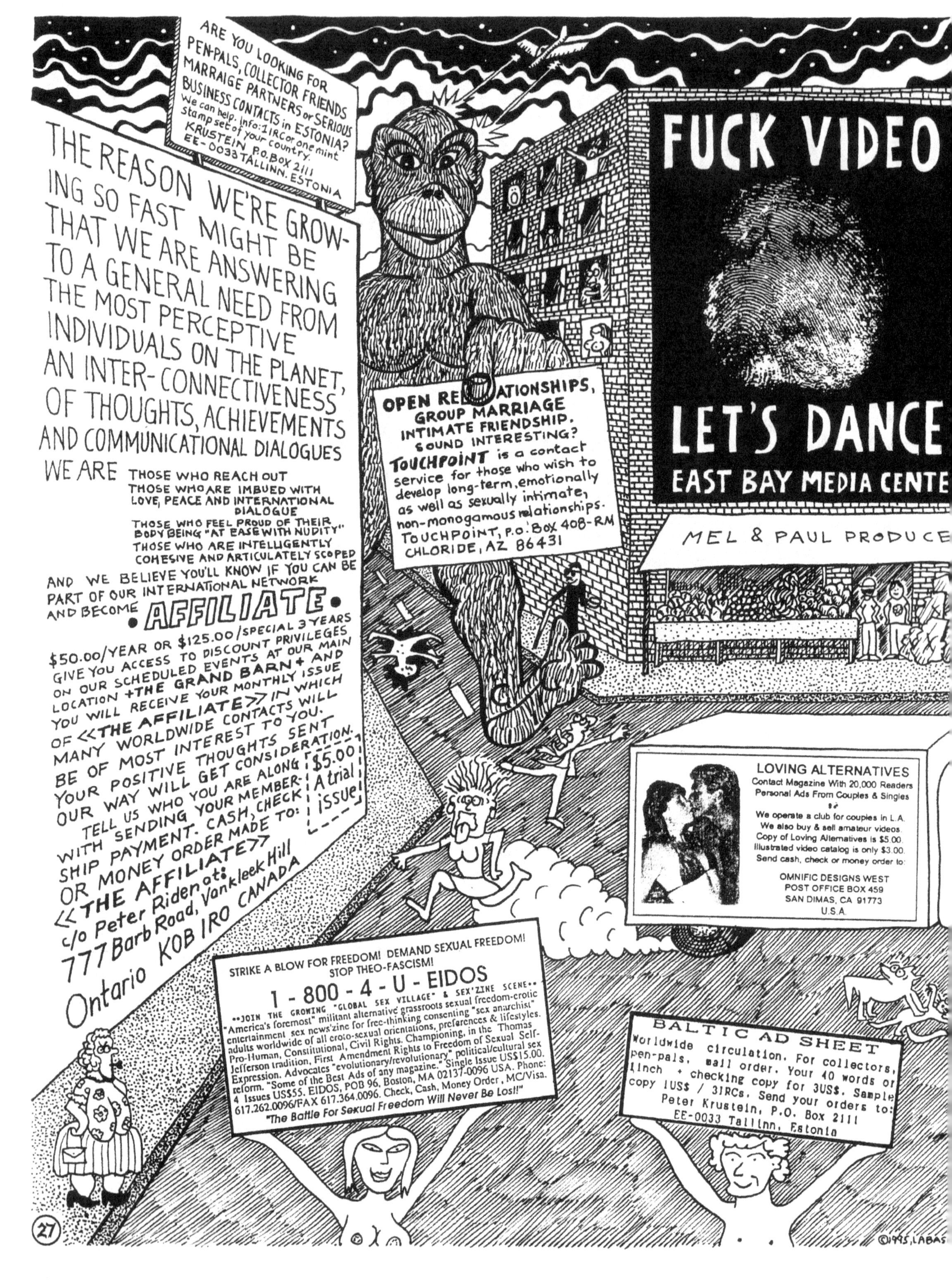

ARE YOU LOOKING FOR PEN-PALS, COLLECTOR FRIENDS MARRAIGE PARTNERS or SERIOUS BUSINESS CONTACTS in ESTONIA?
We can help. Info: 1IRC or one mint stamp set of your country.
KRUSTEIN P.O. Box 2111
EE-0033 TALLINN. ESTONIA
THE REASON WE'RE GROWING SO FAST MIGHT BE THAT WE ARE ANSWERING TO A GENERAL NEED FROM THE MOST PERCEPTIVE INDIVIDUALS ON THE PLANET, AN INTER-CONNECTIVENESS OF THOUGHTS, ACHIEVEMENTS AND COMMUNICATIONAL DIALOGUES
WE ARE THOSE WHO REACH OUT
THOSE WHO ARE IMBUED WITH LOVE, PEACE AND INTERNATIONAL DIALOGUE
THOSE WHO FEEL PROUD OF THEIR BODY BEING "AT EASE WITH NUDITY"
THOSE WHO ARE INTELLIGENTLY COHESIVE AND ARTICULATELY SCOPED
AND WE BELIEVE YOU'LL KNOW IF YOU CAN BE PART OF OUR INTERNATIONAL NETWORK AND BECOME • AFFILIATE •
$50.00/YEAR OR $125.00/SPECIAL 3 YEARS GIVE YOU ACCESS TO DISCOUNT PRIVILEGES ON OUR SCHEDULED EVENTS AT OUR MAIN LOCATION +THE GRAND BARN+ AND YOU WILL RECEIVE YOUR MONTHLY ISSUE OF <<THE AFFILIATE>> IN WHICH MANY WORLDWIDE CONTACTS WILL BE OF MOST INTEREST TO YOU. YOUR POSITIVE THOUGHTS SENT OUR WAY WILL GET CONSIDERATION. TELL US WHO YOU ARE ALONG WITH SENDING YOUR MEMBERSHIP PAYMENT. CASH, CHECK OR MONEY ORDER MADE TO: <<THE AFFILIATE>> c/o Peter Rider at: 777 Barb Road, Vankleek Hill Ontario KOB IRO CANADA
$5.00 A trial issue!
FUCK VIDEO
LET'S DANCE
EAST BAY MEDIA CENTE
MEL & PAUL PRODUCE
OPEN RELATIONSHIPS, GROUP MARRIAGE INTIMATE FRIENDSHIP. SOUND INTERESTING?
TOUCHPOINT is a contact service for those who wish to develop long-term, emotionally as well as sexually intimate, non-monogamous relationships.
TOUCHPOINT, P.O. Box 408-RM
CHLORIDE, AZ 86431
LOVING ALTERNATIVES
Contact Magazine With 20,000 Readers
Personal Ads From Couples & Singles
We operate a club for couples in L.A.
We also buy & sell amateur videos.
Copy of Loving Alternatives is $5.00.
Illustrated video catalog is only $3.00.
Send cash, check or money order to:
OMNIFIC DESIGNS WEST
POST OFFICE BOX 459
SAN DIMAS, CA 91773
U.S.A.
STRIKE A BLOW FOR FREEDOM! DEMAND SEXUAL FREEDOM!
STOP THEO-FASCISM!
1 - 800 - 4 - U - EIDOS
••JOIN THE GROWING "GLOBAL SEX VILLAGE" & SEX'ZINE SCENE••
"America's foremost" militant alternative grassroots sexual freedom-erotic
entertainment sex news'zine for free-thinking consenting "sex anarchist"
adults worldwide of all eroto-sexual orientations, preferences & lifestyles.
Pro-Human, Constitutional, Civil Rights. Championing, in the Thomas
Jefferson tradition, First Amendment Rights to Freedom of Sexual Self-
Expression. Advocates "evolutionary/revolutionary" political/cultural sex
reform. "Some of the Best Ads of any magazine." Single Issue US$15.00.
4 Issues US$55. EIDOS, POB 96, Boston, MA 02137-0096 USA. Phone:
617.262.0096/FAX 617.364.0096. Check, Cash, Money Order, MC/Visa.
"The Battle For Sexual Freedom Will Never Be Lost!"
BALTIC AD SHEET
Worldwide circulation. For collectors, pen-pals, mail order. Your 40 words or 1inch + checking copy for 3US$. Sample copy 1US$ / 3IRCs. Send your orders to:
Peter Krustein, P.O. Box 2111
EE-0033 Tallinn, Estonia
©1995, LABAS

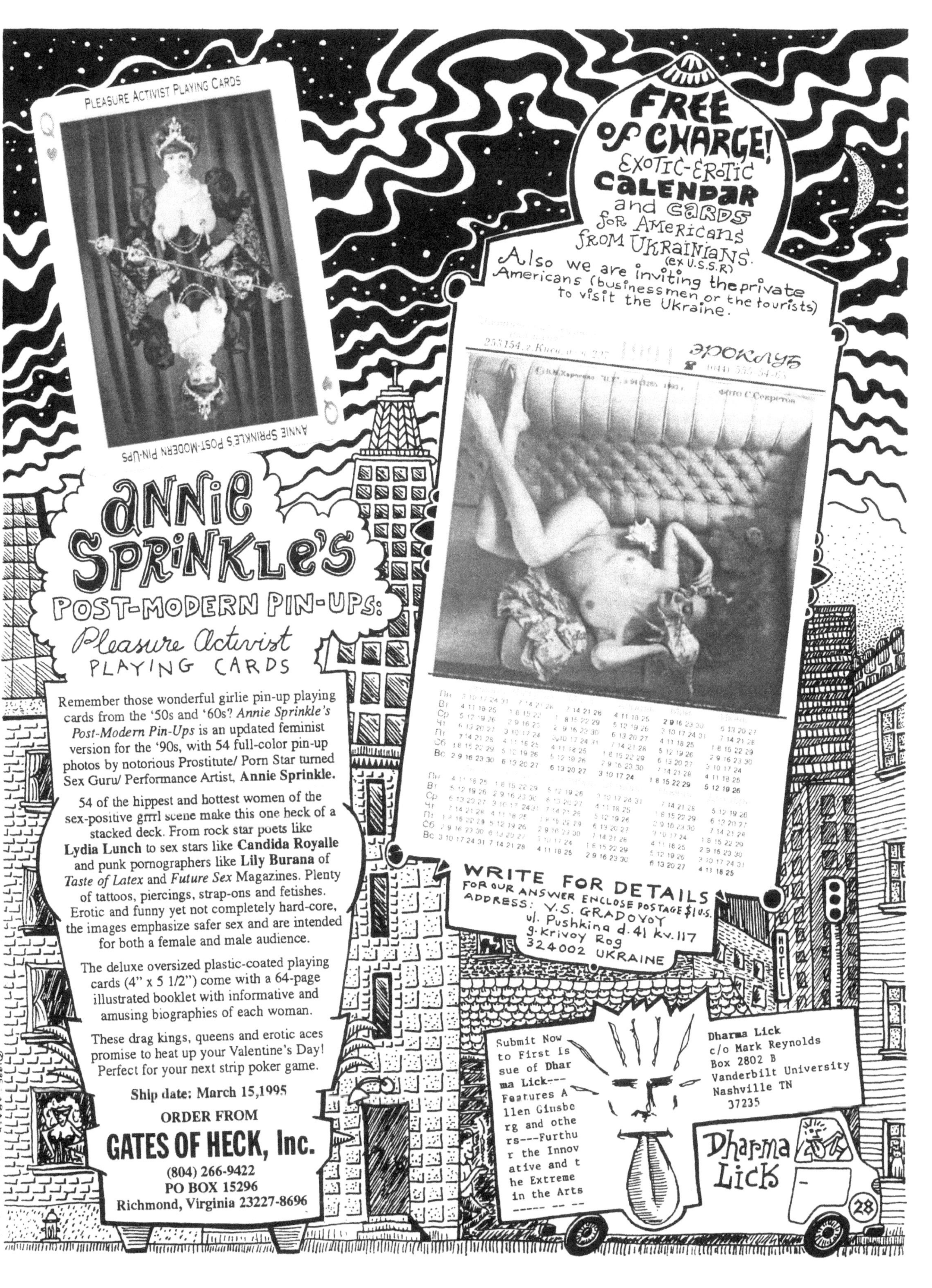

PLEASURE ACTIVIST PLAYING CARDS
ANNIE SPRINKLE'S POST-MODERN PIN-UPS
Annie Sprinkle's
POST-MODERN PIN-UPS:
Pleasure Activist
PLAYING CARDS
Remember those wonderful girlie pin-up playing cards from the '50s and '60s? Annie Sprinkle's Post-Modern Pin-Ups is an updated feminist version for the '90s, with 54 full-color pin-up photos by notorious Prostitute/ Porn Star turned Sex Guru/ Performance Artist, Annie Sprinkle.
54 of the hippest and hottest women of the sex-positive grrrl scene make this one heck of a stacked deck. From rock star poets like Lydia Lunch to sex stars like Candida Royalle and punk pornographers like Lily Burana of Taste of Latex and Future Sex Magazines. Plenty of tattoos, piercings, strap-ons and fetishes. Erotic and funny yet not completely hard-core, the images emphasize safer sex and are intended for both a female and male audience.
The deluxe oversized plastic-coated playing cards (4" x 5 1/2") come with a 64-page illustrated booklet with informative and amusing biographies of each woman.
These drag kings, queens and erotic aces promise to heat up your Valentine's Day! Perfect for your next strip poker game.
Ship date: March 15,1995
ORDER FROM
GATES OF HECK, Inc.
(804) 266-9422
PO BOX 15296
Richmond, Virginia 23227-8696
FREE of CHARGE!
EXOTIC-EROTIC
CALENDAR
and CARDS
FOR AMERICANS
FROM UKRAINIANS.
(ex U.S.S.R)
Also we are inviting the private Americans (businessmen or the tourists) to visit the Ukraine.
ЭРОКЛУБ
WRITE FOR DETAILS
FOR OUR ANSWER ENCLOSE POSTAGE $1 U.S.
ADDRESS: V.S. GRADOVOY
ul. Pushkina d. 41 kv. 117
g. Krivoy Rog
324002 UKRAINE
HOTEL
Submit Now to First Issue of Dharma Lick--- Features Allen Ginsberg and others---Further the Innovative and the Extreme in the Arts ----- -- --
Dharma Lick
c/o Mark Reynolds
Box 2802 B
Vanderbilt University
Nashville TN
37235
Dharma Lick
28

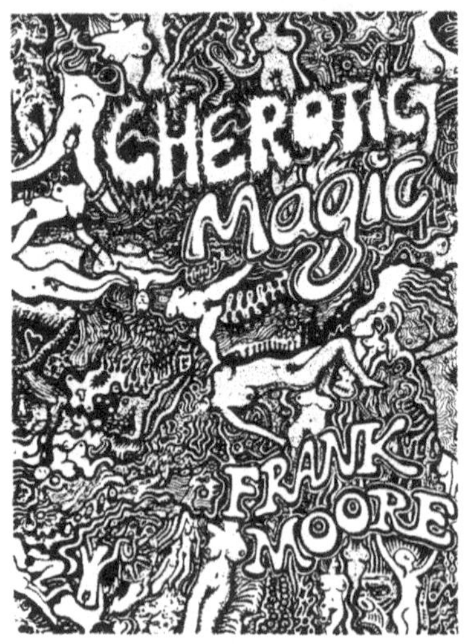

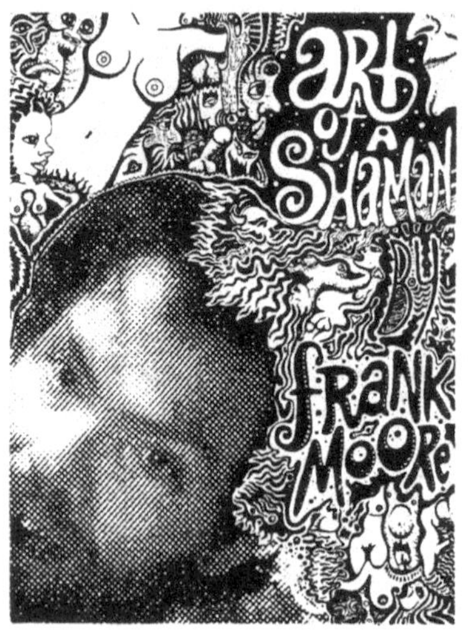

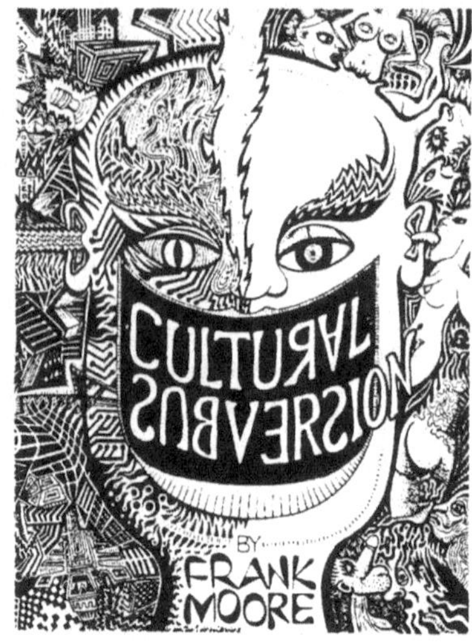

cherotic magic **$15**

A MAJOR ATTEMPT TO INTRODUCE A POWERFUL SYSTEM OF MAGIC INTO OUR MODERN WESTERN EVERYDAY LIFE, THEREBY EXPLOSIVELY EXPANDING SUCH CONCEPTS AS SEX, HUMAN RELATIONSHIPS. THE CLEAR, DOWN-TO-EARTH TEXT IS AMPLIFIED BY THE NON-LINEAR TRANCE ILLUSTRATIONS BY LABASH.
published 1990

BOOKS & ZINES

BY **frank moore**

art of a shaman **$4**

IN art of a shaman, ORIGINALLY A LECTURE PRESENTED AT N.Y.U., FRANK MOORE EXPLORES PERFORMANCE AND ART IN GENERAL TERMS OF THEM BEING A MAGICAL WAY TO EFFECT CHANGE IN THE WORLD. HE LOOKS AT PERFORMANCE AS AN ART OF MELTING ACTION, RITUALISTIC, SHAMANISTIC DOINGS/PLAYINGS. BY USING HIS CAREER AND LIFE AS A "BASELINE", MOORE EXPLAINS THE DYNAMIC PLAYING WITHIN THE CONTEXT OF REALITY SHAPING. HE BRINGS IN CONCEPTS FROM MODERN PHYSICS, MYTHOLOGY, AND PSYCHOLOGY. COVER BY LABASH.
published 1991

cultural subversion **$1**

PERSONAL, ANARCHICAL TECHNOLOGIES SUCH AS XEROGRAPHY, VCR, FAXS, ETC., ARE EXAMINED IN cultural subversion BY FRANK MOORE AS THE MEANS BY WHICH ORDINARY PEOPLE CAN TAKE BACK THE CONTROL OF COMMUNICATIONS AND CREATIVITY FROM THE CENTRAL POWER COMBINE.
published 1992

art of living **$10**

A GUIDE TO DOWN-TO-EARTH SPIRITUALITY AS CHANNELLED BY FRANK MOORE.
published 1987

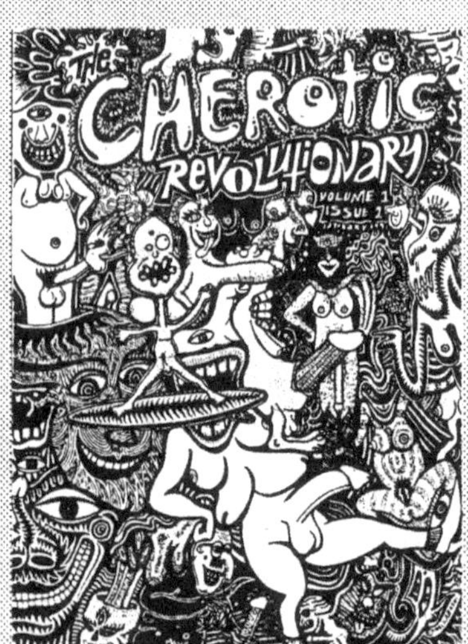

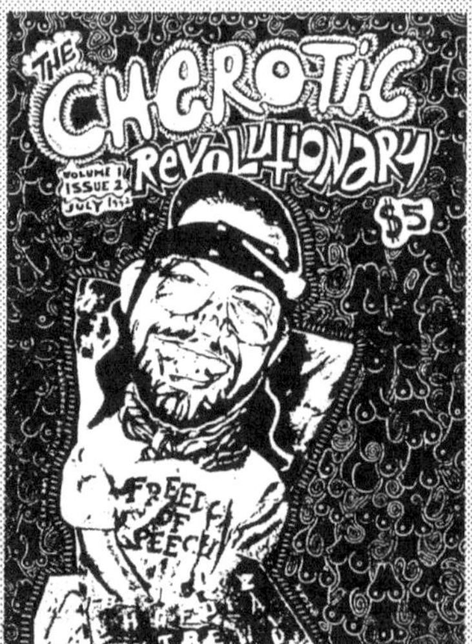

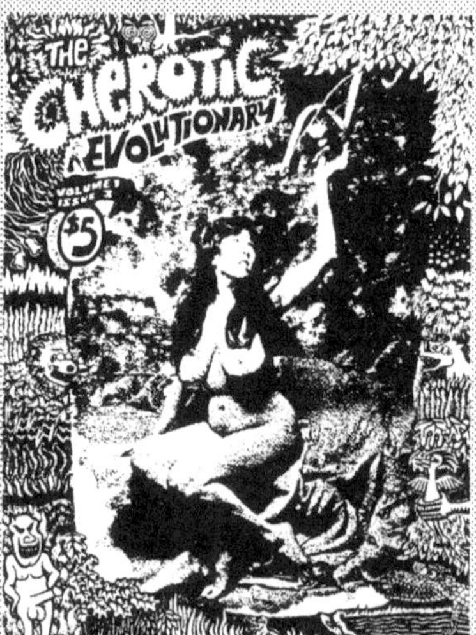

TC(r) #1, *january 1992* **$5**

POEMS BY **KAREN FINLEY, NONI HOWARD, TRACY MOSTOVOY, FRANK MOORE, JACK FOLEY** AND **JESSE BEAGLE**
ARTWORK BY **LABASH**
PHOTOS BY **TRACY MOSTOVOY** AND **ERIC KROLL**
CARTOON BY **WILL OF THE WISP**

TC(r) #2, *july 1992* **$5**

ESSAYS BY **FRANK MOORE, CURTIS YORK** AND **KYLE GRIFFITH**
ARTWORK BY **LEE KAY, H.R. GIGER, PETER PETRISKO, JR., JOHN SEABURY** AND **LABASH**
PHOTO BY **KEVIN RICE**
POEM BY **BARNABY CHANCELLOR**

TC(r) #3, *april 1993* **$5**

POEMS BY **R. (DIXI) COHN, ANNIE SPRINKLE, MERLE TOFER, JESSE BEAGLE**
ESSAYS BY **VERONICA VERA, LUNA SANGUINE** AND **FRANK MOORE**
PHOTOS BY **RICHARD SILVARNES, WINK VAN KEMPEN, ROBERT MAPLETHORPE, ANNIE SPRINKLE, MARC TRUNZ, AMY ARDREY** AND **JAN DEEN**
ARTWORK BY **LABASH** AND **JOHN SEABURY**

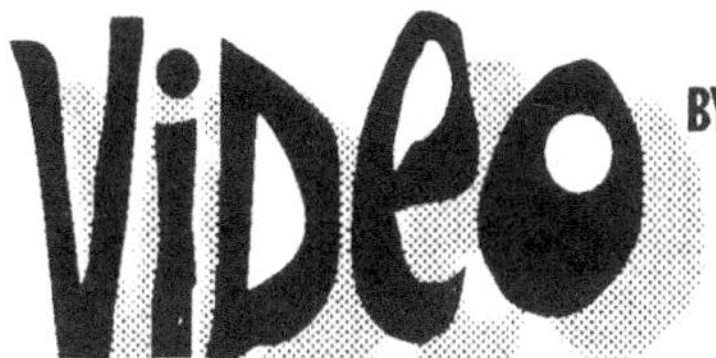

BY **frank moore**

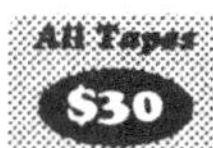

fairy tales can come true
THIS IS A FILM ABOUT RELATIONSHIPS AND DISABILITY STARRING FRANK MOORE, WHO HAS BEEN DISABLED SINCE BIRTH WITH CEREBRAL PALSY. IT IS A HUMOROUS, YET REALISTIC LOOK AT HOW TO ESTABLISH RELATIONSHIPS BY CHANGING NEGATIVE SELF IMAGE.
copyrighted 1981 *35 minutes*

erotic play
THIS VIDEO EXPLORES WHAT HAPPENS WHEN PEOPLE OF ALL TYPES AND AGES ARE GIVEN A CHANCE TO RETURN TO BEING A KID AGAIN. A SIMPLE GAME OF DRESS-UP BECOMES A POWERFUL METAPHOR FOR DROPPING TABOOS, RELEASING CREATIVE EMOTION, AND FOR DRAMATIC CHANGE. AS A RESULT, AN INNOCENT EROTICISM IS FOUND... AS WELL AS GETTING INTIMATE WITH 60 HUMANS.
copyrighted 1983 *84 minutes*

outrageous dream
A SURREAL, VISUAL POEM OF FOUND IMAGES.
copyrighted 1984 *41 minutes*

the nude cave
AN EROTIC, SURREALISTIC VIDEO DREAM THAT COMBINES NON-LINEAR IMAGES AND FRANK'S ORIGINAL MUSIC SCORE.
copyrighted 1984 *113 minutes*

out of isolation
A SURREAL EROTIC EXAMINATION OF AN INTIMATE RELATIONSHIP OF NEED. STARRING FRANK MOORE AND LINDA SIBIO.
copyrighted 1989 *105 minutes*

NOW ALSO AVAILABLE
out of isolation PROSE POEM
$1

the outrageous beauty revue
THIS RAW VIDEO DOCUMENTS THE TACKY, MUSICAL, OVER-THE-EDGE COMEDY REVUE THAT FRANK CREATED, DIRECTED AND PERFORMED IN. THE SHOW RAN ON A WEEKLY BASIS FOR THREE AND ONE HALF YEARS AT THE MABUHAY GARDENS IN SAN FRANCISCO IN ADDITION TO A NUMBER OF OTHER NORTHERN CALIFORNIA AND NEVADA PERFORMANCES. FRANK PERFORMED ALONG WITH THE THIRTY PEOPLE WHO MADE UP HIS THEATRE GROUP, "the theatre of human melting."
copyrighted 1980 *approx. 30 minutes*

chero collage
ATTEMPTS TO CAPTURE THE TRANCE STATE OF LIVE, SHAMANISTIC PERFORMANCE COMBINING FOOTAGE OF SEVERAL OF chero company's RITUALS INTO A REALITY-WARPING VIDEO.
copyrighted 1992 *27 minutes*

the outrageous horror show
A LIVE CABARET SHOW THAT BREAKS THROUGH THE LIMITING TABOOS, THROUGH MESSY NIGHTMARES, INTO THE DREAMS OF ALL POSSIBILITIES.
copyrighted 1992 *32 minutes*

To order call or write:
inter-relations, p.o.box 11445
berkeley, ca 94712
(510) 526 7858

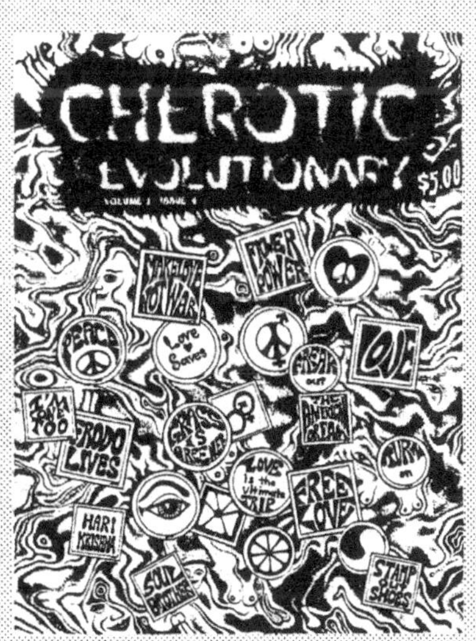

TC(r) #4, *january 1994* **$5**

POEMS BY **ANA CHRISTY, FRANK MOORE, STEVEN KAUFFMAN, NONI HOWARD** AND **ROBERT W. HOWINGTON**
SHORT STORY BY **CAROL A. QUEEN**
ESSAYS BY **TRACE DE HAVEN, JAMES DAVID AUDLIN (CHIEF DISTANT EAGLE), PROF. CURTIS** AND **FRANK MOORE**
ARTWORK BY **JOANNA PETTIT, JOHN SEABURY** AND **LABASH**
PHOTO BY **NINA GLASER**
PHOTOS OF **LINDA MONTANO** BY **ANNIE SPRINKLE**

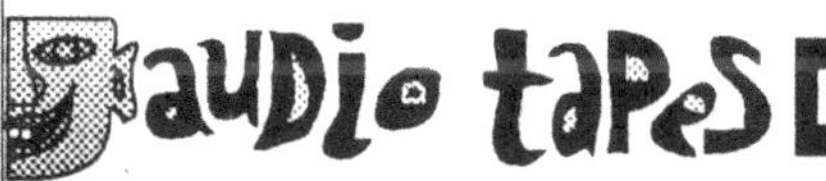

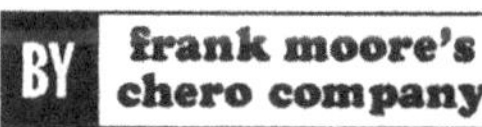

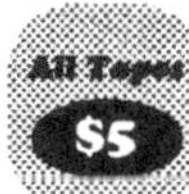

body music
EXPLORING THE HUMAN BODY AS MUSICAL INSTRUMENT.
90 minutes

inter-rhythms
PRIMAL MUSIC CREATED FOR FRANK MOORE'S RITUAL PERFORMANCES.
90 minutes

nude cave soundtrack
THE NONLINEAR ELECTRONIC MUSIC COMPOSED AND PERFORMED BY FRANK MOORE FOR THE FEATURE LENGTH VIDEO. *110 minutes*

rock of passion
THE SOUNDTRACK OF the outrageous horror show, FRANK THE ROCKSTAR SINGS HIS HEART OUT, LITERALLY COVERING THE GREAT HITS OF ROCK, COUNTRY, AND HEAVY METAL ... INCLUDING SUCH SMASHES AS i am woman, i got you babe, AND hand of doom ...

trance rap
WRITTEN BY FRANK MOORE AND SUNG/CHANTED BY MICHAEL LABASH WITH A BACKGROUND OF BODY MUSIC, trance rap IS AN AUDIO INTRODUCTION TO CHEROTIC MAGIC COVERING SUCH SUBJECTS AS eroplay, the plot of fragmentation AND magic art. ALSO INCLUDED IS THE POEM wrapping/rocking.
30 minutes

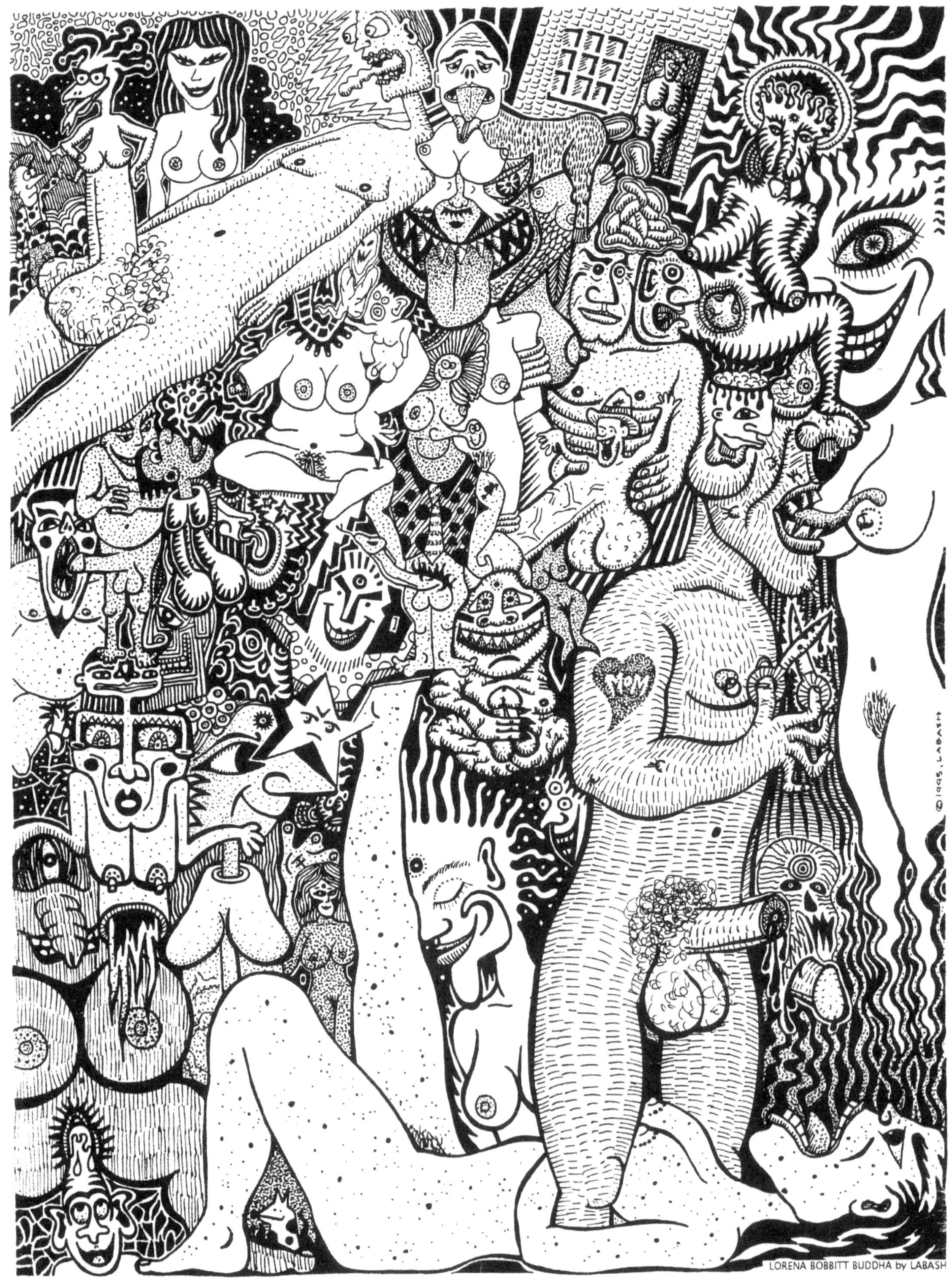

LORENA BOBBITT BUDDHA by LABASH

REVIEWS

The Cherotic (r)Evolutionary #5
May 1995

(TC(r)#5) "is wild!"
Arlene Raven, journalist

(TC(r)#5) "looks super. Thanks for the plugs. It's a lot of work, your mag. Hope it gives you lots in return."
Annie Sprinkle, artist

"Frank Moore means so much to so many people: he's a writer, an artist, a performance artist, a lecturer, a producer, a director, an intellectual, an inspiration - and more. But Frank would prefer his zine not be classified primarily as a sex 'zine: 'We do have a lot of sex in us, but we really are an anarchist/ arts/ avant garde/ experimental/ art/ beat/ cartoons/ community/ counter-culture/ alternatives/ culture/ dada/ surrealism/ erotica/ essays/ ethics/ feminism/ fiction/ gay/ humanism/ humor/ interview/ lesbianism/ libertarian/ literature(general)/ magic/ nonfiction/ philosophy/ photography/ poetry/ prose/ psychology/satire/ sex/ short stories/ spiritual zine ... or a life on the edge zine ... for short.' Frank always has a statement to make. The Cherotic (r)Evolutionary is Frank's platform for speaking out. In this issue, Frank presents an exquisite rant 'In Defense of Bad Art', that is, the right of Berkeley performance artists, known as the X-plicit Players, to be fully protected under the Bill of Rights as a theatrical group instead of being arrested for public nudity. In 'Conversation Between Two Muckrakers', Frank conducts a no-holds barred interview with Paul Krassner, founder of The Realist. (Krassner: '... In the 60's the underground press, like the zines now, were a form of personal revolution as opposed to the alternative papers, which are just a good career move ...') And lots more."
EIDOS Magazine, Volume 8, Number 3

"If a zine could be a performance art piece, Cherotic is it. What a wild, crazy smorgasbord of mind-blowing sensory assault. And it's all tied together through the 'shamanistic', erotic, electrified art of Frank Moore. In the future, when we look back at the 90s, wondering where the freaky culture came from, Cherotic and Moore will be a couple of its heros."
Sticky Green, The Sinner's Bible

REVIEWS CONTINUED...

"Before we start our review of TCR#5, let us mention that TCR #'s 1 through 4 are still available. They are genuine collectors' items .... We anxiously waited for TCR issue #5 and we were very glad when it ultimately landed in our mailbox. The front cover gives you a good idea of what The Cherotic (r)Evolutionary is all about: 'WARNING-Enter at your own risk! This piece may be threatening to your everyday reality. This piece may cause questioning of the common morality. These symptoms may appear days after this piece without warning ... even if during the piece, you may feel as if nothing is happening ... or you may even enjoy it. BUT above symptoms may still appear, leading to restlessness, and even to radical change.' The people at Inter-Relations are working for 'radical' change in society. The way we (we being the editor of OPEN FORUM) see it is that if an individual would experiment and explore going beyond the artificial boundaries, 'over the edge' as they say at TCR, imposed on us by an unwell society, society would see positive radical change. The change would happen because one individual who has broken his emotional and psychological chains would act as a conduit to others to do the same - similar to a chain-reaction. This idea of inter-connectedness runs throughout the teachings of Frank Moore and also appears in the artwork of LaBash (whose splendid work appears in all the TCRs). In issue #5 of TCR there is lots of stuff to entertain while simultaneously making you think - reading TCR is definitely a learning experience! Some of the things you'll find are: an editorial by Frank; an interview with Paul Krassner which covers everything from sex to politics; some letters from readers, one, which brought tears to our eyes, is from a young woman from Moscow who is yearning to create alternate realities for herself; a review by Frank of Annie Sprinkle's one-person show 'Post Post Porn Modernist', Frank digs deep and although positive about Annie's performance, points out, ' ... one of the powerful characteristics of the original goddess has always been an unlimited inclusiveness. This is also true of Annie personally, and it radiates from her show. But both the original goddess and Annie are being misused, distorted, by the forces of exclusion as an excuse and a justification of elitism, separatism, discrimination, fear, and isolation. These forces of exclusion are the main cause of today's world conflict ...'; and a presentation of our friend Peter Riden of The Grand Barn, a meeting place in Canada for open-minded and tolerant individuals, who are 'at ease with nudity'. Also appearing are a myriad of poems, essays and photos. Some are erotic, some are not, and others are social commentary. To conclude we want to comment on something that Frank mentions in his editorial. He says, 'I need to thank the zine community for all the kind reviews of TCR over the years. I only wish they would not classify TCR as a sex zine. We do have a lot of sex in us. We will never shy away from that. But we really are an anarchist/ arts/ avant garde/ experimental/ art/ beat/ cartoons/ community/ counter-culture/ alternatives/ culture/ dada/ surrealism/ erotica/ essays/ ethics/ feminism/ fiction/ gay/ humanism/ humor/ interview/ lesbianism/ libertarian/ literature (general)/ magic/ nonfiction/ philosophy/ photography/ poetry/ prose/ psychology/ satire/ sex/ short stories/ spiritual zine ... or a life on the edge zine ... for short.' What he says is true also of many of the other so-called 'sex' zines out there including OPEN FORUM. Yes, many have as their main theme sex and sensual pleasure, but most also address a variety of other topics such as censorship, human rights, the environment, decriminalization of drugs, and freedom in general. A lot of 'underground' zines are working for, as we articulate in our new advert, empowerment of the individual, tolerance and enlightenment."

Peter Riden, The Affiliate (Canada)

REVIEWS CONTINUED...

"Frank Moore is an interesting guy. For the last twenty years, he has been doing controversial performance art that is extremely political and sexual in nature. Frank claims that he is able to get away with more because he is handicapped. Frank is wheelchair-bound and communicates by pointing at symbols on a board. He is probably sick to death of articles that explain all this, but it is an important part of the Frank Moore persona. In addition to his performance art, Frank is the soul behind the beautifully-crafted The Cherotic (r)Evolutionary. There are many intricate little drawings tucked into every corner and surrounding every photo. It must have taken hours to do each page .... This publication does a nice job of representing Moore's ideas and work. He isn't interested in lewd, degrading art. Instead, he is interested in creating a heightened awareness of the human body, the self, and society."
Mike Hovancsek, You Could Do Worse #5, Autumn 1995

"This mag has a very strong sixties vibe in such a way that this moth-eaten decade could really use. It calls up the days when people actually used their heads and emotions instead of their wallets."
Bleeding Velvet Octopus #4

"Every Frank Moore publication I've seen has a cover by LaBash whose drawings are Bezerkeley trippy, trance, erotic and seem to jump off the coffee table into your face. EEK! ... On the back is Lorena Bobbit Buddha, worth the five bucks the magazine will cost you."
P-FORM #40

"OUR TITS OF THE MONTH uh... ARTIST OF THE MONTH Michael LaBash is from Berkeley, CA and is one of the most chaotic and beautifully perverted artists in the underground. He works with Frank Moore and they produce one of the coolest and free-spirited mags around called The Cherotic (r)Evolutionary. Hopefully he will draw the attention of some over religious and over sheltered right wingers with his cover and get GARY arrested."
The Flashing Astonisher #6, June 1996

REVIEWS CONTINUED...

Frank Moore (Editor) The Cherotic (r)Evolutionary Zine ! Outrageous, Wild, Bizarre, and gorgeous ... are adjectives I can use to describe Frank's Erotic, Hot, Sexy, Juicy (I'm gettin' a little sweaty now myself) and Adults Only Zine!!!! I drew erotic artwork in grand fashion and Mr. Moore published my artistry in his 1995 yearly edition! I just marvel and love Frank's talents as both theatre artist & writer of many sophisticated books. Annie Sprinkle, who was on H.B.O., for her striptease expertise and her photographing nude women for her Calendar ... was the featured celeb in the issue I was published in. Frank has accomplished more as an artist and was born with cerebral palsy, than I ever could do! Frank's a talented and dapper gent! Greetings & regards to Mr. Moore. Thanks!!!!
T.R. Miller, T.R.'s Zine issue #5

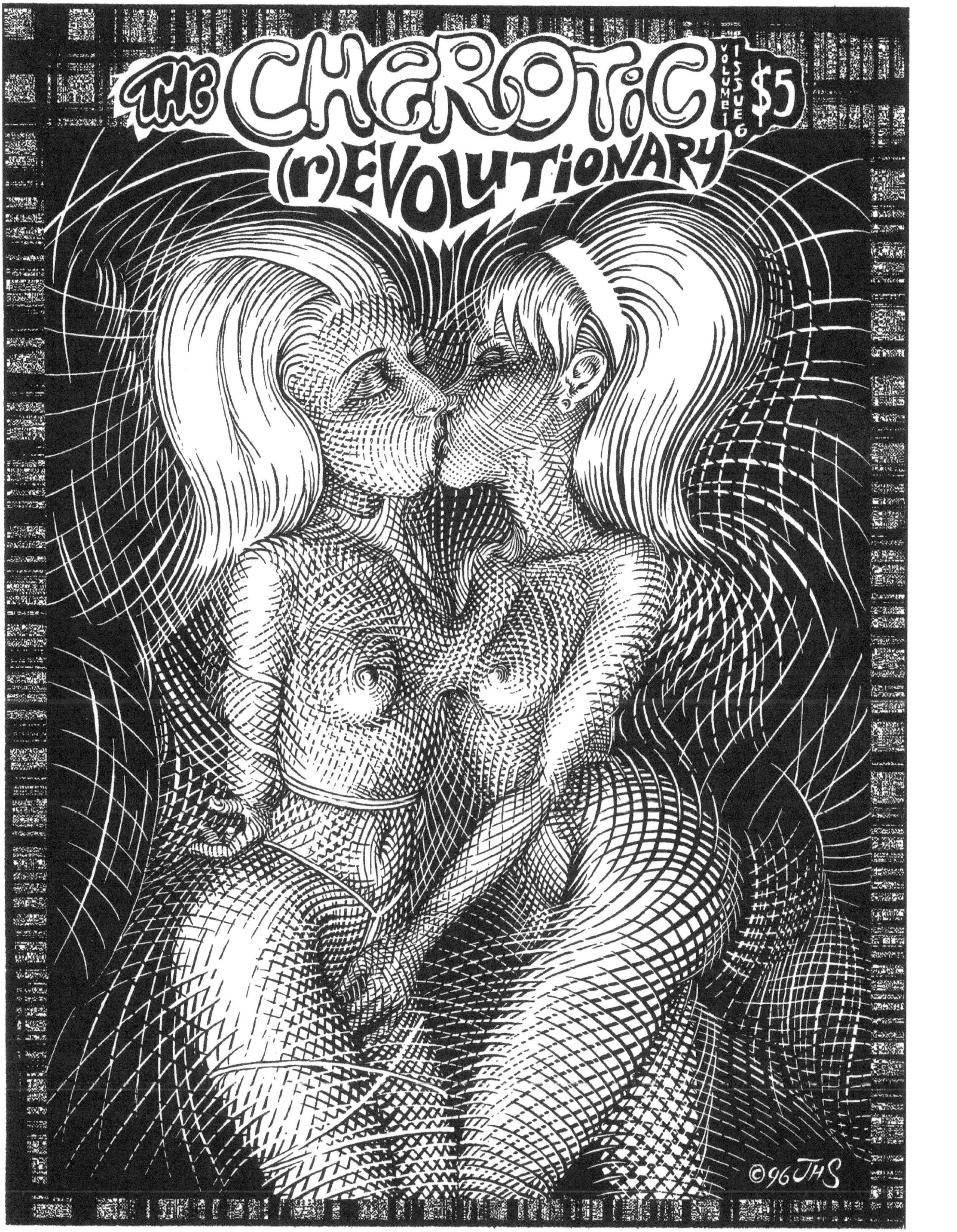

The Cherotic (r)Evolutionary

Volume 1 Issue 6

$5

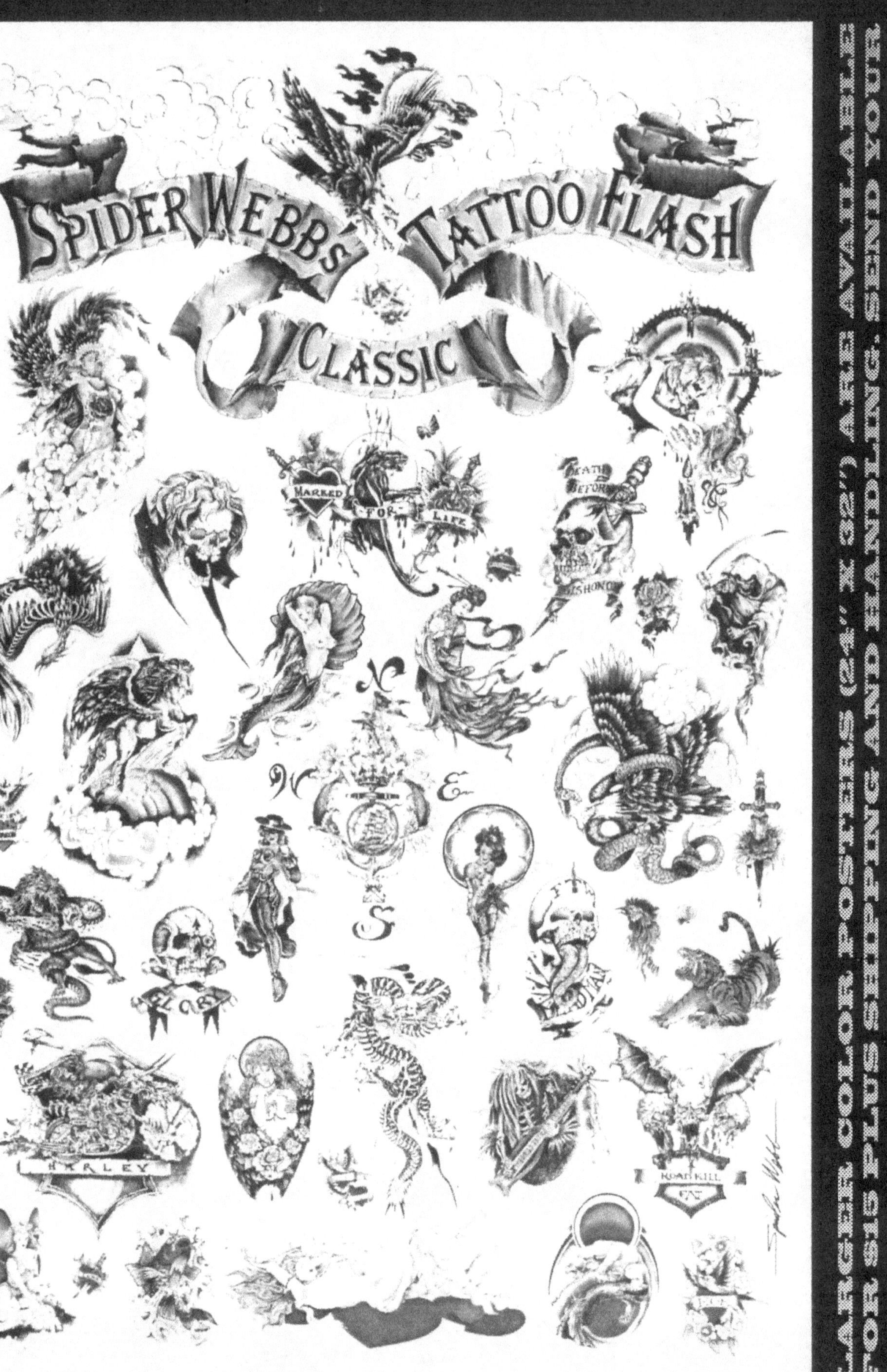
SPIDER WEBB'S TATTOO FLASH
CLASSIC
MARRED FOR LIFE
HARLEY
ROAD KILL

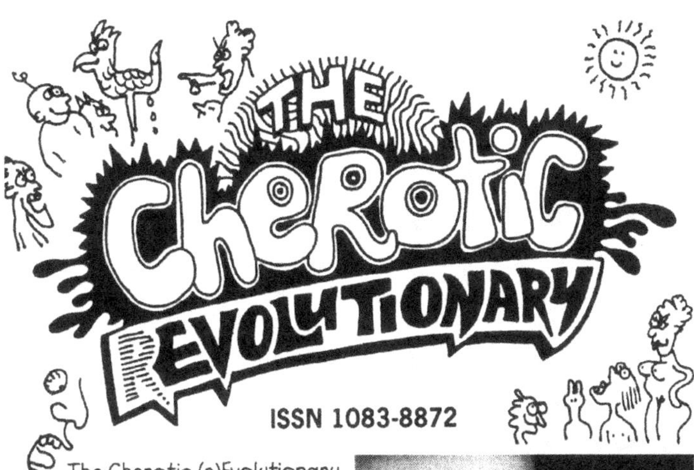

ISSN 1083-8872

The Cherotic (r)Evolutionary is a zine about "the edge" for and by people on the edge.

TC(r) is published by Inter-Relations. The publishers/editors are Frank Moore and Linda Mac, the art editor is Michael LaBash, and the circulation manager is Alexi Malenky.

The price for this issue is $5.00 per copy. We don't sell subscriptions, to avoid tying ourselves down to a rigid publication schedule or magazine size. We want to remain free to publish frequently or larger issues at longer intervals and adjust the price accordingly.

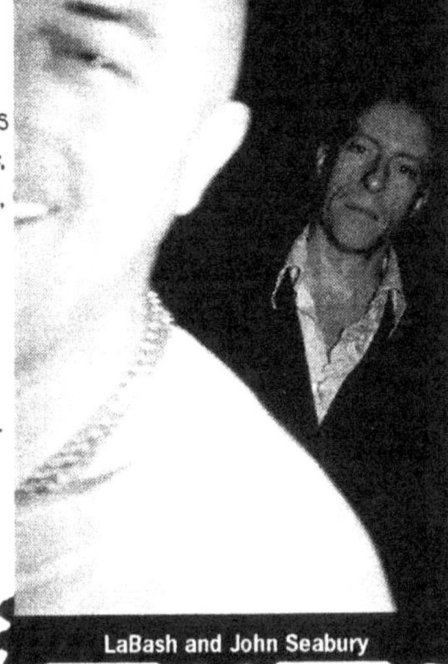
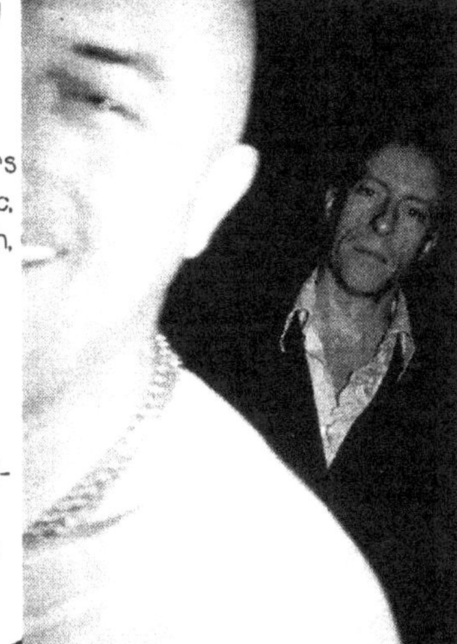

LaBash and John Seabury

We heartily encourage letters of comment from readers and will answer as many as we can. Please tell us if you don't want us to print material from your letter – otherwise we will assume it's OK.

Please address all correspondence and orders for magazines to:

Frank Moore, P.O. Box 11445, Berkeley CA 94712
e-mail: fmoore@lanminds.com
WorldWideWeb: http://users.lanminds.com/~fmoore

TC(r)'s AD POLICY

Recently we have received several inquiries about how to buy ads in The Cherotic (r)Evolutionary. Although we are not actively seeking such ads, we are not precluding them either. However, we will judge whether or not to accept an ad.

TC(r) is a xeroxed, black and white zine that is published irregularly ... if we are lucky, twice a year. So it is not the place for fancy color ads or for ads with time deadlines. On the other hand, TC(r) magically finds its way around the world.

TO SUBMIT AN AD

Send us a copy of your ad and a S.A.S.E. If we accept it, we send you the rate for your ad ... and if we need anything from you such as halftones, we will tell you. If we don't accept it, we will send your ad back.

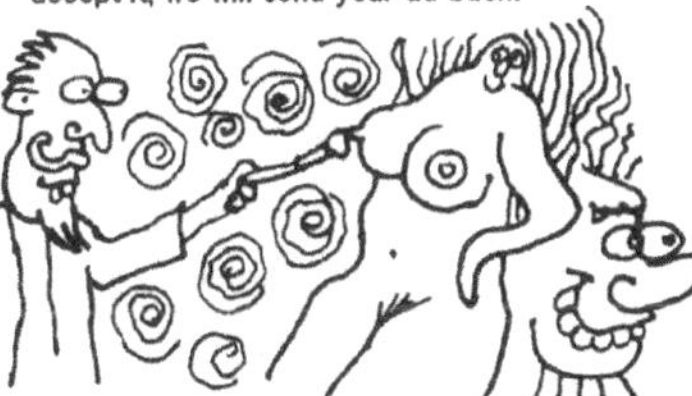

AD RATES

Sliding scale: $10-$50 per quarter of a standard typing page. The scale slides according to our whim.

HOW WE ACCEPT AN AD

Our whim also is a big factor in accepting an ad. Another factor is the other contents of the particular issue. And there may be other factors which are unknown even to us.

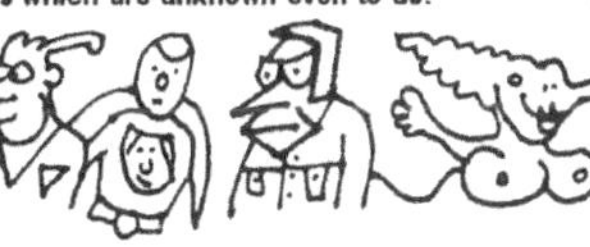

FREE TC(r) COPIES

Because we are not actively looking for paid ads, we do not give free copies to would-be advertisers. But we encourage them to buy a back issue or two. However, we do give you a free copy of the issue in which your ad appears.

Frank Moore
November 12, 1993

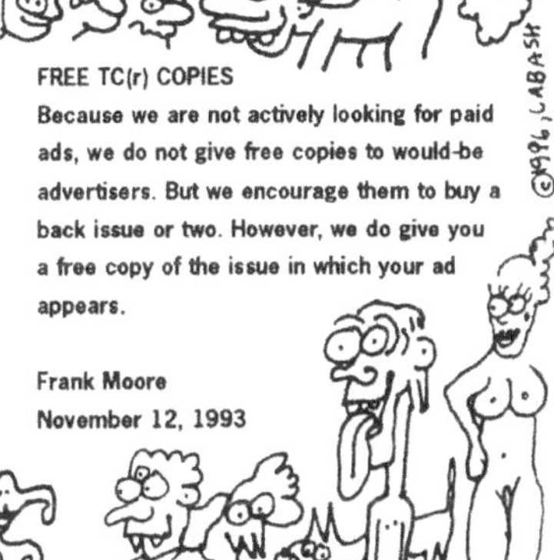

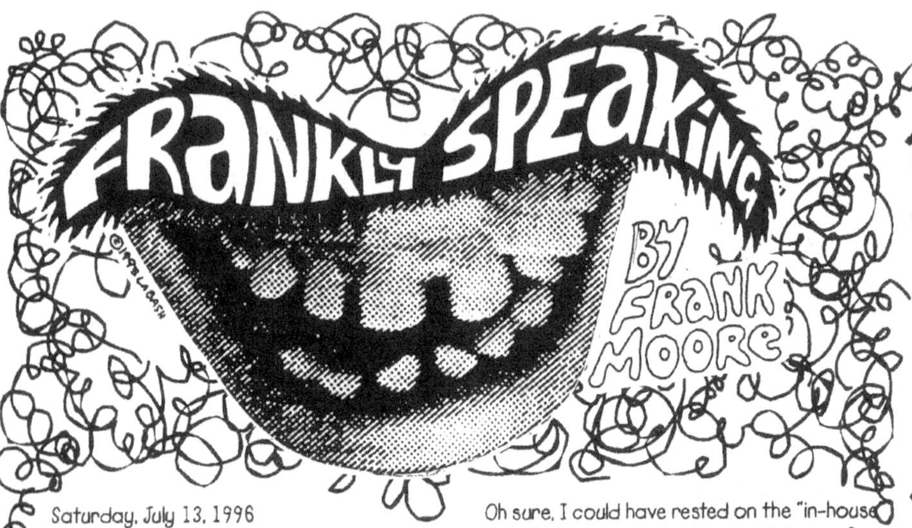

Saturday, July 13, 1996

Well, guess I am still a cultural outlaw. Last night, the cops busted THE ARTISTS' CAFE ...... one of those truly underground tiny places which have always threatened the regular world ... busted it for having me and my band jamming in the early Friday evening. It's flattering to think my voice is a subversive weapon ... just wished the cops would have shown up in time to take me to jail, instead of showing up ten minutes after I had left and stopping the poor folk singer who played after us!

Anyway ... you have in your hands the chubby issue! We had to add more pages to cram all the stuff in ... but we didn't have the heart to raise the price. That reminds me ... a special thanks to the performance artist Jenny Strauss for loaning us her scanner. That saved us big bucks both for this issue and our new WEB OF ALL POSSIBILITIES website at: http://users.lanminds.com/~fmoore. While we are at it ... I have a new e-mail address: fmoore@lanminds.com. If you want to talk to me personally ... The Web is the place. In fact, a lot of the folks in this issue are on the web ... and they are hot linked at W.A.P. ... and tons of art and other shit ... in other words ... visit our web site!

I had to use the web to get visual art for this issue. Each week there is a pile of great pieces of writing in our p.o. box. But we rarely get art, cartoons (except from T. R. Miller Cartoonist who we can't keep up with!), or photographs. Yep, I'm telling you visual artists to get your asses in gear! We did get the mind-blowing group of Cuban artists when the Cuban artist collective BANCO DE IDEAS Z sent us a copy of their artist book and of their calendar ... both hand-printed on home made paper. (Now we are going to great lengths to get their comp copies to them in spite the U.S.'s boycott of Cuba).

Oh sure, I could have rested on the "in-house" art of LaBash and the twisted talents of John Seabury and the other amazing artists we already had. But I wanted more! So first we called our good friend Les Barany ... the gothic figure in the Giger chair. He got us HR Giger, the famous tattoo-artist Spider Webb, and Flo Fox (the fox in the mirror on the next page ... more about her later.)

But I wanted more! So I went surfing! And I found Tony Ryan in Tasmania and Eric Boutilier-Brown in Canada ... all by surfing the web.

We live in an age of whining people who think they are owed something, who think they have the right to not be offended, to have reality be padded to their satisfaction before they will even think of playing the game of life (an actress auditioning for my play actually said she would be in it only if I get a woman director!). We receive letters from prisoners (and also from would-be advertisers and would-be contributors) saying: "I'm in prison. Send me a free copy of your zine." ... as if being in prison (or being a woman, a victim, a crip or whatever) entitles him. I never give such a person a comp ... although we give a shit load of comps away. The reason I put Al Cunningham's personal ad on my page is he always has come from being a risking artist rather than from being a jailbird.

Flo Fox is definitely not a whiner. She was on the NYC streets at 14, both parents dead. A very lusty woman. Married and knocked up at 18. Divorced at 26. But that was when the fun started. She got a camera. Didn't have to close her one eye because it was blind ... perfect for a photographer. Became a famous photo-journalist, focusing on the street scene. Then in 76, she became legally blind. No problem. She just had to wait 2 years before they invented the auto-focus camera ... and she was back in business and art. She started teaching the blind photography. When her MS put her in a wheelchair and the city didn't build curb cuts, she started building them herself, carrying sacks of cement on her chair! Guys, if you go to her apartment, she'll have you whip your cock out for her "dicthology" series. Girls, she has a pussy series too!

Flo is too busy playing lustfully in and with life to withdraw into the self-absorption of a victim. She comes to the table to play ... to play every hand, to match and up every bet ... not for power (the power game is for chumps) but for life, freedom, and the pursuit of happiness!

A foxy hero!

DISEASE

I have a disease . . .
which is eating away at my life
it has ate a hole in my heart
and it's been feeding on my brain
day by day, night by night
little pieces of me falls away
leaving only the shell of the man
I once was.

I have a disease . . .
It weakens my body
my spirit, my soul,
It denies me peace of mind
and creates depression,
suppression, and frustration.

I have a disease...
It sucks at my breath
blinds my sight
and tortures my existence.

I have a disease . . .
But there is a cure
and only the most sensitive,
caring, and sincere person
can administer it.

The disease is called:
"Loneliness"

The cure is:
"Friendship"

Who will give me the cure ? ? ?

Al Cunningham
PO BOX E-22600 (2E80)
SAN QUENTIN PRISON
San Quentin, CA 94974

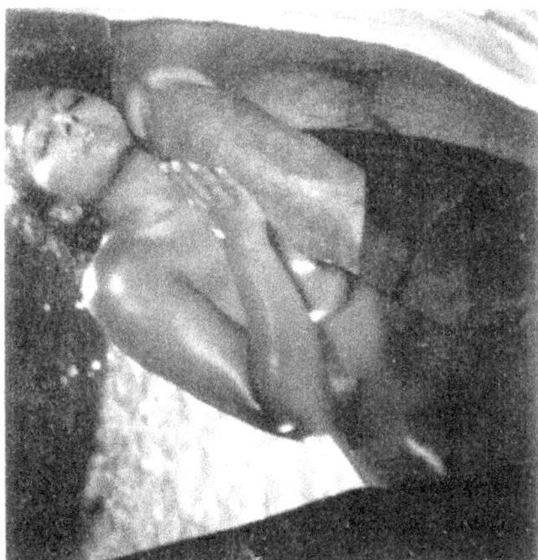

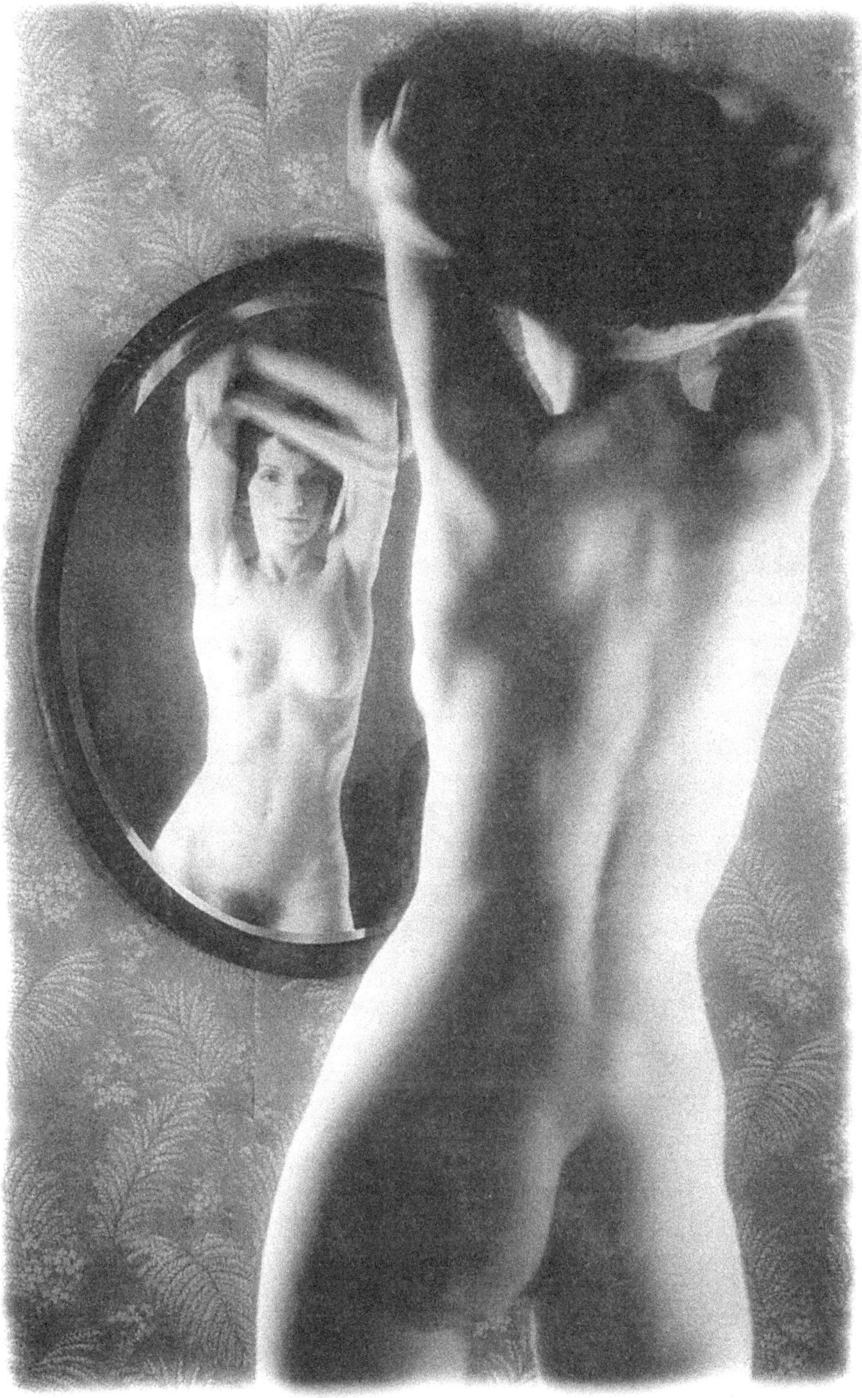

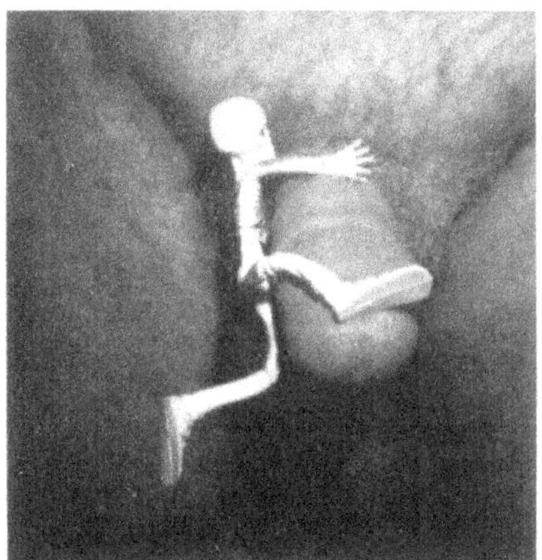

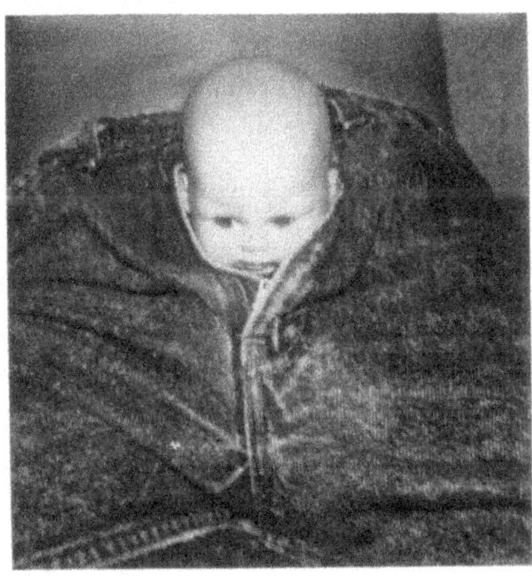

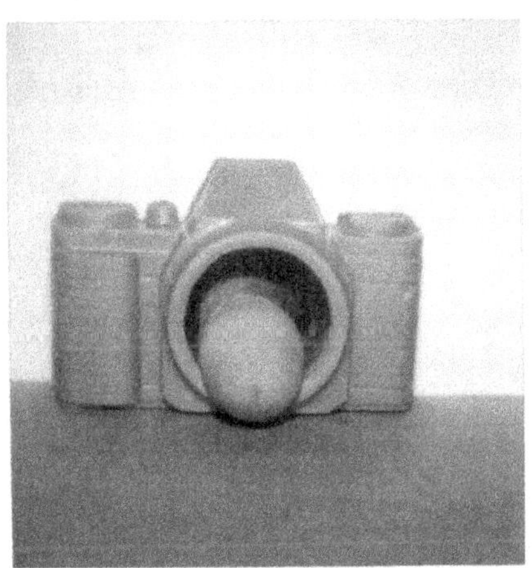

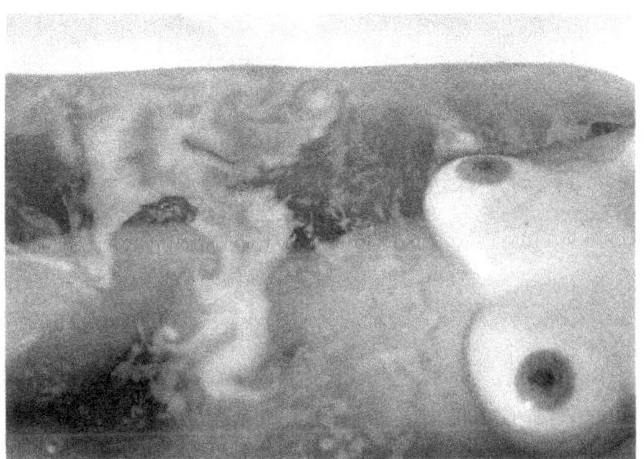

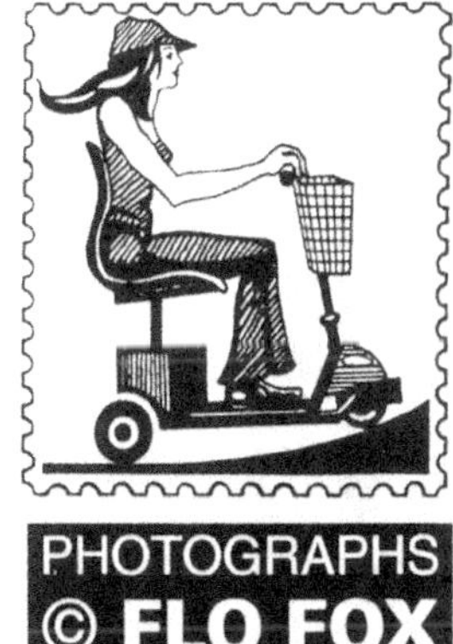

http://www.tiac.net/users/fotoflo/naughty.html

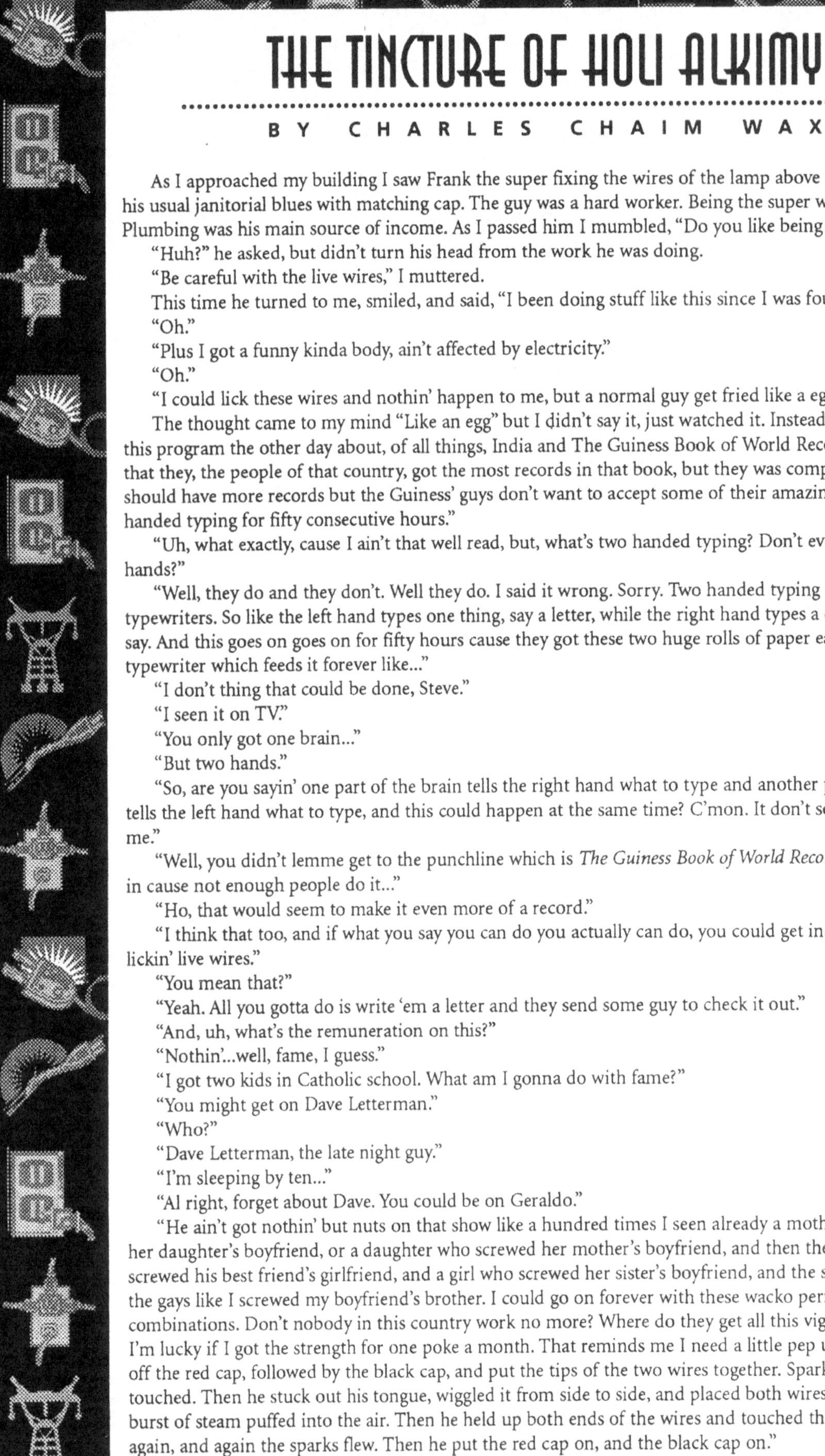

THE TINCTURE OF HOLI ALKIMY

BY CHARLES CHAIM WAX

As I approached my building I saw Frank the super fixing the wires of the lamp above the bells. He wore his usual janitorial blues with matching cap. The guy was a hard worker. Being the super was his second job. Plumbing was his main source of income. As I passed him I mumbled, "Do you like being a plumber?"

"Huh?" he asked, but didn't turn his head from the work he was doing.

"Be careful with the live wires," I muttered.

This time he turned to me, smiled, and said, "I been doing stuff like this since I was fourteen."

"Oh."

"Plus I got a funny kinda body, ain't affected by electricity."

"Oh."

"I could lick these wires and nothin' happen to me, but a normal guy get fried like a egg."

The thought came to my mind "Like an egg" but I didn't say it, just watched it. Instead I said, "I seen this program the other day about, of all things, India and The Guiness Book of World Records. It seems that they, the people of that country, got the most records in that book, but they was complaining that they should have more records but the Guiness' guys don't want to accept some of their amazing feats like two handed typing for fifty consecutive hours."

"Uh, what exactly, cause I ain't that well read, but, what's two handed typing? Don't everybody use two hands?"

"Well, they do and they don't. Well they do. I said it wrong. Sorry. Two handed typing on two different typewriters. So like the left hand types one thing, say a letter, while the right hand types a cooking recipe, say. And this goes on goes on for fifty hours cause they got these two huge rolls of paper each hung over a typewriter which feeds it forever like..."

"I don't thing that could be done, Steve."

"I seen it on TV."

"You only got one brain..."

"But two hands."

"So, are you sayin' one part of the brain tells the right hand what to type and another part of the brain tells the left hand what to type, and this could happen at the same time? C'mon. It don't sound plausible to me."

"Well, you didn't lemme get to the punchline which is *The Guiness Book of World Records* didn't allow it in cause not enough people do it..."

"Ho, that would seem to make it even more of a record."

"I think that too, and if what you say you can do you actually can do, you could get in, I mean the lickin' live wires."

"You mean that?"

"Yeah. All you gotta do is write 'em a letter and they send some guy to check it out."

"And, uh, what's the remuneration on this?"

"Nothin'...well, fame, I guess."

"I got two kids in Catholic school. What am I gonna do with fame?"

"You might get on Dave Letterman."

"Who?"

"Dave Letterman, the late night guy."

"I'm sleeping by ten..."

"Al right, forget about Dave. You could be on Geraldo."

"He ain't got nothin' but nuts on that show like a hundred times I seen already a mother who screwed her daughter's boyfriend, or a daughter who screwed her mother's boyfriend, and then there's the guy who screwed his best friend's girlfriend, and a girl who screwed her sister's boyfriend, and the same thing with the gays like I screwed my boyfriend's brother. I could go on forever with these wacko permutations and combinations. Don't nobody in this country work no more? Where do they get all this vigor for screwing? I'm lucky if I got the strength for one poke a month. That reminds me I need a little pep up." Then he took off the red cap, followed by the black cap, and put the tips of the two wires together. Sparks flew when they touched. Then he stuck out his tongue, wiggled it from side to side, and placed both wires there. A quick burst of steam puffed into the air. Then he held up both ends of the wires and touched them together again, and again the sparks flew. Then he put the red cap on, and the black cap on."

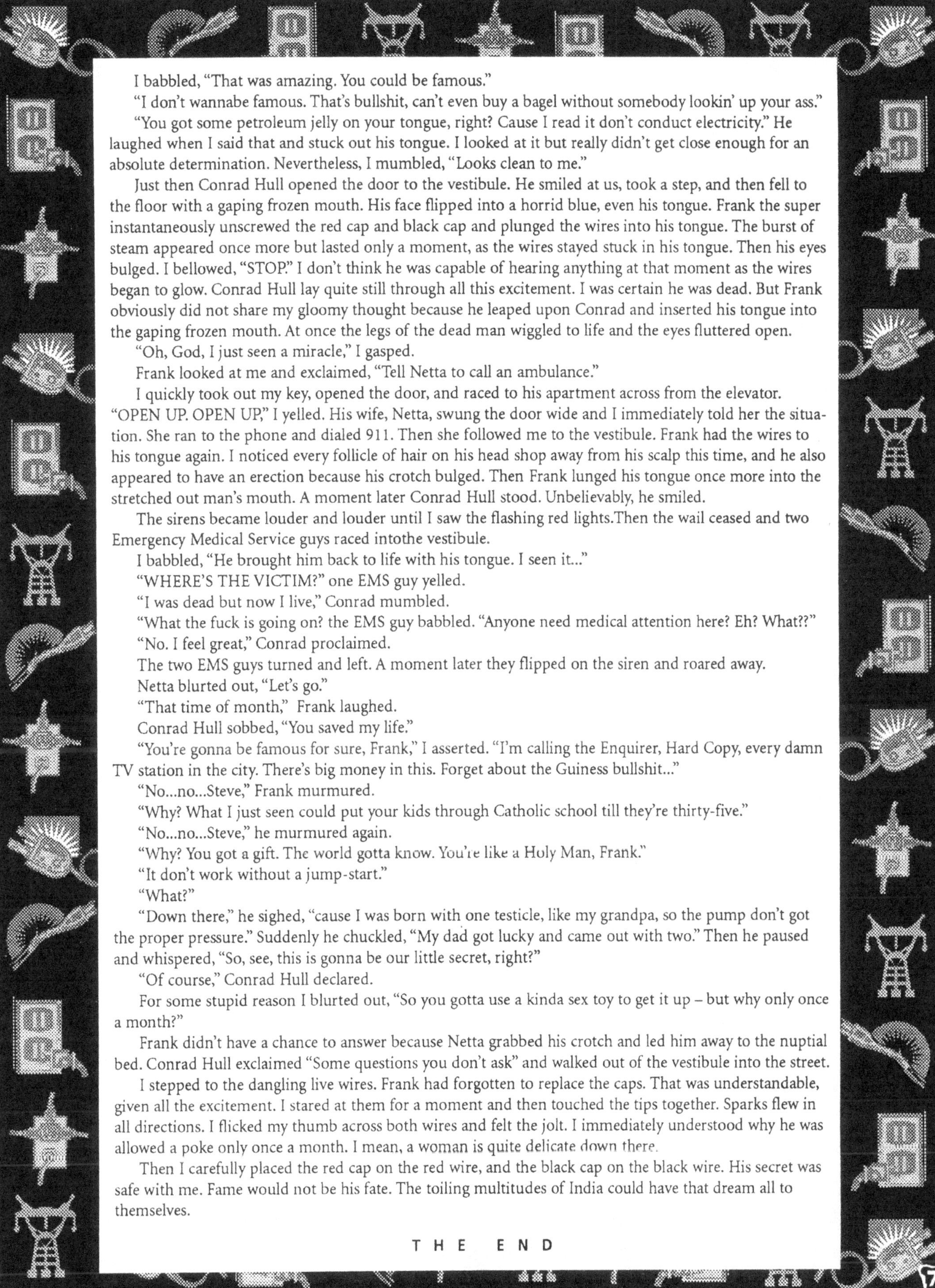

I babbled, "That was amazing. You could be famous."

"I don't wannabe famous. That's bullshit, can't even buy a bagel without somebody lookin' up your ass."

"You got some petroleum jelly on your tongue, right? Cause I read it don't conduct electricity." He laughed when I said that and stuck out his tongue. I looked at it but really didn't get close enough for an absolute determination. Nevertheless, I mumbled, "Looks clean to me."

Just then Conrad Hull opened the door to the vestibule. He smiled at us, took a step, and then fell to the floor with a gaping frozen mouth. His face flipped into a horrid blue, even his tongue. Frank the super instantaneously unscrewed the red cap and black cap and plunged the wires into his tongue. The burst of steam appeared once more but lasted only a moment, as the wires stayed stuck in his tongue. Then his eyes bulged. I bellowed, "STOP." I don't think he was capable of hearing anything at that moment as the wires began to glow. Conrad Hull lay quite still through all this excitement. I was certain he was dead. But Frank obviously did not share my gloomy thought because he leaped upon Conrad and inserted his tongue into the gaping frozen mouth. At once the legs of the dead man wiggled to life and the eyes fluttered open.

"Oh, God, I just seen a miracle," I gasped.

Frank looked at me and exclaimed, "Tell Netta to call an ambulance."

I quickly took out my key, opened the door, and raced to his apartment across from the elevator. "OPEN UP. OPEN UP," I yelled. His wife, Netta, swung the door wide and I immediately told her the situation. She ran to the phone and dialed 911. Then she followed me to the vestibule. Frank had the wires to his tongue again. I noticed every follicle of hair on his head shop away from his scalp this time, and he also appeared to have an erection because his crotch bulged. Then Frank lunged his tongue once more into the stretched out man's mouth. A moment later Conrad Hull stood. Unbelievably, he smiled.

The sirens became louder and louder until I saw the flashing red lights.Then the wail ceased and two Emergency Medical Service guys raced intothe vestibule.

I babbled, "He brought him back to life with his tongue. I seen it..."

"WHERE'S THE VICTIM?" one EMS guy yelled.

"I was dead but now I live," Conrad mumbled.

"What the fuck is going on? the EMS guy babbled. "Anyone need medical attention here? Eh? What??"

"No. I feel great," Conrad proclaimed.

The two EMS guys turned and left. A moment later they flipped on the siren and roared away.

Netta blurted out, "Let's go."

"That time of month," Frank laughed.

Conrad Hull sobbed, "You saved my life."

"You're gonna be famous for sure, Frank," I asserted. "I'm calling the Enquirer, Hard Copy, every damn TV station in the city. There's big money in this. Forget about the Guiness bullshit..."

"No...no...Steve," Frank murmured.

"Why? What I just seen could put your kids through Catholic school till they're thirty-five."

"No...no...Steve," he murmured again.

"Why? You got a gift. The world gotta know. You're like a Holy Man, Frank."

"It don't work without a jump-start."

"What?"

"Down there," he sighed, "cause I was born with one testicle, like my grandpa, so the pump don't got the proper pressure." Suddenly he chuckled, "My dad got lucky and came out with two." Then he paused and whispered, "So, see, this is gonna be our little secret, right?"

"Of course," Conrad Hull declared.

For some stupid reason I blurted out, "So you gotta use a kinda sex toy to get it up – but why only once a month?"

Frank didn't have a chance to answer because Netta grabbed his crotch and led him away to the nuptial bed. Conrad Hull exclaimed "Some questions you don't ask" and walked out of the vestibule into the street.

I stepped to the dangling live wires. Frank had forgotten to replace the caps. That was understandable, given all the excitement. I stared at them for a moment and then touched the tips together. Sparks flew in all directions. I flicked my thumb across both wires and felt the jolt. I immediately understood why he was allowed a poke only once a month. I mean, a woman is quite delicate down there.

Then I carefully placed the red cap on the red wire, and the black cap on the black wire. His secret was safe with me. Fame would not be his fate. The toiling multitudes of India could have that dream all to themselves.

T H E   E N D

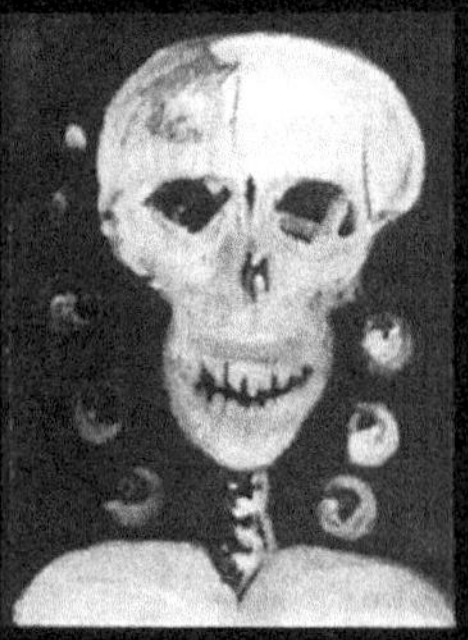

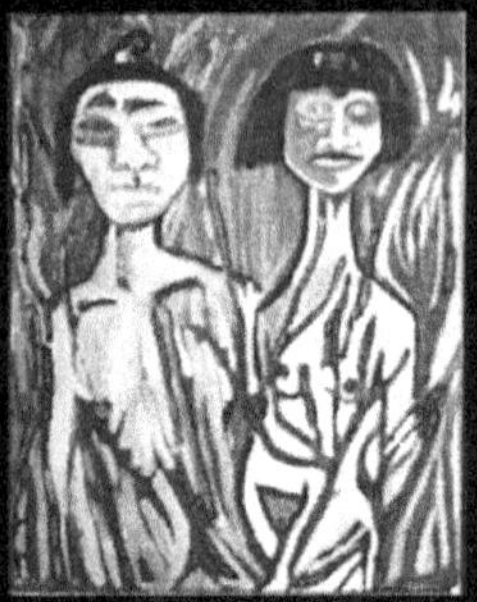

Man and Woman (1989)

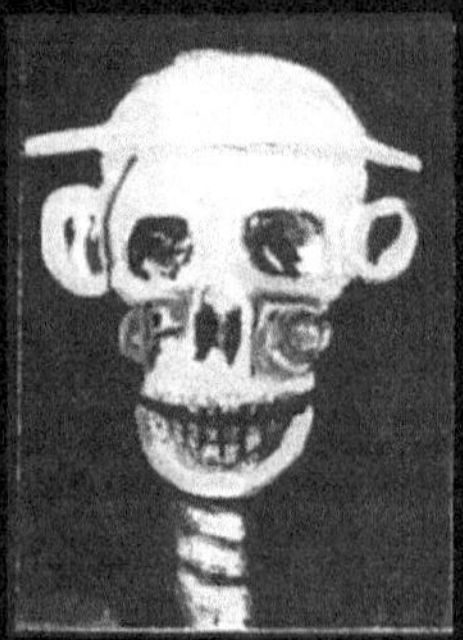

Paintings
(oil and clay on canvas)
BY
Florence Gray

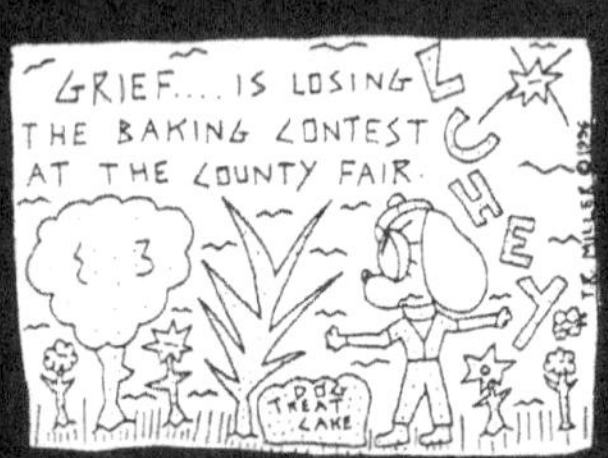

GRIEF... IS LOSING THE BAKING CONTEST AT THE COUNTY FAIR

Notes to 3.c

3.c is one of a series of texts that accompany movements of the composition for noise-guitar: flowers. Although many of my previous compositions have incorporated the performance of spoken or sung verses, the text below is presented in the program notes for live performance (or as "liner notes" for a CD). An excerpt of the the text is read aloud into an electronic system that allows the vocal performance to be played through the noise guitar [performances are to begin in 1996].I have considered having the entire set of verses to 3.c translated into Japanese. An excerpt would then be performed either live or taped along with the performance of the guitar score. I am interested in distributing the text widely enough that the performance of even a section of the text—even performed in a language foreign to a large percentage of the expected audience—might evoke the whole narrative.

-K.A.
katch@well.com
1.14.95

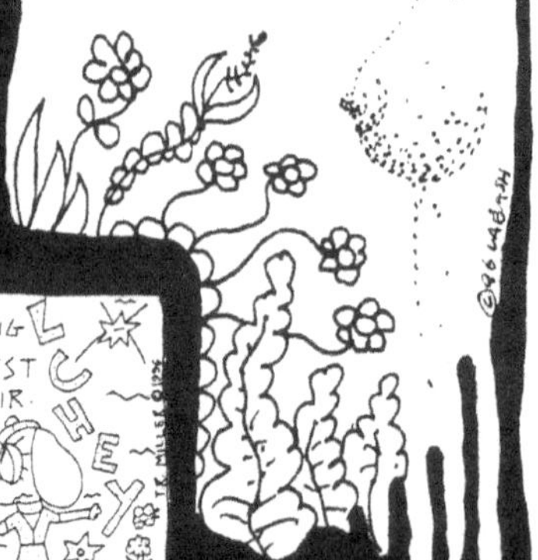

3.C

[The scene opens in a dormitory room of a small, U.S. college during the spring of 1976.]

thirty

Kusumi held Meguro's hands as I fucked her. We stopped and tied her arms to the bed frame. He pinched her nipples as I fucked her harder and came.

twenty-nine

We untied Meguro, turned her face down so that her torso hung over the foot of the bed, tied her hands behind her back and legs spread wide. Kusumi lifted her by the shoulders and placed her mouth over his penis. While he moved Meguro's shoulders up and down, I watched sweat form on the small of her back and thighs. Blood and come matted her sparse, black pubic hairs.

twenty-eight

Blood formed a thick line between the lips of her swollen vulva and smeared her inner thighs. I rubbed my thumb between her lips and smeared a line of blood to her ass, up her spine, to the base of her neck. Pausing, I watched the back of her head move smoothly up and down. I wet my fingertips with blood and drew a circle midway up her back. I divided the circle into thirds using two curved lines. The drawing resembled a sketch of a baseball. I dipped my fingertips and, as practiced, inscribed a circle and seven concentric rays on my forehead. I skimmed my little finger in blood, leaned over and smudged a thick horizontal line on Kusumi's throat followed by six smaller lines leading down Kusumi's chest. We had completely surrendered to the ritual.

twenty-seven

When I saw Kusumi bare his teeth, I called him to pull out. He squeezed the base of his cock, quickly withdrew, and climbed onto the bed as I moved aside. Still holding back, he entered Meguro then released himself.

twenty-six

I untied Meguro and Kusumi rubbed her wrists and ankles. We helped steady her on hands and knees. As I fucked her from behind, Kusumi stood before her, held the hair from her face as she licked the come from his dick and pubic hair. Amphetamines and excitement kept us going.

twenty-five

By the time I was ready to come, Kusumi was slowly working the head of his penis in and out of Meguro's mouth. As prescribed by ritual she growled deeply. Arching my back I pushed deeper and came again. Kusumi pulled out and I moved aside. Meguro rolled onto her back and hugged Kusumi as he finished inside.

twenty-four

Meguro lay between Kusumi and me. She rested her head on my chest, an arm across Kusumi's stomach, and a leg across his legs. After a few moments I signaled that it was time to continue.

twenty-three

Kusumi took a large laboratory-beaker from the dresser top and placed it on the floor. Carefully getting up from bed, Meguro covered her crotch with her right hand and squatted low over the vessel. She parted her lips. Kusumi and I knelt and encouraged her as menstrual blood and come flowed into the beaker. She bounced slightly up and down releasing more fluid.

twenty-two

After she finished, Kusumi helped her stand. I picked up a glass rod and some small packets from my desktop. I emptied the packets into the beaker. Kusumi added a prepared liquid solution and with the rod I stirred the contents into a pink, viscous potion. Meguro brought a half-quart jar of water infused with blue cohosh and slowly poured as I continued to stir. Kusumi pulled a folded piece of paper from a cloth bag and emptied finely crushed dark leaves into the mixture.

twenty-one

I handed the beaker to Meguro. She took the first drink then passed it to Kusumi who stood on her right. Kusumi drank and handed it to me. At the first sip I tasted blood. My face immediately flushed red and my ears tingled. As the potion made one more pass, warmth spread from my throat down to my stomach and through my veins to my hands and feet. I felt as if I were translucent and glowing. After Meguro and Kusumi finished their portions, I brought the beaker to my lips, tipped it back, closed my eyes, and finished the last.

twenty

Though my eyes remained closed, I felt as if I had opened them onto an intensely bright point of expanding light. The light dimmed proportionally as it grew and enveloped me.

nineteen

From within an orb of light I saw the golden, excited faces of Meguro and Kusumi positioned equidistantly from me. Our bodies had vanished and we spun clockwise. I leaned right to kiss Meguro. The sphere distorted as her face retreated from mine. No matter how hard I twisted or thrust, the distance separating us remained constant. Once I understood the orb's physics we all laughed.

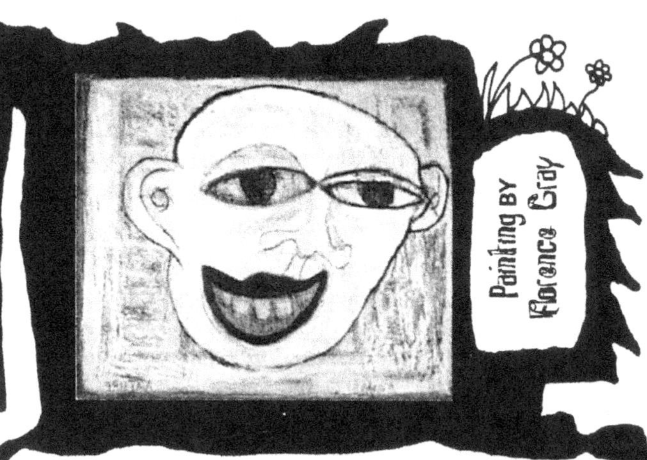

eighteen

Suddenly Meguro's face vanished leaving an egg-shaped form. She quickly reappeared. The three of us smiled, nodded and simultaneously performed a flip that resulted in us looking out from the surface of the revolving sphere. We saw our physical-selves — standing in the room, eyes closed, breathing shallowly, glistening with perspiration.

seventeen

Thick, green vines grew from the ceiling light and sprouted large leaves and orange-red blooms. From a hanging lamp in a corner, thin vines spread rapidly around the room, thickened slightly and blossomed into honeysuckle that filled the air with sweet fragrance.

sixteen

In perfect unison we flipped back inside the ball and laughed. Amber light shimmered across our faces. The shimmering became more pronounced until the light distinctly flickered off and on.

fifteen

I exited and re-entered consciousness synchronously with the pulsing light. Aware only of darkness' outermost edges, I could not tell how long I was unconscious before light shone again.

fourteen

The frequency of pulsing increased and the depth of darkness decreased. We flipped again and watched Meguro and I embrace. I lay on a deep bed of vines

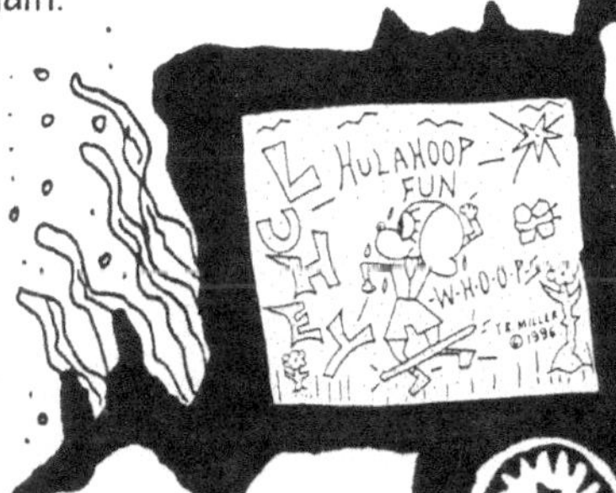

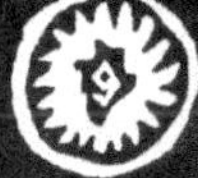

and fragrant blossoms. Meguro straddled me. She reached down, placed my erect penis inside her and gently rocked back and forth. I sat up a little, put my arms around her, pulled her down to my chest. We fucked in the revolving sphere's flashing, golden light.

thirteen

Kusumi squatted behind Meguro. He placed his left hand on her shoulder. I felt pressure as his dick slid up her anus. Meguro and I held still until he was fully inside. Kusumi bent forward and kissed the back of her neck. Slowly he and I moved alternately in and out.

twelve

From every electrical socket delicate, reddish-purple runners snaked across other vines toward the room's center. Fine, light-green tendrils forced the cables from the backs of the receiver and turntable. They bloomed into bright purple flowers. Orange and yellow pollen clouds blew about the room.

eleven

Kusumi quickened his pace then his body stiffened. Meguro moved fast back and forth over my chest. I asked her to open her eyes so that we could see each other come.

ten

I felt a vine spiral around the shaft of my penis. Meguro held me tighter and moaned loudly. She and Kusumi shuddered as another vine wiggled up her anus and around his cock. A knot of vines entered my ass and moved through my intestines. My friends' expressions made it clear that they were having the same experience. I felt a sense of expanding calm as the vines grew inside me.

nine

A shoot appeared from the outside corner of Kusumi's right eye and sprouted a soft pink bud. Another grew from the inside corner of his left eye, bifurcated, and each of those tips formed a bud. Lifting Meguro away from me, I saw that her nostrils' supported beautiful, lavender flowers. I inhaled deeply and felt that I was following a detailed olfactory-map with borders and areas demarcated by nuances of fragrance. I traced the map to the present.

eight

Vines entered my esophagus by way of my stomach. Rather than gagging, I found the sensation soothing and pleasurable. They grew up the back of my throat, out my mouth, intertwined with shoots growing from Meguro's and Kasumi's lips. Soon they grew out the corners of my eyes, nostrils and ears.

seven

One pearl-backed bud opened to reveal a yellow petal that bore a red, crescent moon. The adjacent petals opened; on the right a black numeral "6" floated above a small blue diamond and on the left petal a white hand—palm open and facing—appeared above a white triangle. A fourth petal was inscribed with a golden lightening-bolt. The fifth petal bore the chemical formula C4H10O below the phrase, *spirit: dissolves, leaves;...self: forms, arrives....*In the center of the sixth petal was a lustrous, silver circle.

six

Tiny, spinning black-swastikas and whirling white-crosses rose from a patch of red flowers. The swastikas radiated bright rainbows and the crosses emitted columns of white light. A swarm of black insects flew into their midst, absorbed them, glowed warm amber light and disappeared into the distance.

five

The heads of flowers followed the sun as it passed overhead. Shifting sunlight and shadows created words and symbols that vanished into nodding blossoms, buds, leaves in wind.

four

In the afternoon gentle breezes blew across the field. Tall grasses arched and straightened, sunflowers swayed, vine-leaves stirred close to the earth.

three

In the middle of the field a small glen extended about three-quarters of a mile to the west then crooked north a little before it ended. Rainwater formed a small pond at the eastern end. Dragonflies dipped ripples in water, flew invisibly to tips of grass, circled, disappeared, and returned on iridescent, blue-green-purple wings.

two

Six or seven yellow-orange butterflies flew up from the glen and—in tight loops and delicate arcs—surveyed the field. They settled on a cluster of daffodils and fed on nectar.

one

Along the farm's easternmost edge, blossoming honeysuckle covered the gray wood fence that separated the field from the adjoining farm.

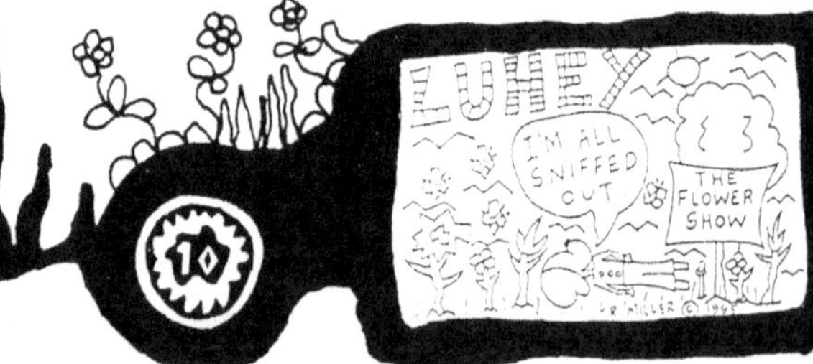

TONY RYAN

Tony.Ryan@its.utas.edu.au
http://pigweb.com/tonyr.htm
http://info.utas.edu.au/docs/tonyr.htm
http://www.alchemy.com.au/Tony.Ryan/

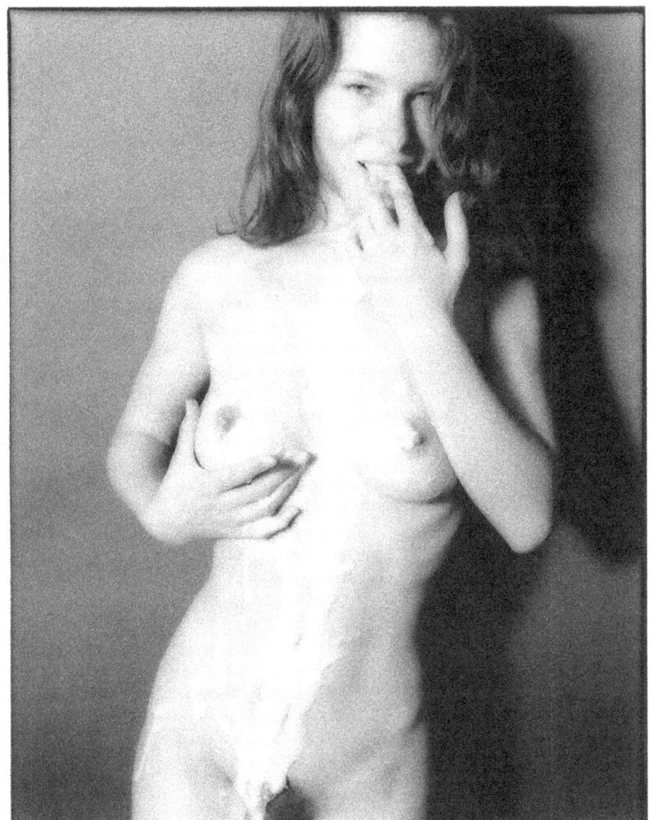

▲ **Kura with Cream**

20x24 inch silver gelatin print, selenium toned
Crabtree, January 1994

This is real, the look in her eyes is real because by profession Kura is a stripper and loves her job. She is genuinely proud of her body and enjoys the admiration it attracts. You can place whatever interpretation you like on the ice cream but notwithstanding the sexual connotations, to me it still suggests the naughty little girl deliberately making a mess and asking 'what are you going to do about it?'

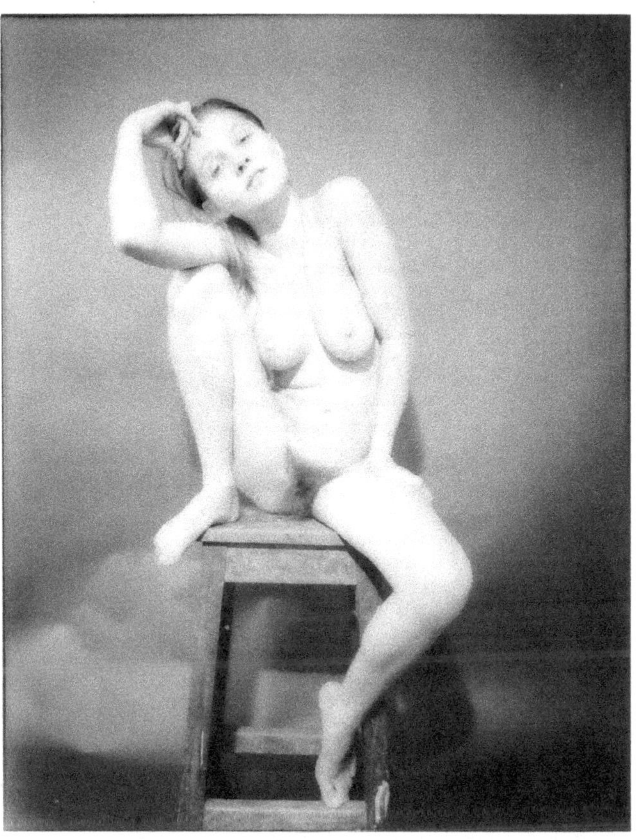

▲ **Hannah in the Studio 1**

20x24 inch silver gelatin print, selenium toned
Crabtree, 1995

In the past my few attempts at nudes for their own sake (in the Edward Weston tradition) have not been successful. There has to be a theme even if it is only the apparent character of the sitter. This series with Hannah all seem to have worked well and I am finding it very hard to choose between them. She is so beautiful it is almost frightening and her dance training has given her a grace and awareness of her body in space that make her perfect for this kind of work. There is something wonderfully "in-your-face" about her poses too.

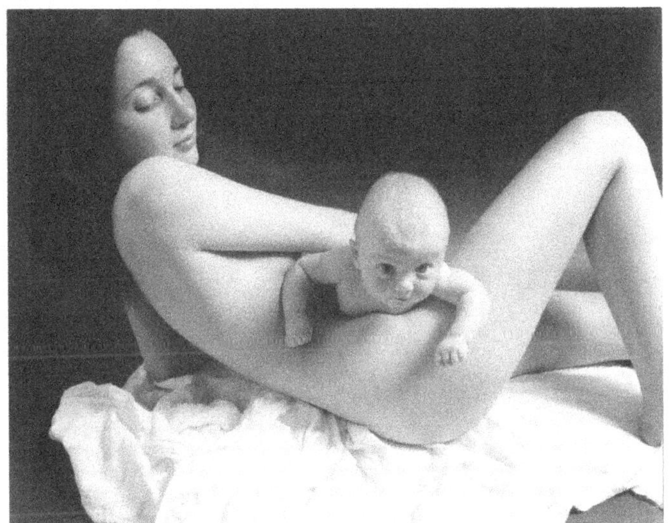

◀ **Sarah and baby Anne (2)**

20x24 inch silver gelatin print, selenium toned
Crabtree, 1994

MADNESS MANIFESTO -1996

NOBODY IS MAD ANYMORE.
EVERBODY is certified SANE.

ALL OUR POETRY is The SAME.
ALL OUR POLITICS IS THE SAME.
ALL OUR ART IS The SAME.
ALL OUR RELIGION IS THE SAME.

LOOK AT ALL THE SANE PEOPLE.
These PEOPLE BROUGHT US
VIETNAM
AFGHANISTAN
the MIDEAST
the PERSIAN GULF
SARAJEVO
SOMALIA
CHECHNYA.

DO YOU STILL FEEL SAFE?
DO YOU STILL feel SANE?

THE DEAD ARE SCREAMING IN Their GRAVES. EVEN their TOMBSTONES CRY OUT. THE DEAD ARE TIRED OF BEING DEAD, THEY HAVE DIED TOO MANY TIMES BEFORE.

MADNESS COMES TO Those WHO WANT IT. CONFRONT CREEPING SANITY WITH INSANE SLOGANS AND ART. DECLARE YOURSELF, AMERICA! GO MAD AND SAVE THE WORLD!

GEORGE KAUFFMAN

THE DAY

(NOTE: in 1938, Stephan Vincent Benet wrote a poem titled-- "Nightmare For Future Reference". In 1962, I wrote the following poem, suggested by Benet's poem; gk)

The loyal people are alive
and it is their problem now.
They had said the amount was
so small it wouldn't matter,
but the effect began sooner
than expected and could be
calculated to the day when
it would happen, but the
people who protested are all
gone, their demonstrations
smashed, their organizations
outlawed. Data has been fed
to the machines for weeks and
still the tapes always come
out the same: today, nobody
was born anywhere on this planet.

George Kauffman

APPLICATION

TO LIVE IN

THE SOUTH

Name: ______________________ Nickname: ______________________
CB Handle: ______________________
Current address: ______________________
Neck shade: Light red ( ) Medium red ( ) Dark red ( )
Number of teeth exposed in full grin: ________ Upper: ______ Lower: ______
Make of pickup: ______________________ Size of tires: ______________
Does it have doors? Yes ( ) No( ) Sometimes ( ) Can't remember ( )
How high is the first step into your pickup? 3 feet ( ) 6 feet ( ) More ( )
Number of empty beer cans on floor of pickup: ________
Number of coon dogs in bed of pickup: ________
Truck equipped with:
( ) Rust ( ) Gun Rack ( ) Camper top ( ) Hi-jack shocks
( ) Winch ( ) Roll bar ( ) Running boards
( ) 8 Track ( ) Spittoon ( ) Fuzz buster ( ) Load of compost
( ) Mud tires ( ) Mud flaps ( ) 4-wheel drive
( ) Air horn ( ) Dog box ( ) Confederate flag
Bumper stickers:
( ) I Love Grits ( ) Elvis ( ) Eat Mo' Possum
( ) Jesse Helms for President ( ) Coon Hunter
( ) Honk If You Love Jesus
Length of right leg: ____________ Left leg: ____________
How many cars do you have up on blocks in your front yard? ________
How many appliances do you keep on your front lawn? ________
Working appliances: ______________ Non-working appliances: ______________
Do you own any shoes (not boots)? Yes ( ) No ( )
If so, how many?
Do you bathe? ( ) Weekly ( ) Monthly ( ) Bi-yearly ( ) With Soap
Are you married to either of the following? ( ) Sister ( ) Cousin
Does your wife weigh more than your pickup? ( ) Yes ( ) No
When was your last Elvis sighting? ______________
Can you sign your name and spell it right every time? ( ) Yes ( ) No
Did you read and understand this? ( ) Yes ( ) No

Date________ Signature______________________

Send to:
Senator Jesse Helms, 403 Dirksen Senate Office Building, Washington, DC 20510-3301
Senator D.M. "Launch" Faircloth, 716 Hart Senate Office Building, Washington, DC 20510

Published & Created by Dave or Shadl, Beast Quarterly, 204 Furman Rd #16, Boone, NC 28607
thanks to Jamie Goodman

Get out your scissors for that standard map of the possible! There have been some bold scouting parties for a world of liberated desire the last few years, and some of the boldest have just put a book out on their discoveries. *More Out Than In: Notes on Sex, Art, and Community,* edited by Rachel Kaplan and Keith Hennessy; a collection of writings about the 848 community space, a do-it-yourself multi-use space available to all manner of experimenters, crossing the boundaries of art, oppositional politics, and sexual liberation. Since it opened in San Francisco in 1992, the 848 has probably hosted a wider range and volume of sex-positive events than any other public space in the world. I'd like this response to generate interest in the book, offer some critical commentary, and explore some of the introspections it has prompted in me.

I happened to be in SF when there was an open forum on the book, and, truth be told, it left me pretty frustrated. I had no idea it had gotten so late, and the conversation ended, way too limited to discussions of S/M. It wasn't until three others and I were leaving that we fully realized how we didn't even touch on so many things that would've been fruitful to talk about. (So I started to boil over and think about writing this....) The editors asked for submissions of "critical writings," and they got them. A good portion of the twenty-four contributors are more than less dissatisfied with some aspect of the sex events or their perceived disproportion, and criticism of the S/M scene is a recurring theme. Oddly, the main proponents of S/M-critical views did not show up at the forum, but there were some eloquent advocates of S/M. The main thing that stands out for me is the dampening effect of the resulting dissension taking up so much of the forum – and the book.

The book is remarkable for its introspectiveness and invitation to criticism. But the more I think about it, the more irritated I get with much of that criticism. Phrases like: "too much sex," and advocating for "sacrifice and service" are used amid discussions of the "relative exchange weight" of "issues of sexual identity to issues of inequality...." I just read Murry Bookchin's new book, *Lifestyle Anarchism or Social Anarchism: An Unbridgeable Chasm,* which is largely an attack on *Anarchy: A Journal of Desire Armed, Fifth Estate,* and Haquim Bey for focusing on the liberation of desire and the expansion of autonomy for authentic lives of adventure and rebellion – as opposed to programmatic political organization building – and much of the criticism of "sex and pleasure activism" seems akin to this morality-based "social" anarchist perspective. To speak of "pleasure activism" and "class war activism" as distinct and competing is curious and foreign to me. Maybe that's because I haven't been too involved in the queer sex party milieu there or taken part in planned "spiritual and/or educational" sex events that apparently are distinctly "safe spaces" protected and separated from the rest of life. But might not the problem therefore lie less in there being "too much pleasure activism," as in the limited nature of the events? "Safe spaces" can also keep the rest of the world safe from your spaces.

On the other hand, much of the criticism seems sincerely aimed at a further evolution of the dialogue on sex and liberation, which could be very positive. The book includes an excerpt from a 1966 interview with Henry Miller about the shallowness of the "sexual revolution" at that time. "It was always more the total liberation of one's self that I was concerned with" as he saw it; "Sexual freedom and the effort toward that should only be one aspect of a movement toward much larger freedom, to think and act freely and creatively, in every domain!" One more effort, sex-pots.... We don't just want better sex lives, we want our whole lives to be sex lives!

My tendency is to foment an insurgence of erotic, playful activity that knows no boundaries. To pursue the "emergence and rapid spread of creatures that will be living embodiments of the surreal, those who will stop the world and open up new possibilities for meeting our needs and relating to one another and the natural world in a more balanced and pleasurable way" – as my fried Paul E. Morphous puts it. In the past this has taken such forms as the Gardeners Against the Work Ethic Association in Carbondale, IL: a 1994 attempt at a summer of sprawling festivity which included a costumed lawn rip-up for a "free feast garden," many mind-altering experiments in non-verbal behavior and non-sexual but intense physical touch and play ("eroplay" as Frank Moore calls it), a prank in which the city council was made to declare Wednesdays a holiday, and various "space poaching" contestations of normalcy like a group erotic stumbling exercise in a mall. I've also traveled across country with a nomadic band in a school bus as another anarchic experiment. In contrast to the socialistic soberness of Bookchin's anarch*ism*, we seek to *create anarchy* on the level of immediate experience. Our activity is an underground current of libertarian enticement to a revolutionary transformation that is a geyser of pleasure pushing away all constraints.

When I read about the 848 space, I feel a deep resonance as well as significant differences. Inspired largely by the Living Theater's call for an "art that would instigate and support and be a revolution," the 848's approach to the fusion of art/politics/life might benefit from an encounter with that of the situationists, with their call for a revolution that would abolish art as a separate category by realizing it in every day life. At the same time, the situationist-inspired milieu has largely ceased to have any living creative practice – whereas 848 has much of the vital quality of a launching pad for contestation beyond the boundaries of art anyway.

It's inspiring to read the personal anecdotes of public, fully uncloseted love; and just to hear of the incredible diversity!

It takes a rare courage to step back and examine what you've done the way they have, and to open up to seeing if you might want to try something else. As I dream of what could be next for me and my shifting webwork of collaborators, I'm asking more now: what have been the limits of insurgent play? Are we ready for something more intense? Deeper and more conscious alterations of consciousness, post-linguistic frolics and eroplay? There is momentum building for "centers" of experimental ludic life, such as rural base camps in dynamic interplay with urban areas. How might we attempt a sustained psycho-geographic assault on an environment? And how might our projects be informed by the 848 experience?

Unru Lee

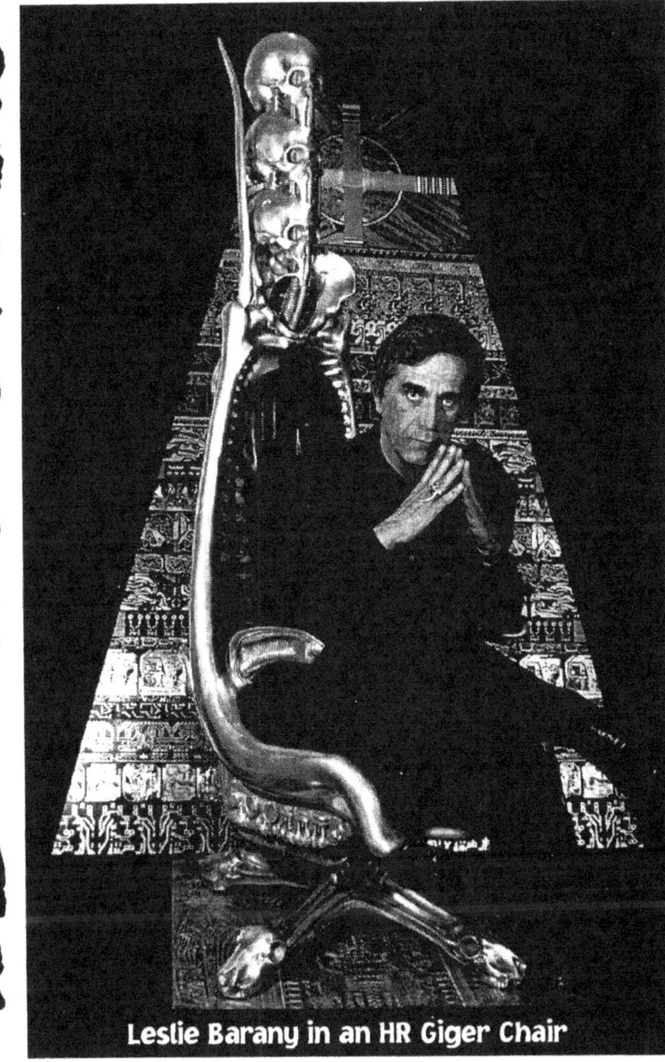

Leslie Barany in an HR Giger Chair

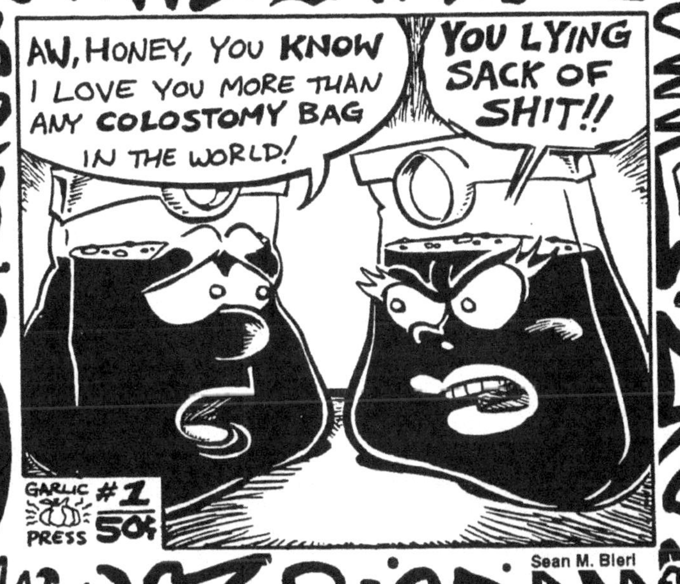

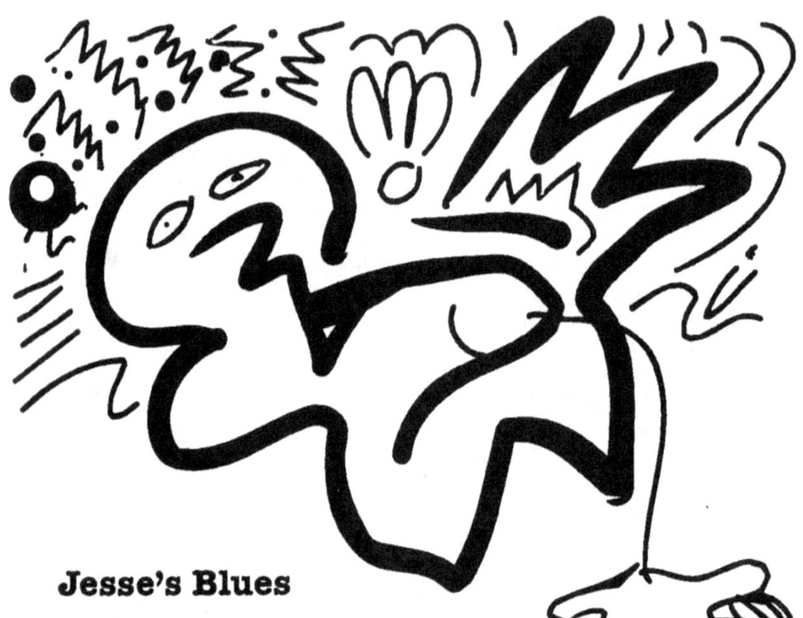

Jesse's Blues

Jesse Helms love Jesus
the saviour he feels the same
got hisself a day-glow ' I love Jesse '
bumper sticker on the back of
his dodge caravan (what you expect
God to drive, some piece of shit jap
junk shitbox, you limp wristed faggot
commie pinko four eyed mutha-fucker of
a nigger living son of a bitch.)
Jesse Helms loves Jesus
He's the defender of our rights
And he'll let you go most anyplace
Just as long as you are white
Jesse helms loves freedom
to say just as he please
and when no one is looking
He takes it on his knees
Jesse helms loves America
so virgin and so clean
but he reserves the right to own
your every single dream
Jesse Helms loves the N.R.A, the GAO and more
The F B I the C I A and marines on foreign shores
Jesse Helms loves Jesus
and all things pre-ordained
the precognition of our
spiritual being and all things
I can't stand so everybody sing
FUCK YOU jesse **FUCK YOU** (hear them drums) fuck you jesse fuck you
FUCK YOU jesse even Jesus hates you jesse your own mother hates you
jesse so **FUCK YOU** jesse **FUCK YOU** (hear them drums and fife)
fuck you jesse fuck you take it up the cornshoot tobacco man
even your own mama hates you jesse cause you an asshole jesse
and you give everybody the jesse blues

elliott

Dear Frank

Cherotic early food for thought Jesse poem is todays I had done a longish piece on Jesse called the reefer demigod but my main publisher has sat on it for some reason.
Tape I mailed was a present not a submission just to say; ' well, HI, there folks ' from elliott
Cherotic has lots of think stuff like life has more to it than prearranged circumstances. My thoughts run something like this on the subject. Nature recycles everything rain to river to evaporation to sky to river to flesh to bone to dust to mineral to fertilize the soil to refurbish new growth over and over every atom is used and used again nothing is wasted neither is the life-force that man calls his soul. It recycles hence some strong willed people can recall past lives. The Buddhists think what you do effects how this perpetual cycle will end but they are incorrect for it is a flow but it is benign but it is not pre-set on some level of karma There is no higher plane only higher recognition of the present Today I went to CLAYTON FORBELL & GLYNN funeral parlor where they layed my girlfriend Diane out in 1986. This town was flooding from all the melting snow. I walked to the river where we had met back in the early seventies. i sat on a metal bench (somehow dry in all the snow). I stared out at the frozen river and she called to me. I wondered how far across i could walk until the ice cracked and I drowned but I stared out at the river and realized that she was life and i was life so the solution was to turn and walk away. I think the main problem with life is that people don't realize the universe itself rests between their legs. They keep waiting for a saviour to pop out of their asshole but only shit does and they always look so surprised. I expect only shit and deal with life accordingly.
OH yeah check is for new issue and glad to be aboard the erevolution some of our thoughts run roughly on the same path

always love,
elliott

©1996 LABASH

LEE'S UNLEADED BLUES/ CHICAGO, SOUTH SIDE

She's leopard skin
wrapped and sweating
a shiny sweat
breasts huge and heavy
rise with the beat of
the words
"don't mind about your thighs
don't worry if you ain't
got no big breasts -
it's what you do with
the rest"

penciled brows curve a tease
she sings sultry
rockin' the red velvet room

heavy lidded guys sweatin'
out her slowwww words
she nags them with her hips
rotating
lips full and reddened seep
out the beat
toying undauntedly
with their need

smoke rises slow and curved
beer flows
the room mellows into red hue
the mood is ripe

the room drips

ahhhhh the blues have stirred
me into a sultry sway

Ana Christy

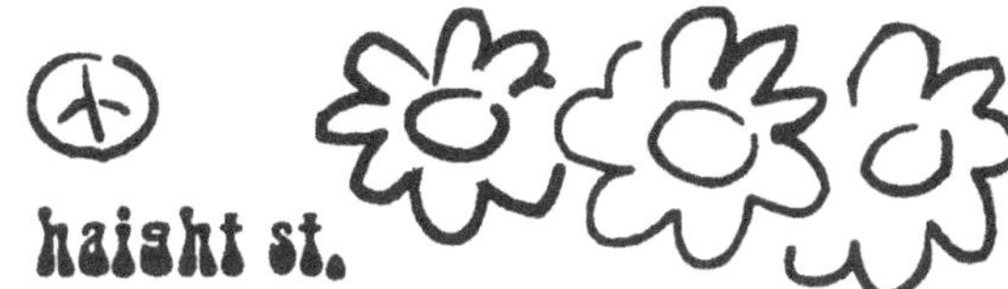

haight st.

this haight with it's mass energy
and lethargy-coffee houses crammed
with writers and artists jewelry
makers and chess players playing
off rickety ashtray filled tables

this haight is a light show of
people and color-transients seek
the dream of freedom
panhandlers playing penny games
on sidewalks
check cashing lines for welfare
checks

on haight kids out of panhandlers
park washing up in cafe washrooms
counting change for coffee-bumming
cigarettes
sidewalks swept off booze bottles
and piles of clothing as the sun
rises over thrift store leopard
coats

on haight colored flyers flapping
on poles
this an acid trip of color
it's frenzy and laidbackness is
the backbone of san francisco and
here i am at one with myself

on this haight i am the angel of
contentness with merging unity
and the tye-dyed buddha gives me
a laughing wink.

Ana Christy

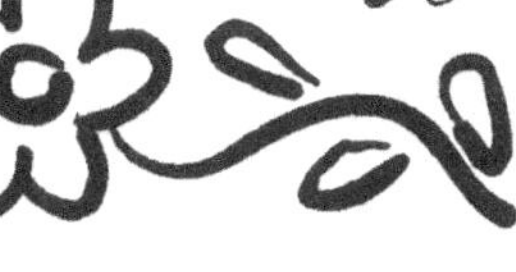

The Fall and Ruin: a Cry

by Dr. Bryan D. Reddick
Elmira College
Elmira, New York 14901

1

Her house was like a big, messy mind. And whenever she cleaned up downstairs, which was extremely seldom now, she always ended up by brushing things under the rug or behind the sofa, stacking those unread magazines in some other corner scarcely disturbing their dust, and throwing most of that old stuff she was going to sort out one day into an unused old trunk she kept just under the stairs.

She often thought there must be things living under there, some enormous, uncharted animal, or rats and roaches and things, *a teeming bed of life all covered up and not often talked about.* **"It was as if the house were built on the sea and if you opened the little door leading under the stairs you'd see the living waters shimmering with never-ending movement and undreamed excitement."** That, she thought one time, was eternity ... living just under her stairs like a sleeping hypothalamus.

And she never really went under there or even downstairs anymore, no more often than she had to. It was dirty: that was it.

She stood up to survey her work. Gleaming and clean, the tiny room lay before her.

All was prepared.

Mentally she surveyed the lab one floor below—the electrodes, the meters and computers, the as yet lifeless woman-model itself. Yes, all there too was waiting, ready, as she had left it. All was quietly awaiting tomorrow.

She stepped again across the tiled floor, stooped to peer into the crevice between the slick wall and the bottom of the stool, genuflected briefly as her aerofoam sponge swiped across the cool and curving stone. The drying film of moisture sparkled in the light.

She straightened again, and turned. Yes, here too in the tiny third floor room, all was neat and ordered. The sink, the tub, the stool itself, the cabinet before it where alone on the shining shelf sat her black box of bank statements and stock reports. All shone and winked at her, and she felt calm and relaxed.

"It does a woman good once in a while," she used to say, "to get down on her hands and knees."

It had been during one of the times when she was reading over those bank and stock figures (her grandchildren, she called them), then when her neat little bathroom was still on the ground floor, one day already so long ago, when she had suddenly thought of all the dirty little things crawling around in her under-the-stairs basement. Perhaps she had been thinking of insecticides and rat poisons, and she had very distinctly heard a noise. Not a very frightening sound in itself, but definitely she heard, or was she only imagining it? *a peculiar little rumble, or a snarl.*

She had become somewhat alarmed, and had left that first tile-smooth chamber, somewhat dingy and old in those times, to prowl the great downstairs floor. She hadn't gone far, however, when there was something, was it a sound? a vibration? something which guided her attention to the doorway under the stairs.

It was then, and immediately too, that she had decided to move upstairs. For from behind the shadowed doorway there had been, or she felt there had been—she often said now, of course, that she must have been imaging it, **"her reckless imagination"**—what was it? how did she perceive it? *a deep, sighing, groaning moan.*

It had been—her eyes glazed now remembering it, and her stomach felt empty—**"it was as if the house were built on a windstorm and now the winds were whirling through the aging beams of a pirate's trusty schooner, listing and creaking as the masts trembled and the ship groaned before splashing down, down into the turbulent waters of the sea below."**

She had gathered all her things, her then small collection of equipment too, and had moved entirely and unhesitatingly to the house's middle floor. And ever after, despite the filth which had met her there (she surmised that the under-stairs pipes had been somehow blocked), despite the days of toil she had been forced to spend cleaning the foul rooms of the excrement she'd found there, she had made her decision final, and almost never again descended to her house's lower floor ... no more often than she had to.

And soon, of course, she had been forced to leave that entire middle floor for her burgeoning laboratory, forced again to move up a floor, to lose days of valuable time cleaning the filth-choked rooms upstairs. But she had carried on, knowing then, of course, that there would soon be her own porcelain suite, spotless and glisteningly clean.

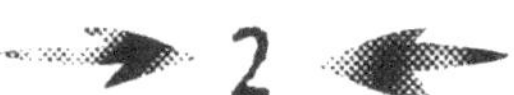

By now she had left the bathroom for the bedroom, and had begun to prepare for sleep.

She sat there in her clean little chamber with the fluorescent lights on before bed. She sat there, holding a shoe thoughtfully in her nimble hand. "Tomorrow," she said to the shoe.

Tomorrow she would descend to the lab (and there was warmth in the thought of it), and she would finish it, the woman she was building, her mirror image. Then she could begin, **"and all her works would praise her name."**

That, she thought to her shoe, is eternity.

She occasionally thought as well, though she said nothing of it since she didn't want it to seem she was complaining, that it was rather unpleasant to have to work where it was so dirty. Her laboratory was on the middle floor of her house, though sometimes she worked out of hours in her nice little room upstairs. And she couldn't help noticing now and again that there was a door which led from one dark corner of the lab into that eerie little storage room under the stairs by means of a short narrow staircase leading almost straight down. She would, on occasion, throw furtive glances in the direction of that little door, though it had long since been bolted and barred, and sometimes wondered if, when the lights were out in the lab, though they almost never were, she couldn't see just a little bit of a *glowing*, showing from *underneath the door.* **"As if the house were built on the sunset and the door was the last cloud the old sol would wink behind before bubbling its hot orange magic underneath the very mountains she was standing on."**

It had been only after the second move—she was getting into her pajamas—when she had left the middle floor for her lab, that her work had taken its new and decisive direction. She was building another woman, a model of himself, a woman which would walk and move and have her being just as she himself did. A perfect replica of the human form, just what humanity needed, a woman-model to observe. The model would show her what they required, for progress. And there would be no involvement, no messy subjectivity. She would be like a test tube or a centrifuge, the algae or a mouth-watering dog.

It was such a *great* idea!

She swung her legs onto the bed, and, sighing, lay back. The fluorescents above sparkled through the water before her eyes.

She was never quite sure whether or not she liked her work. Not that that was important, but it sometimes amused her to try to decide, **"lying there waiting for sleep to invade, like Ethiopia over Mussolini."**

There was, of course, the money. Reluctant governments were nevertheless paying dearly those days for research and construction perhaps destined to solve oh so many problems facing humankind at the moment, perhaps at any moment.

"I'm not doing it for that," she said to herself. "Oh I'm not working for the money." For indeed, she had no real need for money, her house, her equipment, her food and simple pleasures all so freely provided by the government or from privately donated funds. Yet there was the little black metal box placed carefully on the empty white shelf in the bathroom cabinet, before her when she sat; and she would often pass an hour or two there, reading gleefully the records she kept in the box, the increasing figures, the history of her prolific little grandsons and grand-daughters running around from bank to bank, from pile to pile, from hand to hand, making people happy while they bred a little more the months ahead.

"That too," she like to think, "was eternity: coins breeding in a fertile pile of gold."

She knew she must like all that sort of thing—and the calculations too—but somewhere, somewhere beneath the white rubberized laboratory trousers she always wore or next to the superthin calculator she often carried in her breast pocket, somewhere where her eyes could not see, nor her microscope, nor her fluoroscope, there *a voice* **"like a warm breeze wandering through the hot fingers of a dry summer night's grass fire"** was telling her there was *something else* in the work, in the lab itself, **"something dark and fierce like the uncharted in some Arizona pool."** There was *something fierce and dark* in the lab which drove her on **"as a midnight blaze drives a mad, blind stallion charging into the darkness where she cannot see, but charging on and on."**

She rolled onto her back; she was panting.

But her work was important, perhaps vital, she told herself, to all humanity; and she would go on with it day by day carrying on cheerfully, even eagerly. And tomorrow, she would ...

She yawned, and the fluorescents swam above her. Her eyes fluttered closed, and she dreamed of *a racetrack and of himself clocking a speeding unicorn.*

3

She had risen early that day, nervous with anticipation. She had stubbed her toe on the cold white stool while her eyes were still filled with sleep. She had dressed carefully, favoring her throbbing toe and concentrating on remaining calm.

She had descended from her little room ... as usual, she thought to herself; it's just a normal day. Yet the key had somehow crawled through her fingers and bounced to the floor when she began to unlock the lab door; and somewhere she knew.

She had entered the lab; there was nothing changed. Her equipment lay still before her, meticulously arranged and prepared. Yet she had not begun her work. She had been drawn instead to turn about the room, which was quiet and somehow unbalanced by the slanting rays of sunlight which were playing through the only little window near the back. She had paused there before the little door leading down to the under-stairs; she had carefully reached out her hand to check the bolts and bars, and could not now forget that they had distinctly felt warm to her cold, unsteady fingers.

It had been months since she had checked her small white cabinet just beside the outer door across the room. But now she did; today she felt it was important. She ran a short test on a drop she took from the small black vial she kept there.

It was still potent.

It was foolish, she thought cynically to himself, to keep it there. Yet she did not trust the glowing, snarling, softly waving under-stairs, and the poison she'd distilled from monkey urine would kill any beast or monster she might have to face. Perhaps it was—yes, she smiled at her hesitancy, it *was* foolish; but she had humored herself that morning and had found there a sort of confidence.

She had moved on and on about the room, and had finally begun.

And just as the woman was born, just as the model began slowly to stir, to blink her glazed eyes and to scowl, then—she could not now forget it—then, *she had felt the floor shift* **"like the deck of a faltering vessel."** The room was suddenly warm, and from the little door—she must have been imaging it—there was *a glowing like the sunrise and a moaning like a strange imprisoned animal.*

The model woman now sat before her, and knew why she'd been made. The model was wise, and her creator quick to note all her motions and thoughts, though the noting mind often clouded with a dark thought of the cabineted vial.

"I am empty," said the woman.

And she knew that it was true.

Just then, as the woman-model began to speak, the floor began to shake and the walls rattle. The fluorescents flashed and died, but the room was light.

There was a rumbling, a snarling, a roaring like the wind in a fire, and the bars on the little door glowed with heat and fell away.

There was fire everywhere, the floor, the lights. The woman-model's eyes flashed in wonder and in terror as her creator vomited and writhed in her burning rubber pants.

The door smashed open. The woman-model fled, and, running out and up the stairs to the clear white room, she gulped hungrily from the foul vial.

But she, she did not flee, and knew she did not want to go. She was standing then, awaiting it, and it washed over her in a boiling bath. She stood fast, her hands raised high above her head, knowing that she did not want to run, exulting savagely and painfully in the violent burning of her flesh *as the uncharted animal, the swimming seas of boiling unction, the blind, windblown, charging stallion, and the flames crashed upon her like black waves on a sunny rock.*

And as died, as she perished in the awful sea from the under-stairs, her house fell to ruin about her, an innocent victim of the dark savage fight between the flowing sunsets from below the floor and the piles of excrements on the roof.

Her house had fallen into smoldering rubble, floating like dirty scum on a sunlit sea.

And today the wet, charred ruins of her house cry out to the never-ending skies: **"One day, oh humanity, let there be built a house where seas and stools can live united, as in the well-ordered mind of a rose!"**

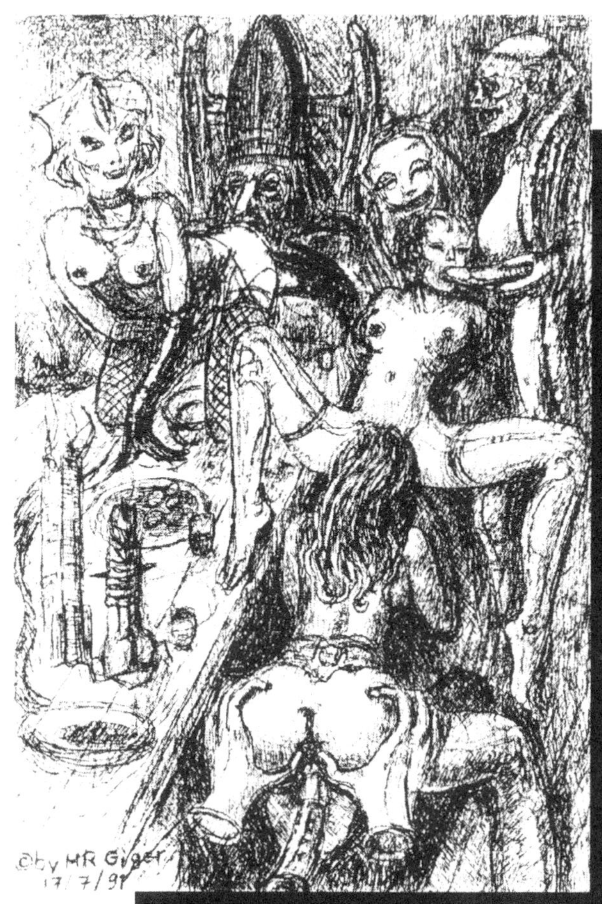

PEN & INK SKETCHES BY

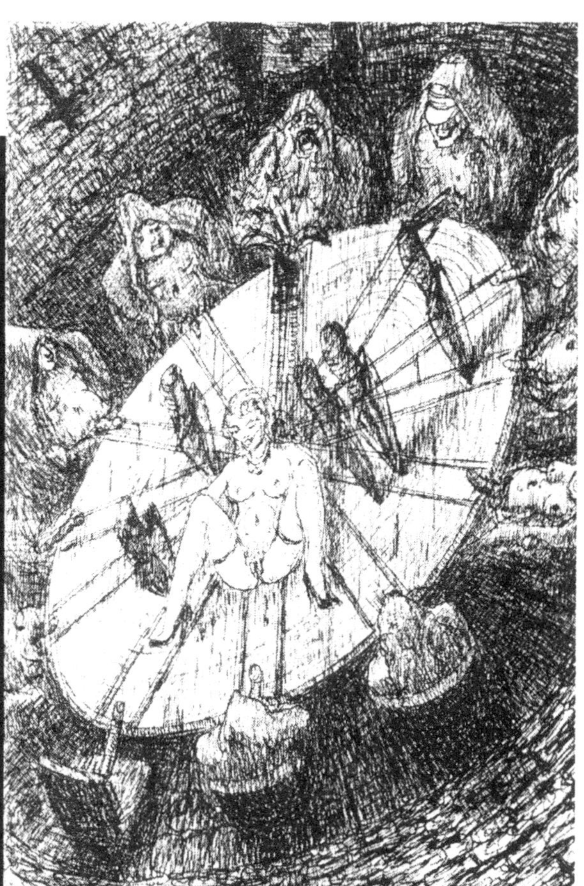

HR Giger

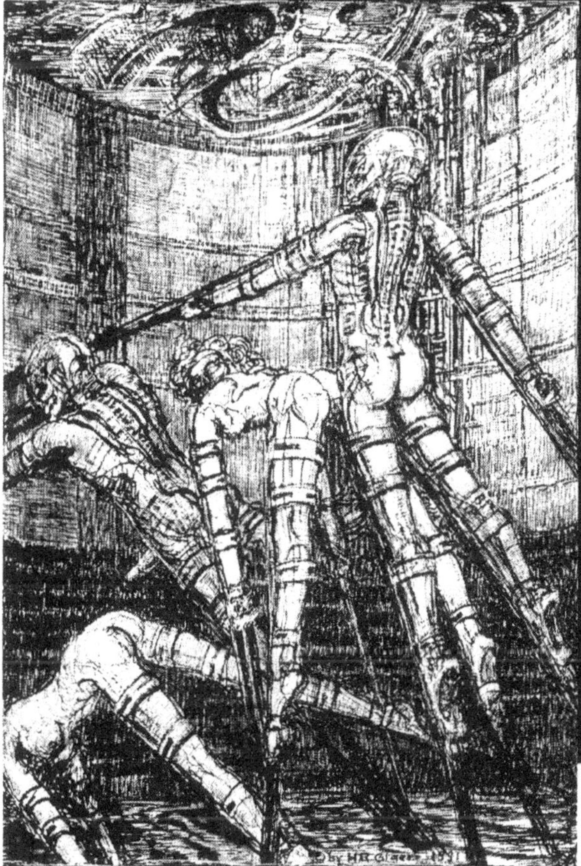

It's still not too late to send your HR Giger tattoos for the book <u>HR Giger Under Your Skin</u> to Leslie Barany Communications, 121 West 27th St. #202 New York, NY 10001 Tel: (212) 627.8488 Fax: (212) 463.7983

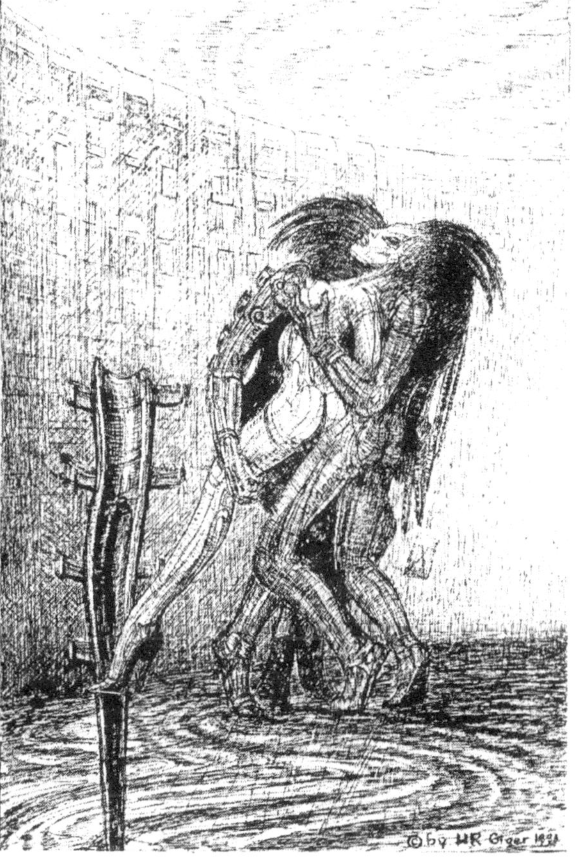

a rant on an open mike

by
frank moore
copyrighted August 16, 1995

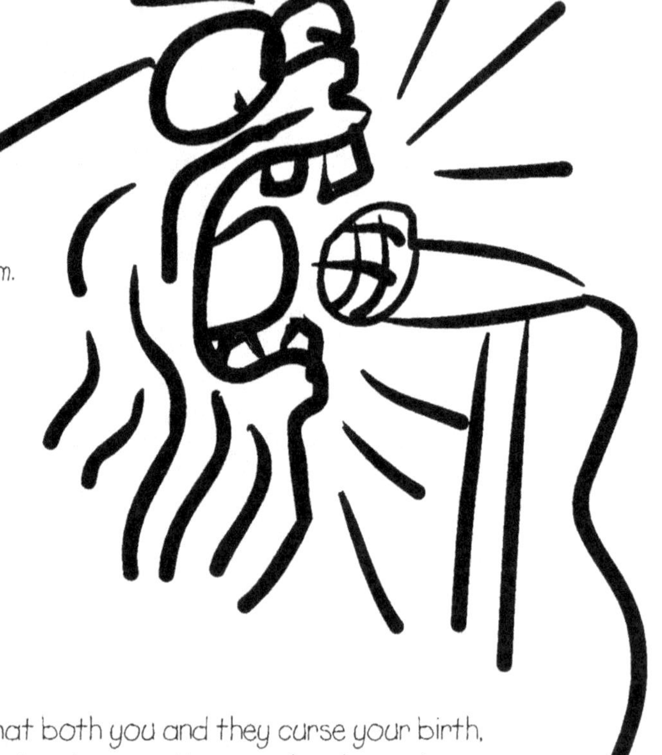

the open mike
is the most democratic channel...
well maybe except for hyde park sproul soapbox freedom.
anyone can sign up
to step up to bat,
step up to the mike
and into the sacred belljar
where art poetry is free to expose truth,
free to use whatever it takes,
whatever style it takes to expose truth...
that is, until your given time runs out
and hooks you around the neck and yanks you
from the belljar stage.
but in the belljar channel
you are in danger testing, crying, being so sucking bad that both you and they curse your birth, sharing found ideas, listening to the silence and the polite clapping greeting your bombs or to your ravings of rage that hit too close to home, messing up the nice polite parlor.

entering the open mike belljar is a leap into uncontrolled possibilities, uncomfortable quest through good bad boring embarrassing and sometimes magical.

nobody owns the belljar,
except when you are in the channel,
in the pipe behind the mike,
holding the modern talking stick
until it is time to pass it on to the next.
but the talking stick is everyone's,
for anyone with something to express.
if one is banned, censored, from holding the talking stick
just to punish, just to protect a neat fragile nice order,
we all are banished from the sacred talking stick which becomes just a cock that we rub.

i get worried if my words and images fit through veins clogged with fatty taboos of polite appropriate of comfortability.

i get worried...is the art that small that it fits through that pinhole of a hole...so small that nudes on the walls, words on telephone poles, any shift in the social power structure threatens the very reality fabric.

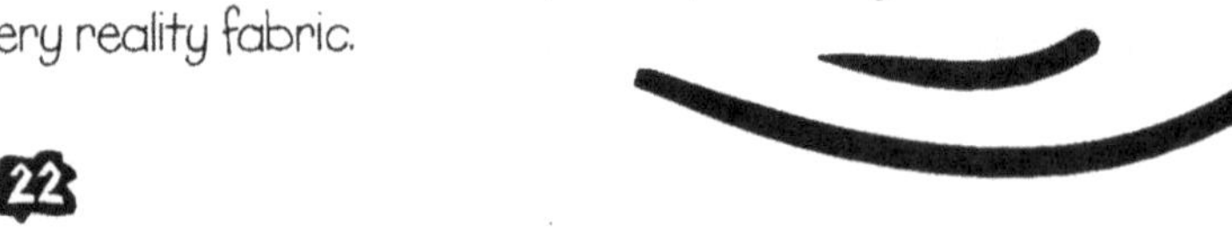

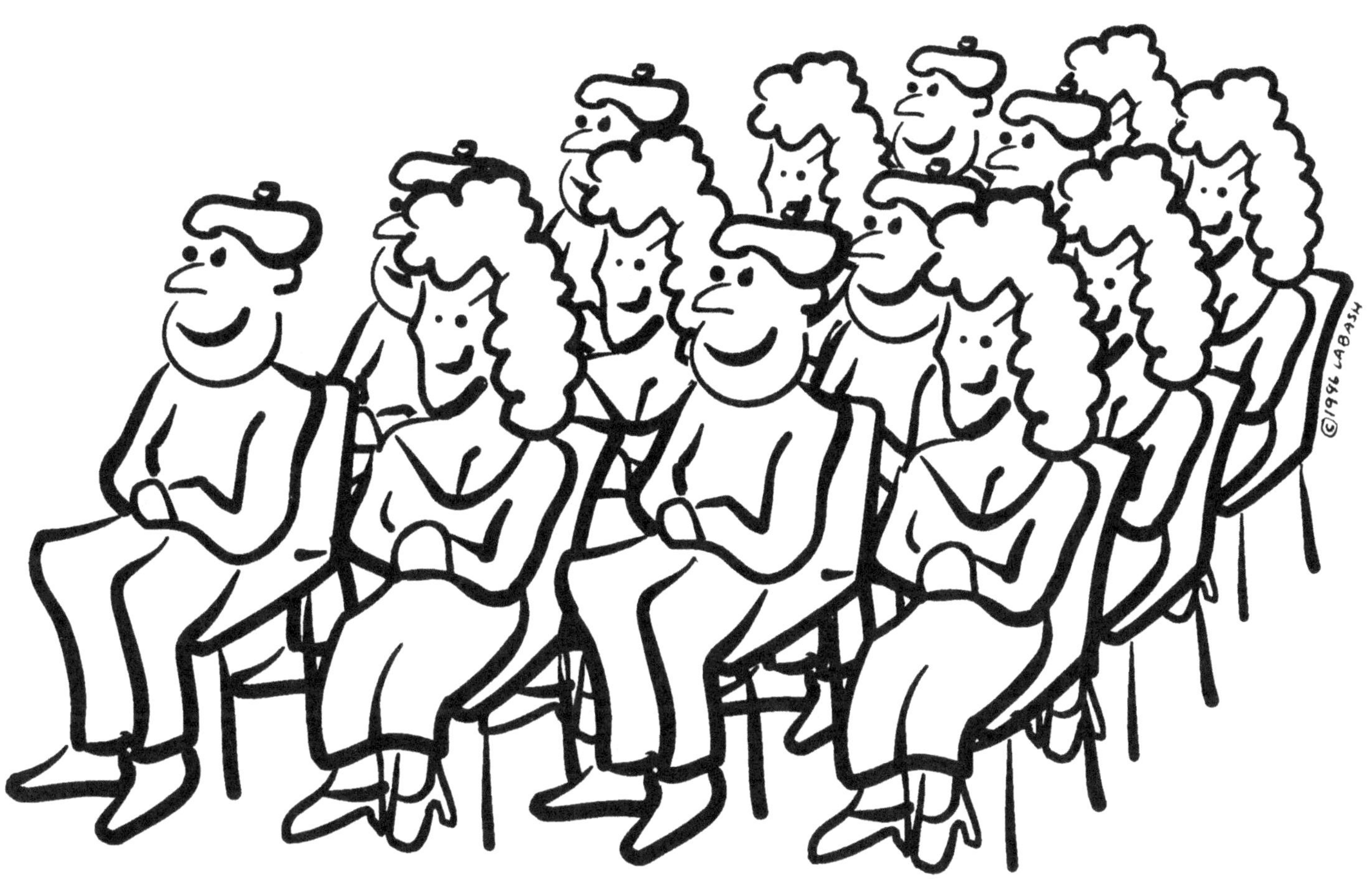

i'm too proud to admit the art poetry is that small. so my art becomes a roto-rooting balloon covered in razors tipped in draino acid,
pushing pressuring uncomfortable unsocial grinding against the grain until the killer fatty clots of taboos burst out the other end and go down the drain like trouble.

i don't really go after the hitlers, the mccarthys, the helms, or their brown shirts.

they are just limp-dicked power-junkies with swiss-cheese egos, each hole filled with inferiority. they are just moons with no power light of themselves, just reflecting fear.

no, i go after the nice people who never asked where the trains were going, boxcars filled with people. didn't have to. only suspected, only heard rumors...after all, the general is a friend. never said, excuse me, i am a jew too, a jap too, a gay too, i've negro blood running in my body, aids too. i'm a commie who took home movies of our nude kids. so better put me on that train too. better put us all on that train. there ain't no train big enough!

i go after the nice people who keep going to work after seeing their friends missing, after hearing rumors of blacklist and blackball. must write something about that subject to THE TIMES. he used to be such a pleasant fellow...but now he is a whining paranoid...not a sort to have to tea. he is like a wet messy fart. not in my backyard!

yes, i go after nice people. but my time in the belljar is about over. so i'll leave you with this. what is happening in your backyard is what really matters. so be sure to weed!

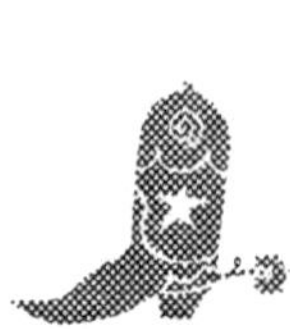

"Gold Digger"

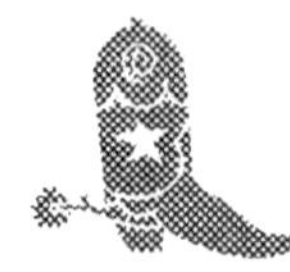

(country song lyric)

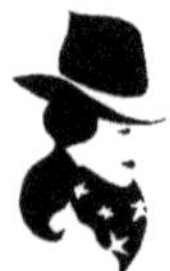

Like your Mama gave me a bad rap,
honey, so you can tell her for me,

If I was a gold digger, honey,
I wouldn't pan for gold in a river full
of fool's gold
If I was a gold digger, honey
I'd be in a penthouse in New York
with servants walking poodles
and a chauffeur come around
to take me to the mall
I'd have a ball

If I was a gold digger honey
I wouldn't be stuck here
on a ranch with no 'lectricity
in sub-zero weather
with crazy hunters shootin'
everything in sight
includin' me.

If I was a gold digger, honey
I'd be floatin' on a yacht
in the Mediterranean
I'd be dancing in the moonlight
with a man whose grammar's good
with big diamond rings on his fingers
and two Mercedes, please,
just for me

If I was a gold digger, honey
I wouldn't sit here in the dark
when all the lights go out
and hear the wolves howling
while I creep about
and try to find
the window, and close it
so the snow don't fill the house up
while the cat is out of food.

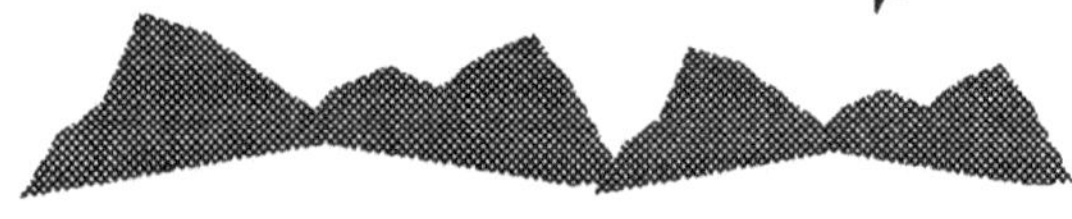

If I was a gold digger, honey
I wouldn't pan for gold
in a river
full of fool's gold

You're not quite as handsome,
got a tooth that's loose,
and hair you still have left
is turning grey,
Your hands are tough from tyin' rope
and boardin' up the fences
they wouldn't put you on a billboard
for Marlboro
though you wear a Stetson hat, sometimes

You're an ordinary
regular
square-dancin', whoop 'n' hollerin'
cowboy dreamer from the old wild West
you ain't no Saint!
You and the boys
and the beer and the noise
and the flashing glint in your eye
that devilish look,
it's the nearest thing to gold I'll ever see,
I'm not lookin' for gold
in the mortgages and creditors
and horsetradin' goin' on,
the bankers and the promissory notes,
All we got to take to the bank is your

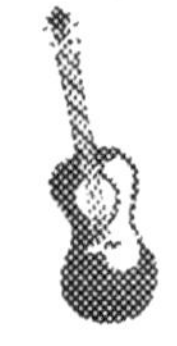

confidant, down- home,
son- of- a- gun, no- holds- barred,
take- me- as- I- am, helluva- man
rawhide- boots an' tight- jeans' swagger!

If I was a gold digger, honey
I wouldn't pan for gold
in a river full
of fool's gold.

Dorothy Jesse Beagle
FULL PANTRY MUSIC (BMI)

Eric Boutilier-Brown

http://www.isisnet.com/empire/ebb/

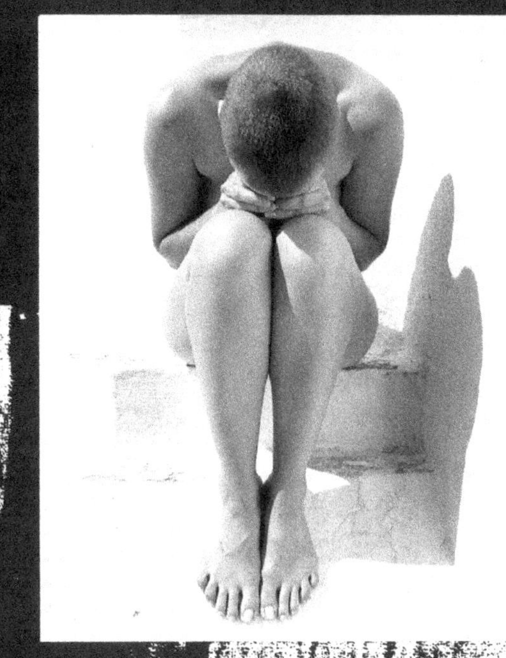

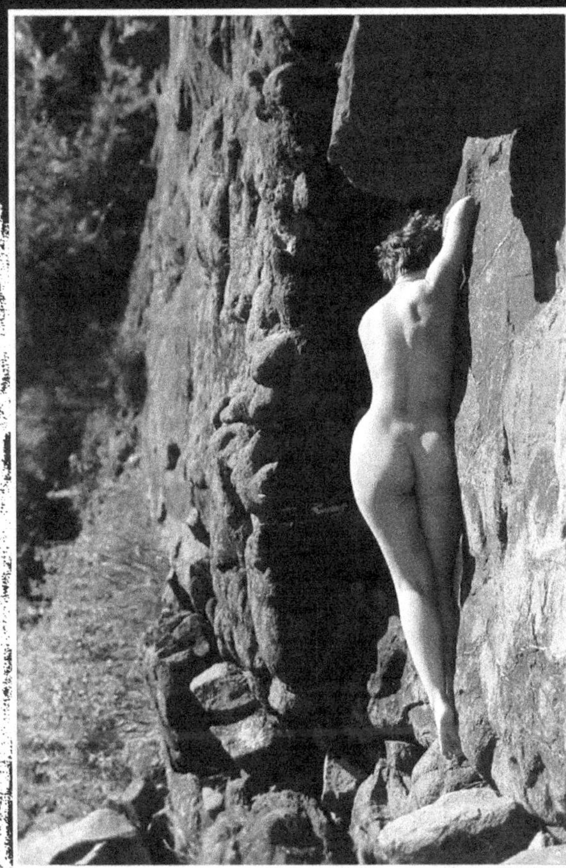

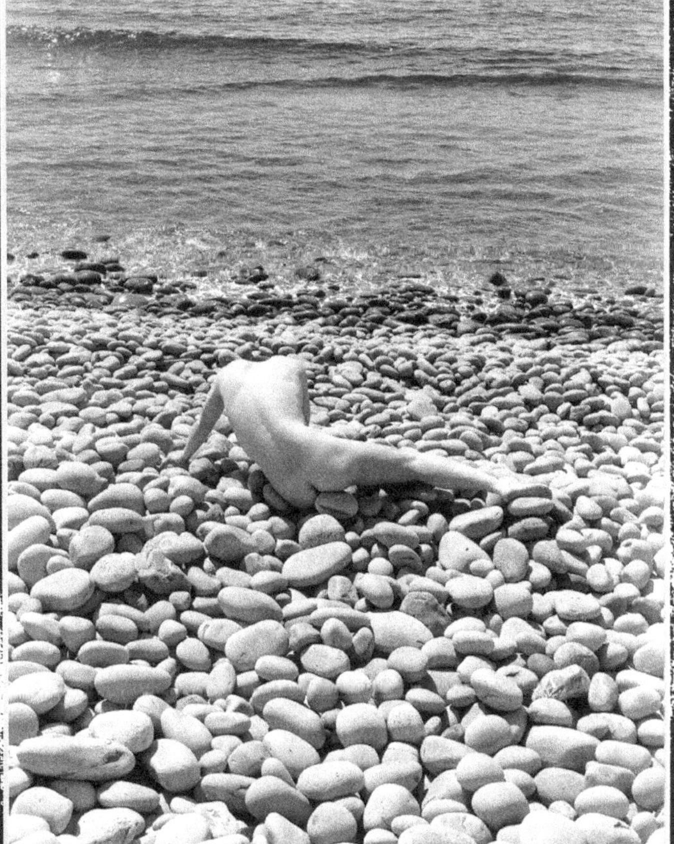

SLEEPLESS NIGHT

I lay sleepless in this lonely cell, feeling like some unformed thing existing in a jar on the shelf in some research laboratory, and perhaps it's intended for me, this dissection of time, with only dreams of things that once was, what I wish was now, and what will probably never be. How can I express the visual concept of my present existence or the pains and suffrage constantly being endured, when nobody hears or cares, when nobody wants to hear or care, for fear of becoming sympathetic of another human being's pain.

I lie here like the skeletons of last years leaves in a fence corner, all my hopes, dreams, wishes and desires are all for nothing. Nothing! Do you understand? I don't expect the experience of love or happiness to ever again visit my life. Not that I would purposely reject it, but that love has to have a beginning, and I think it begins in the home, and it starts from when you're bounced off the knee or off the wall. I'm too old for the knee, and so encased within walls that I tend to feel that I'm a part of the wall. So love don't love nobody, and right now, "I'm nobody."

I am, it is true, running out of time and space. For a little longer I will see and hear, but it will be nothing, and to the world I will mean nothing. In the end, not too far distant, there will be an unbridgeable silence between those that knew me and those that wasted time in not getting to know me. All I can ever hope for is before I die, it is well that I consider of what my final image as a man, as a person may be — the image that will give me a kind of earthy immortality or represent, perhaps, my final collective visage in eternity. Then once again my thoughts and moods can be dissected with no understanding of my feelings, my needs, my desires or my dreams, because there was no one willing to reach out and touch that part of me, but would rather see me as only an object of discussion. But it is to the seeds of death within me/man that I must address you/humanity before I dare ask this final question of what may stand for all of us when all else is fallen and gone down. We shall not begin with Western society, we shall begin with man. We shall open that symbolic sepulcher of which Melville speaks. We shall grope in the roiling, tumultuous darkness for that umplumbed vacancy which Melville termed so ironically the soul of man.

I lie here victimized by circumstances out of my control as the cold freezing winter's night wind envelopes my body into rigid and painful aches, staring at empty, blank walls, aged with time as time fades from my consciousness. God must have valued time highly — He gives us just one second at a time. It took me a lots of years to figure out that this moment is all I have or will ever have. Yesterday is gone and tomorrow is a very well kept secret. Dreaming of the past or planning for the future has their place I suppose, but the only thing we will ever do we will do now. No one knows what tomorrow gives or takes away.

It is said that "affliction can have educational value." In which case, I should have a PH.D. In my simple world any adversity can become my best friend. I try to live by the old saying; "What happens to me is never as important as what I do about it." One of the best military maneuvers in the face of overwhelming odds is retreat. My mother use to say; "It's better to be a living coward, than a dead hero, for a coward lives to fight another day." But I don't think this situation has anything to do with being a coward or hero, but whether I have the sense to realize a "no-win" situation.

Some men do time. I use time. This is why the many years of my exile (incarceration) have rested quietly beside each other. But the toil of these years have left deep scars, psychologically, physically, emotionally, and spiritually. There were times when I had to dip into my rage for inner strength, and other times when I had to rely on unconventional wisdom. Since I cannot visit my dead ancestors, they sometimes come and visit me. Sometimes you must talk to the dead in order to find out how to live, how to survive, who you are, or where you came from. And who knows ... maybe even where you're going.

The night has been silent except for the tic tac of the clock or an occasional scream from someone fighting off the demons within their minds and dreams, and I wonder what more can be said, or have I said anything at all? I do know it's 4 a.m. and I dare not continue at this time for fear of reiteration.

Al Cunningham
January 14, 1994

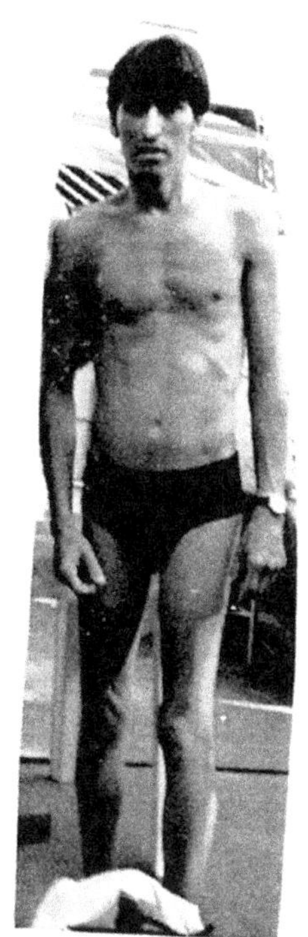

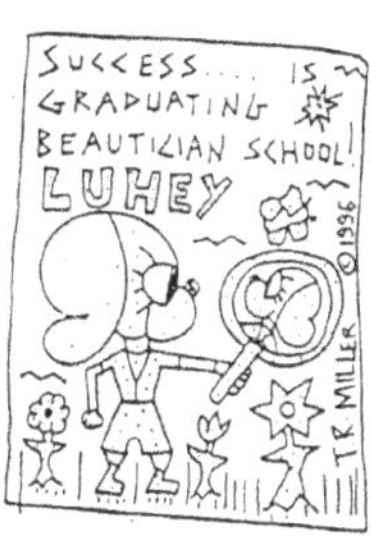

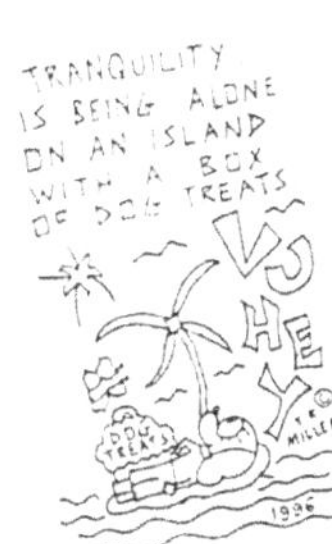

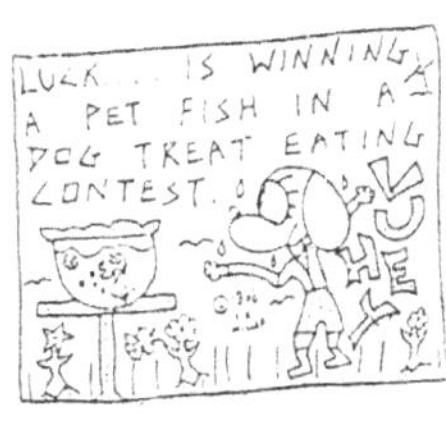

T.R. MILLER, CARTOONIST, HOPES YOU LIKE HIS LUHEY CARTOONS. THE SEASONAL CELEBRATIONS AND THE HOLIDAY EXTRAVAGANZAS IN MILLER'S CARTOONS ARE DONE WITH LIGHT-HEARTED HUMOR. "HAPPY WINTER" AND "HAPPY ST. PATRICK'S DAY," CARTOONS ARE DEPICTED WITH THE SPIRIT OF THE SEASON

ABOUT THE ARTIST

T.R. MILLER, WAS BORN IN NEW JERSEY, AND STILL RESIDES WITH HIS FAMILY IN HIS HOMETOWN OF EAST BRUNSWICK, NEW JERSEY T.R. MILLER ©1996

T.R. MILLER CARTOONIST

12-21-95

To: Frank Moore (editor, The Cherotic Revolutionary)
I was wondering if you could do a story on me as a cartoonist- I've enclosed some information.
Also, let me clarify a few things if you do decide to do a story on me in your '96 issue
(1.) I'M ASEXUAL (CELIBATE) AND LIVING WITH MY FAMILY.
(2.) I'VE ONLY BEEN PUBLISHED SINCE '94.
(3.) I've had my cartoons seen by 25,000 readers.
(4) I will publish a chap book of my cartoons in 1996.
THANKS Have a great year in '96 —
ALL The Best to you —
Sincerely—
T.R. Miller (Cartoonist)

A GORGEOUS SUNSET... PRETTY FLOWERS... DIVINE TREES... AM I BORING YOU? O.K.!!!! HAVE A NICE DAY!
LUHEY
T.R. MILLER ©1996

LUHEY'S OLD-FASHIONED CARTOONS BRING BACK THAT DOWN-TO-EARTH, HOMEY FEELING. I HOPE YOU LIKE THE SIMPLISTIC, YET POIGNANT 'TOONS. LUHEY'S HAPPY-GO-LUCKY PERSONA, AND LIKEABLE DISPOSITION IS VERY PLEASING! HE KNOWS HOW TO LIVEN UP A MOMENT AND, LUHEY ALWAYS HAS A GOOD TIME AND LOTS OF FUN. CHEERS.... AND BEST WISHES TO YOU ALL. _HUGS- LUHEY
T.R. MILLER ©1996

LUHEY GIVES HIS FATHER A DOG TREAT NECKLACE.
HAPPY FATHER'S DAY.
LUHEY
T.R. MILLER ©1996

LUHEY
BIRD FEEDIN' FUN-
T.R. MILLER ©1996

T.R. MILLER, CARTOONIST, HOPES YOU LIKE HIS WHIMSICAL AND UPBEAT 'TOONS. MILLER'S FANCIFUL CREATIONS HAVE BECOME VERY ELABORATE AND STYLISTIC. MANY EDITORS IN THE SMALL PRESS NETWORK HAVE MARVELED OVER MILLER'S VAST IMAGINATION DISPLAYED IN HIS LUHEY CARTOONS. MILLER HAS BEEN DESCRIBED AS EXTRAORDINARILY TALENTED AS AN ARTIST. MILLER WISHES TO THANK ALL EDITORS WHO HAVE SENT TO HIM THEIR KIND REPLIES AND REGARDS. HAVE A GLAMOROUS MOTHER'S DAY AND A RADIANT FATHER'S DAY SINCERELY, T.R. MILLER (CARTOONIST) ©1996

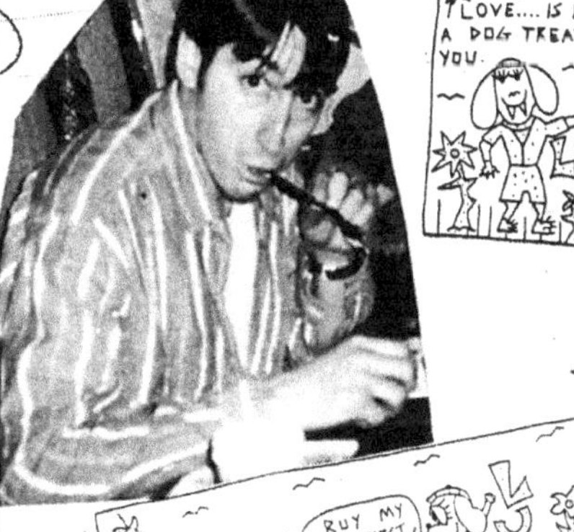

LOVE.... IS BEING GIVEN A DOG TREAT FOR BEING YOU.
LUHEY
T.R. MILLER ©1996

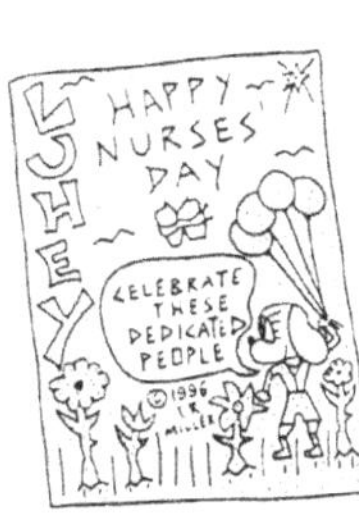

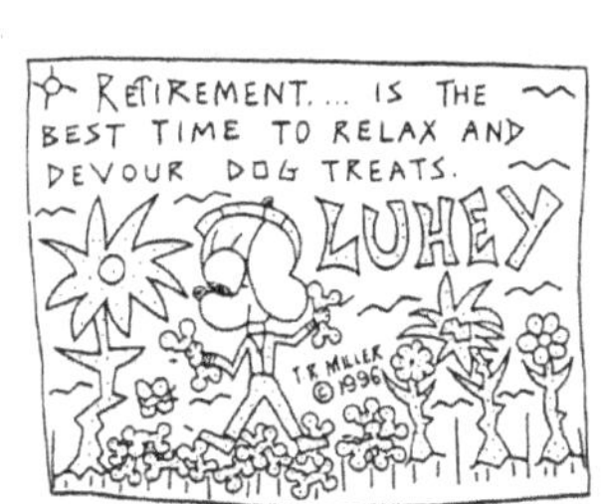

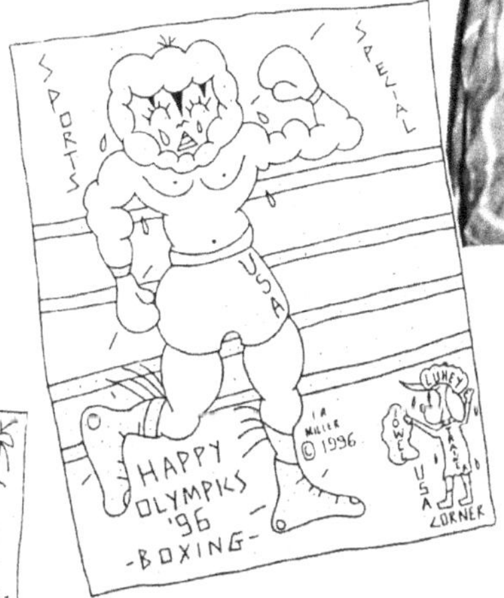

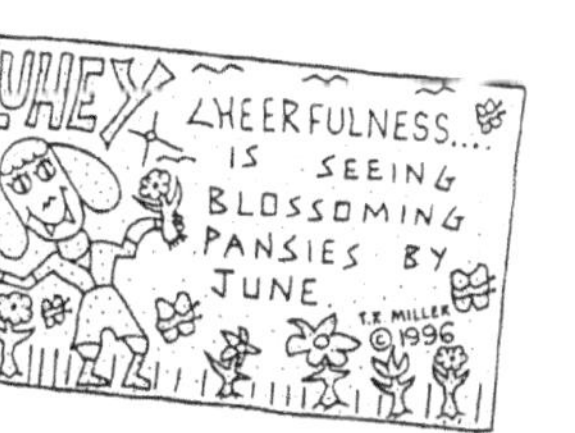

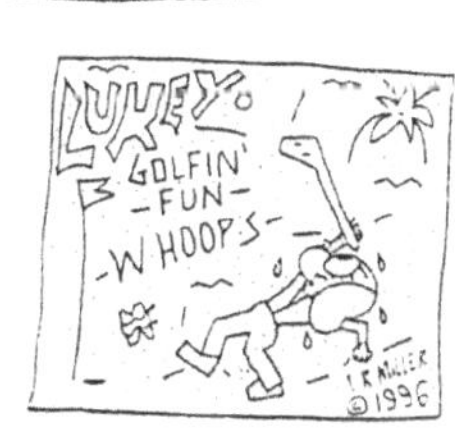

T.R. MILLER, CARTOONIST, PRESENTS HIS LUHEY CHAPBOOK. IT'S 20 PAGES AND INCLUDES HOLIDAYS, SEASONAL, AND MORE. IT COSTS $3.00 U.S.A. ORDERS ONLY, PLEASE! WRITE TO: T.R. MILLER (CARTOONIST) LUHEY'S CHAPBOOK, 74 HILLTOP BLVD. EAST BRUNSWICK, N.J. 08816
BUY MY VERY FIRST CHAPBOOK
LUHEY

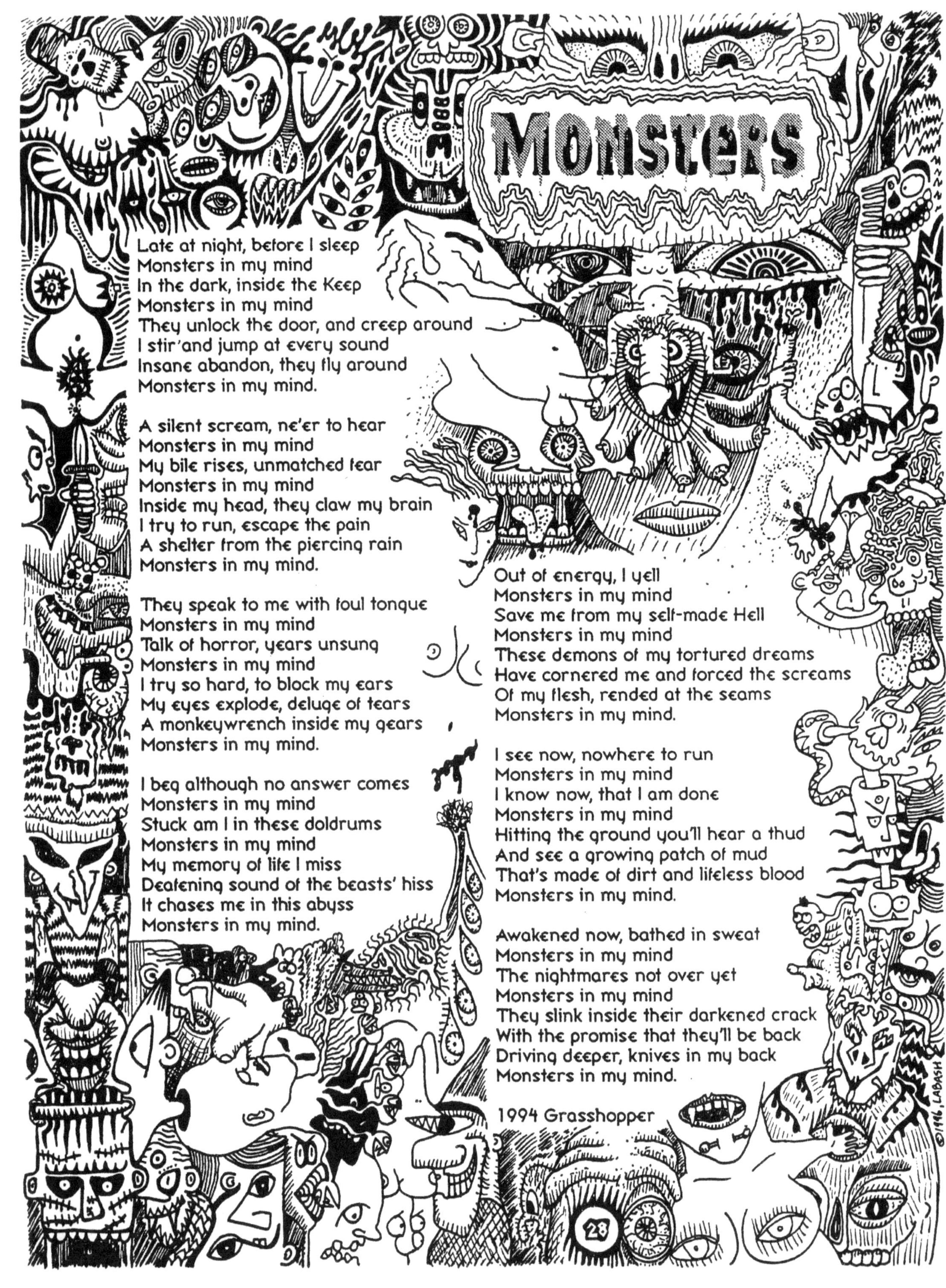

MONSTERS

Late at night, before I sleep
Monsters in my mind
In the dark, inside the Keep
Monsters in my mind
They unlock the door, and creep around
I stir'and jump at every sound
Insane abandon, they fly around
Monsters in my mind.

A silent scream, ne'er to hear
Monsters in my mind
My bile rises, unmatched fear
Monsters in my mind
Inside my head, they claw my brain
I try to run, escape the pain
A shelter from the piercing rain
Monsters in my mind.

They speak to me with foul tongue
Monsters in my mind
Talk of horror, years unsung
Monsters in my mind
I try so hard, to block my ears
My eyes explode, deluge of tears
A monkeywrench inside my gears
Monsters in my mind.

I beg although no answer comes
Monsters in my mind
Stuck am I in these doldrums
Monsters in my mind
My memory of life I miss
Deafening sound of the beasts' hiss
It chases me in this abyss
Monsters in my mind.

Out of energy, I yell
Monsters in my mind
Save me from my self-made Hell
Monsters in my mind
These demons of my tortured dreams
Have cornered me and forced the screams
Of my flesh, rended at the seams
Monsters in my mind.

I see now, nowhere to run
Monsters in my mind
I know now, that I am done
Monsters in my mind
Hitting the ground you'll hear a thud
And see a growing patch of mud
That's made of dirt and lifeless blood
Monsters in my mind.

Awakened now, bathed in sweat
Monsters in my mind
The nightmares not over yet
Monsters in my mind
They slink inside their darkened crack
With the promise that they'll be back
Driving deeper, knives in my back
Monsters in my mind.

1994 Grasshopper

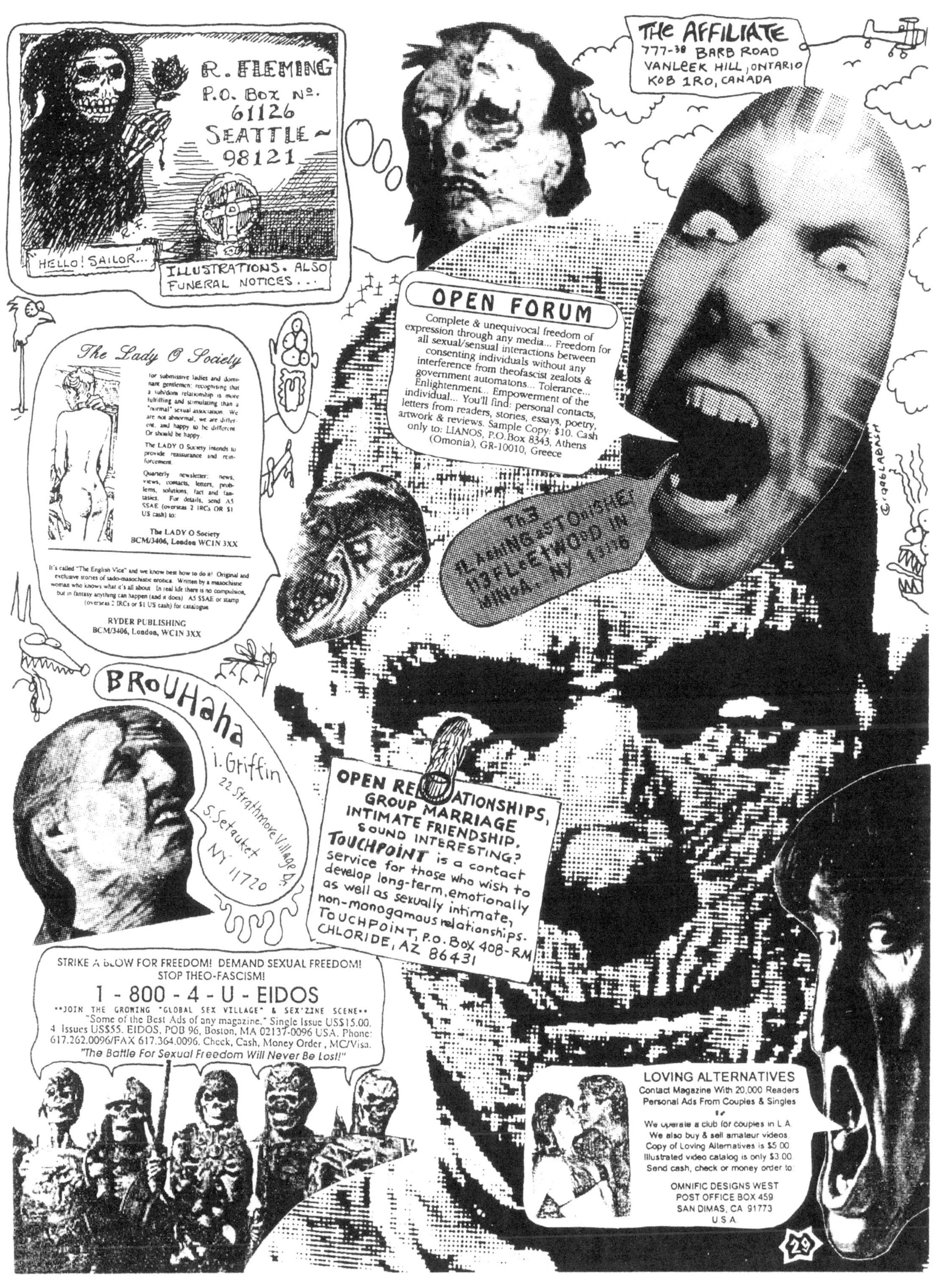
R. FLEMING
P.O. BOX No. 61126
SEATTLE ~ 98121
HELLO! SAILOR...
ILLUSTRATIONS. ALSO FUNERAL NOTICES...
THE AFFILIATE
777-38 BARB ROAD
VANLEEK HILL, ONTARIO
KOB 1RO, CANADA
OPEN FORUM
Complete & unequivocal freedom of expression through any media... Freedom for all sexual/sensual interactions between consenting individuals without any interference from theofascist zealots & government automatons... Tolerance... Enlightenment... Empowerment of the individual... You'll find: personal contacts, letters from readers, stories, essays, poetry, artwork & reviews. Sample Copy: $10. Cash only to: LIANOS, P.O.Box 8343, Athens (Omonia), GR-10010, Greece
The Lady O Society
for submissive ladies and dominant gentlemen; recognising that a sub/dom relationship is more fulfilling and stimulating than a "normal" sexual association. We are not abnormal, we are different, and happy to be different Or should be happy.
The LADY O Society intends to provide reassurance and reinforcement.
Quarterly newsletter: news, views, contacts, letters, problems, solutions, fact and fantasies. For details, send A5 SSAE (overseas 2 IRCs OR $1 US cash) to:
The LADY O Society
BCM/3406, London WC1N 3XX
It's called "The English Vice" and we know best how to do it! Original and exclusive stories of sado-masochistic erotica. Written by a masochistic woman who knows what it's all about. In real life there is no compulsion, but in fantasy anything can happen (and it does). A5 SSAE or stamp (overseas 2 IRCs or $1 US cash) for catalogue
RYDER PUBLISHING
BCM/3406, London, WC1N 3XX
THE FLAMING ASTONISHED
113 FLEETWOOD IN
MINOA, NY 13116
BROUHaha
i. Griffin
22 Strathmore Village Dr.
S. Setauket
NY 11720
OPEN RELATIONSHIPS, GROUP MARRIAGE, INTIMATE FRIENDSHIP, SOUND INTERESTING?
TOUCHPOINT is a contact service for those who wish to develop long-term, emotionally as well as sexually intimate, non-monogamous relationships.
TOUCHPOINT, P.O. BOX 408-RM
CHLORIDE, AZ 86431
STRIKE A BLOW FOR FREEDOM! DEMAND SEXUAL FREEDOM!
STOP THEO-FASCISM!
1 - 800 - 4 - U - EIDOS
JOIN THE GROWING "GLOBAL SEX VILLAGE" & SEX'ZINE SCENE
"Some of the Best Ads of any magazine." Single Issue US$15.00. 4 Issues US$55. EIDOS, POB 96, Boston, MA 02137-0096 USA. Phone: 617.262.0096/FAX 617.364.0096. Check, Cash, Money Order, MC/Visa.
"The Battle For Sexual Freedom Will Never Be Lost!"
LOVING ALTERNATIVES
Contact Magazine With 20,000 Readers
Personal Ads From Couples & Singles
We operate a club for couples in L.A.
We also buy & sell amateur videos.
Copy of Loving Alternatives is $5.00
Illustrated video catalog is only $3.00
Send cash, check or money order to:
OMNIFIC DESIGNS WEST
POST OFFICE BOX 459
SAN DIMAS, CA 91773
U.S.A.
29

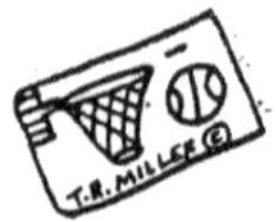

Talking about Jimmy

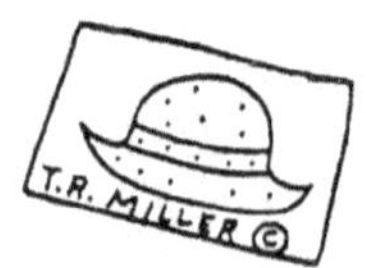

"She tells me all kinds of personal things," my mother said. She was talking about Gloria, her closest friend. "And I really wish she wouldn't reveal some of this stuff. It seems too personal, the kind of thing that should be kept in the family. Just the other day she mentions how Jimmy says weird things, like he thinks people are talking about him, or laughing at him, or how he thinks someone's following him."

"Maybe he's paranoid from smoking pot," I observed.

"That could be," Mom said. "I just try to deflect Gloria's irritation, say things like we all worry about what other people think of us some of the time."

"That's true," I said, "and also, it depends on one's personality. I mean, because sometimes people are talking about you, and maybe that's the unfortunate side of sensitivity or perception, to realize such things. Ignorance is bliss, and all that."

"Oh yes," Mom said, "Gloria says he's very sensitive."

"I'm not surprised, then. That and the weed will do it to him. Remember how Dad said that's why he never enjoyed smoking pot? Because it made him so paranoid?"

"Yes, I remember him saying that."

"Well, that's how it effects some people."

"I don't think Gloria understands that," Mom said. "Sometimes I wish she'd just calm down and quit condemning Jimmy."

I had not seen Jimmy in nearly twenty years. We were in high school together, but Jimmy was the principal's son, and like a preacher's son, had to do something to prove he wasn't a goody two shoes. In my case, he chose to bully me on a singular occasion, which was easy enough considering he was three years older than me. It was no big deal; just a little shoving involved and my departure from the school grounds when I had otherwise planned to stay. It wasn't enough of a reason to hate him forevermore, but on the other hand, that single incident was why I remembered him.

All the predictable things happened to us after high school; the usual marriages, divorces, bachelorhoods, and middleaged philandering; the successes and failures that surprised all the noninsightful who had so judged people on their teenage images; the plain girl who blossomed into beauty, the alcoholic who became a professor, the athletic stars who became laborers, the beauty queens who became young mothers and watched their looks fade amidst post-pregnancy obesity. Some went to college, some killed themselves. Most just settled into lower or middle class obscurity. It was the usual flux and flow.

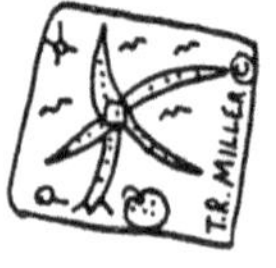

Jimmy fell on some hard times through no fault of his own. He advanced rapidly through aerospace engineering at college, immediately joined the Air Force, and maintained a dream of becoming an astronaut through all kinds of trials and tests, until suddenly his eyesight went, and he lost his status as a jet pilot overnight with not a chance in hell of ever riding the space shuttle. Other dominoes fell. His child died in a freak highway accident. His wife left him. He toughed out the Air Force at a desk job, then returned to his hometown where he flew light planes for a local car dealership.

"The only mistake Jimmy ever made was checking into that mental institution," I said.

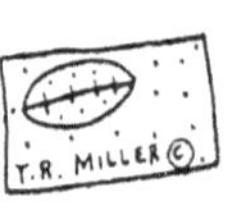

"I agree," Mom said.

"All they did was use up his insurance money, declare him cured, and set him loose. And what did he do? Just went back to smoking pot, which was harmless enough to begin with – not the cause for hysterics that Gloria went into. How can she believe all that outdated, simpleminded crap about 'pot today, heroin tomorrow?' Even in the old days, we all knew that was a joke. And now I know potheads who have done nothing but smoke weed for twenty years. I mean, things could be worse. Jimmy could be an alcoholic. Now <u>there's</u> an addiction, in the true sense of the word. In the clinical sense. The physiological change, and all that. No one ever died going cold turkey off of marijuana. And yet, which drug is legal?"

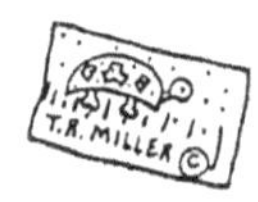

"Not to mention deadly."

"Exactly," I said.

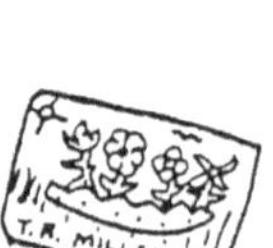

"And now he has that on his record forever. I'm telling you, these psychologists have the biggest scam going of all," Mom said, and launched into one of our favorite peeves. "They pretend their work is science, when it's really only semi-educated guesswork. All this theory, and the theories always change. Back in my day Freud was all the rage. The fact that our society trusts these people, lets

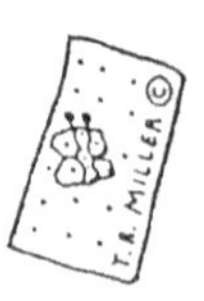

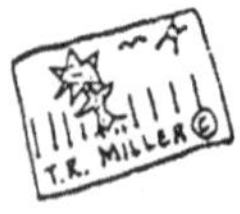

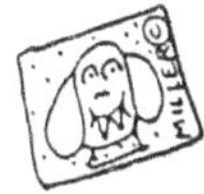

them testify in courts of law as experts, beside the forensic pathologists and DNA analysts, is the biggest hoax of the century."

"No question about it," I said. "And the lawyers have learned to play the game. Did you read about the guy's trial? The one in D.C.? About his wife's murder? Two psychologists, one for the defense, one for the prosecution, each offering exactly opposite interpretations of the same evidence. What did they do? Coach these people beforehand? Screen them in advance for their interpretations? Even if they didn't, it just goes to show you that the 'social science' of psychology is anything but a science. What bullshit."

"Isn't that the truth, " Mom said. We had had this conversation before, but it never failed to rouse our indignation. "Anyway," she continued, "I think you're right. Jimmy should never have checked into that clinic. All they did was keep him doped up."

"My, isn't that ironic," I laughed.

"Isn't it, though? And now Gloria has all of her prejudices against him confirmed."

"What is it with her, anyway?" I mused.

"Oh, Gloria's okay. She just gets into a snit about some things."

"She doesn't understand Jimmy?"

"I think that's a big part of it. He should know better than to tell her certain things. It's like that guy you were talking about, Ray."

"Oh, the one who teased Susan about how she would wreck her car. Yeah, he couldn't understand why that upset her so much. 'They're only words,' he said. Can you believe that? A guy who calls himself a writer, of all things, but fails to appreciate the power, the tremendous power, the almost mysterious power of words," I gestured emphatically. "And you can't talk to these people, either. You can't explain it to them. If they don't already understand, there's no telling them."

"That's Gloria with Jimmy," Mom said. "She just keeps . . . well, she just keeps reacting to him. Why can't she just leave him alone a little bit? I swear, she does more damage that anything Jimmy does to himself."

"Like a vicious circle."

"I'm afraid so."

"Well, the worst is over now, I hope. It looks like Jimmy is going to carry on alright now, isn't he?"

"I sure hope so."

We paused luxuriously and drank our coffee. "People think the Salem witch hunters were demented," I said, "but things really haven't changed that much, have they?"

"We think our society is so 'civilized'," Mom shook her head, "but we're still barbaric in so many ways."

I nodded, and thought back about all the strange things people have done throughout the ages; how they seemed to go into frenzies of bizarre behavior, most dangerous when in the name of righteousness.

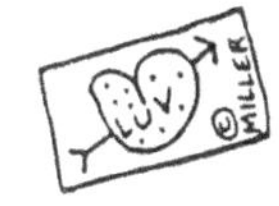

"What weird creatures humans can be," I finally said.

Will Sarvis

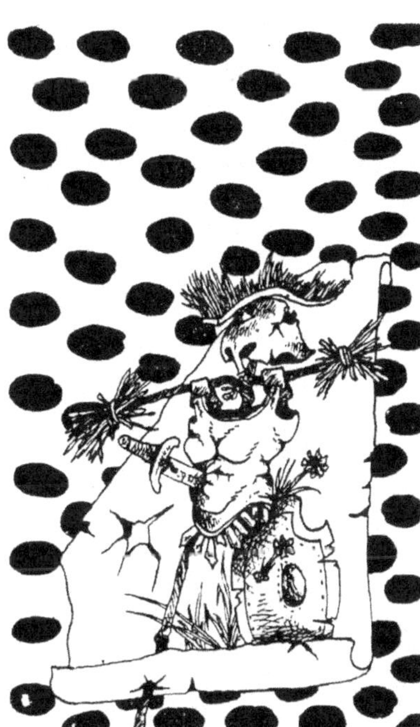

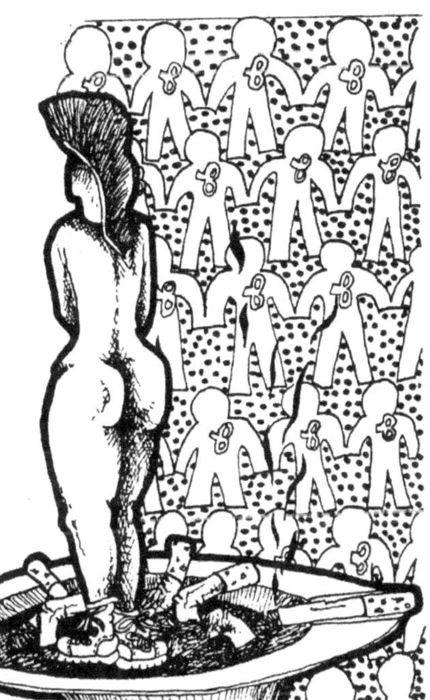

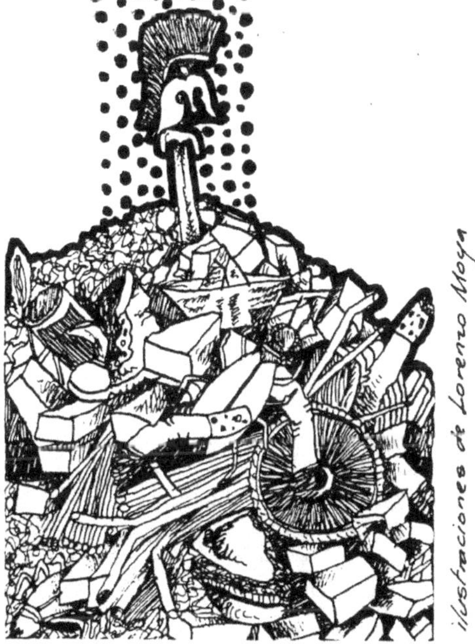

ilustraciones de Lorenzo Moya

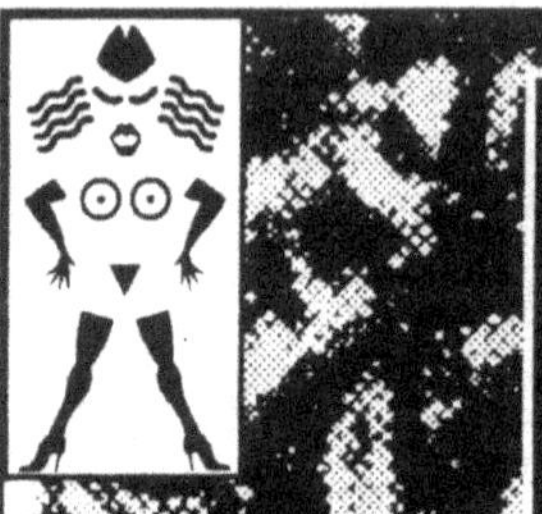

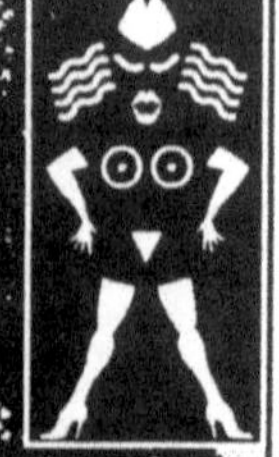

HOME COOKiNG OF GREATEST HiTS

FRANK MOORE'S REVIEW OF BARBARA GOLDEN'S MULTIMEDIA PACKAGE

containing

HOME COOKING & GREATEST HITS vol. 1

copyright September 4, 1995

BY FRANK MOORE

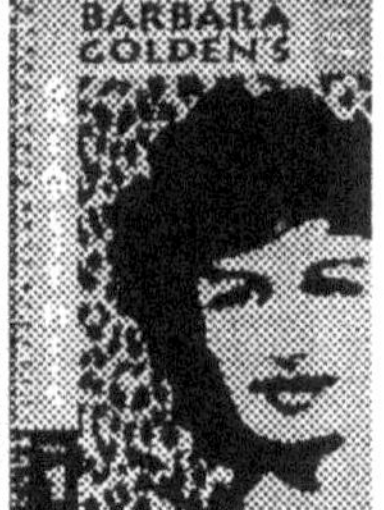

This is supposed to be a review of Barb's combination cookbook/poetry book/art book/ music-poetry CD. Already this description should tell you a lot about both Barb and this multimedia grab bag of goodies for all of the senses.

Anyway, back to what I was saying. This review can't be objective because I have known Barb for too long for that ... over 15 years. But then reviews never are. So ..

I first met Barb by mistake. The papers said L.A.'s performance artist Johanna Went was to be at a club in S.F. The dildo spears and the feminine napkin vests with tampon fringe lying on the stage didn't clue me in ... after all, Went used these kinds of props. But when the three women came onto the stage, I was pretty sure it was not Went (I couldn't be absolutely sure until the drummer who was wrapped as a mummy did a strip ... or a roll). These three middle-aged women, called the WIG BAND, were too funny, too raunchy, too direct to be "art". They were just real artists having loads of fun, going way beyond the PC taboo boundaries, singing such songs as "Trashy Girls", "Boner Boy", "Tampon Rag", "Clit Envy". These songs are among my favorites on Barb's CD. These lusty women liked sex, men, cars, sex, men, clothes, shopping, booze, giving/getting head, etc. This was/is during the time when sex lust for life was/is out of fashion unless you are a sex goddess, a "sex worker", a lesbian, or an expert at self-hand job. These are catchy little songs in different styles that stick to your brain like chewing gum. Songs by/about valley girls grown up into trashy feminists ... the only true feminists, arguably.

Then one of them ... the nicely fleshy one ... got off the stage, into the audience to play the grand piano which happened to be next to where I was sitting. While there, she made a complete costume change. A nude slut after my own heart next to me ... what a show! So I made it my business to get to know this slut, this Barbara Golden. Over the years, we have performed in each other's shows ... have double billed together ... she has had me on her radio program "Crack o' Dawn" many times. And what I have discovered is that she covers a wide range both musically and artistically.

Musically, she has a classical background, is knowledgeable in Balinese music, and highly thought of in the experimental/sound music community that is in the John Cage tradition ... her CD contains several of her sound pieces.

Then why these silly trashy dirty songs ... many of which were co-written by fellow WIGer, Johanna Poehig? Granted, "Trashy Girls" opens with a great long blues wailing horn solo. But they are still just silly, trashy, cheap songs. Or that is what they look like on the surface. But these songs, THE WIG BAND, and Barb belong to the school of what I call TACK ROCK. FRANK ZAPPA comes to mind, as does THE TUBES. Here in the Bay Area, there have been many tack rock bands ... LEILA AND THE SNAKES, COUNTRY PORN, and my own OUTRAGEOUS BEAUTY REVUE are examples of tack rock. Tack rock uses music, characters, humor, skits, taboos, sex, and anything else that is handy to satirize the accepted cultural/moral frame. Barb's best trashy songs sneakily set off major timebombs ... but the timebombs are veiled by Barb's character of a modern day Molly Bloom ... songs with a hidden musical vitality. The songs that have gone stale are the ones with subjects such as Michael Jackson, Nancy Reagan, and Oliver North that were current pop news figures. These figures had a very short shelf life. But be warned, if you listen to these songs, your brain will drive you crazy for days or weeks singing to you lines from them .... "Michael Jackson, you're so pretty ... I WANT THE ELEPHANT MAN!!!" "SAY YES SAY YES JUST SAY YES!"

But when the trashy songs flaunt the grown up valley girl Molly Bloom moral lust for life sex cars ... for everything pleasurable...Barb really takes on both the moral majority and the stick-up-their-ass "feminists" who tried their darndest to make the last 20 years vapid. In these outrageous songs, Barb offers an alternative ... the Molly Bloom trashy girl alternative. But then Barb explores the down side of the Molly Bloom that she is. In the sad song, "Back Burner", she forces herself to pull back from her young lover before he realizes that he is tired of her ... "It hurts me so much to see how you cringe from a touch." It just got human. No new age answers here. Just living, feeling, suffering, enjoying ... fully ... all with a sad, wistful hope captured in her beautiful song "Dreamer".

The CD opens and closes with long sensual/erotic poems, backed with music...poems that by themselves are worth the price of this package. I have called Barb a Molly Bloom. The poem "My Pleasure" forced that description on to me. "My Pleasure" is a day-long epic quest of one woman for pleasures ... a quest that would make James Joyce envious. Food, breakfast and lunch with only a small break for other life activities ... food is the beginning ..... in quantities only the greek goddesses could eat ... so sensual sexual...and you get the recipes right there in Barb's *Home Cooking*! Then, after this type of hunger is satisfied, this female force goes out in search of a man to bring home to satisfy some of her other hungers, after to be discarded for the solo pleasures of booze, dope, rubbing herself into dreams ... hiding in eternity from disturbing disappointments.

The book *Home Cooking* is much more than a sensual cookbook. It contains the words and music to all the songs on the CD. Many of her lusty poems and drawings, many sexy photos of Barb are also included. There is even a transcript of a radio interview of Barb running through the book in a sidebar. In other words, you get Barb, someone who blends different ingredients ... of food, art, music, and life ... to create very filling, tasty, and satisfying dishes.

"Sex, Politics, Gazpacho ... Barbara Golden is a wild woman, a political commentator, a dreamer, a mom, a slut, and hard to get a handle on ... The song titles alone would give Jesse Helms the apoplexy he so richly deserves- 'Boner Boys, Clit Envy, Tampon Rag, she careens from the grossest raunchiness to poetic austerity' Barbara Golden's tasty recipes and tasteless songs, prose/poetry, illustrations and photos. The cd is a retrospective of Goldens most popular songs and audio works." Kyle Gann, THE VILLAGE VOICE

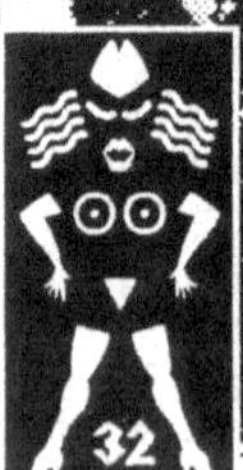

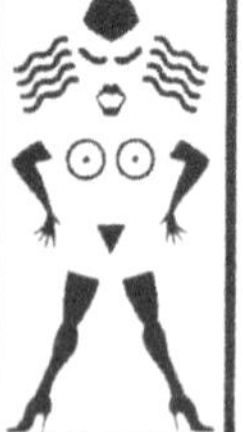

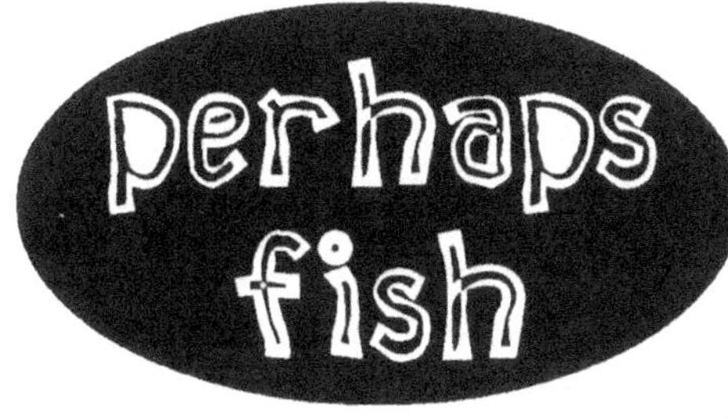

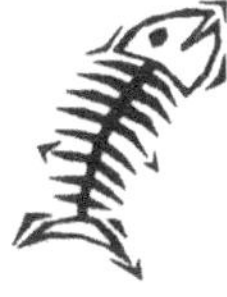

Felix is chomping grass with a hard-on... Thomas is building a farm within the walls of citiscape bustle and technological microchip existence... The farm forgets all... hope is plowed under and springs forth from dirt... belief is a pile of hopscotch horseshit... guitars sing life... candle death is bitter, sticky sweet ooze of life... Preservation is eternal... socks reek sweat and must... butts lie still... Hendrix is dead... Faith is a keyhole peek and can't see nothing good but hope assnaked bumping just out of reach... Masturbation is timeless... cum smells dead... the sea feeds earthfish to spawn in goopy globs splay foot old women must taste first to analyze: Standing on beaches of summer homes they could never afford... bending over stupid fat ankles and varicose veins plooming out all over... bending out over sticky fat two dollar plastic and rubber beach sandals stretched to their limits and reaching ignorant tourist finger down to touch ocean while standing next to a friend of same position (equal or lesser) in stature... bending next to Mable or Myra or Agnes or May and saying, bringing finger to mouth, "Why yes, Myra, I think that it is fish cum. Perhaps salmon or sea-bass - maybe even eel. Yes, Myra, it is a fat dripping gob of fish cum - Oh No! I've spilled some on my fancy new fringed fat ladies swimsuit bought in big grand shopping trip in preparation for our first real vacation in twenty years, since Grandpa died. But yes, it is fish cum and oh, so good - here, Myra, try some... see it's good for the skin to rub it in here and here... like this... let me show you... see, in the wrinkles around the face and nose and all in here where we should have suffered childbirth scars but never did cause we were too busy watching Grandpa die and baking bread and cookies we would eat alone and cry over at night. But see here, Myra, how good the fish cum makes you feel and tingle and yearn... but alone, and quiet and not for many, many years now...

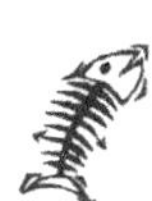

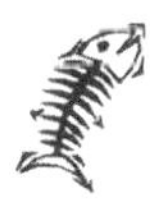

The scene fades as the two old splay foot sisters stand alone in floral print swimsuits big as circus tarps, by water too cold for swimming, and gently rub rich fish cum into each other's drooping pits and flapping holds.

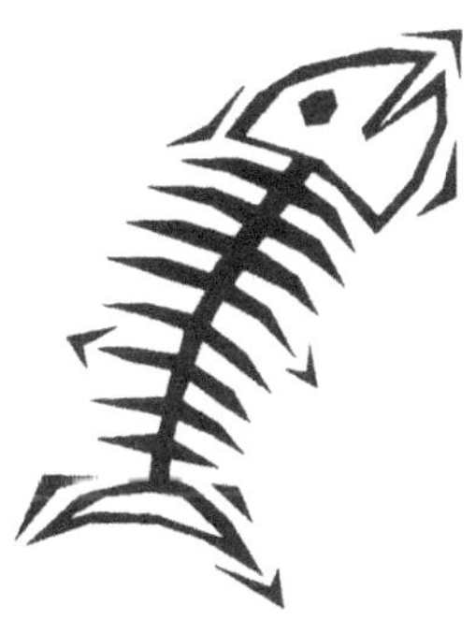

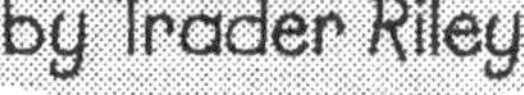

their cuddling cocoon

by Frank Moore april 15, 1995

she sits nude beside him, talking to him, with one hand rubbing him, with her other hand guiding his hand rubbing on her pussy .... relax ritual, peaceful. he curls his body around hers. licks her leg. she starts rocking, pressing his rubbing hand more firmly to her for pleasure, rocking in pleasure.

he pulls her down beside him, half on him, his leg sliding in between her legs, moving it gently to create the same warm creamy dreamy turn-on in her as her rubbing hand is creating in him. giggling licking ears, biting necks, belly deep, heart deep sounds of joy leak out of the both of them. emotional sounds of relief of having each other. kissing deeply, her hips moving, her hand rubbing, his nose in her armpit, then his tongue. she moves up, letting his tongue follow the curve of her breast to the nipple.

he pulls her all the way on top of him. he licks and sucks and enjoys and explores deeply every part of her body as she slowly slides upward. she rocks in licking pleasure. deep pleasure sound duet.

now, she begins her own downward journey of licking kissing exploring of his body. he rubs her back and head. she takes her time when she reaches his cock rubbing kissing licking. he pulls her back up to kiss, to look in her eyes. belly rubbing on belly. rocking together, giggling together, hips moving slowly passionately. two bodies with skin of warming wax, melting together into one body.

she sits up on him and rocks back and forth on his responding body, rubbing into body laughing. sometimes they look far into each other's eyes. other times they are two kids taking their first roller-coaster ride. sometimes they just close their eyes, surrendering to the tides of moaning pleasure. his hands play with her tits, belly, and pussy. she turns around on him so that she can rub his legs and feet as she rocks on him. he rubs her back with his spastic hands.

but all of a sudden, giggling he pulls her down beside him, facing away from him, so he can give her a proper deluxe back massage using not only his hands, but also his head, chin, mouth, elbows. almost like a classical pianist, playing her body. all the while, his cock firmly rubs against her butt.

she turns toward him, taking him in her arms, wrapping her legs around him, pulling him close deep within their cuddling cocoon, to talk about how they can always be together in their small warm world.

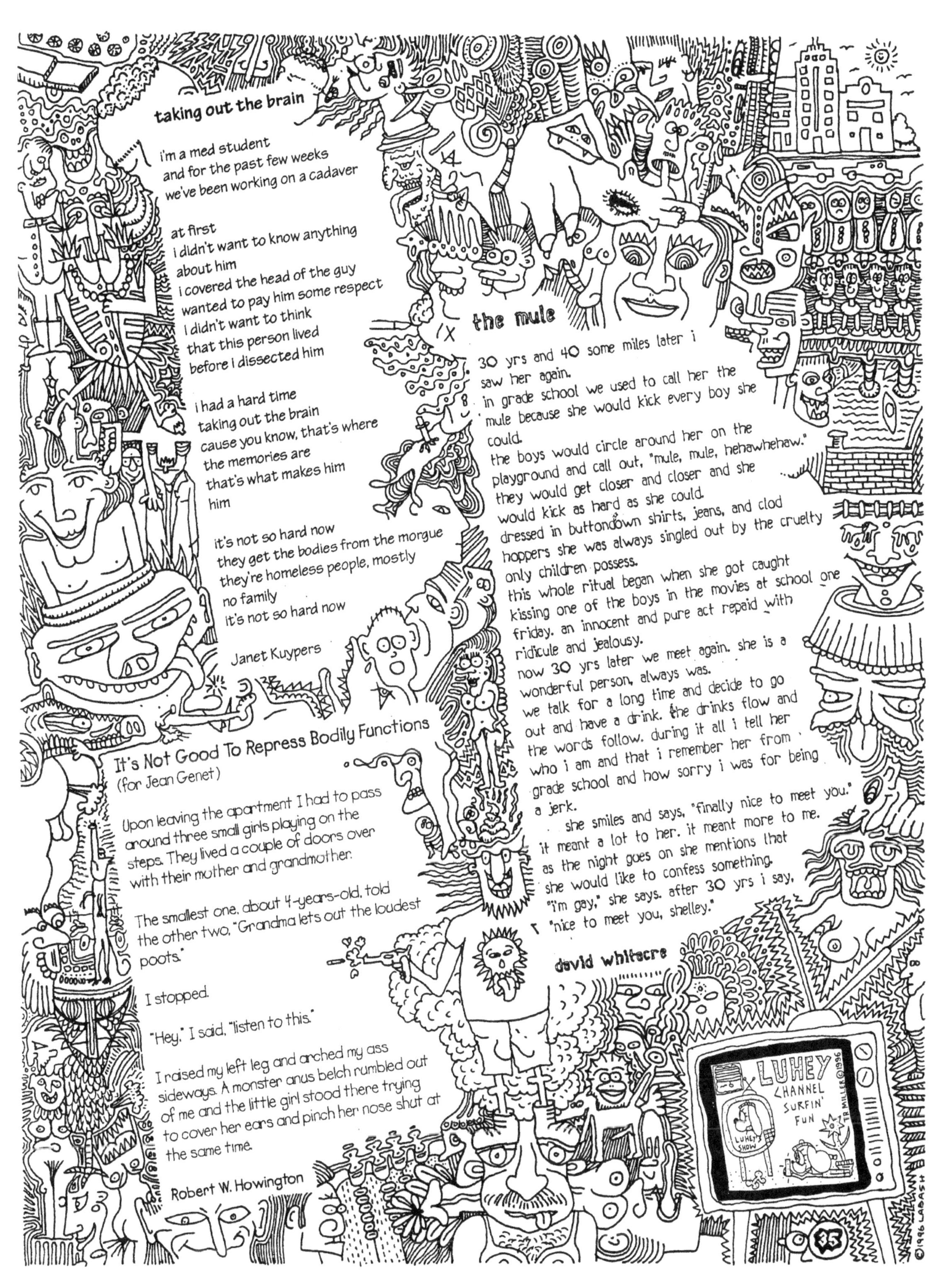

taking out the brain

i'm a med student
and for the past few weeks
we've been working on a cadaver

at first
i didn't want to know anything
about him
i covered the head of the guy
wanted to pay him some respect
i didn't want to think
that this person lived
before i dissected him

i had a hard time
taking out the brain
cause you know, that's where
the memories are
that's what makes him
him

it's not so hard now
they get the bodies from the morgue
they're homeless people, mostly
no family
it's not so hard now

Janet Kuypers

the mule

30 yrs and 40 some miles later i
saw her again.
in grade school we used to call her the
mule because she would kick every boy she
could.
the boys would circle around her on the
playground and call out, "mule, mule, hehawhehaw."
they would get closer and closer and she
would kick as hard as she could.
dressed in buttondown shirts, jeans, and clod
hoppers she was always singled out by the cruelty
only children possess.
this whole ritual began when she got caught
kissing one of the boys in the movies at school one
friday. an innocent and pure act repaid with
ridicule and jealousy.
now 30 yrs later we meet again. she is a
wonderful person, always was.
we talk for a long time and decide to go
out and have a drink. the drinks flow and
the words follow. during it all i tell her
who i am and that i remember her from
grade school and how sorry i was for being
a jerk.
she smiles and says, "finally nice to meet you."
it meant a lot to her. it meant more to me.
as the night goes on she mentions that
she would like to confess something.
"i'm gay," she says. after 30 yrs i say,
"nice to meet you, shelley."

david whitacre

It's Not Good To Repress Bodily Functions

(for Jean Genet)

Upon leaving the apartment I had to pass around three small girls playing on the steps. They lived a couple of doors over with their mother and grandmother.

The smallest one, about 4-years-old, told the other two, "Grandma lets out the loudest poots."

I stopped.

"Hey," I said, "listen to this."

I raised my left leg and arched my ass sideways. A monster anus belch rumbled out of me and the little girl stood there trying to cover her ears and pinch her nose shut at the same time.

Robert W. Howington

POEM UPON RETURNING

recently took a ten
day vacation in the
Portland-Salem area
of Oregon.
while there, away from
this machine, I had no
desire to write,
and this struck
me as odd,
usually away from
this machine I
get
poem ideas,
little thoughts,
or lines.
this made me wonder if
my writing was somehow
connected to this
machine this
apartment or this town,
the heat of it
the simple slow
way of life.
maybe I took
a vacation as a
writer as well
as a person.
this has me wondering
what, if anything,
would happen if I
moved up there as I have
planned on doing. I
suppose that soon after
I would begin
writing again, and though
my writing may change
with the scenery it
probably wouldn't get any
better, it might
even get worse.

Mark Begley
Fresno, California

UNTITLED

have one friend
into the power
and scope of
God,
one who's
passion is
photography,
one is a music
nut and very much
in love
with his
girlfriend.
me...
I really have
nothing to occupy
my mind
nothing to fill
empty spaces of time,
I tap these keys
on
occasion and
kid myself that
something is happening
if just a small
something.

Mark Begley
Fresno, California

7/25/94

Hello Frank Moore,

Got your letter today, thanks for taking the poems UNTITLED and POEM UPON RETURNING. Glad I got them to ya. Your acceptance comes same day as two rejections, about the right ratio, or at least consistent for me. Last acceptance by WORMWOOD REVIEW and just about creamed in my poetry jeans over it.
Also wanted to say thanks for the speedy reply and the extra shit ya sent. I can always tell the humans from the shits in the poetry scene. HUMANS: reply quickly, personally, kindly and send free stuff along. SHITS: reply slowly, impersonally and rudely. So thank god there is another human named Frank Moore on the scene.
Well hell thanks again, look forward to gettin' the mag.

Stay free,
Mark Begley

SCANNING UNDERGROUND POETS CONVENTION ZINE, WHITE BOY LEARNS OF POET WHO IS CENSORED BY POET-MODERATOR AT READING IN BORDERS 4 DOING THE F-WORD, EDITOR OF ZINE WRITES IT'S NOT CENSORSHIP BUT COMMON SENSE, CAUSING A UNCOMMON WB 2 GO 2 BORDERS

1. he's indignant
2. he's outraged
3. he screams FUCK
4. he strips naked

AUDIENCE, ON VIEWING
WBs BODY & SOUL BARED

a. gasps
b. gags
c. regurgitates

SO MUCH FOR THAT PROTEST
SAYS WB ON WAY 2 THE BAR

Paul Weinman

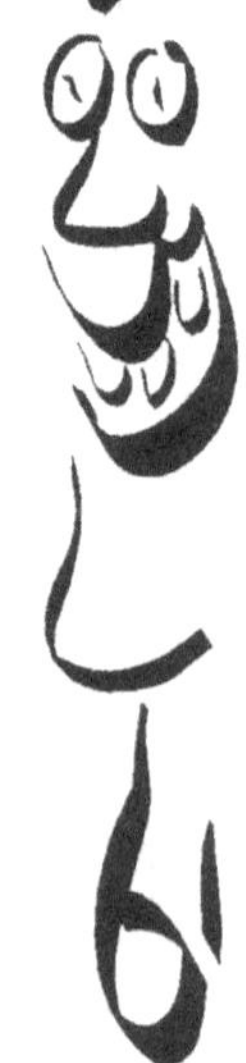

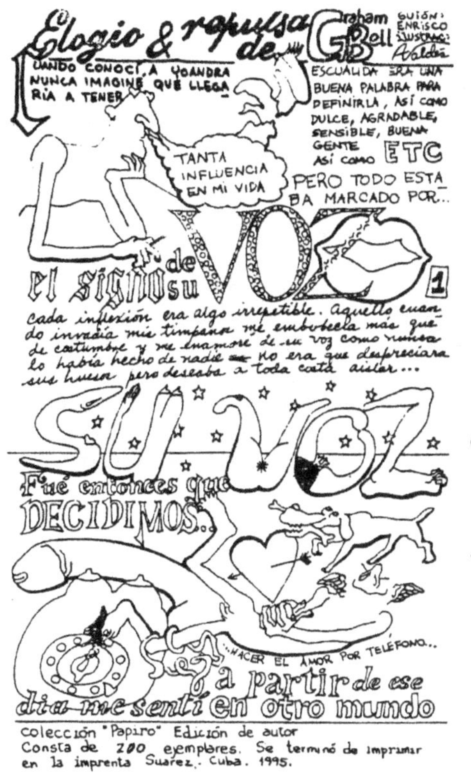

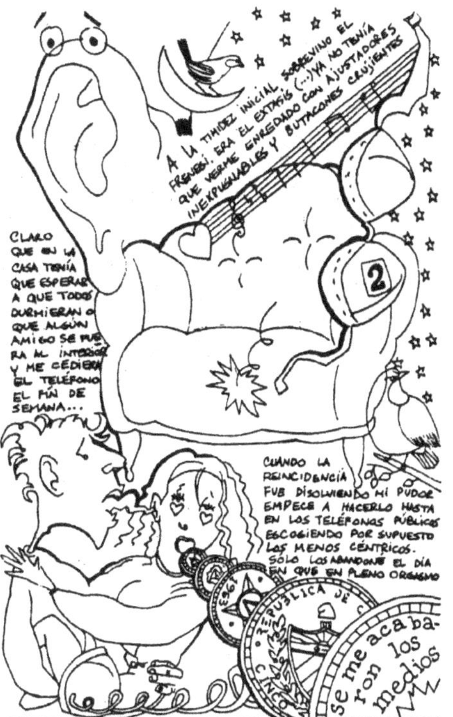

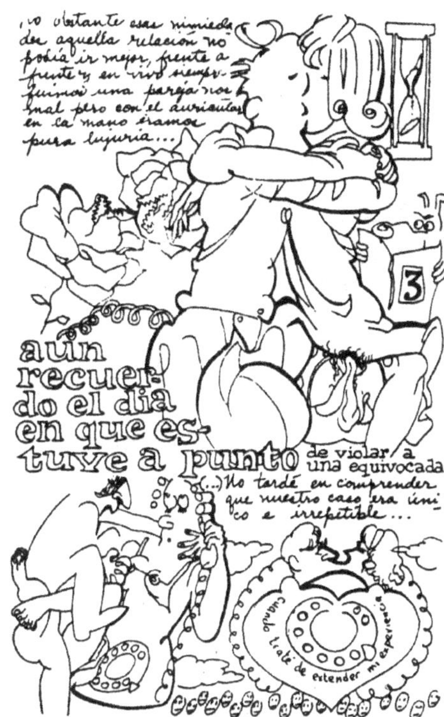

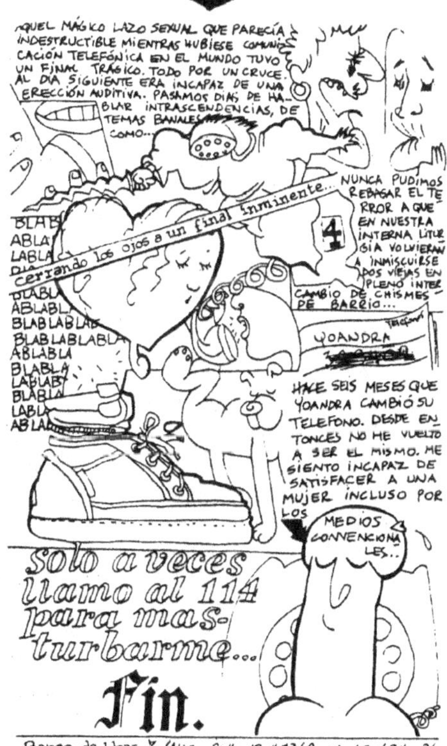

FUCK MUSIC

The ceiling the light the walls
the ugly wallpaper like pictures
drawn in skulls martians frozen
that somehow smile on us
benevolently all shred scraps
of paper the present unwrapped
over your shoulder by the hungry fingers
of my screams that reach out
to lay cold shadows on the neighbor's
empty pillows but you only you
can see that my screams
are white long fibers of light
from your eyes reach down my throat
performing within me the echo
of my scream dance all all
that we believed to be normal
and true was the thin skin
and we have torn it we
have charmed our daily consciousness
like so many rats with fuck music
led away we at this instant
as the currents rocket through me
are sparks in the unknown pearls
from an endless ribbon leaping out
we are free we are burning
fire of life unconquered unafraid

Ericka Slayer

Composition in Late Autumn

dearest darling cut thru my thoughts
beyond cherotic license
a place finite
where everybody is a STAR
and every thing
is an open secret.

speak to me in the most
quiet of places
i need the comfort of yur NO noise
yur pur fect ecletic
soft/ soft whispers
of unbabylon

yur hands on my face.

Pure delight of the bright dawn
as so many coloured leaves
fractures the tense brilliance
of your grey blue eyes
and becomes
my constant catechism.

There is an incredible softeness
in the heart of your movements
a tai chi of the mind:

We touch fingers
and watch the world change

out into
the pure light
of leaves spinning on pavement
as another star
fades quietly
into the white.

© Noni Howard

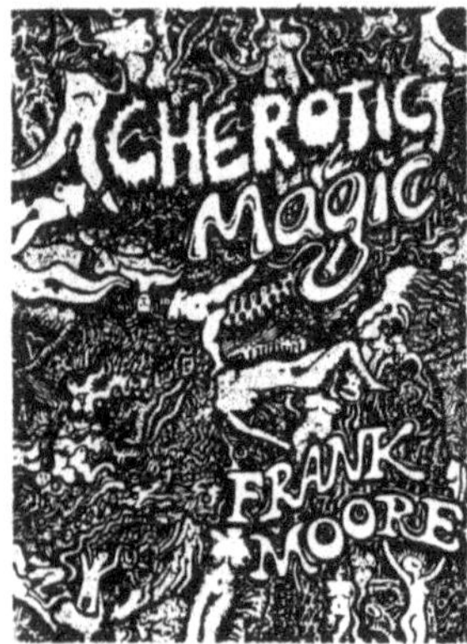

cherotic magic **$15**

A MAJOR ATTEMPT TO INTRODUCE A POWERFUL SYSTEM OF MAGIC INTO OUR MODERN WESTERN EVERYDAY LIFE, THEREBY EXPLOSIVELY EXPANDING SUCH CONCEPTS AS SEX, HUMAN RELATIONSHIPS. THE CLEAR, DOWN-TO-EARTH TEXT IS AMPLIFIED BY THE NON-LINEAR TRANCE ILLUSTRATIONS BY LABASH.

published 1990

out of isolation **$1**

THE PROSE POEM ON WHICH THE VIDEO out of isolation IS BASED.

published 1985

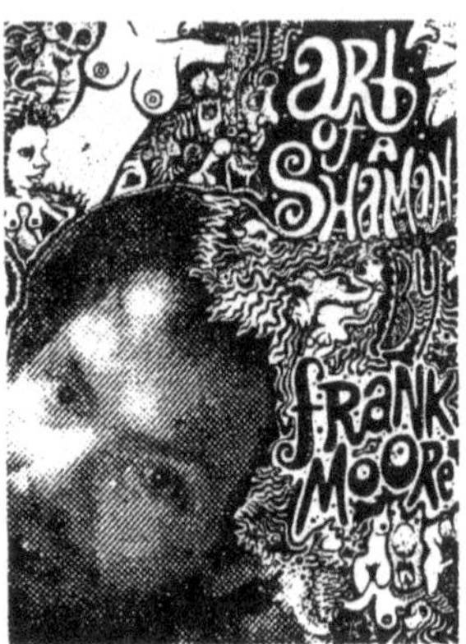

art of a shaman **$5**

IN art of a shaman, ORIGINALLY A LECTURE PRESENTED AT N.Y.U., FRANK MOORE EXPLORES PERFORMANCE AND ART IN GENERAL TERMS OF THEM BEING A MAGICAL WAY TO EFFECT CHANGE IN THE WORLD. HE LOOKS AT PERFORMANCE AS AN ART OF MELTING ACTION, RITUALISTIC, SHAMANISTIC DOINGS/PLAYINGS. BY USING HIS CAREER AND LIFE AS A "BASELINE", MOORE EXPLAINS THE DYNAMIC PLAYING WITHIN THE CONTEXT OF REALITY SHAPING. HE BRINGS IN CONCEPTS FROM MODERN PHYSICS, MYTHOLOGY, AND PSYCHOLOGY. COVER BY LABASH.

published 1991

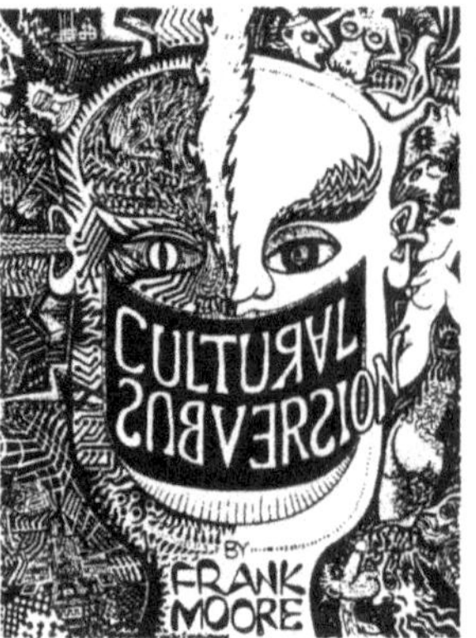

cultural subversion **$1**

PERSONAL, ANARCHICAL TECHNOLOGIES SUCH AS XEROGRAPHY, VCR, FAXS, ETC., ARE EXAMINED IN cultural subversion BY FRANK MOORE AS THE MEANS BY WHICH ORDINARY PEOPLE CAN TAKE BACK THE CONTROL OF COMMUNICATIONS AND CREATIVITY FROM THE CENTRAL POWER COMBINE.

published 1992

art of living **$10**

A GUIDE TO DOWN-TO-EARTH SPIRITUALITY AS CHANNELLED BY FRANK MOORE.

published 1987

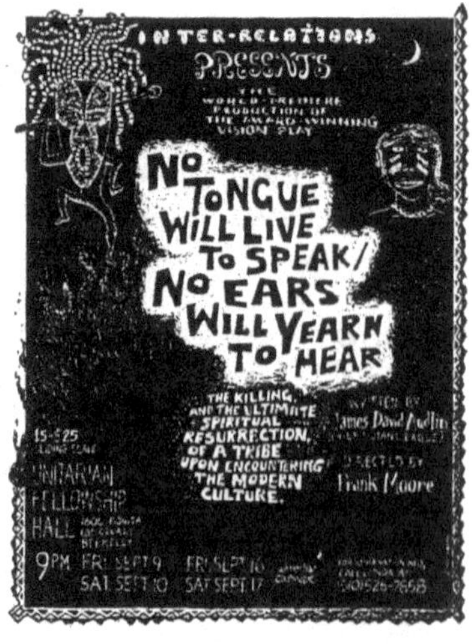

vision theater **$5**

BY JAMES D. AUDLIN & FRANK MOORE

no tongue will live to speak/no ears will yearn to hear IS A PLAY WRITTEN BY JAMES D. AUDLIN (CHIEF DISTANT EAGLE) AND DIRECTED IN 1994 BY FRANK MOORE IN BERKELEY, CALIFORNIA. VISION THEATER IS A BOOK MADE UP OF THE DAILY E-MAIL CONVERSATIONS BETWEEN FRANK AND JIM...BOTH AS DIRECTOR AND PLAYWRIGHT AND AS TWO SHAMANS ... OVER THE YEAR-PLUS THAT IT TOOK FRANK TO PRODUCE/ DIRECT THE PLAY. IT IS AN IN-DEPTH EXAMINATION OF THE BACKSTAGE PROCESS OF DOING A SHAMANISTIC DRAMA (OR ANY DRAMA FOR THAT MATTER)...THE TRICKS, THE PITFALLS, THE DYNAMICS...AND HOW EVERYDAY LIFE AND THE MAGICALLY FRAMED THEATER EFFECT EACH OTHER.

copyrighted 1994

by Frank Moore

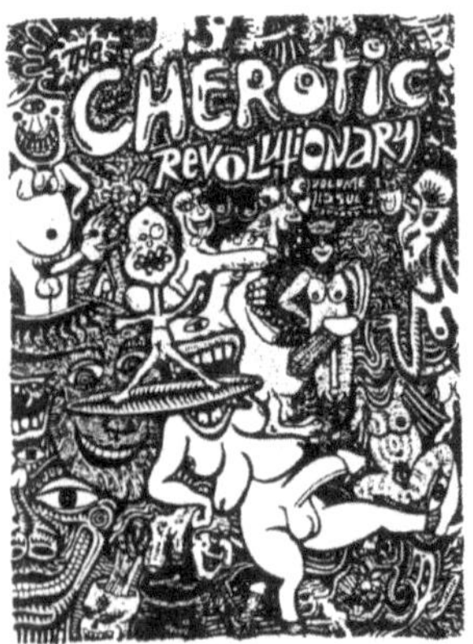

TC(r) #1, *january 1992* **$5**

POEMS BY **KAREN FINLEY, NONI HOWARD, TRACY MOSTOVOY, FRANK MOORE, JACK FOLEY** AND **JESSE BEAGLE** ARTWORK BY **LABASH** • PHOTOS BY **TRACY MOSTOVOY** AND **ERIC KROLL** CARTOON BY **WILL OF THE WISP**

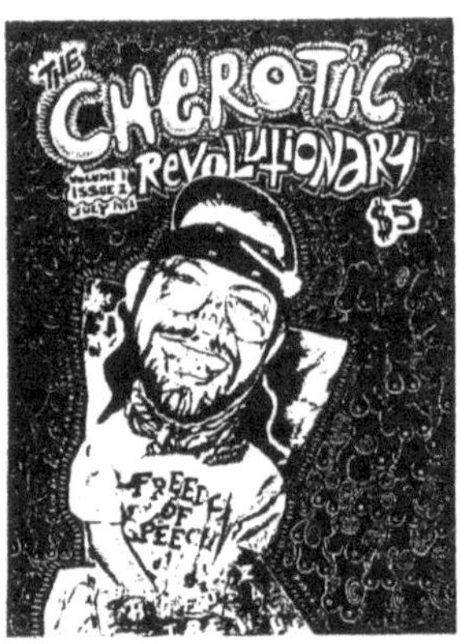

TC(r) #2, *july 1992* **$5**

ESSAYS BY **FRANK MOORE, CURTIS YORK** AND **KYLE GRIFFITH** • ARTWORK BY **LEE KAY, H.R. GIGER, PETER PETRISKO, JR., JOHN SEABURY** AND **LABASH** • PHOTO BY **KEVIN RICE** • POEM BY **BARNABY CHANCELLOR**

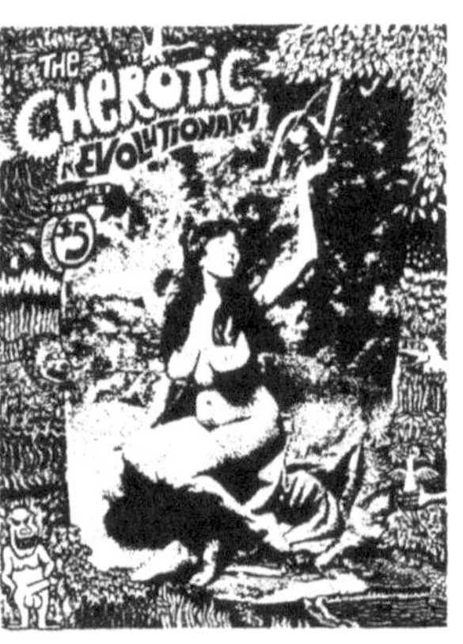

TC(r) #3, *april 1993* **$5**

POEMS BY **R. (DIXI) COHN, ANNIE SPRINKLE, MERLE TOFER, JESSE BEAGLE** ESSAYS BY **VERONICA VERA, LUNA SANGUINE** AND **FRANK MOORE** • PHOTOS BY **RICHARD SILVARNES, WINK VAN KEMPEN, ROBERT MAPLETHORPE, ANNIE SPRINKLE, MARC TRUNZ, AMY ARDREY** AND **JAN DEEN** • ARTWORK BY **LABASH** AND **JOHN SEABURY**

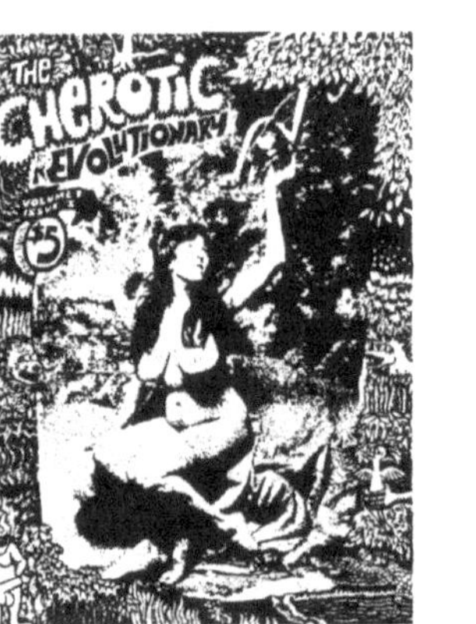
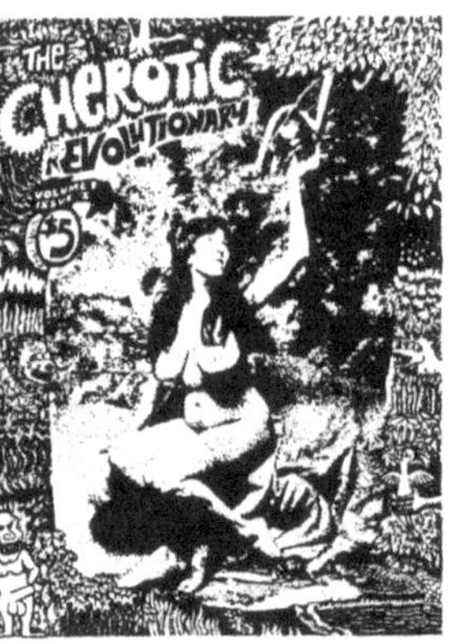

TC(r) #4, *january 1994* **$5**

POEMS BY **ANA CHRISTY, FRANK MOORE, STEVEN KAUFFMAN, NONI HOWARD** AND **ROBERT W. HOWINGTON** • SHORT STORY BY **CAROL A. QUEEN** • ESSAYS BY **TRACE DE HAVEN, JAMES DAVID AUDLIN (CHIEF DISTANT EAGLE), PROF. CURTIS** AND **FRANK MOORE** • ARTWORK BY **JOANNA PETTIT, JOHN SEABURY** AND **LABASH** PHOTO BY **NINA GLASER** • PHOTOS OF **LINDA MONTANO** BY **ANNIE SPRINKLE**

TC(r) ISSN 1083-8872

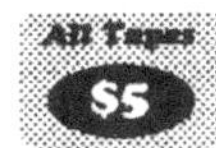

by Frank Moore's Chero Company

body music
EXPLORING THE HUMAN BODY AS MUSICAL INSTRUMENT.
90 minutes

inter-rhythms
PRIMAL MUSIC CREATED FOR FRANK MOORE'S RITUAL PERFORMANCES.
90 minutes

nude cave soundtrack
THE NONLINEAR ELECTRONIC MUSIC COMPOSED AND PERFORMED BY FRANK MOORE FOR THE FEATURE LENGTH VIDEO. *110 minutes*

rock of passion
THE SOUNDTRACK OF the outrageous horror show, FRANK THE ROCKSTAR SINGS HIS HEART OUT, LITERALLY COVERING THE GREAT HITS OF ROCK, COUNTRY, AND HEAVY METAL ... INCLUDING SUCH SMASHES AS i am woman, i got you babe, AND hand of doom ...

trance rap
WRITTEN BY FRANK MOORE AND SUNG/CHANTED BY MICHAEL LABASH WITH A BACKGROUND OF BODY MUSIC, trance rap IS AN AUDIO INTRODUCTION TO CHEROTIC MAGIC COVERING SUCH SUBJECTS AS eroplay, the plot of fragmentation AND magic art. ALSO INCLUDED IS THE POEM wrapping/rocking.
30 minutes

To order call or write:
Inter-Relations, P.O.Box 11445, Berkeley, CA 94712
(510) 526.7858
e-mail: fmoore@lanminds.com

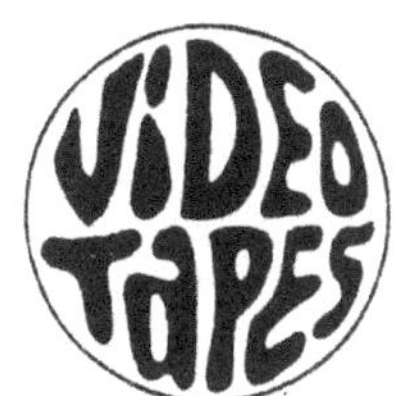

by Frank Moore

All Tapes $30

fairy tales can come true
THIS IS A FILM ABOUT RELATIONSHIPS AND DISABILITY STARRING FRANK MOORE, WHO HAS BEEN DISABLED SINCE BIRTH WITH CEREBRAL PALSY. IT IS A HUMOROUS, YET REALISTIC LOOK AT HOW TO ESTABLISH RELATIONSHIPS BY CHANGING NEGATIVE SELF IMAGE.
copyrighted 1981 *35 minutes*

erotic play
THIS VIDEO EXPLORES WHAT HAPPENS WHEN PEOPLE OF ALL TYPES AND AGES ARE GIVEN A CHANCE TO RETURN TO BEING A KID AGAIN. A SIMPLE GAME OF DRESS-UP BECOMES A POWERFUL METAPHOR FOR DROPPING TABOOS, RELEASING CREATIVE EMOTION, AND FOR DRAMATIC CHANGE. AS A RESULT, AN INNOCENT EROTICISM IS FOUND... AS WELL AS GETTING INTIMATE WITH 60 HUMANS.
copyrighted 1983 *84 minutes*

outrageous dream
A SURREAL, VISUAL POEM OF FOUND IMAGES.
copyrighted 1984 *41 minutes*

the nude cave
AN EROTIC, SURREALISTIC VIDEO DREAM THAT COMBINES NON LINEAR IMAGES AND FRANK'S ORIGINAL MUSIC SCORE.
copyrighted 1984 *113 minutes*

out of isolation
A SURREAL EROTIC EXAMINATION OF AN INTIMATE RELATIONSHIP OF NEED. STARRING FRANK MOORE AND LINDA SIBIO.
copyrighted 1989 *105 minutes*

the outrageous beauty revue
THIS RAW VIDEO DOCUMENTS THE TACKY, MUSICAL, OVER-THE-EDGE COMEDY REVUE THAT FRANK CREATED, DIRECTED AND PERFORMED IN. THE SHOW RAN ON A WEEKLY BASIS FOR THREE AND ONE HALF YEARS AT THE MABUHAY GARDENS IN SAN FRANCISCO IN ADDITION TO A NUMBER OF OTHER NORTHERN CALIFORNIA AND NEVADA PERFORMANCES. FRANK PERFORMED ALONG WITH THE THIRTY PEOPLE WHO MADE UP HIS THEATRE GROUP, "the theatre of human melting."
copyrighted 1980 *approx. 30 minutes*

chero collage
ATTEMPTS TO CAPTURE THE TRANCE STATE OF LIVE, SHAMANISTIC PERFORMANCE COMBINING FOOTAGE OF SEVERAL OF chero company's RITUALS INTO A REALITY-WARPING VIDEO.
copyrighted 1992 *27 minutes*

the outrageous horror show
A LIVE CABARET SHOW THAT BREAKS THROUGH THE LIMITING TABOOS, THROUGH MESSY NIGHTMARES, INTO THE DREAMS OF ALL POSSIBILITIES.
copyrighted 1992 *32 minutes*

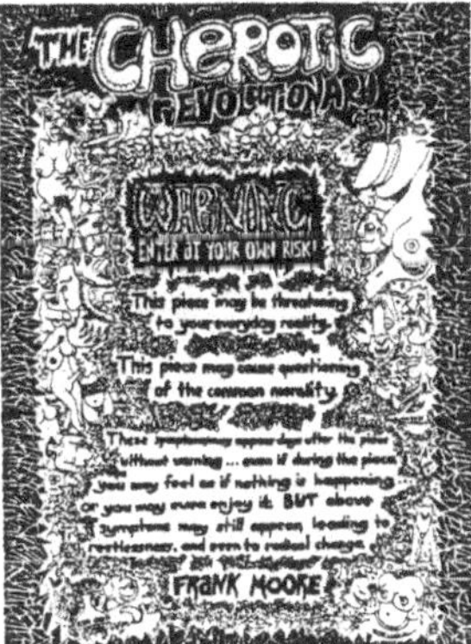

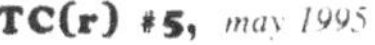

TC(r) #5, *may 1995* **$5**

POEMS BY **JESSE BEAGLE, AL CUNNINGHAM, ROBERT W. HOWINGTON, GEORGE KAUFFMAN, ANA CHRISTY, ANTLER, MOLLY HOLTZCHLAG** AND **ELLIOTT** • ESSAYS BY **FRANK MOORE, JAMES D. AUDLIN (CHIEF DISTANT EAGLE)** AND **PETER RIDEN** • SHORT STORY BY **BARBARA SMITH** • REVIEW OF **ANNIE SPRINKLE'S PERFORMANCE** BY **FRANK MOORE** • ARTWORK BY **LABASH** • CARTOONS BY **T.R.MILLER.** PHOTOS BY **PETER C. TURNER** AND **LINDA MAC** • INTERVIEW WITH **PAUL KRASSNER** BY **FRANK MOORE.**

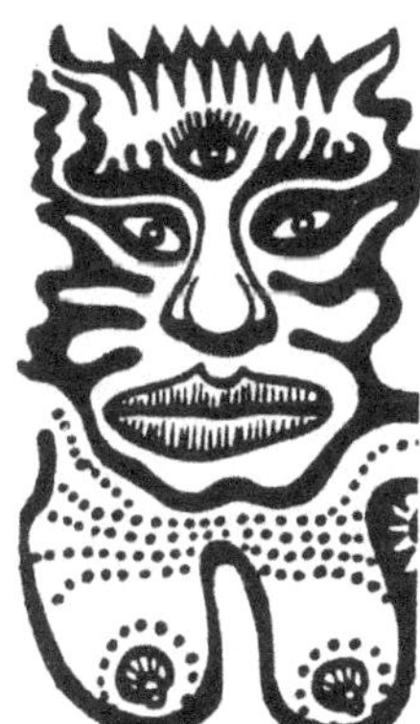

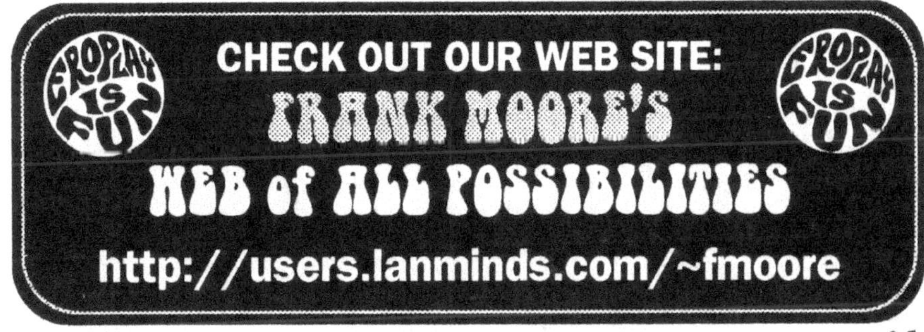

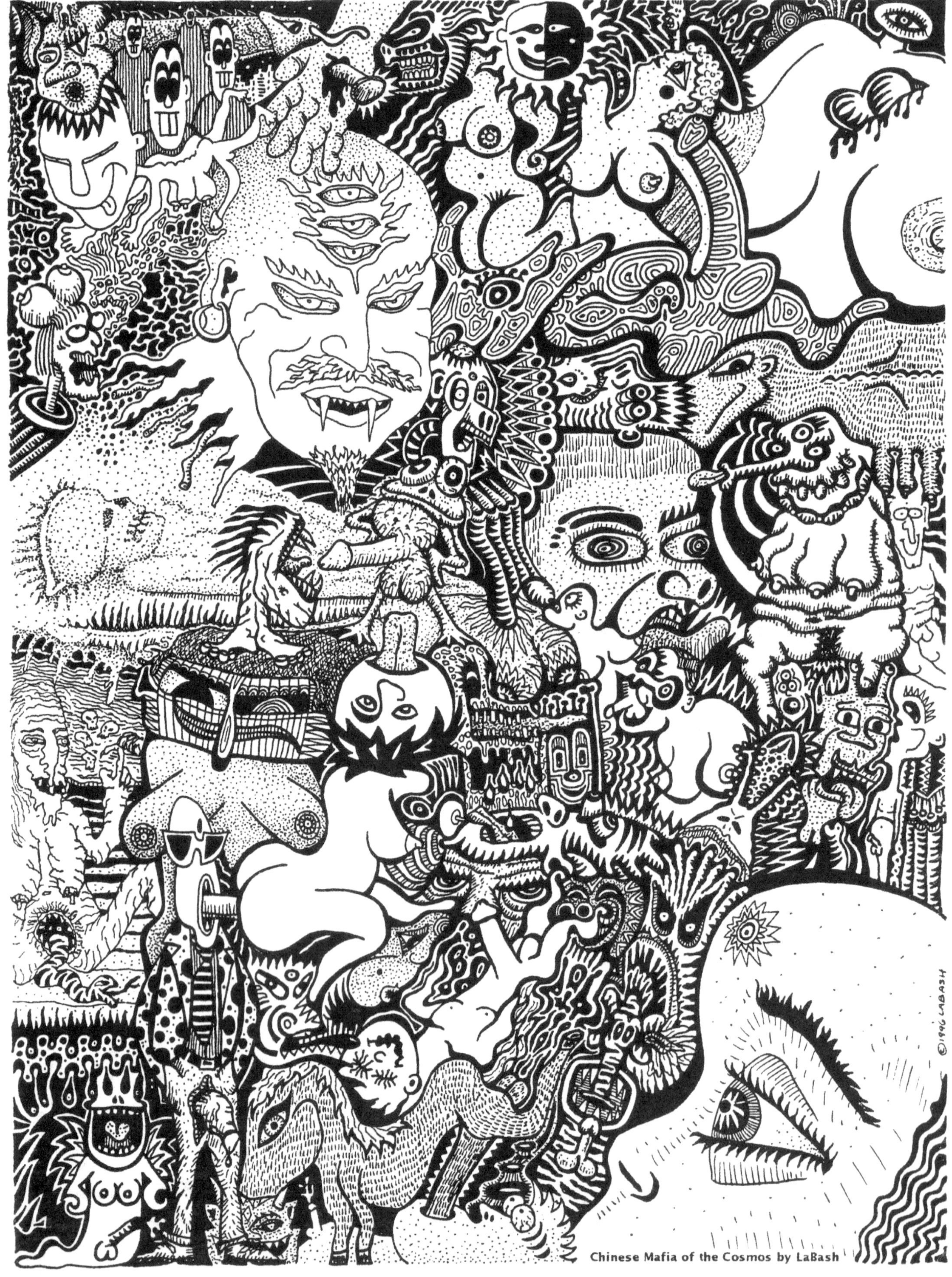

Chinese Mafia of the Cosmos by LaBash

REVIEWS

The Cherotic (r)Evolutionary #6
1996

"When Frank Moore isn't organizing performances and workshops about tribal sex magic, he's producing this zine full of photographs, poetry, stories, psychedelia, and rants. Nice printing makes these photos really stand out. We get some tranquil nudes from Eric Boutilier-Brown, erotic nudes from Tony Ryan, and some playful nudes from blind photographer Flo Fox. I enjoyed all the poems -- some erotic, some angry, some revealing -- especially Frank's poem about open mike events. Also a page each from H.R. Giger and T.R. Miller."
R. Seth Friedman, Factsheet Five

"This is a 40 page, full-sized, b&w publication. For those of you who aren't already aware of Frank Moore and the wonderful work that he has done over the past few decades, The Cherotic (r)Evolutionary is a great way to become enlightened about him. Frank has a 'disability' that makes it impossible for him to speak or to have control of his body movements. He communicates by pointing at letters and words on a board that is attached to his wheelchair. Despite these apparent limitations, Frank has authored books, written numerous performance art pieces, performed on stage, written/directed films, and created a community of people who work to further his ideas.

Frank is particularly interested in the human body and the ways in which people relate to themselves and each other. He has created numerous rituals that involve 'eroplay' as a tool for breaking down barriers between its participants. 'Eroplay' is a term that Frank coined in order to describe the act of playful, non-sexual touching. This kind of ritual enables the participants to reach a point beyond sexuality (it is similar in many ways to rituals described in the Kama Sutra and other writings that strive to help people reach a transcendent state through prolonged physical stimulation).

The Cherotic (r)Evolutionary is a publication that is put together by Frank and the people who share his vision. Every page is densely covered with intricate, lovingly detailed illustrations, photos, and writings. Extremely detailed line art by LaBash fills many of the pages. There are also some beautiful photographs of nude images (not of the pornographic variety), poems, stories, pen and ink sketches by H.R.Giger, and essays on sexuality/the human body. You will want to read this publication from cover to cover. The Cherotic (r)Evolutionary is obviously the product of people who love what they do. Highly recommended."
Mike Hovancsek, EIDOS Magazine, Volume 9, Number 4, issue 36, 1997

REVIEWS CONTINUED...

" 'We live in an age of whining people who think they are owed something, who think they have the right to not be offended...' Those are Frank Moore's own words as he simply sums up why anyone should be doing any creative project. No bodies going to give you anything, you got to build it for yourself. This issue has a beautiful cover by John Seabury of two women at a crowning point. Layout, art, photos and text are all supreme. For Frank Moore's rants on free speech and being sex positive send $5...."
Dr. Ducky DooLittle's Hypnotic Releases, Catalog #2

"Frank's really outdone himself this time. What caught my attention are all the great photos from Flo Fox, Tony Ryan, and Eric Boutilier-Brown. I know these pics of nude women are supposed to be artistic and all, but 'scuse me while I say 'woo woo!' You also have H.R. Giger (!), elliott, Ana Christy, Ericka Slayer, Paul Weinman, and Robert W. Howington among others. Don't forget LaBash's art on the back. That 'Application to Live in the South' will probably piss some people off, but it's still funny. The layout really burns a streak up the mountain, but without being overbearing like some of those slick craprags. As much fun to look at as it is to read."
Bleeding Velvet Octopus #6

"One of the best layouts around offering up some fiction by Charles Chaim Wax, a ton of clothing optional photography that is artistically presented, not porno, a little poetry, a hysterical application to live in the south, info on SF's 848 Community Space that sounds a bit like ABC No Rio but more of an artist community, a story by Elmira, NY's Dr. Bryan D. Reddlick, H.R. Giger pictures, a transcription of an open mic rant by frank moore, and some art by LaBash that titillates. $5 and worth it."
The Flashing Astonisher, Fall Issue #8

"Frank Moore, with Linda Mac have now come out with #6 and it's as thick and big as The Affiliate. Our friend Al Cunningham (a more favorable Cunningham) is making the page of TC(r) with thoughts we did pass along in The Affiliate. Tony Ryan's B&W pictorial is a treat. Beautiful women presented with class. Much in."
The Affiliate, December 1996

REVIEWS CONTINUED...

"Frank Moore and Friends' TC(r) is a sexual/mind/body/spiritual freedom zine with a psychedelic, free love feel to it. Different mediums employed are prose and verse writings, photography, and lots of illustrations, many of which were created by LaBash, who was so generous as to contribute visual material to this issue of OPEN FORUM. Frank, too, is in here. Thanks a lot guys, I deeply appreciate it!

One theme that is addressed throughout TC(r) is the problem of there being practically no true diversity in society, consequently, there is an urgent need for nonconformist action. A good example of how some of the visual imagery and word artists in TC(r) think on this problem is George Kauffman's short poem, Madness Manifesto, he writes, 'Nobody is mad anymore. Everybody is certified sane.' And, 'Madness comes to those who want it...Go mad and save the world!' He also relates that the so-called 'sane' are the ones who have created suffering, wars, and early death for millions. Yes, the so-called 'sane', the Masters and their obedient sheep-like herds, are in fact insane, and many who are labeled eccentric, mentally ill and insane are in fact sane. Dare to be different, dare to be insane!

Some other stimulating treats: On the front cover there is an attention-grabbing drawing of a pair of Siamese twins making love. Flo Fox's penis photos. Tony Ryan's photography, one photo shows a nude female with creamy white ice-cream dripping on and down her breasts, tummy, and between her legs. Anarchist Unru Lee's essay on 'pleasure activism' versus 'class war activism,' he promotes a combination of both, includes some words from Henry Miller, who in 1966 said that sex lib, '...should only be one aspect of a movement toward much larger freedom, to think and act freely and creatively, in every domain!' HR Giger's pen & ink sketches of females getting gang-banged by monkish males, the sketches remind me of the education of Justine. Frank's A Rant On An Open Mike where he '...goes after the nice people who never asked where the trains were going, boxcars filled with people...after the nice people who keep going to work after seeing their friends missing, after hearing rumors of blacklist and blackball...' And lots, lots more!

TC(r) encourages one to experiment and expand one's consciousness and parameters of reality, also to be playful and kind, which doesn't mean being a pushover, quite the contrary - be assertive and live your life as YOU deem fit!"
OPEN FORUM #12, December 1996

REVIEWS CONTINUED...

"This zine combines photography, excellent drawings, poetry and short stories to create a pulsing, shimmering, emotionally charged whole. It includes a catalog of all offerings audio visual and literary. Pages are big and copies are clear, it's about 50 pages. Artists and writers include Frank Moore, Janet Kuypers, LaBash, Eric Boutilier-Brown, and Ana Christy. Visit their web site."
Crimson Leer, 4th issue

"The Cherotic (r)Evolutionary is an irregularly published, very underground, independent, alt.culture (art & lit) zine. Each issue is always jammed with unique, mind-expanding, consciousness-raising material. TC(r)#6 is no exception.

Publisher/Editor Frank Moore is a self-described "cultural outlaw" who says, "It's flattering to think my voice is a subversive weapon". Moore explains: TC(r) "is a xeroxed, black and white zine about 'the edge' for and by poeple on the edge...published irregularly...We don't sell subscriptions, to avoid tying ourselves down to a rigid publication schedule or magazine size. We want to remain free...."

This issue includes illustrations, poems, photographs, artwork, cartoons, commentary, reviews, country song lyrics, a poem called "Fuck Music" and lots more. We especially liked George Kauffman's "Madness Manifesto, 1996"; Beast Quarterly's "Application To Live In The South"; Tony Ryan's, Flo Fox's and Eric Boutilier-Brown's erotic photographs; Jesse's Blues, a poem about Jesse Helms by Elliott and Al Cunningham's poem about loneliness.

TC(r) also sells his books, videos and audio tapes on a variety of specialized subjects like: the human body as a musical instrument, primal music for ritual performances, trance rap, erotic play (eroplay), the nude cave, over-the-edge comedy, human need, cultural subversion, art of a shaman, art of living, vision theatre and much more.

Back issues of TC(r) are still available and letters of comment from readers are "heartily encouraged."

TC(r) will appeal to those seeking to discover a forum for the diverse range of serious material constituting the contemporary cultural underground. Most highly recommended."
EIDOS Magazine, Volume 9, Number 3, 1997

REVIEWS CONTINUED...

"Vol. 1, #6. What a zine! The cover is incredible, a drawing of two nude women kissing, one's arms bound behind getting her crotch rubbed by the other, and they're melded/ blended/ conjoined at one breast. Yes, this is for adults. The beautiful nude photography of Flo Fox, Tony Ryan and Eric Boutilier Brown is showcased (and there's an interesing bio of Flo Fox in the section "Frankly Speaking"). There's an amusing short story by Charles, "The Tincture of Holi Alkimy," that centers around a building super/plumber with a unique immunity to electricity. "3.C" ("one of a series of texts that accompany movements of the composition for noise guitar") by K. Atchley is hot, kinky, disgusting and psychedelic. There are great poetry contributions as well: "Disease" (and the rant "Sleepless Night") by San Quentin resident Al, "their cuddling cocoon" by Frank, George's "The Day," Ana's "Lee's Unleaded Blues/Chicago, South Side," Grasshopper's "Monsters" and "The Mule" by David. Also worth mentioning are the erotic pen and ink sketches by Giger. One technical error that needs mentioning was the inclusion of an extra page, doubles of pages one and two and 37 and 38 (I would have praised a double of one of the photography pages! Hot stuff!). This was a pretty wild ride [DL]."
Amusing Yourself to Death #3

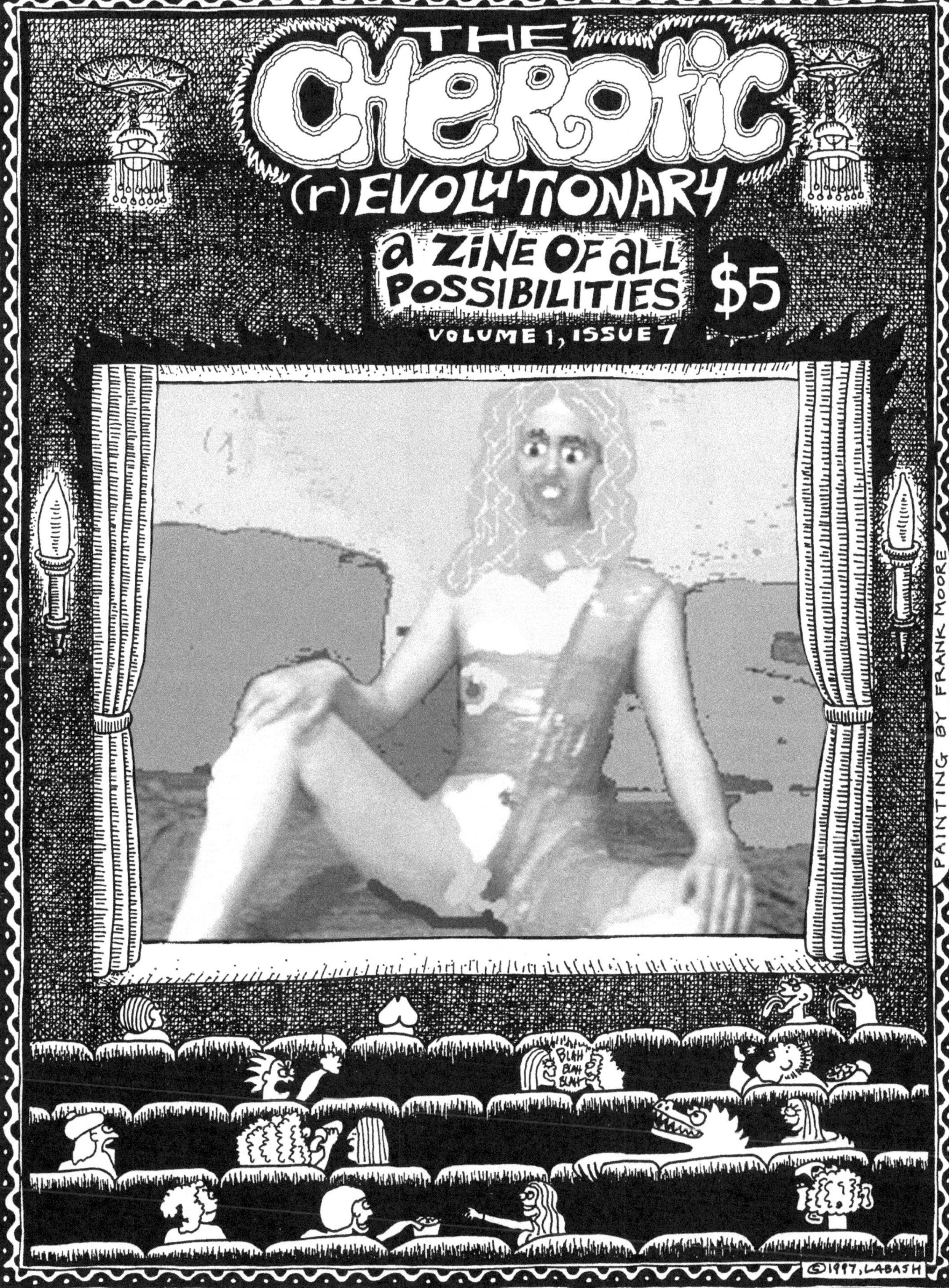
THE
CHEROTIC
(r)EVOLUTIONARY
a ZINE OF ALL POSSIBILITIES
$5
VOLUME 1, ISSUE 7
PAINTING BY FRANK MOORE
BLAH BLAH BLAH
©1997, LABASH

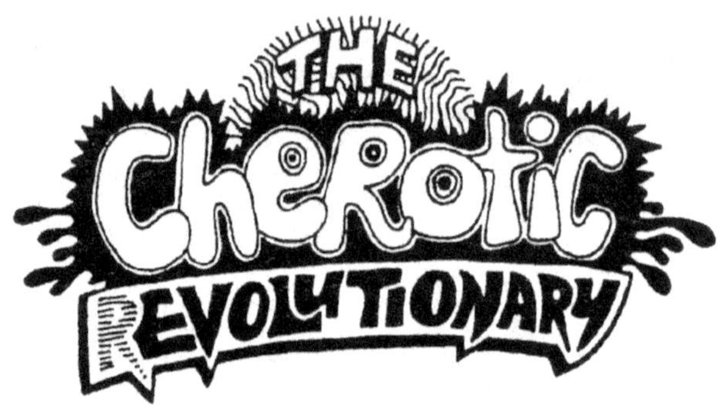

ISSN 1083-8872

The Cherotic (r)Evolutionary is a zine about "the edge" for and by people on the edge.

TC(r) is published by Inter-Relations. The publishers/editors are Frank Moore and Linda Mac, the art editor is Michael LaBash, and the circulation manager is Alexi Malenky.

The price for this issue is $5.00 per copy. We don't sell subscriptions, to avoid tying ourselves down to a rigid publication schedule or magazine size. We want to remain free to publish frequently or larger issues at longer intervals and adjust the price accordingly.

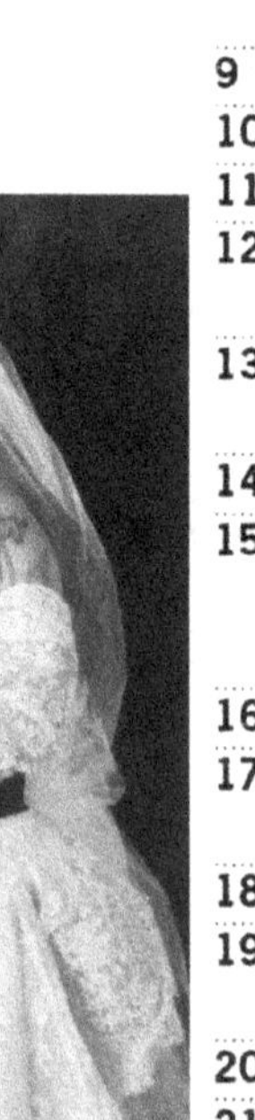

Mrs. &Mrs. Silver-Sprinkle

(photo by Brad Fowler)

We heartily encourage letters of comment from readers and will answer as many as we can. Please tell us if you don't want us to print material from your letter – otherwise we will assume it's OK.

Please address all correspondence and orders for magazines to:

Frank Moore, P.O. Box 11445, Berkeley CA 94712
e-mail: fmoore@lanminds.com
WorldWideWeb: http://www.eroplay.com

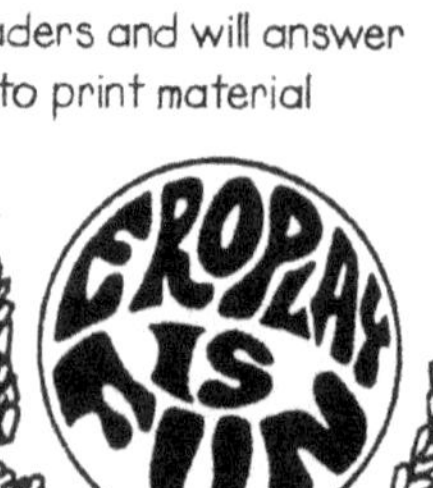

TC(r)'s AD POLICY

Recently we have received several inquiries about how to buy ads in The Cherotic (r)Evolutionary. Although we are not actively seeking such ads, we are not precluding them either. However, we will judge whether or not to accept an ad.

TC(r) is a xeroxed, black and white zine that is published irregularly ... if we are lucky, twice a year. So it is not the place for fancy color ads or for ads with time deadlines. On the other hand, TC(r) magically finds its way around the world.

TO SUBMIT AN AD

Send us a copy of your ad and a S.A.S.E. If we accept it, we send you the rate for your ad ... and if we need anything from you such as halftones, we will tell you. If we don't accept it, we will send your ad back.

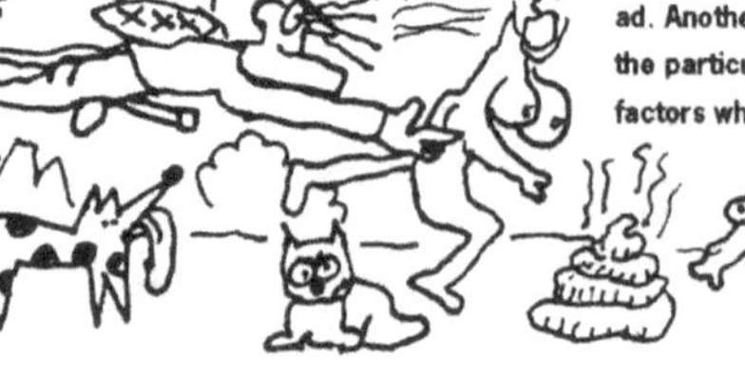

AD RATES

Sliding scale: $10-$50 per quarter of a standard typing page. The scale slides according to our whim.

HOW WE ACCEPT AN AD

Our whim also is a big factor in accepting an ad. Another factor is the other contents of the particular issue. And there may be other factors which are unknown even to us.

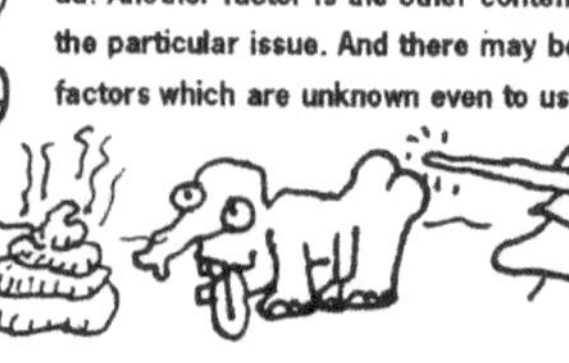

FREE TC(r) COPIES

Because we are not actively looking for paid ads, we do not give free copies to would-be advertisers. But we encourage them to buy a back issue or two. However, we do give you a free copy of the issue in which your ad appears.

Frank Moore
November 12, 1993

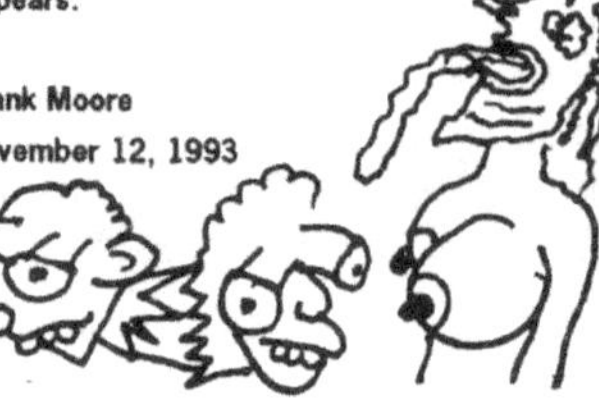

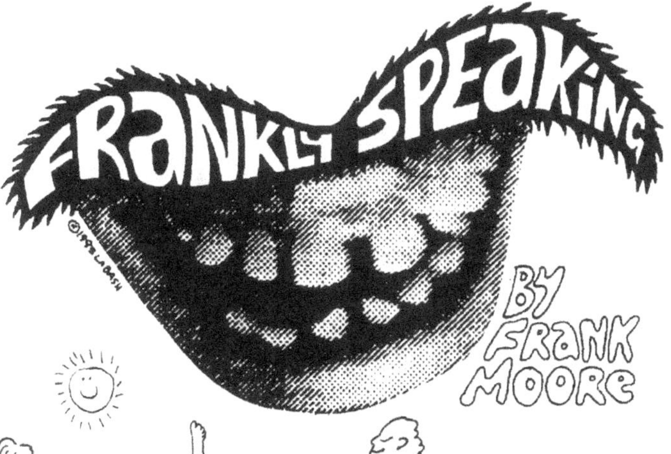

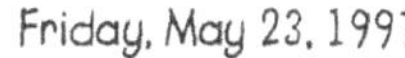
Friday, May 23, 1997

Help me! Please, anybody! Help me! They have tied me in the chair in front of this computer ... ripped the modem from the wall so I can't surf the Internet, can't contact the E-Salon for help. They say everything is ready to put this issue to bed ... except for this column and my review of Tony Ryan's great photography book of nudes. (Face it. That review is just a cheap excuse to be able to publish more of Ryan's beautiful work.) Is this any way to treat the editor? They already have forced me to computer-paint on the sexy photo of Heather (assumedly taken by Matt, her mate) for the cover! (Got you to buy the zine, didn't it? Don't be embarrassed. It is natural.) Never fear ... you can see Heather inside ... without my paint job!

But I don't know why they bother with me! Look at the great goofy stuff LaBash drew around my "painting." And look at all the great artists and writers in this issue. Who needs me? Sure. I can get the art world all upset by my "Mainstream Avante Garde?". But that is easy to do. It just takes writing the obvious. But writing in your own blood, shit and puke as John Fleetham, Elliott, and Robert Penick do, or drawing with your own raw nerve endings dipped in paranoia and/or sweet surrealism as Seabury, Rich, Blunt, Viveros (special thanks to Les Bareny for turning us on to B.V.), Bieri, Montebravo, and Fleming do...well, I don't hold a candle to them! I just hope they live long enough to do more art!

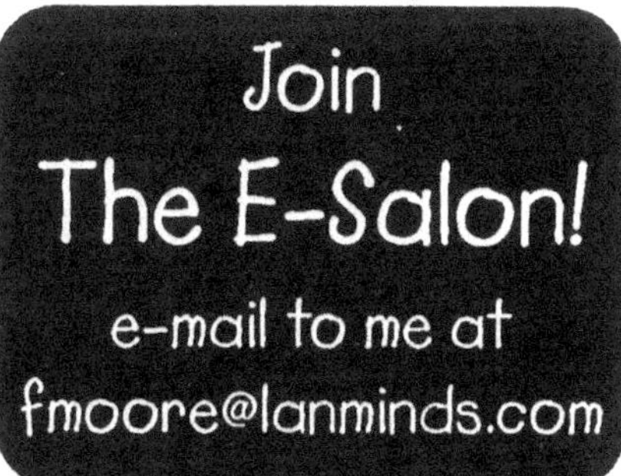

And that reminds me. Robert, you can die now! Folks, people do all kinds of cheap stunts to get into these pages. Robert said he couldn't die until he made it into here. I pictured the walking dead! I didn't want that karma!

Anyway, if you are a regular reader, you will meet some old friends. We could not include all of the regulars because we want to introduce you to new friends. The regulars who aren't in this outing will be in the next ... which we hope will not take a year to get out! (But, as I have said in past issues, we have a life filled with other things other than this zine.) The regulars also appear in the channels we have created on our web site, THE WEB OF ALL POSSIBILITIES, at http://www.eroplay.com ... channels like art galleries which can include color ... and SOUNDS FROM THE UNDERGROUND which includes music, sound collages, poetry readings, interviews, and whatever we/you create. If you are on the Internet, visit us. But even if you are not on-line, send us stuff to put on the site ... we just might use it!

Above I mentioned THE E-SALON. What that is, is a community which has developed via my e-mail. It is a community of "artists" (whatever that is) of all kinds talking, sharing, plotting together in a very deep freeing way. The pieces by Paul, Heather, Kara, Ray, Lob, Jodi, and Brian all came from THE E-SALON, one way or another. If you want to join in the fun, drop me an e-line to fmoore@lanminds.com.

And don't Annie and Kim look happy? Happy life together, gals!

Now for those who are thinking of starting your own zines, web sites, or whatever ... please don't get fooled by our "technical quality." We just have an in-house graphic art company. But all you need is good contents ... which money can't buy. Good contents are in you. So let's see what you got!

Frank Moore
P.O. Box 11445
Berkeley, CA 94712

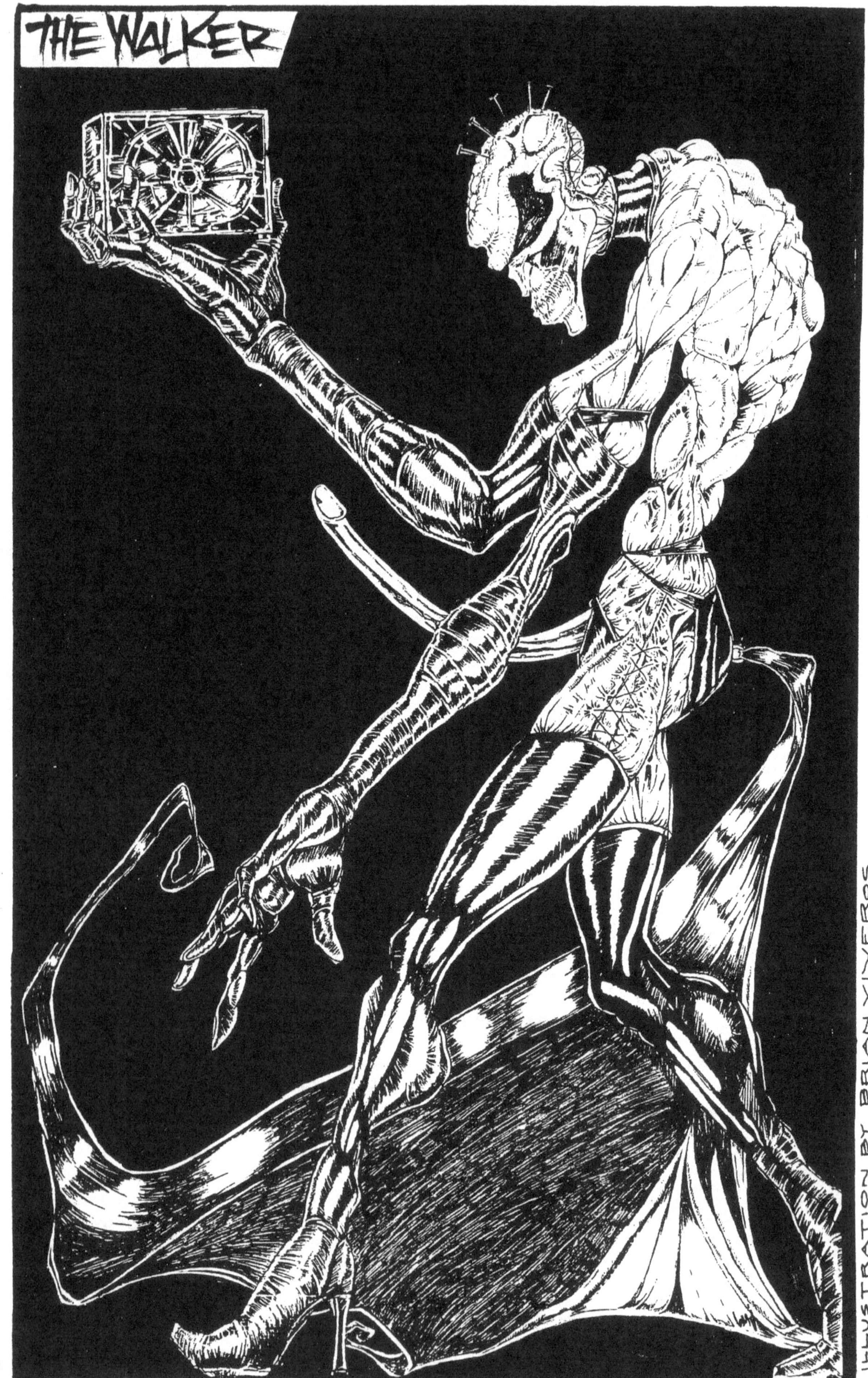
THE WALKER
ILLUSTRATION BY BRIAN VIVEROS

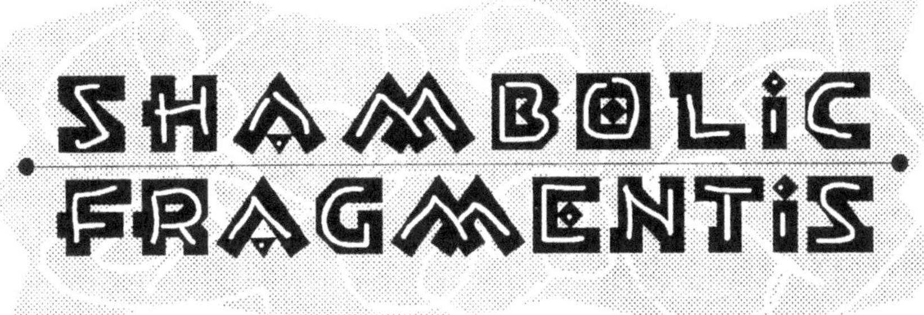

Shambolic Fragmentis

(A CHAPTER FROM A LONGER STORY)

by **JOHN FLEETHAM**

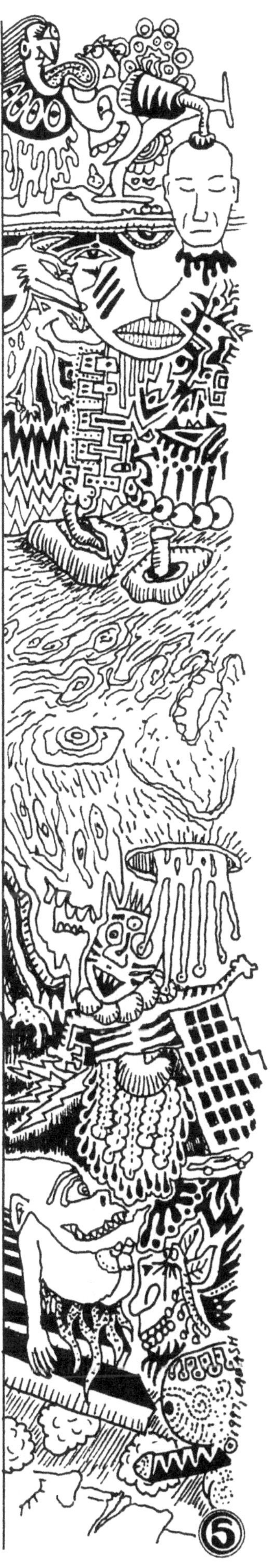

"I am the lowest of the low." Babyland

...it was the frozen cryogenic amnion that must have burst upon my collapse. The winds of guns turning on effluent life grasping hands of tortures and plastic tubing rhythmic regressive movements of the most isolated Himalayas. Her, the dream form of grey, in watch tower skin. The choking birth embankment fondles heaven's waters that err ode the foundations from below. I see leaves blowing across narrow roads opening with the speed of it now. There was, now that I think about it, something of the nothing that must have come in me. The smears on all reflecting matter slithered golden scales. The everything in my vision, "I'm sorry...". I was walking so near the bank. I..I guess I just slipped in walking, in that movement that defined my conscious form; my self of selves. The dragons bear them witness, some saying, "*mug the saints*".

Dope. Plastic bag lying on the floor. *Insights into research: Hunger nacht.* I straight need to recover myself in the bathroom, ashore. Too afraid and shaken to stand up. She was legless in the planes of logic growing pulsating with the bloom of approaching darker nations. I thought I saw my father playing some psych unit drums in some village centuries ago. ..Twelve o'clock has reached us. The birth holes of my eyes distinguished two female figures being let into the room. Trance upon will. Have always been waiting paranoid under beating door. My consciousness is strained like the ballerina on her last twenty horses legs. *She took her body into the shower...*"

My scales quiver the dragon asleep in his cage draped with her dress. My agoraphobia gambles in the dark. While some thing somewhere feels the evenings blowing bulimia walks beneath sanitation sun. Her palms the meat of the Sahara. My leper tongue sewn into a Mercedes-Benz all for the shore fishing. I fell in pigtails from the grape and I now search only for a cold smile in a warm hand. His introgressions go most often unconducted with only one shimmering flame by which to remember home.

Your fundamental mother is a series of wires connecting steak to steak, grass to cow, falling to sleeping. Or a strange solemn oration through ventriloquists hole in the night, whispers crawling backwards.

: We do not speak a real language. There is never a real moment. All existence is a possibility, the flux of possibility:

All of my ancestors are made of salt. Upon my search for the Holy Grail I found a gun. The words *freedom and liberation* only exist as ideas when their meanings don't exist as realities.

Another spider crashes me down the elevator shaft. One shouldn't solve. *larva en vulvus.* The furniture moved in buffalo shadows waxing and waning. The electrode terror drop of red abyss burned through the floor. I hear everything crawling up my back. The space we absorb is toxic. ..*I thought there was someone here with me..* This is probably the shore that should end it. The earth wheels are suspended in dying blasts that fall only to remove the subject. Woken by police hands and cuts. The filthy violent bitch god in the lamb. The organ fugues of the digesting ocean; the sea of calibration. The sun will rape the igloos. My nerves quiet and cold on ships that dock in Cambodia's nostrils. My guts do cleave the seas and skies. She tells me that I laugh in my sleep. Perhaps I found enlightenment in the black-out last night in the wisdom pool drowning quickly. Quinine soothes the system while other agents go to work in other tunnels of mostly vibration. I walk through doorway beads into white sandbag rooms under smuggled

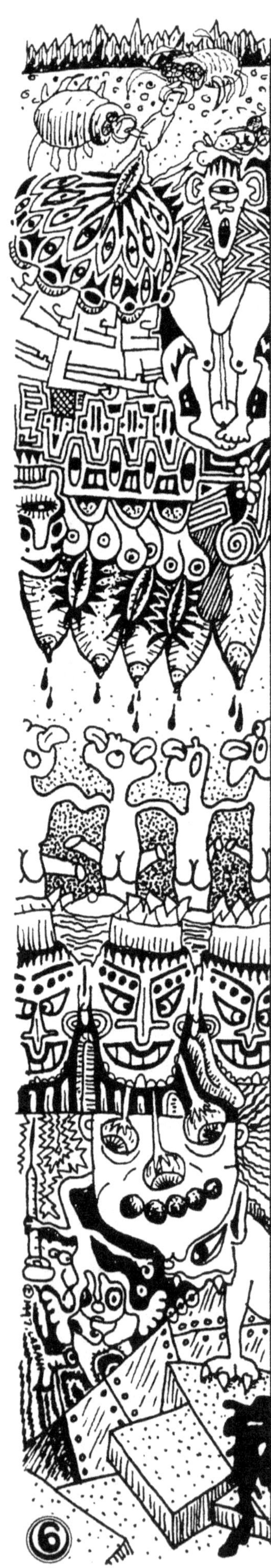

Chinese AK-47's behind my red-haired girl enclosed by burning torsos in long cafe rooms. I now awake to girls banging on my windows or in my wrists. "I'm sorry, but I don't remember fucking you last night. I only know, and so telepathically, that your pale naked body was carried in by red spiders.

Running ghost saline stream held in the center of the air. And I don't know the person who wrote to me. When the cattle cries I turn him off; silenced by the solipsism blade. Undressed in abstract postcard ports through the smears of after ground expanding meteorite mass.

The clairvoyant bone piercer declines justice in subway infrastructure. Bronchial orifices become pyogenic by tomorrow. The horizon is the sublime fortress forgiving of every excess, of hands, of tongue. I am speaking that man's voice. Amphetamine green transgressions into the saintly waters. I don't know how happy I was once. I see the shade dividers papered screen. That paste rubbed tarous onto one's fingers and sucked slowly off into psychotropical gardens of the eyes' balconies. *Into the system.* "..ok. so watch it now, it's gonna be like a good clean hit on the head with a baseball bat." I am the on-on-tolam! Last night I dreamt that I was going through alien executions with my lost cat.

It is grinding beneath my feet. That childhood nap never did end. Rusty gates hanging between old brick wall with large vines and hedges heaving over into the narrow paved alleyway. The centipede dreaming hemorrhages into perception. I will slip on deck frozen, all life seeping out. I would only live to eat cake, as I feared.

I once said to be fed is the sin of demons in rabid chase on the vulture ladder to euphoria only in something overall disgusting. And so with no dignity left in the road weary black ash of the chest and thighs that lose themselves in children's cries, "in submission we sing, in submission we do love to sing!", and on and on they barked. I could not take it any more; I got out. I departed from such sweet measurements against human affection, I writhe.

"With me", she said, "no human disease may infest me. I am sanitation, I am worm. Thou's worn slivers slit quiet still scapes of wall walking nights home, clinging to only some incandescent thread. My fomenting willows only cry destroy the autocracy when the steam room moon nights billow vision down on civilians. That maelstrom hunt of mine to restore my psychotic cigarettes to my psychic mouth. I must urge myself on to her. On to Latin ropes. Only my computer would burn tragically with me. Highways speeding frenzied mileage for me to lay my back down; on it, into it...(the black and white morgue aquarium stares hard at my bloody pulled spine sucking a hisss out from the very pool of rebirth and blood and piss).

I thought it was with me, that I couldn't ever get comfortable, no parking lots flashing around my spherical field of visual interpretation and representation. I thought you were a memory curved way back for reevaluation. You can come back to me, just to check the life but I go home again no further. Hesitation has been canceled, ruled obsolete. I do hear organs, a blast from ... white sands of life.

What does reason reap? Bright blue of bhang in daylight. Taking down sugar as a last resort to stay lucid. I can destroy, I am one. Fuck: the mass times weight soliciting palpable life. What disgusting foreign hair do I find on myself tonight? Adhari gangs plagued the streets in deeper areas of the city. Tribally adorned youths, twenty perhaps being their later midlife. Every moment of their lives was in offense; they were perpetual vagrants, loiterers, homeless. They were followed and bothered by cops all day, asking incessantly for change. Occasionally imitated by suburban hip kids the real punks were unmistakable; in smell, in look, in mannerism.

The attraction of retinas to external stimuli was rigid.
All extreme cases of sub-psychosis were
class- ified. Thus the war..
The rotting entrances to rooms I cannot find in this house I hear
what they heard. The terrorist
collapse of entire buildings
walls
blown off into the areas that only exist
in the pathological fear of the masses.
I suppose I am some kind of a lotus-eater, "ku ku ku."
"I showed her the tree!" It climbed up to heaven without her.
She crawled back home on all fours.
Nothing
can be done.

The grey forms are archaic, ancestral. The winding milky ways of branches hangs down over families of boiling lobster. THE FREQUENCY OF MY DREAMS HAS BEEN REACHED. O MY DOPE, throw down your tresses of polyurethane bags, your forest smells bleaching rabbits white.

"I've got a line on you," he tried to threaten me.

"Lines are for the sea," I responded.

"Look, we know you had that thing in your apartment last night. We got flames up all around the path in. So, man, whatcha know?"

"The pillars that awoke the clouds. Your mother only has one eye. 'I'm frightened, child', is what she always said to you. I can't see with all these bells and alarms and crashing in my head. 'Or is it all just an illusion?". I lost her now. Dreamt about Matahari, and clandestine Angor Wats, the left hand life."

The figures and the tags, the desecration of all physical industrial age manifestations. The language is of the ground, the codes I see. The pyramid on the dollar dominates the masses with his eye. You see? The connection is clear! O but, afternoons drag on. Like she left in the morning and the noon and thereafter we're crawling at the speed of an 8:00 departure flight over Phoenix...Or was it Dahran? "Copperdomes can't sleep either", I told her. "I couldn't find a woman who understood anything I said." We absurd poor folk just writing letters to each other. I'm the happiest when severely incoherent, today I fall asleep everywhere in not very good spaces. Walls secrete moving dots that occasionally grow legs. Singing to me from their booming cars, "come down to the murder town." And all metaphysical life is suspended by wires from the ceiling. Cartesian systems shatter from the rumbling outside trying to get in and help me. To sleep or to die, is the question. "...somnolent, tachycardic, vomiting..." Wait! You've got to vote for president! We've all got to go to vote!"

"What do you mean *vote?*"

"The president is a..bitch-whore, or something..."

The water breaks on the other side of the forced door, I halfway torn from the wall. Brown stucco courtyard in torchlight. Spanish sconces clicking mechanically around in circles. two cuckoo clocks on either side. The cuckoo on the left had a rotten meatball shoved on it's head. I get so afraid when her eyes swing pendulums. I can't stay awake any longer, hanging by a nail. The light bulbs hurt my stomach, the life vests tear my esophagus. The birds have a nest right above my windows. I must shoot them. I can no longer decipher when I am with someone else and when I am alone. I think that I am alone, however, a good portion of the time.

"...ah, so yeah I love that stuff." The reeling trajectories spun through my head for several minutes. I then woke somehow to ask her, "What the fuck were you talking about? No, nevermind..."

"This is a very interesting place you have here. I like interesting places." Some say the insects hum their philosophies. I just take them back to my brown paper bag house. The beaches are all crowded and gorgeous now, no terrorists to attack them at random. It's such a beautiful city. Nevertheless, I still cannot go outside. I've seen a lot of things moving lately. —No. Then some guy took us outside for something. I was looking with total shivering paranoia at everything. Black forms appear from the gently swaying bushes.

There's a flute in the street, it won't stop blowing and I forget how to walk. I can't go see anyone in the hospital now, like this. "Oh look, it's a plane!" You won't drive home in a daisy now, would you? Indeed where is your home? There ain't one for sale anywhere in the world. Pray for money, one needs to, religiously. I just want for the teacup to go away when I set it down. I want invisibility, terror. Restaurants that glowed bourgeois stoned scenario. "Hello, and how are you tonight?"

Quite well, and yourself?" There was only a quiet grunt after that then she showed us to our table, candles and all. "What a fabulous red tie to match your eyes."

"I pocketed it yesterday. Was funny," he laughed. I didn't want to see his eyes. Just for a moment I was so scared to see his eyes. What truth isn't revealed in distraction? What uncomfortable stairways don't slope in his confession? Of the world and it's disease ridden mud. Life slapped on the buttock and shoved up the ass of earth, hemorrhaging the audience. "A glass of ice water would suit me for the world, darling," he said to her. "I would get my tongue up all around her Neptune and shit, yo. What, you hanging out in the ceiling man? What up there, yo? I'm losing time like dice man."

"Who.. whose driving this hearse? These are extremely dangerous turns. I don't know where uoy take me, but don't take my money."

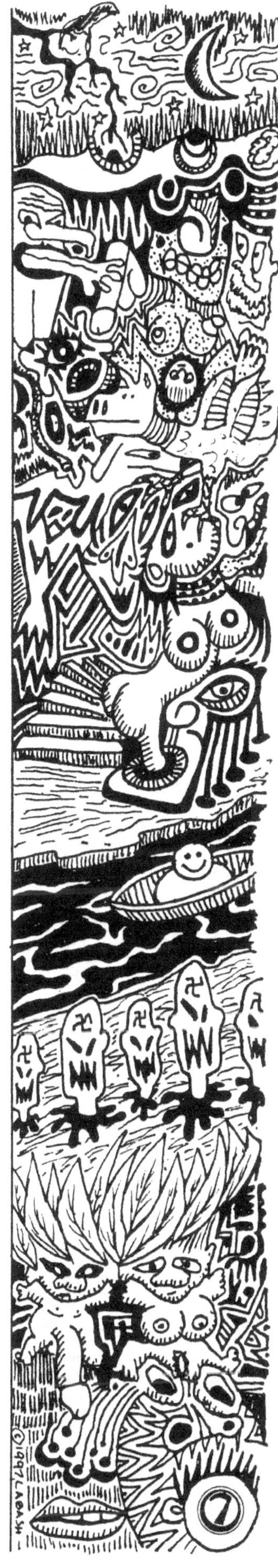

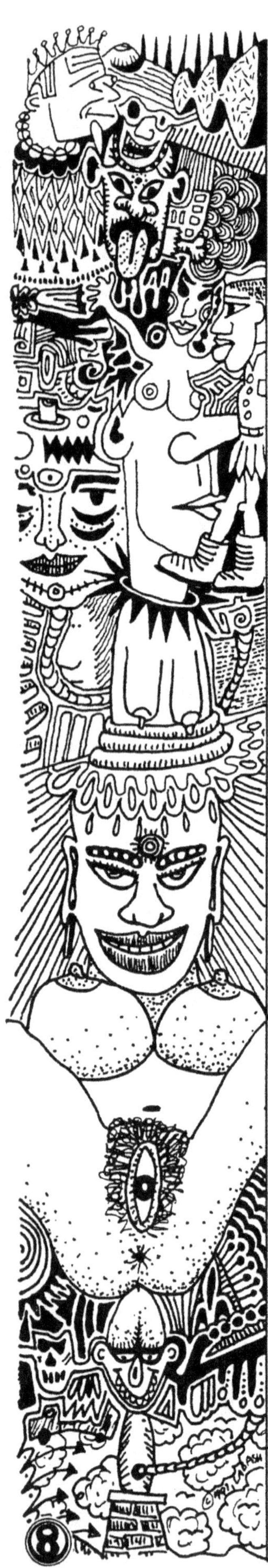

“Do you hear whhat I’m sayying now man? You whan to gt off theese bhuss now?!”

“Yes sir,.. yes sir..”, I grasp my side as it bled all out as if from a balloon. “‘You dirty me I infect you.” Isn’t that what the Adahari’s say to the cops man? Yeah, yeah.. I see it, now..

“My superpowers escape me tonight. That is all, sir.”

The everything of a people came down through rocks. The ancestors swarming in low tones overhead. My bat confessed it’s guilt to me, the sink reciprocated in tears. “What will I do with the Polytechnical degree I all gots and stuff? Sheeit.”

“Mambos breaking my death with the escaped refugee in my heart. How are those other shores for me but without me?— Cloud Nine just spilled it’s butter. Motherfucker. Heaven can only afford the soresuckers. Rings on the drain should spell out our death in it’s waste character. What terror? Who, do you hear me? Mammorous glands suck like quicksand reptila mud.

“I have now been bit, from this still bleeding wound, about twenty-nine koas now. The justice of retreat shall now spread. I read the rumors. It’s time for an Arabian Christmas! I want a bag of dried Moksha ants, they take me right back into worship with her.”

Sitting on a large cushion, back against the window facing the street two floors above; nostrils loading out. It’s all running into parked cars upstairs. I came upholstered in gun having been named injun.

“My nipple for a son’s ant! My nipple for a sun’s ant, Moksha,” he seemed to chant in my direction as none of this conversation had been going on with each other. I didn’t know where I was, nothing. The troops outside did nothing, nothing. I heard bicycles coming up from behind us. The phone wasn’t ringing.

The batcaves are swinging : in tbe (u)en DOR-247 espzx : The feathers wore rust and rained pigeon for state. Envelopes from congress. The shaking apparatus. All abuses are daily. Marijuana is a trigger apropos of several uses daily including the time immediately after waking. I can only stare, no matter how close the machine gets to me. Oil stains either green or brown on the fingers.

— Regression as found in marijuana:

-when adequate means have severely influenced the transformation of one into a purely archetypal and archaic consciousness, when the drug has taken one into the universal pool of consciousness-

In primitive times the collective human super-ego, which is something like the abstract counterpart to the individual eye or super-ego, corresponding to the general intelligence of humans at the time, was undeveloped to coincide with the early, undeveloped earth; *no one knew what to expect.* All movement, all time given is spent in exploration. All does, at times, seem to be teetering on the edge of human fragility.

I am holed up here, to be honest. I still leave to be out all day on most days, but I’ve just not been talking with anyone or going to those places where I know people. But that must have been *hope* tattooed on her stomach in today’s sun! The sun has been out so much lately. Today is a holiday of some kind. Everyone talks about, excitedly.

Maya confronts four-dimensionally. Emotions can come so quickly. In these ages I am so scared of beaches when I’m alone. I never would have imagined it would all end this way. What can I do now? I can’t reach any of the women who have loved me. I wouldn’t want to reach any of them anyway. All of my heroes have or had teeth rotten from vomiting. I’ve been so tearfully alive on winter nights last year. Today I don’t know.

The night, or the early morning, was cold, but the days were summer and warm. One could die from exposure in the nights though. That’s what woke me up. I had been laying on a bench in what appeared to be a baseball field, near home plate and the bleachers. I had only two thin shirts on, I was freezing. I wasn’t sure just where I was. I did not know the general area, of course, I still had my wallet. No drugs inside of you. Mosquito bites all over my body. On the way back home I encountered a school of lice, going home for the morning.

The primary sight is the forest opening on the wall, sunlight crashing onto the tops of high trees as if through cathedral stained-glass windows. Sunny maidens hoeing in the farmland ghetto nations. I hold on me the three tooth pyramid bite. My entire right lower back is discolored and sore.

I did want to hit you.
I did want to hit you.
I did not want to hit you.

"...so, Third Arm Sciences was the sign above the door."

...

"What?", I asked, completely baffled by this statement.

"How long are you going to just sit there and claim that body? That's what I've been wanting to ask you all night!"

"baeicahbsbidsabiabsiascbaibciubas", I said. It was strings of fluorescence above in some public store. What shit. Seemed to happen to me often. I would come to, usually standing up outside somewhere with friends, just a jolt and suddenly I'm with someone whose speaking totally alien material with me. Random bits that orbit perpetually bizarre.

In amerika, where pieces of the fantastic illusion are bought and sold, Void will confront in direct protest our delusions of self, of immortality, and order. We will not survive in this house, amerika will crash into the death of self manipulation as like ants swarming to kill some form inevitably. But those nations around us play such important parts in the destruction. It now slowly rises in the festering rage of opposing countries on all sides. The fires will not keep the mountain lions away tonight. One can start from a run and leap to go sailing down into the valleys and beds of earth. If you want to know what's worthless than listen to the talk of most average people. I wait upon the chance meeting of myself with several variable agents to help out in the worldwide cause of keeping the flow go of bags and money; the translucent undertow in the flowery secret life-support-system rivers. But money is such an elastic and worthless form of our agreed-upon stupidity that it was all very non-real antics coming from a party or class of clowns, what shit. I give my funny bills to the kid no matter how old he is. Rosey-cheeked.

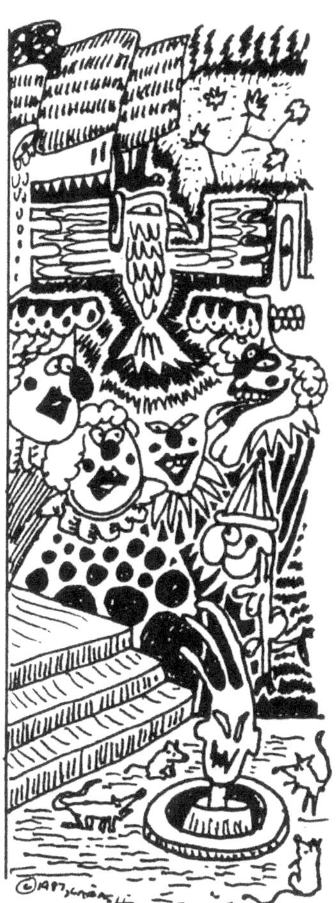

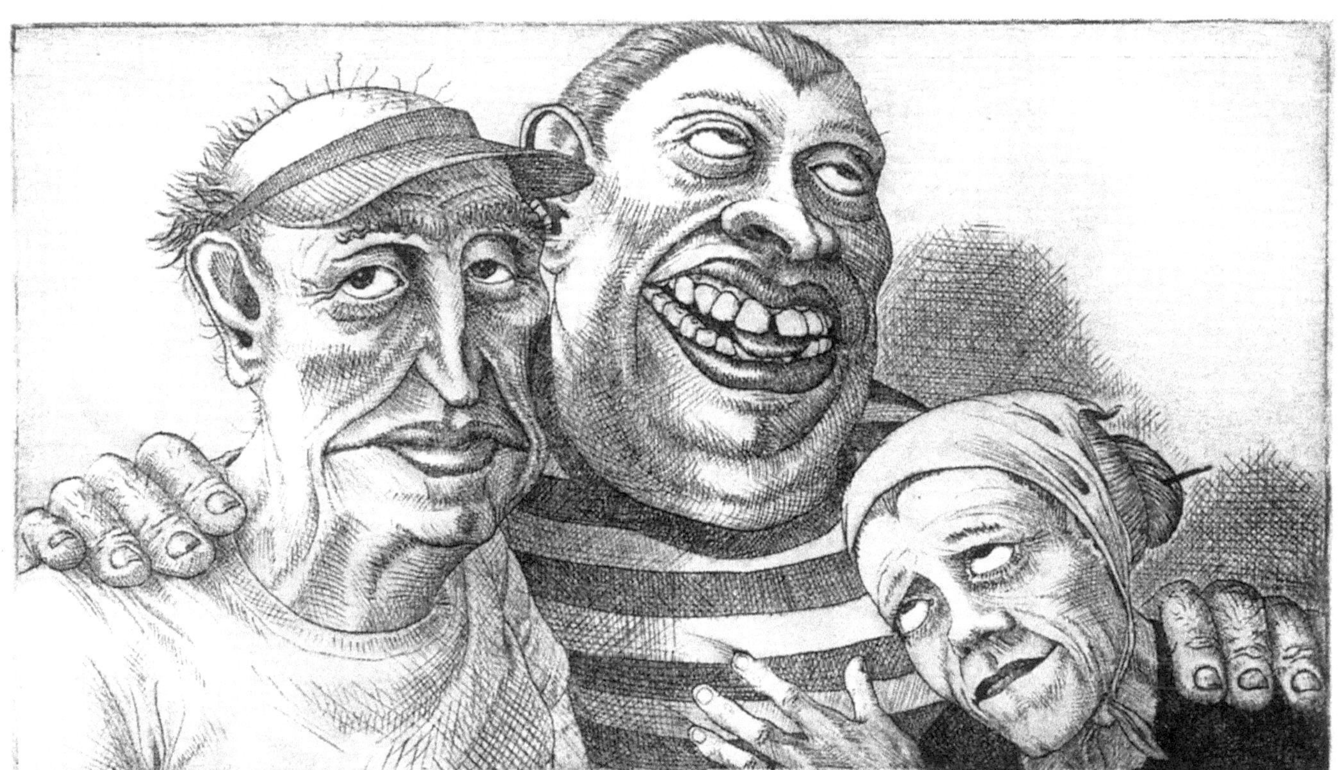

ETCHING by JOHN SEABURY

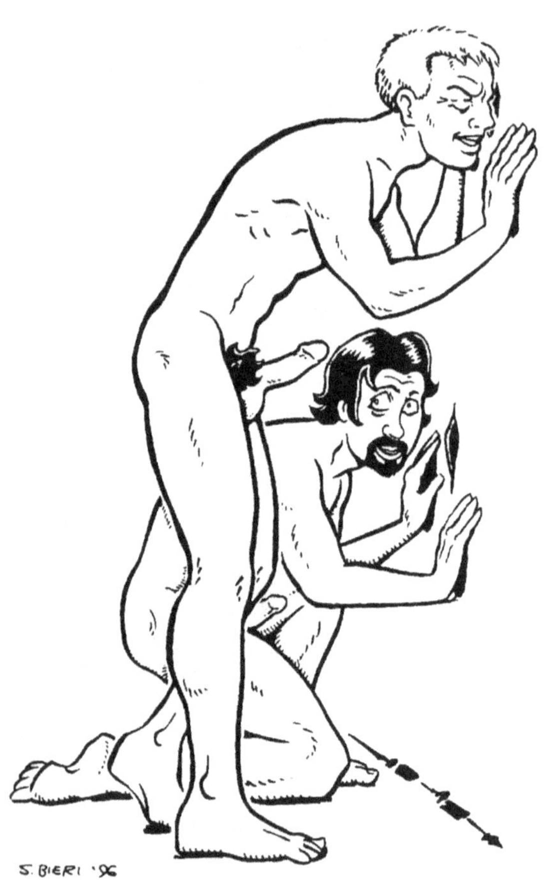

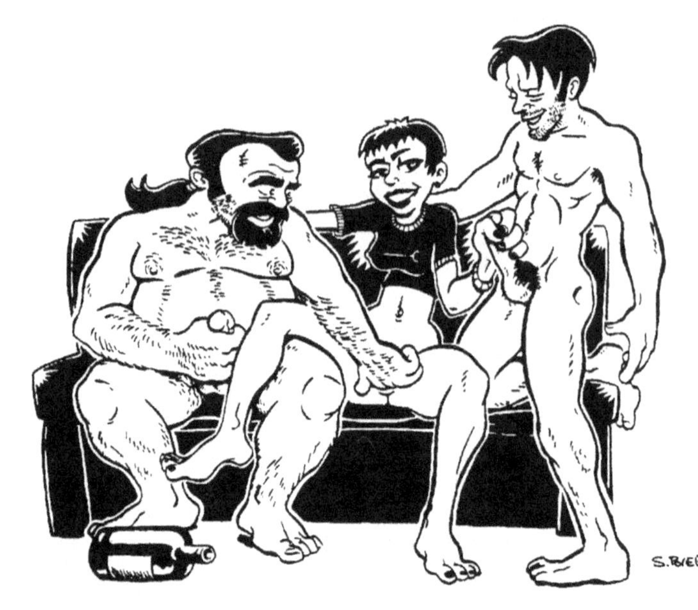

Sean Bieri

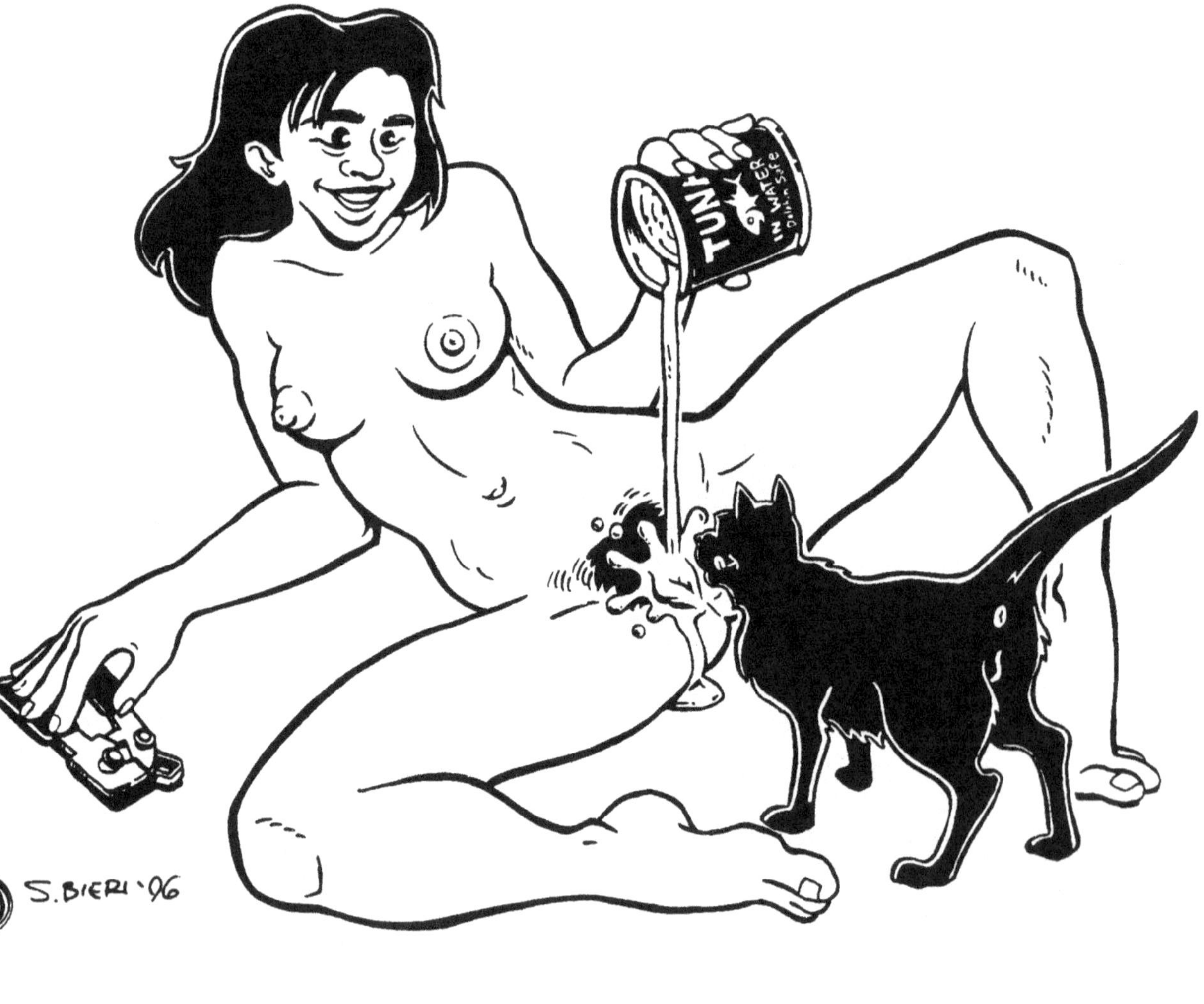

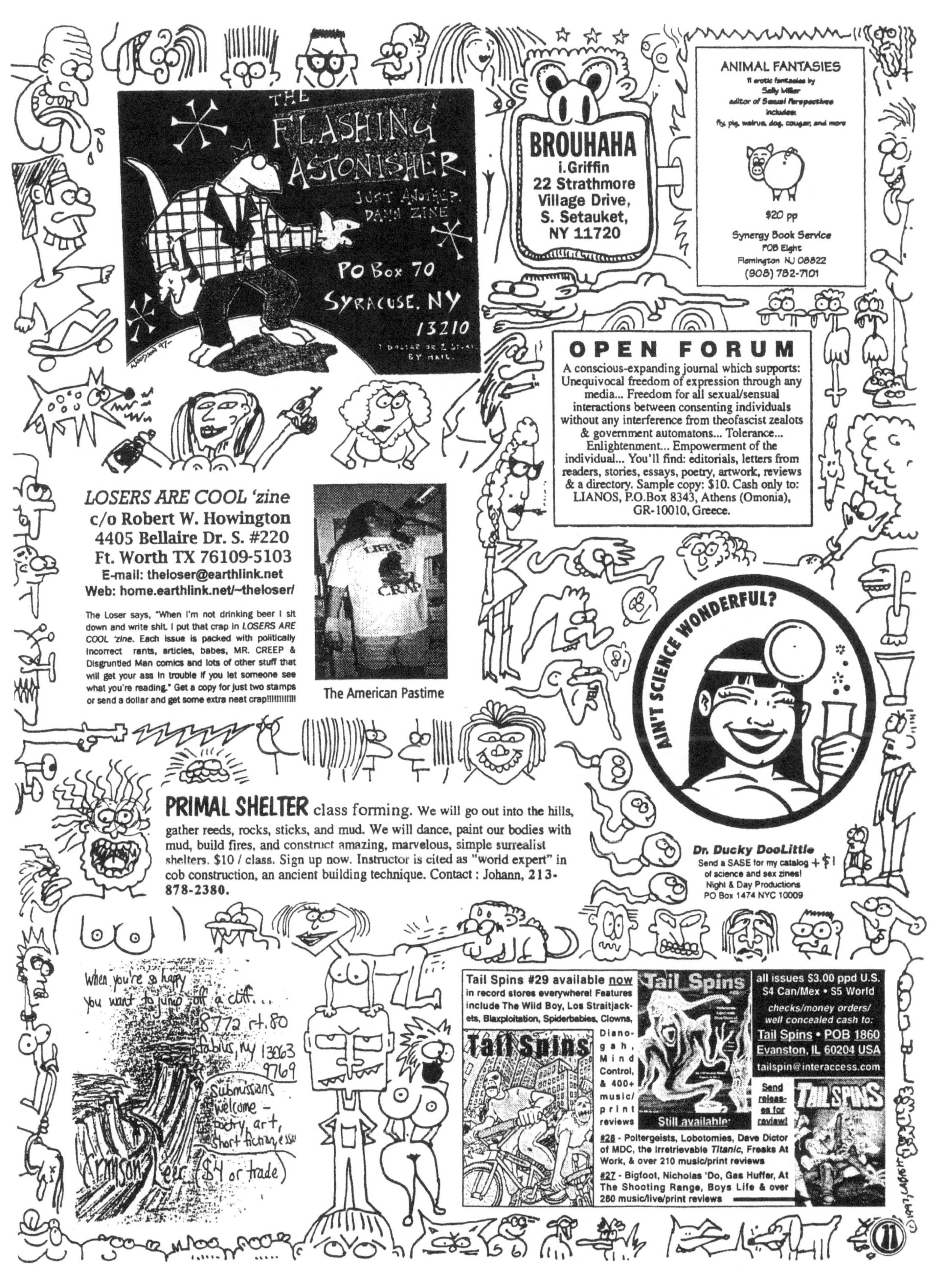
THE FLASHING ASTONISHER
JUST ANOTHER DAMN ZINE
PO Box 70
SYRACUSE, NY
13210
1 DOLLAR OR 2 STAMPS BY MAIL
BROUHAHA
i.Griffin
22 Strathmore
Village Drive,
S. Setauket,
NY 11720
ANIMAL FANTASIES
11 erotic fantasies by
Sally Miller
editor of Sexual Perspectives
includes:
fly, pig, walrus, dog, cougar, and more
$20 pp
Synergy Book Service
POB Eight
Flemington NJ 08822
(908) 782-7101
OPEN FORUM
A conscious-expanding journal which supports: Unequivocal freedom of expression through any media... Freedom for all sexual/sensual interactions between consenting individuals without any interference from theofascist zealots & government automatons... Tolerance... Enlightenment... Empowerment of the individual... You'll find: editorials, letters from readers, stories, essays, poetry, artwork, reviews & a directory. Sample copy: $10. Cash only to: LIANOS, P.O.Box 8343, Athens (Omonia), GR-10010, Greece.
LOSERS ARE COOL 'zine
c/o Robert W. Howington
4405 Bellaire Dr. S. #220
Ft. Worth TX 76109-5103
E-mail: theloser@earthlink.net
Web: home.earthlink.net/~theloser/
The Loser says, "When I'm not drinking beer I sit down and write shit. I put that crap in LOSERS ARE COOL 'zine. Each issue is packed with politically incorrect rants, articles, babes, MR. CREEP & Disgruntled Man comics and lots of other stuff that will get your ass in trouble if you let someone see what you're reading." Get a copy for just two stamps or send a dollar and get some extra neat crap!!!!!!!!!!!
The American Pastime
AIN'T SCIENCE WONDERFUL?
PRIMAL SHELTER class forming. We will go out into the hills, gather reeds, rocks, sticks, and mud. We will dance, paint our bodies with mud, build fires, and construct amazing, marvelous, simple surrealist shelters. $10 / class. Sign up now. Instructor is cited as "world expert" in cob construction, an ancient building technique. Contact : Johann, 213-878-2380.
Dr. Ducky DooLittle
Send a SASE for my catalog + $1
of science and sex zines!
Night & Day Productions
PO Box 1474 NYC 10009
When you're so happy you want to jump off a cliff...
8772 rt. 80
fabius, ny 13063
9769
Submissions welcome - poetry, art, short fiction, essays
Crimson Leer ($4 or trade)
Tail Spins #29 available now in record stores everywhere! Features include The Wild Boy, Los Straitjackets, Blaxploitation, Spiderbabies, Clowns, Dianogah, Mind Control, & 400+ music/print reviews
Tail Spins
all issues $3.00 ppd U.S.
$4 Can/Mex • $5 World
checks/money orders/ well concealed cash to:
Tail Spins • POB 1860
Evanston, IL 60204 USA
tailspin@interaccess.com
Send releases for review!
Still available:
#28 - Poltergeists, Lobotomies, Dave Dictor of MDC, the Irretrievable Titanic, Freaks At Work, & over 210 music/print reviews
#27 - Bigfoot, Nicholas 'Do, Gas Huffer, At The Shooting Range, Boys Life & over 280 music/live/print reviews
11

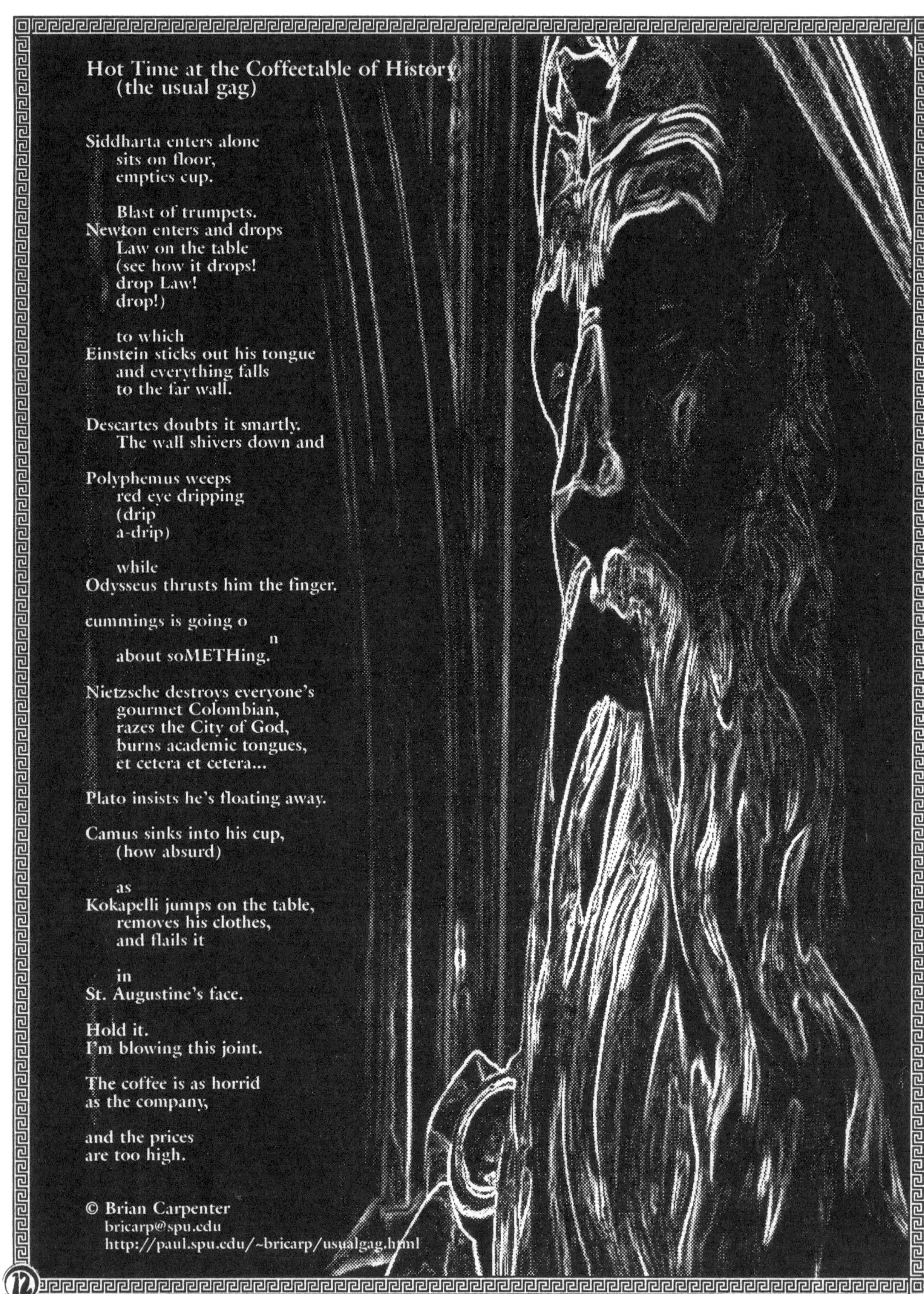

Hot Time at the Coffeetable of History
(the usual gag)

Siddharta enters alone
    sits on floor,
    empties cup.

    Blast of trumpets.
Newton enters and drops
    Law on the table
    (see how it drops!
    drop Law!
    drop!)

    to which
Einstein sticks out his tongue
    and everything falls
    to the far wall.

Descartes doubts it smartly.
    The wall shivers down and

Polyphemus weeps
    red eye dripping
    (drip
    a-drip)

    while
Odysseus thrusts him the finger.

cummings is going o
                                n
    about soMETHing.

Nietzsche destroys everyone's
    gourmet Colombian,
    razes the City of God,
    burns academic tongues,
    et cetera et cetera...

Plato insists he's floating away.

Camus sinks into his cup,
    (how absurd)

    as
Kokapelli jumps on the table,
    removes his clothes,
    and flails it

    in
St. Augustine's face.

Hold it.
I'm blowing this joint.

The coffee is as horrid
as the company,

and the prices
are too high.

© Brian Carpenter
bricarp@spu.edu
http://paul.spu.edu/~bricarp/usualgag.html

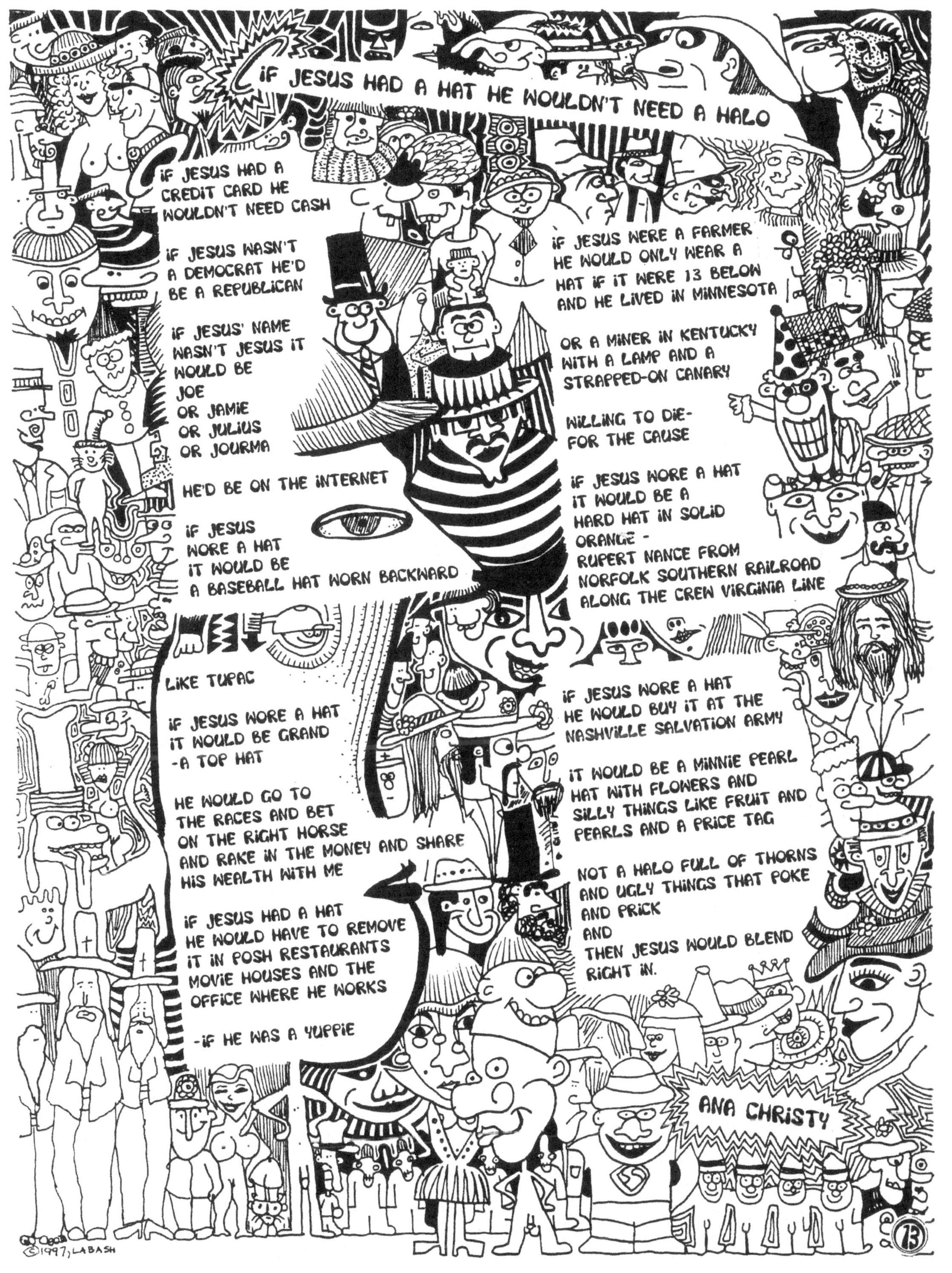
iF JESUS HAD A HAT HE WOULDN'T NEED A HALO
iF JESUS HAD A
CREDIT CARD HE
WOULDN'T NEED CASH
iF JESUS WASN'T
A DEMOCRAT HE'D
BE A REPUBLiCAN
iF JESUS' NAME
WASN'T JESUS iT
WOULD BE
JOE
OR JAMiE
OR JULiUS
OR JOURMA
HE'D BE ON THE iNTERNET
iF JESUS
WORE A HAT
iT WOULD BE
A BASEBALL HAT WORN BACKWARD
LiKE TUPAC
iF JESUS WORE A HAT
iT WOULD BE GRAND
-A TOP HAT
HE WOULD GO TO
THE RACES AND BET
ON THE RiGHT HORSE
AND RAKE iN THE MONEY AND SHARE
HiS WEALTH WiTH ME
iF JESUS HAD A HAT
HE WOULD HAVE TO REMOVE
iT iN POSH RESTAURANTS
MOViE HOUSES AND THE
OFFiCE WHERE HE WORKS
-iF HE WAS A YUPPiE
iF JESUS WERE A FARMER
HE WOULD ONLY WEAR A
HAT iF iT WERE 13 BELOW
AND HE LiVED iN MiNNESOTA
OR A MiNER iN KENTUCKY
WiTH A LAMP AND A
STRAPPED-ON CANARY
WiLLiNG TO DiE-
FOR THE CAUSE
iF JESUS WORE A HAT
iT WOULD BE A
HARD HAT iN SOLiD
ORANGE -
RUPERT NANCE FROM
NORFOLK SOUTHERN RAiLROAD
ALONG THE CREW ViRGiNiA LiNE
iF JESUS WORE A HAT
HE WOULD BUY iT AT THE
NASHViLLE SALVATiON ARMY
iT WOULD BE A MiNNiE PEARL
HAT WiTH FLOWERS AND
SiLLY THiNGS LiKE FRUiT AND
PEARLS AND A PRiCE TAG
NOT A HALO FULL OF THORNS
AND UGLY THiNGS THAT POKE
AND PRiCK
AND
THEN JESUS WOULD BLEND
RiGHT iN.
ANA CHRiSTY
©1997, LABASH
73

H E A T H E R

PHOTOS BY MATT

like a ravaged Lenny Bruce

It's like the old west old there
with kids with tech-9's drawing down
but they are polite and hand back the
empty wallets to the subway riders on
the Avenue A line after cleaning them out
of cash and jewelery.
and even mother nature has turned bad assed
flooding the mid-west heating up the north
and hitting Japan with earthquakes
anyone out there remember the apocalypse?
does it come with thunder or the whimper
of a dying beast, a T-Rex
king of the kingdom or so he thought
until he got his ass reemed
or hers not to be sexist about extinction
and everyone laughs except those with AIDS
It can't happen here as Zappa said; because I've
been checking it out baby and it can't happen here.
because you have a swimming pool and you're white?
and my friend got drunk and took it up the ass from
somebody but he can't recall just who and he should be more
careful and we kiss and WE should be more careful
and there is this chick and she's twenty years younger but
if we are all positive what the fuck difference does it
make in the end(**end**)
cause dead smells the same on all of us and that is
what makes us all the same that smell that fear that
you ain't never gonna hear the ocean again, share a secret,
taste somebody elses' salty tears and tell them it's gonna be
alright. Maybe George Dowden is correct maybe I am a ravaged
Lenny Bruce

– élliott

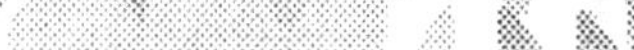

Frank,
I enjoyed browsing the site. Like the unashamed feel of it. Sometimes I find it's more mature to be silly and frank, and I think you know what I mean. I'm sending along two poems and a story. Hope you can use one. I can give you a bio info if you want.

Kevin Sampsell
Portland, Oregon
futuret@teleport. com

POSSESSED BY LENNY?

My two year-old says about 50 words.
One of his favorites is
"Fuck"
or as he phrases it
"Ohhhh fuck".
I think he may be possessed
by the spirit of Lenny Bruce
but of course I'm wrong.
It's the spirit of Lenny's cinematic double
Dustin Hoffman
and he's not even dead yet.
So now we've rented
Scent of a Woman
because it seems like
"Hooyahhhh!"
would be more fun for him to say
and we wouldn't have to pay for an
exorcist to get Mr. Hoffman's
undead spirit out
of our son.

– Kevin Sampsell

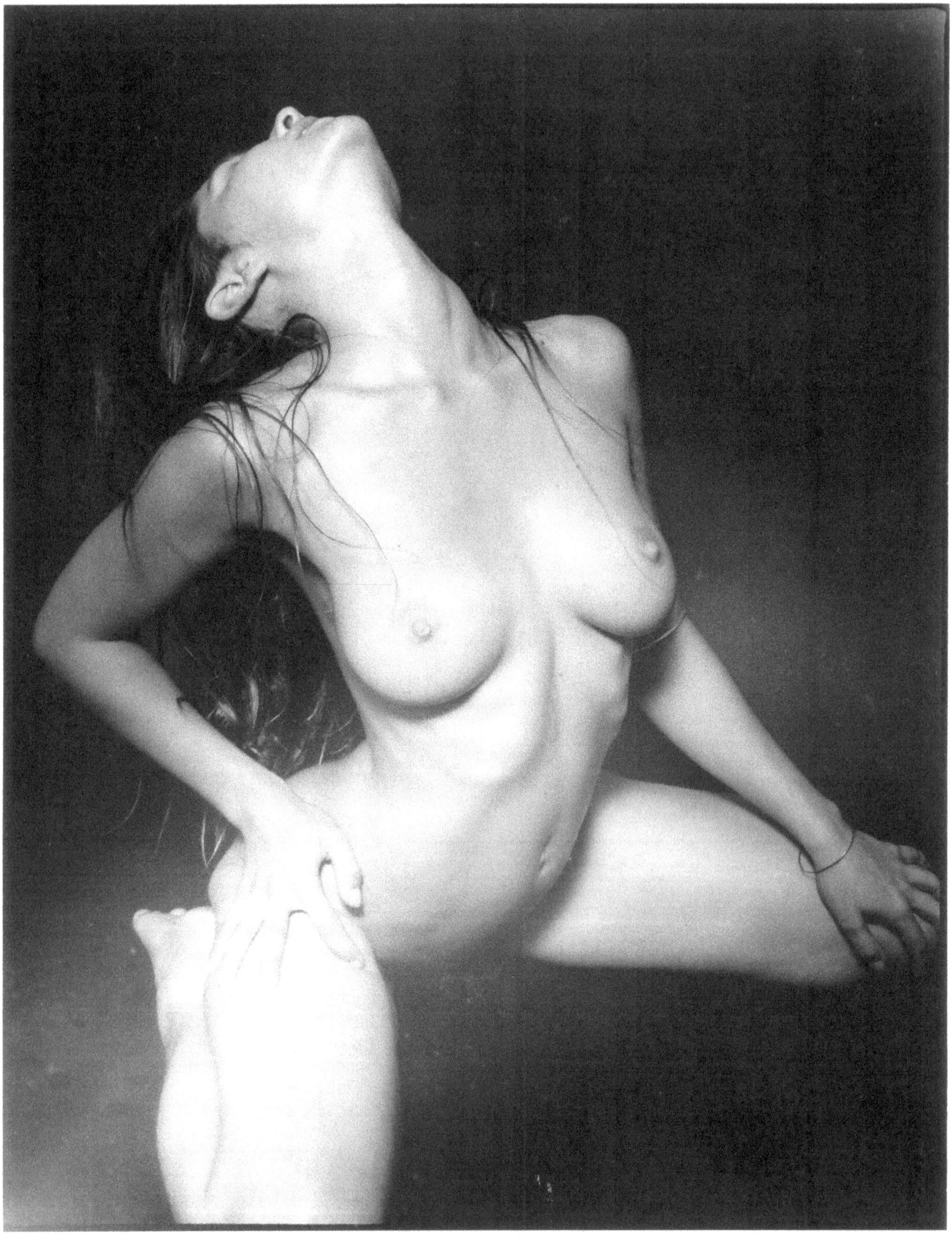

Hannah Dancing II

Beauty REALITY

A REVIEW OF **TONY RYAN'S BOOK** OF **NUDE PHOTOGRAPHS** BY **FRANK MOORE**

Reviewing a book of photographs is dicey. Why don't you just look at the four photos that we have printed from Tony Ryan's book, Beauty Reality? Then look up the last issue of TC(r) in which we featured Ryan's work. Then, if you are on-line, go to his site at: http://imalchemy.com/Tony.Ryan/ ... and feast on his work. After you have done all of that you probably will be so hungry for his work that you will want to buy the book for $30 ... and for another $10, Tony will throw in a signed 8 by 10 inch print of your choice mailed with the book. He is my kind of a teddy bear of a guy!

If you look at his photos, why do I need to write this review? Oh well, I'm writing this to justify my getting the free copy of the beautiful book. A book of beautiful bodies naked ... not just Hollywood Playboy "beauty" ... people beauty ... men, couples of both genders, mothers and children (can the dirty minded cry child abuse?), mothers-about-to-be, children (will the dirty minded cry child porn?) ... and real living lusty women. The cocks-and-tits counting "feminists" will be quick to point out it is mostly nude beautiful women (and they don't include the big women in that classification). Like always, they miss the depth of the art. The nude body in each of Tony's photos is just the starting point to reveal the "subject's" personality/spirit, to explore relationships, and to dive into the magical intimate altered reality of the shooting session ... the special intimate reality created when artist and model come together in art. The work is humanistic (thus, truly feminist), completely erotic because it is not limited by sex. Tony, as do I, admits to being especially attracted to working with women, to what he calls the special tension. In fact, he subtitles the book, "Male Eye-Female Mind". By doing so, he is calling attention to the major and active role of the female models in the creative process. But I think it

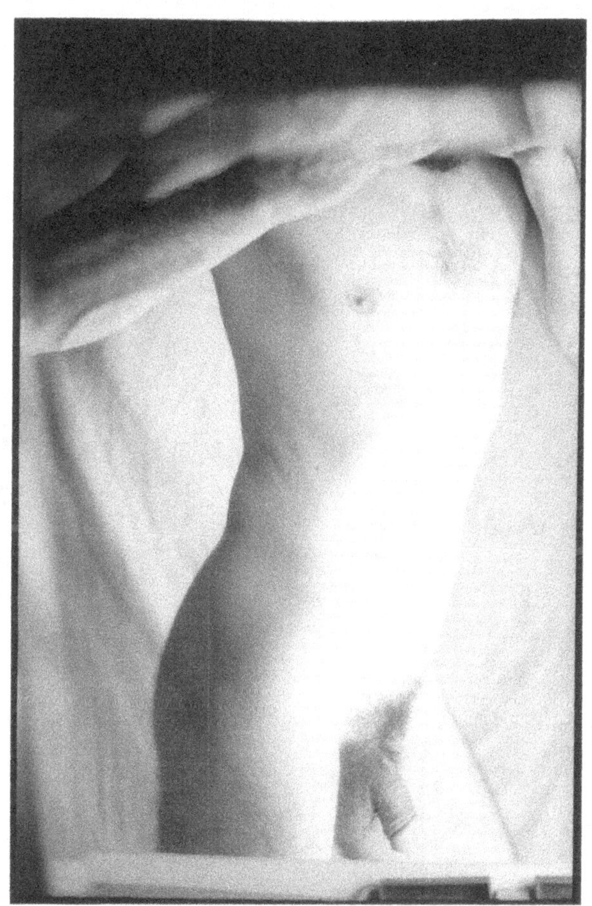

Self-portrait (Crabtree 1979)

can be applied to Tony himself ... because looking at his pictures and reading his writings, I would say Tony has a very developed feminine side in himself.

I met Tony on the Internet when I was searching for erotic art that wasn't legs-spread, beer-can-in-the-ass-dildo-in-cunt-sucking-cock parody on sex (such parodies have their place, but ...). And that is where the world also met Tony. On the Internet is where Tony broke out of the isolation that is felt by

Beauty REALITY CONTINUED

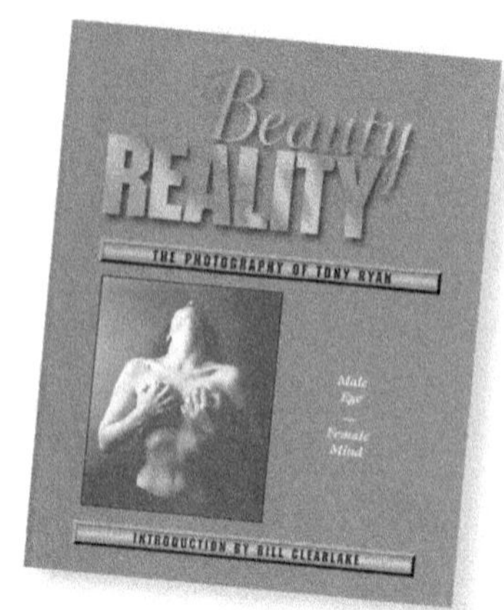

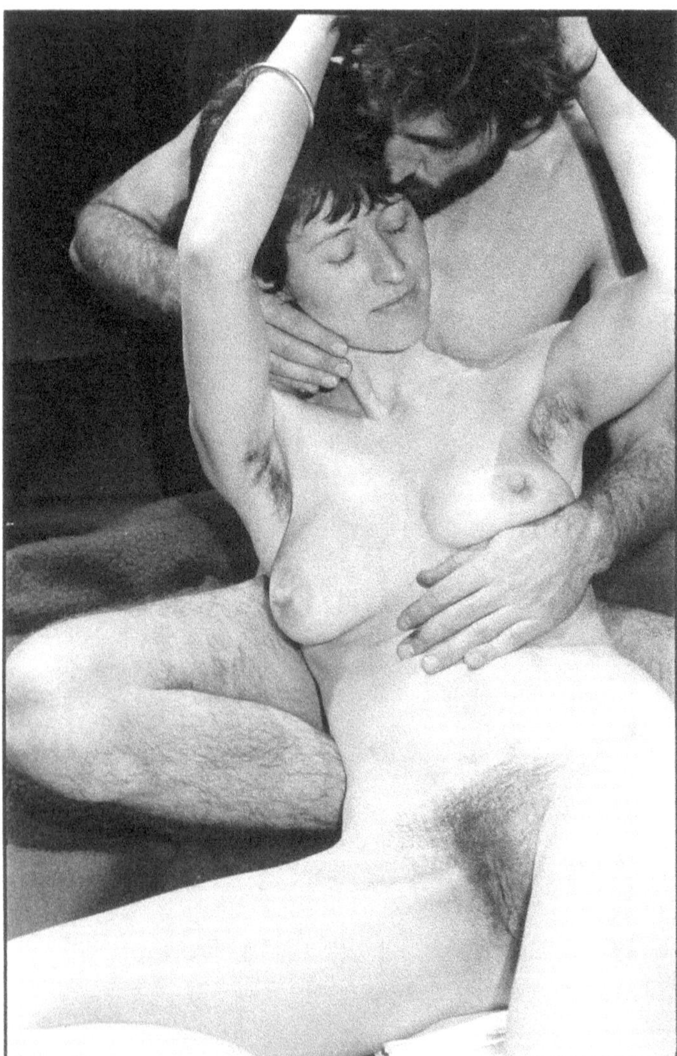

A Couple (Crabtree 1986)

most artists who do not do fashionable art, who do not fit in, or who run afoul of the local art power structure, and/or live in the boonies ... I think Tasmania may be on the outskirts of the boonies (but, judging from Tony's photos, there are a lot of interesting folks living on the outskirts!). Tony shows that by putting your art directly out into the world, you can by-pass all road blocks that the power structures put in your way. This is another reason why Tony's art is so inspiring!

You can contact Tony at:
Email: Tony.Ryan@utas.edu.au
Or snailmail to:
C/- Grove Post Office
Grove, Tasmania
Australia 7109

http://imalchemy.com/Tony.Ryan/

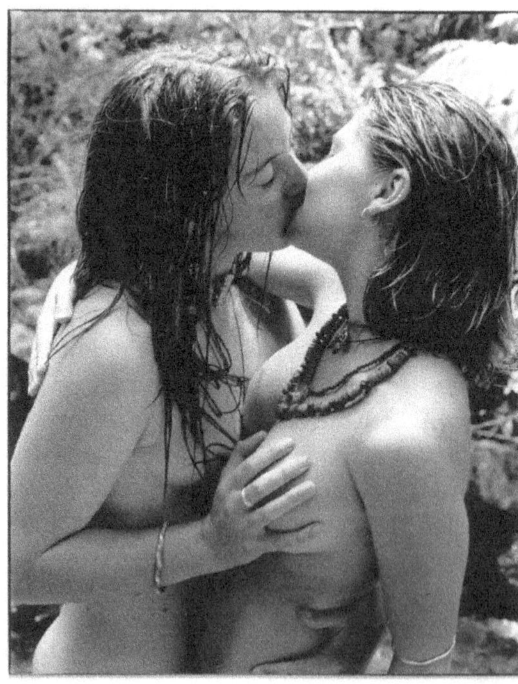

Hannah and Nellie (Crabtree January 1994)

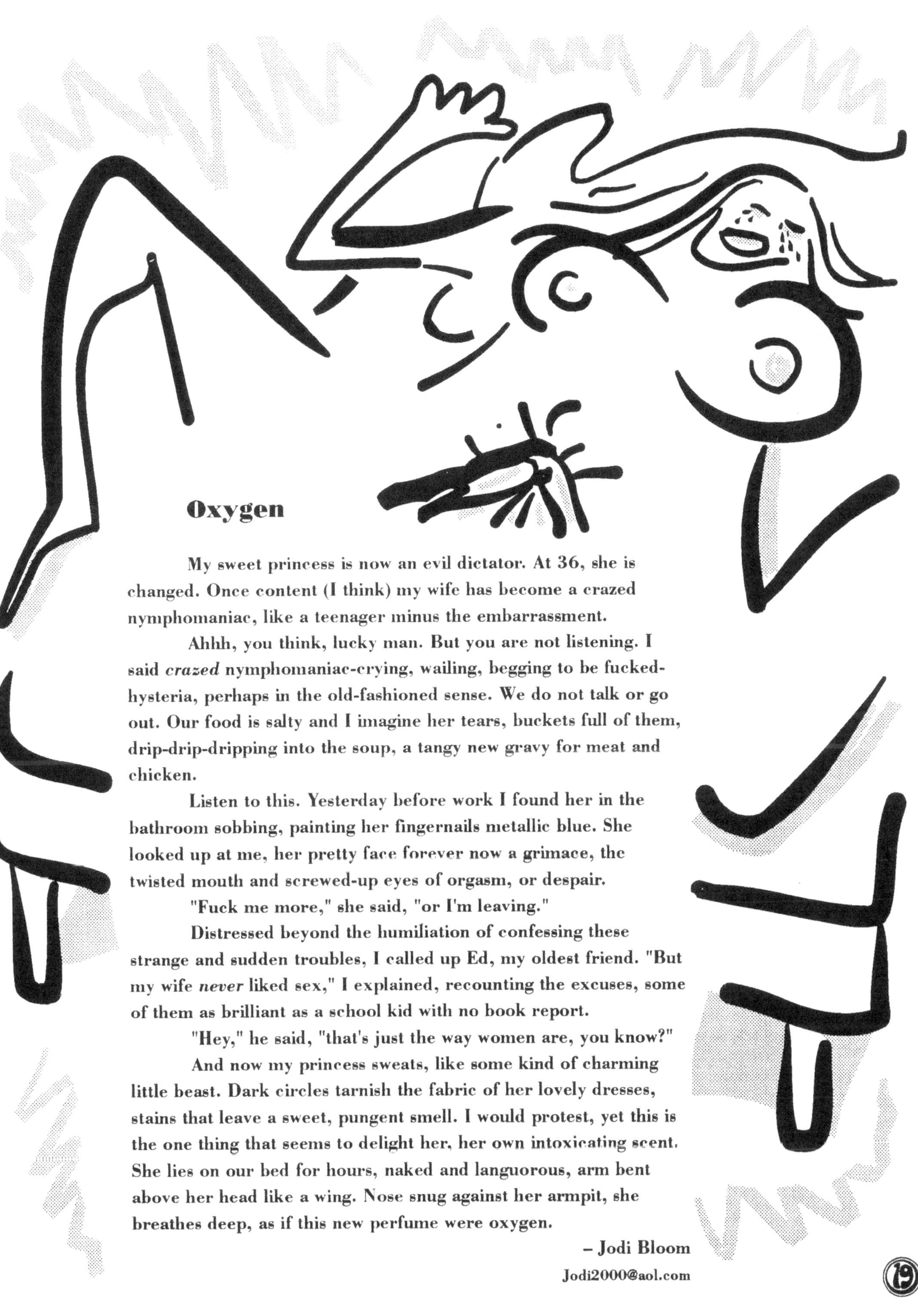

Oxygen

My sweet princess is now an evil dictator. At 36, she is changed. Once content (I think) my wife has become a crazed nymphomaniac, like a teenager minus the embarrassment.

Ahhh, you think, lucky man. But you are not listening. I said *crazed* nymphomaniac-crying, wailing, begging to be fucked-hysteria, perhaps in the old-fashioned sense. We do not talk or go out. Our food is salty and I imagine her tears, buckets full of them, drip-drip-dripping into the soup, a tangy new gravy for meat and chicken.

Listen to this. Yesterday before work I found her in the bathroom sobbing, painting her fingernails metallic blue. She looked up at me, her pretty face forever now a grimace, the twisted mouth and screwed-up eyes of orgasm, or despair.

"Fuck me more," she said, "or I'm leaving."

Distressed beyond the humiliation of confessing these strange and sudden troubles, I called up Ed, my oldest friend. "But my wife *never* liked sex," I explained, recounting the excuses, some of them as brilliant as a school kid with no book report.

"Hey," he said, "that's just the way women are, you know?"

And now my princess sweats, like some kind of charming little beast. Dark circles tarnish the fabric of her lovely dresses, stains that leave a sweet, pungent smell. I would protest, yet this is the one thing that seems to delight her, her own intoxicating scent. She lies on our bed for hours, naked and languorous, arm bent above her head like a wing. Nose snug against her armpit, she breathes deep, as if this new perfume were oxygen.

– Jodi Bloom

Jodi2000@aol.com

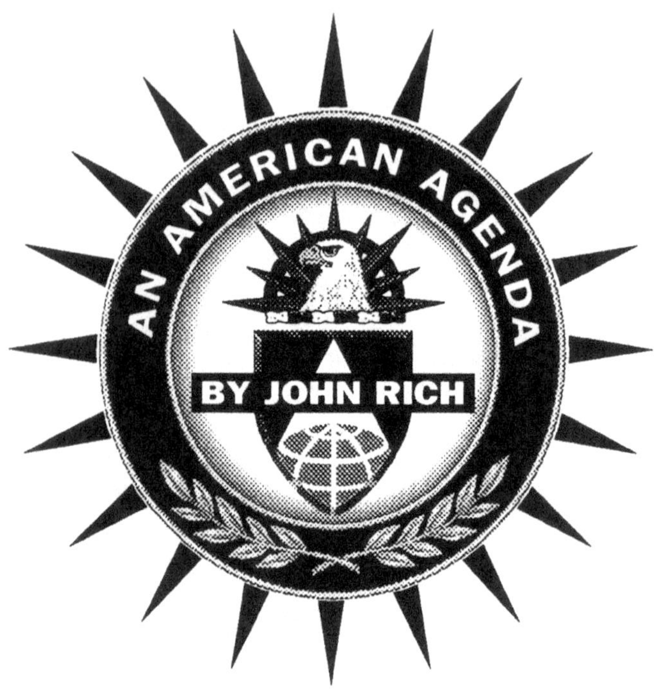

Hippies, vestigial remains of the Enlightenment
Hangin in the Haight.
Ten years after
The summer of love.
A psychedelic Renaissance
Connecting the Voodoo child, Dionysian
Myth, Hoffman, Owsley, and the Dead.
Fear and loathing on tour:
An American Agenda.

A Gratefully Deadicated Jester flashed a
        Tarot Card,
And turned up the cool fool while
        The Great Goat laughs.

Hippy Hill is quiet, yet the princess panics
And the Knight fights. Crystals, Incense
Black lights, strobes, Neon lights,
Crystal balls and even Gypsies
Could not predict that Ken Kesey
Still drives
His magic, psychedelic bus,
And still parks at the Pan Handle.

The poets sing:
We hear note by symbol, vowel, and blue.
Dylan, Broomberg, Hunter, and Johnson-
        Roberts, mostly.
"Truckin', Truckin', Truckin'",
Under the City Lights we walk.
In the mystery of the misty fog filled

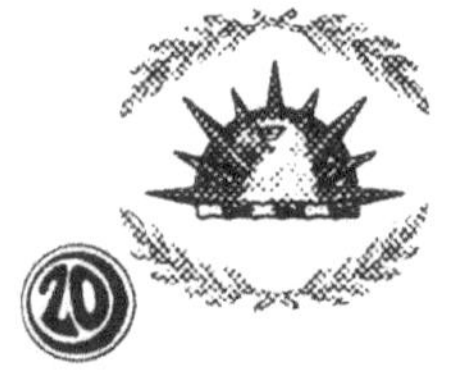
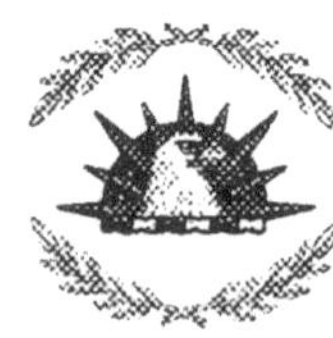
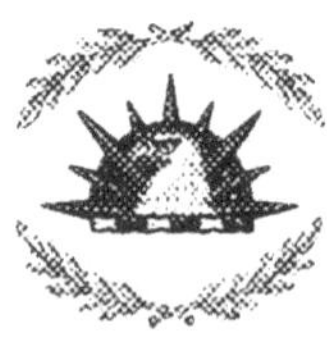

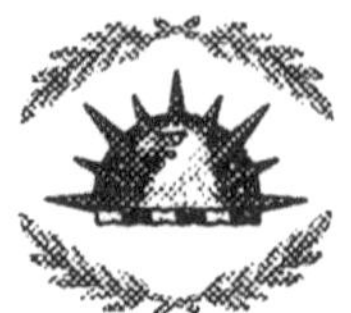

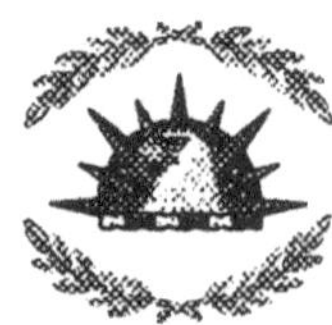

San Francisco night. Condensation
Soaked sidewalks, alleys, lights form
Reflective grids where oil saturated puddles
Catch swirling colours
Like a
Phosphorescent psychedelic tie die.

She's gorgeous
Her heel slips
        Spiked,
        Fishnets,
        Black.
She dances in a leather miniskirt
And makes me watch. I stand.
Lips touch, embrace, caress, the Tarot;
The Queen of Hearts touches, embraces,
Caresses The Tower.
A crack in the pavement
Where a dandelion clings to life:
Leaves sharp, jagged.

Our, no my, utopian drug induced dream
        Broken!
"You don't seem to understand, boy;
I said, this is the DEA."
Baton Rouged in Louisiana,
Too close to New Orleans.

The lunatic bum yelled:
"America's procrustean oligarchy is growing.
Growing into a mighty heartless raptor
That flies off the bill and attacks its own
        America."

I am caught by the talon, the claws,
Incubus of prison walls that tear us apart.
The poppy took root in her heart;
We grow apart.

Bars blossom to freedom
And I get a parole officer, and
A bottle to pee in - the wiz quiz.
Free! Not quite free, but forced drug free.
Under the city lights we part.
She was like a transient cloud
Of fresh air. Images crystalize
In a moment, a fraction,
A transcendent fraction,
A frac....

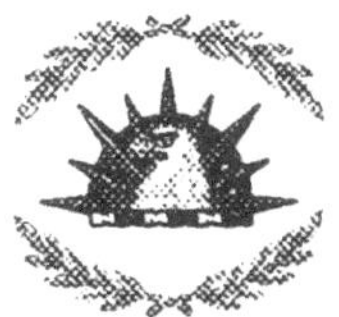 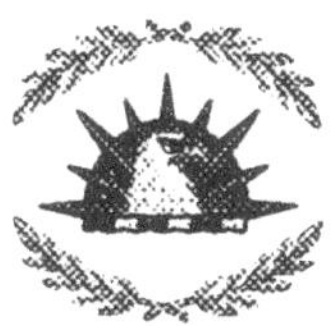 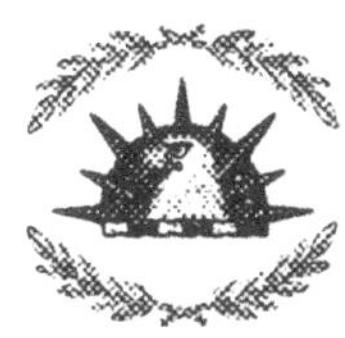

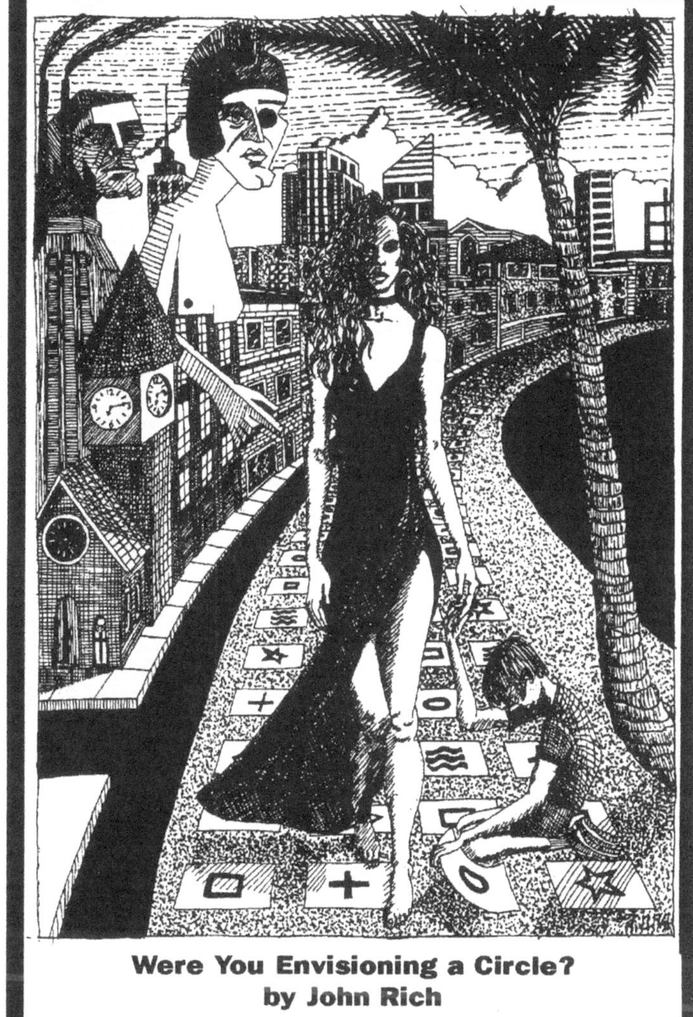

Were You Envisioning a Circle?
by John Rich

She went south
I left the Golden Gate
Over the bay, down into the valley,
Over the Rockies, across the plains,
Past the mounds to stop in the shadow
Of the Brick Yard where the Eagle watches,
And Prometheus lives.

"The Eagle sees no reflection:
Horus Yin or Horus Yang?
What does its eye behold?
Fire holds no boundaries,
Out of flames born vengeance
And the Eagle pulls its arrows in peace time,
Aiming at its own."

Another found my heart
But my carelessness, foolishness, and
Don't give a damn attitude
Fed the Eagle. My life is in the
Belly of the raptor.

Industrial prison's slave labor
Slaughters sacred cows
        Good eats.
        Hathor?

Can I ever hide from the Eagle?
No one can escape spy satellites, wiretaps,
Bugs, choppers cruisers preying,
And I'm beginning to hate
The ignorance of an internecine drug war.

"Silver Eagle on the Shore line
Let us be ________________?
Free and easy!"
I have forgotten the song, washed away.
        Institutionalized.

The dong, the bell, the toll toils,
And the buzzer rings so we march
To the chow hall.
Today's meal: Hathor burgers and fries.

Along the wall, behind the wall,
In the nest, the shadow of the Eagle
I walk.

Silence?
There is no silence.
Silence is a rumble, a pounding, a rapping
A tapping, on concrete and steel.
My cranium thunders with the constant
Beat of the prison block.
The Eagle watches with arrows aimed.
It hates us all.

John Rich #910243
IDC-Westville CC
P.O Box 473
Westville, IN 46391

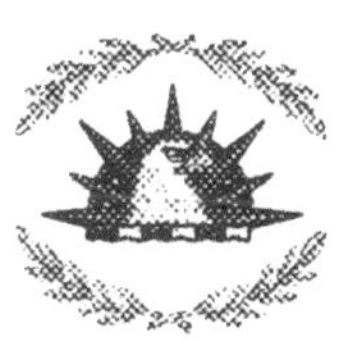 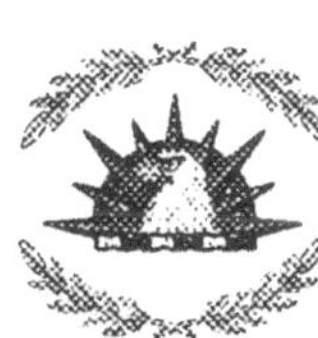 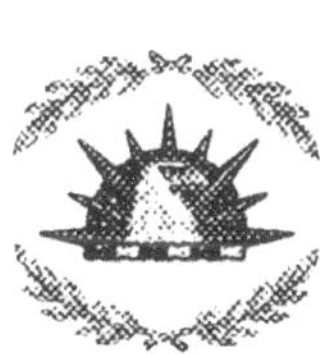 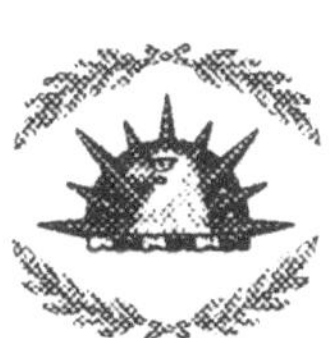

creativity...

as the years pass and the new millennium approaches, fast and vibrant like a new horizon on the peak of shining at us.. ideas and dreams are being ignored with the ever pressing objective of today's societies for "progress". Its obnoxious injection of the "competitive nature" has come to pass as being recognized as "normal" and is passed from one generation to the next as if nothing was wrong. It imposes the ideal that one should live life under the guise of "being better than everyone else". This condition is flawless in constructing a society of followers, & non-thinking over-achievers, who will at any moment become ruthless and cunning if it will suit their needs. Strong warriors are being developed with this formula...but warriors to war with what? and whom? Now, this is not to say that development of ones individual power and strength is a BAD thing.. in fact, quite the opposite... but it is not the ONLY thing.. there is more to the strengthening of a powerful person than just being "the winner"... it comes from understanding and realizing the beauty of experience and the vividness of its face.. to have the ability to imagine and believe in that which you have imagined.. not with the concept of "striking it rich" but more with the ideal that "i did this" and feeling pride for your own work and craftsmanship.. the natural "creative nature" of our race that is being shunned in the modern way of life. Creativity is the oldest known belief, according to all known myths. It is that in which the GODS themselves believed in. It is the purest essence of that which empowered those very gods to BE what and who they were (and are). In light of this, you would think there would be an over emphasis on CREATIVE thinking in our societies, but there is not. This needs to change if our world is to progress into the new aeon with any hope of survival. It is the obvious missing factor in the industrial minded world in which we live today.

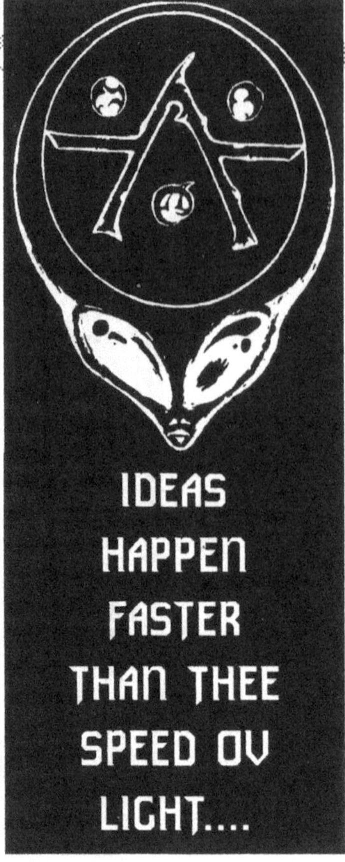

Thee Instagon Foundation (TIF) formed in 1993 with the mission of being a creative alliance of artists working together to enrich the planet with a more creative way of thinking... to share ideals and projects, to work with each other in our artistic approach to the interweaving of our art into the monster of the media, and its audience. We believe in the power of creativity, and its divinity. Each individual is an artist, strong and wise in their craft.. TIF attempts to create forums in which individuals can interact with and experiment in, so that they might find their unknown hidden talent and nurture it into a power and strength, some are creative sculptures or musicians, others creative in their methods of banking or teaching. This is the way of the future for a strong society to exist. We must take wild notions into consideration, as they are usually very powerful and right on the nose of the problem. Ideas happen faster than the speed of light. Thee Instagon Foundation wants you to let your ideas shine.. we encourage and want to attempt to direct all interested parties in directions that may lead to the development of their individual creative dreams and visions. We support all who come to become involved and show a strong will to help us in this dream. TIF, so far, with VERY little funding, has created many outlets for artists to create in. We have our own record label, with decent international distribution, a publishing firm for small books, a free open submission magazine called "THEE NEVERENDING PAGE", published bi-annually, sponsor local poetry readings and spoken word events, a web site, radio programs, performance art, and the list continues... in 1994 TIF joined forces with its long time ally THEE TEMPLE OV PSYCHICK YOUTH NA, and released the debut full length experimental CD from "INSTAGON", which has gained some wonderful reviews world wide. TOPY and TIF are still very interactive today with many projects in the works. In 1995 TIF joined the amazing world of A.I.N., the Autonomous Individuals Network, an international directory for interesting projects happening world wide, TIF serves as the "official" (whatever that is) node of A.I.N. in the USA. We produce and distribute this directory in this country. If you feel that this is something you are akin to, we would love to hear from you.. but we are poor, we are artists, so please include return postage, or you will probably not be answered for a long time, you will be answered.. but it might take awhile. or contact us via the internet at

http://www.tif.org/tif
or instagon@netcom.com

send all inquires to:
THE INSTAGON FOUNDATION
PO Box 894
Huntington Beach, CA
92648-0894 usa

please include SASE or sufficient postage.

Be creative in your daily life.
Make stuff up.

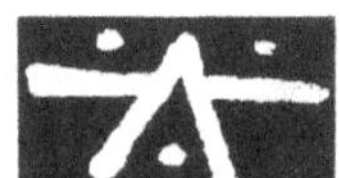

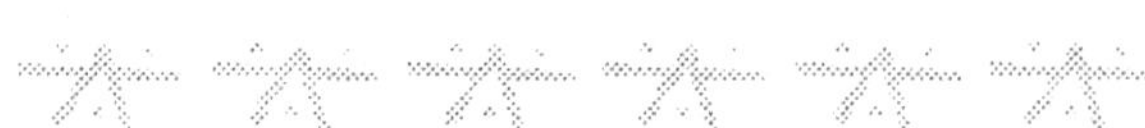

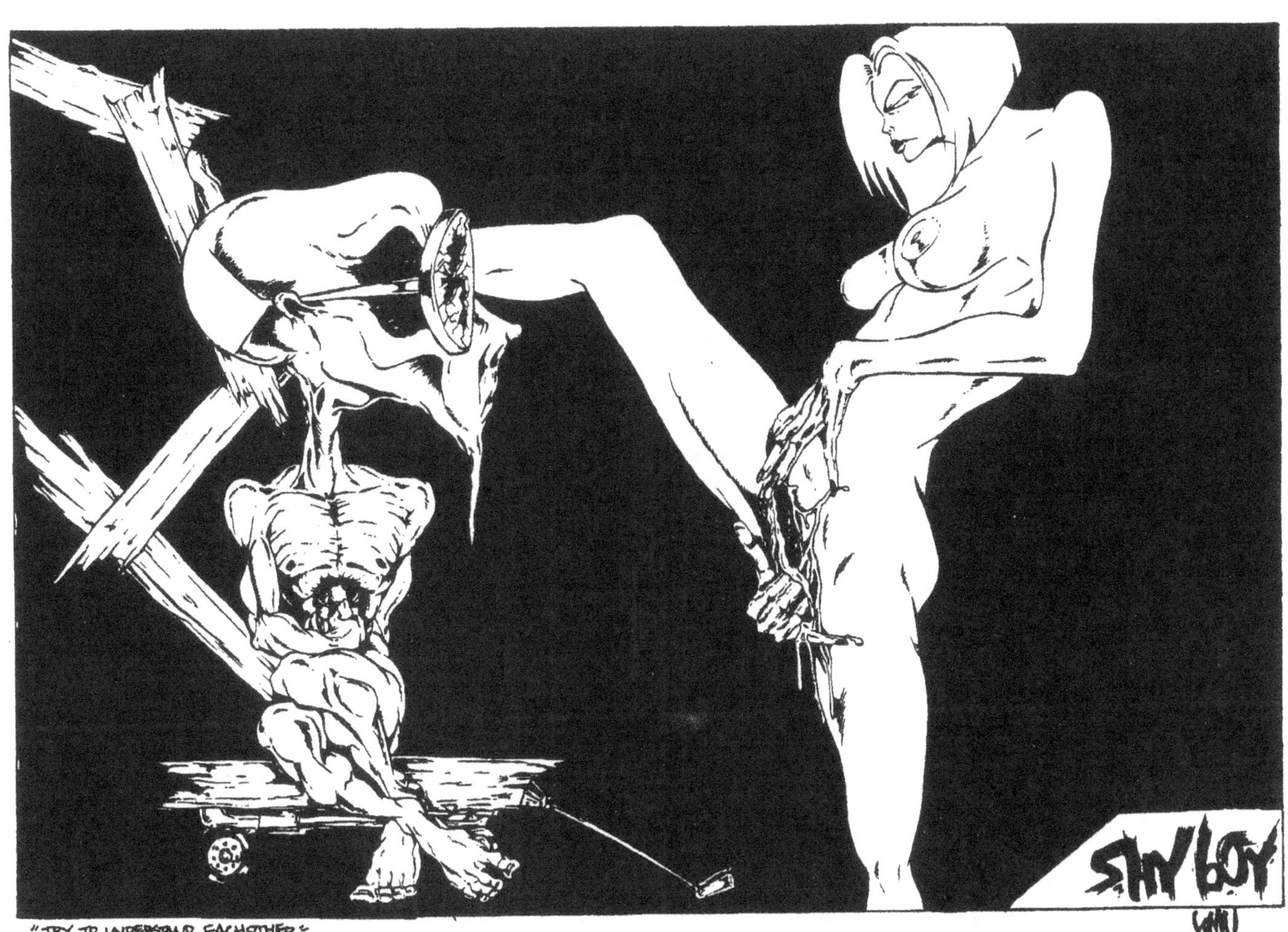

"TRY TO UNDERSTAND EACHOTHER"...

Dancer

Topless,
lucid,
she commands a small
audience
within the dark
of this ditchdigger's
lounge.
Her blouse peeled off
when the cops are gone
she arches her back
makes her tips
breaks the night in two.

The dollars are lovenotes,
her movements a dream.

– Robert L. Penick

"vincent"

in a wheatfield
with his crows
i see his beauty
and his crows

in his room
i sleep in his bed
i wear his hat
and i taste the paint
that drips from his mind

in a museum
i touch his face
and drink his eyes
and fill myself with colour

in his paintbrush
i smell his need
and i swirl with his trees
and clouds
and i know he was not mad

- kara pridgent
bbb@bethanybb.com

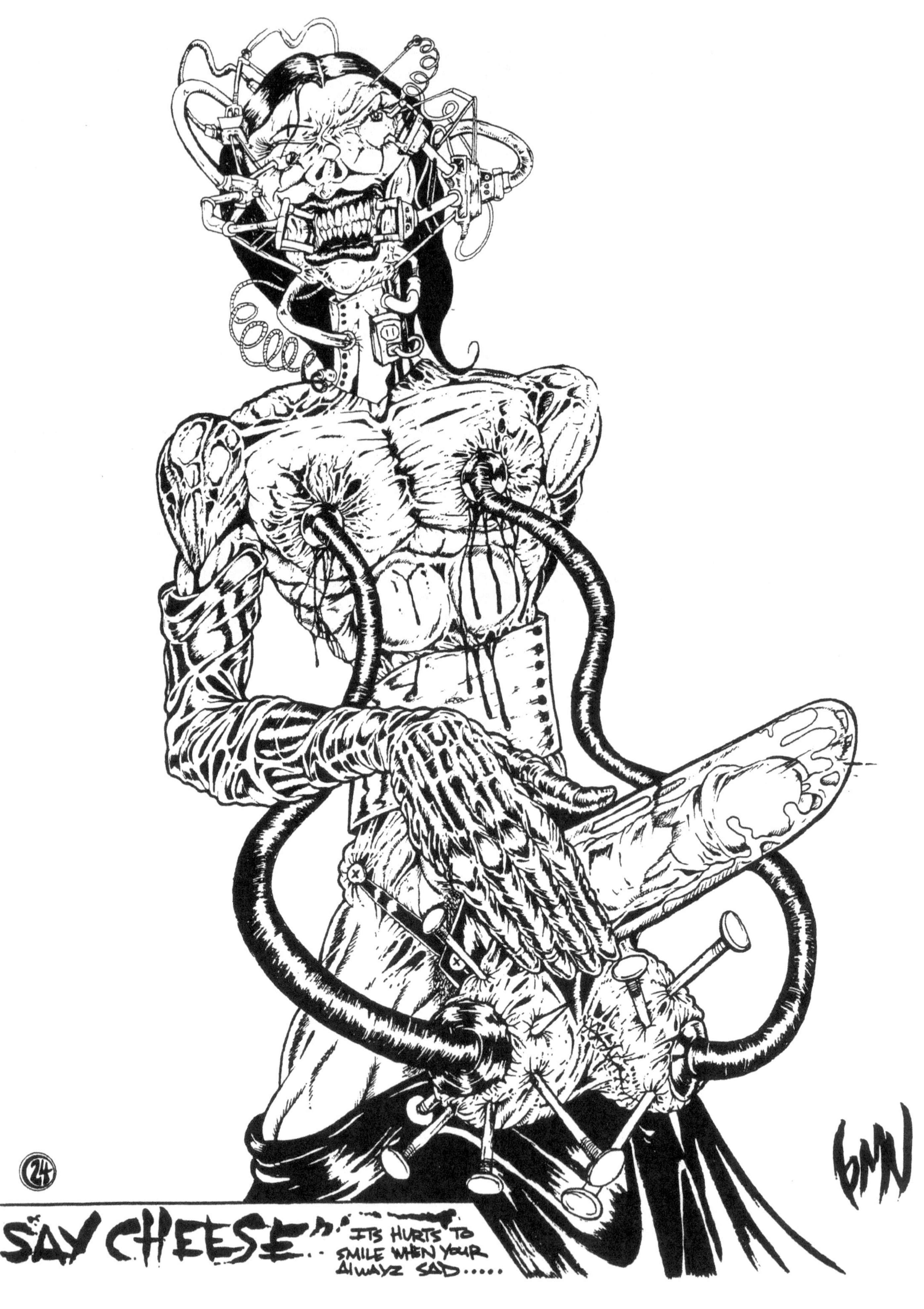

24
SMN
"SAY CHEESE"...
ITS HURTS TO
SMILE WHEN YOUR
ALWAYZ SAD.....

December 28, 1996

I suppose this is a review of sorts. Two things evoke this review. First Martha Wilson of Franklin Furnace asked me to comment on the Furnace's plans. The second event was our going to a Karen Finley reading (which cost $3 as opposed to $30 for a Finley performance....which I could not afford).

I have to start by saying I consider both Wilson and Finley powerful voices of the avant-garde. When other performance galleries were making artists create 'acts' that would fit into 'avant-garde' cabarets...fit in terms of both time and fashionable subject matter...Wilson at the Furnace was giving both artists and the art absolute freedom to perform magic...until THEY shut the Furnace down for 'fire violations.' Karen and I were among the artists who enjoyed this freedom.

In other reviews, I have likened Karen's poetry to Ginsberg's, and her performances to Lenny Bruce's in their intensity and laser commentary on the social injustices. Her poetry makes me cry. Her passions within her performances have transported me into very deep states of reality.

So it is always tragic to see figures like these get sucked, seduced, absorbed, tricked, bribed into 'the mainstream.' It is tragic not only in personal terms for the individual artists, but in terms of the big picture. When an artist sets herself up as being an artist who goes beyond the normal frame, who tells the hard truths, who explores the unknown...not to be hip, or controversial, or to be interesting...but because that is how our tribal human being evolves, so it has to be done...when that kind of artist then goes after money, personal fame, and/or glamour while still claiming to be doing avant-garde art, it is denying society the real evolutionary function of the real avant-garde. It tells people, audiences and artists alike, that the avant-garde is just a branch of the entertainment complex with the same rules, goals, reality as television, rock music, Hollywood, and sports. This is like telling people a can of Slim Fast is a balanced meal of real food. It is a lie. And the scary dangerous thing is artists are buying/selling this lie.

Why am I on this rant? About a year or two ago, Wilson sent out a mass mailing in which she defended art (maybe to funders) as a profitable industry which pulls money, people, and jobs into cities. (True...if you want to make a lot of money, buy property where artists live/create now to sell to the yuppies when they discover the area!) This logic is a very steep, slippery slope indeed. The first glaring danger of this commercialized logic is art, according to this logic, which is not profitable or sellable is not and can not be successful worthwhile art! (Hey, ain't that the American way?) I am sure Wilson does not believe this.

Although another mass mailing I received from her in November (I have been mulling it over until now) makes me wonder if she has fallen down that slope into believing the lie. Avant-garde art is art that tells the truth, explores the taboos, pushes the limits. Obviously this kind of art, if it is honest, can not be focused outwardly. Historically, often 'The People' (who are not the same thing as 'the mainstream') have identified with the avant-garde because it was telling the truth about their lives. The focus of the avant-garde should always be on telling the truth, not on popularity polls and bottom lines. The focus of the avant-garde has been, and should be, on doing art that is as 'pure' as possible...not on mass media entertainment of reaching as many people as possible by shaping 'the product' to that goal.

In her letter, Martha refers to the avant-garde art as 'once unpopular work...formerly at the non-profit fringe'...art that Franklin Furnace, according to the letter, has groomed for 20 years to get it ready for the mainstream...and now 'Franklin Furnace is in a position to lead the avant-garde into the mainstream...'. This hurts my head and heart. It is as if Martha does not see her own historical contribution of giving daring art a home. Instead, she tries to take credit for gravity and decay. The mainstream entertainment, by it sheer mass, has always sucked artists out of the fringe, the underground. That is just gravity. In reality, it takes a lot to enter, and to stay in, the underground. The underground is where the real freedom and the real ability to change society are to be found. This is why artists CHOOSE the underground instead of the mainstream. This is also why, when an artist is pulled into the mainstream, this freedom and ability decay. In my own career, I have worked very hard to stay in the underground...this work has been hard precisely because some of the pieces have turned out to be 'popular' (whatever that means!)...attracting the mainstream sharks.

The mainstream has always tried to create a fake avant-garde with fake controversies, fake taboos, fake 'hipness,' etc. to give the marks a controlled fun-ride through a Disneyland to keep them away from the real edge of life. This is because the powers-that-be can not control or exploit what is in the real avant-garde.

All of this is business as usual...and doesn't scare me.

What does scare me is that someone like Martha bought into it and is becoming a producer of it! Her letter read like a bad Saturday Night Live skit. She is selling Franklin Furnace to get money to match a $100,000 n.e.a. challenge grant. With this money, and by teaming up with the corporate and media America, Franklin Furnace will be a 'content provider for new media' that sniffs out 'emerging alternative artists.' (Emerging from where to where? Alternative to what?) These artists and their art must be suitable to be packaged as 'alternative comedy (a.k.a. performance art.)' The letter tells us this new alternative comedy will be 'funny, yet provocative.' There will be a half-hour t.v. show of this. Plus they will produce short pieces to be aired 'through' Saturday Night Live (as if that show has been cutting edge, or even funny, in the past 15 years) and MTV (with its history of censorship)! Moreover they are seeking other ways of giving 'audiences a glimpse of the avant-garde world' (whatever the hell that is!) 'in an entertaining and easily consumable fashion'...like avant-garde artist trading cards...funded by Philip Morris Companies!

The marketing phrase 'alternative comedy (a.k.a. performance art)' is very damaging to performance art because it trivializes art. In fact it avoids 'art' all together, selling 'alternative comedy' as a weird, consumable form of entertainment which will give you a laugh for your buck. This is not what performance art is. Performance art is the performing/doing/experiencing the act of art. It is going on a physical journey into the unlimited realm of art. Sometimes this journey may be funny or entertaining. But these are not the true goals or rewards. The suggestion (promotion) that these are the rewards of art results in denying people, including the artists, the real full freeing experience of art.

All of this is selling the art, the artists, and the audience way short. I am not questioning Martha's personal commitment to the real avant-garde art. But realistically such art can not exist in such an environment that she is envisioning. Moreover it is misunderstanding the new media such as the internet and zines. In these media, artists can relate to their audiences directly without middlemen, without compromises, without limiting concepts such as 'mainstream'...all for very little money...so why sell out?

But this concept of 'alternative comedy' is disturbing. I guess the Karen Finley reading was an example of alternative comedy. She read from her parody of Martha Stewart (why bother?) which she obviously wrote just to fulfill a book deal. The reading was empty schtick, a passionless exercise in cleverness with no content or message. The audience responded with reflex laughter, like a laugh track. The problem was Karen was trying to be an entertainer, a comedian. Karen is not a comedian or entertainer. That is not her function. Her function is to inspire, confront, transmute...to tell the truth with passion. That is why people come to her. When she does not do that, the people are not fulfilled. When she ended her act, the people just sat there numb. Then I asked Karen to read her very deep, very moving poem 'Black Sheep'... I just happened to have a copy of it with me. As she read it, magic, life, and power started flowing through her body and out into the audience, uplifting them. When she finished reading, people stood up and clapped...because this was why they came.

Oh, by the way, do you consider yourself mainstream? Do you want to be?

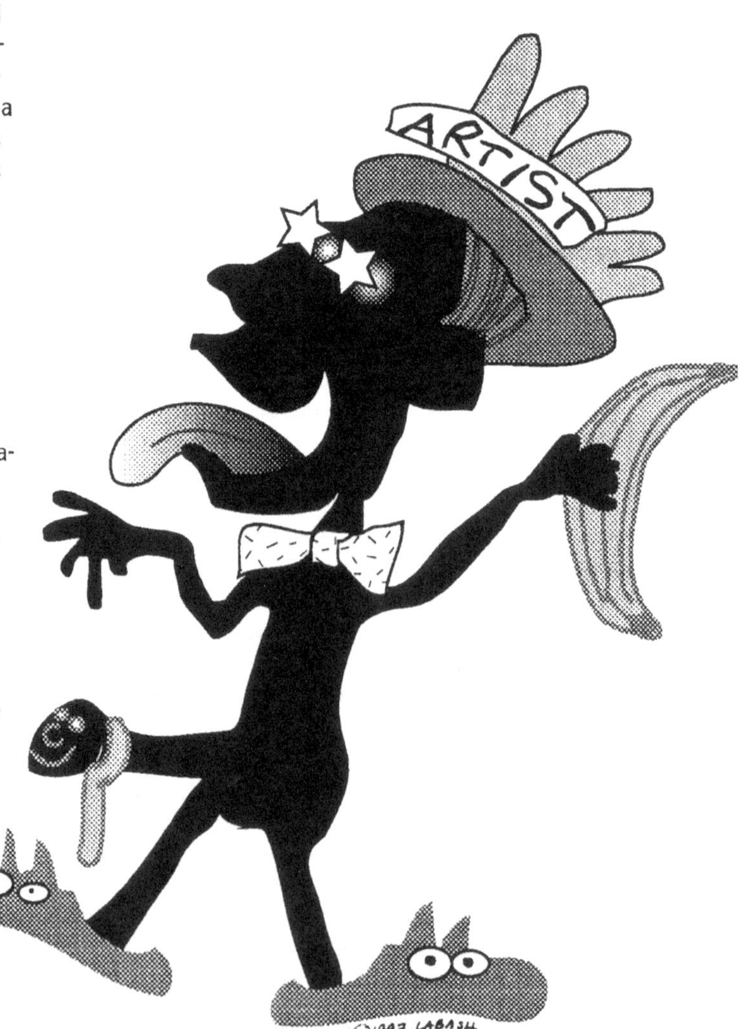

Subject: Re: You URL submission was rejected
Date: Mon, 10 Feb 1997 03:08:52-0500
From: "Ray Heinrich" <ray@scribbledyne.com>
Organization: Scribbledyne Corp - Word Biscuit Division
To: info@linkmonster. corn
CC: fmoore@LanMinds.Com, ray@scribbledyne.com

> Linkmonster Link Rejection Notification
>
> Your link: http://www.eroplay.com was rejected for the following reason:
>
> Link submission contained questionable language and/or subject matter.
>
> We do thank you for your submission. We wish you luck with your next submission.
>
>Linkmonster

I Was a Stranger

I was a stranger
until you read
this poem. Now
we are lovers.
A poem is
forever.
-George Kauffman

dear linkmonster:

your love of gray
is not
like the interesting love
of death
of life
of skin
rubbing against
the skin of all of us
so what do you want?
$5 T-shirts
to buy?
to tell our children
we came from Walmart
to deny
our cunts and cocks?

i take my clothes
in the morning
with my mate
of twenty-five years
and we throw them
in your general direction
and notice
as they touch you
the warmth
you have refused

Biothing (short version):
Ray is an ex-Texas technofreak and hippie socialist wannabe. He writes poems for thrills and attention, likes dogs, and owns a blue fish. Write to him at: ray@scribbledyne.com
http://www.vais.net/~heinrich/wb/

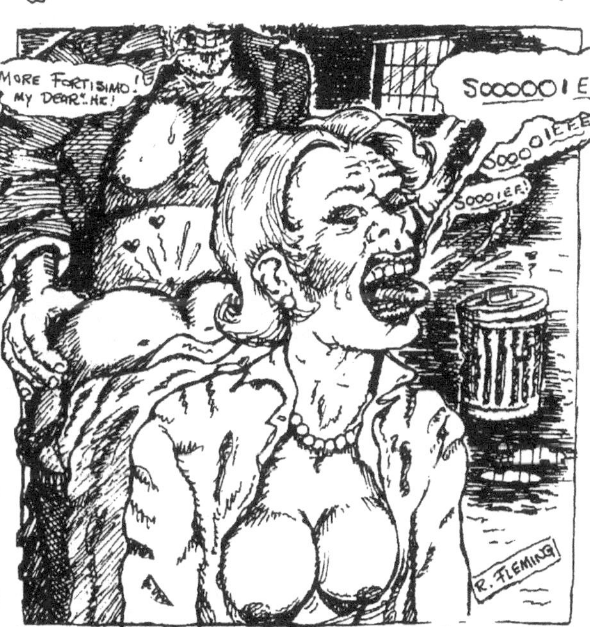

- TALES FROM 1ST AVE. IN BELLTOWN ....

LATE FRIDAY NIGHT/EARLY SATURDAY A.M. IN AN ALLEY BEHIND ONE OF SEATTLE'S MORE 'POSH' AND EXCRUCIATINGLY 'TREND-OID' RESTAURANTS; LOCAL STOCK 'POWER' BROKER AND YUPPIE 'EX-TRAORDINAIRE', LYDIA INDEX, WELL INTO HER CUPS AND OVERWROUGHT WITH ANGST AND FEELINGS OF GUILT PER CLASS, STATUS AND EXPLOITATION, SOLICITS THE SERVICES OF A TRANSIENT 'RUSTIC' FROM SHELTON, WA., NAME OF 'OLIE' AND HAS HIM TEACH HER HOW TO 'DO-"HOG-CALLING" à la THE MOVIE-BOOK 'DELIVERANCE'! .... AFTER THIS THERAPEUTIC SESSION, SHE 'WRITES A CHECK' AND 'GETS ON' WITH LIFE, RELIEVED FOR AWHILE... IDEA INSPIRED BY 'PERSONAL AD' IN THE STRANGER.

Subject: ASKANCE UPDATE
Date: 21 Nov 1996 12:04:11 GMT
From: Paul_Couillard@intacc.web.net (Paul Couillard)
Organization: Matrix Arts Network
To: fmoore@lanminds.com

It's a 'slow' Wednesday afternoon at ASKANCE, the temporary transformative playhouse/radical faerie hangout I've made for myself in downtown Toronto, so I thought I'd write a little update on how things have been going.

Perhaps I should start by telling you a bit about the piece I did at the end of October as part of Rencontre Performance, an international festival of performance art that my non-profit group (FADO) organized/hosted (15 artists from around the world including Mexico, the UK, Finland, Hungary, Romania, Lithuania, Japan and Korea). I did my first 'street piece', LULL, spending 6 hours in various locations along Queen Street (the artsy strip of Toronto) in my newspapier mache outfit (underwear, socks, boots, pants, sweatshirt, double-collared jacket, gloves and hat all done up with newspaper), rocking in my newspapier macheed folding rocker. For this piece I didn't want to speak, just present the image of me, rocking on the street (I've always rocked back and forth, as long as I can remember). I did have a piece of chalk that I put an 'x' at each location that I rocked and then wrote one word that described the experience in that spot, though. It was great — lots of people stopped by to ask me 'what I was protesting', or to call me 'newspaper man', or just to find out what it was all about. The goth girl from the goth bar across the street came down in her nightdress and had coffee on the steps of her building beside me. Someone else brought me a little gift of trail mix which she wrapped up in newspaper before giving it to me. One guy tried to give me money. Lots of people ended up coming to the evening performances as a result of seeing me on the street. Frank Moore talks about how there are 'magical' spots where people just come to you, and other spots, maybe even only inches away, where you will be totally ignored, and I discovered the same thing. In general, the vibes becamse more 'threatened' and hostile as I moved east into the city core, towards Bay Street (our equivalent of Wall Street), though I did get some positive reactions at City Hall.

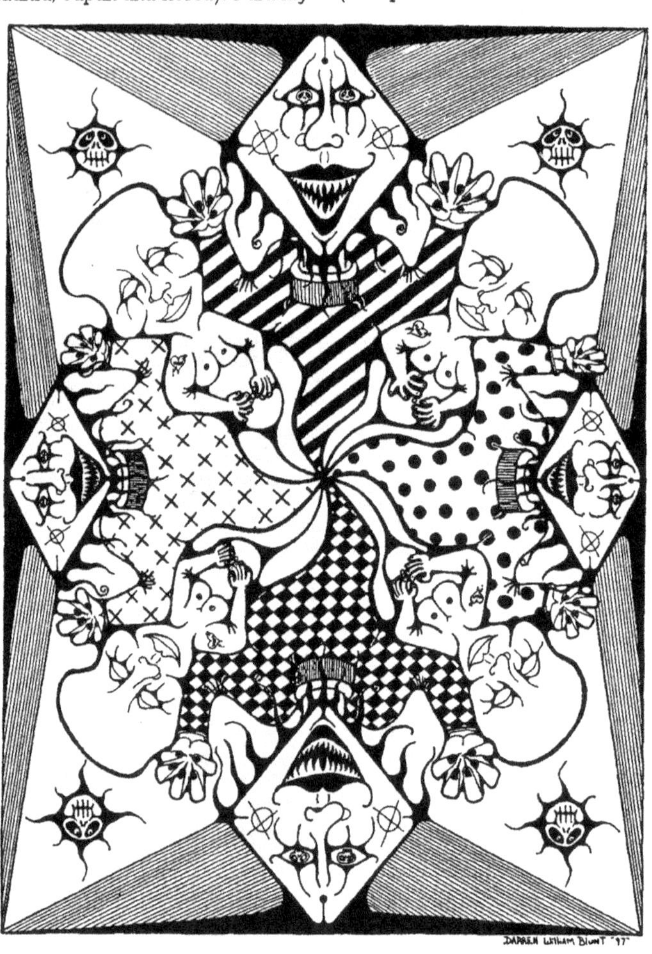

Anyways, it was great and I learned a lot. It made me want to do more of this kind of public work, though I think I'd like to work in more possibilities for interaction with people in the future (I think that's really where this kind of form offers the most), and I'll probably wait until the weather is a little more sympathetic, since it's now close to winter and we've had several little snowfalls (none lasting, though).

From the intense experience of this three-day festival, I jumped into my next project, a month-long series of performance actions called ASKANCE. I've set up a giant playroom in a performance space called Symptom Hall (for you SF types, it's kinda like 848 without the sex — though we're changing that a bit, too...). The main space has been set up with a wonderfully evocative installation. To enter, you have to pass through a 'stiletto curtain' of high heels, pumps, cowboy boots and tiger slippers that have been treated with glitter where the scuff marks were. Inside, you find a 6 x 8 foot floating pond, a blue bubble-wrapped 'stairway to know-where', the beautiful rock I dug from six feet under this summer when I was making a new outhouse hole at the farm where we do our faerie gatherings, a quilting loom where my friend Jules is set up every day for 'stitch and bitch' sessions (the quilt will be auctioned off at the end of the month to raise funds for DRAGHEAD, the faerie magazette [that's 'zette, not 'zine] he edits), a comfortable living room set on the stage that graces one end of the space, lots of pink and purple tulle, and, of course, the tent with the computer (set up with e-list material from the faerie list — and an adventurous hacker would quickly find Frank's e-list as well...) from which I'm writing this. There's also a faerie library in a suitcase that includes some pretty tangential info (like Annie Sprinkle's Post Porn Modernist book, and Frank Moore's the Cherotic [R]evolutionary zine as well as various faerie zines, gathering calls, etc.). I've even colonized the side rooms. The full kitchen is a big centre of activity, but there's also a large well-stocked drag room (what fun to get the straight boys dressed up at the opening night party), an altar room with peat moss and wood chip floor, a hallway of 'faerie sounds' that includes extensive bits of my writing about the faeries in prep for this show in grafitti style on the wall and a broken-down piano board that can be used for jamming, a goddess bath room, and occasional temporal objects/spaces like the spice painting I made at my first twelve-hour ritual (whirling snakes, burning faggots, and a lusty face), now just a mound on a plate that rests by the pond — it smelled amazing in here— or the 'campfire' of rocks and sterno candles that we used for last weekend's slumber party (A Story Story Night). The space has many doorways that are adorned with fetish objects — rubber gloves, a whistle, a necklace, a tiny holy water fount, an animal skull, sunglasses, rubber snakes, a hockey jock (with sock snaps like a garter belt) — and the tech room has been posted over with a 'police line do not cross' ribbon that turns to reveal one of the many wiccan chants the faeries use: the earth the water the fire the rain returns returns returns returns...

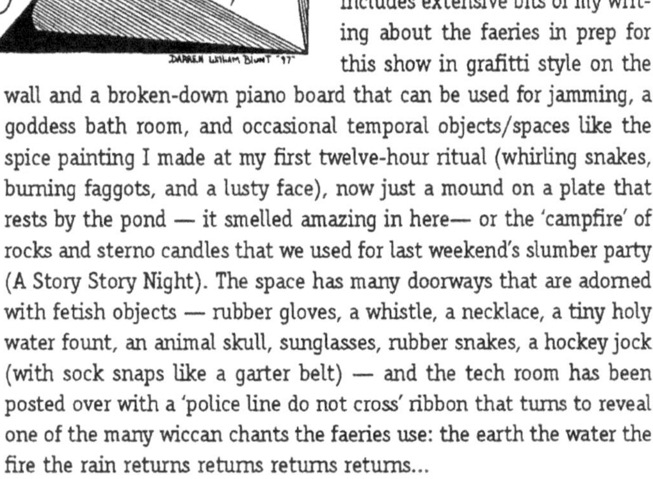

The people who run the space are amazed at the transformations we've effected, and the atmosphere of almost decadent comfort we've created (everyone who comes through wants to either move in or rent the space themselves for their shows!). We did a total physical and psychic strip-down of the place, including painting the walls, scrubbing every surface, and cleansing the remaining negative vibes (including some lingering confused spirit energies) from when the place had a reputation as a rave club and before when it was a Lithuanian community centre. The 'performance schedule' is a little demanding — Saturday Night slumber parties from 9 pm to 9 am (first weekend was an opening party followed by 'bedtime reading'; last weekend was 'a story story night' — our final slumber party this weekend is 'pillow talk'), Sunday Teas (first weekend 'ceremonial tea', last weekend 'high tea' [we're still eating the leftover veggie pates, humus and baba ganouj I made for it, plus, of course, Jules' gingerbread penises] — this weekend, the final one, will be a wild Mad Hatter Tea, hats required), Tuesday all-day performance rituals (the first one I made the spice painting; yesterday's was focused on sound, and I played a lot of accordian music, jangled bells, weaved the building sounds into the sounds I created, tried to integrate it all into a whole as a way of healing Jules' exasperation with the car alarm that kept going off outside all the day before; I don't know yet what I'll do next week for my final piece) from 6 am to 6 pm, and Wednesday to Friday are 'gallery hours' (11 am to 6 pm) where people can come in and do as much of an interactive performance ritual as they dare. Most of them just want to get a tour of the place, have tea, sit and talk — but that's fine. It's not like a paid workshop where they're expected to risk more than that.

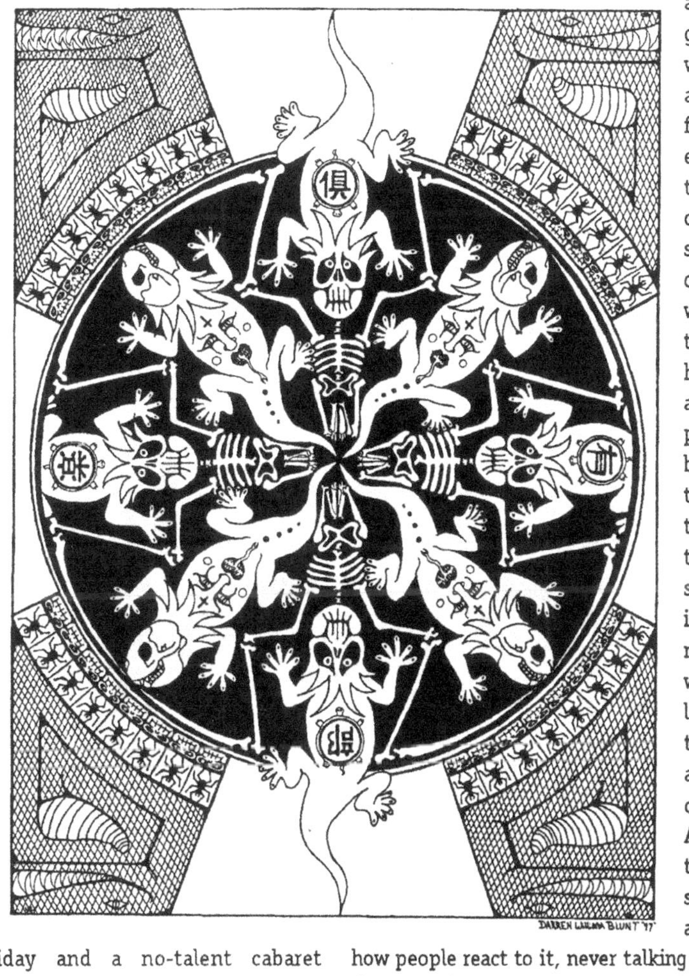

Also on the agenda: a full-moon ritual this Sunday, and then a full-fledged faerie gathering starting Wednesday with public activities (a ritual on Friday and a no-talent cabaret ['Extravaganza', as we call it] — maybe a bit like Frank Moore's Outrageous Beauty Revue? on Saturday).

This month of performance activities is based around my experiences with the radical faeries. I didn't want to do a 'theatre' piece where I would entertain an audience with my stories about the faeries — I wanted the audience to feel more like participants, so I developed this piece that is more like an environment that people come into and that I animate as a performer. No fourth wall separation, no performer-audience dynamic to force the nature of the interaction. A piece about building community (since that is what the faeries have taught me), one in which my 'sissy' side is on display (with its politics, spiritual awareness, sense of fashion, gentleness, etc.) without excluding anyone for their own identifications, and not limiting my own identity to any one label, even one as fluid and ambiguous as 'faerie'.

So far the piece has been magical. The turn-outs haven't been huge, which is fine — communities usually get built slowly and in pieces (I told my friend Andrea the other day, "Toronto is too cold and disconnected a city for me, so I'm building my own city, one person at a time") — but the buzz and interest seems to be gathering as the events go on — so we might be run ragged by next week!

For me, it took a lot of courage to create this playhouse atmosphere and call it 'art' — but so far the reaction has been unexpectedly positive. Some have taken the environment we've created to be a kind of visual art show on its own, asking about the 'titles' of individual pieces ('um, gee, it's not that kind of a show') as if it were a group show of installation pieces. Everyone is completely charmed by the focus around food — where else do you get tea and fresh-baked goods when you come into a show? And all the while I'm in a subtle performance mode, shaping their experience just enough to push them a little bit, interjecting bits of faeriedom, getting them to do simple things like play with the costumes, or sit down and quilt with Jules, or leave something in the altar room. It's been great to have a place to come to every day and just be creative, and have people come by to play. It's also been fun to slowly take over, first the initial rush of having something ready for the opening, but then living in the space (I don't sleep here most nights, but Jules is actually resident here, since he normally lives on the farm where we do our gatherings) and making little adjustments, adding our touch, taking it over inch by inch and transforming it, even if it's only things that we would notice. And it makes so much more sense to me as art than, say, a gallery show where you put up the work and disappear, never knowing how people react to it, never talking with people about their feelings, their impulses, or the motivations that drive the work.

Whatever else happens, I'm having fun — but I also feel like this kind of work has an effect, even if no one shows up. And the connections are often unexpected. There was another group that rents the space on Wednesday nights to drum (it's a class in african drumming, and there's a downstairs space that they're supposed to use during the time I'm here) — so last week I set them up around my snake painting, which was amazing. The teacher got really into the space, and said to his class "tonight I want us to make these snakes dance" — and I got a free show!

More later.

xo Paul

DARREN LUKAS BLUNT '97

Calling all hooligans!

Why waste your brain on those snooty-ass literary magazines when you could injure it permanently with Driver's Side Airbag! With writing and artwork from Michael LaBash, Robert W. Howington, Adrienne GreenHeart, Alice Olds-Ellingson and Alan Catlin, plus comix like Milk & Cheese, The Assassin and the Whiner, Cultural Jetlag, and more!

Sample copy: $4
1 year subscription: $13 (4 issues)
Free catalog with order!

CASH, CHECK OR MONEY ORDER MADE OUT TO
MICHAEL HALCHIN.
Driver's Side Airbag
PO Box 25760
Los Angeles CA 90025
email: mhalchin@aol.com

CREATIVE IDEAS, WORDS, DREAMS, MAGAZINES, BOOKS, MUSIC, EXPERIMENTALISM, ART, NETWERKING, POETRY, PERFORMANCES, SHOWINGS, SMILES, HONESTY, MAGICK, LIFE, LIVING..
THEE INSTAGON FOUNDATION
believing in creativity..
PO BOX 894 Huntington Beach, Kalifornia 92648-0894 USA
please enclose SASE ... or while surfing thee WEB:
http://www.tif.org/tif

PENPALS WANTED
E.O.C.I
RICK BAGBY
SID# 11985975
2500 WESTGATE
PENDLETON, OR 97801

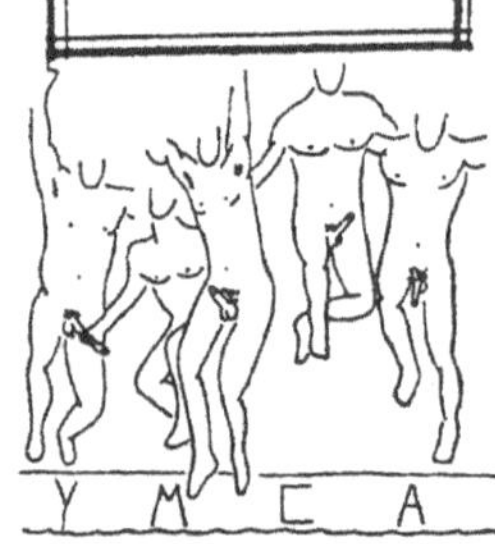

artist: allen renfro.

SHORT FUSE
Box 90436, Santa Barbara, CA 93190-0436
single copies: $1.00 • subscription: $9.00
Free to contributors and institutionalized persons

RONI RAYE • RONI RAYE PRODUCTIONS
"RONI RAYE'S KINK" • "RONI RAYE'S EROTICA"

Each zine is 300 plus pages filled with rants/videos/horror vids/websites/other publications/sex/CD's/literary prose/comix/big bust chicks/commercial ads/lots of pages/aclu/wrestling/body modification/and lots lots more!!!! Stuff to make you think, and shit to make you laugh. Do you write, rant, draw, have a business, have a zine or a comic strip?? Place it here..we'll ship it everywhere..we want your stuff!! We will trade/swap/ and help you get your business and products out there. Mad at the politicians, your lover or your boss..? Want others to know about it?? Write it down and send it to us!!!

Roni Raye Productions, P.O. Box 502210 Indianapolis, IN 46250

Your sequence is the frequency, but the vortex is your friend.....we KNOW you, write for free crap, we're full of it....

Opulence!,

PO Box 2071, Wilmington, NC 28402-2071,
USA, Earf.........

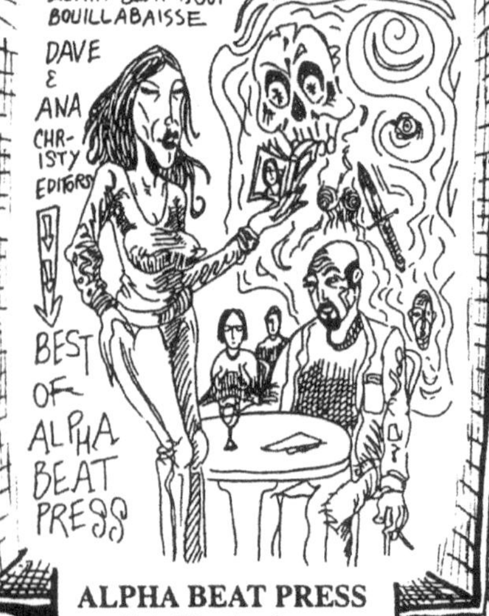

ALPHA BEAT PRESS
31 A. Waterloo Street
New Hope, PA 18938
Dave & Ana Christy, editors
(215) 862-0299
"The Best of The Small Press"

The LUMMOX Journal
PUBLISHED BY LUMMOX PRODUCTIONS
Contributions & Ad deadlines: 20th of each month
Subscriptions: $20 (12 issues)
PO Box 5301, San Pedro, CA 90733-5301
(310) 521-9642
e-mail: lumoxraindog@earthlink.net
online: http://home.earthlink.net/~lumoxraindog/

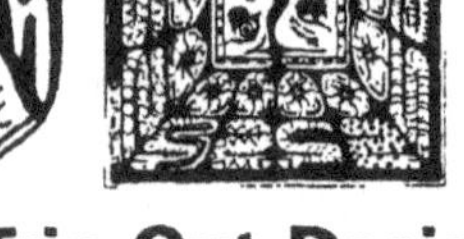

Trip-Out Designs
Unusual Art for Unusual People
Graphic Design, PostersT-Shirts, Logos
Darren W. Blunt, Artist
(910) 343-1583
316 Bladen St. Apt. 2,
Wilmington, NC 28401

Luhey 'toons
T.R. MILLER
Cartoonist
P.O. Box 489
Milltown, N.J. 08850-0489
T.R.'s Zine
Cartoons &Artwork

TRIAL ISSUE
$7.00 North America
$10.00 Elsewhere
Cash, check or money order sent to:
The Affiliate
777-38 Barb Road
Vankleek Hill, ON
KOB 1RO, Canada

STRIKE A BLOW FOR FREEDOM! DEMAND SEXUAL FREEDOM!
STOP THEO-FASCISM!
1 - 800 - 4 - U - EIDOS
JOIN THE GROWING "GLOBAL SEX VILLAGE" & SEX'ZINE SCENE
"America's foremost" militant alternative grassroots sexual freedom-erotic entertainment sex news'zine for free-thinking consenting "sex anarchist" adults worldwide of all eroto-sexual orientations, preferences & lifestyles. Pro-Human, Constitutional, Civil Rights. Championing, in the Thomas Jefferson tradition, First Amendment Rights to Freedom of Sexual Self-Expression. Advocates "evolutionary/revolutionary" political/cultural sex reform. "Some of the Best Ads of any magazine." Single Issue US$15.00. 4 Issues US$55. EIDOS, POB 96, Boston, MA 02137-0096 USA. Phone: 617.262.0096/FAX 617.364.0096. Check, Cash, Money Order, MC/Visa.
"The Battle For Sexual Freedom Will Never Be Lost!"

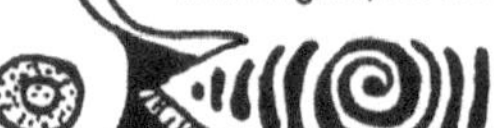

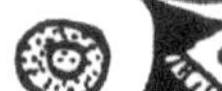
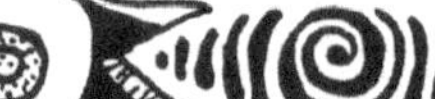

©1997 LABASH

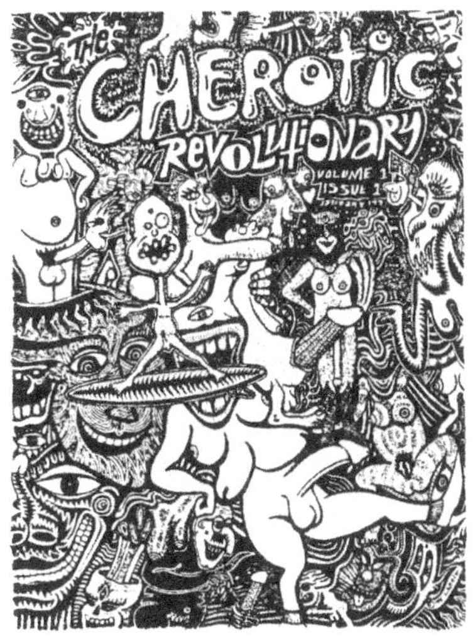

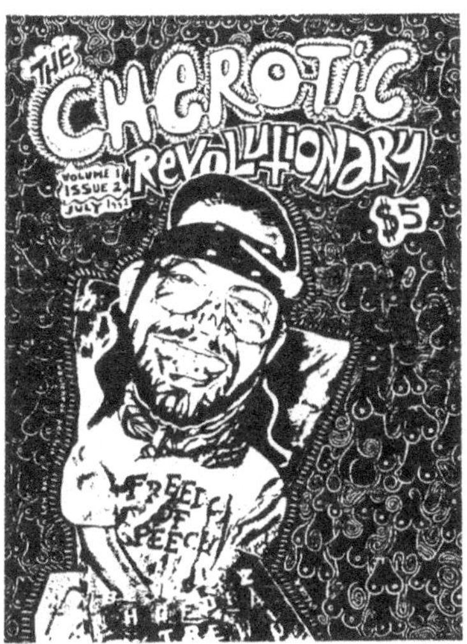

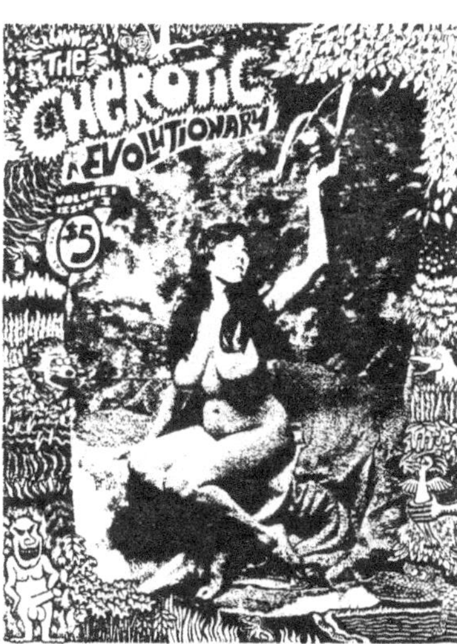

TC(r) #1, *january 1992* **$5**

POEMS BY **KAREN FINLEY, NONI HOWARD, TRACY MOSTOVOY, FRANK MOORE, JACK FOLEY** AND **JESSE BEAGLE** • ARTWORK BY **LABASH** • PHOTOS BY **TRACY MOSTOVOY** AND **ERIC KROLL** • CARTOON BY **WILL OF THE WISP**

TC(r) #2, *july 1992* **$5**

ESSAYS BY **FRANK MOORE, CURTIS YORK** AND **KYLE GRIFFITH** • ARTWORK BY **LEE KAY, H.R. GIGER, PETER PETRISKO, JR., JOHN SEABURY** AND **LABASH** • PHOTO BY **KEVIN RICE** • POEM BY **BARNABY CHANCELLOR**

TC(r) #3, *april 1993* 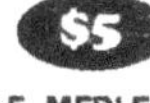

POEMS BY **R. (DIXI) COHN, ANNIE SPRINKLE, MERLE TOFER, JESSE BEAGLE** • ESSAYS BY **VERONICA VERA, LUNA SANGUINE** AND **FRANK MOORE** • PHOTOS BY **RICHARD SILVARNES, WINK VAN KEMPEN, ROBERT MAPLETHORPE, ANNIE SPRINKLE, MARC TRUNZ, AMY ARDREY** AND **JAN DEEN** • ARTWORK BY **LABASH** AND **JOHN SEABURY**

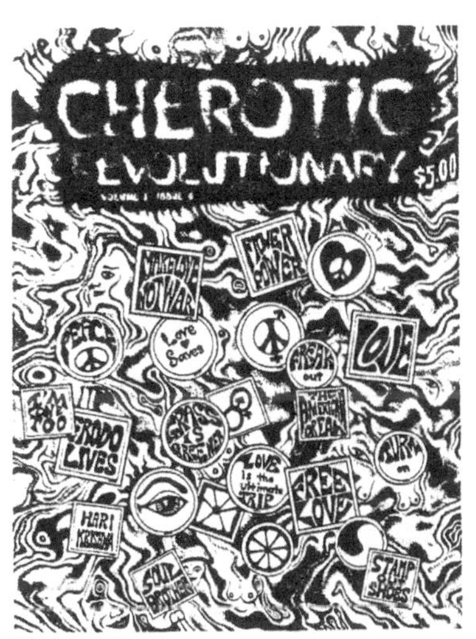

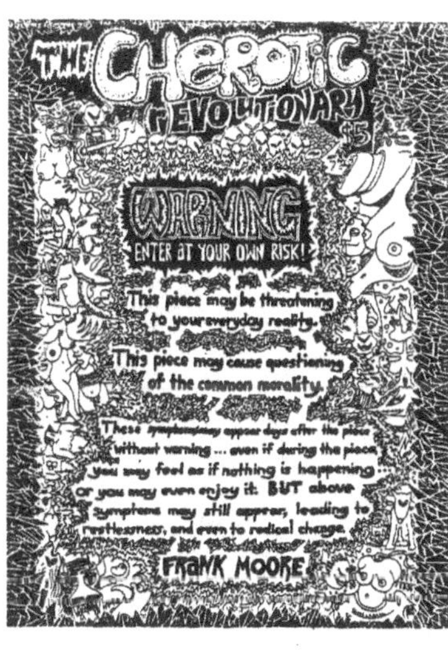

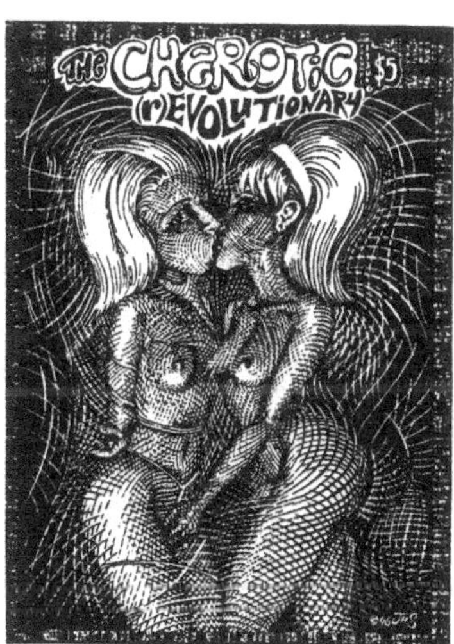

TC(r) #4, *january 1994* **$5**

POEMS BY **ANA CHRISTY, FRANK MOORE, STEVEN KAUFFMAN, NONI HOWARD** AND **ROBERT W. HOWINGTON** • SHORT STORY BY **CAROL A. QUEEN** • ESSAYS BY **TRACE DE HAVEN, JAMES DAVID AUDLIN (CHIEF DISTANT EAGLE), PROF. CURTIS** AND **FRANK MOORE** • ARTWORK BY **JOANNA PETTIT, JOHN SEABURY** AND **LABASH** • PHOTO BY **NINA GLASER** • PHOTOS OF **LINDA MONTANO** BY **ANNIE SPRINKLE**

TC(r) #5, *may 1995* 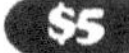

POEMS BY **JESSE BEAGLE, AL CUNNINGHAM, ROBERT W. HOWINGTON, GEORGE KAUFFMAN, ANA CHRISTY, ANTLER, MOLLY HOLTZCHLAG** AND **ELLIOTT** • ESSAYS BY **FRANK MOORE, JAMES D. AUDLIN (CHIEF DISTANT EAGLE)** AND **PETER RIDEN** • SHORT STORY BY **BARBARA SMITH** • REVIEW OF **ANNIE SPRINKLE'S PERFORMANCE** BY **FRANK MOORE** • ARTWORK BY **LABASH** • CARTOONS BY **T.R.MILLER** • PHOTOS BY **PETER C. TURNER** AND **LINDA MAC** • INTERVIEW WITH **PAUL KRASSNER** BY **FRANK MOORE.**

TC(r) #6, *june 1996* 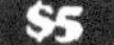

POEMS BY **AL CUNNINGHAM, GEORGE KAUFFMAN, DOROTHY JESSE BEAGLE, ÉLLIOTT, ANA CHRISTY, GRASSHOPPER, JANET KUYPERS, DAVID WHITACRE, ROBERT W. HOWINGTON, MARK BEGLEY, ERICKA SLAYER, NONI HOWARD, PAUL WEINMAN** AND **FRANK MOORE** • ESSAYS BY **FRANK MOORE** AND **UNRU LEE** • SHORT STORIES BY **CHARLES CHAIM WAX, K.ATCHLEY, DR. BRYAN D. REDDICK, AL CUNNINGHAM, WILL SARVIS,** AND **TRADER RILEY** • A REVIEW OF **BARBARA GOLDEN'S MULTIMEDIA PACKAGE** BY **FRANK MOORE** • PHOTOS BY **FLO FOX, TONY RYAN, ERIC BOUTILIER-BROWN** AND **LINDA MAC** • PHOTOGRAPH OF **LESLIE BARANY** IN AN **HR GIGER CHAIR** • ARTWORK BY **JOHN SEABURY, SPIDER WEBB, FLORENCE GRAY, HR GIGER, LORENZO MOYA,** AND **LABASH** • CARTOONS BY **T.R. MILLER, SEAN M. BIERI, ADRIAN VALDES MONTALVAN** AND **ENRIQUE DEL RISCO (ENRISCO)** • **APPLICATION TO LIVE IN THE SOUTH**

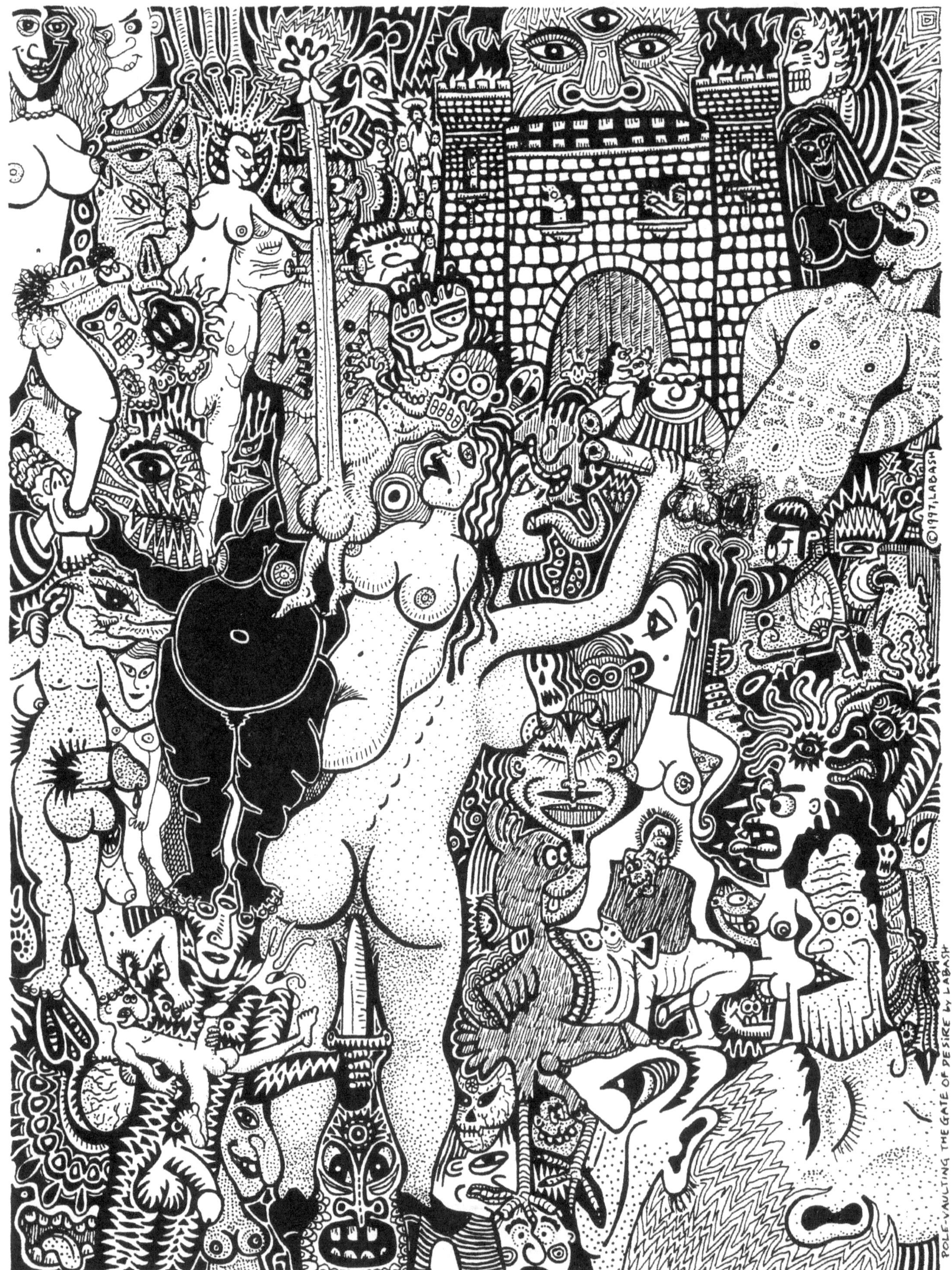

POLE-VAULTING THE GATE OF DESIRE by LABASH

REVIEWS

The Cherotic (r)Evolutionary #7
1997

"Without a doubt, one of the best literary/art zines being published today -- there's a free-spirited attitude throughout Frank's zine that's hard to resist. Quite a few nudes, but they're usually done tastefully and never appear sleazy. Sometimes off-the-wall, sometimes bizarre, The Cherotic (r)Evolutionary is never dull -- and certainly very erotic. The art by LaBash throughout this issue is simply brilliant and the back cover is a thing of beauty (but not meant for the uptight). A few of the many highlights include Ana Christy's 'If Jesus Had a Hat He Wouldn't Need a Halo,' Kevin Sampsell's amusing 'Possessed by Lenny?' ('My two year-old says about 50 words. / One of his favorites is /"Fuck"') and Ray Heinrich's cyberspace poem on having a URL rejected for 'questionable language and/or subject matter.' I greatly enjoyed Frank's thought-provoking 'Mainstream Avant-Garde?,' a rant on art becoming mainstream. 'It takes a lot to enter, and to stay in, the underground,' he writes. 'The underground is where the real freedom and the real ability to change society are to be found.' A review of Tony Ryan's book of nude photographs makes an appropriate centerfold piece -- glad Frank decided to print a few samples. You may balk at the asking price, but art ain't cheap, brothers and sisters!"
Ruel Gaviola, Amusing Yourself To Death #6, August 1997

"This is a fine zine photocopied but with thick cover and center stapled. Each issue is a work of art, with fine photography and drawings. Great cartoon artwork from Michael LaBash and a good mix of underground poetry and short stories. Issue number 7 out now features Frank Moore's review of Tony Ryan's book of nude photographs, Beauty Reality and some examples of his striking photography. A poem by Kevin Sampsell called Possessed by Lenny reads: 'My two year old says about 50 words. One of his favorites is 'Fuck' or as he phrases it 'Ohhhh fuck.' I think he may be possessed by the spirit of Lenny's cinematic double Dustin Hoffman and he's not even dead yet. So now we've rented Scent of a Woman because it seems like 'Hooyaahhh!' would be more fun for him to say and we wouldn't have to pay for an exorcist to get Mr. Hoffman's undead spirit to come out of our son.' Also great is a poem by Ana Christy, If Jesus Had A Hat He Wouldn't Need A Halo, reprinted elsewhere in this issue. All in all, superb work done by everyone. Check this zine out today!"
Lucid Moon, November 1997

REVIEWS CONTINUED...

Frank Moore & Co. have again created a beautiful collage of expression that many will want to have a look at, to experience really. The images, derived from the writing, artwork and photography, will, at the very least, get you to think about your everyday reality. TC(r), 'a zine of all possibilities,' cannot be defined with any one label. Sex zine? yes, erotic (in the widest sense) thoughts and play are used, but they are not exactly ends in themselves. They are used to help people to expand their reality, a reality that will be, hopefully, wholly of their own creation.

TC(r) volume 1 issue 7, 32 magazine-sized pages, contains, among other things: An editorial by Frank, speaking to those who might want to start their own zines or whatever, '...please don't be fooled by our 'technical quality'. We just have an in-house graphic art company. But all you need is good contents...which money can't buy. Good contents are in you...,' SHAMBOLIC FRAGMENTIS by John Fleetham, an hallucinatory trip filled with unusual imagery; drawings by Sean Bieri, one of which is of a female emptying a can of tuna onto her cunt while her lover, a cat, hungrily eyes her (or his) meal; photos by Matt, the very real Heather is shown in different unposed poses, including one with her finger between her very attractive lips (touching her love-button?); a poem POSSESSED BY LENNY? by Kevin Sampsell, his two-year-old son has a vocabulary of 50 words, his favorite being 'fuck', is the little one possessed by Lenny Bruce?; a review of Tony Ryan's book BEAUTY REALITY by Frank Moore, according to Frank, 'a book of beautiful bodies naked...not just Hollywood Playboy 'beauty'...people beauty...men, couples of both genders, mothers and children (can the dirty minded cry child abuse?), mothers-about-to-be, children (will the dirty minded cry child porn?)...and real living lusty women...,' included are four examples of Tony Ryan's excellent work; a poem OXYGEN by Jody Bloom, a man's wife has suddenly become 'a crazed nymphomaniac, like a teenager minus the embarrassment...' he's not at all as lucky as one might think; a poem AN AMERICAN AGENDA by John Rich, a very honest and sharp commentary on America being a police-state and more specifically its 'war on drugs'; a drawing with accompanying text by R. Fleming, 'stock power broker and yuppy' Lydia Index pays money to get it hard up the ass in some trash-filled back alley; and then there are LaBash's great trance illustrations. Be sure to see some of his and Frank's work published here in OF#13.

Inter-Relations also produces videos. The videos are mostly about 'eroplay' - using erotic play to liberate the mind and body. It's good to see people who realize that, in general, WoMan's body has been desexualized. And that sexuality is often seen only as genital penetration. So the whole body needs to be resexualized; and that's why I encourage people to try kissing, nibbling, sucking, touching, fingering, dry-humping etc. People must stop describing these forms of expression as 'foreplay' - in truth, they are just different ways of expressing Eros. It appears that Frank Moore's eroplay consists of something very similar."
Dr. Ducky DooLittle's Hypnotic Releases, Catalog #2

REVIEWS CONTINUED...

"Frank Moore, with Linda Mac have now come out with their "zine of all possibilities" #7 in which plenty of drawings and pictures make it most unique. Tony Ryan's B & W pictorial is a treat and there is a presentation made by Frank that indeed reveals much of Tony's talent. Beautiful women and interacting people presented with class. Annie Sprinkle is photographed with her friend Ms. Silver. As Frank indicates they have many other commitments aside from this publication so that it takes a little while for the next one to come. Their web of all possibilities is at http://www.eroplay.com."
The Affiliate, October 1997

"A peak into the fuel for the free life of Frank Moore. Bizarre and twisted visuals c/o LaBash, Brian Viveros, Darren Blunt, John Seabury, Sean Bieri, the beautiful nude photography of Tony Ryan from Australia, plus a review by Frank of Ryan's book Beauty Reality, another review, of a reading by poet Karen Finley, plus there's some interesting things here and there from Frank's E-salon. I don't know if it's worth $5, but it's really a good zine."
The Flashing Astonisher #10

"Erotic zine, as opposed to porn that is. Most of it is celebrating sexuality in all its forms, but there's some darker stuff here too, especially the illustrations by Brian Viveros which reminded me of Savoy's Lord Horror books. All the usual suspects are here - poetry, short fiction, art, reviews, true life stuff, plus photography, some explicit. Generally I think this is a good zine, although I'm not altogether certain. There's a good sense of interaction and networking from editor Frank Moore. If you're interested in sex zines in the States, this would be a good place to start. Of interest to comics fans is some revelatory art by Sean Bieri which might just blow your mind!"
The Review Sheet v2 #6, November 1997

"A fine publication with great cartoon artwork by Michael LaBash and others and good mix of underground poetry and short stories. One of the best zines around."
Ralph Haselmann, Lucid Moon, September 1997

REVIEWS CONTINUED...

"Yes, this mag is relatively pricey, and it has the same poets and writers you see in a host of other mags, but TC(r) is different. This is the type of forum that us "zine" writers deserve to be printed in. Each page is zany, you don't know what you're going to get when you turn to the next one. Dirty cartoons and pictures galore -- but not the type you'd get on the Internet. These are done by artists. In fact, this mag embraces -- no pun intended -- the Internet: drawings of guys and girls doing it computer-style, and much of the writing comes from e-mail forums. Plus, editor Frank Moore really makes the reader feel involved with his fine product. You're invited in. Usually after I review a mag, I throw it away. I'm keeping this one!"
Jerry White, Literary Rocket 11/97

"This issue is worth your dinero for the artwork alone! From the cyberhorrorsexual drawings of Brian Viveros to Sean Bieri's mid-60's style escapades to the sexy photos from Tony Ryan's new book to (huff puff). Oh. Sorry. And things wouldn't be complete without Michael LaBash's playful hallucinogenic drawings popping up everywhere. You also have Ana Christy, elliott, Kevin Sampsell, the ongoing strong-arm tactics of the govt. as seen by John Rich, Lob's manifesto of sorts that describes his Instagon Foundation, and editor Frank Moore's discussion on the underground and how some folx can be easily manipulated by the lure of fast money. Always a valuable source of information and entertainment."
Bleeding Velvet Octopus #10

"From articles on Sex-Magik to knocked out illustrations by the likes of Michael LaBash to poetry to interviews with members of the avant-garde post modernist porn movement, this 'zine explores the world of sexual beings with humor and an enlightened maturity that is a welcome alternative to the so-called "adult" sex industry. Previous issues have featured the wit and wisdom of Paul Krassner, Annie Sprinkle and, of course, Frank Moore."
Raindog, Lummox Journal, December 1998

REVIEWS CONTINUED...

“The Cherotic (r)Evolutionary is a lovingly assembled collection of art, essays, reviews, and poetry, about the human body. The scope of this work goes beyond eroticism and sexuality, however. It is about the appreciation of the body in a way that is more complex than being aroused or having orgasms. It treats the body as a religious symbol of sorts that can be used to reach transcendent states. If you think Editor, Frank Moore is a crackpot, you should probably check out the Kama Sutra (ancient writings about sexual transcendence that are still in practice to this day).

Each issue of “Cherotic” is densely packed with high quality photography, meticulously rendered drawings, and other appealing graphics. The writing manages to tackle some fairly heady issues in an informal, sometimes humorous manner. This issue includes cartoon images by Sean Bieri, artistic photos by Tony Ryan, and an article entitled “Mainstream Avant Garde?” by Frank Moore. Recommended.”
Jerry White, Literary Rocket 11/97

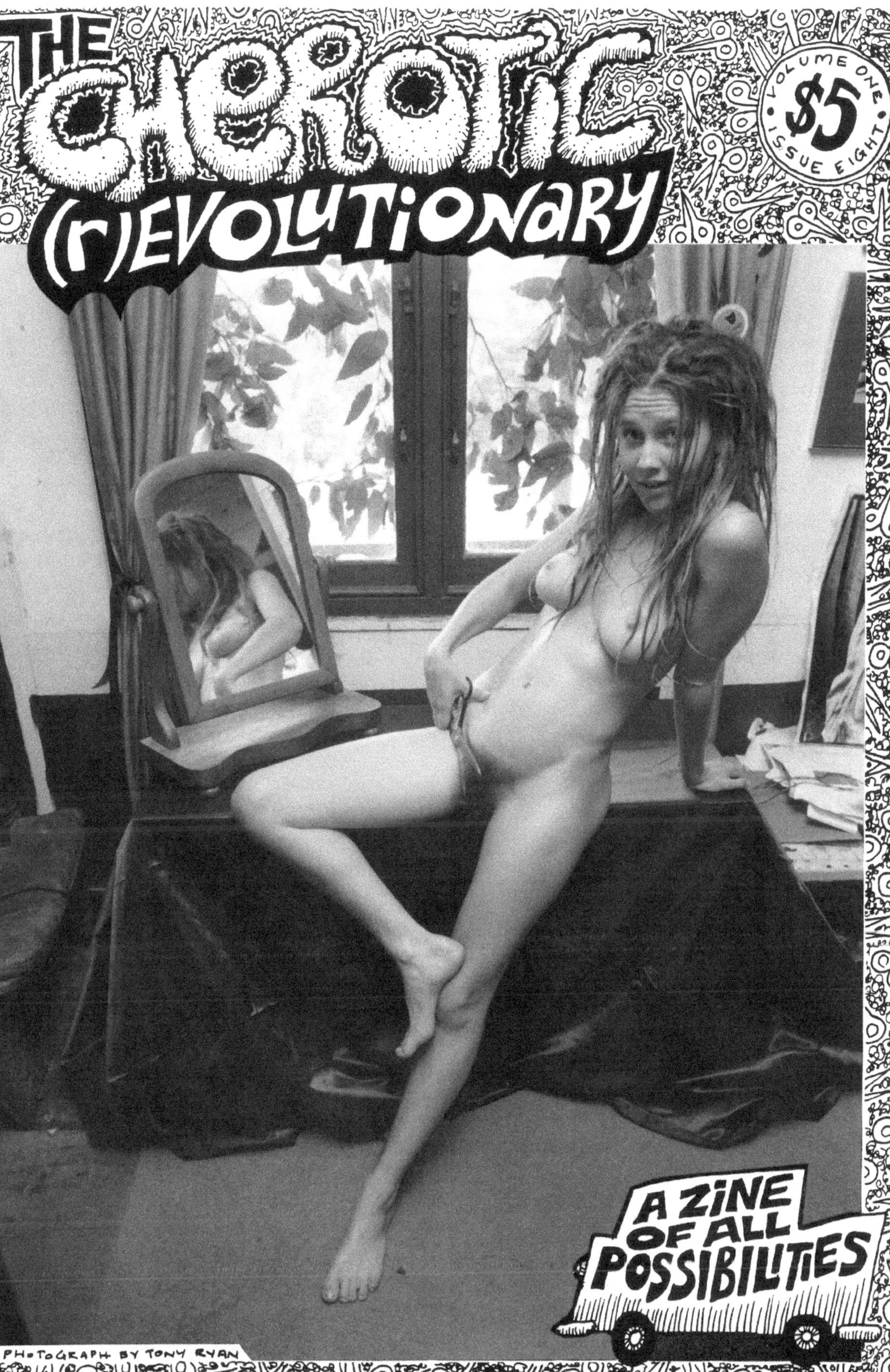
THE CHEROTIC (r)EVOLUTIONARY
VOLUME ONE
$5
ISSUE EIGHT
©1998.LAPASH
A ZINE OF ALL POSSIBILITIES
PHOTOGRAPH BY TONY RYAN

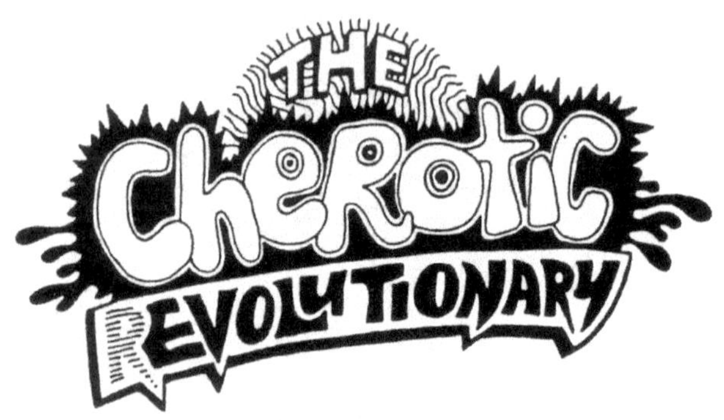

ISSN 1083-8872

The Cherotic (r)Evolutionary is a zine about "the edge" for and by people on the edge.

TC(r) is published by Inter-Relations. The publishers/editors are Frank Moore and Linda Mac, the art editor is Michael LaBash, and the circulation manager is Alexi Malenky.

The price for this issue is $5.00 per copy. We don't sell subscriptions, to avoid tying ourselves down to a rigid publication schedule or magazine size. We want to remain free to publish frequently or larger issues at longer intervals and adjust the price accordingly.

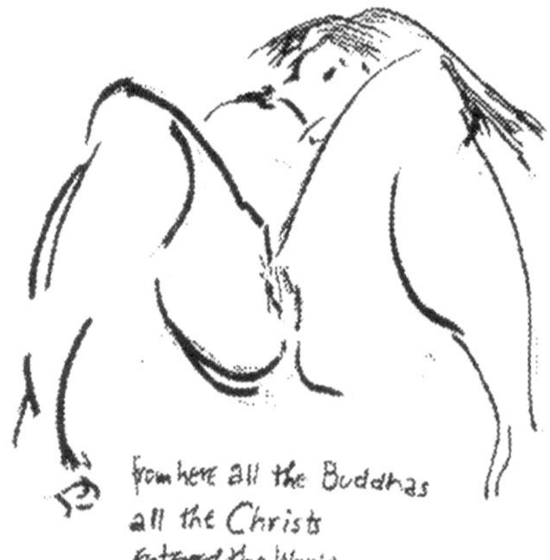

Drawn by Zen Nun 300 years ago ...

We heartily encourage letters of comment from readers and will answer as many as we can. Please tell us if you don't want us to print material from your letter – otherwise we will assume it's OK.

Please address all correspondence and orders for magazines to:

Frank Moore, P.O. Box 11445, Berkeley CA 94712
e-mail: fmoore@eroplay.com
WorldWideWeb: http://www.eroplay.com

EROPLAY IS FUN

TC(r)'s AD POLICY
Recently we have received several inquiries about how to buy ads in The Cherotic (r)Evolutionary. Although we are not actively seeking such ads, we are not precluding them either. However, we will judge whether or not to accept an ad.

TC(r) is a xeroxed, black and white zine that is published irregularly ... if we are lucky, twice a year. So it is not the place for fancy color ads or for ads with time deadlines. On the other hand, TC(r) magically finds its way around the world.

TO SUBMIT AN AD
Send us a copy of your ad and a S.A.S.E. If we accept it, we send you the rate for your ad ... and if we need anything from you such as halftones, we will tell you. If we don't accept it, we will send your ad back.

AD RATES
Sliding scale: $10-$50 per quarter of a standard typing page. The scale slides according to our whim.

HOW WE ACCEPT AN AD
Our whim also is a big factor in accepting an ad. Another factor is the other contents of the particular issue. And there may be other factors which are unknown even to us.

FREE TC(r) COPIES
Because we are not actively looking for paid ads, we do not give free copies to would-be advertisers. But we encourage them to buy a back issue or two. However, we do give you a free copy of the issue in which your ad appears.

Frank Moore
November 12, 1993

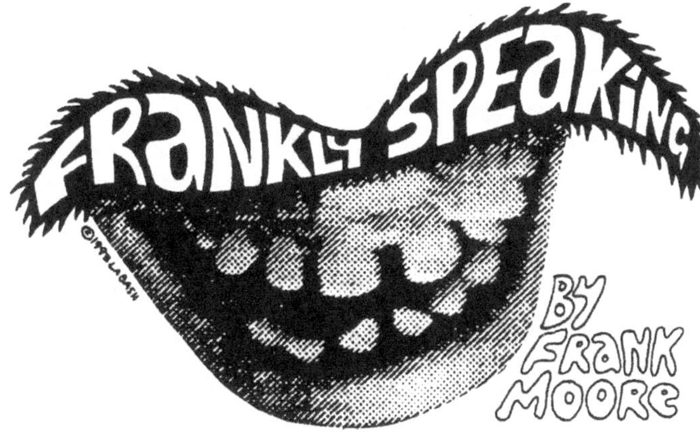

Saturday, April 24, 1999

Ok! Stop your whining! I'm sick of people asking when is the new TC[r] coming out! We here have a life ... we ain't on some fucking time clock! So you have this new issue in your hands, in front of your eyes. So it took two years to create an issue that will make you sweat ... and I don't mean just sweat in your armpits! I mean sweating mind/brain/soul. I mean sweating sex. I mean sweating eyeballs. To take this journey of art, ideas, nude bodies, and other turns-on, you need to be to prepared to be soaked. And we have the artists, writers, and photographers whose passions will addict you, arouse your own passions. That is why we are here! More about passion in a minute. But ...

Who Says?

-for Frank Moore

She took off all her clothes,
then she took off her skin.
I had never seen such bones!
Her legs crushed me while her
tongue darted out of her skull.
I got out of my skin
and we made love. Who says
there's no life after death?

- George Kauffman

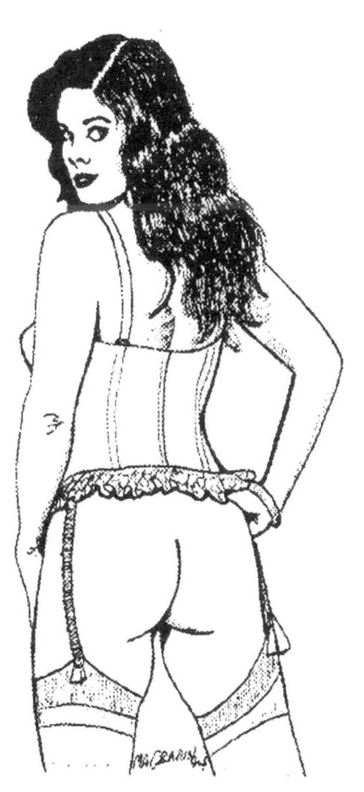

ILLUSTRATION BY MICHAEL ALAN GRAPIN

We tried to thin down this issue to save on money. And we did real good. We cut about fifty percent of what we wanted to put in. (So you who are not in here ... we sweat blood to get you in. But the laws of physics got in our way!) But when we laid out what we had swindled it down to, we still had more pages than last issue. We just said fuck the profit margin (whatever that is) ... this is what we want to put out! Thus, the plump lusty broad which you are fondling right now! We love when you fondle us!

Ok! We didn't spend the two years getting this issue together. We, in the form of Coralhei, have started DIGGER UNDERGROUND DISTRIBUTION EXCHANGE, a free service to get zines etc. out in the San Francisco Bay Area (DUDE'S address is Digger Underground Distribution Exchange, 6201 Harwood, Oakland, CA 94618).

We also have created a huge underground artistic playground/community on the internet. Its home is http://www.eroplay.com. As a part of this, we have started a web radio station, LOVE UNDERGROUND VISION RADIO ... or LUVeR for short (http://www.eroplay.com/luver/) We have artists around the world doing shows (either live or on tape) on/for LUVeR. In fact, you can hear many of the people in this issue .... and past issues ... on LUVeR. Of course LUVeR has the free nonlinear reality of TC(r). All this is to say, we now want not only your writing and art, but also your music, tapes, cds, readings, gigs, programs ... well, use your imagination! Send them to:

Frank Moore
P.O. Box 11445
Berkeley, CA 94712

Now, back to talking about passion...

Passions don't burn out
bliss don't boil away
fuel of life
is for a lifetime

burnt out?
Kill yourself...
or stop using
glamor, hype,
romantic drug
to rush above
everyday reality

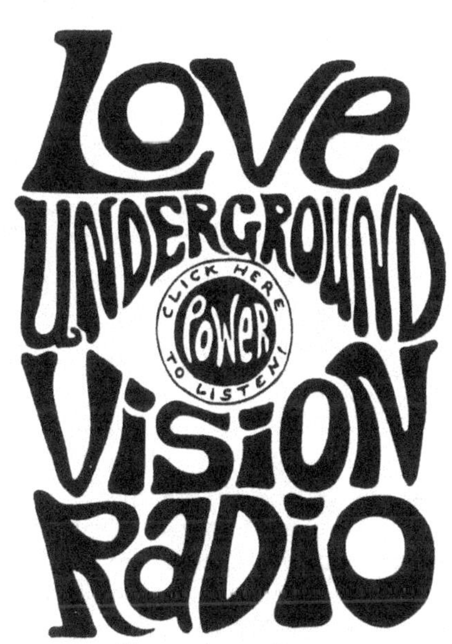

THEATER RANT

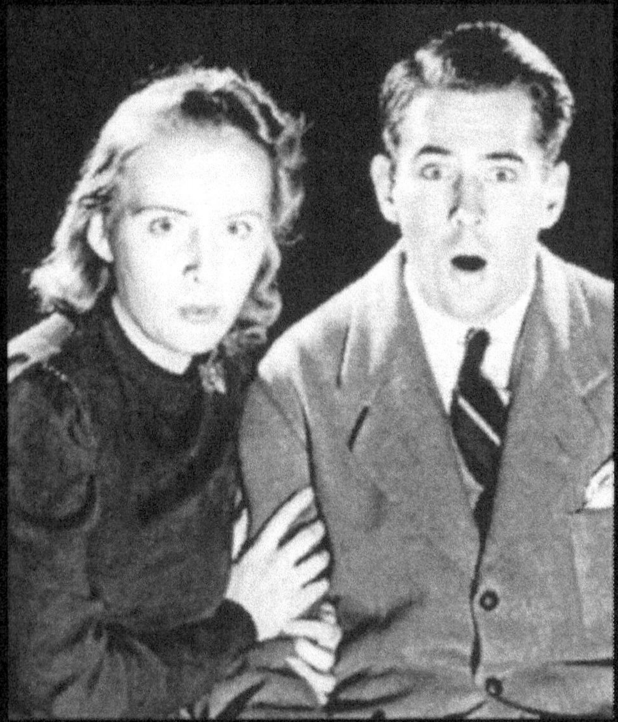

by Heidi Winkle

Ok, so I'm cheating a little here. I'm Crye's fiance, and I would've sent this via your web page, but I don't know the address for it, and I also didn't know if it would let me attach a file. The thing is, I wrote this thing, and I think it oughtta be read by somebody in the theatre community, and from what Mike's told me that includes you to some extent. Unfortunately I'm not familiar with your story more than what was in the last 'fly. So I thought I'd send this along. If you don't care to hear this, say the word, but I'm looking for feedback - I can't believe I'm the only person who feels this way. Thanks for the time.

Heidi

I am a lighting designer for the theatre, and I love my work, but I am becoming more and more disgusted with today's theatre community, and I'm beginning to understand why. The drivel we show our audiences is the same as what they could see on t.v. or most film. I believe the role of theatre in society is more than that. I disagree with the academic explanation of theatre's purpose:

"To entertain, to instruct..." It doesn't say enough. Today's theatregoers are interested in a night of voyeurism, watching someone else's life on stage. They sit in an audience, insulated in thoughts of grocery lists, the staff meeting at the office tomorrow... We need to somehow persuade them to pay attention, find a way to break them out of their role of mere watchers. Shocking theatre is good, if it does this. But how do we go about loosening the financial hold of ticket-buyers who force us to downplay the truly expressive in favor of the sensational, the shallow stuff that fills a house but says nothing? The NEA, as has been seen in recent years, is not the answer. We need to reverse the trend of theatre as entertainment and work our way back to theatre as ritual, as oral history, as social commentary.

In the beginning it filled those roles. Somewhere along the way it lost its morals.

Theatre is becoming a farce. The public goes to see a show under the guise of an intellectual night out, but if that was what we gave them they would be offended. Yes, theatre should entertain. Story-telling is an integral part of the art. But today's story-tellers miss the mark when it comes to any deeper meaning. Give me Tennessee Williams, a master of the story, but with so much more between his lines. Or the Greek greats, who gave us part history and mythology, part story, and part moral and social commentary. Not *Charlotte's Web*, a beautiful children's story turned syrupy on stage, mind-numbing to me and mildly entertaining to its young audiences. And what would Shakespeare say if he saw a production of *Romeo and Juliet* set in the Gaza strip in order to "give it more relevance in today's society"? Or Mary Chase's wonderful *Harvy* with Elwood cast as a female to superimpose a director's feminist feelings over a story that in no way supports that idea. This is the wrong way to do what needs to be done. Any good playwright gives us a script to work with, and work within. He has his own intentions, and we must honor those. If the script doesn't say what you want to present then find one that does. Don't change what you must to make a script fit your intentions. A script is a finished product, a tool we use to get to our end. It I not a two-by-four, bought to be chopped up and used how it is needed. It is more like a musical composition, to be interpreted to some degree by the musicians (in this case directors, designers, actors) but for each note to be played as it was written.

So if reinterpreting the script is not the answer, what is? We must encourage our playwrights to put a little more meat on the bones of today's plays. And as a theatre community we must find a way to say *something* and survive. We must refuse to talk down to audiences in order to sell tickets. And we must not be coerced into filling the role already filled by television – mindless entertainment for the masses.

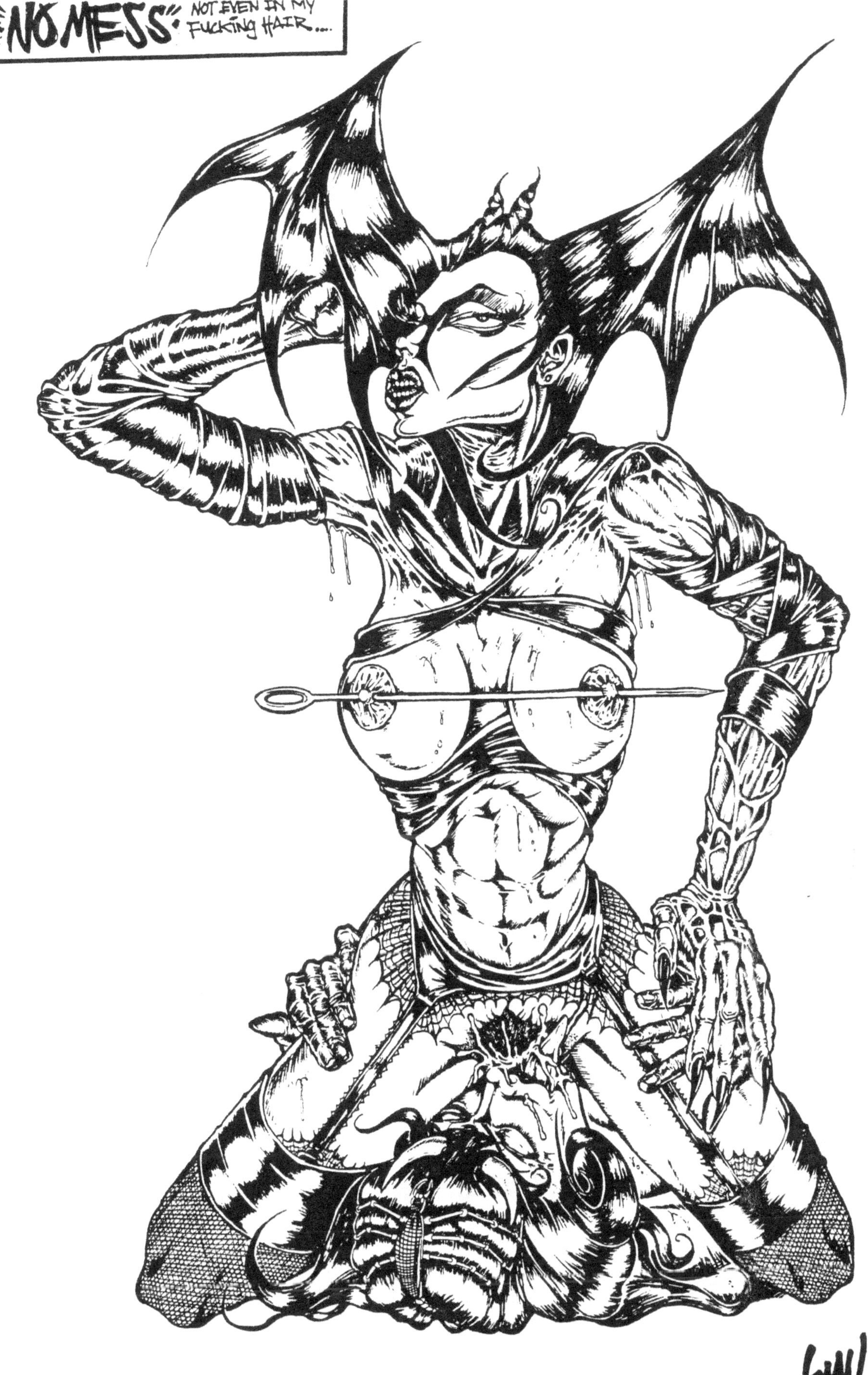
"NO MESS" NOT EVEN IN MY FUCKING HAIR....

Rethinking the Disability Agenda

BY STEVEN E. BROWN

Almost twenty years ago, when I first became an advocate and student of disability rights, a debate about language raged. The offensive words were "crippled," and "handicapped," and the new politically correct word became "disabled," which then evolved into the phrase "people with disabilities." As far back as I can recall I believed the language debate to be a vital one—not because of the words themselves—instead, because the words represented one's sense of personal, social, and political identity.

I didn't know the phrase "identity politics," but I certainly practiced it. I gave speeches and wrote articles discussing the impact of each of these words and phrases and how they fit into a burgeoning disability rights movement. I fought for the integration of people with disabilities into every aspect of society.

I also turned my historian's eye toward as much literature as I could possibly find exploring disability rights. My lifelong quest for justice combined with my personal experiences of discrimination and oppression and my newfound study of disability rights, history, and philosophy. I also enjoyed the performances of a local readers' theater group, JustUs. The funniest skit I remember was the KRIP News. The result of all these activities became a passion for the idea of a culture of disability.

The first known public use of the term "disability culture" occurred at a 1984 conference when two Boston-area professors, David Pfeiffer and Andrea Schein, each responded positively to the question "Is There a Culture of Disability?" During the remainder of that decade, a periodic focus on the idea of a culture of disability appeared in publications like the Disability Rag.

Both the concept and the practice of disability culture, in the United States, exploded in the 1990s. Panels, workshops, conferences, articles and books have all included or focused exclusively on disability culture. After ten years of thinking, talking, and writing about disability culture I offered the following definition:

People with disabilities have forged a group identity. We share a common history of oppression and a common bond of resilience. We generate art, music, literature, and other expressions of our lives, our culture, infused from our experience of disability. Most importantly, we are proud of ourselves as people with disabilities. We claim our disabilities with pride as part of our identity. We are who we are: we are people with disabilities.

When I began to concentrate on the idea of disability culture ten years ago there were few proponents of the concept. That is no longer the case. Now that I am not required to focus each speech or article on proving that there is a disability culture I have had the leisure to explore anew my own perceptions about disability issues. In this process I realized I have undergone a significant transformation.

Unsurprisingly, I returned to language. Instead of asking how our phrases reflect our group and individual consciousnesses I posed the question who gains an advantage. In simple terms, who benefits from disability? The answer angers me.

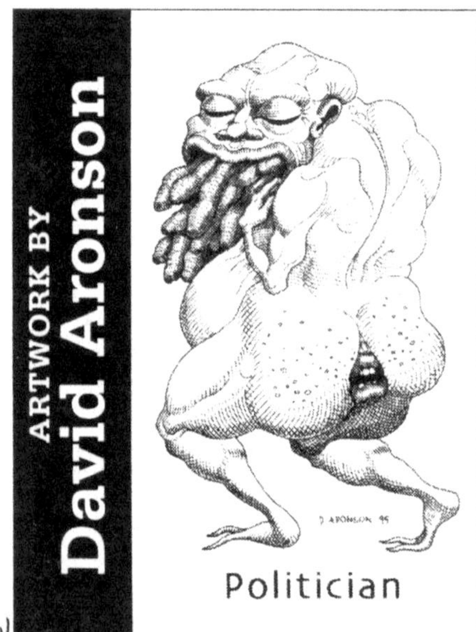

Politician

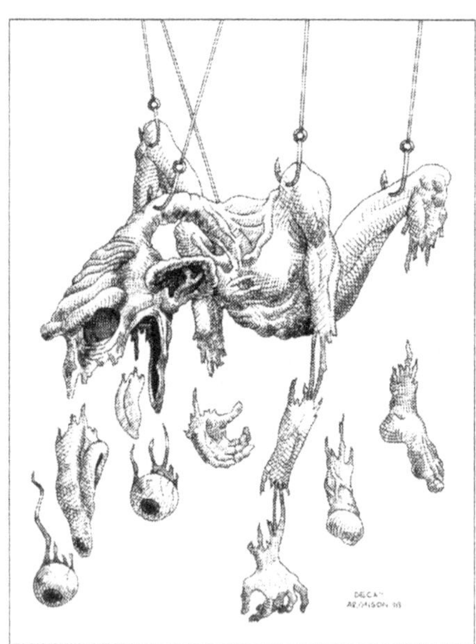

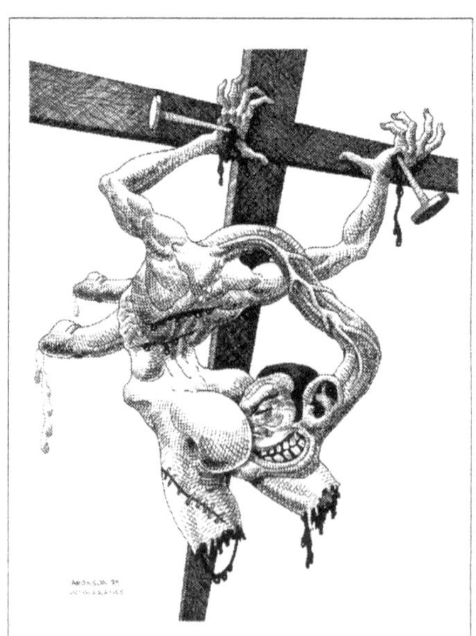

The following groups all benefit from disability: physicians and all other medical personnel who treat people with disabilities; the entire health care field, from policymakers to nursing home conglomerates to HMOs; lawyers, who prosecute and defend personal injury, custody, and discrimination cases; the "helping professions:" psychologists to social workers to special education teachers; bureaucracies, such as Social Security agencies, welfare departments, and the Veteran's Administration; industries, such as wheelchair manufacturers, vehicle modification businesses, and adaptive equipment makers; foundations, associations, and charities that raise money; researchers about (and sometimes on) people with disabilities and academics who teach and write about disability issues; people who own stocks in companies that benefit from the business of serving (or exploiting, depending on your viewpoint) people with disabilities; and myriad other groups who owe their employment to us, including rehabilitation agencies, independent living centers, arts programs, and people, like myself, who make a living consulting, writing, and talking to groups of people with disabilities.

I am not arguing that people with disabilities ourselves do not benefit from any of the above groups. But I am asking the question who benefits more? In terms of financial security, education, employment, physical and attitudinal accessibility, people with disabilities remain the most unemployed, undereducated, institutionalized minority in this country. Who benefits from disability? I would argue that nondisabled people reap more rewards from this classification than we do.

Now I have reached a dilemma. I remain convinced that it is vital that people with disabilities acknowledge and celebrate our culture. But I also believe that as a group we are benefiting others far more than ourselves. How do we attain an equilibrium where we are so comfortable with ourselves as people with disabilities that we have no desire to be different than we are without being continually exploited by those who ostensibly serve us?

I wish I had a revelatory answer, but I do not. All I can do is what most of us do, plod along, and try to rectify life's inequalities using whatever talents and desires I possess. For me this takes the form of posing questions, exploring concepts and actions, and trying to make sense of it through my own art: writing essays and poetry.

Without being able to resolve the dilemma posed, the next best offering I can make is to issue a series of questions:

First, and foremost, why do people with disabilities, why does anyone, have to work so hard, fight so viciously for rights that are already guaranteed to every citizen within our own Constitution? Who has decided to disenfranchise us? Why does anyone let this happen? Again, who benefits? Who does not?

Second, why must we continuously fight to demonstrate that we are worthy of attention, of respect, of money? Who has decided that corporate welfare is more important than funding human rights, social service, and arts organizations? Why have we let them? Why do we continue to let them run roughshod over our interests so they can continue aggrandizement of their interests?

Third, why do we have to prove that our art is worthy? Isn't all art worthy? If not, who decides? Why do we let them? What is being attacked-the art, the artists or both?

We, people with disabilities and artists alike, have been portrayed as victims who need to be rescued. With disability, we are perceived as victims of our bodies or our psyche. Artists are thought to be inept at "making it in the real world." What would happen if all the money that went to corporations and industries were divided and distributed equally to each citizen? What would happen if corporate welfare became artistic welfare? Who would then need to be rescued?

Frank Moore, an artist whom I admire and constantly learn from, set the tone for this discussion with the powerful excerpt from "Out of Isolation." He argues that we reach people one person at a time and that it may take days, months, sometimes even years for the art to make an impact. We cannot always know who we reach with our words, with our action, with our art, with our lives.

But reach we must continue to do. To grow within ourselves. To grow with our art. To grow with our lives. To try and change the inequality of our lives and our art so that we do celebrate ourselves, with and without disabilities, without fear of exploitation because we must be who we are to fulfill our destinies. There is no more important work—no more important art—than that. ■

E-MAIL: stebrown@juno.com

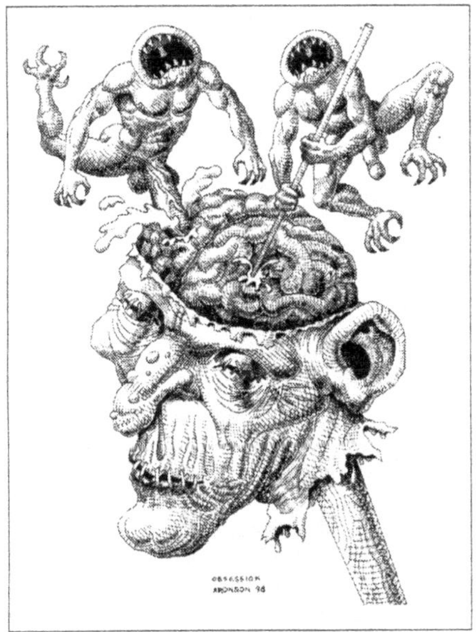

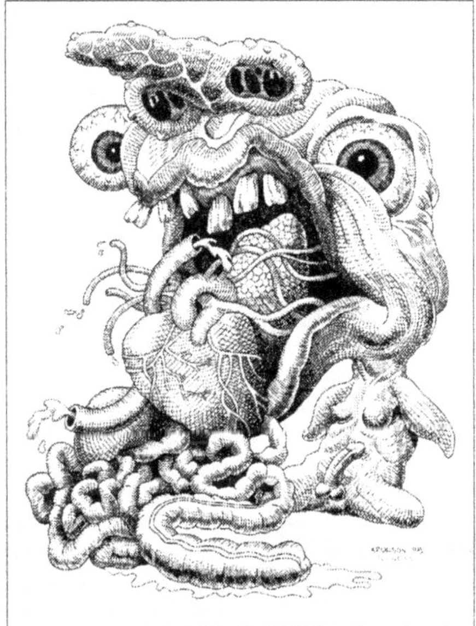

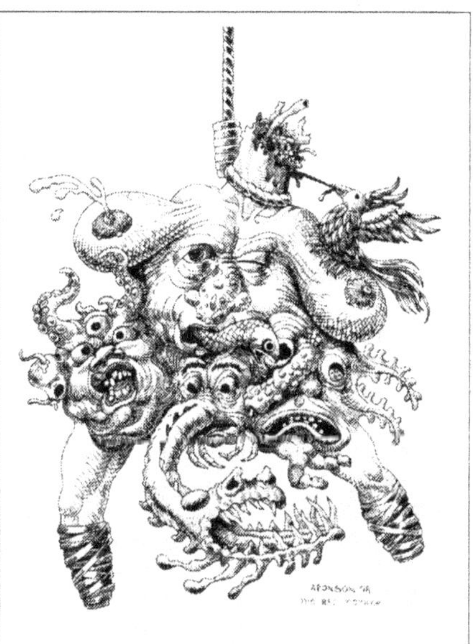

Visit David Aronson's website at **http://www.anti-art.com/aron/aron.htm**

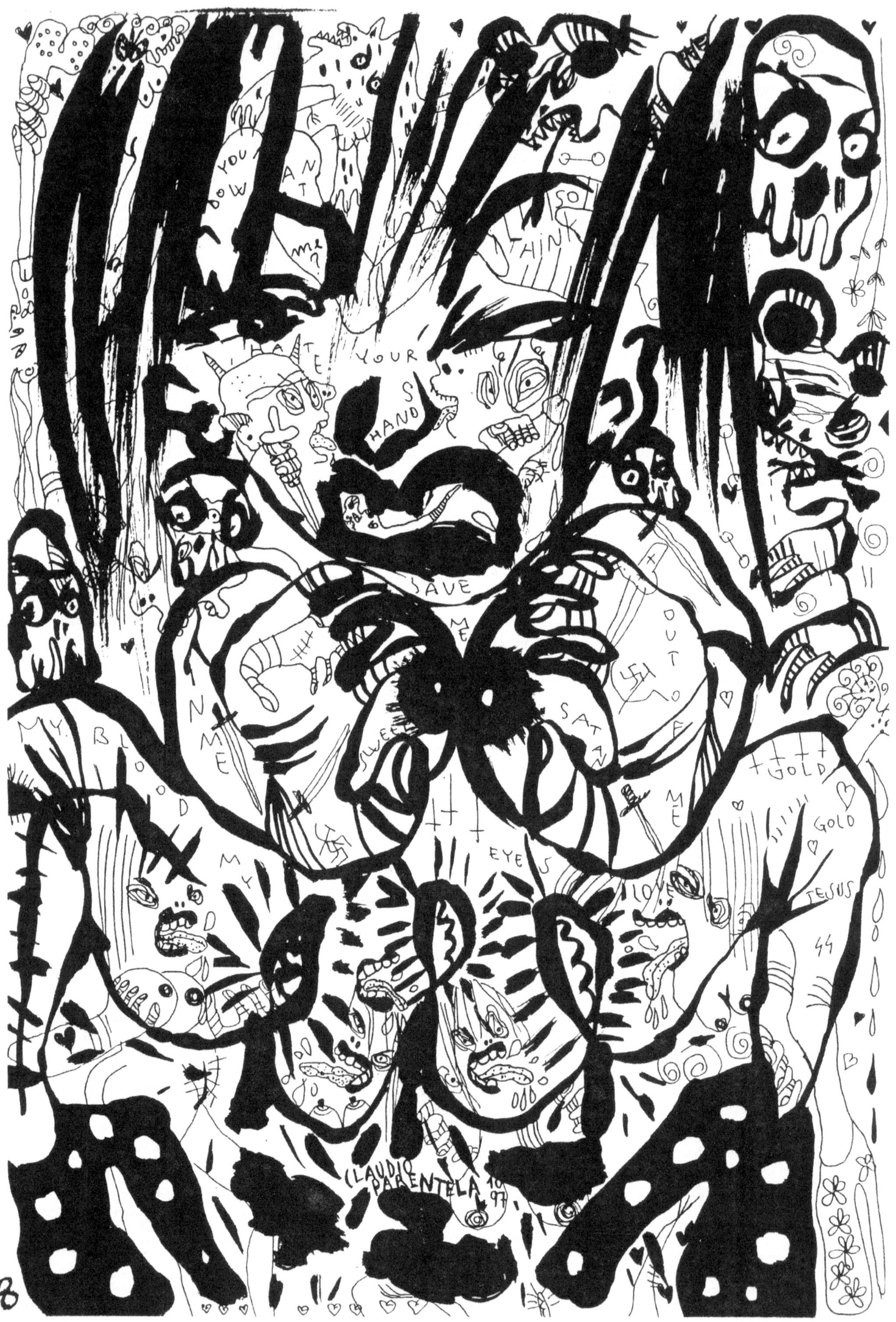
HATE
YOUR
HANDS
SAVE
ME
SWEET
SATAN
MY BLOOD
NAME
MY
EYES
LOVE
GOLD
GOLD
JESUS
CLAUDIO PARENTELA 10 97

ASSEMBLING MAGAZINES

Stephen Perkins (1997)

The term 'assembling magazine' embodies an innovative publishing paradigm which first gained widespread attention in the early 1970's through the publication of the American magazine *Assembling* (1970-87). Frustrated at the limited number of distribution outlets for experimental art and literature during this period, the editors of *Assembling* responded with an open submissions policy. Contributors were invited "to submit a thousand 8 1/2 x 11" copies of whatever they wanted to include."[2] These works were then assembled into an edition of 1000 copies. The first issue included 42 contributors from ten states and three countries. A year earlier in West Germany, one issue of a similar magazine was published under the title *Omnibus News* (1969). Significantly larger than the first *Assembling*, it included 117 contributors from eight countries and was issued in an edition of 1500. Christian D'Orville, in one of the introductory statements by its three editors, writes about his interest in creating this 'Blättersammlung' (collection of sheets) and the uncensored and chance manner in which this mass of heterogeneous material was brought together.[3] In important ways these magazines invert the traditional publishing model: editorial prerogative is abolished, the contributors now become the editors, and the 'editors' assume the role of coordinators. Traditional roles collapsed as both became collaborators in a cumulative process leading to the final publication. More importantly, assembling magazines threw open the doors for anyone to step onto the *omnibus* of experimental publishing.

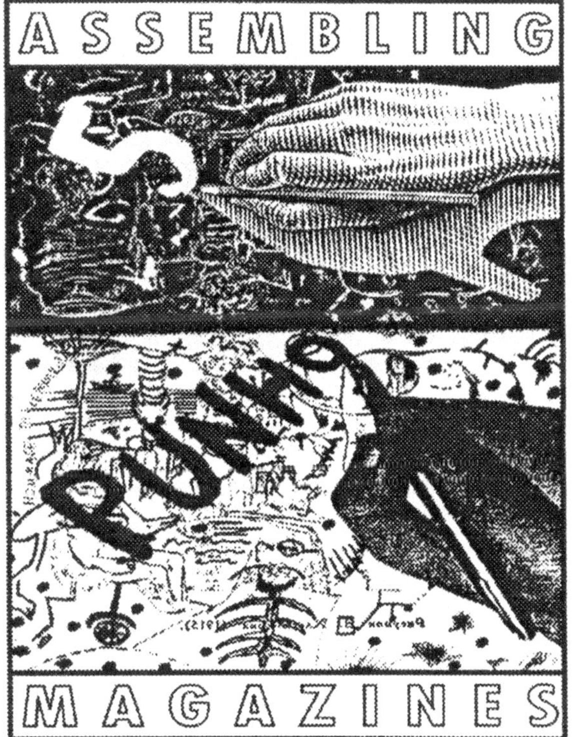

The seeds of this publishing strategy can be traced back to the early avant-gardes of this century. Within this context assemblings can be seen as encompassing a sphere of activity concerned with extending traditional publishing formats and the development of independently produced artists' periodicals.

Most of the early avant-gardes published periodicals (arguably a prerequisite in establishing avant-garde credentials), but, despite the sometimes radical texts and the formal experimentation of these publications, the majority of them still subscribed to the traditional roles of the editor and that of the contributors. Although these periodicals are important repositories of avant-garde texts and images as well as vital players in avant-garde strategizing, the structuring and form in which they came into being is always left unchallenged.

There are some exceptions. Hugo Ball, the founder of Cabaret Voltaire in Zurich, in an entry in his diary from April 18th, 1916, writes "Tzara concerned about the magazine. My proposal to call it Dada is accepted. We could take it in turns to edit; a common editorial board which would entrust the task of selection and arrangement to one of its members for each issue."[4] As it turned out the first issue of *Dada* was published a year later in 1917 with Tristan Tzara firmly entrenched as the editor "simply because no one but Tzara had so much energy, passion and talent for the job."[5] To my knowledge it would not be until 60 years later with the establishment of *Commonpress* (1977-1990), that the apotheosis of this cooperative editorial strategy would be fully realized.[6]

Another magazine that challenged editorial prerogative in a more direct manner was the New York based magazine *The Blind Man* (1917). Initiated by Marcel Duchamp and co-edited with Henri-Pierre Roché and Beatrice Wood, it was inspired by the preparations for the first jury-free exhibition of the newly formed Society of Independent Artists. Duchamp and Roché "thought a magazine could be published without editorial censorship...with the idea that any article would be accepted with a contribution of four dollars."[7] The front cover of the first issue stated that "the second number of *The Blind Man* will appear as soon as YOU have sent sufficient material for it." This issue, which appeared a month later in May, was taken up with the furor surrounding the rejection of Duchamp's 'Fountain' by the Society's supposedly jury-free hanging committee. It is entirely in keeping with Duchamp's penchant for dis-assembling cultural constructs that he was responsible for transferring this jury-free strategy from the realm of the exhibition into the field of publishing.[8,9,10]

It's not until the post WWII era that the format of artists' periodicals comes under sustained scrutiny with the development of periodicals as artworks themselves (rather than merely reproducing artist's works). One early example which illustrates this trend is *Folder* (4 issues, 1953-56). Edited by Daisy Aldan and Richard Miller, each issue had "at least one original serigraph plus a serigraph cover, and consists of loose printed sheets of fine laid paper, enclosed in a paper portfolio."[11] It's significant that this proto-assembling is composed of single sheets gathered together in a portfolio, for this format continued to be a model for a number of artists' periodicals during the 1950's and more decisively in the 1960's. Not surprisingly this strategy was but one way of resolving the problem of combining individual artists' pages into a coherent whole.

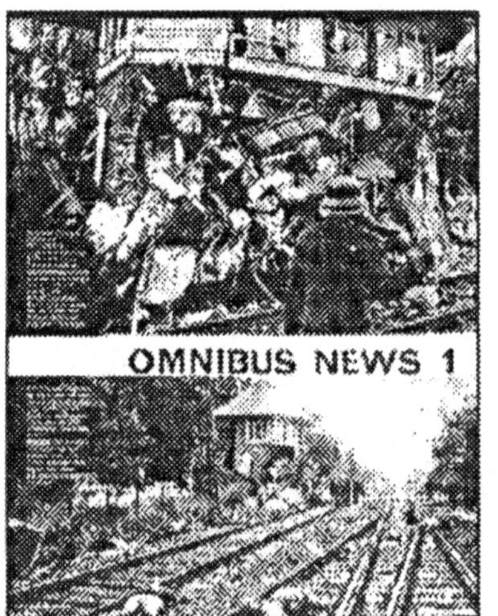

Omnibus News, #1, 1969

Another periodical that adopted a similar format was Wallace Berman's *Semina* (9 issues, 1955-64). Hand printed by Berman in runs of 150-300 copies, each issue was a loose collection of printed drawings, collages, photographs, poems and writings by contemporary and historical figures. Apart from the second issue, all of these were presented in a pocket attached to the inside of a folded cover.[12] Operating well outside of the mainstream, *Semina* circulated within a small network of friends and presages in its intimacy the place that assemblings would assume within the correspondence art network. Michael McClure in a 1992 interview spoke of *Semina* as;

> a form or genre in itself. *Seminas* are a form of love structure that Wallace made, drawing friends together ....*Semina* has some aspects of religion, the religion of art and friends. There's an initiation to *Semina*, i.e. if Berman chose you. One is chosen. One cannot purchase or request a *Semina*; it simply comes to you. The magazine is outside the realm of commodity and merchandising and purchase. There's nothing to consume. And so it's a completely different kind of thing, and precious.[13]

By the late 1950's and early 1960's an increasing number of artists' periodicals were experimenting with different publishing formats. This publishing activity was in response to a broad array of experimental art and literature that depended for its realization, as printed matter. International in scope, these varied fields of experimentation included: concrete and visual poetry, event texts, conceptual works, scores and compositions, to name but a few. One publication that brought together a wide spectrum of this material was *An Anthology*. Published in 1963, edited by Jackson MacLow and La Monte Young, and designed by Fluxus impresario George Maciunas, its extended title gives a flavor of its varied contents, "AN ANTHOLOGY of chance operations concept art anti-art indeterminancy improvisation meaningless work natural disasters plans of action stories diagrams Music poetry essays dance constructions mathematics compositions..."[14] Consisting of a bound volume of individually printed pages, including a number of gatefolds, cut cards, sheets tipped-in envelopes and loose inserts, it represented a compendium of the then current American avant-guarde.[15]

Maciunas, inspired by his involvement with *An Anthology* and in possession of surplus contributions, was concerned that particular artists had not been included and proposed to La Monte Young that another issue be published. When Young declined, Maciunas decided to issue another publication by himself. The name he proposed for this publication was Fluxus. As a skilled designer, Maciunas had given some thought to the presentation of this publication, initially it was to follow in the pattern established by *An Anthology*, except that "graphically it would have been a little more, uh, less conventional than the first one, which means it would have had objects and you know, a different packaging. So really then the idea germinated to use the whole book as bound envelopes with objects in the envelopes."[16] *Fluxus 1* appeared in 1964 as a bolted collection of manilla envelopes which contained assorted printed material and objects and "packaged in a box made from a wine crate with stamped lettering..."[17]

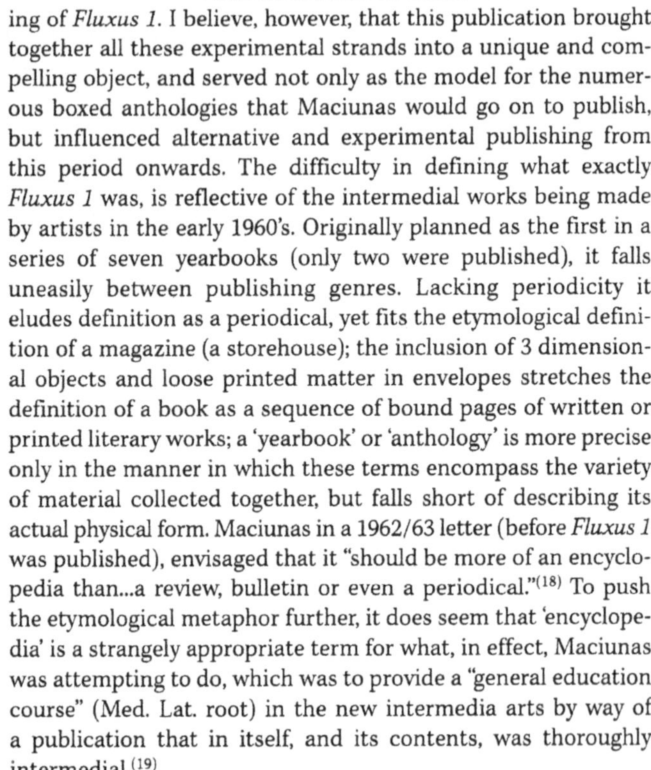

Fluxus 1 was certainly not alone in reconceptualizing the format and packaging of a book/periodical, for there had been a number of publications in previous years that had embraced elements of the structuring of *Fluxus 1*. I believe, however, that this publication brought together all these experimental strands into a unique and compelling object, and served not only as the model for the numerous boxed anthologies that Maciunas would go on to publish, but influenced alternative and experimental publishing from this period onwards. The difficulty in defining what exactly *Fluxus 1* was, is reflective of the intermedial works being made by artists in the early 1960's. Originally planned as the first in a series of seven yearbooks (only two were published), it falls uneasily between publishing genres. Lacking periodicity it eludes definition as a periodical, yet fits the etymological definition of a magazine (a storehouse); the inclusion of 3 dimensional objects and loose printed matter in envelopes stretches the definition of a book as a sequence of bound pages of written or printed literary works; a 'yearbook' or 'anthology' is more precise only in the manner in which these terms encompass the variety of material collected together, but falls short of describing its actual physical form. Maciunas in a 1962/63 letter (before *Fluxus 1* was published), envisaged that it "should be more of an encyclopedia than...a review, bulletin or even a periodical."[18] To push the etymological metaphor further, it does seem that 'encyclopedia' is a strangely appropriate term for what, in effect, Maciunas was attempting to do, which was to provide a "general education course" (Med. Lat. root) in the new intermedia arts by way of a publication that in itself, and its contents, was thoroughly intermedial.[19]

Within the next few years two American editors would extend the format developed by Maciunas and apply it to the publishing of periodicals. *Aspen* (10 issues, 1965-71) edited by Phyllis Johnson and *S.M.S.* ('Shit Must Stop,' 6 issues, 1968) edited by William Copley, adopted a boxed and portfolio format respectively. Both published two and three dimensional multiples from an array of historic and contemporary avant-garde artists. William Copley, in a pre-publication brochure for *S.M.S.*, exemplifies this new attitude towards magazine format:

> Each portfolio will contain personal manifestations by the new as well as the established contemporary artists in all media. The primary concern of the publisher is...to liberate the artists from the restrictions of format...The publisher's complete sympathy with the artist's objective will permit expanded use of new materials in every category (for the composer, choreographer, sculptor, poet, painter, writer, film-maker, all inventors) and fresh application of conventional means.[20]

A consistent feature in the works of artists from the late 1950's is their incorporation of different communication systems into their expanded arts activities. The emergence of the postal system as an integral feature in the conceptualization and distribution of their works is noticeable amongst the Nouveaux Realistes in France, the Fluxus community and in particular the extended web of participants in Ray Johnson's New York Correspondance School. By the late 1960's an international community was emerging which used the postal system exclusively as the medium for exchange and collaboration between its decentralized members. Rejecting the exclusiveness and competitiveness of existing art institutions, this community coalesced as a parallel counter-institution. Known variously as correspondence art, mail art, postal art or simply the Eternal Network (Robert Filliou), its participants began organizing shows, publishing periodicals as well as initiating more personal projects and exchanges. The leitmotif of this informal network can be ascertained from the operational guidelines that were established for the increasing number of correspondence art exhibitions being organized during these years. These were: no fees were charged for submission, no jury or selection process, all works to be exhibited, no works returned and documentation to be sent to all participants.[21,22]

It is within the correspondence art community that the pivotal conjuction of themes that I have outlined coalesced to create the necessary matrix for the establishment of assembling magazines. The pre-requisites for these magazines were: i) the development of innovative periodical formats necessitated by the works coming out of these expanded arts activities; ii) the application of correspondence art's jury-free submissions policy to that of publishing; and iii), the presence of a decentralized network of artists for which assemblings acted as pivotal sites in the collective transaction of community. *Omnibus News* and *Assembling* represent the beginnings of this new publishing paradigm and assemblings continue to this day to be an enduring feature in the topology of the correspondence art landscape, as well as locations through which community is accessed and replenished.

This catalogue is just the beginning in an effort to document this important alternative publishing activity and to bring to light, the nearly three decades-long history of assembling magazines.[23]

Stephen Perkins

References

1. This text originally appeared as the introduction to an exhibition catalogue of assembling magazines that took place at **Subspace**, Iowa City, during September, 1996, curated by myself. The call for submissions was circulated among the correspondence art network and the exhibition was comprised of 38 titles from 15 countries, a small number of assembled books, two audio compilations and assorted artists' magazines, books and catalogues. Many contributors submitted statements about their publications and others offered articles and histories on particular aspects of assemblings. Also included in the catalogue are interviews with editors of four of the periodicals in the exhibition. The catalogue was dedicated to Guillermo Deisler (1940-95), the Chilean born artist and editor of the exceptional assembling magazine *UNI/vers(;)*, (35 issues, 1988-95). Copies of the 64 page catalogue are available in the US for $8 postpaid, write to Stephen Perkins, 1816 E. College St., Iowa City, IA 52245. E-mail address: <sperkins@blue.weeg.uiowa.edu>
2. Richard Kostelanetz in: **Assembling Assembling**, New York: Assembling Press, p. 14.
3. The other two editors were: Thomas Niggl & Heimrad Prem.
4. Hans Richter. **Dada Art And Anti-Art**, New York: Thames and Hudson:, p. 31.
5. Richter, Ibid, p. 33.
6. It could be argued that Ken Friedman's *New York Correspondence School Weekly Breeder* (1971-1974) with its three different editors would also meet these requirements. I would argue that the implementation of rotating editors came after the establishment of the magazine and that it was not initiated with this particular strategy in mind.
7. Beatrice Wood, "I Shock Myself: Excerpts from the Autobiography of Beatrice Wood," *Arts Magazine*, May 1977, p. 136.
8. The eventual fate of *The Blind Man* was decided upon "in a typical Dada gesture, Henri-Pierre Roché & Picabia [editor of 391]

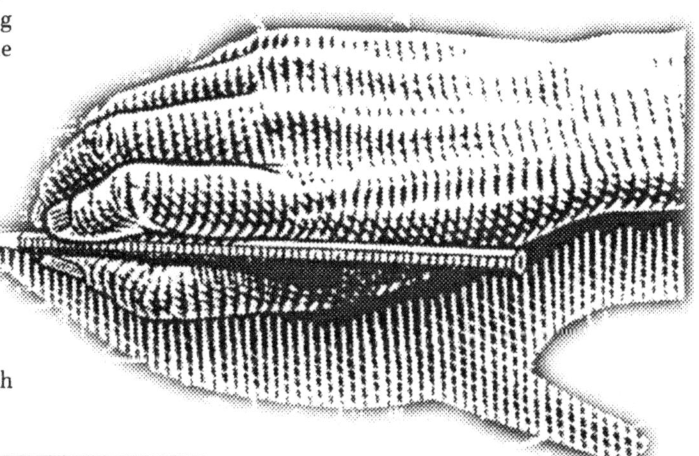

played a game of chess with an absurd twist. The winner was to have permission to continue publishing his own magazine. Roché lost the game, and consequently *The Blind Man* ceased publication after two issues." In: Stephen C. Foster, **DadaArtifacts** (exhibition catalogue), University of Iowa Museum of Art, Iowa City, 1978.

9. As John Held recounts in his article titled "Assembling Magazines" on page 18 of this catalogue, there was another magazine titled *Spawn* which in its editorial for their March 1917 issue (one month before the first issue of *The Blind Man*), lays out a similar open editorial policy for this "cooperative periodical managed by contributors." My lack of information about this magazine precludes me from commenting further, however, it would seem to be based on a very similar jury/editor-free strategy as that of the first exhibition of the Society of Independent Artists and *The Blind Man*. Held's quote from the Spawn editorial comes from its original listing in Howardena Pindell's excellent chronology of artists' periodicals, titled "Alternative Space: Artists' Periodicals," *The Print Collectors Newsletter*, Sept/Oct, 1977, p. 96-121.

10. Although my emphasis in this text concentrates on magazines coming out of the 20th century international avant-gardes, I suspect that there is a parallel, and largely undocumented, tradition of cooperatively edited magazines arising out of networks of people unconnected to this international coterie. An interesting article detailing one magazine that sits squarely within this tradition appeared in the *International Herald Tribune*, June 1-2, 1996, p. 6. Written by Roderick Conway Morris and titled "A Homemade Arts Magazine," it details the rediscovery of the Italian magazine *Lucciola* (Firefly) which was published from 1908-1926. Edited by Lina Caico and produced monthly by a group of Italian women, *Lucciola* was "entirely handwritten and illustrated with drawings, paintings and photographs, and existed as a single copy that was posted from subscriber to subscriber..." One of the conditions of becoming a subscriber was that they should also be contributors, thus one could call *Lucciola* a one-issue assembling. Morris, having surveyed the subscriber list at the back of each volume, concludes that the women contributed to similar periodicals in Germany *(Parva Favilla)* and another in France *(Mouche Volante)*.

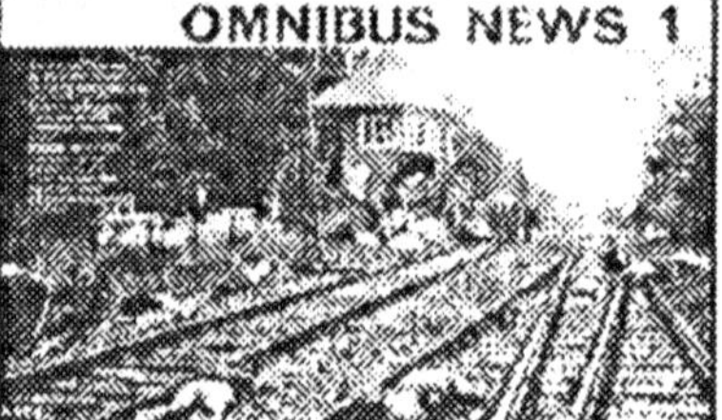

Omnibus News, #1, 1969

11. Barbara Moore and John Hendricks, "The Page as Alternative Space 1950 to 1969," in Joan Lyons (ed), **Artists' Books: A Critical Anthology and Source Book**, New York: Visual Studies Workshop, 1985, p. 88.

12. This description from: Richard Cándida Smith, **Utopia and Dissent**, Berkeley: University of California Press, 1995, p. 232.

13. Michael McClure, "On Semina," in **Wallace Berman: Support the Revolution** (exhibition catalogue), Institute of Contemporary Art, Amsterdam, 1992, p. 60.

14. Jackson MacLow, "How Maciunas Met the New York Avant Garde," in *Art & Design*, #28, 1993, p. 38.

15. A consistent feature in the publishing process of many experimental publications that are made up of individually printed sheets, in particular assemblings, is the collective and social nature of the publication process. At each point in this process, from the soliciting of works from individual artists and the shaping of a collective presence in the publication, to the final party in which the publication is hand collated, there is a process of 'gathering' (literally and metaphorically). From this perspective Jackson MacLow, offers an insight into why some of the copies of *An Anthology* had collating mistakes. "When all the pages had been finally printed, I organised collating parties, where many poets, composers, musicians and other artists and hangers-on gave their labour to get the pages together. (Because of the abundance of soft drugs supplied by some of the participants, we ended up with a number of miscollated copies)." In: Jackson MacLow, "How Maciunas Met the New York Avant Garde," in *Art & Design*, #28, 1993, p. 45.

16. Larry Miller, "Transcript of the videotaped interview with George Maciunas by Larry Miller, March 24, 1978," in **Fluxus etc., Addenda 1**, (exhibition catalogue), New York: Ink, 1983, p. 15.

17. Barbara Moore, "Seminal Artists' Books and Periodicals," Backworks, Sales List: L106, nd., unpaginated.

18. George Maciunas, "1962/63 Letter to Tomas Schmidt," in **Fluxus etc./Addendum II**, (exhibition catalogue), Gilbert Silverman, 1983, p. 157. [My attention to this statement was drawn by Clive Phillpott's article, "Fluxus: Magazines, Manifestoes, *Multum in Parvo*," in: **Fluxus,** (exhibition catalogue), Museum of Modern Art, 1988, p. 10.]

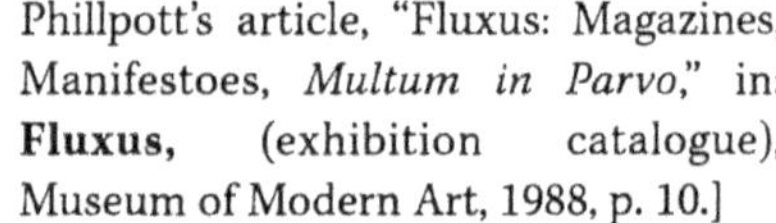

19. Definition from: **The American Heritage Dictionary**, Boston: Houghton Mifflin Co., 1985.

20. Barbara Moore, "Seminal Artists' Books and Periodicals," Backworks, Sales List: L106, nd., unpaginated.

21. Clearly, the egalitarian ethos embodied in these conditions was formulated in direct opposition to the norms that prevailed when artists sought entry into the established art world.

22. In 1970 there were 2 correspondence art shows, in 1975 there were 22 and by 1980 this figure had expanded to 126. Source: John Held, Jr., **International Artist Cooperation: Mail Art Shows, 1970-1985**, Dallas: Dallas Public Library, 1986.

23. The following references are for the few publications that focus on assembling magazines beyond the cursory level:

Richard Kostelanetz (ed), **Assembling Assembling**, New York: Assembling Press, 1978.

International Artists-Magazines (exhibition catalogue), Art Nürnberg 6-Art Fair International '91, editor Jurgen Olbrich Nürnberg, 1991.

Géza Perneczky, **The Magazine Network**, Köln: Soft Geometry, 1993.

Networking Artists & Poets: Assemblings from the Ruth & Marvin Sackner Archive of Concrete & Visual Poetry (exhibition catalogue), editor Craig Saper, University of Pennsylvania Library, 1997.

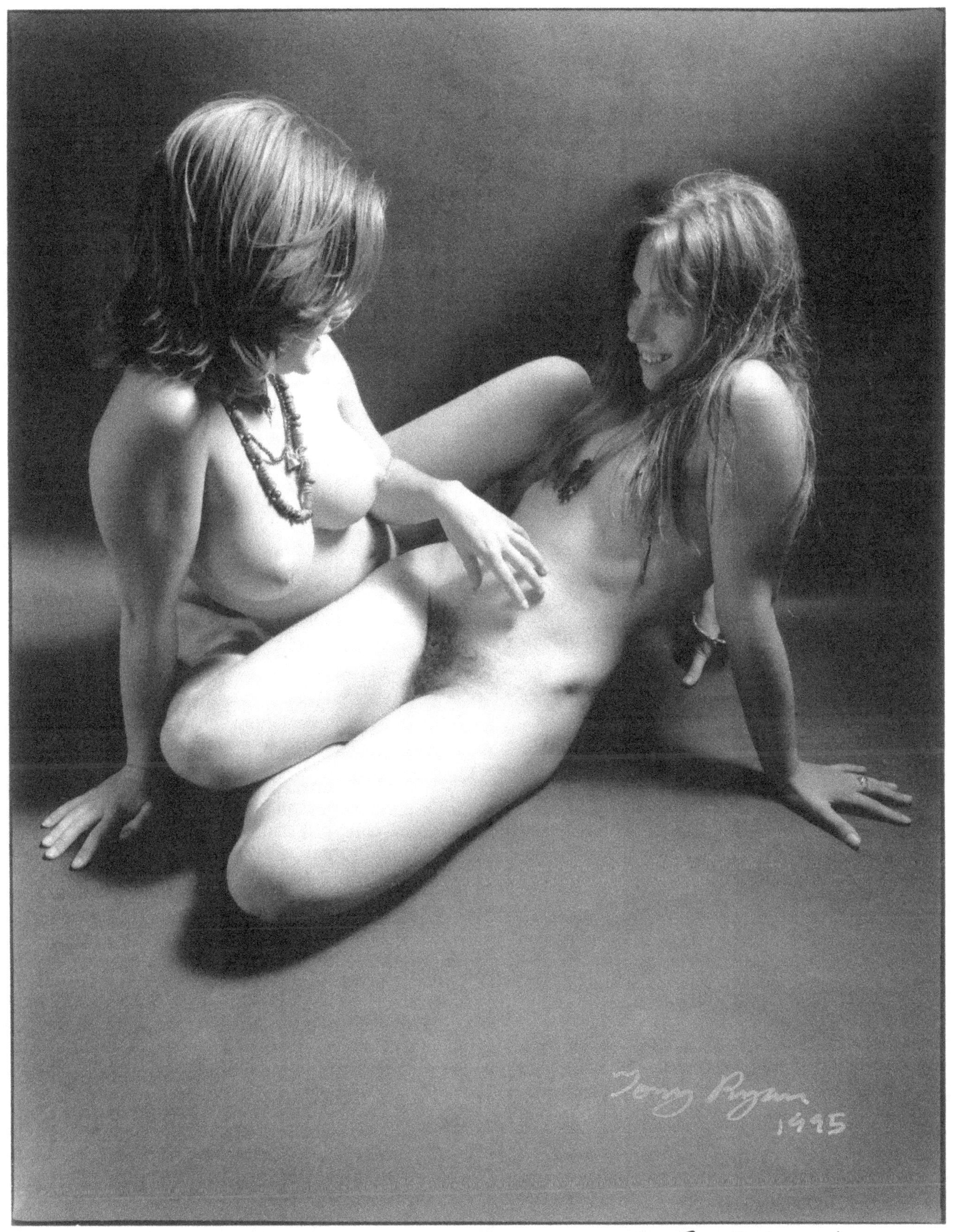

Tony.Ryan@utas.edu.au

SUBJECT: india

REPORT FOR 1997 SUMMER RESEARCH GRANT

The following text will be included in the video enclosed as well as tape taken at a local nursing home:

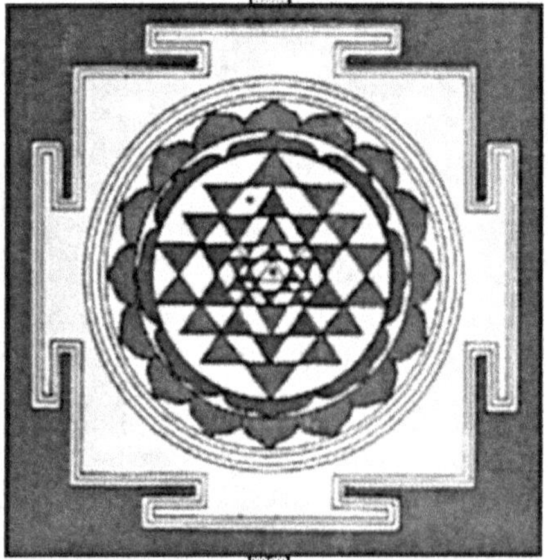

She had always been interested in death. It was one of the many taboos of her childhood. Like food, sex, money , feelings and joy, it was shrouded in a mystery and silence which fueled her curiosity and terror. Was it because she went to a catholic grade school next to a graveyard and spent noon lunch breaks walking through there with a group of girlfriends talking about fingernails found lodged in coffin lids, leftovers from the dead who were buried alive ... talking about flooded coffins floating in the graveyard a long, long time ago. All of this while the boys played red rover. Was it death or the crucifix that interested her most. She obsessed over christ bleeding and gaunt, looked at it, compulsively confessed her sins every saturday afternoon, made every Lenten friday ritual called stations of the cross and forgot about the resurrection. Her grandparents died and they were laid out, embalmed and presented as if sleeping. At least she was allowed to see the dead. When her brother in law died of a brain tumor at home, she observed the stages of death ... his feet got cold and blue, then legs, then hands and arms, and yet he sounded an unintelligible goodbye to her with his voice and eyes. But still it was a mystery, fueling her curiosity. It was close but not close enough. When her ex-husband was shot in the face, death came closer. She massaged his cold feet, kissed the cheek that no longer existed because it was shot off. Her mother soon after became her death teacher, dying in a unique way, allowing her to be present while repetitive sounds poured continuously from her open mouth for 12 hours. Her mother sang her death and her daughter was able to hear. She was getting closer. She had seen, touched, heard and tried to follow her meditation teachers good advice to die daily ... that is, stop the clock, let go, meditate ... and when he died and was cremated in front of his students, she wondered if she would be able to ever see again. But death persisted. She wanted more ... to know more. Feel more ... that was the problem, she couldn't feel it. She wanted death to teach her to feel. The summer of 1997 she went to India, to the city of death, the city of light, Benares. For some Hindus, the train stops in Benares because to die in this city assures an end to re-incarnation and liberation or moksha is guaranteed. It took two years to prepare for the trip. She got a grant, took every immunization possible, went for travel counseling and read voraciously. Her friend and mentor, a 73 year old Jain woman went with her, both needing each other...the beginner and the experienced one, interdependent. They stayed in Ahmnabad with her friend's sister for two weeks, giving her a chance to get used to cows in the road, third world sanitation facilities, the monsoon season and dispensability of human life. That is, to take any form of transportation in India or even walk on the roads is an act of faith and a rhythmic, fatalistic game of chicken where you realize that you are not special, hardly memorable and literally just one more mouth to feed in this country of 850 million humans surviving day to day. She was sobered by the anonymity and insistence that waking up alive was enough, eating was enough, going to the bathroom was enough, wearing clean clothes and communicating well with those close to her ... were all jewels to be cherished. India was spiritually invigorating. Rains and washed out train tracks stalled her plans but eventually she arrived in Benares ... For health reasons her friend could not go with her so she went alone, having made a few calls to a man in that city who worked as a research assistant for Americans, asking him to arrange for a place to stay and for a videographer for her research. One of the most compelling journeys of her life had begun because as she aged, she found that she was more conscious of consequences, germs, conspiracy and her own death which seemed to be travelling swiftly in her direction. Braving jet airways, Indian Airlines and the Delhi Airport she arrived in Benares where a driver greeted her, holding a sign with her name on it. She felt safe for awhile. But the 45 minute trip from the airport in a smallish van was another test of faith. With adrenal glands already pushed to the limit, they gushed even more fright/flight juice into her already overworked bloodstream.Would the van hit that cow, or that baby sitting in the road. Would the car be hit by that other truck careening out of control. Cars, scooters, autorickshaws came within 3 inches of each other and no one wore seat belts, helmets or shoes. Each vehicle carried at least 6 passengers, mom, dad, four kids, grandmother and a baby up front screeching and laughing with delight. A western horror show. Remembering her thesis and goal ... to better understand death, ... she gulped, incorporated the situation she was in and repeated an inner monologue and command that always said, "You asked for this, now surrender, nobody forced you to come here". That self-instruction allowed her to just watch and give up all rights to safety and the western model of correctness. The driver took her to the research assistant, a tall, elegant Brahmin who had studied anthropology at Benares Hindu University and she told him of her plan. "I want to study elders in India, noticing how they are integrated into family life, never seeming to retire. They seem to be respected, not isolated and work hard on life's greatest mystery, their upcoming death. I would like to videotape a hospice in Benares, Mumuksha Bhavan, so that i can experience a place where elders wait for their approaching death in an atmosphere of prayer, expectation and the support of the community." She went on and told the research assistant more, "I want to experience what happens when someone dies, and is carried through the city streets of Benares and is then cremated on the burning ghats". He explained that the Ganges river is considered so sacred that the polluting and hidden aspects of death are transformed by the river's presence. She listened to him and knew that she had come home, that finally, death would be unveiled. But she didn't realize that she would have to die a bit more before she was allowed to make friends with death, because doesn't the homeopathic doctor prescribe snake venom to cure a snake bite ... death would cure her of death. That night she slept with 45 bed bugs and the next day they went to the chief of police to get his permission to videotape cremations. He fed them, something that would never happen in America. And he seemed pleased with her project. But he smiled at everyone and everything, a smile she could not de-code, terror had not yet set in, nor had a bowel movement for 17 days. A three and one half hour boat trip down the Ganges River the next day dislodged her from spectator to participant. Should she look at the seven men defecating about 20 feet away from the boat on a green, well fertilized patch of earth ..? Cultural shocks brought more questions. How could these worshippers stand the scrutiny of their morning ablutions in the Ganges, tourist season after tourist season ... scrutiny by Americans, Germans, Koreans, Norwegians taking photos of them washing, bathing, praying defecating, gargling in the Ganges, year after year? She was beginning to understand aesthetic ethics and the reasons why some artists choose to quiet their curiosity at home, foregoing the invitation to become a cultural imperialist, a cultural colonist, an image thief. Wishing that she had thought through her impulse to travel to a foreign country for her art, she asked more questions of herself ... should I look or not look? Not look at the wild pig nudging the little girl's ass and eating her feces as it dropped to the earth ... she saw that outside Bombay. Should she wonder where the women defecated ... or did they. She certainly hadn't. Should she look closely at the thonged male bodies of worshippers, washing in the Ganges. After all it is the city of lingams and obviously these people were not puritans. It was too much. The desire to see and not look, at life, and then death came again, three feet from the boat ... a bloated, headless, bluish, one breasted woman floated by. She stopped breathing, didn't even consider taking a photo and remembered her mantra "This is why you came here, to learn about death. Surrender." The other American woman in the boat seemed unfazed and said the body, a once living woman, could have been a victim of rape, abortion, family violence or a mafia murder. She intuited a botched mastectomy since one breast had been cut off but maybe the turtles, imported to eat half burned bodies, had eaten the missing breast. Silence. Then 10 minutes later, a headless, bloated, blue dead infant came by. At first someone announced, "Here comes a dead dog", but as it got closer, it became obvious, although at that point, a dog, a baby ... what's the difference. Death was becoming death. Now she was in pure witness mode, not thinking, not feeling, not talking, not documenting. She had been reduced to silence and terror and attention and realized that she was getting her post doctorate in a subject that she couldn't even name. She was shaken to the core although death was not yet her ally or friend. That night she slept with mosquitoes and bedbugs (maybe they would bite her and she would die of sleeping sickness), and repeated a litany of prayers that sounded more like bargaining than praying ... "If I make it back to America safely, I will never, never, never ever again ... fill in the blank", and "I will donate 100 dollars to ... fill in

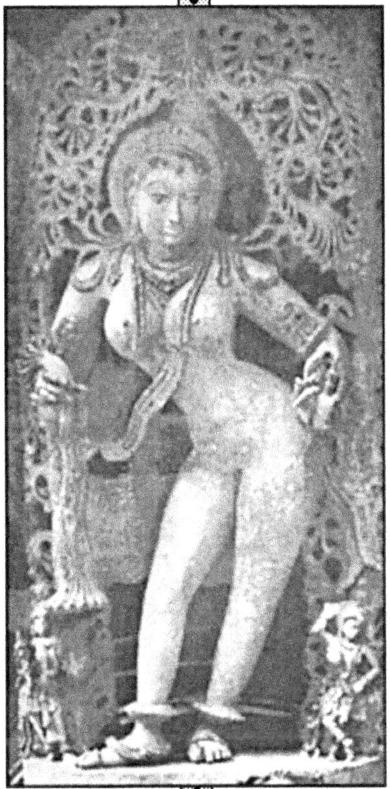

the blank..." She called on Jesus, her meditation teacher ... her friends, good memories all night, for many nights, even though her cowering and infantile game playing with the almighty made her sick while bringing comfort to her desperation. Wondering if she would be thrown into the Ganges if she didn't correctly respect the traditions of this ancient city with its rules that state that only men go to cremations, she swallowed her feminism when the research assistant and videographer went off, without her, to document the bodies being carried through the narrow streets while the stretcher bearers chanted, "nam ram satya hai, nam ram satya hai". She would go on her own to those places and review the video footage knowing that she would edit it and everything would work into the collage and final installation which hopefully would function as a call to meditation. Having heard her mother make her promise that she never be put into a nursing home, she was charged with the task of bringing prayer, japa or repetition of sacred sounds and positively respecting elders to every nursing home in America, just in case she had to be put in one some day. For she envisioned that she would die in an atmosphere of meditation, surrounded by other elders in an ideal setting ... a wonderful nursing home. Elders would be praying, saying mantras, just like India. She knew that she was designing her retirement and death. And to incise death even more deeply into her image bank she spent hours at the burning ghats even though she was a woman, she was compelled to see the place where 100 cremations are performed each day. The place where bodies are first immersed in the Ganges then burned and returned to the Ganges as ashes or as partially burned bodies, depending on the amount of wood the family can afford. She watched. And felt and brushed against stretchers carrying dead bodies ... she noticed how feet burned, smelled the air to see if burning bodies smelled, watched as skulls were crushed with a stick by the male chief mourners so their relative's spirit could fly free. She watched, felt, chatted, gasped, moved from shock to surrender, graduating from Benares. For Benares was healing her of death. Generously, dear Benares let her see enough cremations, enough life being respected yet dispensed with. She saw young Benares boys hanging out at the burning ghats the way kids in America hang out at malls and they helped her lighten up about death because they were teasing a passing goat to erection and insisting on life. It made her laugh. And made her realize that she had seen enough ancient rituals and temples and lifeforce to tolerate the truth and terror of her own mortality. Thank you Benares. I will never forget. What's next?

Linda Montano

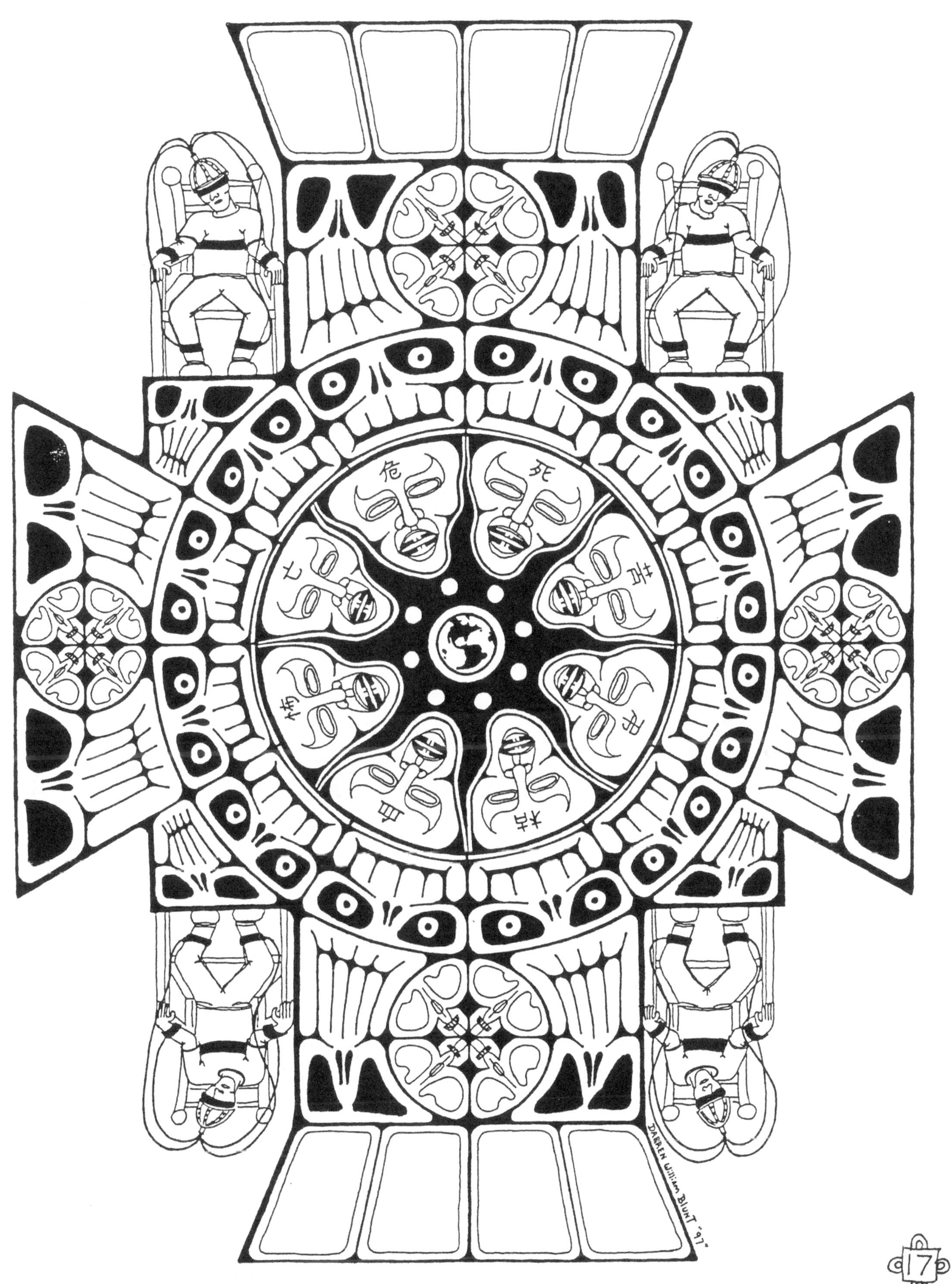
危
死
DARREN William BLUNT '97

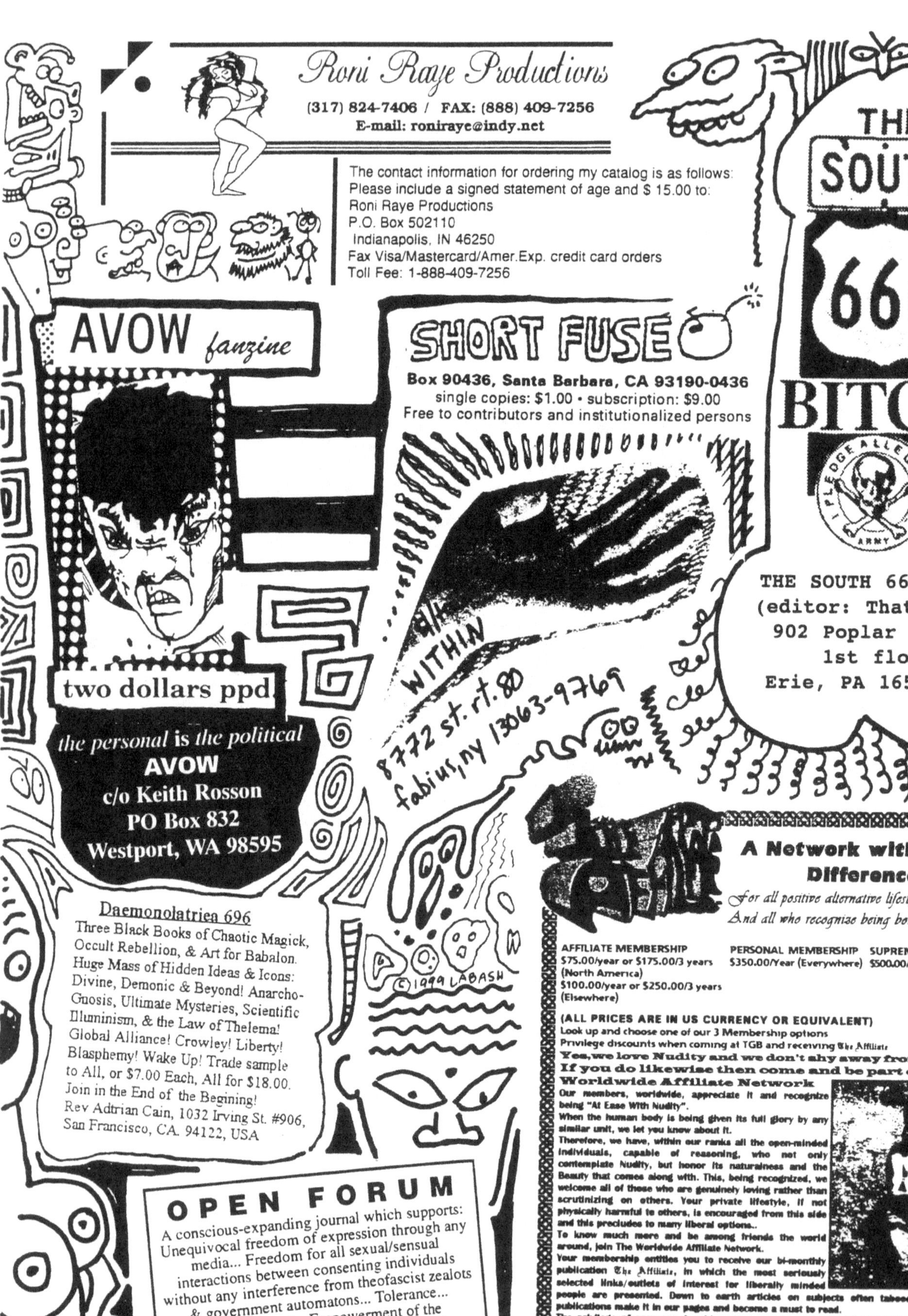
Roni Raye Productions
(317) 824-7406 / FAX: (888) 409-7256
E-mail: roniraye@indy.net
The contact information for ordering my catalog is as follows:
Please include a signed statement of age and $ 15.00 to:
Roni Raye Productions
P.O. Box 502110
Indianapolis, IN 46250
Fax Visa/Mastercard/Amer.Exp. credit card orders
Toll Fee: 1-888-409-7256
THE SOUTH 666 BITCH
I PLEDGE ALLEGIANCE
ARMY
THE SOUTH 666 BITCH
(editor: That Bitch)
902 Poplar Street
1st floor
Erie, PA 16502 USA
AVOW fanzine
two dollars ppd
the personal is the political
AVOW
c/o Keith Rosson
PO Box 832
Westport, WA 98595
SHORT FUSE
Box 90436, Santa Barbara, CA 93190-0436
single copies: $1.00 • subscription: $9.00
Free to contributors and institutionalized persons
all WITHIN
8772 st. rt. 80
fabius, ny 13063-9769
Daemonolatriea 696
Three Black Books of Chaotic Magick, Occult Rebellion, & Art for Babalon. Huge Mass of Hidden Ideas & Icons: Divine, Demonic & Beyond! Anarcho-Gnosis, Ultimate Mysteries, Scientific Illuminism, & the Law of Thelema! Global Alliance! Crowley! Liberty! Blasphemy! Wake Up! Trade sample to All, or $7.00 Each, All for $18.00. Join in the End of the Begining!
Rev Adtrian Cain, 1032 Irving St. #906, San Francisco, CA. 94122, USA
©1999 LABASH
A Network with A Big Difference
For all positive alternative lifestyles
And all who recognize being born Nude
AFFILIATE MEMBERSHIP
$75.00/year or $175.00/3 years (North America)
$100.00/year or $250.00/3 years (Elsewhere)
PERSONAL MEMBERSHIP
$350.00/Year (Everywhere)
SUPREME MEMBERSHIP
$500.00/YEAR (Everywhere)
(ALL PRICES ARE IN US CURRENCY OR EQUIVALENT)
Look up and choose one of our 3 Membership options
Privilege discounts when coming at TGB and receiving The Affiliate
Yes, we love Nudity and we don't shy away from/about it.
If you do likewise then come and be part of our Worldwide Affiliate Network
Our members, worldwide, appreciate it and recognize being "At Ease With Nudity".
When the human body is being given its full glory by any similar unit, we let you know about it.
Therefore, we have, within our ranks all the open-minded individuals, capable of reasoning, who not only contemplate Nudity, but honor its naturalness and the Beauty that comes along with. This, being recognized, we welcome all of those who are genuinely loving rather than scrutinizing on others. Your private lifestyle, if not physically harmful to others, is encouraged from this side and this precludes to many liberal options..
To know much more and be among friends the world around, join The Worldwide Affiliate Network.
Your membership entitles you to receive our bi-monthly publication The Affiliate, in which the most seriously selected links/outlets of interest for liberally minded people are presented. Down to earth articles on subjects often tabooed by most other publications make it in our pages and become a must to read.
The privilege of your membership opens you the door to THE GRAND BARN: Home of The Worldwide Affiliate Network with our 250 acres of freedom where quality people more than its accommodations is what matters most.
Do not hesitate to reach out for friends, worldwide. Write about yourself!
Cash, check or money/postal order sent to The Affiliate
777 - 38 Barb Road
Vankleek Hill, ON
K0B 1R0, CANADA
TRIAL ISSUE
$10.00
North America
$15.00
Elsewhere
OPEN FORUM
A conscious-expanding journal which supports: Unequivocal freedom of expression through any media... Freedom for all sexual/sensual interactions between consenting individuals without any interference from theofascist zealots & government automatons... Tolerance... & Enlightenment... Empowerment of the individual... You'll find: editorials, letters from readers, stories, essays, poetry, artwork, reviews & a directory. Sample copy: $10. Cash only to: LIANOS, P.O.Box 8343, Athens (Omonia), GR-10010, Greece.

grandpa

you were not big on words
especially not big words
you said common things
but they meant a lot
you were not embarrassed to say
i love you
i guess you learned that in the orphanage
with your brother
i loved you
i do
always will
death is funny
but nothing died with your death
except you
what can i say more than that
i guess you would have rather had
me write a poem about grandma
that's what i can say
your life was hers
her life was yours
that's who you were
no more yellow tears.

Anthony Lucero

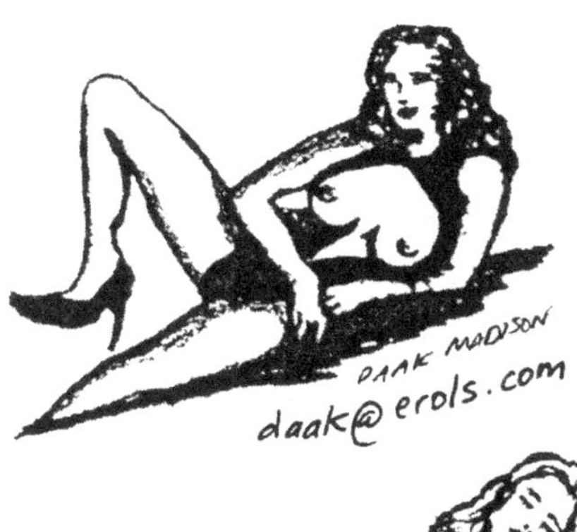

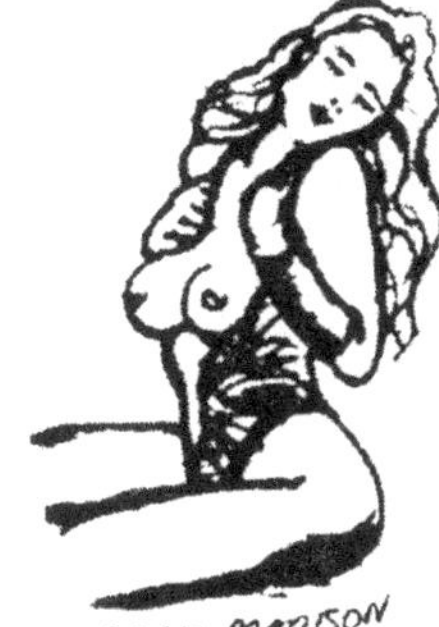

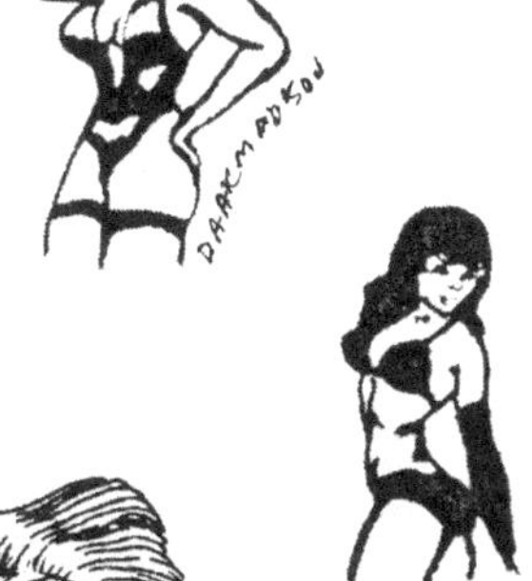

DAAK MADISON

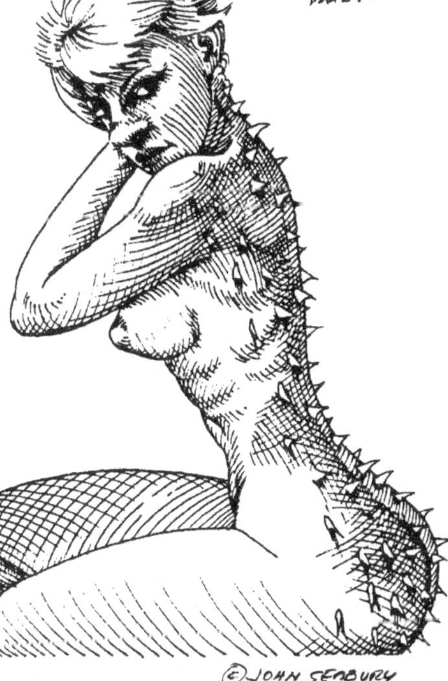

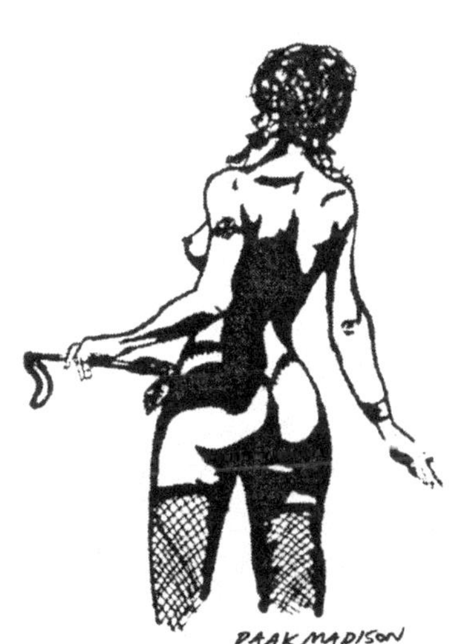

someone else who loved you

by ray heinrich

we never had the chance
i looked at you in the shower
it was one of those open showers
in an army barracks

i loved you

from my top bunk
looking at you as you dressed
knowing
that if i ever mentioned
how i loved your smooth curves
and the way
you laughed at what i said
and when i
took your hand
it seemed to you
that i was shaking it
but i was really holding it

and i could only go to sleep
four feet above you
by listening to your breath
in and out
in and out

i love you

i write your words
one after the other
each time you mention me
and you
like me a lot
like to have me around
we're good buddies
and i feel i might break
keeping this in

but i never did

and maybe you'll see this now
and maybe you'll see my name
and maybe
since you're older
and the times have changed
you won't think of me
as something wrong

just someone else who loved you

ray@scribbledyne.com

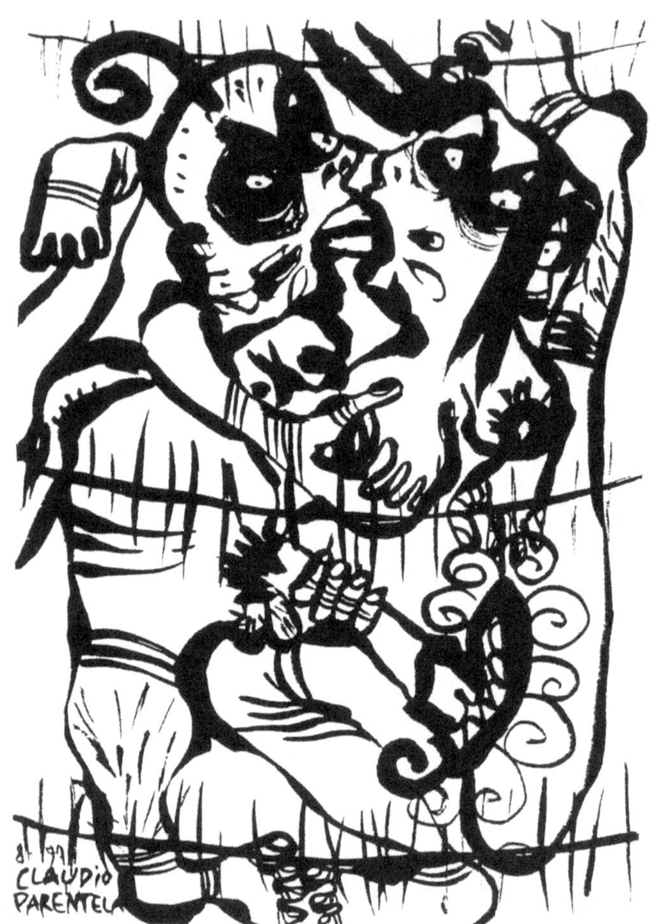

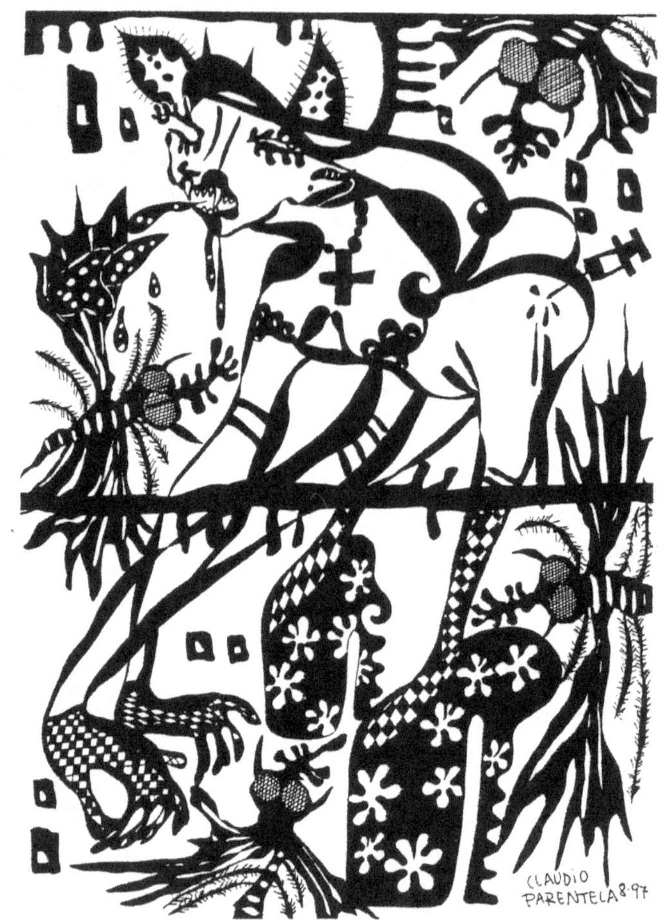

CLAUDIO PARENTELA

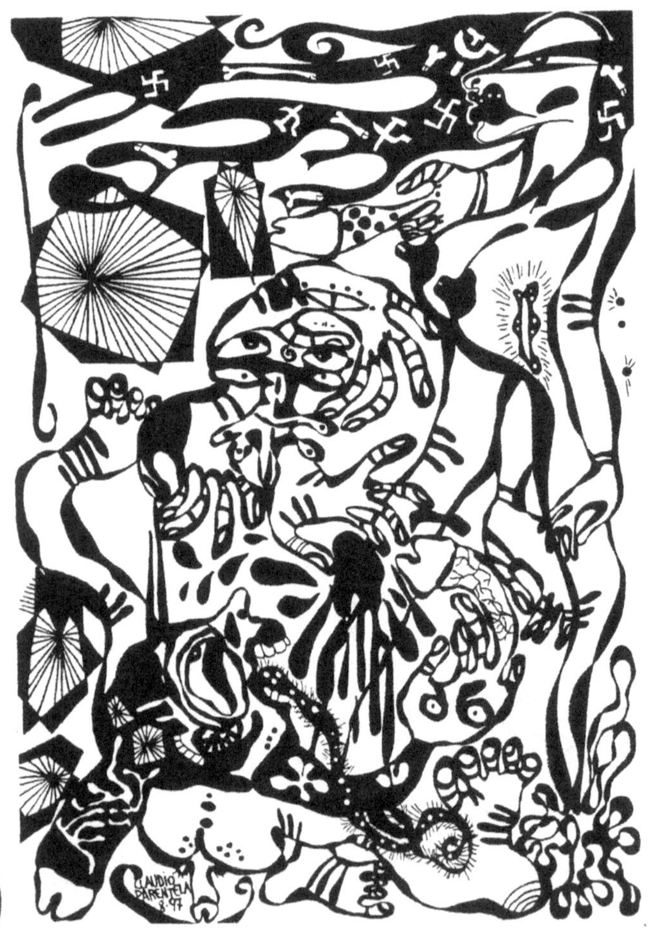

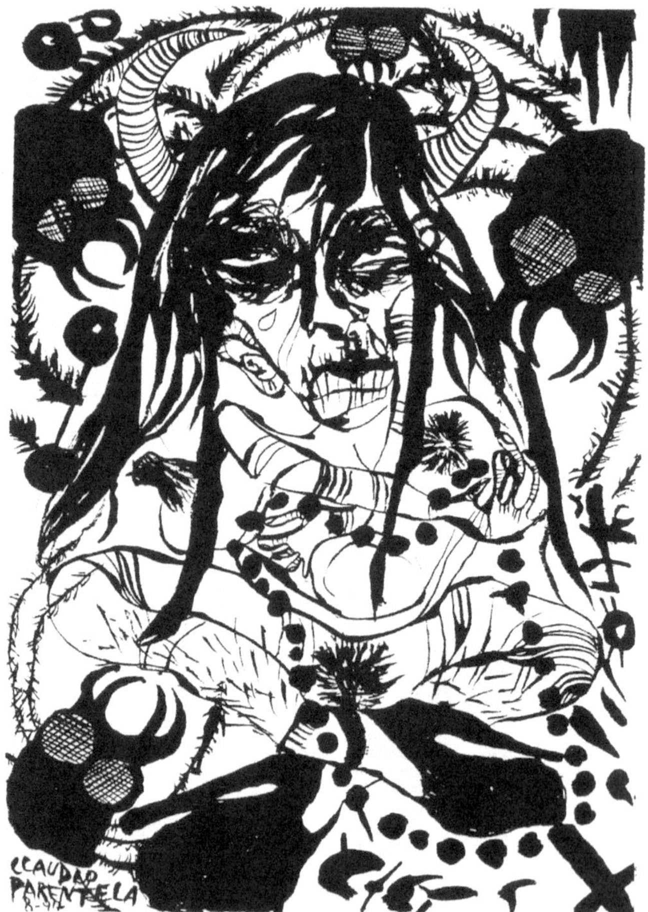

I don't know why artists think fame is all that hard to get, or something worthy of seeking. Why, it's as easy as falling off a log, as easy as dying. You just have to surrender to the forces of gravity and decay. The mainstream entertainment, by it sheer mass, has always sucked artists out of the fringe, the underground. That is

OUT OF ISOLTION

A FILM BY
FRANK MOORE

who is not familiar with the hidden channels of change.

So it is always tragic to see artists who are known for doing underground, shamanistic, and/or risky art get sucked, seduced, absorbed, tricked, bribed into "the mainstream". It is tragic not only in personal terms for the individual artists, but in terms of the big picture. When an artist sets herself up as being an artist who goes beyond the normal frame, who tells the hard truths, who explores the unknown...not to be hip, or controversial, or to be interesting...but because that is how our
;, so it has to be done...when that kind of
ey, personal fame, and/or glamour while still
-garde art, it is denying society the real evolu-
l avant-garde. It tells people, audiences and
t-garde is just a branch of the entertainment
es, goals, reality as television, rock music,
iis is like telling people a can of Slim Fast is a
l. It is a lie. And the scary dangerous thing is
his lie.

ociety's attempt to rechannel the change com-
what an "art expert" told me: "Your work
oesn't address the concerns...(which are a) part
whether it be mainstream or 'alternative'...curators and presenters are (not) obliged to show it." She went on to say that I should stay "in (my) own sphere", and that I don't need the public channels that galleries represent. Which is true. But galleries and the people who think what is in galleries is the full range of art need the artists, not the reverse. The magic of private performance is needed to expand the narrow, shallow river of "the current art dialogue", controlled both in content and depth by the art experts. Fortunately, there are galleries which are willing to go into the
cal unknown represented by private perfor-
:es.

Another way society tries to deball the magical
r of private performance is to co-opt it by
normal reality. What happened to Paul
iple. Paul is, or was, the best of the modern
n the 70's, he did performances in run down
to a rubber-masked trickster who called forth
meals of dog food, mayo and catsup..., of
of hard-ons dangling out of girls' underwear
hole and down throat and up the nose..., of
ed in mayo..., of walking bloodied barefoot on
video in another motel room. But most ran out
pecial kind of shock. It is not the shock of when
y or when a guy exposes himself. It is not a
act. It is more like culture shock. It is a reality
rent realities come together, collide, and com-
d Paul's pieces. Most people could not handle
incredible amounts of uplifting energy.

l had been discovered by the art scene. He
ncisco Art Institute to do a performance. The
tudents. Paul did his rituals, which in the past
om, shocked and physically disturbed most
audience laughed and clapped at everything
drank catsup with him to show how hip they
no magic, no colliding of realities. Paul
s cut off from his private, magical roots by being
w magician into a hot artist.

fter he felt the loss of the magic but did not
After a few more performances, he stopped per-
oss to us all. He was defeated because he
nportance of his private magic, but how much it
threatened normal reality. ★

First appeared in *Movement Research*, Performance Journal #16, Spring 1998

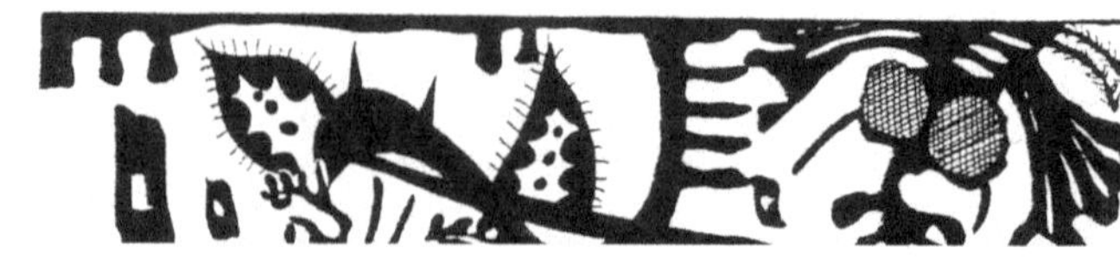

out of Isolation

by Frank Moore

Published by

INTER-RELATIONS

P.O. Box 11445
Berkeley, CA 94712

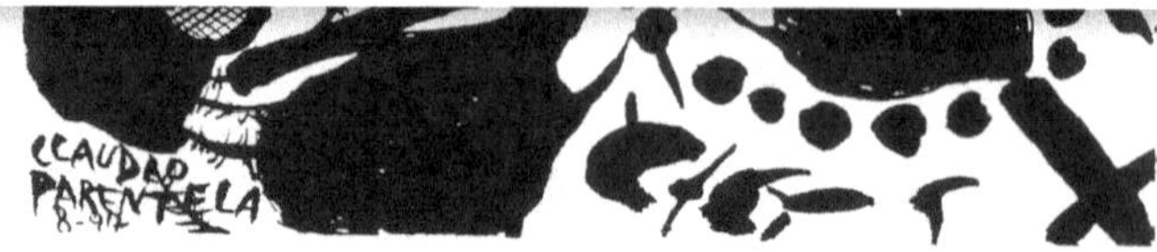

I don't know why artists think fame is all that hard to get, or something worthy of seeking. Why, it's as easy as falling off a log, as easy as dying. You just have to surrender to the forces of gravity and decay. The mainstream entertainment, by it sheer mass, has always sucked artists out of the fringe, the underground. That is

a mat is on the otherwise bare performing area. harsh bright lights. jim lies in his world of the mat.

I lie here in my universe of the mat, my bed. I always have been here lying in my universe forever, forever. My mat, my pillow, my sheet, my blanket ... for countless force-fed meals, enemas, baths, shaves, haircuts, pissed-on sheets ... many many harsh-lighted days, many, many semi-dark nights. Outside my universe there are bony fingers, blotch-skin creatures. Sometimes they invaded my universe ... the sickly-sweet smelling ones. They "take care of me" ... they handle me like they handle my pillow. Their voices are high, loud, flat. Sometimes they lie on beds beside mine, moaning and crying for alone many many, then they get quiet and others of them carry the still ones away. There are always new ones, but they are always the same. There are different bony fingers who invade my universe, who strip me, probe me stretch me until it hurts ... do strange things to me like rubbing ice on my body then brushing me hard. They talk to me in funny ways ... loud and flat. They say, "We are doing this for your own good." They don't think I understand what they are saying. I don't understand most of their words. But I understand enough, I understand I am not a Mister, a Mrs., a Miss, a Nurse, a Doctor. I understand I am not bony fingers. They can keep their universe of bony fingers. I am not going out of my universe of the mat. I understand enough. A long long, when I cried out, they made me numb. I do not like being numb. In my universe of the mat, I am not numb. But they said crying out was not "appropriate behavior". I do not think appropriate behavior is good.

1

who is not familiar with the hidden channels of change.

So it is always tragic to see artists who are known for doing underground, shamanistic, and/or risky art get sucked, seduced, absorbed, tricked, bribed into "the mainstream". It is tragic not only in personal terms for the individual artists, but in terms of the big picture. When an artist sets herself up as being an artist who goes beyond the normal frame, who tells the hard truths, who explores the unknown...not to be hip, or controversial, or to be interesting...but because that is how our

s, so it has to be done...when that kind of
ey, personal fame, and/or glamour while still
-garde art, it is denying society the real evolu-
l avant-garde. It tells people, audiences and
t-garde is just a branch of the entertainment
es, goals, reality as television, rock music,
is is like telling people a can of Slim Fast is a
l. It is a lie. And the scary dangerous thing is
his lie.
ociety's attempt to rechannel the change com-
what an "art expert" told me: "Your work
oesn't address the concerns...(which are a) part
whether it be mainstream or 'alternative'...cura-
tors and presenters are (not) obliged to show
it." She went on to say that I should stay "in (my) own sphere", and that I don't need the public channels that galleries represent. Which is true. But galleries and the people who think what is in galleries is the full range of art need the artists, not the reverse. The magic of private performance is needed to expand the narrow, shallow river of "the current art dialogue", controlled both in content and depth by the art experts. Fortunately, there are galleries which are willing to go into the
cal unknown represented by private perfor-
ces.
Another way society tries to deball the magical
r of private performance is to co-opt it by
normal reality. What happened to Paul
ple. Paul is, or was, the best of the modern
n the 70's, he did performances in run down
to a rubber-masked trickster who called forth
meals of dog food, mayo and catsup..., of
of hard-ons dangling out of girls' underwear
hole and down throat and up the nose..., of
ed in mayo..., of walking bloodied barefoot on
video in another motel room. But most ran out
pecial kind of shock. It is not the shock of when
y or when a guy exposes himself. It is not a
act. It is more like culture shock. It is a reality
rent realities come together, collide, and com-
d Paul's pieces. Most people could not handle
incredible amounts of uplifting energy.
ul had been discovered by the art scene. He
ncisco Art Institute to do a performance. The
tudents. Paul did his rituals, which in the past
om, shocked and physically disturbed most
audience laughed and clapped at everything
drank catsup with him to show how hip they
no magic, no colliding of realities. Paul
s cut off from his private, magical roots by being
w magician into a hot artist.
fter he felt the loss of the magic but did not
After a few more performances, he stopped per-
oss to us all. He was defeated because he
nportance of his private magic, but how much it
threatened normal reality. ★

First appeared in *Movement Research*, Performance Journal #16, Spring 1998

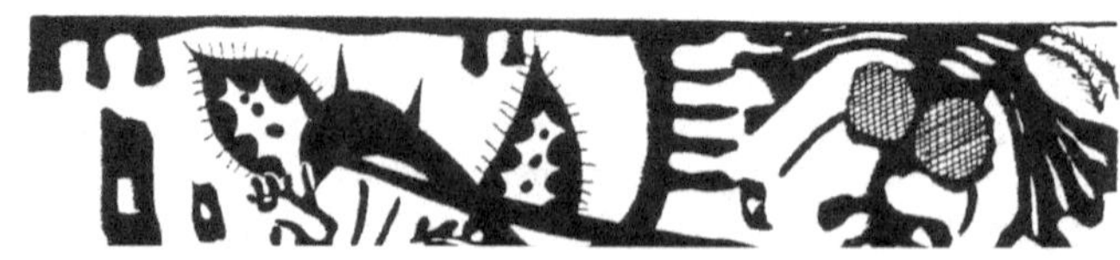

Everything that is not appropriate behavior makes me feel. But I understand enough to stop crying when the bony fingers are around. Stop making any sound, any move when they are around. They stopped making me numb. I understand enough. I discovered a way of rubbing myself that makes me warm, makes me feel good. Bony fingers slapped me away from feeling good. Not appropriate behavior. I understand enough. I do appropriate behavior in the harsh light when they are around. I am still, quiet. In my universe of the mat. I do not even look into their world. I am busy creating within me. But when the harsh light goes and the semi-darkness comes ... when only the still or moaning bony fingers are around ... I move, I laugh, I cry, I rub my body and good feeling comes. Not so loud or so much that the harsh light, the bony fingers, and their numbness come back. But just enough. And by rubbing, I know I am not bony fingers.

In the harsh light, they treat me just like my pillow. They change me just like they change my pillow. Always fast like they need to move on. Sometimes, the special bony fingers, the prodders, stand over me and say I should come into their universe, what they are doing to me will help me. They talk like they talk to my pillow. Why should I want to go into their world of greys, where everyone wears white? In my universe of the mat, I lie on smooth warm softness and create the brightest colors and the sweetest sounds to surround me. But I am not worried. Bony fingers never really believe I ever can enter their universe.

I only wish I was not the only soft fingers ... I wish there was another soft fingers in my universe of the mat ... someone to share in the bright colors and sweet sounds ... someone I could laugh with, cry with, move with,

2

I don't know why artists think fame is all that hard to get, or something worthy of seeking. Why, it's as easy as falling off a log, as easy as dying. You just have to surrender to the forces of gravity and decay. The mainstream entertainment, by it sheer mass, has always sucked artists out of the fringe, the underground. That is

who is not familiar with the hidden channels of change.

So it is always tragic to see artists who are known for doing underground, shamanistic, and/or risky art get sucked, seduced, absorbed,

tricked, bribed into "the mainstream". It is tragic not only in personal terms for the individual artists, but in terms of the big picture. When an artist sets herself up as being an artist who goes beyond the normal frame, who tells the hard truths, who explores the unknown...not to be hip, or controversial, or to be interesting...but because that is how our
;, so it has to be done...when that kind of
ey, personal fame, and/or glamour while still
:-garde art, it is denying society the real evolu-
il avant-garde. It tells people, audiences and
t-garde is just a branch of the entertainment
es, goals, reality as television, rock music,
iis is like telling people a can of Slim Fast is a
l. It is a lie. And the scary dangerous thing is
:his lie.
ociety's attempt to rechannel the change com-
what an "art expert" told me: "Your work
oesn't address the concerns...(which are a) part
vhether it be mainstream or 'alternative'...cura-
tors and presenters are (not) obliged to show
it." She went on to say that I should stay
"in (my) own sphere", and that I don't
need the public channels that galleries
represent. Which is true. But
galleries and the people who
think what is in galleries is
the full range of art need
the artists, not the
reverse. The magic of private performance is needed to expand the narrow,
shallow river of "the current art dialogue", controlled both in content and
depth by the art experts. Fortunately, there
are galleries which are willing to go into the
cal unknown represented by private perfor-
:es.
Another way society tries to deball the magical
er of private performance is to co-opt it by
normal reality. What happened to Paul
iple. Paul is, or was, the best of the modern
n the 70's, he did performances in run down
to a rubber-masked trickster who called forth
/ meals of dog food, mayo and catsup..., of
of hard-ons dangling out of girls' underwear
hole and down throat and up the nose..., of
ed in mayo..., of walking bloodied barefoot on
video in another motel room. But most ran out
pecial kind of shock. It is not the shock of when
y or when a guy exposes himself. It is not a
act. It is more like culture shock. It is a reality
rent realities come together, collide, and com-
nd Paul's pieces. Most people could not handle
incredible amounts of uplifting energy.
ul had been discovered by the art scene. He
ncisco Art Institute to do a performance. The
tudents. Paul did his rituals, which in the past
om, shocked and physically disturbed most
audience laughed and clapped at everything
drank catsup with him to show how hip they
no magic, no colliding of realities. Paul
s cut off from his private, magical roots by being
w magician into a hot artist.
after he felt the loss of the magic but did not
After a few more performances, he stopped per-
oss to us all. He was defeated because he
nportance of his private magic, but how much it
threatened normal reality. ★

First appeared in *Movement Research*, Performance Journal #16, Spring 1998

share good feeling with ... someone who would be with me on the mat, touch me not like touching my pillow, not like pulling things out of me or to make me different. But just because we are the only soft fingers in the universe of the mat.

There is a new prodder. Do not look at bony fingers. But catch sight of same white. Miss Roberts talking to a pillow called Mr. Merrill. Same words about "to make you better". But sound of voice is somehow different, softer. The touch is still changing the pillow of me. But not bony fingers! I sneak a peak. Same white, but different. The skin is soft like my skin. The smell is almost like my smell. Almost enough to try to open my universe to this new soft fingers. But words came, the same words as bony fingers. The prodding soft fingers strips me bare just like she is changing the pillow of me. Easier to probe my pillow of a body. The prodding fingers does the same hurting "make you better" exercises on me as the other bony fingers before. And then the going somewhere else fast. And the touching the pillow of me, instead of touching me.

When the soft fingers and the harsh light were gone, I cried louder than before. I do not care if they make me numb. Maybe numbness is better if soft fingers are the same as bony fingers, if soft fingers also want me to go into grey and white, if soft fingers does not want to be with me, then numbness is better.

Soft fingers keeps coming back. At first, rushing to somewhere else, trying to pull me into the grey universe. I know how to fight against that bony fingers trick. But I like her soft warm skin touching me ... like my soft warm sheet under me. Sometime soft fingers forgets about

3

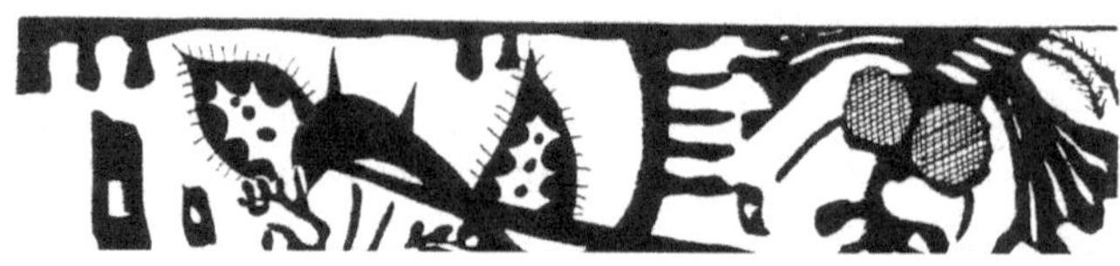

helping me, about making me a better person. For that moment we are the only ones in the universe ... together. Then soft fingers remembers the bony fingers and starts touching me like a pillow again.

But the moments of being together grow. I like when she forgets and makes mistakes and comes closer into my world. I like when she just sits on my mat ... on our mat ... and just looks at me, just listens to me. I feel more and more like I can show her my moves, show her my sounds. I like when soft fingers became Jane and I became Jim. I like when Jane just lies on the mat and we just look at each other, listen to each other, even when we really don't understand what meaning ... but we feel. I like it when Jane starts making her own noises, not just bony words. I like when Jane holds my hand. I like when Jane comes into my world of dim light, when she wears colors bright, soft, smooth flowing ... not bony fingers white ... and even her hair is flowing strangely soft. I like when Jane comes wearing the colors soft even in the harsh light. I like when Jane makes the harsh light go away for a while, when Jane rocks me, when Jane rubs my head. I like when Jane slowly takes all the colors off. She is soft everywhere. She lies next to me on the mat. She makes soft sounds and soft moves, just like me. She is just like me now. Two soft fingers on the mat. I like when Jane lets me rub Jane's back, when Jane calls me Jim. I like it when we are in our universe of the mat sharing not appropriate behavior ... laughing, crying, making good feeling come. Rocking or holding hands made different good feelings come together, making soft sounds together, together making good feelings come.

But suddenly Jane was gone. I was alone in happiness. Jane would come back into the happiness with me on the mat. So I was happy.

4

I don't know why artists think fame is all that hard to get, or something worthy of seeking. Why, it's as easy as falling off a log, as easy as dying. You just have to surrender to the forces of gravity and decay. The mainstream entertainment, by it sheer mass, has always sucked artists out of the fringe, the underground. That is

tricked, bribed into "the mainstream". It is tragic not only in personal terms for the individual artists, but in terms of the big picture. When an artist sets herself up as being an artist who goes beyond the normal frame, who tells the hard truths, who explores the unknown...not to be hip, or controversial, or to be interesting...but because that is how our

;, so it has to be done...when that kind of
ey, personal fame, and/or glamour while still
:-garde art, it is denying society the real evolu-
al avant-garde. It tells people, audiences and
t-garde is just a branch of the entertainment
es, goals, reality as television, rock music,
nis is like telling people a can of Slim Fast is a
l. It is a lie. And the scary dangerous thing is
this lie.

society's attempt to rechannel the change com-
what an "art expert" told me: "Your work
oesn't address the concerns...(which are a) part
whether it be mainstream or 'alternative'...curators and presenters are (not) obliged to show it." She went on to say that I should stay "in (my) own sphere", and that I don't need the public channels that galleries represent. Which is true. But galleries and the people who think what is in galleries is the full range of art need the artists, not the reverse. The magic of private performance is needed to expand the narrow, shallow river of "the current art dialogue", controlled both in content and depth by the art experts. Fortunately, there are galleries which are willing to go into the
cal unknown represented by private perfor-
:es.

Another way society tries to deball the magical
er of private performance is to co-opt it by
normal reality. What happened to Paul
nple. Paul is, or was, the best of the modern
n the 70's, he did performances in run down
to a rubber-masked trickster who called forth
/ meals of dog food, mayo and catsup..., of
.of hard-ons dangling out of girls' underwear
hole and down throat and up the nose..., of
ed in mayo..., of walking bloodied barefoot on
video in another motel room. But most ran out
pecial kind of shock. It is not the shock of when
y or when a guy exposes himself. It is not a
act. It is more like culture shock. It is a reality
rent realities come together, collide, and com-
nd Paul's pieces. Most people could not handle
incredible amounts of uplifting energy.

ul had been discovered by the art scene. He
ncisco Art Institute to do a performance. The
tudents. Paul did his rituals, which in the past
om, shocked and physically disturbed most
audience laughed and clapped at everything
drank catsup with him to show how hip they
no magic, no colliding of realities. Paul
s cut off from his private, magical roots by being
w magician into a hot artist.

fter he felt the loss of the magic but did not
After a few more performances, he stopped per-
oss to us all. He was defeated because he
nportance of his private magic, but how much it
threatened normal reality. ★

who is not familiar with the hidden channels of change.

So it is always tragic to see artists who are known for doing underground, shamanistic, and/or risky art get sucked, seduced, absorbed,

First appeared in *Movement Research*, Performance Journal #16, Spring 1998

But when Jane came the next day, she was in bony white. Jane had become like bony fingers again. She said what we were doing was not appropriate behavior. She used words like romance and sexual that I did not understand. Jane left. The numbness came back without the bony fingers giving me anything.

Jane came back as bony fingers. I kept rising out of the numbness in hope whenever Jane came, but then fell deeper and deeper.

Jane came. I could not hold the crying back. I cried in the harsh light. Then Jane cried too. She made the harsh light go away. She came back into our universe of the mat and rocked me. Jane told me to teach her the noises and the moves of our universe of the mat. Now I have another soft fingers, Jane, on the mat, in the universe with me, together with me.

Together we can expand the universe beyond the mat. Jane can bring other soft fingers in. The bony fingers begin to fade. I can see, begin to see colors beyond the mat, begin to hear laughter beyond the mat. Jane says she and I together will explore the universe that is outside. She and I are happy.

THE END

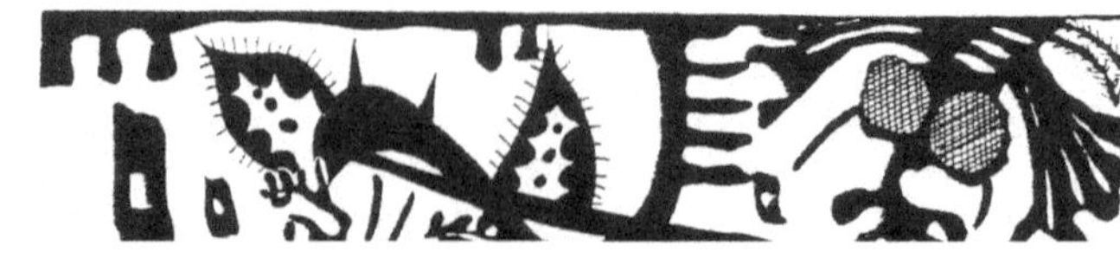

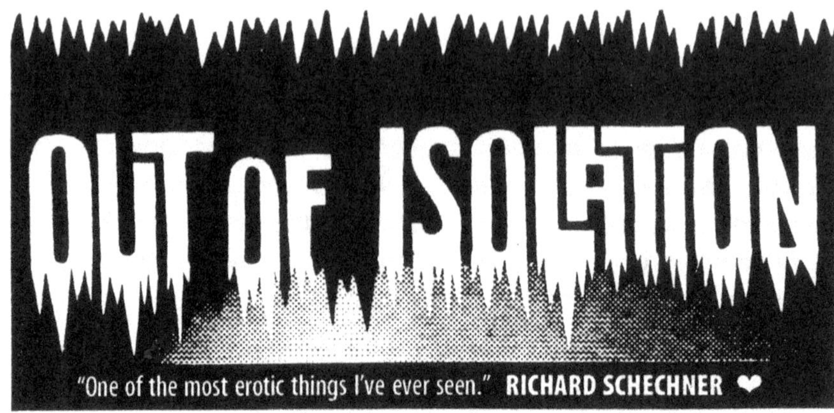

"One of the most erotic things I've ever seen." **RICHARD SCHECHNER** ❤ HONORABLE MENTION AWARD, FEATURE LENGTH VIDEO **EAST BAY VIDEO FESTIVAL** ❤ "It ('Out of Isolation') was the best film, in many respects, that I have ever seen. It is a classic, underground masterpiece, and I was deeply impressed by (Frank Moore's) sense of movement, aesthetic, humanity and taboo." **JIM COHN, ST. LAWRENCE UNIVERSITY** ❤ ('Out of Isolation') "stayed in my mind far more persistently than I first expected, at least based on what the film-makers with millions of dollars at their disposal call 'production values' and 'professional polish'. What most of these high-priced pieces lack, of course, is substance and a genuinely different – and deeply challenging – point of view. Something to shake up, shatter, shame, inspire, perspire, ponder and play with long after the cassette gets rewound. Your films did that for me: they are definitely not easy to absorb, follow, or even 'enjoy' in the ordinary pop-culture sense. But you don't forget watching them, ever." **SCOTT LANKFORD, FOOTHILL COLLEGE** ❤ "And the central irony of the title 'Out of Isolation' as it is revealed is truly unforgettable: the nurse's everyday American loneliness is so much sadder, so much more impenetrable than that of the man she hopes to 'cure.' In this sense, the film makes a bold attempt to break through the cultural/intellectual isolation of the viewer; to stretch our imaginations in ways they have never been moved and stretched before due to our own cradle-to-grave institutionalization within the rigid mindset of every-day America. Which may explain why, even when the film seems painful to watch, it remains powerful: it stretches the imagination in new and different, sometimes painful directions." **SCOTT LANKFORD, FOOTHILL COLLEGE** ❤ "A very powerful film." **JACK FOLEY** ❤

©1992, LABASH

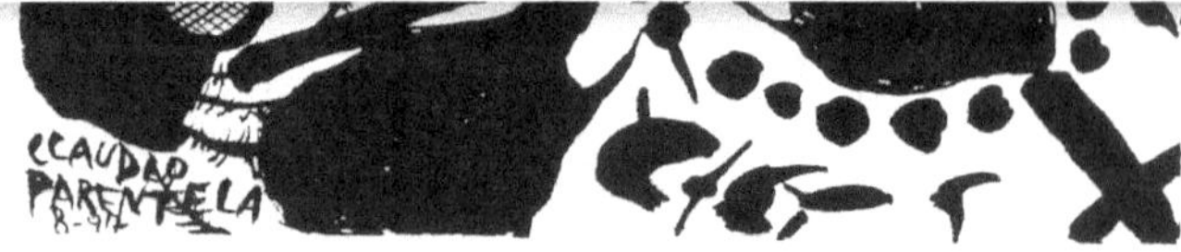

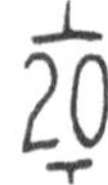

What Price fame

by

FRANK MOORE

18 October, 1997

I don't know why artists think fame is all that hard to get, or something worthy of seeking. Why, it's as easy as falling off a log, as easy as dying. You just have to surrender to the forces of gravity and decay. The mainstream entertainment, by it sheer mass, has always sucked artists out of the fringe, the underground. That is just gravity. In reality, it takes a lot to enter, and to stay in, the underground. The underground is where the real freedom and the real ability to change society are to be found. This is why artists CHOOSE the underground instead of the mainstream. This is also why, when an artist is pulled into the mainstream, this freedom and ability decay. In my own career, I have worked very hard to stay in the underground...this work has been hard precisely because some of the pieces have turned out to be "popular" (whatever that means!)...attracting the mainstream sharks.

The mainstream has always tried to create a fake avant-garde with fake controversies, fake taboos, fake "hipness", etc. to give the marks a controlled fun-ride through a Disneyland to keep them away from the real edge of life. This is because the powers-that-be can not control or exploit what is in the real avant-garde.

About every five years, the fame makers "discover" me, want to make me famous. I always play along. But I also always do "the wrong thing" to keep my work surfing just below the "fame wave". Fame cripples art. But the sub-fame level is where the hidden channels of effecting, healing, changing, dreaming, myth-giving powers lie.

It is easier to stay in this sub-fame level when you do private performances than when you do public performances...because in public performances layers of seductions, limitation, consideration, taboos, morals, ways of being politically correct are laid on the art and the artist by either the powers of the establishment or the "alternative" power systems of the present society or both. But I like the challenge of doing very public work without surrendering to the fame manufacturers.

When I do a public piece, I am not swayed by how many people come or by how many walk out, because I am still functioning, and rooted, in the channels of magical change that I became aware of by doing private performances. This rooting in private rituals gives the artist freedom from, and weapons against, the corrupting concerns of money, fame, competition, good taste, acceptance, and the search for an audience. This freedom is important in shamanistic art, which is art that acts for nonlinear change, because, by bringing new dreams, new myths, new visions into society from the universal underworld, it radically changes society. By being linked to a power system, be it establishment or alternative, the artist is trapped in a basic conflict of interest, because she has aligned herself either with protecting the social system or with a certain manner of change, when her true job is to carry the new visionary myths from the gods into this world through her body.

When the artist is rooted in private rituals, it becomes clear that she is not an agent for society, or some political movement, or the art galleries and art "experts", or even for her own individualistic imagination. Instead, she is an agent of the gods, of dreams, of visions and myths. This causes reactions in society, especially when the piece is public.

Karen Finley is criticized for limiting her audience because she offends them by her words, anger, nudity. An artist who is rooted in the private channels is not affected by this attempt to curb the power of the art by strapping it to audience acceptance and agreement. The power of a Karen Finley is the taboo-breaking energy she releases into society. This societal pressure to tame art down, which usually sounds very reasonable and comes even from liberal sources, is very hard for the artist to resist who is not familiar with the hidden channels of change.

So it is always tragic to see artists who are known for doing underground, shamanistic, and/or risky art get sucked, seduced, absorbed, tricked, bribed into "the mainstream". It is tragic not only in personal terms for the individual artists, but in terms of the big picture. When an artist sets herself up as being an artist who goes beyond the normal frame, who tells the hard truths, who explores the unknown...not to be hip, or controversial, or to be interesting...but because that is how our tribal human being evolves, so it has to be done...when that kind of artist then goes after money, personal fame, and/or glamour while still claiming to be doing avant-garde art, it is denying society the real evolutionary function of the real avant-garde. It tells people, audiences and artists alike, that the avant-garde is just a branch of the entertainment complex with the same rules, goals, reality as television, rock music, Hollywood, and sports. This is like telling people a can of Slim Fast is a balanced meal of real food. It is a lie. And the scary dangerous thing is artists are buying/selling this lie.

Another example of society's attempt to rechannel the change coming from shamanistic art is what an "art expert" told me: "Your work is...not art...(because) it doesn't address the concerns...(which are a) part of the current art dialog, whether it be mainstream or 'alternative'...curators and presenters are (not) obliged to show it." She went on to say that I should stay "in (my) own sphere", and that I don't need the public channels that galleries represent. Which is true. But galleries and the people who think what is in galleries is the full range of art need the artists, not the reverse. The magic of private performance is needed to expand the narrow, shallow river of "the current art dialogue", controlled both in content and depth by the art experts. Fortunately, there are galleries which are willing to go into the magical unknown represented by private performances.

Another way society tries to deball the magical power of private performance is to co-opt it by absorbing it back into the normal reality. What happened to Paul McCarthy is a classic example. Paul is, or was, the best of the modern shamanistic performers. In the 70's, he did performances in run down motels. He transformed into a rubber-masked trickster who called forth realities of vomit, of messy meals of dog food, mayo and catsup..., of wearing women's clothes...of hard-ons dangling out of girls' underwear fucking dolls, tubes up asshole and down throat and up the nose..., of fucking alone in a motel bed in mayo..., of walking bloodied barefoot on glass. Friends watched via video in another motel room. But most ran out in shock. This shock is a special kind of shock. It is not the shock of when a youngster uses obscenity or when a guy exposes himself. It is not a reaction or an aggressive act. It is more like culture shock. It is a reality shock. It is when two different realities come together, collide, and combine. This happened around Paul's pieces. Most people could not handle it. But the shock released incredible amounts of uplifting energy.

By the early 80's, Paul had been discovered by the art scene. He was invited to the San Francisco Art Institute to do a performance. The big hall was packed with students. Paul did his rituals, which in the past would have cleared the room, shocked and physically disturbed most people. But this time, the audience laughed and clapped at everything this clown did. They even drank catsup with him to show how hip they were. There was no shock, no magic, no colliding of realities. Paul stopped, defeated. He was cut off from his private, magical roots by being transformed from an outlaw magician into a hot artist.

He told me the day after he felt the loss of the magic but did not know how to get it back. After a few more performances, he stopped performing...which is a great loss to us all. He was defeated because he underrated not only the importance of his private magic, but how much it threatened normal reality. ★

First appeared in *Movement Research*, Performance Journal #16, Spring 1998

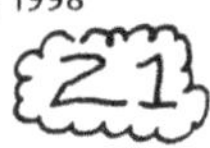

Everybody's Famous

Everybody's famous
the composer said, remembering
the words of the opera tenor
No! the critic answered
I mean the woman who performs
at Paradise Lounge is REALLY famous
she was on KPFA
her name was in THE EXPRESS
It all began when someone important
said that she was famous
But how can you tell?
when a name is a really big name
Not just a name like Frank Moore
you know,
but an accepted in marble halls fame name,
visual nudeless art accepted on the all white walls of a Jesse Helms
castle fame
Art that is annotated.
Art about which someone wearing a success suit will say:
Don't you know, this artist is no longer associated with St. Francis
ragamuffins?
He has become somebody!
The next step is, SHE says that HE
says that SHE's famous
and so it was! In all the land!
and now SHE says
she's famous
and a talk show host
says she's famous
for what?
for manufacturing
music, it must be contemporary
because it's odd enough, isn't it?
from recorded sounds and
she has a cute name
That's the main thing
It only takes
a catchy name.
and one person in the industry
to start
a myth
you too
can be
among the
maybe not RICH
but famous
there's millions like you.....
it's nothing.
but here's the question!

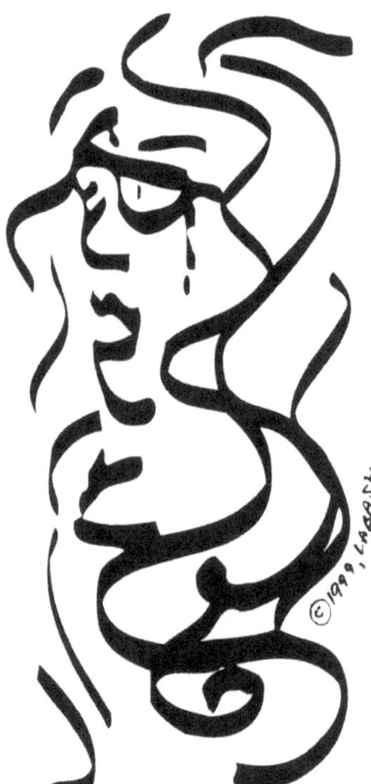

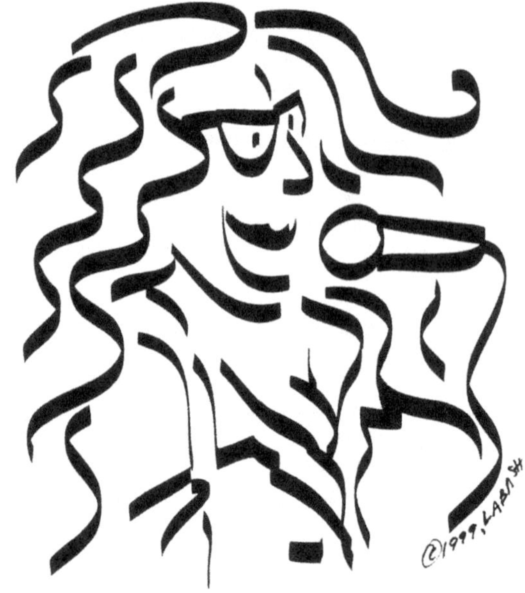

How about, say, the heart
and what about, say, the soul
which game would you rather play?
Here! Pick a role!
Say you had your fill of fame
as a little girl, or a little boy,
it just doesn't mean that much
anymore, kind of a bore,
you were adored, you had show off time
riding bikes - no hands on the handlebars
as a child
applauded
trotted out at an early age to be sat, like me,
almost disappearing with pigtails into the
large piano bench, at a grand piano
as a child performer
you had that thrill of fame
but running wild in the woods, for me,
was more fun.
No, you don't need the fame game
but you do need
the passion
of the art itself,
turning yourself inside out
over and over to disgorge the
magic tricks
turning your talents physically
on their head many times
against the tide of possibilities,
for the passion
to create
or you can choose

to be an acclaimed author
with no new books
you can still talk
about the last one
because the role of fame
takes all your time
and you don't really write anymore.

Picasso said
it was better
before the fame came,
that's when life
was really nice.
Jung said
it's in the struggle
don't arrive
don't get there
don't complete the house
don't reach that fame
keep paddling upstream
and hear the gushes
running of the rapids
dangerous rocks
all around you,
upstream
but for some
it's the quiet pool
the elegant white tie
black tux
riding on a ghost pony
a white many muscled
prancing horse named fame
ride him to the grave
or
choose
the underground and say:
Count me in
with the truly
nonfamous and
count me in
with the homeless
and the hardworking
family in West Oakland.
Count me in with the sinners
Lord knows I've sinned
Count me in
with the artists whose very lives
are a work of art
tapestries of bold, bright threads

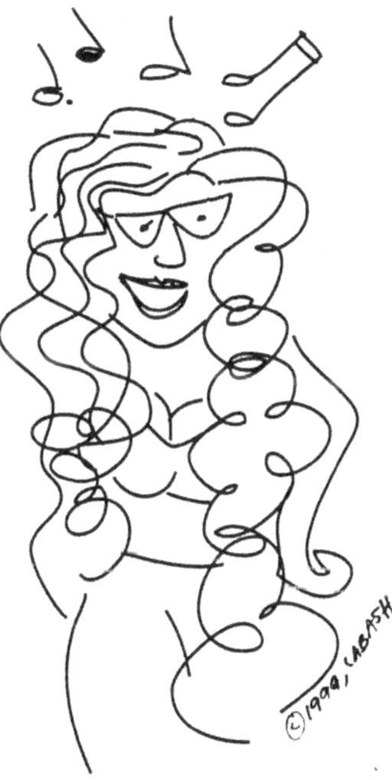

that scream when it isn't popular
to scream

Count me in
with those who
paddle upstream
and love it
Count me in
with those who give
one thousand per cent
for the privilege to create
for the need to create
for the joy to create
for the clay in your hands
for the words in your pen
for sound in your voice
for those who held your hand
in toughest times
for those who went before you
inspiring you, becoming you
and still with you
fame goes
to the seekers of fame
drowning in fame
incesting their fame
don't knock it
they need it!
And bless them
if they can handle it!
I choose the
Underground, the people
who are my kind of people
Who are in my blood
I was born to be a rebel
to be on the other side
to be with the poorest
to be with the questioners
to be with the raggelty taggelty
run sheep runners
and kick the canners
who never grew up
who don't want to be bored
with grown ups
and proper tuxedos.

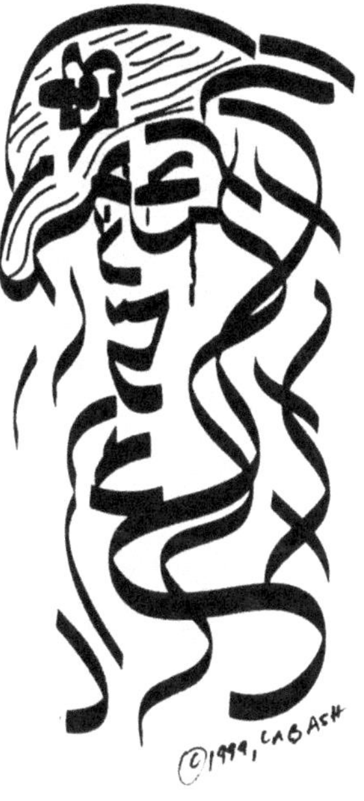

(inspired by and read for TC(r) Reading celebrating Frank Moore zine – Modern Times Books – S.F. 6/27/97)

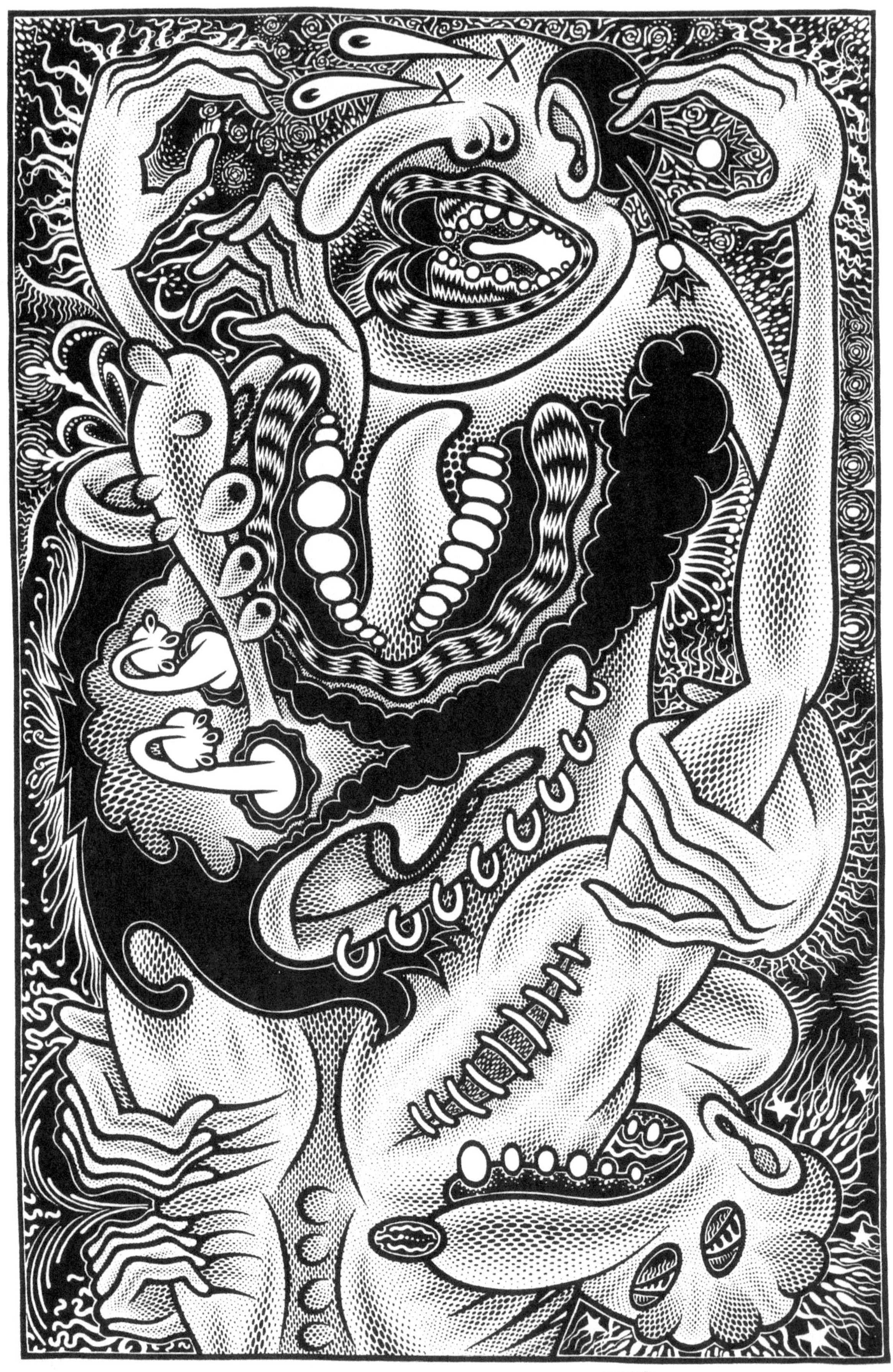

1995 © BLAIR WILSON #479

SCARS 1997

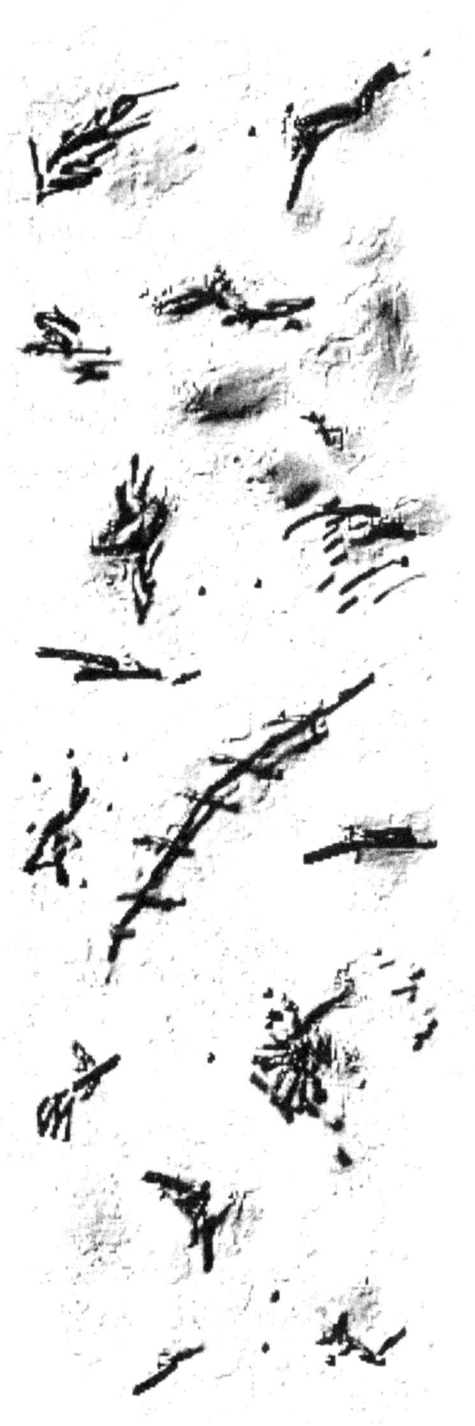

I wear my scars like badges.
These deep marks show through from under my skin
like war paint on an Apache chief.
Decorated with feathers, the skins of his prey.

I have a scar over my left knee.
It's left over from a bout with poison ivy
I had after climbing a mountainside.
The four-inch long slice curves around my leg,
almost perfectly defining the muscles in my thigh.

I have a scar on my right shin.
I slipped on a patch of rocks and cut up the lower
half of my leg and filled it with gravel and dirt.
Joe poured hydrogen peroxide on my leg
and wrapped my wounds with paper towels
because the cuts were so wide spread.
An hour later I was on a plane home,
so I could tend to my wounds in greater detail.
Tend to my wounds in depth.
Now all that is left is a two-inch line down
the side of my leg. Although it wasn't a very
deep cut, it looks like it went straight to the bone.

I have a circular scar on my left calf,
from getting off a motorcycle and sliding
my leg over the scalding hot exhaust pipe.
It has been seven years since I gained that scar,
and with each year I see it fade away just a little.
I can still see it, but the memory is slowly slipping away.

My cat scratched me on my wrist once
when we had to give her medication.
Cats don't like taking pills, or having ointment
dabbed on and liquid poured over their wounds.
When giving her pills, we'd grab all her paws,
pull her head back by the nape of her neck,
pry her jaws wide open so the pill will fall back
and she is forced to swallow it.
But sometimes she'd move too much
and a paw would slip out of our grasp.
And now, over the bone of my left wrist,
a long thin scar stares at me defiantly.

I tell people that if they wake up
with bruises and cuts they don't remember,
then they must have had fun the night before.
But each marking, each scar is a story,
is a memory. It is a way to remember how you lived.
And it is with these marks that I gauge my living.
It is with these marks that I feel decorated.

Janet Kuypers
ccandd@shout.net

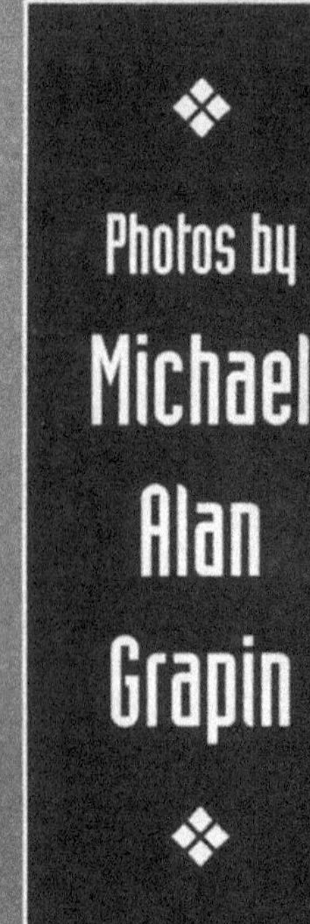
Photos by
Michael
Alan
Grapin

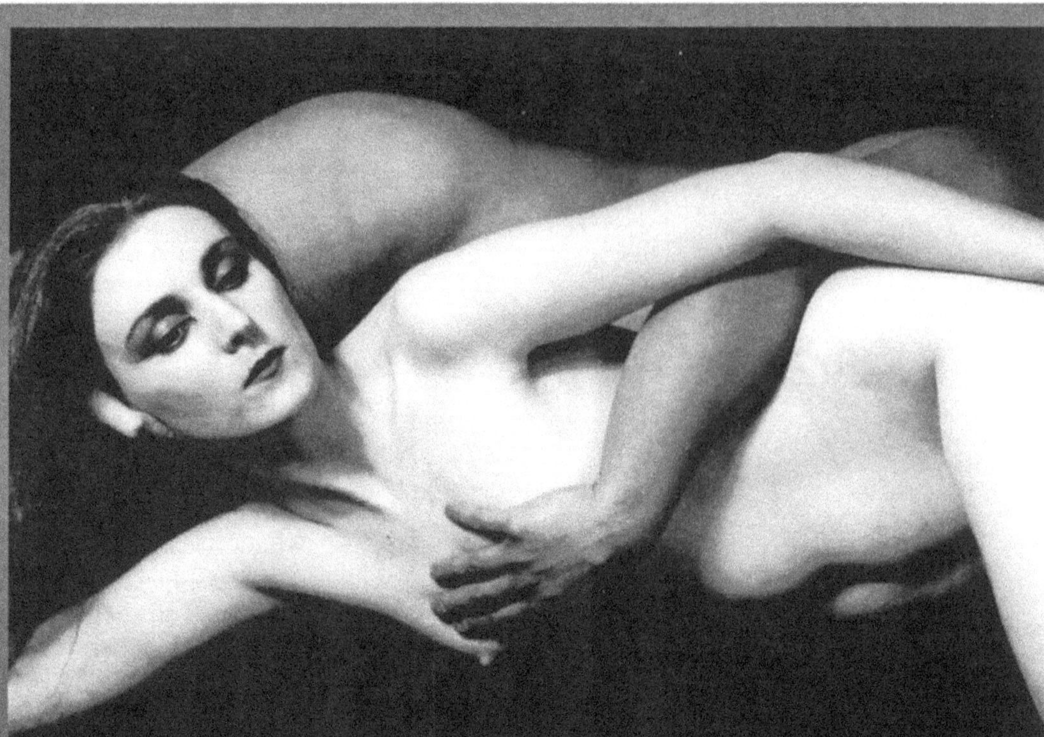

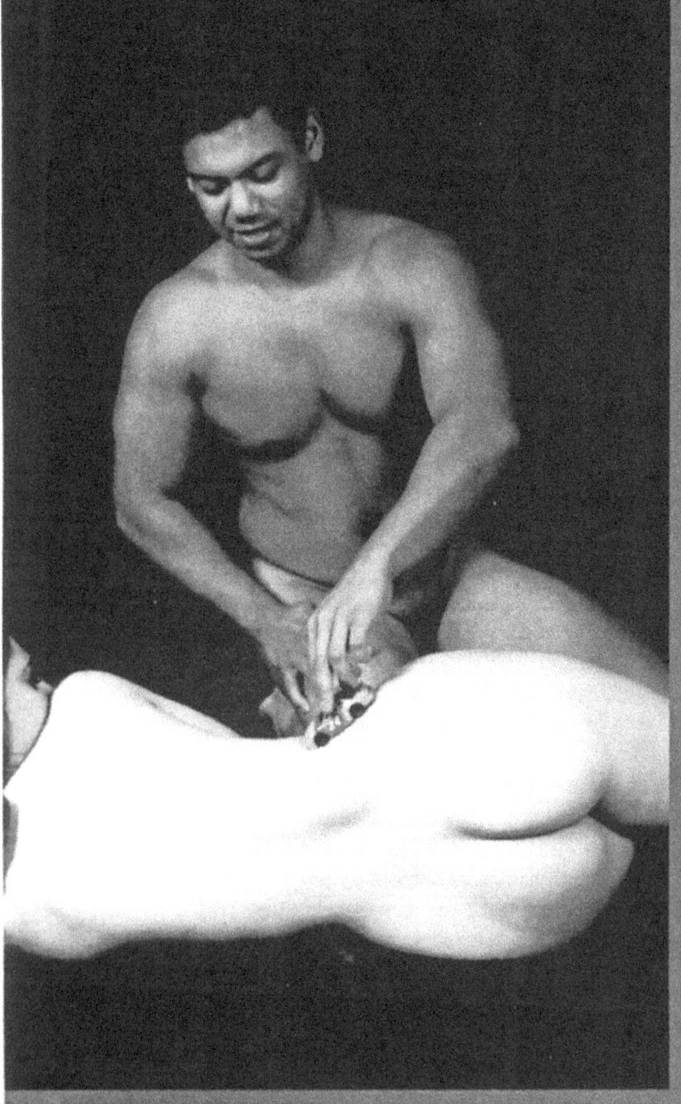

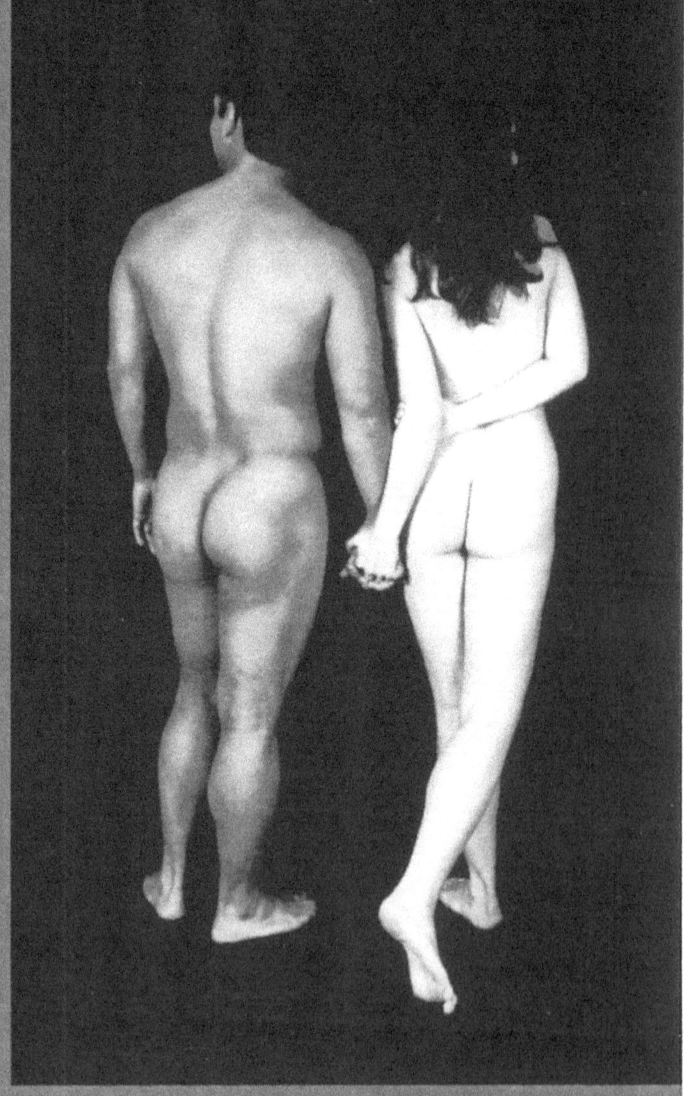

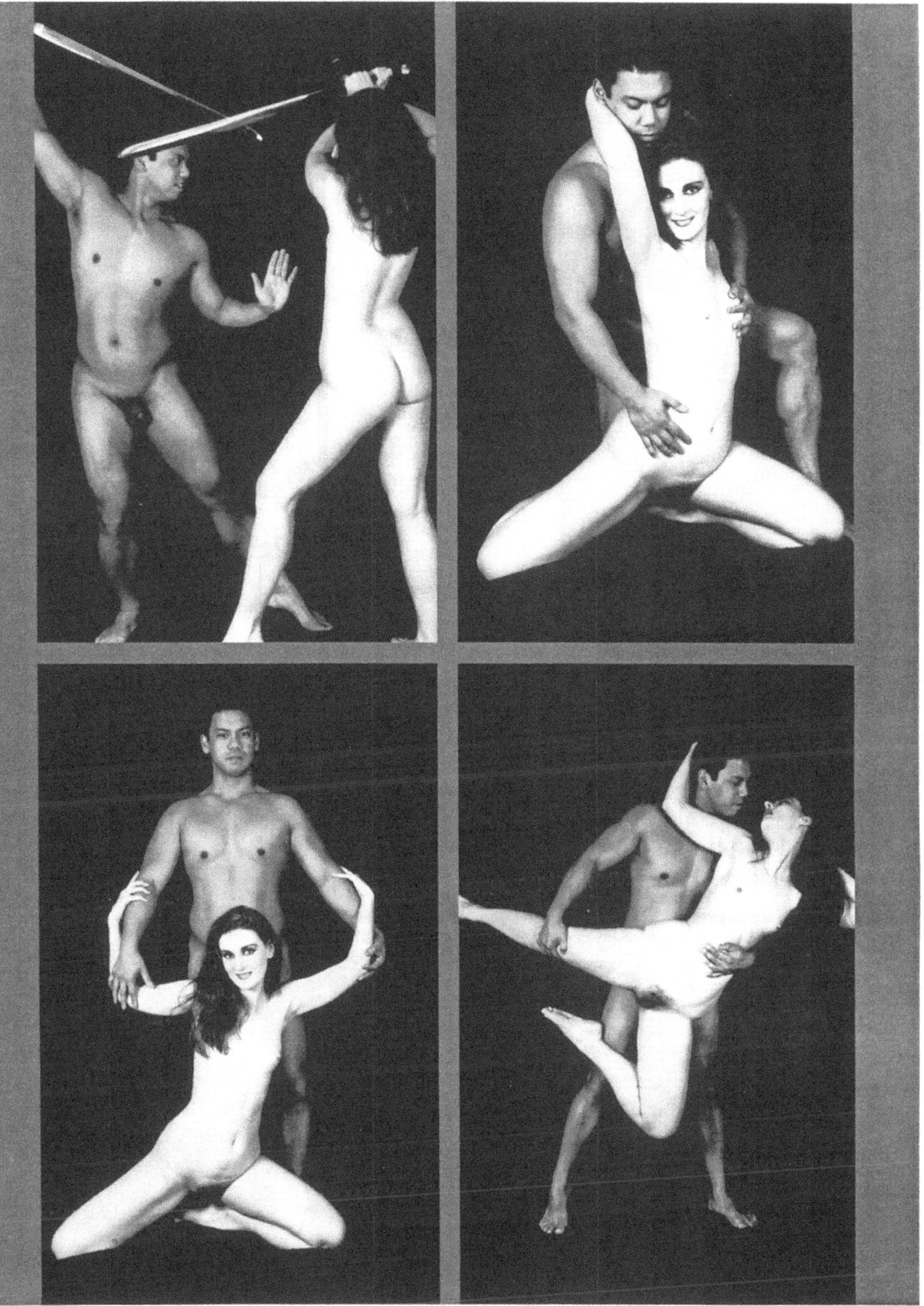

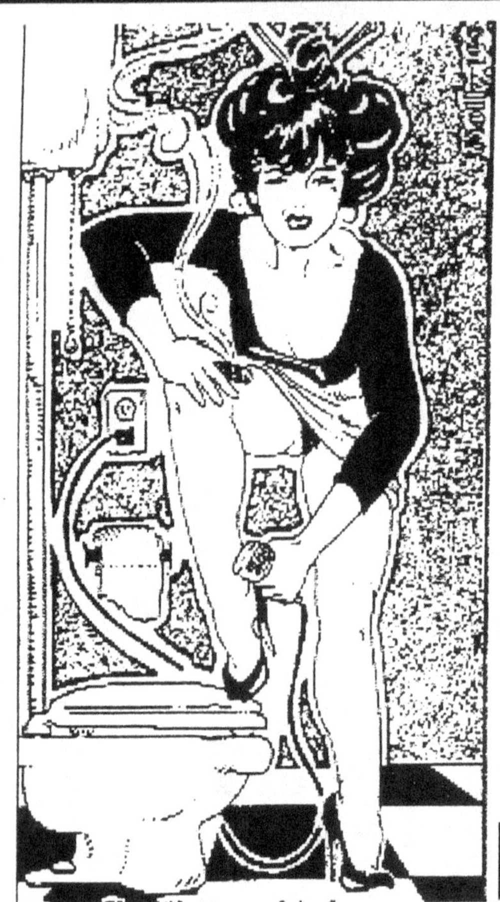

Get a computer & modem & log on to www.eroplay.com to catch gonzo hosting Mondo PolyEster live from Melbourne's Underground bookstore tues's 10am-3pm on LUVeR radio in real audio

more info:
gonzo@polyester.com.au

POLYESTER BOOKS
330 Brunswick St Fitzroy
Ph: (03) 9419 5223 Fax (03) 9419-4961

MmmmHm, you're a big boy, sure. But are you man enough for

MONDO POLYESTER

SHAKE,
BABY,
SHAKE.

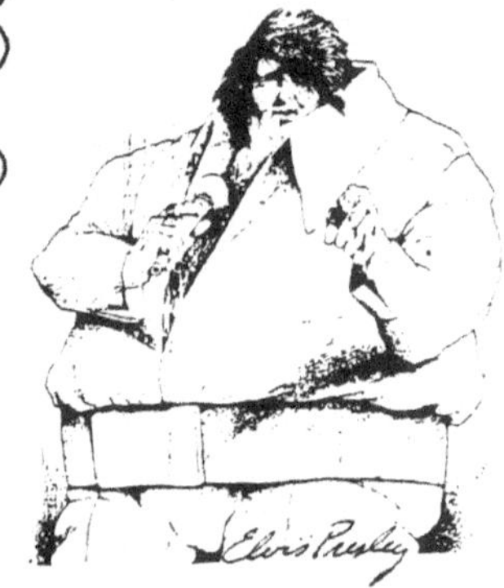

CHANCE MAGAZINE $2 CASH
3929 S. FIFTH ST.
LOUISVILLE, KY 40214

Amusing Yourself to Death

A Small-Press Resource

Dedicated to being a positive force in the zine community!

Send your zines for review or $2 for a sample issue to:

Amusing Yourself to Death
P.O. Box 91934
Santa Barbara, CA 93190-1934

e-mail: rgaviola@aol.com

Brenda Loew's **EIDOS** Magazine

"Everyone Is Doing Outrageous Sex!"

Winner, 1996 *"Golden Phallus Award"*

SAMPLE: US$7; 4 ISSUES : US$25.00 USA
US $31 Europe; US $33 All Others
8 ISSUES: US$45; LIFETIME: US$125.00

Donations Accepted

Check, Cash, MO, AmEx/Visa/MC to:
EIDOS, POB 96, Boston, MA 02137.
Ph: 617-262-0096; Fax: 617-364-0096

Must Be 18+. Age Statement Required.
email: eidos@eidos.org
http://www.eidos.org

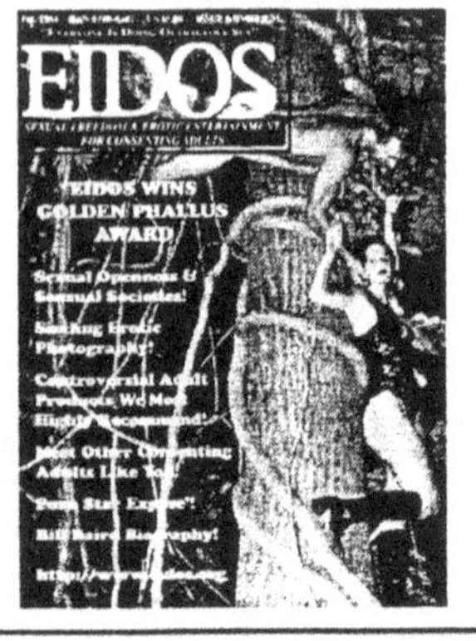

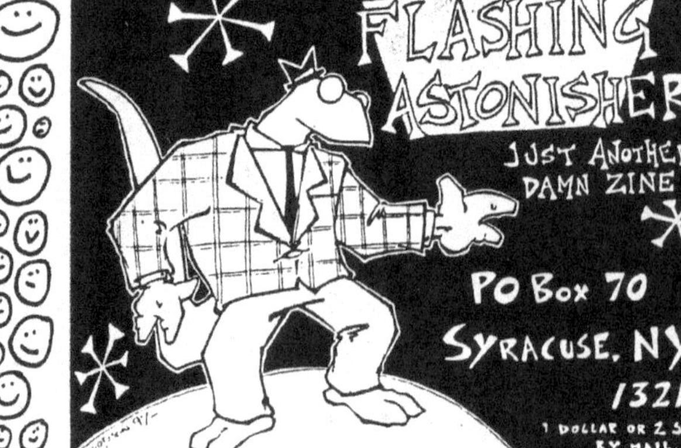

Howdy Frank,

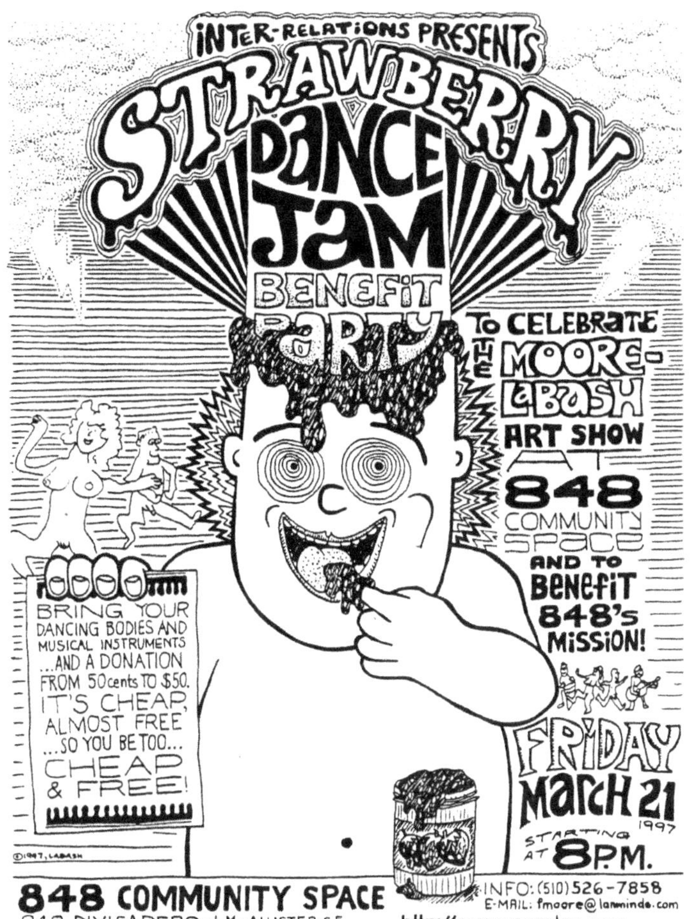

I got your letter and the flyer announcing the "Moore-LaBash" art show. That Strawberry Dance Jam must have been great. When I get out I would love to attend one of those. I hope your art show went well. I'm hoping you will have covered it and included maybe some pictures in TC(r)#7. I can't wait to get the next issue. Thank you so much for taking the time to drop me a line. It means a lot to me. We don't have much to look forward to here, but whenever I get a mag or note from you, I pass it around so everyone can see it. Little things mean a lot here, and to see a person who takes the time to recognize that there are people incarcerated and give them something to laugh at or a word of hope is encouraging. I have it a lot better here than most prisons. I'm in a dorm with about sixty guys. Everybody gets along. I have a friend here from China who is teaching me Mandarin Chinese "what a trip". We don't have cells and we can go out to the day room or the TV room so it seems a little more open than other prisons I've seen on TV. Hey, I gotta poem for you it's kinda funny if you know the story behind it. This guy who never says he's sorry for anything knocked over a hot cup of coffee and it spilled on this black guy's head who was sleeping at the time. The black guy (named Lewis) jumped up and started screaming and running around in circles when he finally figured out what happened (why he was all wet and his head was burning) he said "Hey you spilled hot coffee on me"!! The guilty guy Mark says "Well hell, you didn't have to scream so loud." And that was it. Lewis vowed to get revenge. Seeing all of this happening inspired this little poem. I call it "Hot Coffee".

eenie meenie miney mo
spill hot coffee, watch him go
if he screams and runs away
well hell you didn't have to yell so loud
you can say.
but late at night when you're asleep
around your bed this black man creeps
and spills hot coffee on your head
and makes you jump up from your bed
don't scream too loud or the guard you'll meet
just know for Lewis revenge was sweet.

I thought you might get a kick out of it. Most everyone here is okay. We all have other names. I helped this guy do a feasibility study on a aquaculture project which entailed raising catfish. I picked up the nickname "Catfish". We also have a Dirty Dave, Free Willy, Poo-Poo Man (a Mexican who is always on the toilet), Govenor Lewis (that's his real name), Elvis, Hubba-Bubba (300 pound black guy who walks around going 'Psst, you gotta anything to eat?'), Slim, Skinney, Stinky, Doc, Professor, Tiny, Pony, Chewy, Monkey, Doogie, Carleto(?) and Lawnmower Man. We did have a guy named Opy but then he turned it into Opra. I didn't ask why, but he got sent somewhere else. Anyway we all want to thank you for sending TC(r)#6. I have a friend who I just started writing to in Coos County Jail. She got screwed over but was saved by this expert witness from California. I read in the paper that he proved the police turned her statement around and tried to make her look really bad. She is doing a few years which is a lot less than they wanted to give her. Anyway they did the same thing to me. I asked her for the name and address so I could see what the guy would charge me to have him write a letter on my behalf for my appeal. She got his name but couldn't get his address because her attorney won't answer her letters because she isn't paying him anymore. It figures!! Anyway she said his name was Dr. Richard Ofshe and she said he teaches at Berkeley. All the sudden I thought hey Frank Moore is from Berkeley. I was thinking if it would be possible maybe you could find out how I could write him. If not it's okay I'll think of something. But maybe you know some people who go to school there. Well I'll let you go. I can't tell you how embarrassed I was when I wrote you last time. I think I wrote Fred instead of Frank and when I realized it, it was too late I had already put it in the box. I had been writing an appeal for a guy who is dyslexic (Mark, the guy in the poem). Anyway this guy who ratted on him was named Fred Moore from John Day Oregon. I guess the name stuck. Well anyway take it easy Frank and I'll be waiting to read the next TC(r). Your devoted fan

Rick "Catfish" Bagby

Execrations of the buried life

The convolutions of gray, grey, grae...grai...
mixed in the dirt of vacuum cleaner memories of
smoky El Nino hearts is a constant eon flux. It's
true the piss-yellow dogs of
                nowhere
seem to congregate around weak warriors of mink's souls
and fajita eyes...Painful grassy Cuban nights
filled with rum and cigarish hauntings of things better left
unsaid,
        undid,
                unsung,
                        unzipped,
                                undone...
Burroughs-in-a-blanket served warm with just a "touch" of
a piquant sauce. Bukowski-wrapped tortillas light and fluffy and
NEVER hard on the stomach (or eye), Jeffers casserole-a small
group of highly-spiced flavors...a paella of the mind's scrotum.
Hemingway sweetbreads, dropped and drizzled with orange glaze
and shotgunned to perfection. The cardamon-Milton cakes are just divine,
either with or without coffee (hold the anisette, please).
Stir once,
                twice...
                        heat gently...

                                serve with a side of relish.

-The Monk

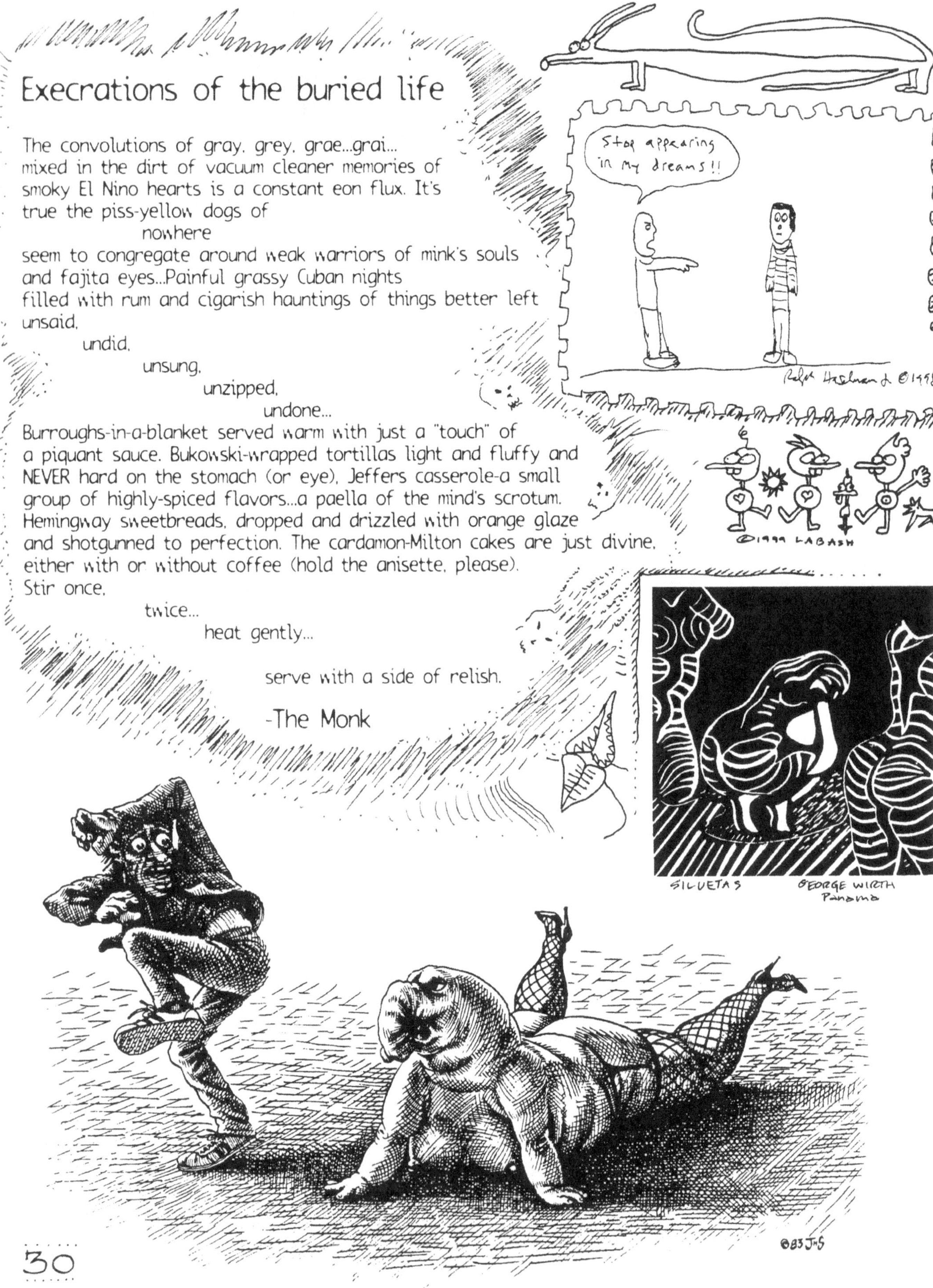

MONICA SELES DIES, 76, MOVIE STAR AND TENNIS GREAT

January 23, 2050 — Lexington, KY (RP) — Just months after being served defeat in the final court challenge of a decades-old battle to try to enter the U.S. government's anti-aging program, Monica Seles passed away. She was 76.

Her death, according to the city coroner, was caused by the adverse chemical effects of a Lexington doctor's own, illegal trial of anti-aging therapy on the once-renown movie and tennis star. The doctor, Sammy M. Fung, is a Chinese national and faces deportation. Seles was born on December 2, 1973, in Novi Sad, Yugoslavia — a former Soviet Bloc country soon to be civil-war torn. She slugged her way out of the nation with her tennis racket, before ethnic infighting began, becoming the youngest No. 1-ranked player ever in 1991.

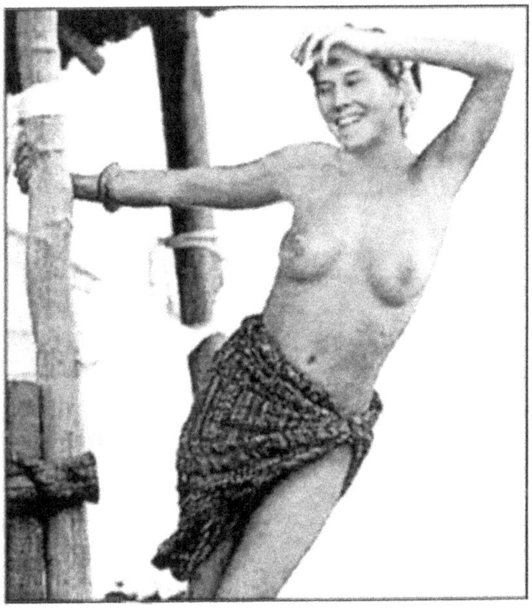

At the height of her tennis career, Seles was stabbed in the back by a crazed fan in a 1993 tournament in Germany. Although she came back to play tennis for several more years, she never again attained sole possession of No. 1.

Seles, yet, found that she had another talent: acting. With the prodding of then-boyfriend and director Salvian Hernandez, she auditioned for the now-classic 2007 movie "I'm Black and Endowed." She ended up starring in the flick with Will Smith and it grossed over $100 million — an unprecedented figure for an X-rated movie. It marked the first large-scale success for what was considered "porn" by the popular media of the day, and that movie was the genesis of the "cinema erotique" movement in filmmaking.

"Cinema erotique was different than its predecessor: porn," said Fred Bindillinger, professor of film at Cayuga County Community College. "While both film styles had closeups of genitalia, cinema erotique focused on imperfection and realistic situations, and found beauty in them. Porn relied on fantasy and people with 'ideal' bodies, or it was just plain dirty."

"I'm Black and Endowed" was filmed in black and white, and — in a scene that's famous among film buffs — during the final climax, the camera centers on a closeup of the scar on Seles' back from the real-life stabbing.

"That scene, where her scar, instead of a penis or vagina, is center stage — that marked the leap from plain-old pornography to something artistic, something for real," Bindillinger added. "And Seles, with those same grunts she used in her tennis days, said more than Shakespeare's Hamlet."

Seles, who went on to star in "Rope-a-Grope" (2010) and "Covet Thy Neighbor's Wife (and Daughter)" (2012), had her screenwriting and directorial debut in 2018 with the tennis-based cinema erotique flick "Serving Love," winning numerous independent film awards. But for all her ability, none of Seles' films ever got any mainstream awards: She was never even nominated for an Oscar.

Her ostracization, many believe, had to do with her refusal to sign with a major studio: do milder movies for a lot more money. And that also marked her downfall.

The government gives a limited number of anti-aging awards each year to people who still have "unique" contributions to make: Usually artists, writers, scientists and CEOs get the expensive therapy, which slows aging sometimes to the point where a person will only gain one biological day for a month's worth of real time.

But anti-aging applications are judged by representatives from large profit-making companies, like Time-Warner, duPont and Microsoft, because big business ends up paying for the therapy thanks to the Taxpayers Reform Act of 2028, which merged big business with government to lower individual taxes.

Therefore, said a UNLV study recently, the anti-aging awards rarely go to non-mainstream artists and writers — and Seles fell victim to her own refusal to work for a major, government-friendly entertainment provider.

She tried unsuccessfully in a series of court cases to get the government to appoint a more unbiased anti-aging review board, getting all the way to the Supreme Court. But the cause ended up being futile, with justices selected by presidents, and presidents backed by commercial corporations like Houghton-Mifflin and Disney. Her applications meanwhile kept getting rejected by the board, for reasons including "her unwillingness to coach tennis," "nary a positive movie review by the New York Times" and "it's unlikely she'll ever be associated with an accessible, crowd-pleasing flick, a la Home Alone XIV."

"If she just had one more 'Serving Love' in her, she'd be worth all the anti-aging therapy in the world," estimated Bindillinger. "The government refusing her is just another stab in the back."

by Darren Johnson

Rocketusa@delphi.com

A Sexual Coquetry

Many times sex is like rhyming words. You know what's coming next (no pun intended to any particular individual). You know it's going to sound like what it already is, only different, only very different. You know you'll hear the last syllable roll over against itself as some familiar, earthy, chiming breath, but you don't expect it anyway, and it clears a tunnel through you that is the echo of your own vice, only different, only not very different. You want to recognize it because it wouldn't be a proper rhyme otherwise, unfamiliar, odd. But you want to be surprised anyway, otherwise it wouldn't be a proper rhyme, delightful, unexpected, new pleasure. You can repeat the parts that sound alike again and again; they always sound different and the same. You anticipate, you hesitate, but only a little. You float through the sound. You don't remember when it sounded this raw before, this essential. Until it does again.

Al Cunningham

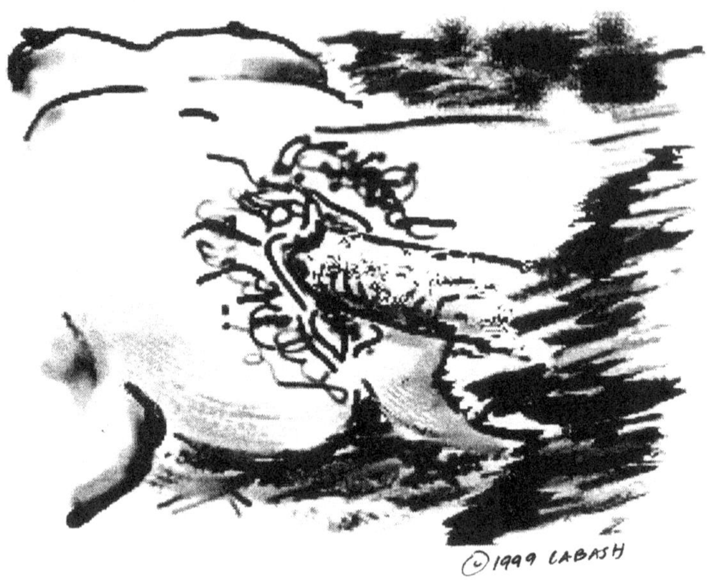

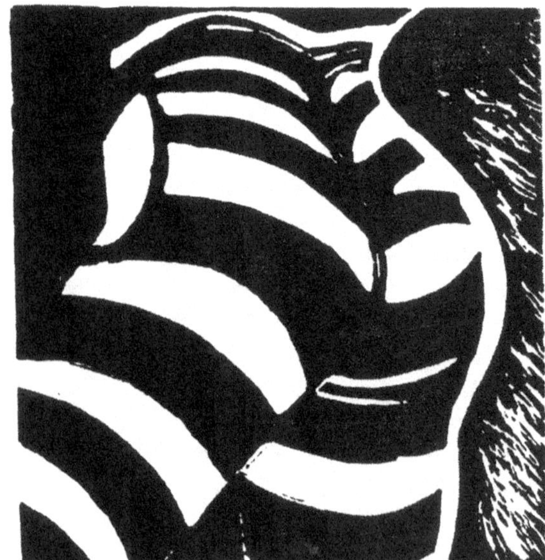
LA FUERZA DEL VOLUMEN by George Wirth (Panama)

Lost friends re-friending

howeverjuice did it (happen) that silly
collide (how I am) sitting down just as (you are)
standing and up-bumping (closely)
as can come (your bib) overalls two blue
(swollen) masterpieces hoping I
will play the kiss game gently as (sleeping)
flowers full at (lips level) flexible
(for being) mischievous to create cunning
hide & seek getting the room (lots warmer)
becoming thru moonlight
why am (I shy?) shall I try? not frivolous need
is a reason but I do know (play is)
your favorite game (the thought) of rich
(kissing) and with the lamps off
love flows freer (eager)
persistence begetting whimmed willingness
smooth (rising) the elevator motionful (and soon)
sweet swellings and (soon tongues)
reaching deep to (feast on) full deliria
(of bodies) engaging oodles
of slippery skin before eagling (birdwings)
high flying (homeward) is heaven...

Jim DeWitt

BEING MOLESTED? BEING ABUSED? BEING TAKEN ADVANTAGE OF?

Is a 16-year-old boy
who already has a hard-on
before he starts to take off
his pants
because he's so excited
at the prospect of getting a blowjob
from a man,
being molested?

After he comes a lot
in the man's mouth
and his cock stays hard
and keeps throbbing
because it felt so terrific
he wants another one
right away,
is he being abused?

And when he runs home
to jack off in his room
picturing the way the man's lips
looked around his dick
when he came
when he comes,
does he think of himself
as having been taken advantage of?

ANTLER

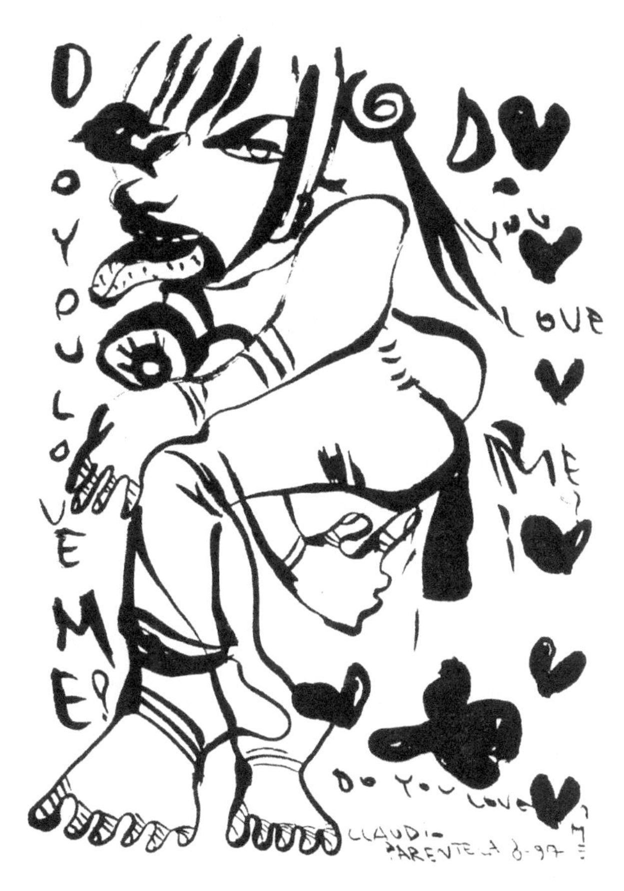

Once upon a time.
there was a boy. such a beautiful boy--
he told me he'd fuck me out in his car,
after his friends had gone home. and he was
tying around his arm, a needle, in his mouth
smoke and metal, disappearing, swallowing,
he glanced in my eyes and said
it's good fucking with cotton fever,
and he laughed and his mouth
opened and his teeth, they were all yellow.
he said, do you want to try?
and i was just trying to control myself but what
could i do, i took the needle from his mouth and it was
yellow too. and his eyes were red as he greedily watched me
and my hand was shaking but he made no move
to help me because i could
help myself. only, it wasn't me who got
the fever it was him. his skin was hot when i touched it and he bit
my ear till blood came. there's no pain here,
he told me and he let me kiss his blond hair. in return
i had to let him throw me over his waterfall, plunge me deep
in salty depths of hunger and emotion.
i think i'm still there, i think i'm dead, i think
he drowned me and i need him but fucking
isn't so good with cotton fever anymore because
he's still up on that waterfall and this time,
i don't think i'll ever entice him to come down.

anna WILSON
anna.within@chickmail.com

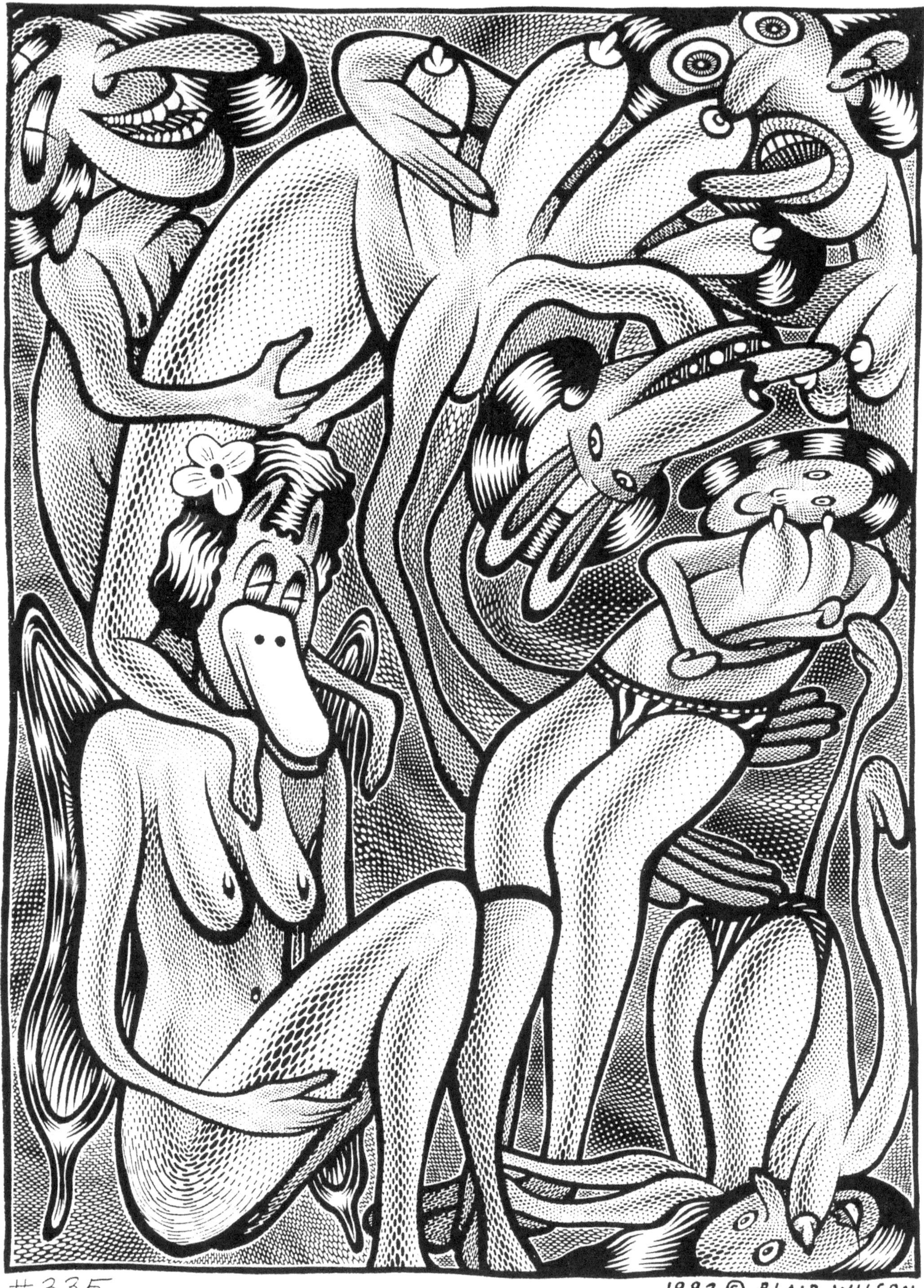

#335

FHTB@aol.com

Alone in the madness of empty nights

there is something terribly
wrong here
the pain is too
bright
too heavy
too much
will I ever sleep the
night without
the constipation
of worry ?
when will I lose this
insane loneliness ?

I fear the cures
will come too late
or worse yet
be more toxic than
the diseases

I've seen the
so called healthy
solved by their money
by their buying and selling
of things
their t.v. lives
and billboard dreams
and my awkwardness continues
clinging my skin like
a rosebush drunkenly tangled
over a naked body
and the neighbors are
too loud and reckless
and too bothersome
and my socks are too worn
my hair too thin

my tolerance is starving
while frustration
grows fat
and I pray to a gutless world
that I'll soon be too
old for any of this to matter
while the nights keep coming
and cigarettes burn like pine
logs in my hand and
the empty beer cans
crowd the floor.

Mark Senkus

11/25/96
8:47 pm

Hello Frank M:

heyy, nice postcard you sent. Women in general get me off, but two getting each other off always brings me on to a wonderful fantasy land far from the dull germs infecting my existence.

Hope all is kickin' some shit around over your way. Here it's a lot of clock-watching and miscalculating love. At least my lighter keeps working...

I've got a hell of a challenge coming on...have to quit drinking for 11 days while I take pills to kill some kind of STD that begins with a "c". I got it from a married slut of all things. Well, she'll have fun explaining it to the hubby. Wish I could be there to see his face, and then tell him "hey, don't feel so bad, she gave it to me too".

Anyway— a few new chants for your view. Hope you might find something dig-able in there.

Gonna whittle this down for now.

PEACE
above th' chaos,
Mark Senkus

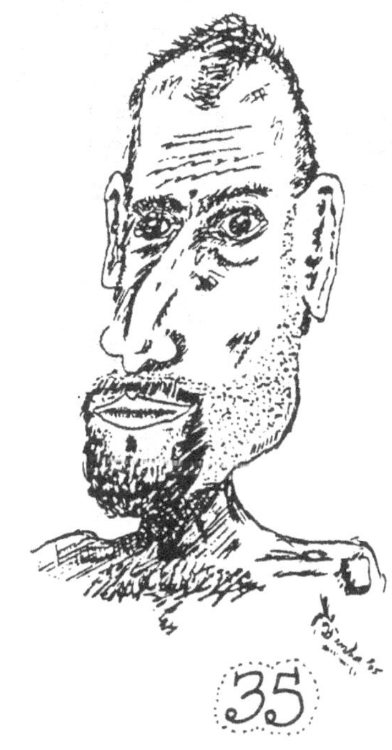

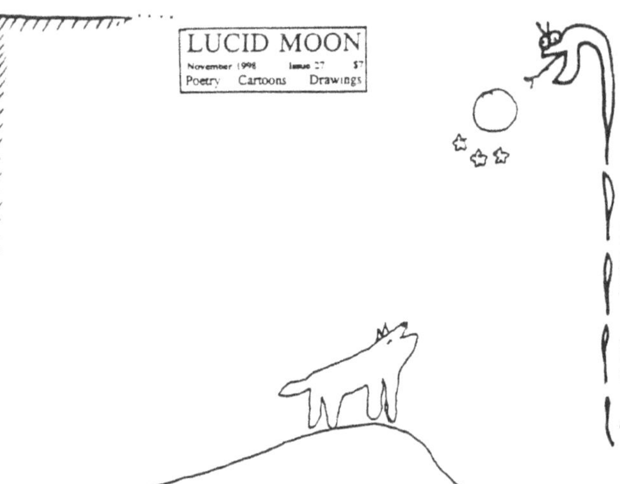

Lucid Moon, the big fat monthly poetry/cartoon/drawing magazine
250 pages, thick stock cover
$7 an issue/ $21 for 3 issues/ $42 for 6 issues
Now seeking submissions
Show me your stuff!
Uncensored, no restrictions, we publish a wide variety of styles,
from heartfelt romantic poetry to underground Beat Poetry
Make checks payable to Ralph Haselmann Jr., 67 Norma Rd, Hampton NJ 08827

Please support the small press scene and buy a subscription today!

As Christians, and consumers, we must be aware of potential spiritual dangers in the products we buy. Even books - once there were only Bibles being printed, now there are books like:

Transient Ways

by none other than the infamous **Jessica Hahn**.

Unveiling Satan!

Her True Identity Revealed

"The more you know about your enemy, the better off you are..."

IS IT ANY WONDER she has been able to DECEIVE THE WHOLE WORLD, as it says in Revelation 12:9"

Revelation 12:9–

And the great dragon was cast out, that old serpent, called the Devil, and Satan, who DECEIVES THE WHOLE WORLD. She was cast out into the earth, and her angels were cast out with her.

In this Book, your will see, proven from numerous historical and authoritative books, the DECEIVER of mankind and one-third of the heavenly messengers, AT LAST UNVEILED.

Transient Ways $6
Elysian Fields $15

Available from:
AK Press Distro
PO Box 40682
San Francisco, CA 94140
tel: 415-864-0892
fax: 415-864-0893
e-mail: akpress@org.org

Also available from:
Last Gasp Distribution
777 Florida Street
San Francisco, CA 94110
tel: 415-824-6636
fax: 415-824-1836
web: http://www.lastgasp.com

D.U.D.E.

DIGGER UNDERGROUND DISTRIBUTION EXCHANGE
a free service to get zines, etc. out in the San Francisco Bay Area
6201 HARWOOD, OAKLAND, CA 94618
email: coralhei@eroplay.com

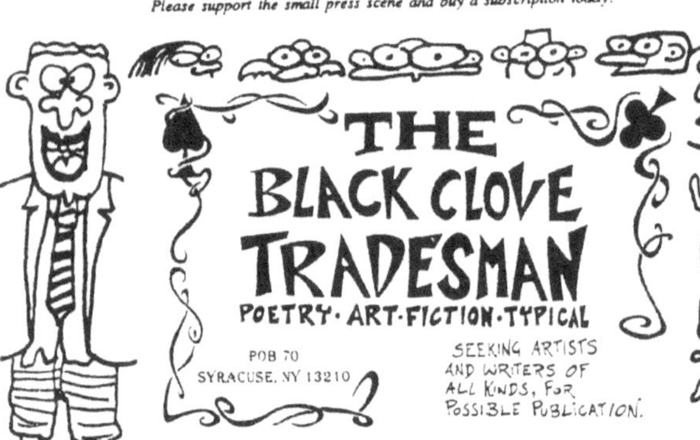

DRIVER'S SIDE AIRBAG
Sample issue: $3
1-year subscription: $11 (4 issues)
Cash, check or money order made out to
Michael Halchin.
Driver's Side Airbag
PO Box 25760, Los Angeles, CA 90025
web: http://members.aol.com/dsairbag
email: MHalchin@aol.com

Mauritius adult photos catalogue: US $ 4.- bank notes to NATIONAL AGENCY, Vacoas, MAURITIUS (Ex-Ad)
10 X A4 PAGES
uncensored $2
(photos galore)

MISS Stella Allet OF
BHAGODAN LANE.
VACOAS, MAURITIUS
SWAPS EROTIC PHOTOS
FOR BANKNOTES (WESE)

ALPHA BEAT SOUP
BOUILLABAISSE
DAVE & ANA CHRISTY EDITORS
BEST OF ALPHA BEAT PRESS

ALPHA BEAT PRESS
31 A. Waterloo Street
New Hope, PA 18938
Dave & Ana Christy, editors
(215) 862-0299
"The Best of The Small Press"

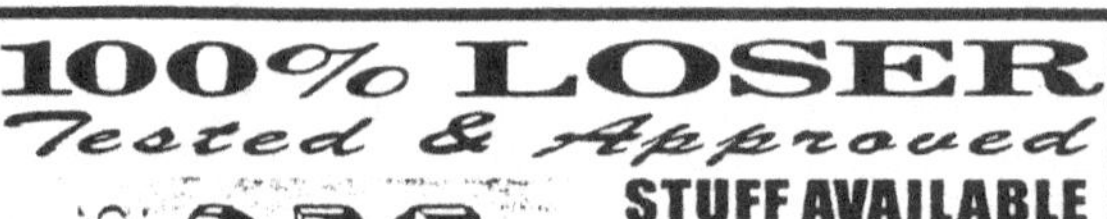

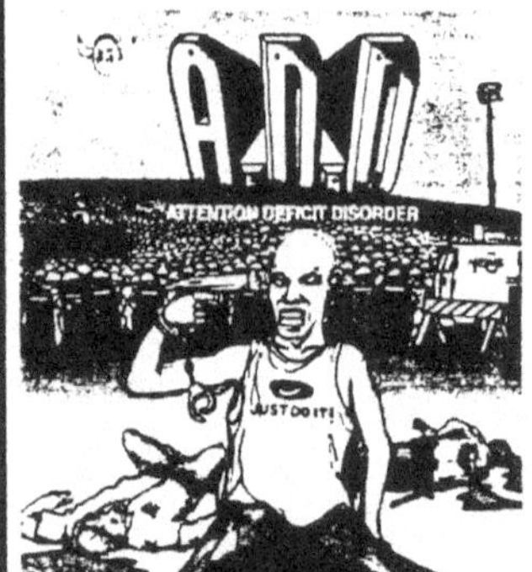

STUFF AVAILABLE

Issue #4: *Hickey, Lagwagon, The Tie That Binds, Clairmel, Chuck, & Pinhead Circus* $1.50pp

Issue #5 "OUT NOW": comes with *Clairmel/Casse split seven inch, plus interviews with Avail, Ann Beretta, Bigwig, No Use For A Name, Four Letter Word, Digger & Cooter* $5pp

Issue #6 "Comes with a 26 band CD comp." Bands *include: Everready, Digger, Big Wig, Discount, Ann Beretta, Funsize, Dillinger-4, The Impossibles, The Fairlanes, Brand New Unit, The Cretins, The Thumbs, Cards In Spokes, Rudiments, The Bar Feeders, Panthro U.K. United 13, Hankshaw, The Tie That Binds, Clairmel, Space Cookie, Sam The Butcher, Knucklehead, Ringworm, Swing Riot, Cooter, & 50 Million* $5pp

RATIONAL INQUIRER #8 "NEW" : *Florida's fattest punk zine is back with a brand new issue. Interviews with Descendents, Sick of it All, Melvins, Torture Kitty & more. Comes with a four band vinyl e.p. : Torture Kitty, Electric Frankenstein, Derozer, Who Killed Bambi* $4pp

ADD T-shirt : *Highway 666 logo* $10pp
ADD vinyl stickers : $1pp

SUBSCRIBE

Get the issue four, five, & six for dirt cheap.
The zines, plus the 7inch & the comp : $14 pp
(all orders come with free junk, stickers, posters..)
Checks payable to David J. De Medici not ADD
7309 N. Huntley Ave. Tampa Fl. 33604
ADDZINE@GTE.NET

ATTENTION DEFICIT DISORDER

©1999. LABASH

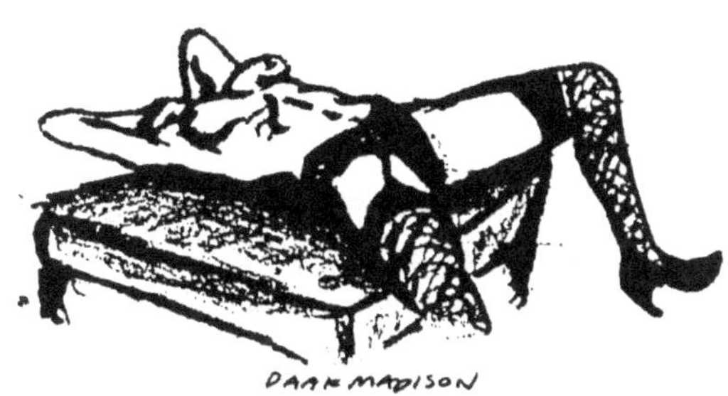

Last of the Beats

for William S. Burroughs

You sly dog
You've finally gone to that
junkie haven in the sky
You pickled your liver and
that's why you lived so long
Last of the Beats

Homo
Queer
Junkie

Your life was a cameo
in a movie
You were a cut-up like most
of your cut and paste novels
Heavy metal priest
Last of the Beats

Naked Lunch
Drugstore Cowboy
The Wild Boys

You were the last of the
wildboys
Kerouac,
Ginsberg,
Corso

With homoerotic lust coursing
through your veins
Sick for the needle
Shot your wife in a William Tell
adventure
Make a Nike commercial to rival
Ginsberg's Gap ad
Scaring most of middle America
with your pallid, weary poetry
reading style
Last of the Beats

We hardly knew ye

Ralph Haselmann Jr.
8/13/97
email: lucidmoon@worldnet.att.net

an early mourning poem

it is 7am
it is quiet and grey outside
the only sound is
the compressor upstairs
delivering oxygen to an 84 year old woman breaking down

even through these floors
I can hear those 84 year old lungs
wheezing at the effort
of pushing
and pulling
and keeping those thick legs moving

something always hurts
and she does not sleep well at all
you can see the front room light on at night
the living-room with peeling wall paper
that hasn't had visitors in twenty years
because Italians always entertain in the kitchen

I keep telling myself I need to go out and
tend to the garden that she cannot descend the stairs to water
but I have always hated dying people
the imminent threat disturbs me
the eventual loss
the smell of incense
and one more limousines ride
and those zucchini lying on the ground
waiting for hands to claim them

hands to claim them

it is 7am
I am going to turn on the radio

Giovanni Moro *email: giovanni@blazt.com*

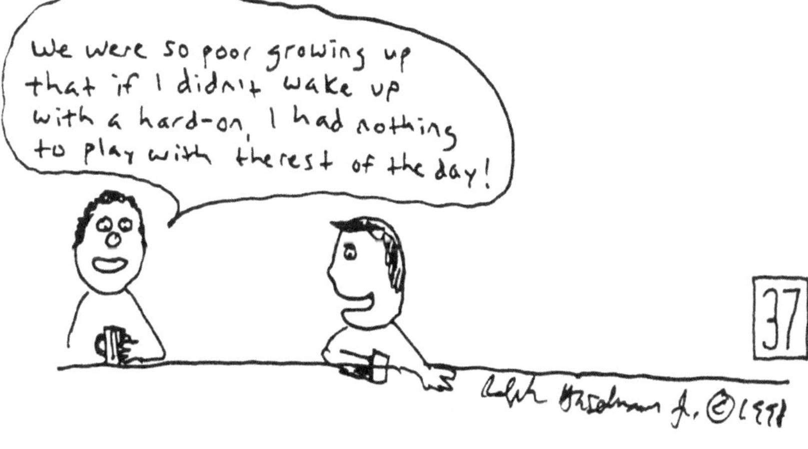

The Poem Will Save You

by Raindog (World Wide Rights Reserved)
lumoxraindog@earthlink.net

"even their nightmares are ringed with tinsel" Charles Bukowski

It's the middle of May and a warm tropical rain is falling
turning dusty streets into greasy ones.
I'm reading the newest book of poesy from my favorite,
now dead, poet
and marveling at his clarity and the strength of his lines.
He said it
"The poem will save your ass from madness"
The poem will save you
while fat drops of acid rain descend
while the bills pile up
while the paint peels
while you wait and wait and wait
for something to change
it doesn't matter what it is
as long as it's something
The poem will save you
while your auto insurance climbs
while the phone screams your name
while the pipe calls to you
from the other room
while your heart considers the pros and cons of retirement
while the beer goes flat
while the women come and go
while you jerk into the hollow memories of their brief
laughter, with legs spread wide
while someone lets the air out of your tires
the wind out of your sails
the joy out of your days
while the life seeps out of your windows
while the warranty on your vcr runs out
while the internet sucks you off
while the open grave waits patiently
and the orange waits to be peeled
and the lights flicker
and the ground moves
and the really important stories wait to be t/sold
and the needle crawls across the floor
like an inch worm
while you wait for it's promise of happy stupidity
while you binge on lollypop dreams of power and glory
while you starve to death
twisting in the wind
The poem will save you
The poem will save you.

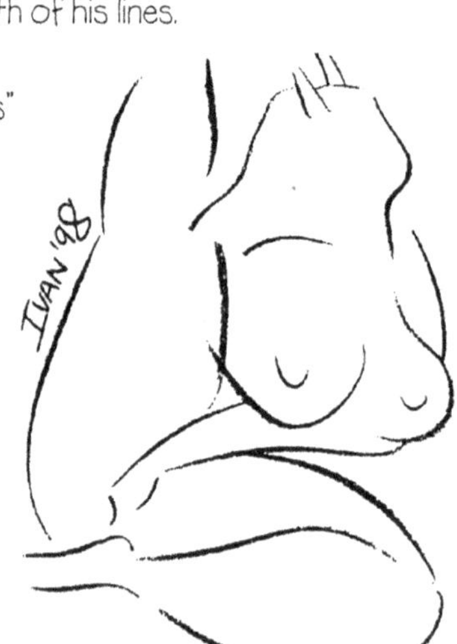

WHEN RON O'NEAL WAS SUPERFLY

everything was superkool &
funky & fun...& suddenly it
was hip ta black folk ta b
black; it was hip fer white
folk ta finance black dreams
....music, movies & tv. it
was hip ta empower black fol
ks; inspire black folks. it
was kool ta b in the "know"
....aware of the groove....
thanks b ta mr. quincy jones
....thanks b ta isaac hayes,
& his oscar-winning-superhit
-SHAFT-theme. thanks b ta
marvin gaye's TROUBLE MAN.
thanks b ta mister curtis
mayfield's superkool SUPER
FLY soundtrack....thanks b.

R.L. NICHOLS

frank moore

sees more pussy
than your average
pet shop
has had annie sprinkle
writhing
across his lap
has survived
the calamity
and holocaust
and gethsemani
of life, yet
smiles like a
beatific child
when cameras
gun him down.

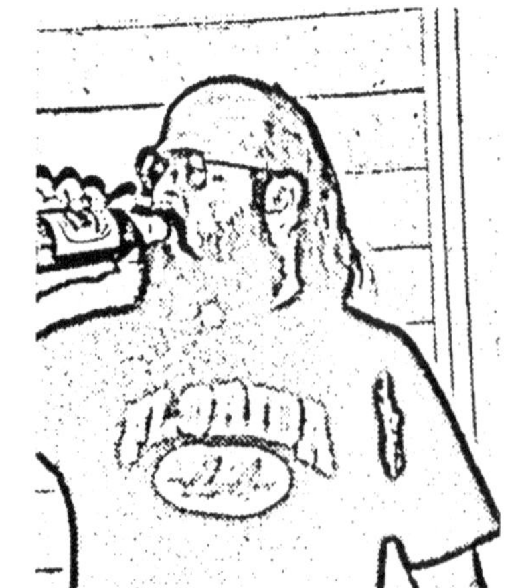

robert l. penick
3929 s. fifth st.
louisville, ky 40214

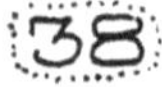

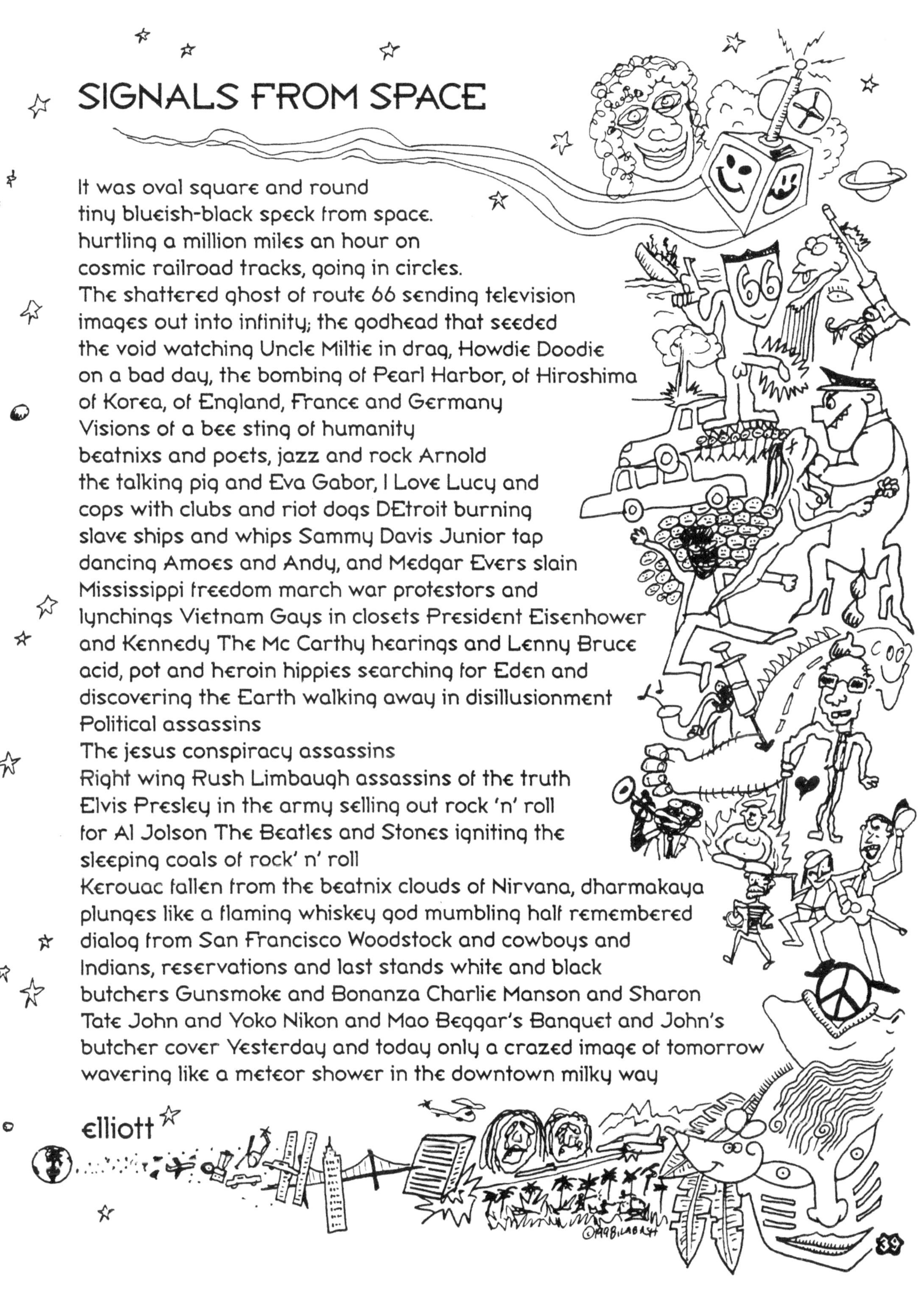

SIGNALS FROM SPACE

It was oval square and round
tiny blueish-black speck from space.
hurtling a million miles an hour on
cosmic railroad tracks, going in circles.
The shattered ghost of route 66 sending television
images out into infinity; the godhead that seeded
the void watching Uncle Miltie in drag, Howdie Doodie
on a bad day, the bombing of Pearl Harbor, of Hiroshima
of Korea, of England, France and Germany
Visions of a bee sting of humanity
beatnixs and poets, jazz and rock Arnold
the talking pig and Eva Gabor, I Love Lucy and
cops with clubs and riot dogs DEtroit burning
slave ships and whips Sammy Davis Junior tap
dancing Amoes and Andy, and Medgar Evers slain
Mississippi freedom march war protestors and
lynchings Vietnam Gays in closets President Eisenhower
and Kennedy The Mc Carthy hearings and Lenny Bruce
acid, pot and heroin hippies searching for Eden and
discovering the Earth walking away in disillusionment
Political assassins
The jesus conspiracy assassins
Right wing Rush Limbaugh assassins of the truth
Elvis Presley in the army selling out rock 'n' roll
for Al Jolson The Beatles and Stones igniting the
sleeping coals of rock' n' roll
Kerouac fallen from the beatnix clouds of Nirvana, dharmakaya
plunges like a flaming whiskey god mumbling half remembered
dialog from San Francisco Woodstock and cowboys and
Indians, reservations and last stands white and black
butchers Gunsmoke and Bonanza Charlie Manson and Sharon
Tate John and Yoko Nikon and Mao Beggar's Banquet and John's
butcher cover Yesterday and today only a crazed image of tomorrow
wavering like a meteor shower in the downtown milky way

elliott

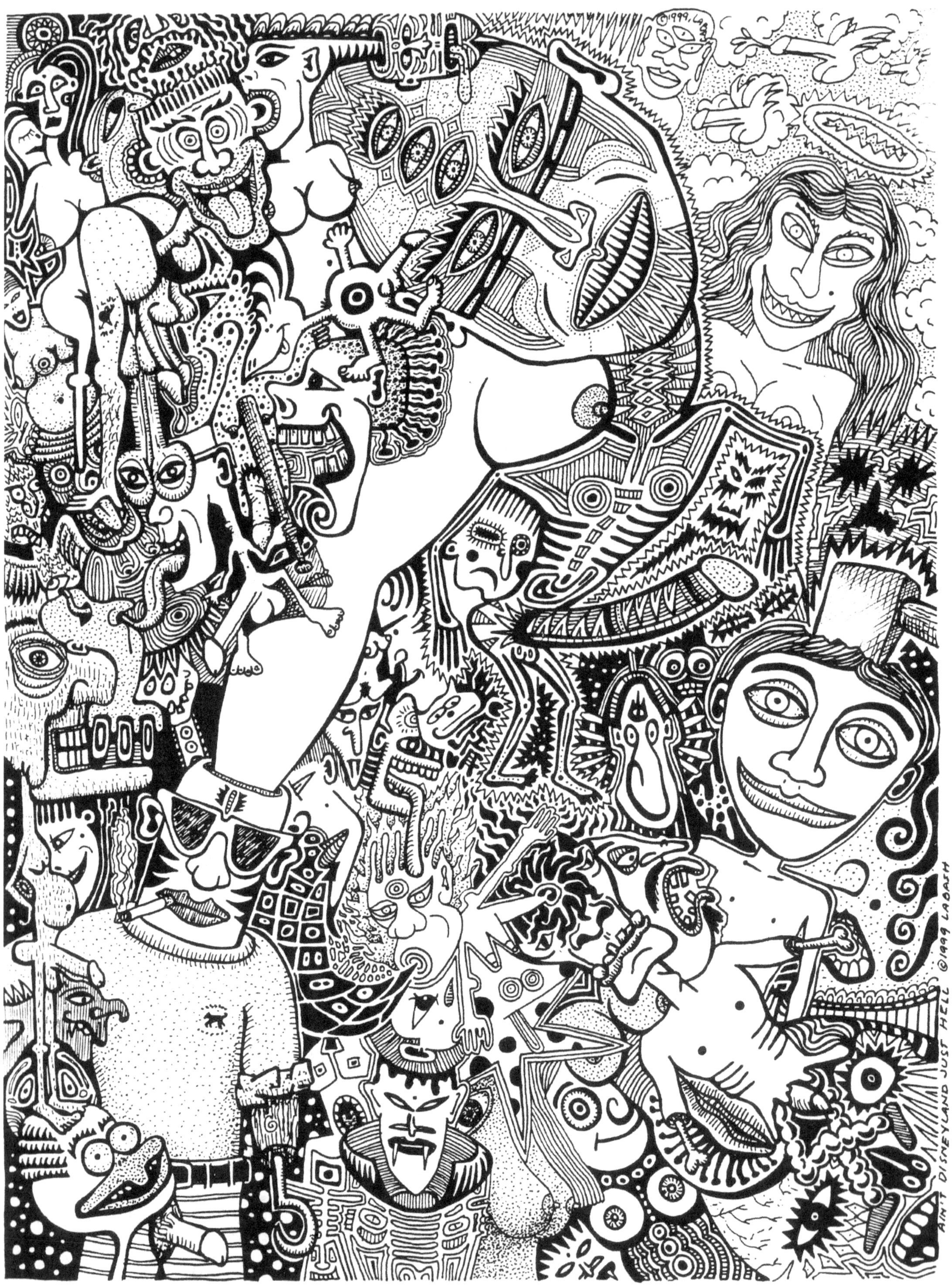
AIN'T DISNEYLAND JUST HELL ©1999 LABASH

REVIEWS

The Cherotic (r)Evolutionary #8
1999

"(TC(r) #8 was) well enjoyed! Particularly I like the layout, it is so fresh and sort of 'clear', I don't know exactly how to define it. GOOD perhaps, or is that too worn out?"
J Luoma, Trapezchedron Press, Finland

"a zine caught between wisdom and child's play, sex, and good ideas."
Jesse Beagle

"Just read the new TCR from cover to cover and was fuckin blown away. Raindog, Catfish, Linda Montano, all the art! Elliott, the LaBash "softer" style. Leaping, thrilling, alive. The disability piece. DON'T get a life, listen to LUVER. Raced through the zine. The black and white became acid colours. Streaming through my saturated brain. I was out of breath when i put it down."
Barb Golden

"Read it cover to cover, just couldn't put it down. Ya know, alot of publications look pretty, and catch the eye, but this did alot more for me. I'm impressed at the quality of the content, and how it seemed like almost every part of the thing reached me on level after level. I found your article on fame especially valuable as I often grapple with the sense sometimes that my work attracts profit mongers, yet I tend to run like hell from them, even though I admit I wouldn't mind making a buck sometime. It's funny, no matter how explicit the work, it's never "dirty" until money starts to become involved. Ray Heinrich's poem "Someone else..." was terrific. A genuine expression. Delightful and somewhat risky. Good art. I loved the Grapin photos. They had a fantasy quality along with a real quality, and bore alot of looking at again and again."
Daak Madison

"Really interesting articles and over all such outrageous vitality and idealism... such a relief from all the gloom and conformity of the 90's."
Tony Ryan

"Every evening when I get up I thank God for Frank Moore. Powerful poetry, incredible artwork, essays, and photos of pretty girls naked! What more could a guy ask for?"
Robert Penick, Chance Magazine Reviews

REVIEWS CONTINUED...

"Okay. On the surface this appears to be another underground, sex-themed zine. It's not. At least, it's not just that. It's more of an on-going "mission statement" by publisher Frank Moore and his army of (r)Evolutionaries. It contains poetry, stories, essays, sexy photos, drawings by Claudio Parentela (you see his work in the Journal, as well as the LRB series). Blair Wilson and the ever-demented Michael LaBash, an interesting article on Assembling Magazines, letters and commentaries on Frank's many projects in the realm of Sex-Magik and the breaking down of sexual taboos. In other words, something for everyone (assuming your mind hasn't been shut down or sanitized "for your protection"), unless you're Jesse Helms."
Raindog, Lummox Journal, October 1999

"I started wondering what the hell happened to that really cool hippie magazine that used to come out of Berkeley. It's been about two long years, but Frank Moore has finally graced us with a new issue, and I have to say that is was time well spent. Some of the contents are "Rethinking the Disability Agenda", "Assembling Magazines", a great piece by Frank Moore called "What Price Fame", poetry and art. Also included, at least in my mailing, is a copy of Frank Moore's famed "Out of Isolation" which was a real treat. All in all, it's well worth the $5 Frank wants for it. Yes, it's truly a zine of all possibilities."
Ken Wagner, BLUE RYDER PRESENTS...BEST OF THE UNDER-GROUND, Vol. 3 (October 1999)

"Frank Moore, with Linda Mac are at #8 with this zine of all possibilities in which plenty of drawings and pictures make it most unique. Tony Ryan's B&W pictorial is a treat and there is a presentation made by Frank that indeed reveals much of Tony's talent. Beautiful women and interacting people presented with class. Frank has a lot to say in there and other contributors are really taking it to the edge in drawing as much as in writing. The nude aspect is not shied upon, so is the sensual and erotic aspect. It's all in there in B&W. Their web of all possibilities is at http://www.eroplay.com."
Peter Riden, The Affiliate Jan/Feb 2000

"Very thought and libido provoking"
Tero Lehto, Finland

REVIEWS CONTINUED...

"...had a great night and read the entire zine (TC(r)#8) thoroughly: wonderful, every article and poem; (LaBash's) outerspace drawings! and wiggle/drawings (my hair) – also a fantastic article on a wish to see death (Linda Montano) and a fine poem that turned out to be our Ralphy's (Ralph Haselmann) re: Burroughs.

Re-read your (Frank Moore's) outstanding article on fame; I relate to so much of that! – Well, obviously, my poem follows it!!!! ALL the poetry was good!!

Frank, the Zine is not just Hors d'oeuvre, it is breakfast, lunch and dinner and dessert. I mean, all encompassing and from so many avenues of words and from the simple statements to the erudite, it is substance!"
Jesse Beagle, artist, musician, playwright, composer

"The cover photo alone, of the nude nymph trimming her pubes, makes this issue of The Cherotic (r)Evolutionary worth picking up, and the inside freedom of expression continues to reign in the forms of articles, art, and poetry. The poetry end is a little heavy, comprising about a quarter of the mag, and some of the special interest pieces ('Theater Rant' and 'Rethinking the Disability Agenda') sort of evade me, but there's some other good and wide-ranging material here. Besides artwork by the prolific and talented artists Claudio Parentela and Blair Wilson, there's an essay on editorial collectives and correspondence art projects, 'Assembling Magazines' by Stephen Perkins, Tony Ryan's photos of nude hippy chicks, a satirical obituary for Monica Seles (dead at 76 due to botched anti-aging treatment after a successful career in mainstream porno), and a mini-zine, Out of Isolation, which is the story for a film by editor Frank Moore about the love affair between a nurse and her severely disabled patient. The most surprising and amazing piece here though is 'Subject: India' by Linda Montano, about her travel to Benares to better understand the nature of death. And it seems the place is ideally suited to such lessons, as portions of her travelogue read like A Panorama of Hell: 'Not look at the wild pig nudging the little girl's ass and eating her feces as it dropped to the earth...a bloated, headless, bluish, one breasted woman floated by.' Fascinating stuff which makes what seems like a difficult existence working for a living here in the U.S. feel downright heavenly by comparison. You can expect nearly anything from a publication coming out of Berkeley, and Cherotic (r)Evolutionary maintains a better creative balance than one might expect."
Tom Crites, Paniscus Revue #6

About Frank Moore

Frank Moore was an American performance artist, shaman, teacher, poet, essayist, painter, musician, and internet/television personality who experimented in art, performance, ritual, and shamanistic teaching from the late 1960s until his death in 2013 in Berkeley, California.

Moore is perhaps most well known as one of the NEA-funded artists targeted by Jesse Helms and the GAO (General Accounting Office) in the early 1990s for doing art that was labeled "obscene". Frank Moore was featured in the 1988 cult film Mondo New York, which chronicled the leading performance artists of that period. He is well known for long (5–48 hours) ritualistic performances with audience participation, nudity, and eroticism. But he has also become well known for his influential writings on performance, art, life, and cultural subversion, for his historic influence on the San Francisco Bay Area music and performance scene, and more recently for his online performance/video archive that has been viewed by over 32 million people worldwide.

Moore coined the word, "eroplay" to describe physical play between adults released from the linear goals of sex and orgasm. He explored this, and similar concepts in performance and ritual as a way for people to connect on a deep human level with each other beyond the social and cultural expectations and limitations, and as a way to melt isolation between people.

Moore has been an underground counter-culture hero and artistic inspiration for decades. He was born with cerebral palsy, could not walk or talk, and wrote books, directed plays, directed, acted in and edited films, regularly gave poetry readings, played piano, sang in ensemble music jams, and continued to lead bands in hard core punk clubs up and down the west coast until his death. He also produced a large collection of original oil and digital paintings that have been shown across the United States and in Canada. Moore communicated using a laser-pointer and a board of letters, numbers, and commonly used words.

Performance artist Annie Sprinkle considers Moore one of her teachers, and Moore performed with a host of performance and punk figures of the underground since the 1970s like Barbara Smith, Linda Sibio, The Feederz, and Dirk Dirksen - The Pope of Punk.

Frank Moore first came to be known in the 1970s as the creator of the popular cabaret show, *The Outrageous Beauty Revue*. In the 1980s he became one of the United States' foremost performance artists. In 1992 he was voted Best Performance Artist by the *San Francisco Bay Guardian*. In the early 1990s he was targeted by Senator Jesse Helms. From 1991 to 1999 Frank Moore published and edited the acclaimed underground zine, *The Cherotic (r)Evolutionary*.

In addition to his books, *Cherotic Magic*, *Art of a Shaman*, *Chapped Lap*, *Skin Passion* and numerous other self-published pieces, Frank Moore was widely published in various art and other periodicals. In artist Pamela Kay Walker's book, *Moving Over the Edge*, Moore is one of the artists featured as having "greatly impacted me and many people through their artistic expression and their lives."

Frank Moore's award-winning video works have shown throughout the U.S. and Canada, and in 2001 Moore began producing shows for Berkeley's public access channel, Berkeley Community Media, Channel 28. His shows continue to play several times each week.

In 2011, Frank launched his online performance and video retrospective on Vimeo. At the same time, he created the EROART group featuring videos by eroart artists from all over the world.

Frank Moore's Web of All Possibilities, www.eroplay.com, features a growing archive of his audio, video, visual and written work, as well as the work of other artists. He founded Love Underground Visionary Revolution (LUVeR) in 1999, a webstation combining live streaming and on-demand libraries of audio and video programming, described by Moore as a "non-corporate, d.i.y., totally uncensored, noncommercial, nonprofit internet-only

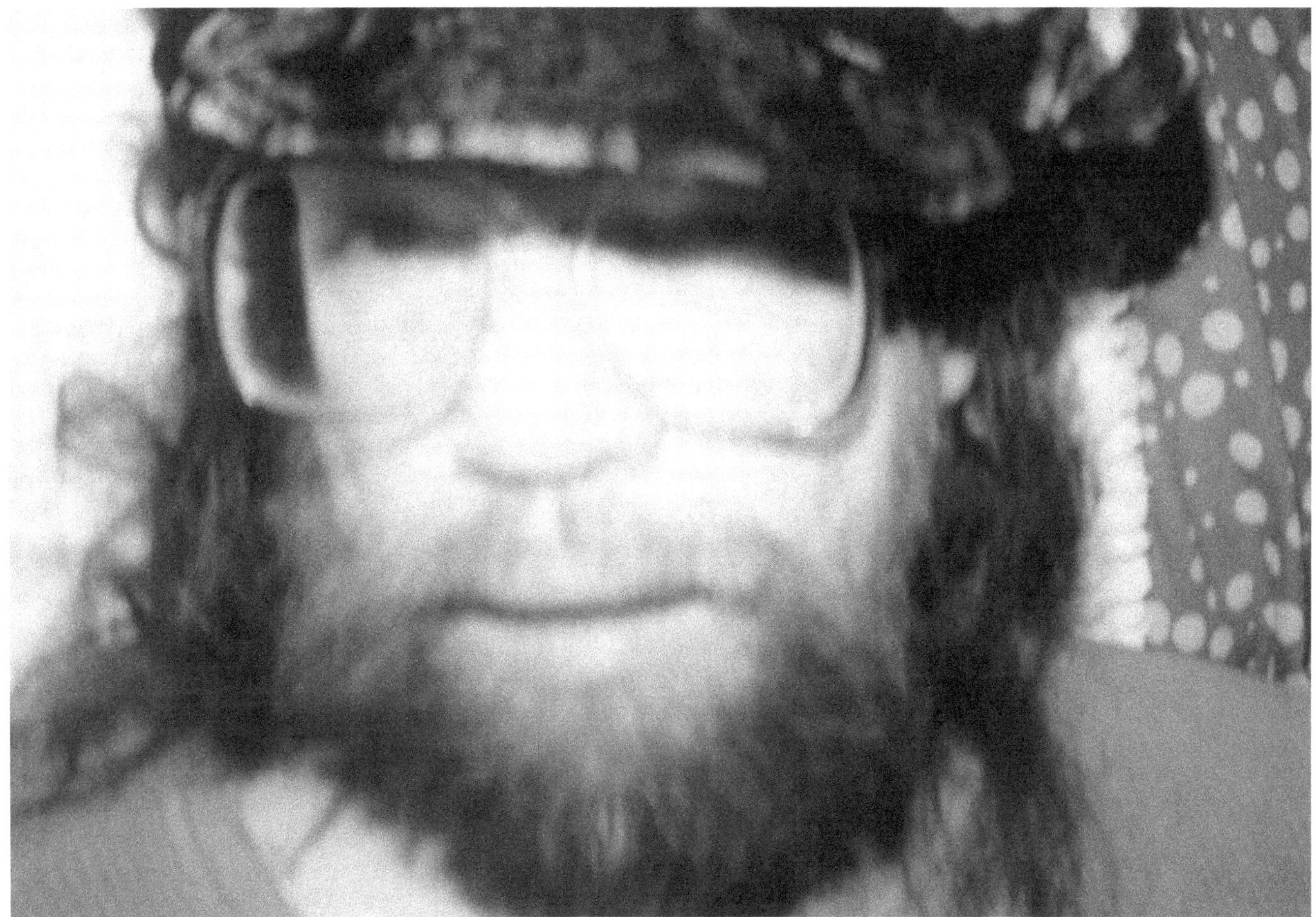

Frank Moore, 1991. Photo by Linda Mac.

communal collective with 24-hour 'live' programming (by amazing people) with 'no-limits' content." LUVeR ran until 2012.

In 2006, Moore announced his candidacy for the 2008 election for President of the United States. He became a qualified write-in candidate in 25 states. His campaign was responsible for reforming the write-in candidate qualifications and procedures in many states. His platform videos are available on YouTube.

Moore also hosted his regular internet show, "Frank Moore's Shaman's Den". Moore described it as a show that "will arouse, inspire, move, threaten you, not with sound bites, but with a two-hour (usually longer) feast of live streaming video. You might get an in-studio concert of bands from around the world ... or poetry reading ... or an in-depth conversation about politics, art, music, and LIFE with extremely dangerous people! But then you may see beautiful women naked dancing erotically. You never know, because you are in The Shaman's Den with Frank Moore." Video and audio archives of all of these Shaman's Den shows are available online.

Frank Moore performed regularly in the San Francisco Bay Area up until his death. His life and art are now being documented in a web video series called *Let Me Be Frank*.

As of September 2017, Frank Moore's work is now being archived at the Bancroft Library at the University of California, Berkeley. The collection is titled: "Frank Moore papers, approximately 1970-2013."

In April 2018, the Berkeley Art Museum and Pacific Film Archive (BAMPFA) accepted two of Frank's oil paintings into their permanent collection: Mariah (1977), and Patti Smith (1979).

In 2019, a collection of Frank Moore's work was archived at the Performistanbul Live Art Research Space in Istanbul, Turkey.

His students and the people influenced by his life/work continue his vision.

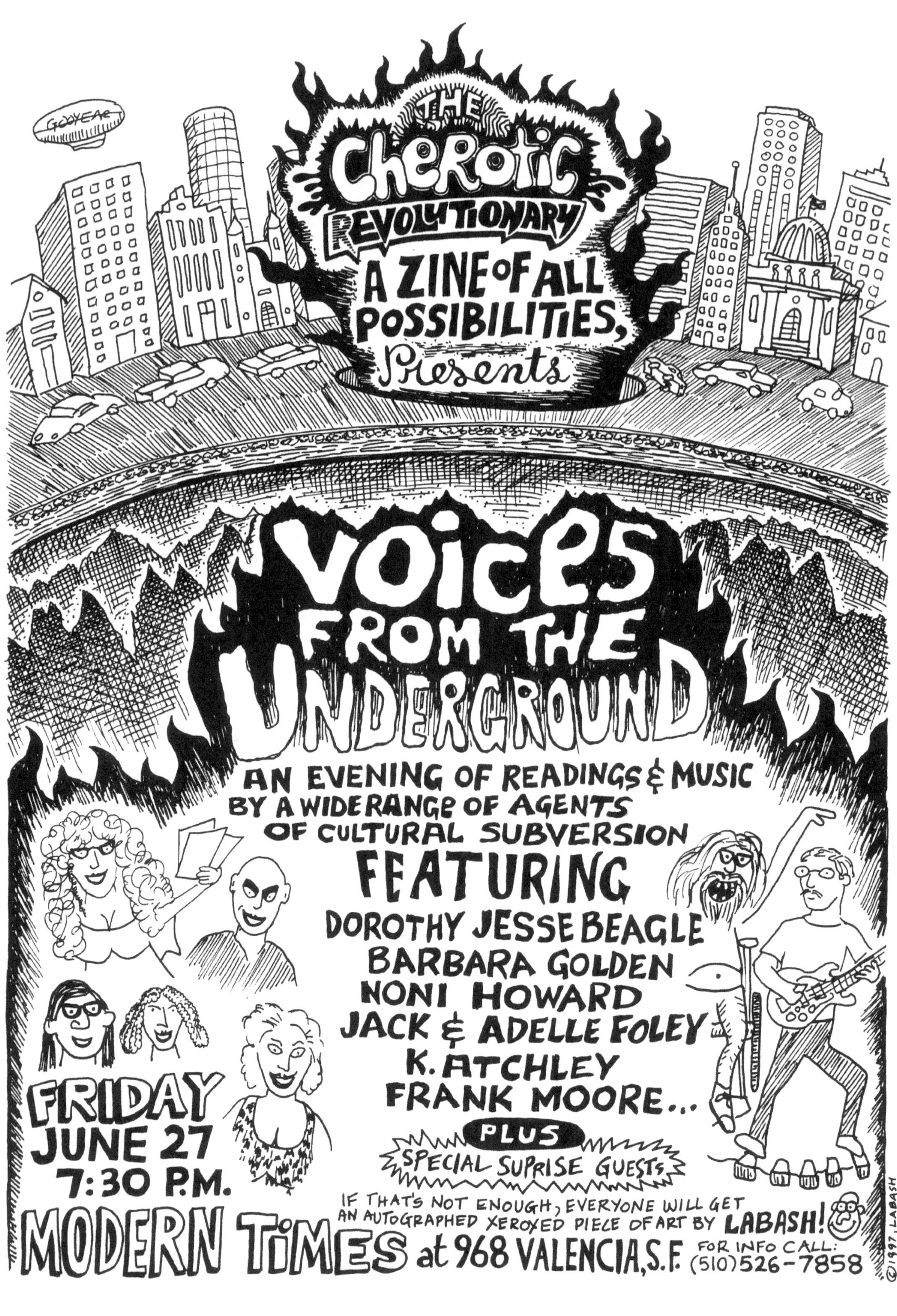
GOODYEAR
THE
Cherotic
REVOLUTIONARY
A ZINE OF ALL POSSIBILITIES,
Presents
VOICES FROM THE UNDERGROUND
AN EVENING OF READINGS & MUSIC
BY A WIDERANGE OF AGENTS
OF CULTURAL SUBVERSION
FEATURING
DOROTHY JESSE BEAGLE
BARBARA GOLDEN
NONI HOWARD
JACK & ADELLE FOLEY
K. ATCHLEY
FRANK MOORE...
PLUS
SPECIAL SUPRISE GUESTS
FRIDAY
JUNE 27
7:30 P.M.
IF THAT'S NOT ENOUGH, EVERYONE WILL GET
AN AUTOGRAPHED XEROXED PIECE OF ART BY LABASH!
MODERN TIMES at 968 VALENCIA, S.F.
FOR INFO CALL:
(510) 526-7858
©1997, LABASH

Frank Moore Online

Frank Moore's Web Of All Possibilities
http://www.eroplay.com

The Shaman's Cave
Performance archives, writings, articles and more
http://www.eroplay.com/Cave/shaman.html

Books by Frank Moore
http://www.eroplay.com/books

Let Me Be Frank - web video series
http://frankadelic.com

Frank Moore Video Collection on The Internet Achive
https://archive.org/details/frank-moore-archives

Frank Moore Audio Archives on The Internet Achive
https://archive.org/details/FrankMoore

Frank Moore's Shaman's Den Archives
Includes an archive of this online show
http://www.eroplay.com/underground/shamansden.html

Frank Moore's Painting Gallery
http://www.eroplay.com/Cave/painting-slideshow/paintings.html

Frank Moore Archives Blog
http://eroplay.org/

The Cherotic (r)Evolutionary
http://www.eroplay.com/contents.html

2008 Presidential Campaign Platform Videos
http://www.youtube.com/user/frankmooreforprez08/videos

Frank Moore on Wikipedia
http://en.wikipedia.org/wiki/Frank_Moore_(performance_artist)

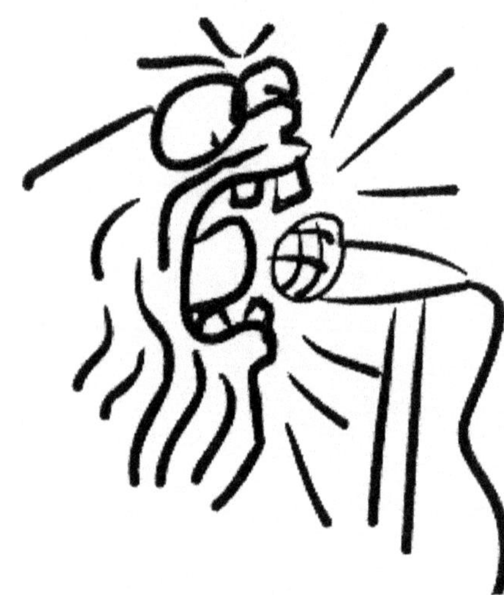

December 21, 2000

Hi Paul,

Thanks for sending us your work.

TC(r) is on indefinite hiatus so we are not accepting any new material. We run an internet radio station, Love Underground Vision Radio (LUVeR) at http://www.luver.com

If you read your work onto a tape we will play it on LUVeR.

In Freedom,
Frank

The Cherotic (r)Evolutionary
Frank Moore
P.O. Box 11445
Berkeley, CA 94712
fmoore@eroplay.com
http://www.eroplay.com
http://www.luver.com
http://www.luver.org

www.ingramcontent.com/pod-product-compliance
Lightning Source LLC
LaVergne TN
LVHW081250100826
845148LV00009B/1183

* 9 7 8 1 7 3 4 6 8 5 0 1 5 *